THE COLLECTED LETTERS OF
JOSEPH CONRAD

GENERAL EDITOR:
FREDERICK R. KARL

VOLUME I

THE COLLECTED LETTERS OF JOSEPH CONRAD

VOLUME I 1861–1897

EDITED BY

FREDERICK R. KARL

AND

LAURENCE DAVIES

CAMBRIDGE UNIVERSITY PRESS

CAMBRIDGE

LONDON   NEW YORK   NEW ROCHELLE

MELBOURNE   SYDNEY

Published by the Press Syndicate of the University of Cambridge
The Pitt Building, Trumpington Street, Cambridge CB2 1RP
32 East 57th Street, New York, NY 10022, USA
296 Beaconsfield Parade, Middle Park, Melbourne 3206, Australia

Volume I of the Cambridge Edition of the Letters of Joseph Conrad
first published 1983

Printed in Great Britain at the University Press, Cambridge

Library of Congress catalogue card number: 82-14643

British Library Cataloguing in Publication Data
Conrad, Joseph
The collected letters of Joseph Conrad.
1. Conrad, Joseph – Biography
I. Title   II. Karl, Frederick R.
823.'912   PR6005.04
ISBN 0 521 24216 9

CE

This volume is dedicated to the memory of
John Dozier Gordan, late curator of the
Berg Collection of the New York Public Library,
and a true Conradian.

CONTENTS

PLATES

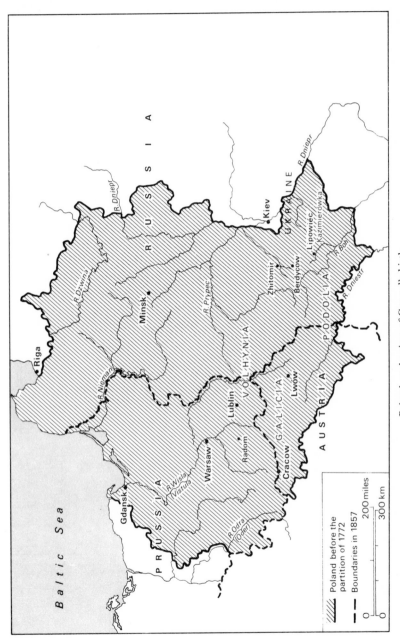

Poland at the time of Conrad's birth

Baltic Sea

Riga

Gdansk

R Odra
(Oder)

R Wisla
(Vistula)

PRUSSIA

Warsaw

Radom

Lublin

Cracow

GALICIA

AUSTRIA

Lwow

VOLHYNIA

PODOLIA

R.Niemen

R.Dzwina

Minsk

R U S S I A

R.Prypec

Zhitomir

Berdycow

Lipowiec
Kazimierowka

R.Boh

R Dniestr

Kiev

UKRAINE

R.Dniepr

R Dniepr

Poland before the
partition of 1772

Boundaries in 1857

200 miles

300 km

0

0

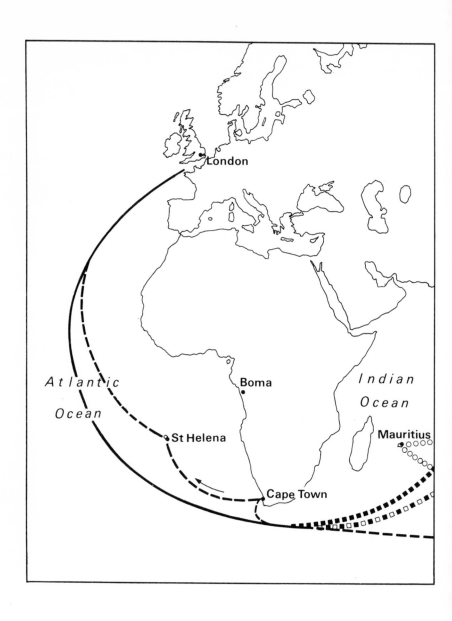

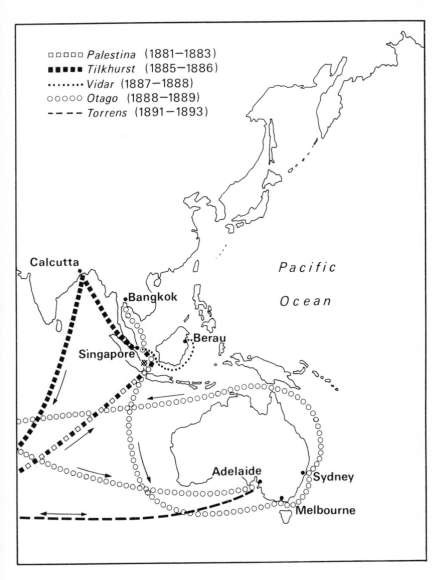

Conrad's sea voyages, 1881–93

Legend:
- □□□□□ *Palestina* (1881–1883)
- ▪▪▪▪▪ *Tilkhurst* (1885–1886)
- ·······*Vidar* (1887–1888)
- ○○○○○ *Otago* (1888–1889)
- – – – *Torrens* (1891–1893)

Calcutta
Bangkok
Berau
Singapore
Pacific Ocean
Adelaide
Sydney
Melbourne

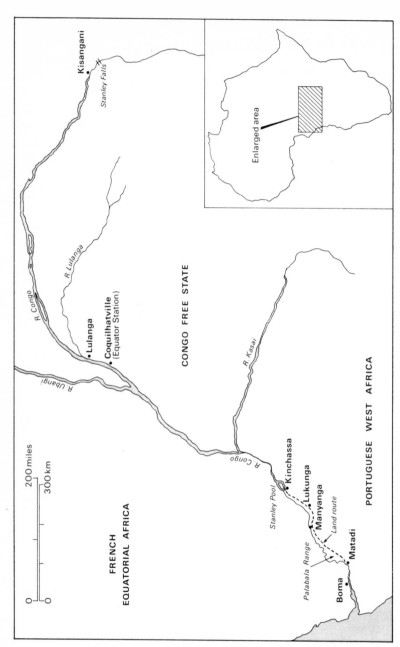

Conrad in the Congo, 1890

GENERAL EDITOR'S ACKNOWLEDGEMENTS

The general editor is deeply grateful to the following foundations and organizations for their support in the preparation of the edition: the Guggenheim Foundation and the Fulbright Commission, for making it possible for me to spend two years abroad; the National Endowment of the Humanities, for freeing me from teaching for a year; the American Council of Learned Societies, the American Philosophical Society, and the City College Fund, for generous annual grants-in-aid; the Research Foundation of the City University of New York, for annual grants to cover travel and related expenses.

This edition, whose planning began in 1960, could not have gone forward without the complete co-operation and help of J. M. Dent, Publishers, who handled the interests of the Conrad Estate in the area of his correspondence; in particular, Mr E. C. Brown, who was unfailingly courteous and encouraging, and his successor, Mr John Sundell, who combined tact with support.

I wish to thank Dr Zdzisław Najder of Warsaw, Poland, for his invaluable aid at nearly every stage of this edition. Besides providing letters in the original Polish and French and helping with translations, he has prevented the commission of many inaccuracies in the text. Of equal help has been Dr Cedric Watts, of the University of Sussex, England, whose sharp editorial skills have been of great aid in preparing Volume One.

Before passing on to the holders of Conrad material who have so kindly and generously made their collections available for this edition, I should like to mention a few individuals whose contributions have been most deeply appreciated by both editors: Dr John D. Gordan, the late curator of the Berg Collection, to whom the first volume is dedicated, whose co-operation and encouragement were matched only by the high standards he demanded of those who entered into literary scholarship; Miss Marjorie Wynne, of the Beinecke Rare Book and Manuscript Library at Yale University, for encouragement and support at every stage of the edition; Mrs Katherine Lamb, the younger daughter of Ford Madox Ford, who so graciously opened her house in Ireland to me, and Professor Richard Ludwig, of Princeton University, who so kindly arranged for my visit and helped unflaggingly in other areas; Mr Ashbel G. Brice, former Director of Duke University Press, who came to my aid at a crucial time; the late Bertrand Russell, who, at ninety-two, welcomed me to his house in Wales; Professor Norman Sherry, of the University of Lancaster, England, for generous help and support; the past and present librarians at the University of Texas Humanities Research Center: Mrs Ann Bowden, Mrs Mary Hirth, Mrs June Moll, Professor David Farmer; the present curator of the Berg Collection, Dr Lola L. Szladits; Mr Bruce Brown, Librarian of Colgate University; Mr Clive Driver and Ms Suzanne Bolan, Directors of the Rosenbach Foundation; the late Signor Ugo Mursia; Mr William R. Cagle; Mr Alfred A. Knopf; the late Professor William Blackburn; Professor Ian Watt; Professor Karl Beckson; Mrs Purd B. Wright III; Professor Arthur Mizener; Mr Robert L. Volz, curator of the Chapin Library, Williams College; Mr Hans van Marle of Amsterdam.

F.R.K.

To the above, the editors would add, alphabetically, with gratitude for their generosity with their time and knowledge: Mr Frederick B. Adams, Jr; Mr John Alden; Ms Elizabeth Anderson; Mr Howard Applegate; Professor Doug Applequist; Mr H. Richard Archer; the late Jocelyn Baines; Mr P. M. Baker; Mr Gordon T. Banks; Mr Julian P. Barclay; Mr George M. Barringer; Mr Paul Bartlett; Mr E. C. Beer; Mr J. Terry Bender; Mr Kenneth Blackwell; Professor Edmund A. Bojarski; Dr W. H. Bond; Mr M. Bosher; Ms Beth Brown; Mr Stanley W. Brown, Special Collections, Dartmouth College; Mrs Jacqueline Bull; Professor Andrzej Busza; Mr William R. Cagle; Mr Herbert Cahoon; Mr John Thomas Casteen III; M. François Chapon; Professor Morton Cohen; Mr John Conrad; Mr Philip N. Cronenwelt; the late Richard Curle; Dr Mario Curreli; Mrs M. L. Danilewicz; Mr Rodney G. Dennis III; Dr Krystyna Dietrich; Mr R. B. Downs; Mr Philip C. Duschenes; Professor Leon Edel; Mr J. W. Egerer; Mr John A. Feely; Mr Lew David Feldman; Ms Donna Ferguson; Mr G. L. Fischer; Mr Malcolm Forbes, Jr; Professor Monique Frazee; Ms Anne Freudenberg; Mr Louis B. Frewer; Mr J. P. Fuller; Dr Donald Gallup; the late David Garnett; Professor Albert Guerard; Mr A. Halcrow; Mr Irving Halpern; Mr Charles Hamilton; Professor Bruce Harkness; Mr Richard Hart; Mr Rupert Hart-Davis; Mrs Christine D. Hathaway; Mr George H. Healey; Mr P. Henchy; Professor James Hepburn; Ms Deborah Hodges; Mr Mark Holloway; Mr K. W. Humphreys; Mr Jerzy Illg; Professor Peter L.

Irvine; Mr Richard E. Jenkins, Jr; Professor Neill Joy; Ms Deborah Karl; Professor Norman Kelvin; Professor Ben Kimpel; Mr David K. King; Professor Owen Knowles; Professor Mary Lago; Ms Vera Lateiner; Professor Dan Laurence; Mrs C. M. Lewis; Professor R. W. B. Lewis; Mr Kenneth A. Lohf; Mr Matt P. Lowman II; Mr Kenneth Macpherson; Ms Alexandra Mason; Mr Glenise A. Matheson; Mr John S. Mayfield; Mr William McCarthy; Professor Frederick P. W. McDowell; Mr David C. Mearns; Mr Robert F. Metzdorf; Dr Bernard Meyer; Ms Lucille V. Miller; Miss Irene Moran; Professor Thomas Moser; Mr Archie Motley; Professor Christopher Mulvey; Mr Edward Naumberg, Jr; M. Jacques Naville; Mrs Mark B. Packer; Mrs A. Parry Jones; Ms Janice Plante; Mr D. S. Porter; Professor Dale Randall; Ms Doris M. Reed; Mr Paul C. Richards; Mr Kenneth W. Riley, skilled cartographer; Mr Stephen T. Riley; Sir John Rothenstein; Professor Blair Rouse; Mr Paul R. Rugen; Ms Mattie Russell; Ms Elizabeth Ryall; Professor Robert Ryf; Mr R. H. Sauter; Ms Marion Savage; M. Jean Schlumberger; Professor Tom Schultheiss; Science Museum, London; Mr Joseph W. Scott; Mrs Margaret Scott; Mr Thomas L Sears; Professor Alessandro Serpieri; Mrs Susan D. Shattuck; Mrs Elizabeth M. Sherrard; Mr S. M. Simpson; Mr T. C. Skeat; Mr Joseph W. Slade; Mr David R. Smith; Mr R. J. Smith; Professor Robert Stallman; Mr Raymond Sutton, Jr; the late Frank Swinnerton; Ms Josephine M. Tharpe; Mr Lawrence S. Thompson; Mr Robert M. Trent; Mrs Elizabeth B. Tritle; Mr H. G. Tupper; Mr D. H. Turner; Professor Renee Waldinger; the late Herbert F. West; Mr Thomas M. Whitehead; Mr Brooke Whiting; Mr Lawrence M. Wilson; Ms Mabel Zahn; Mr Sheldon Zalaznick.

F.R.K.
L.D.

The illustrations appear by permission of: The Jagiellónian Library, Cracow (1 and 2); The Mansell Collection (3, 5, 15 and 16); Humanities Research Center, University of Texas at Austin (4); The National Maritime Museum, London (6); Mrs A. Parry Jones (7); Widener Library, Harvard University (8); Professor Norman Sherry (9); Baker Library, Dartmouth College (10); The Beinecke Library, Yale University (11 and 12); Mr Richard Garnett (13 and 14); Cambridge University Library (17); Laurence Davies (18); The National Portrait Gallery of Scotland (19).

HOLDERS OF LETTERS

Berg	The Berg Collection: Astor, Lenox and Tilden Foundations, New York Public Library
Birmingham	University of Birmingham Library
Chichester	Cobden MSS, West Sussex County Record Office, Chichester
Colgate	Colgate University Library, Hamilton, New York
Columbia	Special Collections Division, Columbia University, New York
Cracow	Library of the Polish Academy of Sciences, Cracow
Dartmouth	Baker Library, Dartmouth College, Hanover, New Hampshire
Duke	Duke University Library, Durham, North Carolina
Free	The Free Library of Philadelphia
Harvard	Houghton Library, Harvard University, Cambridge, Massachusetts
Illinois	University of Illinois Library, Champaign-Urbana
Indiana	Lilly Library, University of Indiana, Bloomington
Korniłowicz	Ms M. Korniłowicz
Leeds	Brotherton Library, University of Leeds
McMillan	Mr S. Sterling McMillan
Meykiechel	Mme Françoise Meykiechel
Morgan	The Pierpont Morgan Library, New York
NLS	The National Library of Scotland, Edinburgh
Northwestern	Northwestern University Library, Evanston, Illinois
NYU	The Fales Collection, New York University Libraries
Ogilvie	Mrs Beatrice Ogilvie
Quiller-Couch	Ms Foy F. Quiller-Couch
Rosenbach	The Philip M. and A. S. W. Rosenbach Foundation, Philadelphia, Pennsylvania
Smith	Mr R. J. Smith
Sutton	Mr Raymond B. Sutton, Jr

Texas	Humanities Research Center, University of Texas at Austin
Virginia	Tracy W. McGregor Collection, University of Virginia Library, Charlottesville
Warsaw	The National Library of Poland, Warsaw
Williams	Chapin Library, Williams College, Williamstown, Massachusetts
Yale	The Beinecke Rare Book and Manuscript Library, Yale University, New Haven, Connecticut

We offer renewed thanks to the individuals and institutions listed above.

PUBLISHED SOURCES OF LETTERS

Blackburn   William Blackburn, ed., *Joseph Conrad:
                     Letters to William Blackwood and David S.
                     Meldrum*. Durham, N.C.: Duke University
                     Press, 1958

Curreli   Mario Curreli, ed., 'Four Unpublished
                     Conrad Letters', *Conradiana*, VIII (1976),
                     209–17

CWW   Norman Sherry, *Conrad's Western World*. Cam-
                     bridge University Press, 1971

G.   Edward Garnett, ed., *Letters from Joseph Con-
                     rad, 1895–1924*. Nonesuch Press, 1928

G. & S.   John A. Gee and Paul J. Sturm, trans. and ed.,
                     *Letters of Joseph Conrad to Marguerite Poradowska,
                     1890–1920*. New Haven: Yale University Press,
                     1940

Illg   Jerzy Illg, '"Polish Soul Living in Darkness"':
                     Letters ... to Wincenty Lutosławski', *Con-
                     radiana*, XIV (1982), 3–22

J-A   G. Jean-Aubry, ed., *Joseph Conrad: Life and
                     Letters*. 2 volumes. Heinemann, 1927

Keating   George T. Keating, *A Conrad Memorial Library:
                     The Collection of George T. Keating*. Garden City,
                     N.Y.: Doubleday, Doran, 1929

L.fr.   G. Jean-Aubry, ed., *Lettres françaises*. Paris:
                     Gallimard, 1929

Najder   Zdzisław Najder, ed., Halina Carroll, trans.,
                     *Conrad's Polish Background: Letters to and from
                     Polish Friends*. Oxford University Press,
                     1964

Najder (1970)   'Joseph Conrad: A Selection of Unpublished
                     Letters', *Polish Perspectives* (Warsaw), XIII
                     (1970), no. 2, 31–45

Najder (1972)   'Conrad in Love', *Polish Perspectives*, XV (1972),
                     no. 11, 26–42

Nouvelles	*Les Nouvelles Littéraires* (Paris), 6 August 1964
Rapin	René Rapin, ed., *Lettres de Joseph Conrad à Marguerite Poradowska*. Geneva: Droz, 1966
Ruch	*Ruch Literacki* (Warsaw), 1927, no. 5
Stallman	R. W. Stallman and Lillian Gilkes, ed., *Stephen Crane: Letters*. New York University Press, 1960.
Watts	C. T. Watts, ed., *Joseph Conrad's Letters to R. B. Cunninghame Graham*. Cambridge University Press, 1969

Magazine publications of single letters are not listed here but cited in the provenance notes in the text.

OTHER FREQUENTLY CITED WORKS

Baines, Jocelyn	*Joseph Conrad: A Critical Biography*. Weidenfeld and Nicolson, 1960
Conrad, Jessie	*Joseph Conrad and his Circle*. Jarrold's, 1935
Conrad, Jessie	*Joseph Conrad as I Knew Him*. Heinemann, 1926
Gordan, John Dozier	*Joseph Conrad: The Making of a Novelist*. Cambridge, Massachusetts: Harvard University Press, 1940
Jean-Aubry, G., ed.	*Twenty Letters to Joseph Conrad*. First Edition Club, 1926
Karl, Frederick R.	*Joseph Conrad: The Three Lives*. New York: Farrar, Straus and Giroux, 1979
Morf, Gustav	*The Polish Shades and Ghosts of Joseph Conrad*. New York: Astra Books, 1976
Sherry, Norman	*Conrad's Eastern World*. Cambridge University Press, 1966

Unless otherwise noted, page references to Conrad's works refer to the Kent Edition, published by Doubleday, Page in twenty-four volumes (Garden City, New York, 1925).

CHRONOLOGY, 1857–1897

3 December 1857 (new style)	Józef Teodor Konrad Korzeniowski (coat of arms Nałęcz) was born, at Berdyczów or Berdichev in Podolia (the Ukraine), to Apollo and Ewelina or Ewa (née Bobrowska) Korzeniowski (married 8 May 1856).
21 October 1861	Apollo Korzeniowski arrested and imprisoned for clandestine political activities against Russia.
8 May 1862	Apollo, Ewelina and the young Conrad forced into exile in Vologda, later in Chernikhov.
18 April 1865	Death of Ewelina Korzeniowska.
Summer 1868	Young Conrad entered a period of ill-health.
23 May 1869	Death of Apollo Korzeniowski, in Cracow.
1869–74	Conrad placed under the guardianship, in turn, of Stefan Buszczyński, Apollo's friend; Teofila Bobrowska, Conrad's maternal grandmother, and Count Władysław Mniszek; finally, Tadeusz Bobrowski, his maternal uncle.
Summer 1870	With his tutor, Adam Pulman, Conrad went to Krynica.
Autumn 1870	Conrad possibly attended the gymnasium of St Anne in Cracow, at a time when the Polish curriculum and language were being replaced by the German.

May 1873	Again with Pulman, who was expected to dissuade Conrad from a sea career, he toured Switzerland for nearly three months.
Summer 1873	Conrad came under the care of Antoni Syroczyński, a distant cousin, and went to live in Lwów, before returning to Cracow in the late summer or early autumn of 1874.
October 1874	Conrad left Poland for Marseilles, France.
1874–8	Years in Marseilles: friendship with the Delestangs, Royalist and pro-Carlist; Richard Fecht; Baptistin Solary; Dominic Cervoni; and a rich assortment of Marseilles bohemians.
25 June – 23 December 1875	Sailed on the *Mont-Blanc*, from Marseilles to West Indies, as apprentice.
8 July 1876 – 15 February 1877	Sailed on the *Saint-Antoine*, from Marseilles to South America, as steward and junior officer.
March – December 1877	May have sailed on the *Tremolino*, gun-runner from Marseilles to Spanish Coast, Dominic Cervoni as captain. (This entire episode is suspect.)
Late February – early March 1878	Conrad attempted suicide.
24 April 1878 – 18 June 1878	Sailed on the *Mavis*, from Marseilles to Sea of Azov, back to Lowestoft, England, as ordinary seaman.
18 June 1878	Conrad first set foot on English soil.
11 July – 23 September 1878	Sailed on the *Skimmer of the Sea*, round trip between Lowestoft

	and Newcastle, as ordinary seaman.
12–19 October 1879	Sailed on the *Duke of Sutherland*, from London to Sydney, Australia, as ordinary seaman.
12 December 1879 – 30 January 1880	Sailed on the *Europa*, from London to Mediterranean ports, as ordinary seaman.
28 May 1880	Applied for examination for second mate, which he passed on 1 June.
21 August 1880 – 24 April 1881	Sailed on the *Loch Etive*, from London to Sydney, Australia, as third mate.
5–13 June 1881	Possibly sailed on the *Annie Frost*, injured, served for only eight days. (More likely, Conrad made up the entire episode.)
21 September 1881 – 15 March 1883	Sailed on the *Palestine*, from London to Far East, as second mate. (Basis of 'Youth'.)
10 September 1883 – 17 April 1884	Sailed on the *Riversdale*, from London to Madras, India, as second mate.
3 June – 16 October 1884	Sailed on the *Narcissus*, from Bombay, India, to Dunkirk, as second mate. (Basis of *The Nigger of the 'Narcissus'*.)
17 November 1884	Failed his examination for first mate.
3 December 1884	Passed his examination for first mate.
27 April 1885 – 17 June 1886	Sailed on the *Tilkhurst*, from Hull, England, to Singapore and Calcutta, as second mate.
28 July 1886	Failed his examination for master.
19 August 1886	Became a naturalized British subject.

11 November 1886	Passed his examination for master (his certificate is so dated).
1886	Writing of 'The Black Mate' for a competition in the magazine *Tit-Bits*, apparently Conrad's first attempt at fiction.
16 February – 1 July 1887	Sailed on the *Highland Forest*, from Amsterdam to Java, as first mate. Injured by a falling spar and sent to hospital in Singapore.
22 August 1887 – 4 January 1888	Sailed on the *Vidar*, from Singapore to Borneo, as chief mate. (Basis of impressions for *Almayer's Folly*, *An Outcast of the Islands*, *The Rescue* and *Lord Jim*.)
19 January 1888	Received notice of appointment to the command of the *Otago*. Sailed from Bangkok to Sydney, and for several months in Australian waters; returned to London after fourteen months as captain, in June 1889.
Autumn 1889 – 1894	Writing of *Almayer's Folly*. In November 1889, interviewed by Albert Thys of the Société Anonyme Belge pour le Commerce du Haut-Congo.
February – April 1890	Conrad returned to Poland for the first time in sixteen years, calling on Aleksander and Marguerite Poradowski in Brussels on the way.
May 1890	Conrad left for the Congo, serving on the *Roi des Belges*, a Congo River steamship, from 4 August to 14 September 1890, as first mate and temporary

	master. Spent four months in all in the Congo.
January 1891	Arrived back in England ill, needing hospital treatment in London and convalescence at Champel, Switzerland.
20 November 1891 – 26 July 1893	Sailed on the *Torrens*, from London to Australia, several passages, as first mate. On one return passage, Conrad met John Galsworthy and Edward ('Ted') Sanderson, and on the journey to Adelaide he showed the manuscript of *Almayer's Folly* to a young Cantabrigian named Jacques. (Conrad stayed with the *Torrens* until 17 October 1893.)
Autumn 1893	A second visit to Poland, staying about a month.
November 1893	Conrad signed as second mate on the *Adowa* but never sailed. This ended his maritime career.
10 February 1894	Death of Tadeusz Bobrowski, Conrad's maternal uncle, former guardian, and benefactor.
20 April 1894	Completion of first draft of *Almayer's Folly*.
August 1894	Began *An Outcast of the Islands*.
November 1894	Met Miss Jessie George.
19 April 1895	Publication of *Almayer's Folly* by T. Fisher Unwin. Beginning of friendship with Edward Garnett.
14–17 September 1895	Completed *An Outcast of the Islands*.
16 March 1896	Publication of *An Outcast of the Islands* by T. Fisher Unwin.

March 1896	Began 'The Sisters' (never finished). Began *The Rescue* (called 'The Rescuer' in early manuscript, completed in 1919).
24 March 1896	Married Jessie George and left for Île-Grande, near Lannion, in Brittany, where they stayed until September 1896.
May 1896	Completed 'The Idiots' (*Savoy*, October 1896).
June 1896	Began *The Nigger of the 'Narcissus'*.
July 1896	Completed 'An Outpost of Progress' (*Cosmopolis*, June–July 1897).
August 1896	Completed 'The Lagoon' (*Cornhill*, January 1897).
September 1896	Returned to England and moved to a semi-detached house in Stanford-le-Hope, Essex, where the Conrads remained until 12 March 1897.
January 1897	Completed *The Nigger of the 'Narcissus'*.
13 March 1897	Moved to Ivy Walls Farm, Essex, remaining until October 1898.
April 1897	Completed 'Karain' (*Blackwood's Magazine*, November 1897).
August – December 1897	Publication of *The Nigger of the 'Narcissus'* in the *New Review*, with the Preface following the December instalment.
September 1897	Completed 'The Return' (never serialized).

2 December 1897   Publication of *The Nigger of the
                                        'Narcissus'* by Heinemann in
                                        England (on 30 November by
                                        Dodd, Mead & Co. in the
                                        United States under the title of
                                        *The Children of the Sea: A Tale of
                                        the Forecastle*).

GENERAL EDITOR'S INTRODUCTION

A collected edition or long sequence of letters by a major author is a publication of great dramatic appeal. No other medium can take us so intimately into both his personal life and his way of working. Letters are more effective than journals, memoirs, or diaries, for these are conscious efforts, written out of what the author understands to be his intentions' and motivations. Letters, however, provide patterns and schemes which move beyond conscious planning. A large number of letters grouped around a particular event or book gives us the contradictions and ambiguities which are the very substance of a writer's creative materials.

When the writer in question is as original as Joseph Conrad, the play of mind is particularly compelling. No writer was more reluctant to become a 'central consciousness' or a focus of modernism. None was more hesitant about offering himself up for display; no writer more forcefully denied his role as a contemporary. His points of conscious departure were nearly always the past, the pull of tradition, the sense of the individual caught by history, circumstance, determined by nature. No writer fought harder against labels, whether that of man of letters, critic, or even professional author. And yet few writers were more meticulous in their demands upon themselves, few more conscious of their craft, more aware of their calling, more priestly in their devotion. The roll-call of priests of fiction is brief – we recognize Flaubert, James, Mann, Proust, Joyce, perhaps Beckett, perhaps Turgenev – and Conrad is firmly among them.

As in his novels and tales, Conrad in his letters brought together a myriad contradictions, ambiguities, ambivalences. He held fast both to his personal doctrines and to his working aesthetic, which was akin to Keats's injunction about the artist's need for negative capability: the imperative to keep oneself open to everything so that one never stands, creatively, for something fixed at the expense of alternative experiences.

When we read Conrad's letters – well over 3500 in the present counting – we become aware how essentially they record his development. Whether to his patron–editor (Edward Garnett), a political opposite (Cunninghame Graham), a non-literary friend (Ted Sanderson), or a major author (André Gide), his letters paralleled every aspect of his thinking and working life. Like his creative work, his letters became for him the public shaping of the private imaginative act. Conrad's correspondence impresses us repeatedly with his delicate stance as a writer, his devotion to an unattainable ideal, his insistent need to recreate the language in order to say something distinctive and unique.

In those early years of fiction writing, in the 1890s, Conrad used his letters as ways of testing out his linguistic abilities and reaffirming the ideals which he hoped to bring to literature. The letters reflect an author still learning English even as he was preparing novels and stories for publication. Word and phrase gripped him like a vice at every turn of plot, scene, and character development. The letters just as compellingly mirror his intellectual growth as he grappled with the ideas that would inform his fiction. As his intellectual and imaginative range began to broaden and deepen, so did his circle of correspondents, in a kind of sympathetic relationship.

Chronological arrangement of the letters in a collected edition displays the expansion of Conrad's interests in a way his biographer, Jean-Aubry, in his *Life and Letters*, could hardly do. Conrad's early correspondents, up to the mid 1890s, were mainly relatives, some distant indeed: the Zagórskis, Maria Tyszkowa, Gustav Sobotkiewicz, or a friend of his father's, Stefan Buszczyński. Unfortunately, many of these early letters have been lost, including potentially the most valuable collection of them all: Conrad's Polish correspondence with his maternal uncle, Tadeusz Bobrowski, which vanished in the 1917 revolution. Seventy-one of his uncle's letters to Conrad remain, however, reprinted in Zdzisław Najder's *Conrad's Polish Background*. The only extended group from this period not lost consists of Conrad's letters to Aleksander Poradowski, a distant cousin, and (chiefly) to his wife, 'Aunt' Marguerite Poradowska.

This collection, in French (in Polish to Poradowski), is of particular value since these letters were numerous and quite regular and contain nearly all we know directly of Conrad in the years when he was writing *Almayer's Folly* and still pursuing a sea career. These were momentous years for Conrad, including his visit to the Congo, his apprenticeship to writing in English, the eager pursuit of a command even as his interests were shifting, the movement toward marriage. It was a time of terrible anxiety and intermittent breakdown indicated by at least three visits to Champel (late May 1891, August 1894, May 1895) for hydrotherapy.

The correspondence with Marguerite Poradowska, which has been freshly translated for this edition, is a miniature of his entire life, with his complaints about illness, anxiety over present and future choices, physical breakdown, despair about his inability to work steadily, loss of faith in himself, and, through it all, a strong intellectual and imaginative development. What makes the correspondence so significant in purely personal terms is its continuity; ten letters in 1890, twenty-four in 1891, six in 1892, nine in 1893, thirty-two in 1894 (which ends with Conrad's having received the proofs of *Almayer's Folly*), eleven in 1895, in which year the correspondence is suspended.

At this point, in the mid 1890s, Conrad's other correspondence begins to develop, and we can now follow his writing career in letters to Edward Garnett (first letter on 4 January 1895); to his publisher, Unwin; to E. L. Sanderson, a young man he met on the *Torrens* with Galsworthy; to Edward Noble, an acquaintance starting out as a writer. This year, 1895, provides relatively few letters, although it was crucial in Conrad's development as a novelist, as he moved from *Almayer's Folly*, which was ready to appear, to the writing of *An Outcast of the Islands* and his first short stories. While we understand his immersion in his fiction, the paucity of extant correspondence unfortunately comes at precisely the time when we would like more information about his imaginative processes.

From 1895, however, we can trace the opening of a creative personality. Even though Conrad continued to the end of the century to seek a naval command, his correspondence after 1895 indicates a new career, and a man fully serious, almost grim, in his determination to succeed. By 1895, the letters to Edward Noble, of 17 June, 28 October, and 2 November, suggest matters that only a committed author could have been concerned with. By suggesting to Noble that he should squeeze out of himself 'every sensation, every thought, every image – mercilessly, without reserve and without remorse', Conrad was indicating the terms of his own creative life. Except for his letters to Marguerite Poradowska, this correspondence affords us our most intense insight into Conrad in the mid 1890s, and these are the first literary letters in English.[1]

After his two novels were published, however, this situation rapidly changed. In 1896, the correspondence extended to H. G. Wells, addressed as anonymous reviewer of *Almayer's Folly* and *An Outcast of the Islands*; and to Henry James, though most letters on both sides are

---

[1] Those to Spiridion Kliszczewski in the 1880s, while of great biographical interest, are unrelated to Conrad as a writer.

destroyed or lost. Moreover, we see a widening of the correspondence with Edward Garnett, tracing progress on both the 'Rescue' manuscript and *The Nigger of the 'Narcissus'*, as well as negotiations with his publisher, Unwin. By the end of 1896 and the beginning of 1897, Conrad was established, with his circle of friends and acquaintances extending to Wells, James, Stephen Crane, Galsworthy, Cunninghame Graham, with Garnett and the Sandersons firmly at the centre of it, broadening professionally to Blackwood of the prestigious *Blackwood's Magazine*, and to Meldrum, his editor. By now we are entering Conrad's life as a writer.

After 1897, the circle spread further to include Quiller-Couch, William Ernest Henley, and Ford Madox Hueffer (Ford), with whom Conrad's collaboration was to begin in the following year. The year 1899 was notable for the beginning of Conrad's relationship with James Brand Pinker, who was to become his literary agent and extraordinarily devoted friend. The exchange of letters with Pinker covered nearly the whole of Conrad's creative life and extended to almost 1200 items (most of them unpublished). After this, the list of new correspondents within the next ten years includes Edmund Gosse, George Gissing (most letters lost), Arnold Bennett, William Rothenstein, James Barrie, W. H. Hudson (all lost), the Colvins, Norman Douglas, and, eventually, Huneker, Gide, Edith Wharton, Mencken, Bertrand Russell, John Quinn, Hugh Walpole, Alfred Knopf, Thomas Wise, as well as less illustrious men who became friends and helpers, such as Richard Curle, G. Jean-Aubry, and Francis Warrington Dawson, a minor American novelist.

In addition to the Pinker correspondence, which is the longest and most detailed, Conrad carried on major exchanges throughout most of his life with Garnett, Galsworthy, Graham, Hueffer, and, in a more limited sense, Wells. These letters remain the source of much of what we know of Conrad's mind, apart from what his fiction tells us. Earlier exchanges with Marguerite Poradowska, Blackwood and Meldrum, and Unwin ceased for personal and professional reasons; later exchanges with Dawson, Curle, Jean-Aubry, and Hugh Walpole are compelling chiefly for the biographer. Letters to Quinn and Wise, particularly those to the former, reveal a good deal of Conrad on the threshold of popular success. And the lengthy correspondence with Douglas that runs through Conrad's middle years, beginning in 1905, is of interest for the light it casts on his connection with the *English Review*.

PREVIOUS COLLECTIONS

After Conrad's death in 1924, Jean-Aubry assembled 2000 of his letters and made a selection for his proposed *Life and Letters*. At the time when he was providing the first selection from the entire range of Conrad's letters, other correspondents were beginning to publish their own collections. In this category, Edward Garnett (in 1928) published virtually all the letters Conrad had written to him, including the thirty-one used by Jean-Aubry, and did so with few omissions or errors in transcription. Also in 1928, Richard Curle, Conrad's friend and a sympathetic critic of his work, published 150 letters sent to him, having omitted only minor items. Curle's editing is generally careful, although he tended to delete passages which he felt were detrimental to his own reverent view of Conrad the man and writer. In addition, both correspondents feared that since several persons mentioned in Conrad's letters were still alive, references even to slight irregularities of behaviour would have to be deleted. Belonging to the same period, the late 1920s, is Jean-Aubry's selection of Conrad's letters in French in *Lettres françaises* (1929), a potentially valuable volume seriously flawed by unprofessional editing and omissions.

In 1940, John A. Gee and Paul J. Sturm, two Yale professors, published translations of Conrad's letters to Marguerite Poradowska (110 in all), although the French text was not to appear until 1966. The holographs, however, were (and are) available at Yale. The translations are themselves uneven: at times idiomatic, but often too free with Conrad's own rather loose French usage. The editing is careful and usually accurate, and in most instances became the basis for the placing and dating of these letters. After that, no further editions of the more than 2000 still unpublished letters appeared for nearly two decades, a hiatus coinciding with the drop in interest in Conrad's work in the 1940s and 50s. During this time, however, John Dozier Gordan purchased most of the Conrad letters to Pinker that came on the market, hoping eventually to edit this vast group himself. His untimely death prevented what would have been a meticulous edition, and the Pinker material will now appear as part of this Collected Edition.

Toward the 1960s, when interest in Conrad once again quickened as a result of critical studies by Zabel, Guerard, Moser, Karl and others, and with Jocelyn Baines's carefully researched biography about to appear in 1960, editions of individual collections of letters began to be prepared for publication. In 1958, William Blackburn published his intelligently thought-out edition of Conrad's important correspondence with William Blackwood and David Meldrum. These letters, a bundle of nearly 150, are particularly relevant to Conrad's early writing years, and Professor Blackburn's edition is usually reliable as to transcription and editing.[1]

Zdzisław Najder's *Conrad's Polish Background: Letters to and from Polish Friends* (1964) provides an extremely significant sequence for any student of Conrad's Polish sympathies and influence. No matter what critical approach one takes with Conrad, the Polish background – especially its presence in his literary imagination – cannot be ignored. Dr Najder brought together many scattered items, reconstituted others, provided translations, consulted original texts which were not destroyed during the Second World War, placing all in perspective in a valuable introduction. With the arrival of the Blackburn and Najder editions, editing reached a level of professionalism not found in Conrad studies thirty years earlier.

Professor René Rapin's edition, in 1966, of Conrad's letters in French to Marguerite Poradowska helped fill another gap. Of equal value with the carefully edited letters is a long chapter on Conrad's French usage, entitled 'Le français de Joseph Conrad'. It was the first systematic attempt to examine Conrad's French, and to show the extent of his errors and misconceptions in grammar, punctuation, and idiom. Professor Rapin's essay provides an invaluable corrective to Jean-Aubry's attempts to regularize Conrad's usage.

The last two editions to appear in the late 1960s are C. T. Watts's most informative edition (1969) of Conrad's especially important series to Cunninghame Graham, eighty-one letters that are among the best Conrad wrote; and Dale Randall's publication (1968) of a hitherto unknown group of Conrad letters (fifty-eight in all) to Francis Warrington Dawson. The latter group is unusual because Dawson was not ordinarily the sort of man for whom Conrad had much time, and part of the value of the edition lies in the revelation of another side to Conrad.

---

[1] A point of additional interest is that Professor Blackburn included Blackwood's letters to Conrad from the company's files and memoranda from Meldrum to Blackwood, materials the Collected Edition will not repeat.

THE UNPUBLISHED LETTERS

What, then, is still uncollected and unpublished? Strikingly, more than a third of Conrad's extant correspondence – close to 1500 letters – has not yet been made available, and this unpublished material includes many large collections which are only fitfully represented in Jean-Aubry or elsewhere. The 200-odd letters to Galsworthy provide an excellent case in point. Jean-Aubry printed seventy-nine in part or in full, and the Polish Library in London has published another small group – leaving almost half of the 200 unpublished. Another group, Conrad's correspondence with Ford, especially in the early years around 1900, is only sketchily represented in Jean-Aubry. However, since Ford's younger daughter, Mrs Katherine Lamb, made the letters available (and later sold them to Yale), we find that Conrad's side of the correspondence includes over 100 items, all of which help fill out the years of their collaboration on three novels, their often stormy meetings over the *English Review*, and their various quarrels, not the least over Ford's indiscreet romantic attachments.

There are, equally, other large collections of letters: fifty to Norman Douglas, forty-one to H. G. Wells, twenty-seven to Stephen and Cora Crane (some published), the exchange of forty (twenty-four from Conrad) with Gide – many of them inaccessible, the eighty-odd items to William Rothenstein, twenty-eight to Stephen Reynolds, the sizeable group to Hugh Walpole and G. Jean-Aubry, the long, extraordinarily detailed series to John Quinn, the several dozen to Thomas Wise – there are hundreds of unpublished letters here, many of them addressed to a single correspondent and, therefore, capable of opening up fresh areas of Conrad study.

Conrad's relationships with his various publishers and editors provide a still further source of unpublished letters. During his lifetime, he was published by, and wrote to, Unwin, Blackwood and Meldrum, Methuen, Heinemann, Doubleday, Dent, Knopf (at Doubleday), often in long series of correspondence. Some of these letters have been published, but only those to Blackwood and Meldrum with any careful attention being paid to the text. If we add to this already large number those to Pinker, we have an entire area of Conrad studies that has been curiously neglected.

THE SIGNIFICANCE OF THE LETTERS

Once we have noted the impressive bulk of the letters, we must ask what, precisely, they focus upon and what, exactly, they meant to Conrad. In his edition of George Eliot's correspondence, Professor Gordon Haight comments that her letters are 'not like those of a Walpole or Chesterfield, planned and composed with care, revised perhaps and copied with an eye on posterity'. Unlike theirs, hers will not engage us as independent literary achievements, but must be read for what they tell us about her life and books. Similarly, Conrad was not a self-conscious correspondent. Yet since he wrote more than 3500 letters, we cannot dismiss their significance as the *obiter dicta* of a writer committed to other means of expression. On the contrary, their importance must be measured in terms of what they suggest to us about Conrad's mind at any given stage in his career, as well as what, by direct comment and implication, they tell us about his novels and stories. Conrad is frequently not a writer whom one can approach directly, and the indirection, as it were, of his correspondence suddenly becomes of a piece with the man.

No matter how we read them, the letters present, often dramatically and intensely, the several careers of Joseph Conrad. Normally, we think of three main periods or staging areas in his life: the Polish background, the French and English maritime career, and the novelist's achievement. But each period has, in addition, its subdivisions, its categories, its major and minor interests, its distinctive themes. Thus, while we stress Conrad's role as novelist, we still must respect the Polish nationalist, the anti-Russian patriot; while we emphasize his literary themes, we must never forget those many years at sea; and while we marvel at his ability to assimilate English, we must never minimize the heavy overlay of French and Polish literature resting on his language and thought. Moreover, there are many other facets of Conrad: the recluse who knew almost every important Edwardian writer, the kindly man who also carried on long exchanges with virtual unknowns, and the proud literary man who nursed a friendship with André Gide, while Gide undertook the extremely delicate job of putting Conrad's work into a French edition.

The usual three periods or divisions, then, break down, and it is preferable to see Conrad's letters under five main headings which often overlap: (1) personal exchanges; (2) letters of biographical interest and (3) literary–historical import; (4) those pertaining to aesthetic matters; and (5) letters to Pinker, publishers, and editors.

(1) *The personal letters* form, obviously, the largest division, since they cut across nearly every other category. The bulk of Conrad's correspondence – with Galsworthy, Garnett, Graham, the Sandersons, Rothenstein, Douglas, Walpole, Curle, and Jean-Aubry – is basically but not exclusively of a private character. Other letters to Ford, Wells, Bennett and Crane, and some to Graham and Galsworthy, are a mixture of aesthetic and personal matters, or, rather, aesthetic matters made personal. Since the biography of a writer provides data which are meaningful in a critical reading of his fiction, this accumulation of epistolary detail will suggest several adjustments of perspective and, even more, supply documentation in areas at present subject to conjecture and speculation.

(2) *Letters of biographical interest* are, of course, often difficult to separate from those personal exchanges referred to above. 'Biographical' here refers to those elements in Conrad's life which have taken on new meaning, or elements we have discovered for the first time, as a consequence of the full record of the correspondence. We gain, for example, considerable biographical detail and different perspectives in the extended correspondence Conrad carried on with Gide, beginning in 1911 and lasting until Conrad's death in 1924. Both of Conrad's previous biographers, Jean-Aubry and Jocelyn Baines, underestimate the friendship, recorded in an exchange of at least forty letters in that thirteen-year period. Yet the series of letters underscores an extremely important relationship for Conrad in his later years. For even as his energies began to flag, or as it became increasingly difficult for him to drag material out of himself, Gide undertook the translation of early Conrad into French, keeping before the latter's eyes his most important work and, as it were, creating an ideal mirror image for Conrad in his declining years. We have, of course, known in the past of the translation and the general relationship, but the letters in their entirety demonstrate the subtle attitudes which resulted in the intertwining of Gide's work with Conrad's, with Conrad looking to Gide for rejuvenation in French.

Not all biographical matters are so dramatic or compelling, although the group to Roger Casement has its own fascination, and the letters to Pinker allow us to track the composition of Conrad's fiction in great detail. Is it presumptuous to suggest that nearly every detail in Conrad's biography is of interest even when it does *not* lead to altogether new perspectives? We do not necessarily have this avid desire for detail about every writer, especially for those novelists like George Eliot or Tolstoy whose literary development seems natural and unforced. For Conrad, however, as for Dickens and Dostoyevsky, we are repeatedly obliged to make leaps of understanding that, seemingly, no amount of detail will ever bridge. His movement from seaman to novelist of international stature, his involvement in three languages and three literatures, the acts of will that drove him relentlessly ahead in each career, the sheer resolution of the man sitting at his desk day after day for 300 words at a time, for 2000 words a week, for 75,000 to 100,000 for the year, year after year – all of these factors make us want to seek out every possible detail that will enable us to comprehend the human spirit and the creative process. Since Conrad's career defies easy categorization, we turn to each letter in the hope that it will expand our knowledge, give understanding, move us (as Conrad would have said) 'to see', knowing, of course, that no single letter or sequence can do that; that understanding is cumulative and that comprehension of a life and a method comes only after we have sifted almost infinite minutiae.

(3) *Letters of historical import* provide, perhaps, an ambiguous category. In one sense, Conrad's letters do not suggest any major shifts in our knowledge of Edwardian literary history. In another way, however, they do create something of a change in focus. Normally, we have categorized as Edwardian such writers as Galsworthy, Wells, Bennett, Gissing, Hudson – making this a period of fine writers of less than major significance.

We may retain that view of the Edwardian but we must redefine it after looking at Conrad's relationship to Edwardian fiction.

First of all, there was Conrad himself, by the turn of the century very much a Modernist. Historically, the documentation by letters allows us to see more clearly how Conrad was moving beyond his correspondents' concept of fiction even as he cultivated them as friends. The interchange with Wells, for example, suggests that Conrad accepted his friend's work even as he was himself formulating ideas that transcended Edwardian literary canons. His comments to Galsworthy, interspersed with personal matters, indicate a counterthrust to Galsworthy's flat realism and moderation. In his correspondence with Bennett, as well, Conrad was motivated not by idle praise, but by the desire to make Bennett see his own limitations as a Realist, those limitations that Virginia Woolf was also to expose.

In still another historical sense, Conrad's letters help establish a network of Edwardian correspondence of a density hitherto unrealized. We recognize how central Conrad was both as correspondent and as friend/acquaintance of most of the significant British writers of the period. And we recognize, further, how small this Edwardian world was. The circle of correspondents was indeed a circle: Bennett and Wells, Wells and Conrad, Conrad and Bennett, Bennett and Galsworthy and Conrad, Conrad and James, James and Wells, Wells and Gissing, Gissing and Conrad (letters now mainly lost), Conrad and Garnett, Garnett and Galsworthy. This is only a partial listing, omitting Ford, Hudson, Douglas, Graham, Barrie, later Gosse, Gide (who, in turn, corresponded at length with Gosse and Bennett, as well as with Conrad), among many others.

The letters of this diverse group run into the thousands. Remarkably, they all, except for Conrad and James, carefully saved each other's letters, even in the years before the correspondents' major achievements. For our purposes, this round robin of exchanges has Conrad as its centre, in that for most correspondents he was *the* major writer in their midst, the one who set a particular kind of standard – even when, like Galsworthy and Wells, they did not usually agree with what he was doing. Also, historically and biographically, the extensive correspondence suggests that Conrad considered himself less of a recluse than he normally gave out. Although he kept himself physically and geographically beyond most social circles, his exchanges with these writers, his reading of their novels and stories, his desire to criticize when he felt their work warranted it, his wish nevertheless to be judged part of the scene, all indicate his immersion in Edwardian literary matters.

(4) *Letters of aesthetic interest* are those which say something significant about Conrad's creative powers, his view of himself as a writer, his philosophy or theory of fiction, his sense of the literary moment and his own role as a novelist at that time and place. When we have weeded out inessentials, we can find more than enough to understand Conrad's working aesthetic. He made valuable comments on others' work, on literature in general and his own fiction. But *caveat lector*: Conrad disclaimed the role of critic, disdained literary men (as distinct from writers), and eschewed even the role of self-critic. Indeed, his letters repeatedly and explicitly reject a literary role for himself. But the working novelist had reached deep within to his own creative processes, and these comments scattered among the letters are his critical legacy rather than any clearly defined aesthetic.

We find them in various modes and places: in comments upon other writers in general; in his reactions to the working methods of a given correspondent such as Galsworthy, Bennett, or Graham; in remarks on his own way of working; in his recognition of specific influence upon his work, and of how these influences shaped his thought and method; in his attempts to forge a personal working aesthetic. The letters to Galsworthy, Wells, and Bennett, as well as those to Ford, Douglas, Graham, Noble, Ernest Dawson, Clifford, F. Warrington Dawson, and his several publishers provide the raw materials.

In a related sense, the letters in their cumulative power take us deeply into Conrad's way of working and furnish, often, a day-to-day record of his work. The group to Pinker, for instance, tells us much about *Victory* that we did not know before, including something about its inception and development; and for other works as well, we must redate beginnings and redefine development. Even more compelling, perhaps, are the references to the *Rescue* manuscript at stages in Conrad's career when we thought he had struck it from his mind.

(5)   *Pinker, publishers and editors*: with the letters, notes, and telegrams addressed to James Pinker and his son Eric numbering almost 1200 items, this collection is the keystone of Conrad's middle correspondence, as we have noted. This vast and important group was assembled in the main by the late John D. Gordan and bequeathed at his death to the Berg Collection of the New York Public Library. The letters to Pinker provide an invaluable insight into Conrad's way of working and into the daily organization of his life. Since most of the letters are concentrated in Conrad's middle years, they constitute, in some weeks, every second or third letter he wrote. Pinker became Conrad's agent in 1899, and the first letter from Conrad was written on 23 August. Correspondence was slim for the next five or six years (one Conrad letter in 1899, four in 1900, twenty-two in 1902, eighteen in 1903, thirty in 1904, nineteen in 1905, twenty-six in 1906) and then jumped from fifty to one hundred and fifty in a given year.

Conrad never wrote a proper autobiography, although *A Personal Record*, *The Mirror of the Sea* and *Notes on Life and Letters* form a loose episodic narrative. Nevertheless, the letters to Pinker from 1899 to his death in 1922 constitute a much more revealing and intimate narrative, recording most aspects of Conrad's personal and professional life, from his monetary needs, his marriage and children, and his friendships, to the development of much of his significant longer fiction, including his fears about his imaginative powers, his growing sense of decline, his need to hold on to his reputation as a major author even when his work suggested otherwise. If autobiography records an internal world, rather than simply the external data of one's existence, then these letters to

Pinker are Conrad's true autobiography, an inner journey related in the epistolary style.

In addition to the letters to Pinker concerning publishers and publication, Conrad wrote hundreds of letters directly to publishing firms, the early ones to Unwin and Blackwood and Meldrum being most important. He could be brutally candid, sarcastic, ironic, and occasionally witty. Unlike those of many other writers whose exchanges with their publishers focus almost solely on business matters, Conrad's frequently reveal both his manner of working and his views of his own creative talents. In his letters to his publishers, we find Conrad becoming increasingly more certain of his reputation and very consciously moulding his career, not only in correspondence with Methuen and Dent but even earlier with Unwin, Heinemann, and Harper's. We discover the rage he harboured toward publishers who, he felt, had taken advantage of him by imposing unusual or difficult terms which, when younger, he had had to accept. Bitter towards Unwin for driving miserly bargains, resentful towards Blackwood for not selling more, angry at Methuen for his mean terms and failure to advertise his work, fearful that Dent was going to distribute his work in penny weeklies, hopeful that the young Alfred Knopf and the firm of Doubleday were his ultimate saviours, Conrad presented another whole aspect in these mainly unpublished exchanges.

This facet of Conrad's personality, ignored in most studies, helps balance our view of an author so immersed in his daily grind that he was otherwise naive in business matters. On the contrary, the Conrad we see in his dealings with editors, publishers, and his literary agent is very much a realist, an author taking great care that the talent he had so carefully husbanded would not be wasted. Even as he protested that Fate was controlling his destiny, he very firmly attempted to control his own life.

The letters, as a whole, in their sweep of over thirty-five years, confirm Conrad's place in the pantheon of twentieth-century novelists. Thomas Mann, who sensed in Conrad a fellow conspirator, called his work 'ultra-modern, post-middleclass' because it plumbed the grotesque, the 'genuine anti-bourgeois style'. It is questionable whether Conrad would have agreed with this assessment of his work – he disagreed with nearly all such judgements – but he would have sensed in Mann's comments the sympathetic tones of another votary, another priest of literature. Toward that kind of spirit Conrad's letters are profoundly sympathetic.

TEXTUAL AND EDITING PROBLEMS[1]

Conrad corresponded in three languages – French in the earlier parts of his career, English and some French in the later, occasional Polish throughout. Each language created its separate problems, so that we may speak of Polish textual problems, those in the French and, of course, those in the English. At times Conrad's letters in all three languages share common properties, but there are so many variables in his correspondence that it is difficult to generalize. To be safe, the editor must concentrate on the individual letter rather than on a language or period grouping, although these categories on occasion prove useful.

Individual editing procedures are necessarily related to the textual difficulties an editor faces in Conrad's correspondence, Polish, French, and English alike.

1. The originals of numerous Polish letters have been lost. Of the 13 letters to the Zagórskis, for example, three were published in the original Polish before the originals were destroyed in the Warsaw uprising of 1944. For those three, a printed text is the sole source. For the 10 that were lost before they could be printed, there are English translations in G. Jean-Aubry's *Life and Letters* and a manuscript of a French translation in the Jean-Aubry papers at Yale's Beinecke Library. From these two versions, it was necessary to construct a text that was more accurate than either Jean-Aubry's French or English versions. The alternative was to rely solely on the French translation, which is not what Conrad wrote, or on the English version, which was not Conrad's either.

In other instances of Polish letters which have been lost, the only recourse has been to print from published sources, even though the text may well be inaccurate. In some cases – the Polish letters to Bruno Winawer, for example – one finds it necessary to choose between texts. That is, faced by the disappearance of the originals, one must decide whether to use Winawer's copies or Jean-Aubry's published versions. Whenever such a choice is necessary, the general policy has been to avoid Jean-Aubry's versions.

Considerations of economy prevent inclusion of the Polish texts, which are available in Z. Najder's *Listy – Conrad, J.* (Warsaw: Ars Polona-Ruch). These letters will be printed only in translation; Halina

---

[1] An early version of this section appeared in *Conradiana*, the journal of Conrad studies (Fall 1973), as a way of interesting scholars in the scope of the edition.

Carroll's English versions are taken, by permission, from Z. Najder's *Conrad's Polish Background* (Oxford, 1964).

2. The letters in French are no less problematic; for here too the editor must decide whether to use an evidently imperfect copy when the original cannot be discovered. These letters number well over 400, the chief correspondents being Marguerite Poradowska, André Gide and Jean-Aubry. Those to Mme Poradowska are, of course, extremely valuable for an understanding of Conrad's early career, and those to Gide for the middle-to-late period when Gide supervised the French translation of Conrad's work. Fortunately, the original texts of the 110 to Marguerite Poradowska are available, at the Beinecke Library; and the entire group of Conrad's 24 letters to Gide is at the Bibliothèque Littéraire Jacques Doucet in Paris. The third large group of Conrad's letters in French, to Jean-Aubry, is available in the original or in copies at the Beinecke. Where copies are involved, the editor must either reproduce what he knows to be a defective text or attempt reconstruction.

For many of the remaining letters in French, we are dependent on Jean-Aubry's collection of Conrad's French correspondence, *Lettres françaises* (1929), in itself a valuable enterprise. This selection contains a broad range of correspondence, from early business notes to Albert Thys, newsy letters to Polish relatives and friends, on to literary matters with Henry James, Gide, Blasco Ibáñez, Davray, Larbaud, Schlumberger, de Smet and other translators. Two-thirds of the original texts of these letters are available, but for the remaining third (53) we face the familiar problems.

In the letters for which originals exist and which can be compared with the printed text, we find some or all of the following problems: deletions, not all of them concerned with what might have been thought sensitive matters; haphazard transcriptions from Conrad's holograph; mispunctuation based on misreading of the original and misconceptions of the correction itself, even in French; whimsical transpositions; misnumbered pages; extraneous comments introduced; and attempts at regularization of Conrad's French usage – especially in the suppression of his capitalization of 'Vous' and 'Votre'. Since one-third of these letters were scattered after Jean-Aubry used them, and are now irrecoverable, we are forced to print inaccurate texts from his edition.

Moreover Conrad himself made numerous errors in French; so that even when the editor knows that a correction is in order, he is uncertain what Conrad may have written and must leave the primary text untouched, so reprinting the many errors of Jean-Aubry.[1]

The letters in French are followed in this edition by an English translation (by Frederick R. Karl and Laurence Davies).

3. When we turn to the 3000 letters in English, the editor's task is easier, although some of the original texts still remain undiscovered. The single largest group, almost 1200 letters, beginning in 1899, is to James Brand Pinker, Conrad's agent, and the manuscripts of nearly all of this important group are located in one place, the Berg Collection of the New York Public Library. Other major exchanges are also available in original manuscript: 41 to Wells, 215 to Galsworthy, more than 100 to Ford, over twenty to Stephen and Cora Crane, 81 to Cunninghame Graham, well over half of the 221 to Garnett, and the large correspondence with William Rothenstein, Hugh Walpole, Richard Curle, E. L. Sanderson, Norman Douglas, Thomas Wise, Francis Warrington Dawson; plus smaller exchanges with Gosse, Knopf, Russell, Newbolt, Symons, Bennett and Shorter. To this we may add Conrad's lengthy correspondence with his publishers: Unwin, Dent, Methuen, Blackwood, Doubleday and Heinemann. The opening of the John Quinn papers at the New York Public Library has made available this large group of Conrad letters, especially valuable for his later years when sales of his manuscripts and typescripts to Quinn and Wise helped to supplement his income. Unfortunately, only three-fifths of the 104 letters to the Colvins have turned up, although copies of many of the others do exist.

Rich as these groups are, the editor finds several lacunae. Until now, Jean-Aubry's selection, published in 1926, has been the only collection

[1] See Professor René Rapin's invaluable essay, mentioned above, on Conrad's French usage, 'Le français de Joseph Conrad', in his edition, *Lettres de Joseph Conrad à Marguerite Poradowska* (Geneva: Librairie Droz, 1966). An excellent example of Jean-Aubry's own editorial and textual errors arises in a letter Conrad wrote to Gide, on 21 June, 1912 (reprinted on page 119 of *Lettres françaises*). Although there is no misdating, errors of transcription abound, phrases are omitted, letters are capitalized without plan, words are changed for no apparent reason, some errors in the original are corrected, others ignored, accents are shifted, punctuation is revised consistent with neither French nor English usage. Worst of all, Jean-Aubry inexplicably omitted a final paragraph, although not for the usual reasons of tact. The passage is not sensitive. It is, indeed, light chatter that fits well into this newsy letter that touches on several matters: Gide's invitation for the Conrads to visit the Abbey of Pontigny, Conrad's disclaimers about the value of *Nostromo* and his pleasure at hearing Gide is working on a major novel (*Les caves du Vatican*), and, finally, family news about John and Borys Conrad.

in English (Z. Najder has published his own selection in Polish) which covers the whole of Conrad's life. In pointing out the errors and omissions of Jean-Aubry's work, we should stress that his conception of an edition of letters was very different from our own. For example, he omitted all those letters to Galsworthy which pointed to Conrad's financial dependence on his friend, and deleted passages from the letters he did print to hide this aspect of their relationship. Jean-Aubry's selectiveness plays down Conrad's real plight and indicates how he, as editor, attempted to shape Conrad's image.

Although we can excuse him for his over-protectiveness in a more genteel era, especially since both Galsworthy and Jessie Conrad were alive at the time, the fact remains that many, possibly most, of the letters as printed in his edition are unreliable. None of this would ultimately matter except that the letters placed at Jean-Aubry's disposal for his biography and selection were later scattered, without, as far as one can discover, anyone making a note of who owned the letters and where they went. As a result, the later editor often has to print from Jean-Aubry without recourse to all of the originals. In all, 66 (from *Life and Letters*) are missing, chiefly to Sir Ralph and Lady Wedgwood, J. St Loe Strachey, Scott Moncrieff, Sir Hugh Clifford, Barrett Clark and Christopher Sandeman. Moreover – and this is potentially more damaging – some of the letters Jean-Aubry decided *not* to use, perhaps including some to Bronislaw Malinowski, George Gissing and W. H. Hudson, cannot be located over fifty years later. Although we are certain that Conrad corresponded, however infrequently, with these men, only one letter, to Gissing, has turned up.

In one other instance we must print from published collections for which not all the originals are available. Edward Garnett in 1928 published 221 of Conrad's letters to him, including the 31 used by Jean-Aubry, although without the latter's errors. Though we are forced to print from Garnett's text some letters for which Conrad's manuscripts are unavailable, we can do so on the assumption that we are reprinting a basically correct letter, with usually accurate dating and a minimum of material deleted for personal reasons.

PRINCIPLES OF SELECTION

This edition includes every letter, telegram, postcard, note or brief written message by Joseph Conrad. The minor items are few; the majority of Conrad's letters are of some length, not brief messages. When the original or photocopies of the original are unavailable, we print from books, magazines, other editions, including transcripts which we know are not free from error. This reproduction of unauthentic texts is considerably less than one-tenth of the total number, about 250 letters at most. We have not, however, printed excerpts from catalogues or extracts from biographies when the Conrad material is clearly outside the given context.[1] The text reproduced in the edition will be the full text so far as it can be established. Excerpts in biographies or in catalogues are certainly not representative of the letters Conrad originally wrote. Likewise, we have avoided reproducing all marginal scribblings when they are not themselves part of a letter, such as brief inscriptions in books: these are different kinds of documents. If an excerpt in a catalogue or in a book does appear to be of interest, it is included not as part of the text but as an annotation.

What, then, is missing besides excerpts? An edition of this kind can only be comprehensive, not complete, for some holders of letters will not permit access; or, permitting that, they will not allow copying. Then, too, there are those letters which have been followed through auctions until the material vanishes, the purchaser refusing to come forward. Fortunately, their numbers are not great. The active search for Conrad letters began in 1960, so that the first volume (covering 1861–97) has received more than twenty years of attention. By the time the edition is completed, the search will have continued for considerably longer, and those letters which turn up out of their chronological order will be included in the final volume. Missing are exchanges with Gissing, Hudson, and Malinowski, possibly with Shaw and Kipling, and we can only speculate about their ultimate value. Those to Malinowski, a countryman of Conrad's, could have been of considerable value. There is also the further chance that private holdings include more than the 8 letters to Hugh Clifford published in Jean-Aubry, and that other Christopher Sandeman letters are extant as well. On the other hand, Conrad did not carry on long exchanges with people such as Clifford or Sandeman, who glanced off his life; and even those missing groups to Hudson or Gissing or Shaw, we can infer from Conrad's own remarks, would be limited and occupy only a very few years.

One additional question involves letters _to_ Conrad and their effect upon the edition. Only about two hundred such letters exist. Unfortunately, Conrad destroyed most of the letters addressed to him once

---

[1] Professor Schulteiss has printed, in _Conradiana_, some of those catalogue and book excerpts for which the full text is still unavailable.

he had responded. Of the two hundred or so, the most valuable is the group of 71 from his maternal uncle, Tadeusz Bobrowski (available in Z. Najder's *Conrad's Polish Background*). Others are from Edward Garnett and André Gide, with a scattering also from Blackwood, Ford, Huneker, Bennett, Crane, Gissing, James, Kipling, Drinkwater, Muirhead Bone, Wells, E.V. Lucas, as well as a small non-literary group from Jessie Conrad to her husband when he was away in America. Although these return letters are few and widely spaced, they are of value as supplementary material for Conrad's own letters and will be referred to in the annotation. In the best of all worlds, they might have appeared interwoven into the text, but such luxuries are no longer practicable.

EDITORIAL PROCEDURES

Editing principles have been kept simple. The overall plan has been to transcribe Conrad's more than 3500 letters as they appear in the original holograph or typescript. The aim throughout is to provide a text representing what Conrad wrote and what his recipients read, with a minimum of alteration or interference.

Unless it appears to be important, we do not reproduce a cancellation. Usually, although not always, Conrad's excisions involved either idiom or else his sometimes faulty grammar. Such changes were not substantive. The same policy applies to accidentals, variants, diagrams, and other such matters: if significant, they are printed, if inessential ignored. The scholar who wishes to study alterations, cancellations, accidentals, variant readings of illegible passages, doodles, diagrams and drawings would in any case need to examine the manuscript. For all other readers, such cancellations are of minimal interest.

Conrad's uncorrected errors of punctuation, accentuation, grammar, spelling and idiom are, however, another question. As the scars of his struggle with languages not originally his own, they have more interest than the absent-minded stumblings of a native-born author. Tacit correction of the letters as he wrote (and his correspondents read) them would water down their characteristic flavour. Yet we do not want to give the general reader literary dyspepsia. In order to reconcile comfort with verisimilitude, we have adopted certain conventions. Missing letters and words are supplied in square brackets. Taking ease of reading as our criterion, we also use square brackets to expand some, but not all, of the profusion of contractions that makes some of

Conrad's letters look like pages from a book of codes. Rather than employ the more obtrusive and possibly disapproving *sic* (one would be proud to have written most of these letters in one's own language, let alone another), we mark other peculiarities with an asterisk. Trifling slips of the pen have been silently corrected but such corrections are listed in a note at the end of the volume. In the case of letters in French, where errors of spelling and accentuation abound, we omit even the asterisks. Both in French and in English, we keep Conrad's erratic but lavish capitalization of personal pronouns as a notable survival of a Polish convention. The capitalization is often obvious in the original, but some borderline cases are a matter of personal judgement; the same holds true of paragraphing, since Conrad sometimes marks what must be intended as a new paragraph by starting a new page or leaving a small gap rather than by indentation. Naturally but unfortunately, not all these conventions can apply to letters whose originals have vanished since such early editors as Garnett and Jean-Aubry saw them.

The dating of Conrad's letters presents occasional problems. Although most of the letters are dated or can be placed by means of content, a few cannot be located by month or even year. Not many postmarked envelopes have survived, and, like James, Conrad did not hold on to his correspondence. Paper, watermarks, and other such clues are almost useless, for Conrad often wrote on whatever scrap of paper was to hand. Changes in handwriting, which prove so helpful in dating Dickens's letters, are useful only when the handwriting indicates illness or a severe attack of gout in the wrist. It is then possible to place the letter during Conrad's more intense periods of suffering, but even this can be self-defeating, because attacks of gout frequently meant sparse correspondence.

As a consequence, some handful or so of letters remains impossible to date, but these are usually brief pieces of correspondence without significant content. These letters are grouped either at the end of a volume marking a particular period, or at the conclusion of the entire edition under correspondent, and left undated. If dated, letters to unknown correspondents are placed in chronological order; if undated, they also appear at the end of a volume. It should be noted that Conrad used the *English* system of all-figure dating, in which (for example) '6.5.1890' means '6 May 1890'. In the notes, the reader will find some dates in both Gregorian (Western) and Julian (Russian) forms. Thus 12 December in the Julian calendar would be 24 December in the Gregorian.

The annotations have been kept as brief as is consistent with making the material accessible to both the intelligent general reader and the specialist. Correspondents are described on the first occurrence of their names and in a separate list. There is, of course, some duplication and cross-referring, since the reader is not expected to absorb the text chronologically or systematically. Annotations are repeated as necessary, both for names and for events. The aim of the edition, throughout, has been to furnish texts and notes useful to the scholar which, at the same time, do not discourage the general reader.

Frederick R. Karl

New York University

INTRODUCTION TO VOLUME ONE

Alas! I have been too far East where not many cultivate the virtue of reticence. (Conrad to E. L. Sanderson, 26 March 1897.)

In a letter which appears in this volume, Conrad tells A. T. Quiller-Couch that 'Writing in a solitude almost as great as that of the ship at sea the great living crowd outside is somehow forgotten; just as on a long, long passage the existence of continents peopled by men seems to pass out of the domain of facts' (23 December 1897). Wherever we turn in Conrad's life, his fiction and his letters, we find solitude: the eleven-year-old boy in Cracow, walking at the head of his father's funeral cortege; the captain whose Cain-like double lurks below decks; Yanko Goorall amongst the uncomprehending villagers; Józef Teodor Konrad Korzeniowski, the only Polish officer in the British Merchant Navy; Decoud, burdened with revolutionary gold, growing quietly desperate on his island; Joseph Conrad, sitting at his desk with a reputation as a writer's writer and the stack of blank paper in front of him that should have been turning into *Nostromo* but was not. Yet we associate Conrad with such scenes because he spent so much time in telling other people about them in essays, short stories, novels and letters. In Conrad, moreover, solitude is framed by a community of some sort – of mariners, Poles, conspirators, relations, scoundrels, fellow-writers.

But Conrad owes his reputation as a connoisseur of loneliness to the constant shifting of those frames, these communities, in his work as in his life. In the same letter to Quiller-Couch, he observes of *The Nigger of the 'Narcissus'*:

It does not belong to the writing period of my life. It belongs to the time when I also went in and out of the Channel and got my bread from the sea, when I loved it and cursed it. Odi et amo—what does the fellow say?—I was always a deplorable schoolboy.

Here, three aspects of his life converge: he writes as author, as sailor and, an adult remembering his studies in a language that represents the westward aspirations of his people, as Pole.

The reader will find an outline of the crucial events in Conrad's first forty years between pages xx and xxvi. Although the details may confuse, the basic patterns stand out clearly. Late in 1857, Józef Teodor Konrad Korzeniowski[1] was born to parents active on the left wing of Polish nationalism. For his clandestine operations against the Russian occupiers, the father was imprisoned and, along with his family, exiled to northern Russia. At the age of seven, Conrad lost his mother; at the age of eleven, his father. Under a succession of guardians, he spent his adolescence partly in the Russian-dominated Ukraine, partly in Austrian-administered Cracow. Pushed by the threat of twenty years' conscription in the Czar's army and the apparent hopelessness of the Polish situation, pulled by a romantic and literary attraction towards the unknown, and very much against the inclinations of his relatives, Conrad decided to go to sea. Between voyages to the Caribbean, he passed the years from 1874 to 1878 in Marseilles. There he flirted with legitimist politics, perhaps (although the evidence cannot be trusted) even running guns for the Carlist insurgents in Spain. The Marseilles period ended in thwarted love, financial crisis, and a botched attempt at suicide.

At that inauspicious point in Conrad's life, he began his service on British ships, a service that, interrupted only by shore-leaves and the four wretched months in the Congo, lasted for fifteen years. Studying his way through the various examinations for ship's officer – second mate's ticket in 1880, first mate's in 1884, master's in 1886 – he worked under sail and steam, with passengers and cargo: an ordinary seaman on the *Mavis, Skimmer of the Sea, Duke of Sutherland* and *Europa*; third mate on the *Loch Etive*; second mate on the *Palestine, Riversdale, Narcissus* and *Tilkhurst*; first mate on the *Highland Forest, Vidar* and *Torrens*; commander of the *Otago*. His voyages took him to India, Malaya, Thailand, Java, Borneo, Australia, Mauritius and Cape Colony.

At the end of the 1880s, the pattern of his life shifted once more. Already he had written a short story and started using Conrad as a surname. In 1889 he began *Almayer's Folly*, his first novel, seeded by his travels in the waters around Borneo. Also in 1889, he visited Poland for the first time in sixteen years and, in Belgium, negotiated an appointment in what was known, utterly inappropriately, as the Congo Free State. His experiences there, the raw material for 'Heart of Darkness', made him sick in body and at heart. *Almayer* was completed in 1894; in the previous year, Conrad had made his last voyage as a professional

---

[1] Commemorating the hero of two patriotic poems by Mickiewicz, the name Konrad was to function both as Christian name and – in anglicized form – as surname. In boyhood, he was often called Konrad rather than Józef (see the first letter from his uncle, Najder, p. 35); in the late 1880s, he started to call himself Conrad rather than Korzeniowski. To avoid confusion, we shall simply call him Conrad from now on.

sailor. Although from time to time he talked about returning to the sea, he only did so as a weekend yachtsman with his friend G. F. W. Hope; the transition from mariner to author had, in one sense, been achieved. In another sense, however, the pen never completely displaced the compass. Conrad, to the end of his days, could own to a multiple identity.

Anyone in search of biographical news of Conrad will be tantalized by mysterious and infuriating gaps in this first volume. It embraces more than half of Conrad's life, starting in 1861 with a note in Polish from a child of three-and-a-half not yet able to manage an unaided pen, and winding up at the end of 1897 with season's greetings to a fellow-Pole, written in French by an author, master-mariner and exile just turned forty. In between, we have letters from Singapore, Calcutta, Cape Town, a country estate in the Ukraine, a pension at a genteel Swiss health resort, the headmaster's house at a boys' preparatory school, a wool and grain port in South Australia, the S.S. *Adowa* interminably confined to a Norman dock, lodgings in Pimlico, a Thames-side warehouse, a granite island off the Breton coast, the Congolese settlement of Kinshasa, and Ivy Walls Farm, near Stanford-le-Hope in Essex. Both in time and space, the range of the first volume is, then, considerably broader than that of the volumes which follow.

But the gaps are broader too. We have nothing from Conrad's adolescence, nothing from his turbulent sojourn in Marseilles, nothing from his earliest years in the Merchant Navy. Such absences must be, to some extent, the result of actual losses, brought about by war and revolution, fire and water, the discretion or the indifference of succeeding generations. Poland has not been the ideal location for family archives. We cannot, however, assume that an abundance of letters from the silent years existed in the first place. Duty, perhaps fondness, and certainly the need for moral and financial support, made Conrad during his time of wandering stay in contact with his guardian and uncle, Tadeusz Bobrowski; in a situation quite the opposite of what prevails elsewhere in his correspondence, the letters *to* Conrad have survived, but not the letters from him. Since this is the only correspondence that we can be sure of Conrad's having conducted in that period, the loss is particularly heavy. But even if it had been temperamentally congenial – we possess no evidence that it was – letter-writing on a large scale and to a plethora of recipients would have been extremely difficult during the years at sea, and especially during that portion of those years spent under sail.

Entirely at the mercy of the weather, the erratic schedule of a sailing ship at sea for months on end does not exactly encourage the exchange of affections or ideas by post. Under such circumstances, letter-writing would be as frustrating as a game of blindfold tennis. We cannot be sure that, until he discovered the epistolary possibilities of his honorary aunt and fellow-spirit, Marguerite Poradowska, Conrad knew or liked anyone but Tadeusz Bobrowski well enough to try a serious and prolonged correspondence. Close friendships were to be the luxury and consolation of his life on shore.

Thanks to the Poradowska correspondence (conducted in French) and a small but important batch of letters to Spiridion Kliszczewski (the earliest surviving letters in English), Conrad's last years at sea are quite extensively represented in this first volume. Once Conrad, having left the sea for good, has endured the completion of *Almayer*, the list of correpondents grows very rapidly. Among the most striking groups, we find those to E. L. Sanderson and Helen Watson, Edward Garnett, R. B. Cunninghame Graham, T. Fisher Unwin, William Blackwood and the Briquel family. Many of these letters are either unpublished – for example, some of those to Sanderson, virtually all of those to Unwin – or, as in the case of the flattering but revealing exchange with the Briquels, published in journals inaccessible to the general reader. Not every friendship that began before the end of 1897 is represented in Volume One. For instance, nothing to G. F. W. Hope has come to light, but since he and Conrad spent so much time together, especially after the move to Stanford-le-Hope, nothing much can have needed putting on paper. The courtship of Jessie George, whom Conrad married in 1896, appears only in comments to others. What does appear here is the record of friendships and professional relationships that, whether because of physical distance or because of emotional and intellectual complexity, did need the written word.

Conrad wrote to Marguerite Poradowska from the ends of the earth, and his letters to her covered the period of his metamorphosis from sailor to writer. She herself was no stranger to ambiguous states or liminal conditions. Simultaneously she belonged to the stuffy world of the French and Belgian *haute bourgeoisie* – one thinks of the clutter of heavy furniture and ideas that entombs Kurtz's Intended – and to the freer, more bohemian world of literature. An independent widow with her own career, she was yet entitled to the privileges, and hobbled by the expectations, of nineteenth-century chivalry. Her family was rooted in France and Belgium; her marriage had made her Polish by affinity and

Austrian by nationality. Her husband (who died soon after the correspondence began) was Conrad's cousin, and nominally she was Conrad's aunt. Nevertheless, the true kinship was intellectual, artistic, and perhaps romantic. Conrad fell into a friendship with a person who was witty, intelligent, well-read, understanding, experienced in the ways of exile – and published. Because her books, although well received in the France of her day, are hard to come by in the English-speaking world (neither the British Library nor the Library of Congress can muster more than token representation), one might easily forget that in the early 1890s, she was the author and her 'nephew' the apprentice. 'Chère Maitre', Conrad calls her when he suggests they publish *Almayer* as a collaboration (30[?] July 1894), a phrase he was later to use to Henry James. The breadth and sophistication of her sympathies and interests made her an excellent confidante. Writing from the Congo, for instance, Conrad freely confessed his disillusionment, unabashed by the fact that Mme Poradowska had helped to get him there:

Decidement je regrette d'etre venu ici. Je le regrette même amèrement. Avec tout l'egoisme d'un homme je vais parler de moi. Je ne peux pas m'en empêcher. Devant qui soulagerai-je mon cœur si ce n'est devant Vous?! (26 September 1890)

The tone of his letters ranges from soulful (22 October 1891) to manically comic; he would even write to her when drunk (7 January 1894). The confidences, however, did not all move in the same direction. Conrad often rallied his friend's spirits or denounced the scheming relatives who gave her no peace; she too must have been confiding in him. In this exchange of feelings there is much affection, a hint of passions kept on the rein, and a dash of flirtatiousness. The situation between the two of them was intellectually, artistically, and emotionally stimulating–and more than a little piquant.

Two other groups of letters in French need special notice: those to the Briquel family and those to Janina de Brunnow. Janina de Brunnow was a boyhood friend who re-established contact in 1897. Whether or not she was the 'first love' recalled in the Author's Note to *Nostromo*, Conrad obviously regarded her with a good deal of affection mixed with curiosity about her present condition (19 August). It was with the air of someone coming to the point at once, because so much time has already gone by, that he gave her a seemingly unguarded estimate of his ambitions as a writer (2 October). Conrad drew a rather different picture of himself as writer in his dealings with the Briquel family. He met them in 1895 when they were staying at a Swiss pension. Émilie was twenty and Paul seventeen; as great admirers of literature, they had no aversion to meeting a freshly published author whose manner was courtly and appearance distinguished. Émilie showed a pleasing enthusiasm for *Almayer* and even wanted to translate it; Conrad responded in a tone that ranged from spirituality to banter:

Et si le Maître de nos âmes, le Maître Miséricordieux et Clément veut bien entendre la voix d'un solitaire et aveugle pécheur, il vous donnera de longues années paisibles et douces. (29 December 1895)

Bien fait! le billard! Vous n'avez pas dit qui gagne aux dominos. Donc vous perdez? Pas vrai? Eh? (10 June 1895)

To Paul, however, the tone is unmitigatedly solemn:

Vous avez lu bien des livres. Moi, je n'ai lu que la grande page, la page, énorme, monotone et remplie d'une vie passée tout en dehors de moi dans l'oubli de l'individualité, au contact avec les forces mystérieuses et variées qui bataillent contre notre volonté. Et voilà! Je conclus que c'est là la seule possibilité du bonheur. Dans la tâche accomplie, dans l'obstacle vaincu, n'importe quelle tâche, n'importe quel obstacle; là est le vrai refuge de l'homme fourvoyé sur cette terre, car la raison est faible, et courte, et la volonté est éternelle et forte. (Before 3 July 1895)

A fine display of attitudes, one might think: eloquent, experienced, and glib—a performance calculated to inspire a young man who has a yearning for knowledge and an attractive sister. If, however, one discounts Conrad's improbable claim that he has neither read very much nor given much attention to matters of the self, what remains is the expression of a typically Conradian wish: the desire to find oblivion in work. The style and not the subject makes this passage sound contrived. Even at his most opulent, he does not forget his fundamental obsessions. Indeed, according to the letter to Émilie of 14 July, in writing to her brother, Conrad was simply carried away by his own ideas.

The early letters to Spiridion Kliszczewski would be noteworthy even if they did not belong to a period (the 1880s) from which very little else has been saved. They have an extra fascination as the oldest surviving specimens of Conrad's English. The son of a Polish émigré, Kliszczewski (or Joseph Spiridion, as he was also known) lived in Cardiff. Although Conrad sailed under her flag, his experience of shore life in Great Britain had been mostly, though not exclusively, gained in sailors' hostels and lodging-houses. As a financially comfortable family man very much at home in the new country, in more ways than one Kliszczewski provided the uprooted sailor with an example of successful domestication. Besides offering business advice and hospitality, he seems to have counselled making the best of exile: 'I agree with you that in a free and hospitable land even the most persecuted of our race may find relative peace and a certain amount of happiness,' Conrad told him, characteristically adding 'materially at least' (13 October 1885). Kliszczewski also supplied newspapers and political comment, both of a conservative disposition. Conrad replied in kind with a jeremiad on the General Election of 1885 that has more to do with denouncing 'the newly enfranchised idiots' than it does with the actual results. With its curious assumption that Joseph Chamberlain, who would shortly desert the Liberals for the Conservatives, is a leftist stooge, it suggests that at that stage Conrad knew the language of England better than her politics. A virulent letter, it advocates coolness and resignation in white-hot terms:

I look with the serenity of despair and the indifference of contempt upon the passing events. Disestablishment, Land Reform, Universal Brotherhood are but like milestones on the road to ruin. The end will be awful, no doubt! (19 December 1885)

In the scornful but passionate denunciation of political passions (Conrad's father, incidentally, had crusaded for land reform), this letter anticipates the political Conrad of *Nostromo*, *The Secret Agent*, *The Nigger of the 'Narcissus'* and the letters to Cunninghame Graham.

Only five of the eighty-one known letters to R. B. Cunninghame Graham appear in this volume, and they all date from the second half of 1897. By the end of that year, however, Conrad has already achieved the intensity of argument that characterizes their correspondence as a whole. On 14 December he envisages self-consciousness as the curse of the thinking classes; on 20 December he compares the universe with a machine that can be neither adjusted nor stopped. With their sense that the world is essentially an inescapable but meaningless nightmare, these ideas express Conrad's darkest metaphysical fears. They are also designed to persuade Graham, a Socialist who had quoted Marx in Parliament and gone to gaol for defying a ban on demonstrations in Trafalgar Square, of the error of his ways: 'You are a most hopeless idealist—your aspirations are irrealisable. You want from men faith, honour, fidelity to truth in themselves and others' (20 December 1897).

Why should Conrad have bothered with this broadcaster of Socialist beliefs, beliefs that he had once assured Kliszczewski (19 December 1885) were 'infernal doctrines born in continental back-slums'? The pleasure of hearing from a notorious character aside, Conrad may have realized that in many ways Graham bore a close resemblance to himself. Graham was an aristocrat who had grown up on a large but impoverished estate; his father's behaviour had jeopardized the family's well-being; his travels (in Africa and the Americas) and his mixed ancestry (Scottish and Spanish) had given him a view of Britain from the outside and sharpened his sense of irony; in his writing, he evoked the memory of personal experience and described a vanishing way of life on the pampas even as Conrad described the declining years of sail. Thus Graham could not be accused of innocence; unlike the good professional men who hear Marlow's African tale, his mind was not 'sedentary'. Clearly he was worth arguing with. Furthermore, Conrad himself knew the desire for 'faith, honour, fidelity to truth', and he may have recognized that behind both his despair and Graham's pursuit of the possible lay the same potentially debilitating scepticism and the same desire to force meaning out of moral and epistemological chaos.

Although intimate, the letters to Ted Sanderson are not so strenuous. When Sanderson and his companion John Galsworthy met Conrad in 1893, Conrad was first mate of the *Torrens*. The *Torrens*, one of the last clippers to carry passengers, was much favoured by convalescents, Sanderson among them, who needed a long sea-voyage. An elder-brotherly solicitude for his physical and mental health continued to figure in Conrad's feelings about him: 'It seems to me You are facing just now a lot of worries and are thinking of lifting a tolerable sack-full of work ... It is more manful to recognise one's own limitations than to ignore them' (16 February [1897]). By invoking the desire to be 'manful', Conrad made a shrewd appeal to his friend's sensibilities. Sanderson taught in an Anglican preparatory school, and he showed every sign of accepting the imperative of duty, loyalty, and service to Queen and country. Unfortunately for him, however, his health and his bouts of depression did not always allow him to pursue these ideals as heartily as he would have liked. The affectionate letters to him and to his fiancée, Helen Watson, reveal a tactful awareness of the problem. Conrad puts up with their idealism much more quietly than he does Cunninghame Graham's, perhaps because the idealism is not so threatened by scepticism, and because the ideals in question are closer to his own conservative instincts. He could most easily contemplate fidelity and solidarity – his two favourite abstractions – in the context of a hierarchical society where captains and headmasters could take their proper place. The warmth and the profuseness of the letters to Ted Sanderson and Helen Watson come from the pleasure of finding true and uncorrupted believers.

Sanderson and Garnett shared a susceptibility to depression and a fondness for reading and writing poetry, but not much else. To Sanderson, Conrad expressed his sense of place and order; to Garnett, an anarchist by temperament, a cynic by experience, and a talented man surviving precariously on the economic margin of society, he expressed his sense of disorientation. When Conrad was most troubled by the isolation that writing entailed and most bewildered by sensations of unreality, he turned to Garnett: 'I feel like a man who can't move, in a dream. To move is vital – it's salvation – and I can't! I feel what you mean and I am utterly powerless to imagine anything else' (8 October 1897). Garnett was the secret patron of modern literature; scores of writers from Robert Frost to D. H. Lawrence enjoyed the benefit of his sympathy, encouragement and painstaking criticism. As a publisher's reader, he took the side of the author rather than the employer. In his gently persuasive way, he helped Conrad to develop a sense of fiction as a calling without neglecting such day-to-day aspects of survival as contracts, proofs, and deadlines. Conrad's letters suggest that Garnett perfectly understood the welter of high aims and low necessities through which the novelist was floundering:

The progressive episodes of the story *will* not emerge from the chaos of my sensations. I feel nothing clearly. And I am frightened when I remember that I have to drag it all out of myself. (19 June 1896)

I haven't got the cheque (how pretty the word looks!) but I shall no doubt receive it tonight or to morrow. (12 March [1897])

The exchanges did not, however, always involve Garnett as doctor and Conrad as patient. Sometimes they reversed the roles. Garnett wanted criticism of his prose poems, and Conrad supplied it, carefully and tactfully. Garnett's gift to Conrad was to take him seriously as a writer and yet not overwhelm him with excessive praise or blame; part of that taking seriously was to consult him as literary authority as well as friend.

The correspondence with his publishers, T. Fisher Unwin and William Blackwood, has much to say about pounds, shillings and pence, but Conrad does not restrict himself to matters of pure business. Primed in advance by Garnett (see, for instance, the letters of 16 and [25]

October 1896), Conrad negotiates rights, royalties and advances with a confident air. Even before Garnett has come to his aid, Conrad's delightful inquiry about the fate of *Almayer* ('put between *two* detached sheets of cardboard': 8 September 1894) shows a certain panache in his dealings with the house of Fisher Unwin. Since Unwin was a self-satisfied Liberal with no great reputation for liberality, some of Conrad's flourishes of artistic and philosophical principle look suspiciously like gestures of defiance against his publisher's parsimonious complacency: 'Bad or good I cannot be ashamed of what is produced in perfect single mindedness' (22 July 1896); 'Our captivity within the incomprehensible logic of accident is the only fact of the universe' (22 August 1896). Working with Blackwood seemed more congenial. The family once broke a printers' strike by running the presses themselves, but William Blackwood could afford to treat his authors generously, even encouraging Conrad to make changes when a story was in proof (Blackburn, pp. 20, 7). Echoing David Meldrum, his sagacious literary adviser, Blackwood had enthusiastic praise for Conrad's work. Nevertheless, the general amiability did not put Conrad's critical independence to sleep. When *Blackwood's Magazine* published a review article which deplored, in passing, 'bloodthirsty ruffians' who sought asylum in Great Britain and 'dirty rascals' who enlisted naïve young men in revolutionary causes, Conrad objected politely but firmly:

Here and there I would take exception to a phrase—to the phrase rather than to the thought. Not every man who "waved a cap of liberty on a pike" was a scoundrel. And England had not only given refuge to criminals . . . the ideas (that live) should be combatted, not the men who die. (29 October 1897)

One ought, in other words, to hate the political sin and not the sinner. As the son of a revolutionary and as a refugee himself, Conrad could hardly accept *Maga*'s high-Tory position. As a letter-writer, he could be tactful but never sycophantic, partisan but never willing to distort the truth as he saw it.

A full account of Volume One would linger over the significance of many other letters. There is, for example, the affable set to the Polish cousins Maria Tyszkowa and the Zagórskis, which includes a very amusing description (to Karol Zagórski, 10 March 1896) of his plans for marriage. Then there are the first, extremely respectful, approaches to Henry James and the beginnings of correspondences with Crane and Wells that will figure much more prominently in later volumes. Moreover, as a striking letter ([17 June 1895]) to Edward Noble bears out, the reader in search of Conrad's comments on his art should not look only for the famous recipients. But although so many other letters deserve attention, a more detailed examination probably would not change the overall picture.

To see letters grouped by recipient (as in Cedric Watts's stimulating and scholarly edition of the letters to Cunninghame Graham) certainly gives one a feeling for the nature and continuity of particular friendships. The pleasures of a collected edition differ in kind. Reading such an edition, one is conscious, above all, of the range of personalities at Conrad's disposal. While remaining essentially Conrad, he seems to reshape himself for each correspondent: subversively cynical for Garnett; sympathetic, encouraging, upright, rather respectable for Ted Sanderson and Helen Watson; soulful for the Briquels; Byronic for Marguerite Poradowska; provocatively nihilistic for Cunninghame Graham; fussily professional for Unwin; good-natured for the Polish cousins; frank for Janina de Brunnow. In these letters, often so personal, yet so much of a performance, an impersonation, we hear not one but many voices.

It is hardly startling to find that a letter-writer modulates his tone to suit the varied interests of his correspondents. Who does not? Sooner or later, courtesy (not to mention guile) makes impersonators of us all. What stands out in Conrad's case is not the fact of his making such adjustments but their extent both in range and in intensity. The personality that informs the letters of, say, D. H. Lawrence feels clearer, more consistent, easier to define; the same is true of Dickens, Virginia Woolf, Byron, or even the suave Henry James.

Suavity, however, is not the point, or not the only point. Admittedly, Conrad's ceremonious politeness colours the whole correspondence. It is the expression both of a Polish gentleman's loyalty to the code of his ancestors and of a ship's officer's conviction that everything must be done in the proper way. For example, he writes to T. Fisher Unwin, the Enlightened Patron of Letters frequently derided in the Garnett correspondence: 'Really Your kindness is unwearied showing itself in great things and in little things with quite a rounded perfection of friendliness which I have done nothing to deserve' (14 August 1896). So intense, in fact, is Conrad's manifest desire to put his reader at ease that it must sometimes have achieved the opposite effect. Nevertheless, he was by no means always on his best behaviour. Even with Unwin, he would sometime plays the fool, as he does in the letter of 12 March 1895, with a 'frivolity of expression' that 'disguises very deep feelings'.

A vigorous willingness to talk about himself often breaks into the correspondence; the corollary of his voluble civility is an equally voluble candour.

Having read the letters in Jean-Aubry's collection, Garnett, the best authority possible, recalled that

It needed a fine ear to seize the blended shades of friendly derision, flattery, self-depreciation, sardonic criticism and affection in his tone. And so with the early letters, many of which show a wonderful chameleon-like quality, sometimes both parodying his own admissions and turning the light of his irony from himself on to his correspondent. (Garnett, p. 20)

Irony at the correspondent's expense may or may not be designed for recognition. When Conrad does design it, the intended reader is normally an intimate who can be trusted to hear the fine harmonics. One therefore expects, and usually finds, more subtlety in a letter to Garnett than in one to Unwin. A common-sense explanation of Conrad's 'wonderful chameleon-like quality' would indeed put it down to the unastonishing circumstance of knowing some people better than others.

Yet unfamiliarity did not stop Conrad from giving a reviewer an especially revealing description of *The Nigger of the 'Narcissus'* (9 December 1897). What is more, the contrasts of thought and tone shine out most strikingly in the letters to good friends:

Only the other day I've re-read Miss Helen's letter—*the letter* to me. It is laid away with some of my very particular papers. It is so unaffectedly, so irresistibly charming—and profound too. One seems almost to touch the ideal conception of what's best in life. And—personally—those eight pages of Her writing are to me like a high assurance of being accepted, admitted within, the people and the land of my choice. And side by side with the letter I found the printed paper signed by the Secretary of State. The form of nationalisation and its reality—the voice of what is best in the heart of people. (to Ted Sanderson, 26 March [1897])

No man can escape his fate! You shall come here and suffer hardships, boredom and despair. It is written! It is written! You—as a matter of fact— have written it yourself (at my instigation—very rash of you) and I shall be inexorable like destiny and shall look upon your sufferings with the idiotic serenity of a benevolent Creator ... looking at the precious mess he has made of his only job. (to R. B. Cunninghame Graham, 6 December 1897)

These passages mirror writer and recipient alike. One can see Sanderson in them, and Cunninghame Graham too: the idealistic schoolmaster, proud of his fiancée, proud of being British, and the far-travelled, combative Scot who jests about theology but dearly loves a phrase from the Koran.

Saying that one correspondent or another brings out the *real* Conrad raises certain difficulties. One has to beware of conjuring up imaginary hierarchies of friendship; they are flimsy constructions at best, for they are put together in ignorance of what does not appear on paper – the silence between words, the unrecorded conversations, the ebb and flow of intimacy. One should also beware of assuming that one kind of friendly candour must inevitably be franker than another. Although a late-twentieth-century sensibility may regard the authentic Conrad as an exile adrift in a universe where God is sitting on His hands, there is absolutely no way of being sure. What seems to the modern reader the richest ore may not come from the very bottom of the mine. To give priority in a description of the letters to scepticism over belief, nihilism over a sense of moral order, alienation over a sense of destiny shared with the rest of humanity is more an act of preference than one of total comprehension.

Paralysis and action, solidarity and loneliness, damning illusions and saving illusions, compassion and detachment, futility and usefulness, assurance and despair: in a gathering of the correspondence, or even in individual letters, these antinomies become as visible as they are in the fiction. To the extent that they mask or suppress one aspect or another of Conrad's self, the letters could be considered miniature fictions in themselves, and the early correspondence a series of rehearsals for his performance as a novelist. But thinking of them in that way obscures the character of his writing. When the concept of fiction is used as loosely as has been the case in recent years it is time to find a more discriminating word.

The letters are, in the sense in which Montaigne coined the word, *essays*: trials, explorations, a writer's attempts at understanding his medium and his circumstances. Of course that is not to deny their function as messages: 'How kind you were to write!' 'Thank you for admiring my book.' 'What do you think of this wretched government?' 'Could you, perhaps, lend me five pounds?' Even a brief sampling of this first volume should, however, suggest that something more is involved. The 'something more' undoubtedly includes an element of mystification and concealment, of manoeuvring to preserve Conrad's private territory, and it also includes a great deal of personal revelation. In either case, writing letters gave Conrad a chance to experiment with words and with ideas. Indeed, the distinction between trying on a mask and discovering lost fragments of character becomes hard to maintain, and so the difference between impersonation and self-examination does not finally matter. Both exposure and disguise opened up the possibilities of language.

As he expressed it in a letter to Garnett, Conrad's own sense of identity was decidedly fluid:

When once the truth is grasped that one's own personality is only a ridiculous and aimless masquerade of something hopelessly unknown the attainment of serenity is not very far off. Then there remains nothing but the surrender to one's impulses, the fidelity to passing emotions which is perhaps a nearer approach to truth than any other philosophy of life. (23 March 1896)

These words anticipate several of Conrad's statements about art, among them the Preface to *The Nigger of the 'Narcissus'* and the comments in the Author's Note to *Within the Tides*, about 'scrupulous fidelity to the truth of my own sensations'. But, as their laboriously worked and reworked manuscripts attest, the novels and short stories came with much greater difficulty than the letters. In the correspondence, unhampered by demands of character and entanglements of plot, he could more easily achieve a match of words to feelings and ideas. This convergence of language, intellectual vigour and emotion he brought about in a form that has the spontaneity of a journal without its solipsism. To return to the notion that began this preface, one might say that Conrad's great subject is communicated solitude. 'I'm hanged if I can be mute,' he wrote to Garnett, his 'dear encourager', on 22 February 1896. 'I will not hold my tongue! What is life worth if one can not jabber to one['s] heart's content?'

Laurence Davies

Dartmouth College

CONRAD'S CORRESPONDENTS
1861–1897

William BLACKWOOD (1836–1912), editor of *Blackwood's Magazine* ('Maga'), was head of the Edinburgh publishing house and publisher of some of Conrad's early work, including 'Karain', 'Youth', 'Heart of Darkness', and *Lord Jim*. Conrad's relationship with the firm began in summer 1897 and ended in winter 1903, from the period of *The Nigger of the 'Narcissus'* to work on *Nostromo*.

Maria BOBROWSKA: see TYSZKOWA

THE BRIQUEL family – Madame, her son Paul, her daughter Émilie – became friendly with Conrad when he went to Champel, near Geneva, for hydrotherapy. The Briquels were a bourgeois family from Lunéville in Lorraine. Emilie was twenty at the time of the meeting with Conrad on 2 May 1895; there was, apparently, some romantic attachment between them, broken by her engagement to a local doctor on 10 February 1896.

Minnie BROOKE, a friend of Jane Cobden Unwin, visited the Conrads during their honeymoon. Her husband, the Reverend Arthur Brooke, was the rector of Slingsby in the North Riding of Yorkshire.

Jeanne or Janina de BRUNNOW (née Taube) was a childhood friend of Conrad's. After the death of her father, she and her six brothers and sisters became the wards of Tadeusz Bobrowski, Conrad's uncle and guardian, and Conrad lived in the same building with them in the early 1870s. According to undocumented stories, Conrad was supposedly in love with Janina, and it was she whom he invoked as his 'first love' in the Author's Note to *Nostromo* and in a cancelled opening to *The Arrow of Gold*.

Charles BULS (1837–1914), author of several books on art and a burgomaster of Brussels, was a suitor for Marguerite Poradowska's hand both before her marriage and after her husband's death in 1890.

Stefan BUSZCZYŃSKI (1821–92), a close friend of Apollo Korzeniowski and the one to whom the latter entrusted his manuscripts shortly before his death in 1869, was for a short time the young Conrad's guardian. He was a poet, dramatist, literary critic, journalist and historian. Like Apollo, Buszczyński was a patriot and an opponent of foreign domination of Poland.

W. H. CHESSON was, along with Edward Garnett, a reader at Fisher Unwin when Conrad submitted the manuscript of *Almayer's Folly*. In later years, Chesson came to believe that he, not Garnett, had discovered Conrad. He died in 1953.

Stephen CRANE (1871–1900), the novelist and poet. When he met Conrad in October 1897, Crane was already the author of *Maggie: A Girl of the Streets* (1893) and *The Red Badge of Courage* (1895). Conrad admired Crane's work as that of an impressionist of the highest quality, and when Crane and Cora moved to Ravensbrook, the two families often visited each other.

Constance (Mrs Edward) GARNETT (née Black, 1862–1946) was the well-known translator of Russian literature into English. Conrad admired, particularly, her translations of Turgenev.

Edward GARNETT (1868–1937) was a reader for T. Fisher Unwin, the publisher, when Conrad submitted the manuscript of *Almayer's Folly*. Son of Richard Garnett, biographer and librarian, Garnett and his wife, Constance, lived at the Cearne, near Limpsfield, Surrey, often a gathering place for writers, artists, anarchists, socialists, and Russian émigrés. His early encouragement of Conrad was indicative of his entire career as a discoverer of literary talent and a sensitive critic of literature.

Olivia GARNETT (née Singleton) was the mother of Edward and the wife of Richard Garnett, librarian and man of letters, best known for his work at the British Museum as Keeper of Printed Books. She died in 1903.

Robert Bontine Cunninghame GRAHAM (1852–1936) was a Scottish Laird, a Nationalist and a Socialist. As a young man, he worked and travelled widely in the Americas. From 1886 to 1892 he represented North-West Lanarkshire in Parliament; for his part in the Bloody Sunday demonstration of 1887, he spent four and a half weeks in

Pentonville gaol. A prolific writer of essays, biographies, travel books and short stories, Graham is perhaps best known for *Mogreb-el-Acksa* (1898), *Thirteen Stories* (1900), and *Portrait of a Dictator* (1933). His close and enduring friendship with Conrad began in 1897.

Henry JAMES (1843–1916) was already internationally famous as a novelist and short story writer when Conrad sent him a copy of his second novel, *An Outcast of the Islands*, in October 1896, with a letter–inscription. James, in turn, sent his *The Spoils of Poynton* in February 1897, the exchange of novels beginning the friendship and correspondence.

Spiridion KLISZCZEWSKI (Joseph Spiridion) was the son of Józef Kliszczewski, the Cardiff watchmaker who had emigrated to Britain after the failure of the 1830–1 insurrection in Poland. With their mutual ties to the home country, Conrad became friendly with the entire family, and his extant letters to Kliszczewski appear to be his first in English.

Apollo KORZENIOWSKI (1820–69), Conrad's father, was not only a celebrated patriot and political revolutionary, but a poet and translator of some note as well. He translated Shakespeare and Hugo, among others, into Polish; in 1914, Conrad saw his father's manuscripts in the Jagiellónian Library in Cracow.

Adolf P. KRIEGER was, along with G. F. W. Hope, one of Conrad's first friends in England, the friendship dating back to the early 1880s, when the young seaman stayed in London between voyages. Krieger proved helpful to Conrad in many ways, seeking out positions for him and lending him fairly large sums of money. The friendship began to cool in 1897, apparently over Conrad's indebtedness to Krieger.

Wincenty LUTOSŁAWSKI (1863–1954), was a Polish philosopher and zealous nationalist. He wrote to Conrad while he was studying in London; later he taught in Cracow, Geneva, Lausanne, London, Paris and Wilna, where he held the chair of philosophy from 1919 to 1928. In his work, he attempted to combine Platonism with the belief that Poland is the Messiah among nations. His *The Origin and Growth of Plato's Logic* (Longmans, 1897), published in English, established the chronology of Plato's work. An unstable man, he suffered a number of nervous breakdowns.

George MANSFIELD was a seaman acquaintance of Conrad's.

David S. MELDRUM was a literary adviser in the London office of the firm of William Blackwood, the Edinburgh publishing house, and among the first of those to recognize Conrad's talent as a writer of fiction. He became a partner in the firm in 1903 and retired in 1910. In 1902, he published *The Conquest of Charlotte*.

Edward NEWTON was a director of Methuen, the publishing house with which Conrad had considerable difficulty during his 'middle career'. His father, John Newton, F.R.A.S., had been one of Conrad's tutors for his examination for second mate.

Edward NOBLE was a young seaman friend of Conrad's, just starting out as a writer when their correspondence began in 1895. Noble went on to become the author of many novels, among them *The Edge of Circumstance*, *The Waves of Fate* and *The Lady Navigators*.

Sydney S. PAWLING (1862–1923), a partner of William Heinemann, the publisher, was a sympathetic admirer of Conrad's early work. Pawling acquired *The Nigger of the 'Narcissus'* for Heinemann and tried, unsuccessfully, to place the incomplete *Rescue*.

Marguerite PORADOWSKA (née Marguerite Gachet) of Brussels married Aleksander Poradowski, the first cousin of Conrad's maternal grandmother, and thereafter was referred to by Conrad as 'Aunt', although no blood relationship of course existed. Considered a great beauty, she was much sought after both before her marriage and after Poradowski's death in 1890. By the time Conrad began to correspond with her, in 1890, she was establishing herself as a writer of some small success, with *Yaga* (1887) and *Demoiselle Micia* (1888–9), followed later by *Popes et popadias* (1892), *Marylka* (1895), and several other books. She died in 1937, aged 89.

Aleksander PORADOWSKI (1836–90), the first cousin of Conrad's maternal grandmother, left Poland after the 1863 insurrection against Russia. He lived in exile in Germany and France before moving to Brussels, where he met and married Marguerite Gachet. Before his death in 1890, at the age of fifty-four, Poradowski helped to found a charitable organization for Polish refugees.

Sir Arthur Thomas QUILLER-COUCH (pseudonym 'Q', 1863–1944) a most versatile man of letters, at one time serving as a lecturer in classics, later as an associate editor of the *Speaker*, then after settling in Fowey ('Troy Town') turning out numerous volumes of fiction and other prose. His *The Oxford Book of English Verse* was a standard anthology for many years. Knighted in 1910, he became in 1912 King Edward VII Professor of English Literature at Cambridge.

Edward Lancelot ('Ted') SANDERSON met Conrad when, along with John Galsworthy, he sailed on the *Torrens*, in March 1893, from Adelaide to England. Upon his return, he became Assistant Master at Elstree School, in Hertfordshire, and married Miss Helen Watson in 1898. After service in the Boer War, he remained in Africa, employed in the Transvaal Education Department in Johannesburg and then in Nairobi, returning to England in 1910 as Headmaster of Elstree. He died in 1939.

Katherine SANDERSON, to whom Conrad dedicated *The Mirror of the Sea*, was the mother of 'Ted' Sanderson.

Gustaw SOBOTKIEWICZ was distantly related to the Korzeniowskis on Conrad's paternal side; his friendship with Conrad's uncle Tadeusz Bobrowski lasted for more than half a century.

Joseph SPIRIDION was the anglicized name of Spiridion KLISZCZEWSKI, q.v.

Albert THYS (1849–1915), then Captain and later General, in his role as deputy director of the Société Anonyme Belge pour le Commerce du Haut-Congo, interviewed Conrad in 1889 for a position as the skipper of a steamer, a meeting which led to Conrad's journey to the Congo the following year.

Maria TYSZKOWA (née Bobrowska) was the daughter of Kazimierz Bobrowski and, therefore, Conrad's cousin on his maternal side. She married Teodor Tyszka in 1890.

Jane Cobden UNWIN (1851–1949), active in feminist and Radical causes, was the daughter of Richard Cobden, the apostle of Free Trade. She married T. Fisher Unwin in 1892.

T. Fisher UNWIN (1848–1935) was the publisher of three of Conrad's first four books, *Almayer's Folly* (1895), *An Outcast of the Islands* (1896) and *Tales of Unrest* (1898). With *The Nigger of the 'Narcissus'*, Conrad, already dissatisfied with Unwin's monetary arrangements, moved from Unwin to Heinemann and later to Blackwood.

Helen WATSON was the daughter of the Sheriff-Substitute of Dumfries and Galloway, Scotland, and lived at Corsbie West, Newton Stewart, until she married 'Ted' Sanderson in 1898. Her maternal grandfather was Professor of Moral Philosophy at Edinburgh. Together with her husband, she remained a devoted friend and loyal admirer of Conrad's throughout most of his life.

H. G. WELLS (1866–1946), the well-known novelist, social critic and historian, anonymously reviewed Conrad's *An Outcast of the Islands* in the *Saturday Review*, when he was himself just beginning his career as a writer of scientific romances. Conrad responded to the review and began a friendship and correspondence that lasted for over ten years, until differences of literary attitudes created a division between them. At the height of their friendship, Wells was already turning to social concerns which Conrad considered foolhardy, and Conrad was practising an art which Wells deemed decadent.

Vernon WESTON succeeded his father, J. E. Vernon Weston, as manager of the Sailors' Home, Well (now Ensign) and Dock Streets, London, E.1. In 1886, the elder Weston may have helped Conrad with his naturalization.

Aniela ZAGÓRSKA (née Unrug) was the wife of Karol (Charles) ZAGÓRSKI, Conrad's second cousin once removed and Madame Poradowska's nephew by marriage. The Zagórskis, with their two daughters, Aniela and Karola, lived in Lublin. The younger Aniela was in later years to translate Conrad into Polish, her efforts including *Lord Jim* and *The Mirror of the Sea*.

·

1861

To Apollo Korzeniowski

Text *Kobieta Współczesna* (Lwów, 1931); Najder 205[1]

[23 May 1861]
[Terechowa][2]

Daddy,

I am fine here, I run about the garden—but I don't like it much when the mosquitos bite. As soon as the rain stops I will come to you. Olutek has sent me a beautiful little whip.[3] Please Daddy dear lend me a few pennies and buy something for Olutek in Warsaw.[4]

Have you been to see this Bozia,[5] which Granny [told me about]?[6]

Konrad.

---

[1] Halina Carroll's translations of the Polish letters come, by permission, from Najder.
[2] An estate in the family of Conrad's maternal grandmother, Teofila Bobrowska (née Biberstejn-Pilchowska), who took a great interest in her grandson.
[3] Olutek: unidentified. A picture of Józef holding the whip is reproduced in this volume.
[4] Apollo Korzeniowski (1820–69) was away working for the Red faction of Polish Nationalists, which strove for land reform as well as independence. When his father was in captivity after the uprising against the Russians, Józef wrote on the back of a photograph: 'To my beloved Grandma who helped me send cakes to my poor Daddy in prison—grandson, Pole, Catholic, nobleman—6 July 1863—Konrad' (Najder, p. 8).
[5] 'Little God', a phrase that Polish children apply to divine effigies. According to Najder, Józef probably meant a famous crucifix in Warsaw cathedral.
[6] A conjecture. This little note forms part of a letter from Ewa Korzeniowska to her husband. As he was only three-and-a-half, she guided Józef's hand.

1883

To Stefan Buszczyński

Text MS Cracow; Najder 205

14th August, 1883.
Teplitz [Teplice,
Czechoslovakia].

Dear and Honourable Sir,[1]

We had hoped—Uncle Tadeusz[2] and I—that we would be able to meet you here, in Teplitz; but we have learned upon our arrival of your departure.

Therefore, being unable personally to remind you of myself and to obtain your indulgence for all my faults, I hasten to do it in writing, enclosing my photograph, in the hopes that in memory of the friendship for the father the son will find a friendly remembrance, and for his letter—even after such a long silence—a kind reception.

Although I have been long away from my country and apparently forgetful of those whose favour I once experienced, I have never, in fact, forgotten either the country, the family, or those who were so kind to me—amongst whom I number you, dear Sir, my guardian when I was orphaned, and who amongst them must take the first place.

I, therefore, permit myself to ask you to remember me to dear Kostuś[3]—if I may venture to call him thus. True! I have given him every reason to forget the friendly relations between us in Cracow:—I shall never forget them although they seem so long ago! Perhaps he too will be good enough to remember those old days, and will accept from me my heartfelt good wishes and a friendly embrace.

I am leaving here for London in a few days; from there I do not know where fate will take me. During the last few years—that is since my first examination,[4] I have not been too happy in my journeyings. I was nearly drowned, nearly got burned,[5] but generally my health is good, I am not short of courage or of the will to work or of love for my profession; and I always remember what you said when I was leaving Cracow:

---

[1] Stefan Buszczyński (1821–92), a Polish patriot who had been a close friend and the literary executor of Apollo Korzeniowski. When Apollo died in 1869, Buszczyński became Józef's guardian for a short time.

[2] Tadeusz Bobrowski (1829–94), Conrad's maternal uncle, guardian and benefactor. They were spending a month at health resorts in what is now Czechoslovakia.

[3] Stefan Buszczyński's son Konstanty, who was one year older than Conrad.

[4] For second mate, on 1 June 1880.

[5] Conrad's wretched stint as second mate of the *Palestine* culminated when her cargo of coal caught fire off Sumatra; on 14 March, 1883, the crew had to abandon ship. This incident made the basis of 'Youth'.

'Remember'—you said—'wherever you may sail you are sailing towards Poland!'

That I have never forgotten, and never will forget!

In the hope that my sins will be forgiven me, and commending myself to your kind memory, I remain, with affection, gratitude, and the highest regards,

Your humble servant,
Konrad N. Korzeniowski.

1885

To Spiridion Kliszczewski

Text MS Yale; J–A, I, 79

27th September 1885.
Ship *Tilkhurst*[1]
Singapore.

Dear Sir.

According to Your kindly expressed wish and my promise I hasten to acquaint you with my safe arrival here.—

This globe accomplished almost half a revolution since I parted from you in the station at Cardiff: and old Father Time always diligent in his business has put his eraser over many men, things and memories; yet I defy him to obliterate ever from my mind and heart the recollection of kindness you and yours have shown to a stranger, on the strenght[2] of a distant national connection. I fear I have not expressed adequately to your wife and yourself all my gratitude; I do not pretend to do so now, for in my case when the heart is full the words are scarce, and the more so the more intense is the feeling I wish to express.

I am in hopes of receiving a letter from You some time next month. Besides a natural desire to be assured of Your and Your family's welfare I await with anxiety the news of your Father's health.[3] We had a very fine passage, and my health is comparatively good.

Not wishing to take up more of your valuable time I shall bring this letter to a close, reserving any further intelligence that may be worth communicating for my next—In answer to yours—I hope.—

My compliments to Mme Kliszczewska and a hearty handshake all round for the boys.—Believe me my dear Sir

Yours Gratefully and faithfully,
Conrad N. Korzeniowski

---

[1] Conrad served on the *Tilkhurst*, as second mate, from 24 April 1885 to 17 June 1886, sailing from Hull to Singapore and Calcutta.

[2] Conrad was always to have trouble with the *th* sound in such words as 'strength' and 'length'.

[3] Spiridion's father, Józef Kliszczewski, had settled in Cardiff after the 1830–1 Polish insurrection and established himself as a watchmaker. Conrad met the Kliszczewskis in the following manner: since the *Tilkhurst* was to call at Penarth, near Cardiff, Wales, for a cargo of coal, Conrad was asked by a Polish sailor named Komorowski to repay a small loan to the elder Kliszczewski; this led to the friendship and to what probably were, apart from his response to an advertisement in the *Evening Standard* for a seaman's berth, Conrad's first attempts at letter-writing in English. Although Conrad often addressed envelopes to 'Mr. J. Spiridion', Kliszczewski preferred to use his Polish surname (information from his grand-daughter).

11

To Spiridion Kliszczewski

Text   MS Williams; J–A, 1, 80

13th Oct^{er} 1885.
Singapore—

My Dear Sir.

I need not tell you with what great pleasure I received Your kind and friendly letter. I am exceedingly glad to know that your father, Yourself, and your family are all well—and that Your holiday was a success.—

I also gratefully acknowledge the receipt of the "Daily Telegraph." The Liberal gov^t was defeated on the budget vote a day or so before our departure from Penarth; as soon as we arrived here I looked anxiously t[h]rough the papers expecting great things.[1] Although somewhat disappointed, I saw with pleasure the evidence of improved relations with Germany; the only Power with whom an Anti-Russian alliance would be useful—and even possible—for Great Britain.—No wonder that in this unsettled state of affairs politics—at least foreign politics—are slightly dull. Events are casting shadows—more or less distorted—shadows deep enough to suggest the lurid light of battlefields somewhere in the near future, but all those portents of great and decisive doings leave me in a state of despairing indifference; for, whatever may be the changes in the fortunes of living nations, for the dead there is no hope and no salvation! We have passed t[h]rough the gates where "lasciate ogni speranza"[2] is written in letters of blood and fire, and now the gate is shut on the light of hope[3] and nothing remains for us but the darkness of oblivion. In the presence of such national misfortune, personal happiness is impossible in its absolute form of general contentment and peace of heart. Yet I agree with you that in a free and hospitable land even the most persecuted of our race may find relative peace and a certain amount of happiness—materially at least; consequently I understood and readily accepted your reference to "Home." When speaking, writing or thinking in English the word Home always means for me the hospitable shores of Great Britain.—

We are almost discharged but our loading port is as yet uncertain. At any rate I hope to be in England some time in July, when You may depend—I shall gladly avail myself of your kindness and run down to

[1] On a Conservative amendment to the Budget, Gladstone's government was defeated early in the morning of 9 June, but a general election could not be held until November. Conrad was hoping for a Conservative victory.
[2] 'Abandon all hope [you who enter here]': words inscribed on the gates of Dante's Hell (*Inferno*, III, 9).
[3] Jean-Aubry omitted 'and now the gate is shut on the light of hope'.

Cardiff to see You all. As soon as my exam: is over I shall be at liberty.[1] I had a letter from my uncle, but he does not say if we could arrange an interview in Germany next year as we contemplated.—

Accept a hearty handshake with many thanks for your kindness, and believe me my dear Sir,

Yours very faithfully,

Conrad N. Korzeniowski

To your father my dutiful respects. I am so glad to hear of His better health. My compliments for Mme Kliszczewska and greetings for the boys.—

We are ordered to Calcutta. Agents: Finlay, Muir and C° We leave in 10 days and shall arrive there about end Nov^er

To Spiridion Kliszczewski

Text MS Berg; J–A, I, 81

25th Nov^er. [1885]

Calcutta

My dear Sir

The second number of the "Standard" came to hand yesterday via Singapore.[2] I suppose You are now in receipt of my second letter from Sing: advising You of our departure for this place, where we arrived—after a tedious passage—only four days ago.

Everything is well with me and I am also greatly cheered by the fact that we chartered for Dundee and according to all probabilities we will leave here about New Year's day to be home by the end of May or in the first week of June.[3]

I am afraid this will be a long letter—and moreover entirely taken up with my personal concerns—upon which I want Your friendly advice. You have been so kind to me that I do not feel greatly diffident in ad[d]ressing You—still I wish to apologise before beginning.—

As you are aware I shall pass (I take it for granted) my last exam—on my return—and—I consider—make a fresh start in the wordl.*—In what direction to shape my course? That is the question!—

---

[1] By his unpublished researches in the Registry of Shipping and Seamen, Hans van Marle has shown that Conrad took (and failed) an examination for his master's certificate on 28 July 1886; he succeeded on a second attempt, 10 November 1886.

[2] Conrad began reading the London *Evening Standard* early in his career on British ships.

[3] The *Tilkhurst* actually reached Dundee on 17 June 1886.

That question I have partly answered myself; I wish to start due North!—

In other words and speaking—(as everybody ought) plainly my soul is bent upon a whaling venture.

And now here I must pray You to take also for granted that I am brimfull with the most exhaustive information upon the subject. I have read, studied, pumped proffessional* men and imbibed knowledge upon whale fishing and sealing for the last four years. I am acquainted with the practical part of the undertaking in a thorough manner. Moreover I have the assurance of active help from a man brought up in the trade—and although doing well where he is now—ready to return to his former pursuit (of whales). Finally I have a vessel in view, on very advantageous terms. And now for ways and ways and means![1]

Upon that question I want Your advice—or rather your opinion upon my plan to raise the necessary capital. From my uncle I cannot possibly ask the sum I require: £1,500. for reasons You no doubt understand. I do not know a man willing and able to advance me that amount of hard cash for the sake of my distinguished appearance, or any other sentimental consideration; having no tangible securities to offer I have hit upon the idea of creating the same by insuring my life.

—For—You see—altho' I cannot ask my uncle for the capital, I receive from Him and from the London business (which I am advised is daily improving)[2] yearly a sum, sufficient for the payement* of premium on Life policy for £2000 and the interest on the loan I *suppose* I could ra[i]se on the security of the said policy (supposing the interest to be at the rate of 10%) even should the venture for which the loan is destined to turn out a dead failure—And I have special reasons to believe that such would not be the case.—But let that pass! Now, where I want your advice is on these points:

1° Is such a transaction—for a man in my position—at all possible?

2° If it is—what is the proper way to go about it?—(for I am a very infant in business matters)

3° Supposing the plan feasible do you think—as a cool business man not interested in the matter—that it would be sound to embark upon an undertaking (highly paying *if successful*—as You know whaling is) on a capital borrowed at 12%—For it will come to that with the premium and interest. (*NB* My idea is to pay the premium for the first year in advance and then pay it every six months).—always in advance.—

---

[1] Nothing came of Conrad's efforts.
[2] The uncle was Tadeusz Bobrowski; for his help in buying Conrad a partnership in the London firm of Barr, Moering, see Najder, p. 200.

This is all the advice and "Counsel's opinion" I require; but with my natural modesty I boldly ask for actual—mental—help in carrying the matter t[h]rough—should it turn out to be something more than the ravings of an unbusinesslike lunatic. I have thought over it in all its aspects.—Believe me it is not the desire of getting much money that prompts me. It is simply the wish to work for myself—I am sick and tired of sailing about for little money and less consideration. But I love the sea; and If I could just clear my bare living in the way I suggested I should be comparatively happy. Can it be done? And if so: should it be done?

I intended to ask you all those questions "viva-voce" on my return, but I received here letters from Peterhead advising me of a sealing schooner—just the thing!—This together with the fact of us going actually to Dundee (next door to Peterhead)[1] decided me to write to you on the matter. According to Your answer I shall—or shall not, run down to Peterhead before going to London; I shall or shall not, give up plans carefully nursed for the past four years—and go on plodding in the old way—any way! And now Dear Sir will you kindly transmitt* to Your Father the expressions of my greatest respect and affection, my sincerest wishes for His good health and general welfare. My dutiful compliment for Mme Kliszczewska and friendly greetings for the boys, and always believe me my dear Sir Yours gratefully and truly faithful[ly]

Conrad Korzeniowski.

My ad[d]ress: M[r] Conrad. 2[d] mate "Tilkhurst" Sailors Home. Dundee. To be delivered on arrival.[2]—Write about end May—say the 20th

To Spiridion Kliszczewski

Text J–A, 1, 83

19th December, 1885
Calcutta.

My Dear Sir:

I received your kind and welcome letter yesterday, and to-day being Sunday,[3] I feel that I could not make better use of my leisure hours than in answering your missive.

By this time, you, I and the rest of the "right thinking" have been

---

[1] About a hundred miles apart.
[2] This is the first known instance of Joseph's using Conrad as a surname.
[3] The 19th was actually a Saturday.

grievously disappointed by the result of the General Election.[1] The newly enfranchised idiots have satisfied the yearnings of Mr. Chamberlain's herd by cooking the national goose according to his recipe.[2] The next culinary operation will be a pretty kettle of fish of an international character. Joy reigns in St. Petersburg, no doubt, and profound disgust in Berlin: the International Socialist Association are triumphant, and every disreputable ragamuffin in Europe feels that the day of universal brotherhood, despoliation and disorder is coming apace, and nurses day-dreams of well-plenished pockets amongst the ruin of all that is respectable, venerable and holy. The great British Empire went over the edge, and yet on to the inclined plane of social progress and radical reform. The downward movement is hardly perceptible yet, and the clever men who started it may flatter themselves with the progress; but they will soon find that the fate of the nation is out of their hands now! The Alpine avalanche rolls quicker and quicker as it nears the abyss—its ultimate destination! Where's the man to stop the crashing avalanche?

Where's the man to stop the rush of social-democratic ideas? The opportunity and the day have come and are gone! Believe me: gone for ever! For the sun is set and the last barrier removed. England was the only barrier to the pressure of infernal doctrines born in continental back-slums. Now, there is nothing! The destiny of this nation and of all nations is to be accomplished in darkness amidst much weeping and gnashing of teeth, to pass through robbery, equality, anarchy and misery under the iron rule of a militarism* despotism! Such is the lesson of common sense logic.[3]

Socialism must inevitably end in Caesarism.

Forgive me this long disquisition, but your letter—so earnest on the subject—is my excuse. I understand you perfectly. You wish to apply remedies to quell the dangerous symptoms: you evidently hope yet.

I do so no longer. Truthfully, I have ceased to hope a long time ago. We must drift!

---

[1] Liberals 335, Conservatives 249, Irish Nationalist Party (Parnellites) 86: the Parnellites, who had been playing the two British parties against each other, thus held the balance of power. Conrad had wanted an out-and-out Conservative victory.

[2] In 1885, the year before he deserted the Liberals, Joseph Chamberlain (1836–1914) had, as President of the Board of Trade, steered the Third Reform Bill through Parliament. Passage of the Bill ensured the principle of 'one man, one vote'; it also enfranchised two million new voters in Great Britain and half a million in Ireland, bringing the total electorate to over four million.

[3] The Conservatives formed a minority government; the Liberals were led by Mr Gladstone; the two Socialist candidates in London constituencies scraped up 59 votes between them.

The whole herd of idiotic humanity are moving in that direction at the bidding of unscrupulous rascals and a few sincere, but dangerous, lunatics. These things must be. It is fatality.

I live mostly in the past and the future. The present has, you easily understand, but few charms for me. I look with the serenity of despair and the indifference of contempt upon the passing events. Disestablishment, Land Reform,[1] Universal Brotherhood are but like milestones on the road to ruin. The end will be awful, no doubt! Neither you nor I shall live to see the final crash: although we both may turn in our graves when it comes, for we both feel deeply and sincerely. Still, there is no earthly remedy for those earthly misfortunes, and from above, I fear, we may obtain consolation, but no remedy. "All is vanity."

Descending to common matters of life I transmit to your wife and yourself my best wishes for the coming year. May you have the winds fair and the seas smooth in the voyage of life. May the sail be long and pleasant, and if I wish your fine boys to walk straight in the path traced by their parents, I can wish them no better, for in the path of rectitude lies the true happiness!

With a hearty shake of the hand, believe me, my dear Sir and kind friend,

Yours very sincerely and faithfully,
K. N. Korzeniowski.

[1] A vocal faction of the Liberal Party favoured disestablishment (separation of the Church of England from the State). Land reform had been an issue in the recent election; Conservative opponents made fun of Chamberlain's scheme of allotments for rural workers with the slogan 'three acres and a cow'.

1886

To Spiridion Kliszczewski

Text MS Indiana; J–A, I, 85

6th of Jan. 86.
Calcutta

My dear Sir.

At last we are going to make a start for home! I am glad of it, being rather tired of the voyage and the ship—altho' very comfortable in all respects.

I hope all my letters reached you; they do get mislaid sometimes as I know by experience. I venture to express the hope that You will kindly write to Dundee and pronounce your verdict upon my scheme. Even should all the arrangements (as I expect) strike you as foolish yet I pray You to opine upon the insurance part—as distinct from the whaling enterprise.—What I should like to know is: Can I reasonably expect to be able to raise a loan upon that security—should opportunity occur (to get command for instance) on moderate terms?

Should you opine that such a proceeding would be inadvisable or impossible I shall not trouble to insure—for not having a family, I do not see any necessity for doing so, unless for my own advantage.—

I shall not—I think—start for Cardiff till I have passed my examination, when I shall be able with my mind free of all immediate cares to enjoy Your society.—

We are leaving to-morrow and a five months passage is before us,[1] then another month and I shall have the happiness to shake Your friendly hand; till then believe me my Dear Sir Yours very faithfully

Conrad.

My compliments to Mme Kliszczewska and friendly greeting for the boys—My dutiful respects to Mr Spiridion. Sen. with the hope of seeing Him in good health on my return.—

CK.

Address:
Mr J. Conrad. 2^d mate
ship "Tilkhurst"—Sailor's Home
Dundee—to be delivered on arrival.

[1] The *Tilkhurst* was a sailing ship.

1889

To Albert Thys[1]

Text L.*fr.* 25

Novembre 4, 1889.
Londres.

Monsieur l'Administrateur-Délégué
Société Belge du Haut-Congo.

Monsieur,

J'ai l'honneur de vous apprendre que j'ai renoncé à faire le voyage du Mexique et aux Indes Occidentales au service de MM. Walford et C[ie][2] —naturellement avec la permission de ces Messieurs.

Je pense que, vu mon séjour prolongé aux pays chauds (d'où je viens de retourner maintenant),[3] et mon probable départ pour l'Afrique dans peu de mois, il serait prudent de profiter du climat européen le plus longtemps possible.

Je m'empresse de vous prévenir de ce changement dans mes projets, car je considère qu'il est de mon devoir à présent de vous tenir au courant de mes mouvements.

Les lettres à l'adresse ci-dessous me parviendront sans délai.

J'ai l'honneur d'être, Monsieur l'Administrateur, avec la plus haute considération votre très obéissant serviteur.

Conrad Korzeniowski.

c/o Messrs. Barr, Moering and C°., 36, Camomile Street, London E.C.[4]

---

[1] Although Baines must have seen this letter somewhere, it is not at Yale as he says it is (pp. 107–8; 467, n. 17). Baines records Thys's comment, written on the letter: 'Bon capitaine quand nous en aurons besoin pour le Haut-Congo. Demandez renseignement (à Walford [and Co.])'. The portly Captain (later General) Thys, an explorer and administrator, was closely involved with the exploitation of the Congo Free State, King Leopold's private domain.

[2] An Antwerp shipping company.

[3] After fourteen months as captain of the *Otago*, he had returned to London in June. He was now lodging in Bessborough Gardens, off Vauxhall Bridge Road, and working on the early stages of *Almayer's Folly*.

[4] Factors and shipping agents. Thanks to his friends Krieger and Hope, and with financial help from his uncle, Conrad had a small interest in the company and for several years used their office as a forwarding address.

4 November 1889
London

M. Deputy Director
Belgian Company of the Upper Congo
Sir,

I have the honour to inform you that I have withdrawn from the voyage to Mexico and the West Indies in the service of the house of Walford & Co. – naturally with the permission of these gentlemen.

I think that, considering my prolonged stay in the torrid zone (from which I have just returned) and my probable departure for Africa within a few months, it would be wise to profit from the European climate for as long as possible.

I hasten to apprise you of this change in my plans, for I consider that at present it is my duty to keep you informed of my movements.

Letters to the address below will reach me without delay.

I have the honour of being, Monsieur l'Administrateur, with the greatest respect, your very obedient servant

Conrad Korzeniowski

c/o Messrs. Barr, Moering and Co.,
36, Camomile Street, London E.C.

To Albert Thys
Text   MS Yale; *L.fr.* 26

November 28, 1889.
Londres.

Monsieur,

Je viens d'apprendre par une lettre de M. de Baerdemaecker[1] à MM. Barr, Moering et Cie que vous étiez dans l'idée que j'avais servi M. Walford comme capitaine d'un de ses navires.

Je me hâte de m'excuser envers vous pour m'être exprimé si mal dans l'entrevue que vous avez bien voulu m'accorder à Bruxelles. Mon intention était de vous informer que j'étais dans l'emploi de M. Walford pour le moment: j'ignorais même qu'il fut un armateur. J'ose espérer que vous m'accorderez votre indulgence pour ce malentendu, causé simplement par mon manque d'habitude à m'exprimer en français.

Comme sans doute il s'agirait de mes qualifications pour le poste qùe vous avez eu la bonté de me promettre, je prends la liberté de vous

---

[1] Shipping agent stationed at Ghent.

informer que je possède une comission du "Board of Trade" me qualifiant absolument pour commander des navires à voile et à vapeur dans la marine britannique (obtenu par examen à Londres 1885).[1]

Je suis prêt à produire des copies des certificats signés par les Capitaines et armateurs qui m'ont employé pendant mes 15 ans de service sur mer, témoignant de mon habileté en matière du métier et de ma bonne conduite en général.

Je suis aussi—depuis 4 ans—membre de la Société des Capitaines ("Shipmaster's Association", London, 60 Fenchurch Street) où mon état de service est naturellement connu.

G. F. W. Hope Esq., Director of the South African Mercantile C[o]., member London Chamber of Commerce, 39 Coleman Street, vous donnera toute information à mon sujet que vous jugerez nécessaire de lui demander.[2]

J'ai l'honneur d'être, Monsieur l'Administrateur, avec la plus haute considération.

C. Korzeniowski.

28 November 1889
London

Sir,

I have just learned from a letter of M. de Baerdemaecker to Messrs. Barr, Moering & Co. that you thought I had served M. Walford as captain of one of his ships.

I hasten to apologize to you for having expressed myself so badly during the interview which you were kind enough to grant me in Brussels. My intention was to inform you that I was employed by M. Walford for the time being: I was not even aware he was a shipowner. I dare to hope you will grant me your indulgence for this misunderstanding, caused simply by the unfamiliarity of expressing myself in French.

As doubtless there would be the question of qualifications for the post you have been so kind as to promise me, I take the liberty of informing you that I possess a commission from the Board of Trade, qualifying me

[1] Conrad received his Master's certificate in 1886, not in 1885.
[2] The friendship with Hope began in 1880 and was to continue into the period when most of Conrad's friendships were literary. Though not at the same time as Conrad, Hope had served on the *Duke of Sutherland*. When he became a 'Director of Companies' (as Conrad called him in 'Heart of Darkness'), he bought the yawl *Nellie* (later replaced by the cutter *Ildegonde*) and often took Conrad on his sailing expeditions. For Hope's own recollections, see CWW, pp. 122–4.

absolutely to command sailing ships and steamers of the British merchant service (obtained by examination in London, 1885).

I am ready to produce copies of the certificates signed by the captains and shipowners who have employed me during my fifteen years of sea service, witnessing my competence in matters of seamanship and my good conduct in general.

I have also been – for the last four years – a member of the Society of Captains (Shipmasters' Association, London, 60 Fenchurch Street) where my standing is of course known.

G. F. W. Hope, Esq., Director of the South African Mercantile Co., member of the London Chamber of Commerce, 39 Coleman Street, will give you all the information about this matter you may judge it necessary to request.

I have the honour to be, Monsieur l'Administrateur, with the highest respect,

C. Korzeniowski

To Albert Thys

Text L. fr. 28

27 Décembre 1889.
Londres.

Monsieur l'Administrateur-Délégué, Société Belge du Haut-Congo.

Monsieur,

Je viens de recevoir une invitation de la part d'un de mes parents pour passer quelque temps dans ses terres dans le Sud de la Russie.[1]

Il me serait très agréable de l'accepter, mais avant de décider j'aimerais à savoir précisément le temps dont je pourrais disposer.

Les communications dans ce pays sont assez difficiles en hiver, et souvent même le télégraphe ne fonctionne pas régulièrement. D'un autre côté une courte visite ne vaudrait pas le peine et les dépenses du déplacement.

Dans ces circonstances j'ose m'adresser à vous, dans l'espoir que vous voudrez bien me faire la faveur de m'informer (à peu près) de la date où vous aurez besoin de mes services. Je pourrais alors prendre mes mesures pour revenir à Londres ponctuellement où je me tiendrai à votre disposition.

Veuillez, Monsieur, accepter d'avance mes remerciements pour la

---

[1] The invitation came from Tadeusz Bobrowski, Conrad's maternal uncle, who lived at Kazimierówka, an estate in Podolia, Government of Kiev (the western part of the Ukraine).

réponse, ainsi que mes excuses très sincères pour occuper ainsi votre temps.

J'ai l'honneur d'être, Monsieur l'Administrateur, avec la plus haute considération,

Votre très obéissant serviteur,
J.C. Korzeniowski.

27 December 1889
London

M. Deputy Director
Belgian Company of the Upper Congo

Sir,

I have just received an invitation from one of my relatives to spend some time on his estate in Southern Russia.

It would please me very much to accept it, but before deciding I would like to know precisely how much time I have at my disposal.

Communications within that country are rather difficult in winter, and even the telegraph often does not function properly. On the other hand, a short visit would not be worth the trouble and expense of travelling.

Under these circumstances I venture to address you in the hope that you will please do me the favour of informing me (approximately) of the date when you will need my services. I could then take measures to return to London punctually, where I would hold myself at your disposal.

Please, sir, accept in advance my thanks for your answer, as well as my very sincere apologies for thus taking up your time.

I have the honour of being, Monsieur l'Administrateur, with the highest respect, your very obedient servant

J. C. Korzeniowski

1890

To Aleksander Poradowski

Text MS Yale; Najder 206

16th January, 1890
[letterhead: The British and
Foreign Transit Agency. Barr,
Moering & Co., Shipping and
Custom House Agents, 36,
Camomile Street, London, E. C.]

My Dear Uncle.[1]

I have just had a letter from Kazimierówka, in which, in reply to my inquiry, Uncle Tadeusz tells me that you are living in Brussels and gives me your address. I am terribly sorry that I did not know this earlier, as I was in Brussels in October last year. It is possible, however, that before long I shall have to visit Brussels again. The object of this scrawl to you is to remember myself to the relation whose great kindness to me in Cracow I have certainly not forgotten. I do not ask whether you will permit me to visit you—for I permit myself not to doubt it; but I would very much like to be certain that you are in Brussels and that I shall be able to find you there in the course of the next month.

I returned to London six months ago after a three years' absence. Of these three years I spent one among the islands of the Malay Archipelago, after which I spent two years as master of an Australian vessel in the Pacific and Indian Oceans.[2] I am now more or less under contract to the 'Société Belge pour le Commerce du Haut Congo' to be master of one of its river steamers. I have not signed any agreement, but Mr. A. Thys, the director of that Company, has promised me the post. Whether he will keep his promise and when he will send me to Africa, I do not yet know; it will probably be in May.

I intend to visit Uncle Tadeusz soon; that is to say I want to, and he also wants me to; but he says that it is difficult during the winter.[3] I am expecting a letter from him in a few days' time, which will decide the

---

[1] In fact he was a first cousin of Teofila Bobrowska, Conrad's maternal grandmother. Although Aleksander Poradowski (1836–90) came from Galicia (Austrian Poland), the outbreak of the 1863 insurrection found him an officer in the Russian army. He joined the insurgents, was captured and condemned to death, but escaped with the help of a fellow officer. Except for a few years in Lwów (Lemberg) in the comparative safety of Austrian Poland, he spent the rest of his life in exile. While living in Brussels, he helped start a charitable organization for Polish refugees.

[2] Conrad spent fourteen months as a master, of the barque *Otago*, from January 1888 to end of March 1889. He had been away not three years, but twenty-eight months.

[3] Involving an eight-hour sleigh journey from the nearest railway station.

matter. If I do go home it will be via Hamburg—returning via Brussels. If, however, my visit is postponed I shall nevertheless be going to Brussels in March in connection with the post in the Congo. Therefore in any case I shall have the pleasure of seeing you, my dear Uncle, and of making myself known to Aunt Poradowska[1] whom I only know from that portrait of her which you had with you in Cracow.

In the meantime, my dear Uncle, a most cordial embrace from your affectionate relation and servant,

Konrad Korzeniowski.

A letter care of Messrs. Barr Moering will always find me.

To Aleksander Poradowski
Text   MS Yale; Najder 207

20 January, 1890.
[letterhead: Barr, Moering]

Dear Uncle,

My most affectionate thanks to you and to Aunt for the kind expressions contained in your letter. The sight of your handwriting gave me inexpressible pleasure, but, alas, my joy was short-lived! The news of your poor state of health has grieved me greatly.[2] Please, do not trouble to answer this letter. I hasten to inform you that in view of the state of your health, I have decided to come home via Brussels.[3] I realize that after the operation you will need not visits but a complete rest. This morning I received, simultaneously with your letter, one from Uncle Tadeusz that says 'come'. However, those villains in the Russian Consulate do not want to grant me a visa—which means further delay, inconvenience, and visits to the Embassy, perhaps to no avail.

I shall let you know how I am getting on as soon as I settle matters with these pirates. And so, au revoir to you, my dearest Uncle. I kiss the hands of dear Aunt.

Your loving and devoted nephew
and servant.
Konrad.

My apologies for the scrawl, but I have barely time to catch the post.

[1] See notes to the letter of 4 February.
[2] Poradowski was dying.
[3] Conrad arrived on 5 February.

To Aleksander Poradowski

Text MS Yale; Najder 208

31 January, 1890.
[letterhead: Barr, Moering]

My Dearest Uncle,

I am already in possession of all the necessary documents and intend to leave London next Tuesday or, at the latest, Wednesday, but not later, via Brussels of course. I shall, therefore, arrive at your place on Wednesday or Thursday and if you allow me I shall stay there 24 hours. I would not like to cause any embarrassment to dear Aunt—especially as you are not well. I could spend the night at an hotel and the day with you both 's'il n'y a pas d'empêchement'. When I leave you we shall say to each other 'see you soon', for I shall come back again shortly, via Brussels of course. A thousand embraces.

I shall come to you directly from the station.

Your loving,

K. N. Korzeniowski.

To Marguerite Poradowska

Text MS Yale; Rapin 60; G. & S. 3

Mardi, le 4 fev: 1890[1]
[London]

Ma chère Tante.[2]

Merci mille fois pour Votre[3] carte. Je quitte Londres demain. Vendredi[4] a 9ʰ du matin et je dois arriver à Bruxelles a 5½ʰ du soir. Je serai donc avec Vous vers 6 heures. Croyez moi, avec la plus vive reconnaissance Votre neveu très affectionné et serviteur très dévoué.

Conrad Korzeniowski.

[1] Beneath the date, Mme Poradowska added 'Maliszewski', the name of the man who wrote about Poradowski's role in the Polish uprising of 1863.
[2] Marguerite Poradowska (née Gachet: 1848–1937) was the wife of Aleksander Poradowski, who was then in his last illness. French by ancestry, she had grown up in Brussels and returned there with her husband after several years' residence in the Austrian sector of Poland. Drawing on her knowledge of that country, she had already written *Yaga* (1887) and *Demoiselle Micia* (1888–9) and was to continue to publish novels, short stories and sketches. At least until the mysterious interruption of their correspondence between 1895 and 1900, Conrad's 'Aunt' – fellow writer, cosmopolitan link with Poland, and confidante – played an important part in his life.
[3] Frequently, but by no means consistently, Conrad carried over into French (as well as English) the Polish convention of capitalizing *You* and *Your*.
[4] Probably a slip for *mercredi*, Wednesday: cf. the preceding letter.

Tuesday, 4 February 1890
[London]

My dear Aunt,

Many thanks for your card. I am leaving London tomorrow, Friday, at 9 a.m. and should arrive in Brussels at 5.30 p.m. I shall therefore be with you at about six. Believe me, with the liveliest gratitude, your very affectionate nephew and very devoted servant

Conrad Korzeniowski

To Marguerite Poradowska

Text MS Yale; Rapin 60; G. & S. 5

Le 11 Fevrier 1890.
Varsovie.—

Ma Chère et bonne Tante.

Je vous ecris ce mot pour Vous dire que Charles Zagórski à quitté Varsovie pour Lublin de sorte que je n'ai pas encore vu personne de la Famille.[1]

J'etais avec Vous de pensée et de cœur hier partageant, qoique[2] loin de Vous, Votre douleur comme du reste je n'ai cessé de le faire depuis que je Vous ai quitté.[3] Je pars demain soir et j'aurais a trouver Charles avant de me presenter chez les Zagórski. Il n'a pas laissé son addresse a Varsovie—du moins parmis les personnes que je connais.—

J'ai visité la redaction du "Słowo" sans trouver le redacteur.[4] J'ai laissé au bureau la lettre de faire part et ma carte. J'y repasserai demain.

Au revoir. ma chère Tante. Si je ne sais comment exprimer tout ce que je ressens Vous ne m'en croirez pas moins Votre affectionné neveu, ami et serviteur très devoué

C. Korzeniowski.

J'ecrirai de Lublin ou de Kazimierówka aussitôt arrivé. —[5]

---

[1] Charles (in Polish, Karol) Zagórski (d. 1898), nephew of Aleksander Poradowski and Conrad's distant cousin; Conrad felt deep affection for him and his wife Angèle (in Polish, Aniela).

[2] We leave Conrad's French spelling and accentuation as they stand.

[3] Aleksander had died on the 7th.

[4] 'The Word' was a conservative Warsaw periodical for which Aleksander Poradowski wrote, among other things, a series about the Brussels Exhibition; its editor for a time was the novelist Henryk Sienkiewicz, whom Conrad once called 'St Henry'.

[5] Lublin is about 90 miles from Warsaw; Tadeusz Bobrowski's estate lay a further 325 miles SE.

11 February 1890
Warsaw

My dear and good Aunt,

I am writing you this line to tell you that Charles Zagórski has left Warsaw for Lublin, so that I have not yet seen anyone in the family.

I was with you in thought and spirit yesterday, sharing, though far from you, your sorrow, as indeed I have not stopped doing since I left you. I am leaving tomorrow evening, and I shall have to find Charles before paying my respects to the Zagórskis. He hasn't left his address in Warsaw – at least with anyone I know.

I called at the offices of *Słowo* without finding the editor. I left the announcement and my card there. I shall call again tomorrow.

Au revoir, my dear aunt. If I do not know how to express all that I feel, you will believe me none the less your affectionate nephew and very devoted friend and servant

C. Korzeniowski

I shall write from Lublin or Kazimierówka as soon as I arrive.

To Marguerite Poradowska

Text   MS Yale; Rapin 61; G. & S. 5

Samedi. 14 Fevrier 90 [15/16 February?][1]
à Lipowiec. En route pour
Kazimierówka.

Ma chère Tante Marguerite.

Hier j'ai quitté Lublin sans pouvoir trouver un moment de libre pour Vous ecrire selon ma promesse. Pardonnez moi ce délai de 24 heures dans le compte–rendu de ma triste mission.–

Toutes ces bonnes âmes eprouvées tant par la douleur ne cessent de penser a Vous. Ils ont appris la nouvelle quelques heures avant mon arrivéee par la notice obituaire du journal mais il faut la cacher a tante Jeanette et au pauvre oncle Jean qui est—hélas—bien mal.[2]—Et tous ces malheureux accablés par le coup qui les frappe, vivant dans l'attente—presque journalière—d'une autre mort dans la famille se sont empréssés autour de moi demandant "et Marguerite"? "Cette pauvre

---

[1] That year, 14 February fell on a Friday. Gee and Sturm (pp. 4–5) argue for a combination of 15th and 16th. On the 16th, Conrad reached Kazimierówka by sleigh.

[2] Johanna Poradowska, sister-in-law of Marguerite Poradowska and aunt of Karol Zagórski; Jan Zagórski, father of Karol. Both Jan and Johanna died the following year, Jan in April and Johanna in July.

Marguerite". Tante Gabrielle[1] a voulu tout savoir et j'ai eu a faire—le cœur serré—le récit de Votre epreuve douleureuse. Je Vous ai décrit comme je Vous ai connue bonne, aimante, devouée et courageuse. Mais ils Vous connaissent si bien! Vous apprecient tant ! Tous, Gabrielle et Angèle et Charles ce sont des cœurs d'or. L'annonce de Votre arrivée en Pologne a fait comme une éclaircie dans le noir de notre entrevue. Tante Gabrielle Vous attend. Je leur ai dit tout ce que je savais de Vos projets. Ils Vous ecriront. Ils vous attendent a bras ouverts.—

C'est tout chère Tante. Je repars d'ici dans 10 minutes. Mon oncle m'attend. Son domestique—qui m'accompagne me dit que le cher vieillard n'a presque pas dormi depuis la récéption de mon telegramme du mardi passé. Je Vous ecris bientôt.—

Tout a Vous et avec Vous de cœur
Conrad Korzeniowski.

Pardonnez moi chère petite Tante cette lettre. Je Vous ecris en français car je pense a Vous en français; et ces pensées si mal écrites viennent du cœur qui ne connait ni la grammaire ni l'orthographe d'une sympathie raisonnée. Voilà mon excuse. J'ai fini Jaga[2]—deux fois.— Je ne Vous en ecris rien sous le charme de cette lecture. Tantôt, Froidement; mais bientôt

Yours

J.C.K.

Saturday, 14 February 1890 [15–16? February 1890]
at Lipowiec. En route to
Kazimierówka.

My dear Aunt Marguerite,

I left Lublin yesterday without being able to find a free moment to write to you as I promised. Excuse this twenty-four-hour delay in narrating my sad mission.

All those good souls, tried so much by sorrow, never cease thinking of you. Some hours before my arrival they learned the news from the obituary in the newspaper, but they hid it from Aunt Jeanette and poor Uncle Jean, who is, alas, very ill. And all those unhappy people crushed

---

[1] Gabriela Zagórska, wife of Jan.
[2] *Yaga*, a novel of Ruthenian life by Mme Poradowska, appeared serially in *Revue des Deux Mondes* for 1 and 15 August 1887, and was published the next year by Ollendorff, in Paris.

by the blow striking them, living in almost daily expectation of another death in the family, pressed around me asking, 'And Marguerite?' 'Poor Marguerite'. Aunt Gabrielle wanted to know everything, and with a grief-stricken heart I had to give her the account of your sorrowful ordeal. I described you as I have known you, kind, loving, devoted and spirited. But they know you so well! Appreciate you so much! All of them, Gabrielle and Angèle and Charles, possess hearts of gold. The announcement of your visit to Poland was like a lightening in the blackness of our meeting. Aunt Gabrielle expects you. I have told them all that I know of your plans. They will write to you. They await you with open arms.

That is all, dear Aunt. I leave here in ten minutes. My uncle expects me. His servant – who is accompanying me – says that the dear old man has hardly slept since receiving my telegram last Tuesday. I shall write to you soon.

Sincerely and affectionately yours
Conrad Korzeniowski

Excuse this letter, my dear little Aunt. I write to you in French because I think of you in French; and these sentiments, so badly expressed, come from the heart, which knows neither the grammar nor the spelling of a studied sympathy. That is my excuse. I have finished *Yaga* – twice. I shall write nothing to you about it while I am still under its charm. Presently, dispassionately; but soon,

Yours

J.C.K.

To Marguerite Poradowska
Text MS Yale; Rapin 62; G. & S. 6

10 Mars. 1890
Kazimierówka.

Ma chère Tante.

Ce n'est qu'hier que j'ai reçu votre lettre du 15 fevrier par l'entremise de notre bonne tante Gabrielle. Le retard s'explique par notre absence de Kazimierówka ou nous sommes rentrés hier après une excursion dans le voisinage qui a duré 10 jours.—

Merci mille fois pour le bon souvenir que Vous me gardez. Mon admiration et amitié pour Vous s'augmentent d'un sentiment de profonde reconnaissance pour la bonté que Vous me temoignez.—L'idée de Vous revoir a Bruxelles me sera une consolation quand le moment de me separer de mon oncle arrivera. Je le quitterai le 15 d'avril et j'aurai le bonheur de Vous voir le 23 du même mois si tout va bien—

Je suis bien heureux de savoir que la Princesse[1] a été tout ce qu'il y a de bon et d'amical pour Vous, mais j'ose éspérer que Vous ne prendrez aucune decision a la hâte.[2] Du reste Vous n'aurez a Vous decider que vers la fin d'Avril. A cette epoque je serais avec Vous et je serais en état de Vous donner l'information quand au voyage en Pologne de vive voix.—

J'ai lu avec un melancolique plaisir le discours de Mr Merzbach.[3]—Il n'a pas fait des phrases mais il a raconté cette vie si simple et noble en peu des paroles mais provenant du cœur; et il a reconnu (je ne dis pas apprécié)—mais il a reconnu la part que Vous avez eue dans cette vie.—Je Vous demande pardon pour cette lettre si courte. On envoit a la poste aujourd'hui et j'ai reçu un tas de lettres qui exigent des reponses immédiates. Je crois que ma recommandation auprès de la Cie du Congo n'a pas été assez forte et que la chose ne réussira point.[4] Ça me chagrine un peu.

Au revoir chère Tante—et même a bientôt car le temps passé vite. Je Vous baise les mains et je Vous embrasse de tout mon cœur.

Votre affectionné neveu

C. Korzeniowski.—

Mon addresse: M^r. T. Bobrowski. poste Lipowiec. à Kazimierówka. Gouv^t de Kiew. Russie méridionnale.—(pour Conrad)

N'ecrivez que si le cœur Vous en dit car nous pourrons causer un peu dans peu des jours.

---

[1] Princess Hedwige Lubomirska (1815–95), who became the Princesse de Ligne in 1836 when she married Prince Eugène de Ligne. She lived at the Château de Belœil, near Mons.

[2] Apparently the Princess had asked Mme Poradowska to live with her.

[3] Henry Merzbach (1837–1903), Polish poet and journalist living in Brussels after the 1863 Warsaw insurrection, gave the funeral elegy for Aleksander Poradowski. Conrad could have read excerpts in the obituary notice which appeared in the *Journal de Bruxelles* for 12 February 1890. Merzbach was, with M. Poradowski, founder of the Société de Bienfaisance Polonaise.

[4] See the correspondence with Albert Thys.

10 March 1890
Kazimierówka

My dear Aunt,

Only yesterday I received your letter of 15 February, through the agency of our good Aunt Gabrielle. The delay is explained by our absence from Kazimierówka, to which we returned yesterday after an excursion in the immediate area that lasted ten days.

Many thanks for the kind memory you carry of me. My admiration and friendship for you are increased by a feeling of deep gratitude for the goodness you show me. The thought of seeing you again in Brussels will console me when the time to part from my uncle arrives. I leave him on 15 April, and I will have the happiness of seeing you on the 23rd of the same month, if all goes well.

I am very happy to know that the Princess has been altogether so kind and friendly to you, but I venture to hope you will not make any hasty decision. Besides, you will not have to decide until near the end of April. By that time I should be with you and in a position to give you news of the Polish visit in person.

I have read M. Merzbach's speech with melancholy pleasure. He has not made any fine phrases, but he has recounted that simple and noble life in words brief but springing from the heart; and he has recognized (I do not say appreciated) – he has recognized the part you played in that life. I ask your pardon for such a short letter. The post leaves today and I have received a pile of letters which must be answered promptly. I believe that my recommendation to the Company of the Congo was not strong enough and that the matter will not succeed at all. That vexes me a little.

To our next meeting, dear Aunt – soon, for time goes quickly. I kiss your hands, and I embrace you warmly. Your affectionate nephew

C. Korzeniowski

My address: Mr T. Bobrowski, Lipowiec post office, Kazimierówka, Gov't of Kiev, South Russia. – (for Conrad)

Do not write unless you feel so inclined, for we shall be able to chat a little within a few days.

To Marguerite Poradowska

Text MS Yale; Rapin 64; G. & S. 8

23 mars 1890
Kazimierówka

Ma chère Tante.

Je viens de recevoir votre lettre que j'ai lu avec beaucoup de tristesse. La vie roule en flots amers, comme l'ocean sombre et brutal sous un ciel couvert des tristes nuages, et il y a des jours ou il semble au pauvres âmes embarquées le déséperant voyage que jamais un rayon de soleil n'a pu penétrer ce voile douleureux; que jamais il ne luira plus, qu'il n'a jamais éxisté! Il faut pardonner aux yeux que le vent âpre du malheur a rempli des larmes s'ils se refusent de voir le bleu; il faut pardonner aux lèvres qui ont gouté l'amertume de la vie si elles se refusent a prononcer les paroles d'esperance.—Il faut surtout pardonner a ses âmes malheureuses qui ont élu de faire le pélérinage a pied, qui cotoient le rivage et regardent sans comprendre l'horreur de la lutte, la joie de vaincre ni le profond déséspoir des vaincus; a ces âmes qui recoivent le naufragé le sourire de pitié et le mot de sagesse ou de reproche aux lèvres. Il faut pardonner surtout à ceux là "car ils ne savent pas ce qu'ils font!"[1] Voici ma pensée sur Lui,[2] sur Vous, sur ceux qui Vous entourent;[3] mais je Vous prie de reflechir, je vous supplie de comprendre qu'il est permis a une âme habitant un corps tourmenté par la souffrance epuisé de maladies, d'avoir ces moments d'égarement. Sous la pression des souffrances physiques l'intelligence voit faux le cœur se trompe, l'âme sans guide roule dans un âbîme.—Aprésant cette âme est delivrée; elle a connu son erreur. Il lui faut Votre pardon. Il faut le lui accorder, entierement, sans reserves avec l'oubli complet de Votre souffrance personelle, non pas comme un sacrifice, mais comme un devoir. Accordé ainsi, votre pardon approchera quelque peu vers l'ideal humain de la Justice Divine, vers cette Justice qui est le seul espoir, le seul refuge des âmes qui ont combattu, souffert et succombé dans la lutte avec la vie.—

—Et puisque cette lettre est sur le thème du pardon je Vous le demande aussi pour moi. Si cette lettre Vous cause desappointement ou douleur ne me jugez pas.—Attendez! Plus tard vous verrez peut-être que j'ai essayé de vous dire seulement ce je que je croyais être la verité et si je Vous chagrine maintenant Vous me pardonnerez alors. Au revoir ma chère et bonne Tante. Je suis pour toujours votre serviteur et ami, très sincère et très dévoué.

J. C. Korzeniowski.

[1] Luke 23.24.
[2] Presumably her late husband.   [3] Her relatives in Brussels.

J'ai demandé a mon oncle son opinion quand a Vtre visite en Russie. Il n'y aura aucune difficulté.—Vous pouvez retourner comme sujette autrichienne ou française sans la moindre crainte.—[1]
J'hesite a Vous envoyer ceci mais "fiat justicia ruat coelum."[2]
Vous me comprendrez! Tout à Vous
25. *Mars.*[3]

23 March 1890
Kazimierówka

My dear Aunt,

I have just received your letter, which I read with much sorrow. Life rolls on in bitter waves, like the gloomy and brutal ocean under a sky covered with mournful clouds, and there are some days when to the poor souls embarked on the desperate voyage it seems that not a ray of sun has ever been able to penetrate that sad veil; that never again will it shine, that it never even existed! We must forgive those eyes which the harsh wind of misfortune has so filled with tears that they refuse to see the blue; we must forgive those lips which have so tasted life's bitterness that they refuse to express words of hope. Above all, we must forgive the unhappy souls who have elected to make the pilgrimage on foot, who skirt the shore and look uncomprehendingly upon the horror of the struggle, the joy of victory, the profound hopelessness of the vanquished; or those souls who receive the castaway with a smile of pity and a word of wisdom or reproach on their lips. We must especially forgive the latter, 'for they know not what they do!' This is my thought about him, about you, about those who surround you; but I beg you to consider, I beg you to understand that a soul living in a body tormented by suffering and worn out by illness is permitted to have such aberrant moments. Under the pressure of physical suffering, the intellect sees wrongly, the heart deceives itself, the unguided soul strays into an abyss. You must grant it, entirely, unreservedly, with complete disregard of your personal suffering; not as a sacrifice, but as a duty. So granted, your pardon will move a little nearer the human ideal of Divine Justice, nearer the Justice which is the only hope, the only refuge of souls who have fought, suffered, and succumbed in the struggle with life.

---

[1] Consequences of the dismemberment of Poland. Aleksander Poradowski had fled the Russian-occupied area after the 1863 insurrection; his widow, therefore, had good cause to be apprehensive of the Russian authorities. As a native of Galicia, however, he was an Austrian subject. So, by marriage, was Marguerite.
[2] 'Let justice be done, although the heavens fall.'
[3] Date of the postscript.

And since this letter is on the theme of forgiveness, I ask it also for myself. If this letter occasions disappointment or pain, do not pass sentence on me. Wait! Later you will perhaps see that I have tried to tell you only what I believed to be true; and if I annoy you now, you will pardon me then. Au revoir, my dear and good Aunt. I am eternally your very sincere and very devoted servant and friend

J. C. Korzeniowski

I asked my uncle to give his opinion about your visit to Russia. There won't be any difficulty. You can return, as an Austrian or a French subject, without the least fear.

I hesitate to send you this but 'fiat justicia ruat coelum'. You will understand me! Yours.

25 March.

To Gustaw Sobotkiewicz

Text MS Korniłowicz; *Tygodnik Powszechny*, Cracow,
1959, no. 13; Najder 208

17/29 March, 1890
Kazimierówka

Dear and Honourable Sir,[1]

I thank you heartily a thousand times for the kind and friendly words addressed to me in your letter to my Uncle. That I have not forgotten those who in their kindness remembered me may be witnessed by my letters to Uncle, in which I frequently asked after you and your daughter—not out of good manners—a quality which my way of life has not done much to develop—but out of a yearning from my heart which has not forgotten the good old times. And were they really so long ago? My later life has been so different, so unlike the life that I began, that those earlier impressions, feelings and memories have in no way been erased. And now, reading your letter, they are revived more clearly than ever.

I am extremely sorry that circumstances do not permit me to return through Cracow. I came here through Warsaw in order to reach my Uncle as soon as possible, and now I must go back the same way, so as to see the family in Radom,[2] and to get back to London in time.

Although I am sorry to hear you speak of your journey to the last port

---

[1] An old friend of Tadeusz Bobrowski and a distant relation of the Korzeniowskis.
[2] South of Warsaw, about half-way to Lublin.

of call in this life—a port from which there is no return, I have seen so many people living long years on the edge of eternity; indeed I myself have so often seen, as I thought, its portals, that I well know how illusory those presentiments are.

Your health will surely mend, and you will stay fit! Please allow me—as I set out on a long journey, with your blessing—to go away in the hope that in the near future—a year or two—I shall have the joy of seeing you and of thanking you personally for your kindness—which is so dear to me.

I thank Mrs. Dębowska[1]—whom I remember so well as Miss Marya sitting in a highlander's carriage together with you, somewhere on the Hungarian frontier—with all my heart for remembering me so kindly. Of our comrade on that excursion—Pulman—[2] who so determinedly ran from mountain hut to mountain hut asking the way—I have news only from my Uncle, who refuses to accept the tragic story of his death in the flames of the burning Vienna theatre as not being in accordance with the documents in the archives of Kazimierówka. Probably he is living in Sambir,[3] but I do not know how he is getting on.

Hoping that both you, honoured Sir, and your daughter will continue to remember me, I am,

Your grateful and humble servant,
K. N. Korzeniowski.

To Albert Thys

Text   MS Yale; *L. fr.* 28

11 Avril 1890.
terre de Kazimierowka.

Monsieur Alb: Thys.
á Bruxelles.—
Monsieur l'Administrateur.—

Je viens d'être avisé par mes agents que Votre lettre a mon addresse a Londres a été réexpédiée, après moi, pour la Russie—selon mes instructions. Je croyais avoir pris toutes les précautions possibles au sujet de ma correspondence; malheureusement il parait que cette lettre

---

[1] Mrs Dembowska, Sobotkiewicz's daughter.

[2] Adam Pulman, Conrad's tutor in Cracow, had been commissioned by Tadeusz Bobrowski to dissuade Conrad from going to sea.

[3] Pulman lived for some time at Sambor, in Galicia; Sambir, or Berouw, as we can note in *Almayer's Folly*, is in East Borneo. (Conrad was writing *Almayer* at this period: hence his confusion of the two place-names.)

est égarée ou peut-être est-elle absolument perdue?—J'ai réclamé au bureau des Postes de la province mais jusqu'a présant sans aucun succès.—

J'ignore donc le contenu de la communication dont Vous m'avez honoré, mais j'ose éspérer que—si elle contenait une décision favorable a ma candidature—le regrettable accident de sa perte ne me portera aucun préjudice.[1]

Comme j'ai informé Monsieur le Sécrétaire de la Compagnie durant l'entrevue qu'il a bien voulu m'accorder le 5 Fevrier. a[nnée] c[ourante] je serai de retour vers la fin du mois d'avril.

Je serai donc à Bruxelles le 30 de ce mois au plus tard et je me presenterai sans perte de temps aux bureaux de la Société du Haut-Congo, afin d'apprendre Votre décision a mon égard.—

J'ai l'honneur d'être, Monsieur l'Administrateur, avec la plus haute considération,

> Votre serviteur très obéissant,
> J.C. Korzeniowski.

11 April 1890
district of Kazimierówka

M. Albert Thys,
Brussels
M. l'Administrateur,

I have just been advised by my agents that your letter sent to my address in London has been forwarded to me in Russia – according to my instructions. I thought I had taken all possible precautions with my correspondence; unfortunately it seems that this letter has been mislaid, or perhaps it is entirely lost. I have inquired at the Provincial Post Office, but up to now unsuccessfully.

I am unaware, therefore, of the contents of the communication with which you have honoured me, but I dare hope that – if it contained a decision favourable to my candidacy – the regrettable accident of its loss will not carry any prejudice.

As I informed the Secretary of the Company during the interview that he so kindly granted me on 5 February of this year, I shall return towards the end of April.

I shall therefore be in Brussels on the 30th of this month at the latest,

---

[1] Conrad received his appointment and sailed for the Congo on 10 May.

and shall present myself without loss of time at the offices of the Company of the Upper Congo, in order to learn your decision concerning my affairs.

I have the honour of being, Monsieur l'Administrateur, with the highest respect, your very obedient servant

J. C. Korzeniowski

To Marguerite Poradowska

Text MS Yale; Rapin 65; G. & S. 9

14 Avril 1890
Kazimierówka

Ma chère Tante.

J'ai reçu Votre bonne et charmante lettre et cette preuve de Votre amitié que Vous me donnez en Vous occupant de mes projets africains me touche plus que je ne pourrai le dire. Mille fois merci pour Vos bons soins; j'attends avec impatience le moment ou je pourrai baiser Vos mains en Vous remerciant en personne.—

Je quitte mon oncle dans quatre jours; j'ai des visites a faire en chemin (entre autres 48^h a Lublin) de sorte que je ne serai a Bruxelles que le 29 du m[ois] c[ourant].[1]—Alors nous causerons de Vos projets de visite en Pologne et de Vos plans d'avenir qui m'interessent beaucoup—comme Vous pouvez bien le croire.

Avez Vous reçu ma dernière lettre? je me demande. Aprésant j'ai des doutes. Vous ai-je bien compris? Ma reponse Vous a-t-elle déplu? Veuillez en la lisant penser au profond attachement que j'eprouve pour Vous et aussi pour la memoire de mon cher pauvre Oncle Alexandre. Soyez donc indulgente ma chère et bonne Tante.—

Au revoir donc et a bientôt. Il y a du monde et je viens de m'echapper pour un moment pour ecrire ces quelques mots. Ont m'appelle!—

Je baise Vos mains. Votre très devoué ami et neveu.

J. C. Korzeniowski

---

[1] Conrad left Lublin on the 22nd, and apparently arrived in Brussels on the 24th, not the 29th.

14 April 1890
Kazimierówka

My dear Aunt,

I have received your kind and charming letter, and this proof of friendship you give me in concerning yourself with my African plans touches me more than I can express. Many thanks for your kind attention. With impatience I await the moment when I shall be able to kiss your hands while thanking you in person.

I am leaving my uncle's in four days. I have some visits to make on the way (among others, one of forty-eight hours to Lublin) so that I shall not be in Brussels until the 29th of this month. – Then we shall talk of your plans to visit Poland and your future projects, which interest me a good deal – as you can well believe.

Have you received my last letter? I wonder. I have some doubts now. Did I understand you correctly? Has my reply offended you? In reading it, please think of the deep attachment I feel for you and also for the memory of my poor dear Uncle Alexander. So be indulgent, my dear and kind aunt.

Au revoir, then, for the time being. We have visitors and I have just escaped for a moment to write these few words. They are calling for me!

I kiss your hands. Your very devoted friend and nephew
J.C. Korzeniowski

To Maria Bobrowska

Text   *Ruch*; Najder 209

London, 2nd May, 1890.

My dear Maryleczka.[1]

I could not write any sooner. I have been extremely busy and in fact still am so. In four days' time I am sailing to the Congo, and I have to prepare myself for a three years' stay in Central Africa. You can, therefore, imagine how precious each minute is to me. I hope that your Mother is better now and that you, my dear, will soon be writing to me. Probably your letter will be too late to find me in Europe, but it is certain to be forwarded to me. Do not be surprised by the delay in getting a reply; no one can tell where your letter will eventually catch up with me.

---

[1] A first cousin: daughter of Conrad's Uncle Kazimierz.

Please explain to Zunia and Marcia my reasons for not writing to them. I am sorry indeed! My photographs will not be ready till after my departure. I am leaving addressed envelopes ready for posting them. That is why you will find the photographs unsigned and no letter enclosed. So you see, my dear Maryleczka, how sad the situation is. I doubt even if I shall have time to write a few words to Stanis. and Tadzio.[1] Please act as my intermediary with the family. Embrace them all on my behalf and ask for kind remembrances of the wanderer.

My best regards for Mr. and Mrs. Meresch, Mr. and Mrs. Dąbrowski, and Mr. Tyszka.[2] I kiss my Aunt's hands and embrace you a thousandfold, commending myself to your heart.

Your loving,

K. N. Korzeniowski.

To Maria Bobrowska
Text *Ruch*; Najder 210

London, 6th May, 1890

Maryleczka dear,

I am sailing in an hour. As soon as the photographs are ready I shall send a letter.

The second photograph is for dear Marcia. I shall send a separate one for Aunt. Embraces and best regards for all,

Your loving,

K. N. Korzeniowski.

I am sending one separately for Zunia as well.

To Marguerite Poradowska
Text MS Yale; Rapin 66; G. & S. 10

15 mai 1890
Teneriffe.[3]

Ma chère petite Tante.

Si je Vous disais pour commencer que j'ai evité la fièvre jusqu'a présent! Si je pouvais Vous assurer que toutes mes lettres commenceront par cette bonne nouvelle! Enfin nous verrons! En attendant je suis

---

[1] Zuzanna, Marta, Stanisław and Tadeusz were Maria's brothers and sisters.
[2] Teodor Tyszka, Maria's fiancé; they married on 15 July.
[3] First port of call for the *Ville de Maceio*, heading for Boma.

comparativement heureux ce qui est tout ce que l'on peut éspérer dans ce bas monde. Nous sommes partis de Bordeaux un jour de pluie.[1] Jour triste; depart pas bien gai; des souvenirs qui vous obsèdent; des vagues regrets; des éspérances bien plus vagues encore. On doute de l'avenir. Car enfin—je me demande—pourquoi y croirait-on? Et aussi pourquoi s'attrister?—Un peu d'illusion, beaucoup des rêves, un rare eclair de bonheur puis le desillusionement, un peu de colère et beaucoup de souffrance et puis la fin;—la paix!— Voilà le programme, et nous aurons a voir cette tragi-comedie jusqu'a la fin. Il faut en prendre son parti.—

L'helice tourne et m'emporte vers l'inconnu. Heureusement il y a un autre moi qui rôde de par l'Europe. Qui est en ce moment avec Vous. Qui Vous precedera en Pologne. Un autre moi qui se déplace avec une grande facilité; qui même peut être en deux endroits a la fois. Ne riez pas! Moi je crois que c'est arrivé; je suis très serieux. Ne riez donc pas;—je Vous permets cependant de dire: "Qu'il est bête!"—Ceci est une concession. La vie est composée des concéssions et de compromis.—

A propos de ça. Et l'Evéque? Avez Vous compromis avec l'Eveque![2] Un peu avec Votre conscience et beaucoup avec Votre cœur? Donc: avez Vous commencé a vivre?—Dites moi tout quand Vous ecrirez.—

J'adresse cette lettre a Mme Votre Mère a qui je présente mes devoirs très respectueux ainsi qu'a Mme Votre Belle-Sœur. J'embrasse les enfants bien fort.[3] Dites leur que je leur envois "My love."—

Je baise Vos mains et je me recommande a Votre cœur.

                                        Votre tout devoué

                                                      Conrad.—

Mes comp^ts à Mme & Mr Bouillet J'ai peut-être mal ecrit. Je veux dire Rue Godecharles.[4]

                                                      15 May 1890
                                                      Teneriffe

My dear little Aunt,

What if I were to begin by telling you I have so far avoided the fever! What if I could assure you all my letters will start with this good news!

---

[1] Around 10 May.

[2] Unidentified. The tone of Mme Poradowska's own reference to him (G. & S., p. 136), as well as the play here on 'avec' and 'L'Eveque', suggests someone who was a bishop in manner rather than actual rank.

[3] Mme Charles Gachet (née Maud Chamberlin) and her children, Jean and Alice.

[4] M. and Mme Bouillot, friends of Marguerite Poradowska, who lived in the rue Godecharles in Brussels.

Well, we shall see! In the meanwhile I am comparatively happy, which is all one can hope for in this wicked world. We left Bordeaux on a rainy day. Dismal day, a not very cheerful departure, some haunting memories, some vague regrets, some still vaguer hopes. One doubts the future. For indeed – I ask myself – why should anyone believe in it? And, consequently, why be sad about it? A little illusion, many dreams, a rare flash of happiness followed by disillusionment, a little anger and much suffering, and then the end. Peace! That is the programme, and we must see this tragi-comedy to the end. One must play one's part in it.

The screw turns and carries me off to the unknown. Happily, there is another me who prowls through Europe, who is with you at this moment. Who will get to Poland ahead of you. Another me who moves about with great ease; who can even be in two places at once. Don't laugh! I believe it has happened. I am very serious. So don't laugh. I allow you, however, to say: 'What a fool he is!' This is a concession. Life is composed of concessions and compromises.

While on this subject, how is the Bishop? Have you compromised with the Bishop? A little with your conscience and much with your heart? Then – have you begun to live? Tell me everything when you write.

I address this letter to your mother, to whom I present my very respectful regards, as I do to your sister-in-law. I hug the children. Tell them I send them 'my love'.

I kiss your hands and commend myself to your heart.

Your very devoted

Conrad

My compliments to Mme and M. Bouillet. Perhaps my spelling is wrong. I mean the people in the Rue Godecharles.

To Karol Zagórski

Text J–A, I, 126; Najder 211[1]

Freetown, Sierre Leone,
22nd May, 1890.

My dearest Karol!

It is just a month today since you were scandalized by my hurried departure from Lublin. From the date and address of this letter you will

---

[1] The Polish original has disappeared. Najder's text is based on a collation of Jean-Aubry's published English text with a French translation of the original in the Jean-Aubry archives at Yale.

see that I have had to be pretty quick, and I am only just beginning to breathe a little more calmly. If you only knew the devilish haste I had to make! From London to Brussels, and back again to London! And then again I dashed full tilt to Brussels! If you had only seen all the tin boxes and revolvers, the high boots and the tender farewells; just another handshake and just another pair of trousers!—and if you knew all the bottles of medicine and all the affectionate wishes I took away with me, you would understand in what a typhoon, cyclone, hurricane, earthquake—no!—in what a universal cataclysm, in what a fantastic atmosphere of mixed shopping, business, and affecting scenes, I passed two whole weeks. But the fortnight spent at sea has allowed me to rest and I am impatiently waiting for the end of this trip. I am due to reach Boma on the 7th of next month[1] and then leave with my caravan to go to Léopoldville. As far as I can make out from my 'lettre d'instruction' I am destined to the command of a steamboat, belonging to M. Delcommune's[2] exploring party, which is being got ready. I like this prospect very much, but I know nothing for certain as everything is supposed to be kept secret. What makes me rather uneasy is the information that 60 per cent. of our Company's employees return to Europe before they have completed even six months' service. Fever and dysentery! There are others who are sent home in a hurry at the end of a year, so that they shouldn't die in the Congo. God forbid! It would spoil the statistics which are excellent, you see! In a word, there are only 7 per cent. who can do their three years' service. It's a fact! To tell the truth, they are French! Des nevrosés! (C'est très chic d'être nevrosé—[3] one winks and speaks through the nose.) Yes! But a Polish nobleman, cased in British tar! What a concoction! Nous verrons! In any case I shall console myself by remembering—faithful to our national traditions— that I looked for this trouble myself.

When you see—with the help of a microscope, no doubt—the hieroglyphics of my handwriting. you will, I expect, wonder why I am writing to you? First, because it is a pleasure to talk to you; next, because, considering the distinguished personage who is penning this autograph, it ought to be a pleasure to you too. You can bequeath it to your children.

---

[1] Conrad's destination on the *Ville de Maceio*, which began his Congo adventure; he arrived in Boma on 12 June and departed from Matadi, for Léopoldville, on 28 June.

[2] Alexandre Delcommune, an explorer brother of Camille Delcommune, the Congo Company manager at Kinshasa, whose dislike of Conrad was equalled by Conrad's detestation of him.

[3] 'Neurotics! (It's very fashionable to be neurotic).'

Future generations will read it with admiration (and I hope with profit). In the meantime, trêve de bêtises![1]

I kiss my dear uncle's and aunt's hands,[2] and your wife's too. I forget none of you, but can't write the whole list because this abominable lamp is going out.

> Yours very affectionately
> K. N. Korzeniowski.

To Marguerite Poradowska
Text   MS Yale; Rapin 67; G. & S. 11

> 10 Juin 1890.
> Libreville. Gabon.—

Chère petite Tante.

Ceci étant la dernière escale avant Boma ou se termine mon voyage par mer je commence cette lettre ici au moment de partance afin de la continuer pendant la traversée et la terminer le jour de mon arrivée a Boma, d'ou naturellement je vais l'expédier.[3]

Rien de neuf quand aux événements. Quand aux sentiments rien de neuf aussi; et là est le malheur; car, si on pouvait se debarrasser de son cœur, de sa mémoire (et aussi—de sa cervelle) et se procurer ensuite un nouveau service complet de ces choses-là, la vie deviendrait idéalement amusante. Comme c'est impossible, elle ne l'est pas. C'est abominablement triste! Par example: entre autres choses que je voudrai oublier sans y parvenir, je voudrai perdre le souvenir de ma charmante Tante. Naturellement c'est impossible; par consequent je me rapelle, et je suis triste. Ou êtes-Vous? Comment êtes-Vous? M'avez-Vous oublié? Vous laisse-t-on bien tranquille? Travaillez Vous? Surtout cela! Avez-Vous trouvé l'oubli et la paix du travail qui crée, qui absorbe? Enfin voilà! Je me demande tout cela. Vous avez doté ma vie d'un nouvel interet, d'une nouvelle affection; je Vous en suis très réconnaissant. Reconnaissant pour toute la douceur, pour toute l'amertume de ce cadeau sans prix. Je regarde aprésant dans deux avenues taillées dans le l'épais et chaotique fouillis d'herbes malsaines. Ou vont-elles. Vous suivez l'une, moi l'autre. Elle divergent. Trouverez Vous un rayon de soleil, aussi pâle qu'il soit,

---

[1] 'Enough of these stupidities!'
[2] Karol Zagórski's parents, Jan Zagórski and Gabriela Zagórska, née Poradowska. Cf. letter to Mme Poradowska, 14 February.
[3] Conrad had probably arrived in Libreville, Gabon, by 28 May. On 12 June he reached Boma, which is about 60 miles from the mouth of the Congo River; in 1890, it served as administrative capital and chief port of call of the Congo Free State.

au bout de la Votre?—Je l'éspère! Je vous le souhaite! Il y a longtemps que je ne m'interesse plus au but ou mon chemin me conduit. Je m'en allais la tête baissée, maudissant les pierres. Aprésant je m'interesse a un autre voyageur; ça me fait oublier les petites misères de mon chemin a moi.—

En attendant l'inévitable fièvre, je me porte très bien.—Pour rendre l'existence tant soit peu supportable il me faut des lettres; beacoup des lettres. De vous entre autres. N'oubliez pas ce que je Vous dis là chère et bonne petite Tante.

Après mon depart de Boma il se peut faire un long silence. Je ne pourrais ecrire qu'une fois arrivé a Leopoldville. Il faut 20 jours pour y aller; à pied aussi![1] Horreur.—

Probablement Vous ecrirez a mon oncle; c'etait Votre intention je crois. Vous serez bien bonne de lui dire quelque chose de moi. Par exemple que Vous m'avez vu à Bruxelles, que j'étais bien de corps et d'esprit. Ça lui fera plaisir et il en sera plus tranquille sur mon sort. Il m'aime beaucoup et moi je m'attendris comme une vieille bête quand je pense a lui. Pardonnez cette faiblesse.—Quand serez Vous de retour a Bruxelles?[2] Quels sont Vos projets d'avenir? Entretenez moi de tout cela dans Vos lettre et ne Vous mettez pas a Votre ecritoire que quand Vous aurez une bonne envie de causer avec "l'absent". "L'absent" sera mon appelation officielle a l'avenir.—Je serai bien heureux de savoir que l'on ne Vous embête pas; que Vous travaillez l'esprit libre. J'attends Votre nouvelle œuvre avec curiosité et impatience.[3] Il faudra me l'envoyer. N'est-ce pas? J'apprends que ma compagnie a un navire de mer et que probablement ils en construiront d'autres. Si je pouvais en obtenir le commandement ça serait bien mieux que la rivière. Outre que c'est plus sain on a toujours la chance de revenir chaque année au moins en Europe.—Quand Vous reviendrez a Bruxelles je vous prierais de me faire savoir si on en construit de sorte que je pourrai faire ma demande. Vous pourrez savoir par Mr Wauters.[4] Tandis que moi au fond

---

[1] If we can take his words in 'Heart of Darkness' literally, Conrad spent only one night in Boma before departing for Matadi 30 miles upstream. He apparently passed about two weeks in Matadi, having written to Mme Poradowska on 18 and 24 June (the letter of the 24th is lost). Léopoldville is close by Kinshasa, where Conrad expected to take his command; he arrived at Kinshasa about 2 August after an overland journey from Matadi of 230 miles.

[2] Mme Poradowska was then in Poland.

[3] Mme Poradowska's adaptation from the Polish of Ladislas Łozinski's *La Madone de Busowiska*, a novella which appeared in the *Revue des Deux Mondes* for 1 September 1891.

[4] Although a resident of Brussels, A. J. Wauters (b. 1845) was an important figure in Congo affairs, as secretary-general of the Compagnies Belges du Congo, founder and editor of the *Mouvement Géographique* and the *Congo Illustré*, and one of the compilers of the *Bibliographie du Congo, 1880–1895*.

d'afrique je n'aurai pas des nouvelles. Je suis sur que Vous ferez cela pour moi.—

Au revoir chère Tante. Je Vous aime et Vous embrasse
C. Korzeniowski.

10 June 1890
Libreville, Gabon

Dear little Aunt,

This being the last port of call before Boma, where my sea-voyage ends, I am beginning this letter here at the moment of leaving so as to continue it during the passage and end it the day of my arrival in Boma, where of course I am going to post it.

No new events. As to feelings, also nothing new, and there is the trouble. For, if one could unburden oneself of one's heart, one's memory (and also – one's brain) and obtain a whole new set of these things, life would become perfectly diverting. As this is impossible, life is not perfectly diverting. It is abominably sad! For example: among other things I should like to forget but cannot – I should like to forget the memory of my charming Aunt. Naturally, it is impossible. Consequently, I remember and am sad. Where are you? How are you? Have you forgotten me? Have you been left undisturbed? Are you working? That above all! Have you found the forgetfulness and peace of work that is creative and absorbing? So, you see! I ask myself all these questions. You have endowed my life with new interest, new affection; I am very grateful to you for this. Grateful for all the sweetness, for all the bitterness of this priceless gift. I now look down two avenues cut through the thick and chaotic jungle of noxious weeds. Where do they go? You follow one, I the other. They diverge. Do you find a ray of sunlight, however pale, at the end of yours? I hope so! I wish it for you! For a long time I have no longer been interested in the goal to which my road leads. I was going along it with my head lowered, cursing the stones. Now I am interested in another traveller; this makes me forget the petty miseries of my own path.

While awaiting the inevitable fever, I am very well. In order to make my existence even slightly bearable, I need letters, many letters. From you, among others. Do not forget what I am telling you, dear and kind little Aunt.

After my departure from Boma, there may be an extended silence. I shall be unable to write until Léopoldville. It takes twenty days to go there, on foot too! How horrible!

You will probably write to my uncle; it was your intention, I believe. It would be kind if you would give him news of me. For example, that you saw me in Brussels, that I was well in body and spirit. This will give him pleasure and make him easier about my fate. He is very fond of me, and I grow as tender as an old fool when I think of him. Forgive this weakness. When do you return to Brussels? What are your future plans? Tell me all about it in your letter and sit at your desk only when you have a strong inclination to chat with 'the absent one'. 'The absent one' will be my official name in future. I shall be very happy to know that nobody is worrying you; that you work with an untroubled free spirit. I await your new work with curiosity and impatience. You must send it to me. Agreed? I have learned that my company has a sea-going ship and probably will build others. If I could obtain the command of one, that would be much better than the river. Not only is it healthier; there is always the chance of returning to Europe at least every year. When you return to Brussels, I beg you to let me know if any ships of this sort are being built so that I can enter my request. You can learn this through M. Wauters, whereas I, in the depths of Africa, will have no news. I am sure you will do that for me.

Au revoir, dear Aunt. I love and embrace you.

C. Korzeniowski

To Marguerite Poradowska

Text   MS Yale; Rapin 68; G. & S. 14

Matadi. 18.6.90[1]

Merci! Merci mille fois chère Tante pour Votre bonne et charmante lettre, venue a ma rencontre a Boma. Il n'y a qu'une petite Tante cherie pour imaginer des si jolies surprises. Si ca m'a fait plaisir?! J'ai bien envie de dire non pour Vous punir de me l'avoir demandé, pour avoir eu l'air d'en douter!

Je pars demain a pattes. Pas d'âne ici excepté Votre très humble serviteur. Vingt jours de caravane.[2] La temperature très supportable ici

---

[1] The dating 18 June would appear inconsistent with Conrad's words that her letter, received in Boma, made him very happy 'the day before yesterday', since he left Boma, apparently, on 13 June. Conrad, possibly, was speaking loosely, as G. & S. speculate.

[2] Conrad actually left on 28 June, if we can believe his 'Congo Diary'. Along with Prosper Harou, a Belgian agent of the Congo Free State, and 31 porters and guides, he spent 34 days (from 28 June to 1 August) on the trip from Matadi to Nselemba, by Stanley Pool.

et santé très bonne. Aussitot possible j'ecrirai. Apresant je Vous embrasse bien fort et baise la main qui a tracé des mots qui m'ont rendu très heureux avant'hier. Votre neveu très aimant et serviteur devoué

Conrad.—

18 June 1890
Matadi

Thank you! Many thanks, dear Aunt, for your kind and charming letter, which met me at Boma. Only my dear little Aunt could think up such splendid surprises. Has it given me pleasure?! I have a good mind to say No in order to punish you for having asked, for having seemed to doubt it!

I leave tomorrow on foot. Not an ass here except your very humble servant. Twenty days of safari. Temperature very bearable here and health very good. I shall write as soon as possible. Now I embrace you very heartily and kiss the hand that wrote the words which made me very happy the day before yesterday. Your very loving nephew and devoted servant

Conrad

To Maria Tyszkowa
Text *Ruch*; Najder 212

Kinshasa,
Stanley Pool,
Congo.
24th September, 1890.

My dear Maryleczka,

Your letter and the photograph reached me today and I hasten to write and explain to you the long interruption in our correspondence.

I have been on the river Congo, some 2,000 versts[1] from the coast where the post office is, so I could neither send nor get news from Europe. I was pleased to get your letter although at the same time it saddened me slightly. I have lived long enough to realize that life is full of griefs and sorrows which no one can escape, nevertheless I cannot help feeling sad at the thought that people whom I love must suffer, and are suffering. It is nonetheless pleasing to get a proof of the trust you place in me by writing openly about your worries. Indeed, I do not deserve to have a place in your hearts – for I am practically a stranger to you – nevertheless

---

[1] A Russian *verst* is about two-thirds of an English mile.

the affectionate words you have written are most precious to me. I shall carefully preserve them in my heart, and the photograph will be in my album so that I can glance each day at my dear little sister.

Now that you are married and your desires fulfilled my wish for you both is that your lives will be nothing but sunshine with no clouds in the sky.[1] Please, assure your husband of my deep esteem, and of the very friendly feelings I have for him. I accept your invitation with gratitude and I promise to devote as much time as possible to my good lady sister.[2] I trust that Aunt's health will improve steadily now that all the unpleasant contacts are left behind. I have a letter from Uncle Tadeusz, who intended to visit you in August. He is probably back home by now.

I am very busy with all the preparations for a new expedition to the River Kassai.[3] In a few days I shall probably be leaving Kinshasa again for a few months, possibly even for a year or longer. Thus you must not be surprised if you get no sign of life from me for a long time.

My love to dear Zuzia and my apologies for not having written to her. Please send me her exact address – and your new one as well. I kiss dear Aunt's hands. I commend myself to your thoughts and especially to your heart, dear Maryleczka.

Do not forget about me amidst all the new events in your life. I embrace you most warmly.

Your always loving brother,
K. N. Korzeniowski.

To Marguerite Poradowska

Text   MS Yale; Rapin 69; G. & S. 15

26 Sept^{re} 1890.
Kinchassa.[4]

La plus chère et la meilleure des Tantes! J'ai reçu Vos 3 lettres ensemble a mon retour de Stanley Falls ou je suis allé comme supernuméraire a bord du navire "Roi des Belges" afin d'apprendre la rivière.[5]—

---

[1] Maria (née Bobrowska) had married Teodor Tyszka on 15 July.

[2] An affectionate term. Conrad was her first cousin.

[3] Conrad never made this expedition, nor were his plans for a permanent command fulfilled.

[4] Beside Léopoldville, on the Stanley Pool, where Conrad arrived on 2 August; base of the Upper Congo flotilla.

[5] The sequence in 'Heart of Darkness' does not follow what actually happened. Conrad left Kinshasa on 4 August with Camille Delcommune, the station manager, aboard for Stanley Falls, on the Upper Congo; when Conrad had been instructed about navigational dangers by a Dane named Koch, he was to be placed in (temporary) command. He arrived in Stanley Falls on 1 September and returned to Kinshasa on the 24th. For parallels to 'Heart of Darkness', see Rapin, p. 69, n. 6, and *CWW*, *passim*.

J'apprends avec joie Votre succès a l'academie[1] dont—du reste—je n'ai jamais douté. Je ne peux pas trouver des mots assez expressifs pour Vous faire comprendre le plaisir Vos charmantes (et surtout bonnes) lettres m'ont causé. C'était comme un rayon de soleil perçant a travers le nuages gris d'une triste journée d'hiver; car mes journées ici sont tristes. Il n'y a pas a s'y tromper! Decidement je regrette d'etre venu ici. Je le regrette même amèrement. Avec tout l'egoisme d'un homme je vais parler de moi. Je ne peux pas m'en empêcher. Devant qui soulagerai-je mon cœur si ce n'est devant Vous?! En Vous parlant j'ai la certitude d'être compris au demi-mot. Votre cœur devinera mes pensées plus vite que je ne saurai les exprimer.—

Tout m'est antipathique ici. Les hommes et les choses; mais surtout les hommes.[2] Et moi je leur suis antipathique aussi. A commmencer par le directeur en Afrique qui a pris la peine de dire a bien de monde que je lui dèplaisai souverainement jusqu'au a finir par le plus vulgaire mécanicien ils ont tous le don de m'agacer les nerfs—de sorte que je ne suis pas aussi agréable pour eux peut-être que je pourrai l'être. Le directeur est un vulgaire marchand d'ivoire a instincts sordides qui s'imagine étre un commerçant tandis qu'il n'est qu'une éspèce de boutiquier africain. Son nom est Delcommune.[3] Il deteste les Anglais et je suis naturellement regardé comme tel ici. Je n'ai a esperer ni promotion ni augmentation d'appointements tant qu'il sera ici. Du reste il a dit que les promesses faites en Europe ne le lient guère ici tant qu'elles ne sont pas sur le contrat.[4] Celles faîtes a moi par Mr Wauters ne le sont pas. Du reste je ne peux rien esperer vu que je n'ai pas de navire a commander.[5] Le bateau neuf sera fini en Juin de l'année prochaine peut-être.[6] En attendant ma position ici n'est pas nette et j'ai des ennuis

---

[1] Her *Demoiselle Micia, mœurs galiciennes*, which had been published in the *Revue des Deux Mondes*, appeared under the Hachette imprint in 1889 and won one of the six French Academy prizes of 500 francs.

[2] Further evidence appears in the 'Congo Diary' and in 'Heart of Darkness'; for a detailed discussion, see *CWW*, pp. 45ff.

[3] Camille Delcommune (1859–92), first assistant manager of the Société Belge du Haut-Congo, then manager. For a further account of Conrad's relationship with him, see *CWW*, and Jean-Aubry's *Conrad in the Congo* (London, 1926), pp. 58ff.

[4] Upon receiving this letter, Mme Poradowska wrote to Albert Thys indicating that Delcommune had told Conrad not to expect either promotion or rise in salary; further, that Conrad was told that contracts made in Europe were not binding in the Congo. Her letter is dated 29 November.

[5] The *Florida*, which Conrad had intended to command when he arrived in Kinshasa, was given to a man named Carlier at the urging of Alexandre Delcommune. Conrad took his revenge on Carlier by using his name for one of the feckless agents in 'An Outpost of Progress' (1897). For Wauters, see notes to letter of 10 June.

[6] Gee and Sturm mention the launching of two new ships in 1891, the *Archiduchesse Stéphanie* and the *Princesse Clémentine*.

a cause de cela. Enfin!—Pour comble d'agrément ma santé est loin d'être bonne. *Gardez m'en le secret*—mais c'est un fait que j'ai eu la fievre en remontant la riviere 4 fois en 2 mois,[1] et puis aux Falls (qui en est la patrie) j'ai attrapé une attaque de dyssenterie qui a duré 5 jours. Je me sens assez faible de corps et tant soit peu demoralisé, et puis ma foi je crois que j'ai la nostalgie de la mer, l'envie de revoir ces plaines d'eau salé qui m'a si souvent bercée, qui m'a souri tant de fois sous le scintillement des rayons de soleil par une belle journée, qui bien des fois aussi m'a lancé la menace de mort a la figure dans un tourbillon d'ecume blanche fouettée par le vent sous le ciel sombre de Decembre. Je regrette tout cela. Mais ce que je regrette le plus c'est de m'être lié pour 3 ans. Il est vrai qu'il n'est guère probable que je les finirais. Ou l'on me cherchera une querelle d'allemand pour me renvoyer (et ma foi je me prends quelquefois a le désirer) ou une nouvelle attaque de dissenterie me renverra en Europe, a moins qu'elle ne m'envoie dans l'autre monde, ce qui serait une solution finale de tous mes embarras! Et voilà quatre pages que je parle de moi même! Je ne Vous ai pas dit avec quelles délices j'ai lu Vos descriptions des hommes et des choses chez nous.[2] En verité en lisant Vos chères lettres j'ai oublié l'Afrique, le Congo, les sauvages noirs et les esclaves blancs (dont je suis un) qui l'habitent. J'ai été heureux pendant une heure. Savez que ce n'est pas une petite chose (ni une chose facile) de rendre une créature humaine heureuse pendant *toute une* heure. Vous pouvez être fière d'y avoir réussi. Aussi mon cœur va vers Vous dans un elan de gratitude et d'affection la plus sincère et la plus profonde. Quand nous reverrons nous? Helas la rencontre conduit a la separation—et plus on se rencontre plus les separations sont douleureuses. Fatalité.—

Cherchant un remède pratique a la désagréable situation que je me suis fait j'ai trouvé un petit plan—assez en l'air—ou Vous pourriez peut-être m'aider. Il parait que cette compagnie ou une autre affiliée a celle-ci aura—(est[3] même en a déjà un) des navires de mer.[4] Probablement ce grand (ou gros?) banquier qui fait la pluie et le beau temps chez nous aura un large intérêt dans l'autre Comp^ie.—Si on pouvait soumettre mon nom pour Commander un de leur navires

---

[1] Since leaving Matadi.

[2] Mme Poradowska was then in Lublin.

[3] Conrad frequently wrote 'est' for 'et' and vice versa.

[4] Apparently, Conrad was in error, for no Belgian ship moved between Europe and the Congo in the beginning of 1892 (G. & S.). In this connection, Mme Poradowska brought the problem to M. Albert Thys and asked him for a command for Conrad (Jean-Aubry, *Conrad in the Congo*, p. 334).

(dont le port d'attache sera Anvers) je pourrai chaque voy^{ge} m'echapper pour un jour ou deux a Bruxelles quand vous êtes là. Ce serait ideal! Si on voulait me rappeler pour prendre un commandement je payerais mes frais de retour moi même naturellement. C'est une idée a peine praticable peut-être mais si Vous revenez a Bruxelles en hiver, Vous pourriez par M^r. Wauters savoir ce qui en est. N'est-ce pas chère petite Tante?—

Je vais envoyer ceci aux soins de la Princesse (que j'aime parce qu'elle Vous aime).[1]—Bientôt probablement Vous verrez pauvre chère Tante Gaba, ces chers et bons Charles Zag^{ski} et leur charmantes petites.[2] Je Vous envie! Dites leur que je les aime bien tous et que j'en demande un petit brin de retour. Mlle Marysieńka a oublié probablement la promesse qu'elle m'a faite de sa fotographie![3] Je suis toujours son cousin et serviteur très devoué. Je n'ose pas dire admirateur de peur de ma Tante Ołdakowska a qui je me rapelle avec affection.[4] Je Vous charge par tous les dieux de me garder le secret de ma santé devant *tout le monde*, autrement mon oncle sera sur de le savoir.—Je finis. Je pars dans une heure pour Bamou[5] dans un canot choisir et faire couper le bois de construction pour la station ici. Je resterai campé dans la foret 2 ou 3 semaines a moins de maladie.[6] J'aime cela assez. Je pourrai sans doute avoir un ou deux coup de fusil sur les buffles ou elephants. Je Vous embrasse de tout mon cœur. J'ecris par la malle prochaine une longue lettre.[7] Votre affectionné neveu

J.C.K.

26 September 1890
Kinshasa

Dearest and best of Aunts!

I received your three letters together on my return from Stanley Falls, where I went as a supernumerary on board the vessel *Roi des Belges* in order to learn about the river. I learn with joy of your success at the Academy, which, of course, I never doubted. I cannot find words sufficiently strong to make you understand the pleasure your charming (and above all kind) letters have given me. They were as a ray of

---

[1] See notes to letter of 10 March.
[2] Aunt Gabriela Zagórska. The Zagórski daughters were Aniela and Karola.
[3] Marie Ołdakowska, niece of Mme Poradowska.
[4] Mme Poradowska's sister-in-law.
[5] Thirty miles west of Kinshasa.
[6] According to Jean-Aubry, Conrad returned to Kinshasa by October 19.
[7] Possibly written and lost.

sunshine piercing through the grey clouds of a dreary winter day; for my days here are dreary. No use deluding oneself! Decidedly I regret having come here. I even regret it bitterly. With all of a man's egoism, I am going to speak of myself. I cannot stop myself. Before whom can I ease my heart if not before you?! In speaking to you, I am certain of being understood down to the merest hint. Your heart will divine my thoughts more quickly than I can express them.

Everything here is repellent to me. Men and things, but men above all. And I am repellent to them, also. From the manager in Africa who has taken the trouble to tell one and all that I offend him supremely, down to the lowest mechanic, they all have the gift of irritating my nerves – so that I am not as agreeable to them perhaps as I should be. The manager is a common ivory dealer with base instincts who considers himself a merchant although he is only a kind of African shop-keeper. His name is Delcommune. He detests the English, and out here I am naturally regarded as such. I cannot hope for either promotion or salary increases while he is here. Besides, he has said that promises made in Europe carry no weight here if they are not in the contract. Those made to me by M. Wauters are not. In addition, I cannot look forward to anything because I don't have a ship to command. The new boat will not be completed until June of next year, perhaps. Meanwhile, my position here is unclear and I am troubled by that. So there you are! As crowning joy, my health is far from good. *Keep it a secret for me* – but the truth is that in going up the river I suffered from fever four times in two months, and then at the Falls (which is its home territory), I suffered an attack of dysentery lasting five days. I feel somewhat weak physically and not a little demoralized; and then, really, I believe that I feel homesick for the sea, the desire to look again on the level expanse of salt water which has so often lulled me, which has smiled at me so frequently under the sparkling sunshine of a lovely day, which many times too has hurled the threat of death in my face with a swirl of white foam whipped by the wind under the dark December sky. I regret all that. But what I regret even more is having tied myself down for three years. The truth is that it is scarcely probable I shall see them through. Either someone in authority will pick a groundless quarrel in order to send me back (and, really, I sometimes find myself wishing for it), or I shall be sent back to Europe by a new attack of dysentery, unless it consigns me to the other world, which would be a final solution to all my distress! And for four pages I have been speaking of myself! I have not told you with what pleasure I have read your descriptions of men and things at home. Indeed, while reading your dear letters I have forgotten Africa, the Congo, the black savages and the white slaves (of whom I am one) who inhabit it. For one hour I have been happy. Know that it is not a small thing (nor an easy thing) to make a human being happy for an *entire hour*. You can be proud of having succeeded. And so my heart goes out to you with a burst of gratitude and the most sincere and most profound affection. When will we meet again? Alas, meeting leads to parting – and the more one meets, the more painful the separations become. Such is Fate.

Seeking a practical remedy to the disagreeable situation which I have made for myself, I conceived of a little plan – still up in the air – in which you could perhaps help me. It appears that this company, or another affiliated with it, will have some ocean-going vessels (or even has one already). Probably that great (or fat?) banker who rules the roost where we are concerned will have a large interest in the other company. If someone could submit my name for the command of one of their ships (whose home port will be Antwerp) I would be able to get away for a day or two in Brussels when you are there. That would be ideal! If they wanted to call me home to take command, I would naturally pay the cost of coming back myself. This is perhaps not a very practicable idea, but if you return to Brussels in the winter, you could learn through M. Wauters what the chances are. Isn't that so, dear little Aunt?

I am going to send this care of the Princess (whom I love because she loves you). Soon, probably, you will see poor, dear Aunt Gaba, and that dear and good Charles Zagórski family with their charming little daughters. I envy you! Tell them that I love them all and that I ask a little something in return. Mlle Marysieńka has probably forgotten the promise she made me about her photograph. I am ever her devoted cousin and servant. I dare not say 'admirer' for fear of my Aunt Ołdakowska, to whom I wish to be remembered with affection. I urge you by all the gods to keep secret from *everybody* the state of my health, or else my uncle will certainly hear of it. I must finish. I leave within an hour for Bamou, by canoe, to select trees and have them felled for building operations at the station here. I shall remain encamped in the forest for two or three weeks, unless ill. I like the prospect well enough. I can doubtless have a shot or two at some buffaloes or elephants. I embrace you most warmly. I shall write a long letter by the next mail.

Your affectionate nephew

J.C.K.

1891

To Marguerite Poradowska

Text MS Yale; Rapin 77; G. & S. 19

Londres. Dimanche
[1? February 1891][1]

Ma chère Tante.

Arrivé heureusement ici[2] je me suis empressé de courir chez le
medecin qui pour commencer m'a envoyé au lit[3]—a cause de mes
jambes.—Il m'a completement rassuré quand a l'état general de ma
santé. Je suis tant soit peu anémié mais tout les organes sont en bon
état.—

Je me suis levé aujourd'hui exprès pour ecrire. Je viens de finir la lettre
a mon oncle; je me sens beaucoup plus fort et je ne doute pas que dans
peu de semaines je serai parfaitement retabli.—

J'ai honte de l'avouer a Mme Votre Belle-Sœur mais j'ai perdu
l'adresse qu'elle m'a donné pour le paquet confié à ma charge.[4] J'espère
qu'elle voudra bien me pardonner et m'enverra l'addresse nécéssaire.—

Rien d'interessant à Vous dire. Plus je viellis plus je deviens bête. Je ne
saurais même pas inventer des nouvelles. Je ne suis pas très gai enfermé
comme je le suis. J'ai des livres; mais les livres sont bêtes aussi.—

Je pense que je serai en état de me remettre au travail dans six
semaines. Pourvu que j'en trouve?!

Si Vous croyez Pêchet praticable je Vous informe que je suis agé de 32
ans. Possède certificat anglais de Cap^ne marin que j'ai servi a voile et a
vapeur. Commandé les deux—mais principalement a voile.[5] Que je
peux fournir des bonnes references des armateurs et aussi de negociants
a Londres.—Avec tous ces avantages je brule de desir d'avoir l'honneur
de commander un des vapeurs a M. Pechet.—Vous pourrez aussi
ajouter que jugant a l'apparence de mon nez je ne m'enivre qu'une fois
par an, que je n'ai pas l'air d'avoir un penchant vers la piraterie et
que—d'après ce que Vous savez de moi—Vous ne me croyez pas capable
de commettre un detournement des fonds. Je n'ai jamais passé a la police
correctionnele et je suis capable de donner un coup d'œil discret a un joli

---

[1] Under the address, Mme Poradowska wrote 'Fevrier 91'. Gee and Sturm assign
Conrad's letter to 1 February a Sunday, citing an incomplete answer of Mme
Poradowska's, dated 4 February.
[2] In late January.
[3] Possibly the Dr Ludwig mentioned by Jean-Aubry (1, 145), who sent Conrad to Champel
for hydrotherapy.
[4] He had spent two days in Brussels on his way back from the Congo.
[5] Ed. Pécher et Cie of Antwerp were agents for the Prince Steam Shipping Co., Ltd, which
operated ships in the African service. Conrad was 33 (not 32); his certificate was dated 11
November 1886; he had commanded the *Otago* (1888–9) and the *Roi des Belges* (1890).

minois sans loucher. Il est vrai que je boîte, mais je suis en compagnie distinguée. Timoléon etait boîteux et il y a même un Diable qui l'est d'après ce que j'ai entendu dire.[1]—

Si après avoir entendu tout cela il refuse de me confier un navire, eh bien il faudra l'abandonner a son triste sort—et chercher ailleurs.—

Mes devoir a Mme Votre mère et a Mme Gachet Jun: J'embrasse les enfants.[2]—

Je baise Vos deux mains et en attendant de Vos nouvelles je suis toujours—et pour toujours—Votre neveu très devoué et Votre très humble serviteur

K. N. Korzeniowski

Mes comp^ts a Mme et Mr. Bouilhet.[3]
ad: c/o of Barr Mo[e]ring & C°
36 Camomile Street
London E.C.

London, Sunday
[1? February 1891]

My dear Aunt,

Having arrived here safely, I could hardly wait to run to the doctor, who, to begin with, sent me to bed – because of my legs. He has completely reassured me about the general state of my health. I am somewhat anaemic, but all my organs are in good condition.

I got up today expressly to write. I have just finished the letter to my uncle. I feel much stronger, and I don't doubt that within a few weeks I shall be perfectly recovered.

I am ashamed to confess this to your sister-in-law, but I have lost the address she gave me for the package entrusted to my care. I hope she will be kind enough to forgive me and will send the necessary address.

Nothing interesting to tell you. The older I get, the more stupid I become. I would not even know how to make up any news. I am not very cheerful, shut in as I am. I have some books, but the books are stupid too.

I think I shall be able to return to work in six weeks – if I can find any! If you believe Péchet approachable, I inform you that I am thirty-two

---

[1] Conrad confuses Timoleon, the Greek statesman, with Tamerlaine, the lame conqueror. The other allusion is to Lesage's satirical novel *Le Diable boiteux* (1707).

[2] Mme Charles Gachet, sister-in-law of Mme Poradowska, not to be confused with Mme Émile Gachet, Mme Poradowska's mother. The children were Jean and Alice.

[3] Bouillot.

years old, have English master's certificate for my service in sail and steam, commanded both – but principally sail – can furnish good references from shipowners and also from London merchants. With all these assets, I burn with the desire to have the honour of commanding one of M. Péchet's steamers. You can also add that, judging from the appearance of my nose, I get drunk only once a year, that I don't seem to have any leanings towards piracy, and that – according to what you know of me – you do not believe me capable of committing embezzlement. I have never come within the jurisdiction of the police, and I am capable of looking discreetly upon a pretty face without leering. It is true I limp, but I am in distinguished company. Timoleon was lame, and there is even a devil in the same condition, according to my information. If, after having understood all that, he refuses to entrust me with a ship, well then, we shall abandon him to his sad fate – and look elsewhere.

My regards to your mother and to the younger Mme Gachet. I hug the children.

I kiss both your hands and, while waiting to hear from you, I am still – and for always – your very devoted nephew and very humble servant

K.N. Korzeniowski

My compliments to Mme and M. Bouilhet [Bouillot]
Address: Care of Barr Moering & Co.
36 Camomile Street
London E.C.

To Marguerite Poradowska

Text MS Yale; Rapin 79; G. & S. 21

Dimanche soir
[8 February 1891][1]
Londres.

Ma chère Tante.

On avait egaré Votre Carte postale au bureau[2] de sorte que je ne l'ai recue qu'aujourd'hui. Je suis très malheureux de Vous savoir souffrante. Je suis sur que Vous Vous êtes refroidie le soir en me reconduisant.[3] C'etait si bon de causer avec Vous quelques instants de plus que je n'ai pas protésté comme j'aurai du le faire; egoïste que je suis!

---

[1] As in the previous letter, the dating is Mme Poradowska's. Rapin and Gee and Sturm agree.
[2] Barr, Moering's.
[3] In Brussels, the preceding month.

Je ne sais pas comment Vous exprimer ma reconnaissance pour Votre bonté. Malade comme Vous l'êtes Vous pensez à moi! Ce n'est pas encore le fait des services que Vous voulez me rendre qui me touche. C'est surtout de savoir qu'il y a au monde quelqu'un qui me porte interêt, dont le cœur m'est ouvert, qui me rend heureux.—Soignez Vous ma chère Tante et surtout prenez bien garde de sortir trop tôt avant une guerison complète.

Moi je vais mieux; je me sens plus fort et plus disposé a vivre—ou du moins a supporter l'existence. Cette même existence est assez monotone a présant. Je sors peu pour ne pas fatiguer mes jambes. Il peut se faire que la semaine prochaine j'irai a Anvers avec mon ami M. Hope[1]—pour affaires. Dans ce cas naturellement Vous me verrez—si Vous permettez. Je ne vais pas m'infliger pour longtemps. Une visite de 2–3 heures Voulez Vous?!—

En attendant je Vous embrasse de tout mon cœur, je baise Vos mains et je suis toujours Votre neveu

très dévoué

J. C. Korzeniowski.

Sunday evening [8 February 1891]
London

My dear Aunt,

They mislaid your postcard at the office, consequently I received it only today. I am very sorry to learn you are not well. I am sure you caught cold the evening you saw me home. It was so good to chat with you for a few moments longer that I didn't protest as I should have done; egoist that I am!

I do not know how to express my gratitude for your kindness. Ill as you are, you think of me! What touches me is not simply the fact that you want to be of service to me. It is above all to know that there is in the world someone who takes an interest in me, whose heart is open to me, who makes me happy. Take care of yourself, my dear Aunt, and above all beware of going out too soon before a complete recovery.

As for myself, I am getting better. I feel myself stronger and more disposed to live – or at least to endure existence. This same existence is monotonous enough at present. I go out little so as not to tire my legs. Possibly next week I will go to Antwerp with my friend Mr Hope – on

---

[1] The trip to Antwerp was postponed. For Hope, 'the Director of Companies', see letter to Thys, 28 November 1889.

business. In that case, of course, you will see me – if you agree. I am not going to inflict myself on you for long. A visit of 2–3 hours – would you like that?!

In the meantime I embrace you warmly, I kiss your hands, and I am always

Your very devoted nephew
J. C. Korzeniowski

To Marguerite Poradowska
Text MS Yale; Rapin 80; G. & S. 22

17 Fev. [18]91
[letterhead: Barr, Moering]

Ma chère Tante.—

Imaginez Vous j'ai été en Ecosse[1]—toujours pour affaires. Je viens de lire Vos chères lettres. Vous êtes la meilleure des Tantes!—Je me suis fatigué tant soit peu et mes jambes sont enflées de nouveau. J'ai l'intention de me reposer pendant quelque jours.—Le voyage a Anvers est remis pour quelque temps ou peut-être abandonné pour toujours en ce qui concerne les affaires. Mais cela ne m'empêchera pas de venir a Bruxelles sous peu—Vous payer une petite visite. Veuillez m'ecrire un mot au reçu de ce gribouillage pour me dire comment Vous allez. J'ai hâte de rentrer chez moi me coucher voila pourquoi je n'ecris pas plus longuement.

Je vous embrasse de tout mon cœur.

Votre très reconnaissant, et devoué neveu
K. N. Korzeniowski

J'ecris bientôt longue lettre.

17 February 1891
[letterhead: Barr, Moering]

My dear Aunt,

Think of it, I have been in Scotland – on business as always. I have just read your dear letters. You are the best of Aunts! – I am somewhat tired and my legs are swollen once again. I intend to rest for several days. The trip to Antwerp has been postponed for some time or perhaps abandoned

---

[1] In Glasgow, seeking a command.

altogether, as far as business is concerned. But that will not stop me from coming to Brussels soon – to pay you a little visit. Upon receipt of this scribble, please write me a word to tell me how you are. I am hurrying home so as to lie down; that's why I am not writing at greater length.

I embrace you warmly.

Your very grateful and devoted nephew
K. N. Korzeniowski

I shall write a long letter soon.

To Marguerite Poradowska
Text MS Yale; Rapin 80; G. & S. 22

27: Fev 1891
[London]

Chère Tante

Malade au lit a l'hôpital.[1] Rheumatisme de jambe gauche et neuralgie de bras droit. Merci pour Vos bontés. Aussitot possible ecrirais.—

Je Vous embrasse
J. Conrad

27 February 1891
[London]

Dear Aunt,

In bed ill, in hospital. Rheumatism in left leg and neuralgia in right arm. Thanks for your kindness. Shall write as soon as possible.

I embrace you
J. Conrad

[1] The German Hospital in Dalston, London. See Bobrowski's letter to Conrad, 12/24 March 1891 (Najder, p. 137).

To Marguerite Poradowska
Text MS Yale; Rapin 81; G. & S. 24

12: Mars 91
[London]

Chère Tante—
Toujours au lit.[1] Jambes dans mauvais état et estomac aussi. Merci pour Vos lettres—Je suis trés inquiet au sujet de Vos rechutes.[2]—Je suis guère gai—
Je Vous embrasse de tout mon cœur

J. Conrad

12 March 1891
[London]

Dear Aunt,
Still in bed. Legs in bad condition and stomach also. Thanks for your letters. I am very upset by your relapses. I am hardly cheerful.
I embrace you warmly

J. Conrad

To Marguerite Poradowska
Text MS Yale; Rapin 82; G. & S. 24

30 Mars 1891.
Londres

Ma chère Tante.
Je viens de me lever: j'ai fini la lettre a mon oncle[3] et la seconde (celle-ci) est pour Vous naturellement. Je suis assez inquiet de savoir que Vous souffrez d'une laringite; il faut être très prudent avec cela; malheureusement toutes ces maladies là trainent en longueur et je conçois très bien Votre impatience. Moi j'ai été au lit un mois et je crois que c'est le plus long mois de mon existence—et encore je ne suis pas guéri, il s'en faut de beaucoup, mais je suis bien mieux.

Merci, merci, pour Vos lettres. C'est une joie pour moi de les recevoir! Dans le plaisir de les lire j'oublie (egoiste que je suis) ce qu'elles doivent Vous couter a écrire malade comme Vous l'êtes. N'êtes Vous par sortie trop tôt? chère Tante. Nous avons un temps abominable ici.

---

[1] Conrad's shaky handwriting, in pencil, indicates illness.
[2] Into influenza or laryngitis.
[3] A letter to which Bobrowski responded on 30 March/12 April (Najder, p. 139).

Grâce a votre inepuisable bonté pour moi les armateurs du Royaume
Uni se sont mis en mouvement. J'ai reçu une lettre de M. Knott de
Newcastle qui sur la demande de M. Pechêt me fait des ouvertures pour
le commandement d'un vapeur.[1] Malheureusement dans les circonstances presantes je ne puis pas profiter de sa bonne disposition. Je n'ai
pas encore ecrit a M. Pechêt pour le remercier car cela me fatigue trop.
Dans quelque jours nous verrons. Donnez moi de vos nouvelles quand
Vous pouvez. Pourvu qu'elles soient bonnes! J'ai reçu une invitation de
mon oncle[2]—le cher homme.

Je Vous embrasse de tout mon cœur.

Votre neveu et serviteur devoué
Conrad Korzeniowski

Mes devoirs a Mme Votre Mère et Belle sœur.[3]—

30 March 1891
London

My dear Aunt,

I have just left my bed. I have finished the letter to my uncle and the
second (this one) is for you, naturally. I am very disturbed to learn that
you are suffering from laryngitis. You must be very careful with that.
Unfortunately, all these illnesses go on and on, and I understand your
impatience only too well. As for myself, I have been in bed a month, and
I think it has been the longest month of my life – and still I am not cured,
far from it, but I am much better.

Thank you, thank you for your letters. It is a joy to receive them! In the
pleasure of reading them, I forget (egoist that I am) what it must cost you
to write, ill as you are. Didn't you go out too soon, dear Aunt? We are
having execrable weather here.

Thanks to your untiring kindness to me, the shipowners of the United
Kingdom have bestirred themselves. I have received a letter from Mr
Knott of Newcastle who, at M. Pécher's request, is making some
overtures to me to command a steamer. Unfortunately, in the present
circumstances I cannot profit from his favourable disposition. I have not

---

[1] James Knott, of Newcastle-upon-Tyne, controlled the Prince Shipping Co., a line of
small freighters plying between Africa and Europe. Pécher (not Pechêt) et Cie acted as
Knott's agents in Antwerp.

[2] To recuperate at Kazimierówka. (See Bobrowski's letter of 26 February/10 March
[Najder, p. 136].)

[3] Mmes Émile and Charles Gachet.

yet written to M. Pécher to thank him, for that activity tires me too much. In a few days, we shall see. Give me some news of yourself when you can. Provided that it is good news! I have received an invitation from my uncle – the dear man.

I embrace you warmly.

Your devoted nephew and servant
Conrad Korzeniowski

My regards to your mother and sister-in-law.

To Marguerite Poradowska

Text MS Yale; Rapin 83; G. & S. 25

14 Avril 91.

Chère Tante.

Merci mille et mille fois pour Votre lettre. Comme Vous devez être fatiguée! Je suis très fâché et inquiet de la santé de Mme Votre Belle Sœur. Je vois tout avec un tel decouragement – tout en noir. Mes nerfs sont tout a fait detraqués.—

Ainsi pauvre oncle Jean est mort! Quel triste fin de vie! Je devrai bien ecrire a chère Tante Gaba[1] mais je ne sens pas le courage. Le fait est que le travail de rassembler mes idées et de chercher des expressions en polonais est—pour le moment—au dessus de moi.—

Envoyez moi un petit mot chère Tante si Vous en avez le temps. Ne Vous fatiguez pas a ecrire longuement. Rien qu'une carte-postale pour me dire comment ça va chez Vous.

Mes devoirs a Mme Votre Mère.—

Je Vous embrasse et Vous baise les mains.

Votre neveu très devoué
C. Korzeniowski.

14 April 1891
[London]

Dear Aunt,

A thousand thanks for your letter. How tired you must be! I am very troubled and upset about the health of your sister-in-law. I see everything with such despondency – all in black. My nerves are completely frayed.

[1] Gabriela Zagórska, the widow of Jean (Jan), and herself paralysed.

So poor Uncle Jean is dead! What a sad end! I must indeed write to dear Aunt Gaba, but I do not have the heart. The fact is that the effort of gathering my ideas together and seeking the Polish for them is, for the moment, beyond me.

Send me a short note, dear Aunt, if you have time. Do not tire yourself by writing at length. Nothing more than a postcard to tell me how you are.

My regards to your mother.

I embrace you and kiss your hands.

Your very devoted nephew
C. Korzeniowski

To Maria Tyszkowa

Text   Ruch; Najder 213

London
15th April, 1891.

My dearest Maryleczka!

Your letter of the 24th February found me ill, and that sickness of mine lasted so long that it has been impossible for me to answer you sooner. Do not suspect me of indifference – or even of laziness. I was in bed for two months. I got up not long ago and for three weeks my hands were so swollen that I only managed with the greatest difficulty to write a few words to my Uncle. Thank God, you yourself are well again, my dear sister! You say that you will be leaving Elżbiecin, but you do not say why, – I hope you will let me know the reason – that is if I may be permitted to know it. I thought that you intended to stay there permanently. As to troubles – who has not got them? But you, surrounded as you are with the loving care of good and kind Teodor,[1] can bear them more easily than those who have to struggle through life alone.

With my whole heart I congratulate dear Zunia and Marcia[2] on the birth of their children. From afar I participate in their joy, commending myself to the kind thoughts of both their households.

A warm handshake for dear Teodor, and I kiss both your hands. I embrace you a thousandfold.

Your loving brother,
K. N. Korzeniowski.

I kiss Aunt's hand and commend myself to her heart.

[1] Her husband.
[2] Her sisters.

To Marguerite Poradowska

Text MS Yale; Rapin 83; G. & S. 25

1er Mai 1891
London.

Très chère Tante.

J'ai recu votre lettre du 21 il y a quelques jours mais je n'étais pas assez bien pour Vous repondre. Le fait [est] que j'ai de nerfs desorganisés ce qui produit des palpitations de cœur et des accés d'étouffement. Il parait que ce n'est pas dangereux: mais c'est très penible a supporter et m'affaiblit beaucoup.

Je pense que vers fin mai je vais me rendre a un etablissement hydropathique près de Genève.[1] En ce cas je passerais par Paris ou j'aurai le bonheur de Vous voir. Veuillez ne point ecrire a mon oncle au sujet de ma santé. Je lui ecrirais moi même la semaine prochaine.

Pardonnez moi mes lettres—si bêtes. Les Vôtres font mon bonheur. Ne Vous decouragez pas; écrivez; Vous ferez là une bonne et charitable action. Vos lettres sont positivement toniques et c'est ce qu'il me faut.—

Votre égoïste neveu Vous embrasse bien fort
J. C. Korzeniowski.

1 May 1891
London

Very dear Aunt,

I received your letter of the 21st some days ago, but I was not well enough to answer you. The fact is that my nerves are disordered, which results in palpitations of the heart and attacks of breathlessness. Apparently it is not dangerous, but it is very painful to bear and very weakening.

I think that towards the end of May I shall take myself to a hydropathic establishment near Geneva. In that event I should travel via Paris, where I should have the pleasure of seeing you. Please do not write at all to my uncle on the subject of my health. I shall write to him myself next week.

Excuse my letters – so stupid. Yours are my joy. Don't be discouraged

---

[1] At Champel, in the outer suburbs. For this and several subsequent visits, Conrad was to stay at the Hôtel-Pension de la Roseraie. Hydropathy (or hydrotherapy) was a much-favoured cure for nervous disorders; in the form of high-pressure douches, it used the curative waters externally as well as internally.

– write. You will be performing a good and charitable action. Your
letters are positively tonic, and that is what I need.

Your egoist of a nephew embraces you very warmly

J. C. Korzeniowski.

To Marguerite Poradowska

Text   MS Yale; Rapin 84; G. & S. 26

10 mai 1891

Londres

Ma chère Tante.

J'ai reçu avec joie (comme toujours) Votre lettre du 3 Mai. Vous ne
dites pas quand Vous allez quitter Lille definitivement.[1] J'adresse donc
cette Lettre rue de la Barre et je ne doute pas qu'elle Vous suivra si Vous
êtes déjà à Paris.—

J'ai l'intention de quitter ici le 17, Dimanche prochain; donc le 18 je
serai probablement a Paris. Je ne sais par par quelle route j'irai;
probablement par Folkestone–Boulogne.

Je m'arretérai à Paris un jour seulement—cette fois ci. En returnant je
m'arrangerai a rester un peu plus longtemps si Vous y êtes encore. Votre
lettre me fait plaisir par le ton d'espoir et d'interêt dans la vie qui s'y fait
entendre. Le jour commence a poindre pour Vous, et j'espère—je desire
de tout mon cœur, avec toute mon âme—que Vous puissiez realiser tout
vos rêves, voir s'accomplir tous Vos désirs.

Moi je suis encore plongé dans la nuit la plus épaisse et mes rêves ne
sont que cauchemars; cependant j'etouffe moins depuis quelque jours—
il ne faut pas se plaindre

Je Vous embrasse de tout mo[n] cœur.

Votre neveu très devoué

K. N. Korzeniowski

10 May 1891

London

My dear Aunt,

I was glad (as always) to receive your letter of 3 May. You don't tell
me your date of final departure from Lille. Accordingly, I am sending
this letter to the Rue de la Barre, and I have no doubt it will follow you if
you are already in Paris.

---

[1] Mme Poradowska was visiting relatives in Lille, her father's birthplace.

I plan to leave here on the 17th, next Sunday; on the 18th, therefore, I shall probably be in Paris. I do not know by what route I shall go: probably by Folkestone–Boulogne.

I shall stop in Paris for only one day – this time. On returning I shall arrange to remain a little longer if you are still there. Your letter gives me pleasure by the tone of hope and interest in life which I sense in it. Day begins to break for you, and I hope – I wish with all my heart, with all my soul – that you will be able to fulfil all your dreams and see all your desires accomplished.

As for myself, I am still plunged in densest night and my dreams are only nightmares. Nevertheless, for several days I have been breathing more easily – one should not complain.

I embrace you warmly.

Your very devoted nephew
K. N. Korzeniowski

To Marguerite Poradowska

Text   MS Yale; Rapin 84; G. & S. 27

Jeudi soir. [28 May? 1891][1]
[Champel, Switzerland]

Ma très chère et bonne Tante.—J'ai médité longuement le contenu de Votre lettre et malheureusenment sans arriver a aucune conclusion.—Je ne doute pas que Vous m'auriez permis de donner mon opinion au sujet de Votre place de residence mais j'ai a avouer que je ne suis pas compétent d'en former une. Le plan de la Prin[ce]^{sse} ne me deplait pas[2]—mais je Vous connais (un petit brin) et j'ai bien peur que Vous ne l'accepterez pas. Vous êtez un tout, tout petit peu "impraticable" ma tante. Je déplore le fait tout en avouant que ce n'est qu'un charme de plus que possède pour moi Votre chère Personne. Cependant Vous en avez tant d'autres que Vous pourriez très bien Vous passer de celui-là, et Vous laisser conduire (pour une fois dans la vie) par la lumière de la raison pure qui ressembla en cela à l'électrique, qu'elle est froide. Mais dans l'an de grâce 1892 il est trop tard pour revenir a la noble chandelle

---

[1] The date 1892 in the body of the letter is evidently an error on Conrad's part, and the letter fits into the May–June 1891 sequence from Champel. Gee and Sturm point out the similarity of the paper used at this time, but more conclusive is internal evidence placing Conrad at the hydropathic establishment and details which make it precede the letter dated 3 June, 1891. 28 May, a Thursday, is the only likely date, since Conrad arrived in Champel in late May.

[2] Probably the Princesse de Ligne's plan to have Mme Poradowska live part of the year – or even permanently – with her.

de deux sous de nos ancêtres. En attendant je serais dans l'inquietude
jusqu'au reçu d'une nouvelle lettre.

Je Vous embrasse de tout mon cœur.

Votre neveu est serviteur devoué
Conrad.

Cure commencée depuis deux jours par consequent peut pas juger des
resultats. Je la supporte assez bien.—

Thursday evening. [28 May? 1891]
[Champel]

My very dear and good Aunt,

I have thought for a long time about the contents of your letter and,
unfortunately, without arriving at any conclusion. I do not doubt that
you would have allowed me to express my opinion on the subject of your
place of residence, but I must admit I am not competent to form one. The
Princess's plan does not displease me, but I know you (just a little) and I
am afraid you will not accept it. Aunt of mine, you are very, very slightly
'impractical'. I deplore the fact even while confessing that it is yet one
more charm which your dear person possesses for me. However, you
have so many others that you could do very well without this one, and let
yourself be guided (for once in your life) by the light of pure reason,
which, like electricity, is cold. But in the year of grace 1892, it is too late
to return to the noble twopenny candle of our ancestors. In the
meanwhile, I shall be uneasy until I receive another letter.

I embrace you warmly.

Your very devoted nephew and servant
Conrad

Cure begun two days ago, so cannot judge the results. I am bearing it
well enough.

To Marguerite Poradowska
Text MS Yale; Rapin 85; G. & S. 28

Mercredi. 3. Juin 1891.
La Roseraie. Genève

Ma chère Tante.

J'ai lu votre dernière lettre avec joie. Enfin Vous voilà parfaite car Vous êtes raisonnable.[1] Je Vous embrasse bien fort la-dessus; tout ira bien; le succès Vous attend, j'en au le plus fort pressentiment.—La Princesse est très bonne, mais en Vous aimant Elle ne fait que son devoir je pense; et puis Elle ne pouvait pas s'en empêcher—voilà tout.

Mon retour est incertain tant soit peu. Dans tous les cas je ne pourrais que passer une journée a Paris et pour ces quelques heures il ne me semble pas bon de Vous déranger. Vous aurez besoin du repos a la campagne avant de Vous mettre au travail a Paris. J'ai dans l'idée que nous nous reverrons bientôt dans tous les cas. Je me sens beaucoup mieux si-non tout-a-fait guéri.[2]—J'ai écrit plusieurs fois a mon oncle mais il y a longtemps que je suis sans ses nouvelles.[3]—

Je Vous embrasse de tout mon cœur. Vous felicitant de Votre succès. Votre neveu et serviteur très devoué

J. Conrad.—

Si Vous avez le temps pour un petit mot Vous me rendrez très heureux.—

Wednesday, 3 June 1891
La Roseraie, Geneva

My dear Aunt,

I read your last letter with joy. Now you have become perfect, for you are reasonable. I hug you very warmly for that; all will be well. Success awaits you; I have the strongest presentiment of that. The Princess is very kind, but in loving you she is only doing her duty, I think, and then she could not help doing so – that is all.

My return is a little uncertain. In any event I should be able to spend only one day in Paris, and for those few hours it does not seem right to bother you. You will need some rest in the country before going to work

---

[1] In deciding to live alone in Paris, rather than with the Princess.
[2] Apparently, Conrad felt well enough to resume the writing of *Almayer's Folly*, whose Chapter VIII was completed at Champel. (See *A Personal Record*, p. 14.)
[3] Bobrowski's last letter was dated 30 March/12 April.

in Paris. I have an idea we will see each other soon in any case. I feel much better, if not altogether cured. I have written to my uncle several times, but I have been without news for a long time.

I embrace you warmly, congratulating you on your success. Your very devoted nephew and servant

J. Conrad

If you have time for a short note, you will make me very happy.

To Marguerite Poradowska
Text   MS Yale; Rapin 86; G. & S. 29

Mercredi. 10. Juin 91
[Champel]

Chère Tante.

Merci pour Votre bonne et charmante lettre. J'étais serieux a propos de Paris et je suis très serieux aussi en Vous prevenant que j'arriverai là le 15 cou[ran]^t (Lundi) matin, pour repartir le soir.

Donc vers 10^{h}½ je serai a Votre porte puisque Vous avez l'intention de revenir a Paris le 14.—

Je Vous aime bien et Vous embrasse bien fort.

Votre neveu très devoué
J. C. Korzeniowski

Je vais assez bien.

Wednesday. 10 June 1891
[Champel]

Dear Aunt,

Thank you for your kind and charming letter. I was serious about Paris, and I am very serious also in informing you that I will arrive there on the 15th of this month (Monday), in the morning, leaving in the evening.

So I shall be at your door at about 10.30, since you intend to return to Paris on the 14th.

I love and embrace you warmly.

Your very devoted nephew
J. C. Korzeniowski

I am fairly well.

To Marguerite Poradowska
Text MS Yale; Rapin 86; G. & S. 29

22 Juin 1891.
London.

Ma très chère Tante.

Je ne Vous ai pas ecrit plus tot parceque je n'avais vraiment rien a Vous dire. Jeudi dernier j'avais rejoint le yacht de mon ami Hope[1] et je reviens seulement a Londres en ce moment; il y a 2 heures a peine, pour être exact.

Ma santé est assez bonne quoique je ne suis pas encore bien fort. Le petit voyage de mer dans le yacht m'a fait beaucoup de bien.—

Je forme des vagues projets pour l'avenir; très vagues! Du reste a quoi bon projeter puisque c'est toujours l'imprévu qui arrive. Aussitôt que cet imprévu sera arrivé je Vous ecrirai pour Vous en rendre compte. Je suis moi même très curieux de savoir quelle mine il aura.

Ecrivez moi un petit mot Tante cherie quand Vous aurez le temps et pardonnez moi mes lettres si Vides d'interêt.

Je Vous embrasse de tout mon cœur.

Votre neveu très devoué
J. C. Korzeniowski.

22 June 1891
London

My very dear Aunt,

I did not write sooner because I truly had nothing to tell you. Last Thursday I rejoined my friend Hope's yacht, and I have returned to London only now: hardly two hours ago, to be exact.

My health is reasonably good, although I am not yet very strong. The little sea-voyage in the yacht has done me much good.

I am forming some vague plans for the future, very vague! Besides, what is the good of planning, since the unforeseen always occurs. As soon as the unforeseen does happen, I shall write to give you a complete account of it. I am myself very curious to know what it will look like.

Write me a short note, very dear Aunt, when you have time, and forgive my letters, so void of interest.

I embrace you warmly.

Your very devoted nephew
J. C. Korzeniowski

[1] On 18 June. For Hope, see notes on letter to Thys, 28 November 1889.

To Marguerite Poradowska

Text MS Yale; Rapin 87; G. & S. 30

2 Juillet 1891.
[London]

Chère Tante.

Merci de votre bonne lettre. Ce que je suis content de Vous savoir casée quelque part! Vrai, je n'aimai pas a Vous savoir dans l'appartement du Docteur.[1] Ça avait trop l'air cauchemaresque avec ces peintures de l'ecole de Charenton[2] et cette sonnette! On rit bien de tout cela pour le moment mais en somme l'impression finale est penible. Je suis très heureux de Vous savoir a peu près satisfaite. Je brule de desir d'accourir a Passy voir l'appartement[3] (n'allez pas Vous imaginer que c'est pour Vous voir, au moins!) et une fois dedans (l'appartement) manger ce diner dont le menu Vous préoccupe déjà. (Et moi aussi du reste).—Franchement Votre lettre m'a rendu heureux. Le ton était si bon. Et surtout pas de decouragement!—

Ma santé assez bien. Je pars demain dans le yacht de Hope pour la côte Est. Nous reviendrons Lundi prochain.[4]

Tous mes plans ont manqué.[5] Aussi je n'en fais plus. On n'evite pas sa destinée. Nous verrons ce qu'elle apportera.—Je Vous embrasse de tout mon cœur

Votre

Conrad.

2 July 1891
[London]

Dear Aunt,

Thank you for your kind letter. How happy I am to know you are settled somewhere! Truly, I did not like knowing that you were in the doctor's apartment. It had a nightmarish atmosphere, with its paintings of the Charenton school and that little bell. For the moment, we may well laugh at it all, but on the whole, the final impression is painful. I am very

---

[1] Rapin (p. 87) identifies the doctor as Dr Paul Gachet, the friend of Cézanne, Courbet, and Van Gogh.
[2] The lunatic asylum near Paris. Conrad is probably referring contemptuously to the so-called 'crazy' paintings of the Impressionists.
[3] 84 rue de Passy, where Mme Poradowska lived until 1910.
[4] 6 July.
[5] Mainly to obtain a command or some other kind of maritime post. Bobrowski wrote at this time (18/30 July) of his fears that Conrad might be planning a liaison with Mme Poradowska, whom his uncle calls a 'worn-out female' (Najder, p. 148).

happy to know you are well-nigh satisfied. I have a burning desire to hasten to Passy to see the apartment (certainly don't go imagining it's to see you!), and once within (the apartment) to eat the dinner whose menu so preoccupies you already. (And me, too, as it happens.) Frankly, your letter has made me happy. The tone was so good. And above all, no dejection!

My health reasonably good. I leave for the East Coast tomorrow in Hope's yacht. We shall return next Monday.

All my plans have misfired. So I am making no more. No one can escape his destiny. We shall see what it brings. I embrace you warmly.

Your

Conrad

To Marguerite Poradowska

Text MS Yale; Rapin 88; G. & S. 30

8 Juillet 1891.

[London]

Chère Tante. Je viens de lire Votre lettre avec tristesse et indignation. —Indignation contre l'injustice de la souffrance qui Vous poursuit, contre la cruauté des choses et la brutalité de l'inevitable;—puisque tout est inévitable! Et dans le cas des accidents comme celui dont Votre cousin vient d'être l'infortunée victime[1] la douleur est plus poignante et le regret plus douleureux. Car là il y a toujours la pensée de ce qui aurait pu être, le regret des choses non accomplies, le desespoir de la perte inutile, des affections qui faisaient le bonheur de ce[ux] qui restent ahuris dans l'étonnement de la cruauté inexplicable de l'Invisible guidant les choses inanimées vers la destruction d'une existence nécéssaire au bonheur des être innocents, de l'être inconscient encore! En verité nous sommes les esclaves de la fatalité avant de naître, et nous payons le tribut au malheur avant de l'avoir connu. Nous poursuit-il au delà de la tombe? Je me demande avec effroi!—Mais si il y a quelqu'un au monde pour consoler les coeurs brisés c'est bien Vous.—Vous qui avez passé par l'epreuve du feu. Vous qui avez su supporter courage-

---

[1] The letter refers to the death of a male cousin of Mme Poradowska. He was evidently a married man with children, and his wife was pregnant at the time of his death. He perished in a disaster which involved 'inanimate things' – perhaps a reference to a railway crash. Conrad had written to Bobrowski about a 'locomotive' which had 'écrasé son cousin', but the locomotive was taken by his uncle to be a metaphor for his nephew's being in love with Marguerite; as a consequence, we cannot determine whether the 'locomotive' was a literal one or a vast engine of love. (See Bobrowski to Conrad, 18/30 July 1891; Najder, p. 148.)

usement non seulement la mort mais même la vie.—Ils sont heureux
dans leur malheur ceux a qui Votre cœur gracieux et plein de bonté
apporte la consolation, ceux dont Votre main—savante d'une cruelle
experience—panse les blessures. Il y en a qui ont a souffrir et saigner
dans une muette solitude! Ce[ux][1] là sont a plaindre. Vous savez cela
Vous même, helas!—

Je me reproche de ne pas avoir été là quand Votre lettre est arrivée. Je
Vous admire et Vous aime de plus en plus.—

Je baise Vos mains
J. C. Korzeniowski.

8 July 1891
[London]

Dear Aunt,

I have just read your letter with sadness and indignation. Indignation
at the injustice of the suffering that pursues you, at the cruelty of things
and the brutality of the inevitable – since everything is inevitable! And in
the case of accidents such as that which has now claimed your cousin as
an unfortunate victim, the grief is more acute and the regret more
sorrowful. For in that case there is always the thought of what might
have been, the regret for unaccomplished things, the despair over the
useless loss, of affections which brought happiness to those who remain
bewildered by the shock of the inexplicable cruelty of an invisible power
which has guided inanimate things toward the destruction of an
existence necessary to the happiness of other innocent beings and of a
being not yet conscious! Truly, we are the slaves of Fate even before
birth, and we pay tribute to adversity even before making its acquaintance. Does it pursue us beyond the tomb, I ask myself with alarm? But if
there is someone in the world to console broken hearts, it is indeed you.
You who have passed through the ordeal by fire. You who have known
how to endure not only death but even life with courage. Happy even in
their misfortune are those to whom your gracious and kindly heart
carries consolation, those whose wounds are dressed by your hand,
grown skilled by cruel experience. There are others who have to suffer
and bleed in dull solitude! They are to be pitied. You know that yourself,
alas!

I reproach myself for not having been there when your letter arrived. I
admire you and love you more and more.

I kiss your hands
J. C. Korzeniowski

[1] The 'ux' here and overleaf have been added by Mme Poradowska.

To Marguerite Poradowska

Text MS Yale; Rapin 88; G. & S. 31

22^d July [189]1
[letterhead: Barr, Moering]

Ma chère Tante. Je viens de recevoir Votre lettre avec carte geographique ainsi que le passport mortuaire de pauvre Jeannette. Je ne peux pas pretendre a une grande douleur, le fait est que cette mort soulage tout le monde y compris la decédée.[1]—Acceptez, acceptez l'invitation des Ordega![2]—Je suis sur que cela Vous fera du bien car Vous avez besoin de que[l]que chose de ce genre pour Vous remettre après ces jours d'hopital. Moi je suis assez occupé et "yachting" est hors de question pour moi.—Tous mes projets sont manqué et je crois qu'il me faudra rester a Londres pour de bon.[3]—

Pas le temps d'expliquer aujourd'hui. J'ecrirais bientôt
Je Vous embrasse et Vous baise les mains

Votre très devoué

J. Conrad.

22 July 1891
[letterhead: Barr, Moering]

My dear Aunt,

I have just received your letter with the map as well as poor Jeannette's death-certificate. I cannot claim to be very sorrowful; the fact is that this death is a relief to everyone, including the deceased. Do accept the Ordega invitation. I am sure it will do you some good, for you need something of this sort to restore you after those days in hospital. As for myself, I am somewhat busy, and yachting is out of the question for me. All my plans have failed, and I think I shall have to stay in London for good.

No time to explain today. I shall write soon.
I embrace you and kiss your hands.

Your very devoted

J. Conrad

---

[1] Jeannette (Johanna) Poradowska, sister-in-law of Mme Poradowska. In Czarist Russia, the 'passeport mortuaire' – also called 'passport to heaven' – was a death-certificate signed by two priests (G. & S., p. 31).

[2] Family friends of Mme Poradowska.

[3] See note to letter of 2 July 1891.

To Marguerite Poradowska
Text   MS Yale; Rapin 89; G. & S. 32

30 Juillet 1891
Londres.

Tante très chère

Me voilà malade encore—juste comme j'allais commencer a travailler.[1] Une attaque de malaria sous forme de dyspepsie. C'est déséspérant.—

Je ne sais que Vous dire car je ne peux pas penser. Je suis comme abasourdi par ce nouveau desastre—car c'en est un pour moi dans les circonstances.

Ecrivez un petit mot.

Je Vous embrasse de tout mon cœur
J. Conrad.

30 July 1891
London

Very dear Aunt,

Here I am, ill yet again – just as I was going to begin work. An attack of malaria in the form of dyspepsia. It is disheartening.

I don't know what to tell you, for I cannot think. I am stunned by this new disaster – for that is what it is for me under the circumstances.

Write a short note.

I embrace you warmly
J. Conrad

To Marguerite Poradowska
Text   MS Yale; Rapin 89; G. & S. 32

5/8/91
London.

Ma chère Tante.

Merci pour Votre bonne lettre. Mais pourquoi Vous alarmer? Peut-être c'est un peu de ma faute. Je suis toujours a me plaindre et a gémir et ma Tante me prend au serieux.

---

[1] Probably a dual reference, to office work at the Barr, Moering warehouse, and to creative work on the manuscript of *Almayer's Folly*, For the latter, see *A Personal Record* (p. 14), where Conrad refers to the writing of Chapter IX as being 'inextricably mixed up with the details of the proper management of a waterside warehouse'.

J'ai commencé a travailler hier. Pour le moment je dirige l'entrepot appartenant a MM Barr Moering.^{s}fl

Si je vois que je peux me faire a cette vie je resterai a Londres.a8

J'ai un peu de fièvre encore tous les jours; rien de serieux—Seulement cela empêche de regagner les forces. Je me fatigue donc très vite.—Je Vous en prie n'ecrivez pas tout cela a mon oncle. J'ai l'intention de lui ecrire dans 2.3 jours en lui annonçant la guerison en même temps que la maladie.—

Je baise Vos mains

Tout a Vous

J. Conrad.

5 August 1891
London

My dear Aunt,

Thank you for your kind letter. But why are you alarmed? Perhaps I am a little to blame. I am always complaining and groaning, and my aunt takes me seriously.

I began work yesterday. For the time being, I am managing the warehouse of Messrs Barr, Moering.

If I find that I can accustom myself to this life, I shall remain in London.

I still have a little fever every day; nothing serious – only it keeps me from regaining my energy. So I tire very quickly – I beg you not to write about this to my uncle. I intend to write to him within 2–3 days, announcing the cure at the same time as the illness.

I kiss your hands,

All yours

J. Conrad

To Marguerite Poradowska

Text MS Yale; Rapin 90; G. & S. 33

26 Augt [189]1.[2]
[letterhead: Barr, Moering]

Ma très chèr Tante.

Merci pour Votre bonne lettre que j'ai reçue avant hier.—Ma santé n'est pas tout à fait brilliante mais en somme je vais pas mal avec un peu

---

[1] At 95 Upper Thames Street, London E.C.4. Conrad held a sleeping partnership in the firm.

[2] First written as 25 August.

de fièvre de temps en temps. Je Vous ecris ici dans la vaste (et poussiéreuse) solitude de cet entrepot ayant un moment de libre vers le millieu de la journée. Le soir—de retour chez moi—je me sens si paresseux que je regarde les plumes avec horreur, et quand a l'encrier je l'ai banni de ma chambre depuis longtemps.—Après tout je ne suis pas aussi heureux de travailler comme Vous sembler le penser. Il n'y a rien de bien rejouissant a faire un travail qui déplait. Ça ressemble trop aux travaux forcés avec cette différence que tout en roulant la pierre de Sysiphe vous n'avez pas la consolation de penser a l'agrément qu'on a eu en comettant le crime. C'est là ou les forçats ont l'avantage sur Votre serviteur.—Je suis très fâché que mon Oncle se soit mêlé de Vous embêter—avec les autres.[1] Du moins Vous pouvez croire que ces motifs sont moins mercenaires que Vous l'imaginez. Quand a moi je pense que ces questions là sont tellement personelles que je ne peux pas même m'y interesser beaucoup—même pour les plus proches—même si une sœur etait en question je ne crois pas que je pourrai ressentir un vrai interet. Ce qui n'empêche pas que (au risque de Vous fâcher pour toujours) je crois que l'individu qui a le malheur de Vous deplaire tant est un "very fine fellow".[2] On admire ce dont on manque. Voilà pourquoi j'admire la perseverance et la fidelité et la constance.—Et puis j'aime a contempler les bons côtés des hommes, d'autant plus quand il y a une suggestion du "Pathos" dans la situation. Ça complete la chose au point de vue artistique, qui est le mien dans cette affaire.[3] Vous semblez ne pas Vous apercevoir of the characteristic note of sadness of life in all this episode. The weary yet hopeful waiting and the hopeless collapse at the end.[4] Mais après tout quand on y pense ce n'est pas peut-être triste—c'est peut-être très—drole? Enfin je ne sais pas!—Vous voyez que je discute tout cela academiquement. Et ceci pour la dernière fois. Ce qui m'interesse reelement c'est Votre nouveau ouvrage.[5] Je l'attends avec impatience mais en attendant faites moi savoir dans quel N° du Figaro Ill: vous paraissez et aussi la date de la Revue.[6]—Je Vous souhaite

[1] Her Polish relatives, probably in connection with her husband's finances. The uncle was Tadeusz Bobrowski; in a recent letter (Najder, p. 148), he had warned Conrad against becoming too deeply involved with her.
[2] Unidentified.
[3] A pose of Flaubertian detachment.
[4] In his letters in French Conrad sometimes breaks into English, just as in English he will sometimes break into French. By 'the end', Conrad appears to mean an unsatisfactory conclusion to the wrangling over Poradowski's estate.
[5] Possibly *Popes et popadias*, which appeared in the *Revue des Deux Mondes* late in 1892.
[6] Conrad is confusing the *Figaro illustré*, in which Mme Poradowska is not represented, and the *Figaro* 'Supplément littéraire'. In the *Revue des Deux Mondes* (for 1 September, 1891), there appeared the novella *La Madone de Busowiska, mœurs houtsoules*, adapted by Mme Poradowska from the Polish of Ladislas Łozinski.

succès de tout mon cœur, le courage ne Vous manque pas, et le bonheur viendra dans le travail. Amen!

Je Vous embrasse et Vous baise les mains

Tout a Vous

J. Conrad.

Ne nous epargnez pas je Vous en prie. Cela leur fera du bien la bas de se voir un peu comme ils sont![1] Peut-être?! Quoique guerir des maniaques avec de la literature semble un peu improbable. Qu'en pensez Vous. Et puis cela fera plaisir a M. Buloz et les Russes et fera du bien a la grande Alliance.[2]—

26 August 1891
[letterhead: Barr, Moering]

My very dear Aunt,

Thank you for your kind letter, which I received the day before yesterday. My health is not altogether sparkling, but on the whole I am not feeling bad – with an occasional fever from time to time. I am writing to you here in the vast (and dusty) solitude of this warehouse, as I have a free moment toward the middle of the day. In the evening, after returning home, I feel so lazy that I look at pens with horror, and as for the inkwell, I banished it from my room a long time ago. After all, I am not as happy working as you appear to think. There is nothing very cheerful in doing disagreeable work. It is too much like penal servitude, with this difference, that while rolling the stone of Sisyphus, you lack even the consolation of thinking of the pleasure you had in committing the crime. There, convicts have the advantage over your humble servant. I am very disturbed that my Uncle has involved himself with the others in bothering you. At least you can rest assured his motives are less mercenary than you imagine. As for myself, I believe these questions are so personal that I cannot greatly interest myself in them – even for those closest to me; even if a sister were in question, I don't believe I could feel a real interest. Which doesn't alter the fact that (at the risk of offending you for ever) I think that the individual who had the bad luck to displease you is a very fine fellow. One admires what one lacks. That is

[1] Rapin interprets this postscript as an allusion to the *Popes et popadias* on which Mme Poradowska was working. In Chapter xv, three Poles have a violent quarrel over religion, and an Orthodox priest proposes the union of Galicia and the Ukraine in an independent Ruthenia.

[2] An ironic reference to the alliance between France and Russia, then under negotiation, which was further to isolate the Poles. M. Buloz directed the *Revue des Deux Mondes* from 1877 to 1893.

why I admire perseverance, and fidelity, and constancy. And then I like to contemplate the good side of men, the more so when there is a suggestion of 'Pathos' in the situation. That completes the affair from the artistic point of view, which is mine in this business. You seem to be unaware of the characteristic note of sadness of life in all this episode. The weary yet hopeful waiting and the hopeless collapse at the end. But after all, when one considers, it is, perhaps, not sad. It is, possibly, very – droll? Indeed, I don't know! You see I discuss the entire matter academically. And this for the last time. What truly interests me is your new work. I await it with impatience, but in the meanwhile let me know in what Number of the *Figaro illustré* you will appear and also the date of the *Revue*. With all my heart, I wish you success; courage you do not lack, and happiness will come with work. Amen!

I embrace you and kiss your hands.

Yours

J. Conrad

Do not spare us, I beg of you. It will do them some good, down there, if they see themselves rather more as they are! Perhaps?! Though curing maniacs with literature seems a little improbable. What do you think? And then it will please M. Buloz and the Russians and further the Grand Alliance.

To Marguerite Poradowska

Text   MS Yale; Rapin 91, G. & S. 35

15. Sept. 1891
London.

Ma très chère Tante.

Merci de Votre lettre et de la Revue que j'ai recue il y a deux jours. J'ai lu la Madonne[1] et je me felicite de l'avoir lue en français et adaptée par Vous, car je pense cela devait être assez fatiguant en polonais si Łozinski—comme les autres a l'habitude de "pietiner sur place" selon Votre expression. Naturellement je n'y trouve pas le "relief"—la vie distincte que l'on trouve dans "Yaga"[2] mais j'y retrouve avec un bien grand plaisir, le langage le style, enfin presque tout le plaisir purement litteraire que la lecture de Yaga m'a donnée. Le fait est que remis en appetit, (si je puis m'exprimer ainsi) je viens de relire Yaga—que j'aime plus que jamais.—

[1] *La Madone de Busowiska*; see note for letter of 26 August 1891.
[2] Mme Poradowska's novel of Ruthenian life, which appeared in 1887.

Je vais faire bien attention dorenavant a ce que je Vous dis ou vous ecris si Vous prenez la mauvaise habitude de Vous rappeler ce que je dis. Votre sympathie m'est très precieuse mais a Vous dire vrai je me moque pas mal du bonheur. A peine je sait ce que c'est. Je ne suis ni plus courageux ni plus indépendant que les autres; je suis peut-être plus indifferent, ce qui n'est pas une qualité, sans etre cependant une faute. Pourquoi seriez Vous malheureuse? Pourquoi serait-ce bon pour Vous de l'être—et mauvais pour moi? Nous sommes des gens ordinaires qui ont juste le bonheur qu'ils méritent ni plus ni *moins*. Si je Vous laisse entrevoir quelque fois que la vie fait mal de temps en temps c'est une faiblesse a moi dont j'ai tres honte—mais il ne faut pas me prendre trop au serieux. Je supporte très bien le fardeau du monde entier sur mes epaules—comme du reste le font les 5 millions des misérables dont se compose la population de cette ville.—Vous comprenez très bien que je ne me plaint pas. Je Vous dis seulement ce que je ressent, confiant dans Votre amitié.

Ah! Madame ma Tante! "Les hommes sont incroyables"—à propos de forçats—et moi je Vous dirais que les Femmes sont ... bien femmes.—

Mais ma chère Tante si ces forçats trouvaient la consolation dans l'expiation ils ne seraient plus des forçats ils seraient des Anges (Catholiques) tombés dans le malheur. Etant des forçats ils trouvent leur consolation dans le souvenir des crimes commis; dans l'anticipation des crimes a comettre aussitôt la peine finie.—Les forçats sont une classe des gens très mal appréciée. Ils ont toutes les qualités de leur defauts. La seule classe qui leur soit superieure est celle (peu nombreuse) des gens qui ont commis des crimes sans se laisser attraper.—

Après tout comme on se connait peu! Moi je Vous étonne et peut-être scandalise par ma plaisanterie forçatesque tandis que Vous me supposez capable d'accepter ou même d'admettre la doctrine (ou la theorie) de l'expiation par la souffrance. Cette doctrine, produit des intelligences superieures mais sauvages est tout simplement une infâme abomination quand des gens civilisés la prêchent. C'est une doctrine qui mène d'un coté droit a l'Inquisition et d'un autre montre des possibilités de marchandage avec l'Eternel. Il serait tout aussi rationel de vouloir expier un meurtre par un vol! "Two wrongs cannot make a right."—Du reste il n'y a pas d'expiation. Chaque acte de la vie est final et produit fatalement ses conséquences malgré tous les pleurs et les grincements des dents, et la douleur des âmes faibles, souffrant dans l'effroi qui les saisit devant les résultats de leur propres actions.—Quand a moi je

n'aurais jamais besoin d'être consolé pour aucun acte de ma vie, et ceci parce que je suis assez fort pour juger ma conscience au lieu d'en être l'esclave comme les orthodoxes voudrait nous persuader de l'être.—
    Pardonnez tous ce galimatias. Quoique tombé dans la dèche complète je n'en suis pas encore reduit a habiter les bureaux de la maison. Par consequent mon adresse privée n'est pas Rue Camomille[1] mais *17. Gillingham Street S.W.* mais comme je dois changer bientot de logement[2] Vous feriez mieux de m'ecrire au bureau—comme d'habitude.—Mes compliments a Mme Votr[e] mère. Je Vous embrasse de tout mon cœur

                                                                J. Conrad.

                                                    15 September 1891
                                                              London
My very dear Aunt,
    Thank you for your letter and the *Revue*, which I received two days ago. I have read *La Madone* and am pleased to have read it in French and in your adaptation, for I think it must be tiring indeed in Polish if Łozinski – like the others – is in the habit of 'marking time', as you put it. Naturally, I do not find there the 'relief', the distinct life one finds in *Yaga*, but I recognize with very great pleasure the language, style, indeed almost all the purely literary pleasure the reading of *Yaga* gave me. The fact is that, restored in appetite (if I may express myself so), I have just reread *Yaga* – which I like more than ever.
    I shall, henceforth, pay close attention to what I say or write to you, if you form the bad habit of recalling what I say. Your sympathy is very precious to me, but to be honest I don't care a straw for happiness. I hardly know what it is. I am neither more courageous nor more independent than the others; I am perhaps more indifferent, which is not a virtue, though nevertheless not a fault. Why should you be unhappy? Why should it be good for you – and bad for me? We are ordinary people who have exactly the happiness we deserve, neither more nor *less*. If occasionally I let you glimpse my sometimes painful life, that is a personal weakness of which I am very ashamed – but you should not take me too seriously. I bear the weight of the entire world on my shoulders very well – like the other five million wretches who make up the population of this city. You understand perfectly well that I am not

---

[1] Barr, Moering's office in Camomile Street, E.C.
[2] Near Victoria Station. This continued to be his London address until he married in 1896.

complaining. Assured of your friendship, I am simply telling you what I feel.

Ah, Madame; ah, my aunt! 'Men' – turning the subject to convicts – 'are incredible' – and I myself would say to you that women are – indeed women.

But, my dear aunt, if these convicts found consolation in atonement, they would no longer be convicts – they would be (Catholic) angels fallen into adversity. Being convicts, they find their solace in their memory of crimes committed and in the anticipation of crimes to commit as soon as their punishment ends. Convicts are a class of people very little appreciated. They have all the virtues of their vices. The only class which may be superior to them is that (small number) of people who have committed crimes without getting caught.

After all, how little one knows about oneself! I surprise and perhaps scandalize you by my jokes about criminals, while you suppose me capable of accepting or even admitting the doctrine (or the theory) of atonement through suffering. That doctrine, product of superior but savage minds, is quite simply a sordid abomination when preached by civilized people. It is a doctrine that on one hand leads straight to the Inquisition and on the other shows the possibilities of bargaining with the Almighty. It would be quite as rational to want to expiate a murder by a theft! 'Two wrongs cannot make a right.' Moreover, there isn't any expiation. Each act of life is final, and inevitably produces its consequences despite all the weeping and gnashing of teeth, and the sorrow of feeble souls who suffer the terror that seizes them when confronted by the results of their own actions. As for myself, I shall never need to be consoled for any act of my life, and that is because I am strong enough to judge my conscience instead of being its slave as the orthodox believers would persuade us to be.

Excuse all this balderdash. Though I am absolutely broke, I am not yet reduced to living in the company's offices. Consequently, my private address is not Camomile Street, but 17 Gillingham Street S.W., but as I must soon move, you would do better to write to me at the office – as usual. My regards to your mother. I embrace you warmly

J. Conrad

To Marguerite Poradowska
Text   MS Yale; Rapin 93; G. & S. 37

30th Sept. 1891
17 Gillingham St
London S.W.

Ma chère Tante.

J'aurai du Vous remercier depuis longtemps pour Votre bonne et charmante lettre.—Vous me flattez la dedans (ce qui est toujours agréable) et puis Vous êtes satisfaite parceque j'ai lu "Yaga" et puis Vous avez un si joli rêve—celui de Votre devoué neveu arrivant a Passy.[1]—Les rêves ont du bon quelquefois;—on s'oublie.—

Il est extremement probable que sous peu je partirai pour un long voyage; Australie ou ailleurs peu m'importe. Je fais les demarches nécéssaires et je me plait a croire qu'elles aboutiront.

Mon absence ne durera pas plus d'un an—(sauf l'imprévu) et a mon retour je me mettrai a l'œuvre pour realiser Votre rêve. Ah, le beau rêve! Le beau rêve!

Tout ça c'est que des projets—Vous comprenez bien—mais je Vous tiendrai au courant des événements. En ce moment j'ai (excepté le projets ci-dessus) la tête tellement vide que je n'ose pas gribouiller davantage. J'ai remarqué que quand on a rien dire on dit toujours trop; par consequent je m'arrête Je presente mes devoirs a Mme Votre Mère et je Vous embrasse et Vous baise les mains. Tout-à-fait a Vous

J. Conrad:

30 September 1891
17 Gillingham Street
London S.W.

My dear Aunt,

I should have thanked you long ago for your kind and charming letter. You flatter me in it (which is always agreeable), and then you are pleased because I have read *Yaga*, and then you have such a fine dream – that of your devoted nephew arriving at Passy. Dreams are good sometimes; one forgets oneself.

It is highly probable that I shall be leaving soon on a long voyage; Australia or elsewhere, it matters little to me. I am taking the necessary steps, and I like to think they will lead to something.

I shall be away no more than a year (unless something unforeseen

---

[1] Mme Poradowska's new flat in Passy, a fashionable quarter of Paris.

happens) and on my return I shall set to work to make your dream a reality. Ah, the lovely dream! The lovely dream!

All this is only tentative – you realize – but I shall keep you informed of events. At present, I have (excepting the above plans) such an empty head that I dare not scribble any longer. I have noticed that when one has nothing to say, one always says too much; therefore, I leave off. I present my respects to your mother, embrace you and kiss your hands.

All yours

J. Conrad

To Marguerite Poradowska

Text   MS Yale; Rapin 93; G. & S. 38

16 octobre. [1891][1]

Londres.

17 Gillingham St.

S.W.

Chère Tante.

Je me demande si Vous êtes très fachée contre Votre très paresseux neveu? J'aime a croire cependant que Vous avez le sentiment du devoir de l'indulgence, vu que l'existence n'est possible qu'en vertu de ce même sentiment.

Je n'ai absolument rien a Vous dire. Je vegète. Je ne pense même pas;—donc je n'existe pas (selon Descartes). Mais un autre individu (un savant) a dit: "sans phosphore point de pensée."[2] D'ou il semble que c'est le phosphore qui est absent et moi je suis toujours là. Mais dans ce cas j'existerais sans penser, ce qui (selon Descartes) est impossible.— Grand Dieux! Serai-je un Polichinelle? Le Polichinelle de mon enfance, vous savez—l'echine cassée en deux le nez par terre entre les pieds; les jambes et les bras raidement écartés, dans cette attitude de profond desespoir, si pathetiquement drôle, des jouets jétés dans un coin. Lui n'avait pas de phosphore; je sais, car j'ai léché toute la peinture de ces joues vermeilles, embrassé, et même mordu, son nez bien des fois sans m'entrouver plus mal. C'etait un ami fidèle. Il recevait mes confidences d'un air sympathique en me regardant d'un œil affectueux. Je dis d'un œil car dans les premiers jours de notre amitié je lui avait crevé l'autre

---

[1] No year is given, but the letter appears to fall within 1891, although the tone might also suggest middle or late October 1892. Conrad was planning another voyage on the *Torrens* by that time.

[2] Jakob Moleschott, whose maxim 'Ohne Phosphor kein Gedanke' ('Without phosphorus, no thought') appears in his *Lehre der Nahrungsmittel*, II, i. 4.

dans un acces de folle tendresse. Du reste il n'a jamais semblé s'en apreçevoir de peur de me causer de la peine. C'etait un "gentleman". Les autres polichinelles que j'ai connu depuis criaient quand on leur marchait sur le pied. A-t-on l'idée d'une impertinence pareille!? Après tout rien ne remplace les amitiés de notre enfance.—

Ce soir il me semble que je suis dans un coin, l'echine cassée, le nez dans la poussière. Voulez Vous avoir la bonté de ramasser le pauvre diable, le mettre tendrement dans Votre tablier, le presenter a Vos poupées, lui faire faire la dinette avec les autres. Je me vois d'ici a ce festin le nez barbouillé des confitures, les autres me regardant avec cet air d'etonnement frigide qui est naturel aux poupées bien fabriquées. J'ai été regardé comme cela bien des fois par des mannequins innombrables. Ma foi! Je leur pardonne; il y a eu un temps ou j'étais chrétien!—J'avais l'intention en commencant cette lettre de Vous dire que Votre costume de pose (pour le portrait)[1] me plait quoique il m'est difficile de Vous imaginer dedans. Savez Vous que par une de ces charmantes plaisanteries dont le Destin e[s]t si prodigue je ne Vous ai vue qu'en noir? Enfin! Qui vivra verra. Peut-etre je vivrai assez longtemps pour voir Votre portrait.—

> Je Vous embrasse de tout mon cœur. Votre très devoué
> J. Conrad.

16 October [1891]
17 Gillingham Street
London S.W.

Dear Aunt,

I wonder if you are very cross with your lazy nephew. I like to believe, however, that you feel the duty of indulgence, seeing that life is only possible by virtue of that feeling.

I have absolutely nothing to say to you. I am vegetating. I do not even think – therefore I do not exist (according to Descartes). But another individual (a scientist) has said: 'Without phosphorus, no thought'. From which it seems that I am still there, but the phosphorus is missing. Yet in that case I would exist without thinking, which (according to Descartes) is impossible. Good Heavens! Could I be a Punch? The Punch of my childhood, you know – his spine broken in two, his nose on the floor between his feet; his legs and arms flung out stiffly in that attitude of profound despair, so pathetically droll, of dolls tossed in a

---

[1] A pastel done by a Dutch artist, Schaken.

corner. He had no phosphorus; I know, for I licked all the paint from his rosy cheeks, kissed and even bit his nose often enough without being any the worse for it. He was a faithful friend. He received my secrets sympathetically, while looking at me with one affectionate eye. I say 'one eye' because in the first days of our friendship I had put out the other in a fit of mad tenderness. Still, he never seemed to pay it any attention for fear of giving me pain. He was a gentleman. Every Punch I have known since then cried out when anyone stepped on his feet. Have you ever heard of such cheek!? After all, nothing takes the place of our childhood friendships.

This evening I seem to be in a corner, spine cracked, nose in the dust. Would you kindly scrape together the poor devil, put him tenderly in your apron, introduce him to your dolls, make him join the dinner party with the others? I can see myself at that banquet from here, nose besmeared with jam, the others watching me with that air of cold astonishment natural to well-made dolls. I have been looked at like that many times by countless manikins. My word! I forgive them; once upon a time I was a Christian! On beginning this letter, I had intended to tell you that your outfit (for the portrait) pleases me, although it is hard to imagine you wearing it. Do you know that as a result of one of those charming jests in which Destiny is so rich I have seen you only in black? Well, time will tell. Perhaps I shall live long enough to see your portrait.

I embrace you warmly. Your very devoted

J. Conrad

To Marguerite Poradowska

Text   MS Yale; Rapin 94; G. & S. 39

22^d Oct^{er} [189]1
[letterhead: Barr, Moering]

Tante très chère. Je viens de recevoir Votre lettre ce matin comme je sortai.—Je l'ai emportée dans ma poche. je l'ai lue dans le train et je reponds tout-de-suite. Si Votre lettre—comme Vous dites est "assomante" j'aime a être assomé; si elle est "inepte," plut au ciel que le manteau de cette ineptie descendisse sur mes epaules! Si elle est bête c'est donc d'une betise qui vaut un million des sagesses. Elle est si humaine, Votre lettre, dans cette douleur de tous les commencements. Je Vous comprends parfaitement. C'est l'hesitation du seuil, le degout des choses neuves, l'incertitude du noir ou on tatonne du pied avec effroi.—Mes vous verrez. La solitude perd de ses terreurs, quand on la connait; c'est une amertume qui pour les gens courageux, qui ont approché la coupe au lèvres sans sourciller, se change en une douceur dont on n'echangerait pas le charme pour rien dans l'univers entier.

Donc sans sourciller—buvez! et le courage viendra avec l'oubli, ou plutôt l'effacement du passé. Ce n'est pas le manque du feu dans la pièce du millieu qui Vous decourage—Vous doutez sans le savoir de l'Etincelle Divine qui est en Vous. En ceci Vous êtes comme les autres. Leur serez-Vous differente en cette foi qui souffle l'etincelle en un feu brilliant? Du fond de mon cœur, Madame, je le crois! Ne descendez pas du piedestal ou je Vous ai posée même quand ce serait pour Vous rapprocher de moi. Je ne suis pas toujours egoïste. Je Vous embrasse. Ecrirai bientôt

J. Conrad

22 October 1891
[letterhead: Barr, Moering]

Very dear Aunt,

I had your letter this morning, just as I was going out. I brought it along in my pocket, read it on the train, and answer immediately. If your letter is, as you say, 'boring', I like to be bored; if it is 'inept', would to God that the mantle of that ineptitude might descend on my shoulders! If it is 'stupid', then it is a stupidity worth a million wise sayings. Your letter is so human in that sadness of all beginnings. I understand you perfectly. It is the hesitation at the threshold, the distaste for new things, the uncertainty of the darkness where one fearfully inches along. But you will see. Solitude loses its terrors when one knows it; it is a bitterness which, for the courageous people who have brought the cup to their lips without wincing, is changed to a sweetness whose attraction one would not exchange for anything else in the entire universe.

So without wincing – drink! and courage will come with forgetfulness, or rather with the obliteration of the past. It is not the lack of fire in the living-room which discourages you. Without realizing it, you doubt that the Divine Spark is within you. In this, you are like the others. Will you differ from them in faith which fans the spark into a brilliant fire? From the bottom of my heart, Madame, I believe it. Do not come down from the pedestal where I have placed you, even though that would bring you nearer to me. I am not always an egoist. I embrace you. Shall write soon.

J. Conrad

To Marguerite Poradowska

Text   MS Yale; Rapin 95; G. & S. 40

14 Nov: 1891.
36. Camomile Street
London—E C.

Ma très chère Tante.

A Vous la première j'envoie la nouvelle de mon prochain départ. C'est arrivé tout d'un coup.—Hier dans l'après midi j'ai reçu une lettre d'une connaissance a moi qui commande le navire "Torrens"[1] m'offrant la place du premier officier a bord. J'ai accepté, et aujourd'hui (a 7½ heures du matin) j'ai pris mon service des mains de mon prédecesseur. En ce moment il est passé dix heures du soir. Je viens de rentrer dans mon nouveau logement près du bassin ou se trouve le navire. Je rentre assez ereinté de ma longue journée de travail et très disposé a me coucher mais ... a vous la première—il faut envoyer la grande nouvelle.—

Nous partons dans six jours et nous sommes loin d'être prêts pour cela.[2] A partir de Lundi prochain[3] on travaillera jour et nuit probablement, donc je serais très occupé. Il peur se faire que la presente sera ma dernière lettre de Londres. La destination du navire est Port-Adelaide (Australie-du-Sud).—Le passage durera de 70–80 jours.[4] J'ecrirai aussitôt arrivé et la lettre par paquebot via Suez sera 40 jours en route. Donc disons dans quatre mois vous aurez de mes nouvelles.—

Pendant ce temps là Vous me garderez un bon souvenir; un petit coin de cœur, et a mon retour (dans 9 à 10 mois) si Vous voulez bien on tachera de se voir. A quoi bon projeter. Le destin est notre maitre!—

Je baise Vos deux mains et Vous embrasse de tout mon cœur.

J. Conrad.

Si Vous repondez tout de suite a l'addresse comme en tête de cette lettre Vous me trouverez encore ici.—

Addresse australienne. *Mr. J. Conrad*. Chief mate ship "Torrens". Pt. Adelaide. South Australia. (Ecrivez a la mi-Janvier).

---

[1] A clipper of some 1300 tons, captained by Walter H. Cope, famous for its fast voyages to the Southern Seas. See Conrad's 'The *Torrens*: A Personal Tribute' (*Last Essays*, pp. 33–43).
[2] The *Torrens* left London on 20 November.
[3] 16 November.
[4] Actually, 100 days.

14 November 1891
36 Camomile Street
London E.C.

My very dear Aunt,

You are the first to whom I send news of my approaching departure. It happened suddenly. Yesterday afternoon I received a letter from an acquaintance of mine who commands the ship *Torrens*. offering me the first officer's berth. I accepted, and today (at 7.30 a.m.) I took over from my predecessor. Now it is past 10 p.m. I have just returned to my new lodgings near the dock where the ship is moored. I have returned quite worn out from my long day of work and feel like going to bed, but . . . to you first of all – I must send you the great news.

We leave in six days and are far from ready to do so. Starting next Monday, we shall work probably day and night, so that I shall be very busy. Possibly this letter may be my last from London. The destination of the ship is Port Adelaide (South Australia). The passage will take from 70 to 80 days. I shall write upon arrival, and the letter, despatched via Suez, will take 40 days. Let's say, then, that within 4 months you will have some news.

During this time, remember me kindly; reserve a little corner of your heart, and on my return (within 9 to 10 months) if you are willing we shall try to meet. But what is the use of plans? Destiny is our master!

I kiss your hands and embrace you warmly

J. Conrad

If you reply at once to the address in the heading, you will find me still here.

Australian address: *Mr J. Conrad*. Chief mate ship *Torrens*. Pt Adelaide. South Australia. (Write in mid-January.)

1892

To Marguerite Poradowska

Text MS Yale; Rapin 99; G. & S. 41

5 mars 1892.
Ship "Torrens"
Port Adelaide.

Ma très chère Tante.

Nous sommes arrivés ici avant-hier après un long passage.[1] Je me suis précipité sur Vos lettres et je m'empresse de Vous remercier pour le plaisir que leur lecture m'a donnée.—

—Mais rien d'agréable n'est complet en ce monde; les nouvelles de Votre santé m'inquiètent. Je n'aime pas cette persistente bronchite, et j'ai peur que l'esprit de sacrifice ne Vous mène trop loin. Car il est evident que Vous ne Vous soignez pas assez—peut-être pas du tout.

Je Vous avouerai aussi que je comprend mal—peut-être pas du tout—la ligne de conduite que Vous avez choisie. Je ne puis pas imaginer sur quelle fondation ethique Vous basez Votre conduite envers Mme Votre Tante.[2]—Je suppose que le sentiment de famille y est pour quelque chose mais moi je comprends cela autrement. Selon moi les droits et les devoirs en cette relation sont mutuels—tandis qu'ici il me semble que Vous avez tous les devoirs et Mme Votre Tante tous les droits—si nous admettons qu'un être humain peut avoir le droit de meurtrir physiquement et moralement un autre etre humain; ce que je ne puis admettre. Dans mon entourage le sentiment de famille se manifeste par une solidarité absolue entre tous les membres, qui sanctionne par approbation tous les actes des individus—tant qu'ils ne sont pas deshonorables—mais les droits de l'individu a arranger sa vie a sa guise ne sont jamais mis en question pour satisfaire les demandes d'un egoisme plus ou moins mesquin.—Le respect pour l'age y est pour quelque chose sans doute. Mais veuillez reflechir que la vieillesse c'est une infortune— pas un privilège, que la sagesse—quoique on en dise—n'augmente pas avec le nombre des années; que le respect du a la vieillesse n'est réelement au fond que le sentiment deguisé de pitié profonde pour les malheureux que la mort a oublié mais que le Temps a depouillé de l'Espoir. Madame Votre Tante possède sans doute toutes les vertus qui sont le don universel du Createur au genre humain—excepté celle de la Charité qui est un don direct de l'Eternel aux âmes choisies—car la Charité c'est l'Amour eternel et universel, la vertu divine, la seule

---

[1] More precisely, on 28 February (see Basil Lubbock, *The Colonial Clippers*, Glasgow, James Brown and Son, 1921, p. 162). Conrad often used dates approximately.
[2] Unidentified.

manifestation de la Toute Puissance qui peut justifier en quelque sorte l'acte de la création.—

Donc c'est le desir de se sacrifier—de rendre le bien pour le mal—cette poussée mysterieuse vers l'abnégation et la souffrance qui gouverne le sentiment feminin est la principale cause de Votre conduite—apparement si hautement exemplaire—envers Mme Votre Tante.—Malheureusement je ne puis pas mettre a Vos pieds le tribut de l'admiration que Vous avez—a première vue—si richement merité car dans mon opinion l'abnegation poussée dans ses lointaines limites—ou Vous etes en train d'errer—devient non pas une faute mais un crime—que rendre le bien pour le mal est non seulement profondement immoral mais c'est aussi dangereux, en ce sens que cela aiguise l'appetit pour le mal de l'etre malveillant et developpe (inconsciement peut être) cette tendence dormante de l'humanité vers l'hypocrisie dans l'être ... —: disons: bienveillant.

Du reste il me semble que dans cette affaire dans Votre desir de remplir Vos devoirs envers Mme Votre Tante Vous avez manqué a Vos devoirs envers Vous même. Vous avez jété de coté la dignité, les affections, les souvenirs! Et pourquoi? Avez Vous trouvé la paix qui est la recompense des sacrifices acceptés par le maitre de nos ames?

Je Vous dis tout cela car je Vous aime beaucoup, Vous admire immensement et je Vous baise les mains en disant au revoir—si Vous voulez encore me connaitre a mon retour.

Votre très devoué neveu
J. Conrad Korzeniowski

Nous partons d'ici le 10 avril.[1] Si Vous ecrivez a Mr. J. Conrad. Chief officer Ship "Torrens",

Cape Town.

ou nous arriverons vers la fin Mai Vous me rendrez heureux. Je suis très occupé. Je Vous ecrirai d'ici avant notre depart

Mes compl^ts a Mme Votre Mère & Mme Vtre Bellesœur.—

5 March 1892
Ship *Torrens*, Port Adelaide

My very dear Aunt,

We arrived here the day before yesterday after a long voyage. I fell upon your letters and I am eager to thank you for the pleasure which reading them gave me.

---

[1] The *Torrens* left Port Adelaide for the Cape of Good Hope on 7 April.

But no pleasure is complete in this world; the news of your health disturbs me. I do not like that persistent bronchitis, and I am afraid the spirit of sacrifice carries you too far. For evidently you do not take sufficient care of yourself – perhaps none at all.

I will also confess I can scarcely understand – perhaps not at all – the line of conduct you have chosen. I cannot imagine on what ethical grounds you base your conduct toward your aunt. I suppose family sentiment has something to do with it, but I consider all this in another way. In my view, the rights and duties in this relationship are mutual; while here it seems to me you have all the duties and your aunt all the rights – if we grant that one human being has the right morally and physically to injure another human being – which I cannot grant. In my circle, family feeling displays itself by an absolute solidarity among all members, which sanctions by approval all the acts of the individual – inasmuch as these are not dishonourable – but the individual's right to arrange his life as he chooses is never questioned to satisfy the demands of a more or less mean egoism. Respect for age enters into it no doubt. But please remember that old age is an unfortunate condition, not a privilege; that wisdom, whatever one may say, does not increase with years; that really the respect due to old age is at bottom only a veiled feeling of deep pity for the hapless people whom death has forgotten but time has stripped of hope. Your aunt surely possesses all the virtues which are the universal gift from the Creator to mankind – except that of charity, which is a direct gift from the Eternal to the elect. For charity is eternal and universal love, the divine virtue, the only manifestation of the Almighty which can in some way justify the act of creation.

Thus the desire for self-sacrifice – for returning good for evil – this mysterious urge toward abnegation and suffering which governs feminine feeling – is the chief reason for your conduct, apparently so highly exemplary, toward your aunt. Unfortunately, I cannot lay at your feet the tribute of admiration which you have, at first sight, so richly deserved; for in my opinion abnegation carried to an extreme, as you are now trying to carry it, becomes not just a fault but a crime; and to return good for evil is not only profoundly immoral but also dangerous, in that it whets the appetite for evil in the malevolent and arouses (perhaps unconsciously) that dormant human tendency toward hypocrisy in the – let us call them – benevolent.

Moreover, it seems to me that in this affair, while wishing to fulfil your duties to your aunt, you have failed in your duties to yourself. You have thrown aside dignity, affection, memories! And why? Have you found the peace which is the reward of these sacrifices accepted by the master of our souls?

I tell you all this because I love you very much, admire you immensely, and I kiss your hands in saying *au revoir* – if you still wish to know me on my return.

Your very devoted nephew

J. Conrad Korzeniowski

We leave here on 10 April. If you write to Mr J. Conrad, Chief Officer, Ship *Torrens*, Cape Town, where we shall arrive towards the end of May, you will make me happy. I am very busy. I shall write to you from here before our departure. My regards to your mother and sister-in-law.

To George Mansfield

Text MS Indiana; Unpublished.

P[or]t Adelaide

Thursday

31 March [1892][1]

M[r] G. Mansfield.

——Capt Cope[2] desires me to inform You that he is willing to accept your services as O[rdinary] S[eaman] at £1 per month. As the ship is going to leave on the 7th prox: You had better come over at once if you wish to join.——

J. Conrad

mate.

Ship "Torrens"

---

[1] The year is clearly 1892, since Conrad mentions leaving Adelaide on the 7th, and the *Torrens* did leave on 7 April.

[2] Captain W. H. Cope of the *Torrens*.

To Marguerite Poradowska
Text   MS Yale; Rapin 100; G. & S. 43

6 Avril 1892.
à bord du "Torrens"
Port Adelaide

Ma très chère Tante

Nous partons demain pour le Cap de Bonne Esperance d'ou nous irons a Ste Helene et puis a Londres. Je compte être en Europe vers la mi-Août si tout va bien.[1]

J'ai été excessivement occupé pendant notre séjour ici;—ceci, et une espèce de torpeur intellectuelle qui m'oppresse m'a empêché de Vous ecrire plus souvent. Ceci est ma troisième—et dernière—lettre d'Australie.[2] Je compte sur votre indulgence. Du reste Vous savez bien que si je n'ecris pas souvent je ne Vous en aime pas moins.

Vos lettres ont été delicieuses—interessantes et curieuses, car il Vous arrive de rencontrer des caractères qui ne se trouvent pas ordinairement sur le chemin de la vie de nous autres simples mortels—

On vient de m'interrompre. Je reprend:—Donc je veux dire que Vous possedez le coup d'œil de l'auteur—qui voit des traits qui echappent a la vue de gens dont le metier n'est pas d'observer leur semblables. Du reste il y en a qui savent bien observer mais ne savent pas decrire. Vous observez et Vous decrivez. Dans la [   ][3] et saisissante simplicité de vos descriptions Vous me rappelez un peu Flaubert dont je viens de relire Mme Bovary avec une admiration plaine de respect[4]—

On vient de m'interrompre encore. Je reprends:

En voilà un qui avait assez d'imagination pour deux realistes. Il y a peu d'auteurs qui soient aussi créateurs que lui. On ne questionne jamais pour un moment ni ses personnes ni ses evenements; on douterai plutôt de sa propre existence.—Assez de Flaubert.

Votre santé m'inquiète chère Tante. J'aurai bien voulu recevoir une lettre rassurante de Vous avant mon depart. Le paquebot des Messageries[5] est arrivé hier. Rien!—On se resigne—mais on n'est pas plus heureux pour cela.—Rien de mon Oncle mais du moins sa dernière lettre me donnait des bonnes nouvelles.[6]

---

[1] Conrad arrived at the beginning of September.
[2] Mme Poradowska has written 'Une lettre perdue' above the salutation.
[3] In turning the page, Conrad omitted a word.
[4] For Flaubert and Conrad, see Karl, pp. 270–1, 326–7.
[5] Messageries Maritimes, the French mail line.
[6] Probably a reference to Bobrowski's letter of 26 December 1891/7 January 1892, in which he says his health is quite good.

J'ai peur de Vous avoir déplu dans man première lettre.[1] Il faut me pardonner. Vous concevez bien que si je ne Vous aimais pas tant je ne ressentirai pas avec toute cette amertume les tricheries de votre destinée.[2] Il m'est permis de me fâcher quand je vois une nature dans mon opinion digne d'un meilleur sort s'user dans une lutte contre des ennuis, des evenements sans aucune logique—se debattant dans un courant qui prend sa source dans l'egoisme feroce des natures inferieures a celle dont elles font leur victime. Voilà pourquoi je me suis permis de Vous dire que—dans le cas donné—l'abnegation est une faute et presque un crime. Du reste. a quoi bon s'étendre la-dessus!? Les femmes ne comprennent pas cela. On pourrait precher jusqu'a a la fin des siècles. On rage on se tait, et on admire.—Je Vous baise les mains. A bientôt
                                          Votre tout devoué
                                                                  J. Conrad.

Ecrivez a Londres c/o Messrs. Barr Moering
36 Camomile St—E.C.

                                                              6 April 1892
                                                       on board the *Torrens*
                                                            Port Adelaide
My very dear Aunt,
    We are leaving tomorrow for the Cape of Good Hope, from whence we shall go to St Helena and then to London. I count on being in Europe around mid-August if all goes well.
    I have been exceptionally busy during our stay here; that, and a kind of intellectual torpor which oppresses me, has impeded my writing to you more often. This is my third – and last – letter from Australia. I count on your indulgence. Moreover you know very well that if I do not write often I love you none the less.
    Your letters have been capital – interesting and surprising; for it has fallen to you to meet some characters who are not ordinarily found on life's highways by us simple mortals.
    Someone has interrupted me. I resume: therefore, I would say that you possess the author's insight, which sees characteristics that escape the eye of those whose business is not that of observing their fellows. Still there are some who know well how to observe but not how to describe.

[1] 5 March 1892.
[2] The difficulties with the unidentified aunt of the preceding letter.

You both observe and describe. In the [   ] and striking simplicity of your descriptions, you remind me a little of Flaubert, whose *Madame Bovary* I have just reread with respectful admiration.

Another interruption. I resume:

In him, we see a man who had enough imagination for two realists. There are few authors who could be as much a creator as he. One never questions for a moment either his characters or his incidents; one would rather doubt one's own existence. Enough about Flaubert.

Your health worries me, dear Aunt. I would indeed have wished to receive a reassuring letter from you before my departure. The French mail steamer arrived yesterday. Nothing! I am resigned – but not any happier for that. Nothing from my uncle, but at least his last letter gave me some good news.

I fear I displeased you in my first letter. You must pardon me. You can well understand that if I did not love you so much I would not resent so bitterly the tricks that Destiny has played on you. I have a right to be angry when I see a being who in my opinion deserves a better fate wear herself out in a struggle against annoyances, against events devoid of logic – floundering in a current whose source is the ferocious egoism of natures inferior to the one they victimize. That is why I allowed myself to tell you that, in this particular case, abnegation is a fault and nearly a crime. However, why dwell on that!? Women do not understand this point. I could preach until doomsday. I rage, am silent, and admire. I kiss your hands. I shall see you soon.

Your very devoted

J. Conrad

Write to London c/o Messrs. Barr Moering 36 Camomile St, E.C.

To Marguerite Poradowska

Text MS Yale; Rapin 102; G. & S. 45

4 Sept. 1892.
Londres.

Très chère Tante.

Arrivé avant-hier j'ai eu le bonheur de lire Vos charmantes et bonnes lettres ce matin. J'ai trouvé toutes les lettres a Londres car mon ami Krieger[1] etant très gravement malade personne au bureau n'a eu le bon

---

[1] Adolf Krieger, of Barr, Moering.

sens de me les envoyer en Australie ou au Cap ou on savait bien que nous allions faire relâche. Je suis heureux de Votre bonheur (comparatif) ou du moins de la paix que Vous avez trouvée dans cette solitude qui Vous faisait tant peur. Malheureusement j'ai a Vous annoncer qu'il me sera impossible de rompre cette solitude car je serais très occupé et un congé e[s]t tout-a-fait hors de question. Quand a quitter le navire je ne peux pas me permettre ce luxe a cause du pain quotidien—vous savez—celui qu'on mange a la sueur de son front—et quelquefois a celle d'autrui quand on a l'intelligence de rester a l'ombre et laisser les autres s'evertuer au soleil. Moi je ne possède ni cette intelligence ni cette chance—par conséquent Vous ne me verrez pas cette année ci a Passy.—Je Vous dis cela tout de suite car je Vous crois capable de deranger tout Vos pour Votre vaut-rien (pas vaurien) de neveu.—Ce que Vous me dites de Jean m'attriste.[1] Vous pensez déjà aux conquêtes qu'il fera et cœurs qu'il brisera. Comme c'est caracteristique individuellement et nationalement! Moi je pense qu'élévé de cette façon il grandira et mûrira sans realiser la significance de la vie avec une fausse idée de sa place dans le monde. Il se croira important. On se croit toujours important a 20 ans. Le fait est cependant que l'on ne devient utile que quand on [a] realisé toute l'etendue de l'insignificance de l'individu dans l'arrangement de l'univers. Quand on a bien compris que par soi même on n'est rien et que l'homme ne vaut ni plus ni moins que le travail qu'il accomplit avec honnêtété de but et des moyens et dans les strictes limites de son devoir envers la société ce n'est qu'alors que l'on est maitre de sa conscience et on a le droit de se dire un homme. Autrement serait-il plus charmant que le prince Charmant, plus riche que Midas plus savant que le docteur Faust lui même l'être a deux pattes sans plumes n'est qu'une loque meprisable pietinée dans la boue de toutes les passions. Je pourrais gâter bien du papier sur ce thême là mais Vous me comprenez sans doute aussi bien que je me comprends moi même sans plus d'explications.—

Mon oncle a été plus ou moins malade tout l'hiver En été il se sentit mieux mais j'ai bien peur que cela ne durera pas. Du reste je me trompe peut-etre car je vois tout en noir depuis que ma santé n'est plus bonne. C'est bête mais c'est comme cela.

Nous avons arrangé ma visite en Russie pour l'année prochaine et alors je passerais par Paris.[2] J'espère donc Vous voir en même temps. Mais faire des plans est une occupation bien ingrate. C'est toujours l'imprévu qui arrive.—

[1] Mme Poradowska's nephew, Jean Gachet.
[2] Conrad went via Holland.

Presentez mes compliments a Mme Votre Mère et a Mme et M. Bouillot[1] Je presume que Mme Votre Belle sœur et les enfants sont en Angleterre en ce moment.—

Je Vous remercie mille et mille fois du bon souvenir que Vous me gardez. Je ne sais vraiment comment j'ai merité Vos bonnes grâces, mais je les accepte comme on accepte les dons du Ciel; avec une humble gratitude, avec la conscience de mon indignité, sans tâcher de comprendre la Sagesse Eternelle.

Votre très dévoué

J. Conrad

4 September 1892
London

Very dear Aunt,

Having arrived the day before yesterday, I had the pleasure of reading your kind and charming letters this morning. I found all your letters in London, for my good friend Krieger was very gravely ill and no one at the office had sense enough to send them on to me in Australia or at the Cape, where they knew perfectly well we had our port of call. I am glad to hear of your (comparative) happiness or at least the peace you have found within the solitude you so feared. Unfortunately, I have to tell you that it will be impossible for me to break this solitude, for I shall be very busy and leave is altogether out of the question. As for quitting the ship, I cannot permit myself that luxury – daily bread, you understand, which one eats by the sweat of one's brow – and sometimes by that of another's, when one has the intelligence to remain in the shade and let others exert themselves in the sun. As for me, I have neither such intelligence nor such luck – and so you will not see me at Passy this year. I tell you this at once, for I believe you are capable of upsetting all your plans for your 'unworthy' (not worthless) nephew. What you say of Jean saddens me. You are already thinking of the conquests he will make and the hearts he will break. How characteristic, individually and nationally! Personally, I think that, raised in this way, he will grow and mature without realizing the meaning of life, with a false notion of his place in the world. He will consider himself important. At twenty, one always thinks oneself important. The fact is, however, that one becomes useful only on recognizing the extent of the individual's utter insignificance within the arrangement of the universe. When one has fully understood that, by oneself, one is nothing and man is worth neither more nor less than the

[1] Mme Poradowska's friends.

work he accomplishes with honesty of means and purpose, and within the strict limits of his duty to society, only then is one master of one's conscience, only then has one the right to call oneself a man. Otherwise, were he more charming than Prince Charming, richer than Midas, wiser than Dr Faust himself, the two-legged, featherless creature is only a contemptible rag trampled in the mud of all the passions. I could indeed waste some paper on this theme, but you doubtless understand me as well as I understand myself without more explanation.

My Uncle has been more or less ill all winter. During the summer, he felt better, but I am afraid it will not last. However, perhaps I am mistaken, for ever since my health deteriorated, I have looked gloomily at everything. It's stupid, but that's how it is.

We have arranged my visit to Russia for next year, and then I shall pass through Paris. I hope, therefore, to see you then. But to make plans is a thankless business. It is always the unforeseen that happens.

Give my compliments to your mother and to Mme and M. Bouillot. I assume that your sister-in-law and the children are now in England.

I thank you again and again for the kind remembrance you have of me. Truly I do not know how I have merited your great kindnesses, but I accept them as one accepts gifts from Heaven. With humble gratitude, with awareness of my unworthiness and without trying to understand Eternal Wisdom

Your very devoted

J. Conrad

To Maria Tyszkowa

Text Ruch; Najder 214

London, 8th September, 1892.

Dear Maryleczka,

Thank you for your very kind letter which I found here on my return. I can't imagine why they did not forward it to me in Australia,—anyway that is what has happened and so through no fault of mine the reply is delayed.

I am sad to learn of your troubles and worries. From Uncle's letters I already knew of Stanisław's unhappy case[1] and I can well imagine your anxiety and sorrow. Generally the news from home is far from cheerful.

---

[1] Her brother's imprisonment, for political reasons. For details, see Tadeusz Bobrowski's letter to Conrad for 2/14 May 1892 (Najder, p. 162). The chief charge appeared to be that Stanisław had been doing unauthorized teaching of artisans in the Polish language.

I congratulate you both on the arrival of your daughter, and I shall endeavour to come as soon as possible in order to have the joy of making her acquaintance. I am afraid, however, that it will not be possible until next year. You did not say what name you have given to the young lady?

I am myself, dear Marylcia, such a bad correspondent that I would never dream of blaming anyone for not writing. But I am always glad to receive a token that I am not forgotten and I value it all the more because I feel myself unworthy of it.

I returned from Australia on the 3rd of this month and I am going back there again on the same ship, on the 20th October. At the end of July I shall probably return from that voyage and shall then take 6 weeks' leave to visit Uncle and all of you. Till then I shall live in the hope of finding you all healthy and happier than you have been this year. My own health is not at all bad, but still rather uncertain, and the less we say about my happiness, the better. From the worthy Tadeusz I have also received a letter written in May like yours. I am answering it today. I thank your husband for remembering me so kindly and I shall send him a warm handshake—My brotherly embraces to you and many kisses for Miss Tyszka.

Your brother,

Konrad Korzeniowski.

Kiss Zunia for me and give my regards to Mr. Meresch.[1]

To Marguerite Poradowska

Text   MS Yale; Rapin, 103; G. & S. 46

13 Sept. 1892.

Londres.

Ma chère Tante—

Votre lettre du mois d'Avril ne m'est parvenue qu'hier. On l'avait oubliée quelque part. Je m'empresse de Vous dire combien je suis heureux de voir que l'offre de Hachette vous convient.[2] Vous voilà en bonne voie et personne n'en est plus content que Votre neveu—

Cette note est ecrite exprès pour Vous dire cela. Je suis très occupé. Je me couche tard—je me lève de bonne heure et je tourne la manivelle

---

[1] Maria's brother-in-law and sister.

[2] Rapin suggests the acceptance of *Popes et popadias* (Hachette, 1893).

toute la journée. J'en devient positivement bête. Je Vous embrasse bien
fort. Ecrivez petit mot

Toujours votre

J. Conrad.

13 September 1892
London

My dear Aunt,

   Your April letter reached me only yesterday. Someone, somewhere,
had forgotten it. I hasten to tell you how happy I am to see that
Hachette's offer suits you. You are making progress, and no one is
happier about it than your nephew.

   I am writing this note expressly to tell you that. I am very busy. I go to
bed late – I get up early and work at the treadmill all day long. I am
becoming absolutely stupid. I embrace you most warmly. Send a note.

Always yours

J. Conrad

To Marguerite Poradowska

Text   MS Yale; Rapin 104; G. & S. 47

4.10.92.
Londres.

Ma très chère Tante.

   Je viens de recevoir Votre lettre ce matin et j'en suis tout regaillardi;—
tout joyeux de votre bonheur.[1] Enfin! Vous avez ce que Vous méritez. Et
moi—qui parle en connaissance de cause—je suis sur que ce n'est pas
d'un moment trop tôt.

   Je ne demande pas mieux que d'oublier le contenu de Vos lettres de
l'année dernière car elles m'ont causé bien du chagrin et de la colère,
seulement je Vous demanderai: est-il bon d'oublier ainsi? et je me
demande a moi:—est-il possible d'oublier? Du reste c'est très marin ça,
cet oubli des injures des peines et des tempêtes. C'est aussi une des
charmantes qualités de l'enfance; a présent que j'y pense, c'est même
très chrétien ce manque de memoire. Et puis c'est si commode pour cette
bande de braves gens qui s'en vont de par le monde empoisonnant la vie
a droite et a gauche, vous presentant la coupe amère.—"Buvez donc
miserable pêcheur. Cela ne vous tuera pas.—Cela ne fera que vous

---

[1] Gee and Sturm suggest a satisfactory settlement of her late husband's financial affairs.

tordre le cœur—une misère! Allons buvez—et oubliez!"[1] On boit. On oublie. Et puis ça recommence; la torture et les larmes; les sanglots et la revolte; le courroux et la lutte indignée et honnête. Mais la memoire est courte. Oubliez! on vous crie. Et la lutte finit dans l'effondrement mou des espérances deçues; des affections trichées; de saintes indignations profanées; de la dignité renoncée, jetée au vent pour ce mot fatal prononcé sur l'air faux du sentiment religieux. Et voilà. C'est Vous qui avez raison! Oublions bien vite.—

Mes félicitations de l'honneur qui Vous arrive derechef d'etre mise a cheval (shocking!) sur les deux années.[2] Vous m'enverrez le Figaro [ill.3] en Australie n'est-ce pas? Je Vous enverrais l'addresse. Il faudra ecrire directement. Du reste j'espère avoir encore une lettre de vous avant de partir.

Mes occupations ne sont pas très variées, mais elles n'en sont pas moins absorbantes pour cela. Elles ne pourrait avoir aucune espèce d'interet pour Vous. Je me porte assez bien. Je Vous baise les mains et suis Votre très devoué toujours C.K.

4 October 1892
London

My very dear Aunt,

I have just received your letter this morning, and I am altogether delighted by it – really happy at your good fortune. At last! You have what you deserve. And I – and I know what I'm talking about – I am sure it is not a moment too soon.

I ask nothing better than to forget the content of your last year's letters, for they have indeed caused me much concern and anger. However, I would ask you: is it right to forget like that? And I ask myself – is it possible to forget? But it is very sailor-like, this manner of forgetting offences, pains and storms. It is also one of the charming qualities of childhood: and, now I think of it, this lack of memory is positively Christian. And then it is so convenient for that band of worthies who travel about the world poisoning life to right and left, handing you the

---

[1] We omit the three pairs of punctuation marks that Conrad, as if to show that these lines should be read as dialogue, placed in the margin.

[2] The publication of *Demoiselle Micia* in the *Revue des Deux Mondes* had straddled 1888 and 1889. Although Mme Poradowska expected a similar arrangement for *Popes et popadias*, both parts had appeared by the end of 1892. Ladies, of course, rode side-saddle.

[3] Once again, Conrad confuses the *Figaro illustré* with another publication (in this case, the *Revue*).

bitter cup – 'Drink, then, miserable sinner! It won't kill you. It will only wring your heart – a trifling thing! Come, drink – and forget!' One drinks. One forgets. And then it begins again: torture and tears, sobs and revolt, rage and indignant, honest struggle. But memory is short. 'Forget!' they shout at you. And the struggle ends with the limp collapse of misguided hopes, of deceived affections, of righteous indignation polluted, of dignity abandoned, thrown to the winds for that fatal word enunciated with the false air of religious sentiment. And there it is! You are right! Let us forget very quickly.

My congratulations on the honour that falls to you once again of being mounted astride the two years (shocking!). You will send me the *Figaro illustré* in Australia, won't you? I shall forward the address. You will have to write directly. Still, I hope to have another letter from you before leaving.

My duties are not very diversified, but they are no less engrossing for that. They could not have any interest for you, whatsoever. I feel fairly well. I kiss your hands and am always your very devoted.

C.K.

To Marguerite Poradowska
Text   MS Yale; Rapin 104; G. & S. 48

19.10.92.
Londres.

Ma très chère Tante.

Vous vous moquez un petit brin de Votre Neveu en le comparant a feu Hamlet (qui était fou je crois). Du reste je me suis laissé dire qu'a part son etat de demence c'etait une personne tout-a-fait estimable. Je ne suis donc pas offensé par la comparaison. Je ne sais pas ou Vous avez trouvé les signes de mon mépris des hommes. Ceci me prouve qu'en generalisant on peut bien dire que même ceux qui nous connaissent le mieux nous connaissent bien peu. Le philosophe qui a dit: "Connait toi même" était je pense probablement gris (après un souper avec des demoiselles grecques—ce qui etait dans les habitudes philosophiques du temps—) puisque je ne puis pas admettre qu'il était bête. Un philosophe ne peut pas être bête. N'est-ce pas? On se connait bien vite soi même. La difficulté est de connaitre les autres. Je me hate de Vous assurer (avant mon depart qui aura lieu le 25 courant) que j'aime l'humanité autant que Vous sans doute mais d'une autre manière peut-etre. Du reste— Vous savez!—l'Humanité s'en moque. Je ne méprise personne car je n'ai pas envie d'être payé de retour. Je ne suis pas assez philosophe pour endurer (avec calme) le mepris de mes dissemblables. Et notez bien que les coups de pied de l'âne font très mal. Une des études constantes de ma vie a été de les eviter. Veuillez prendre connaissance par la présente que je respecte l'ane (avec un grand A). Je saisis cette occasion pour prononcer ma confession de foi. Les longues oreilles sont éternelles—le commencement et la fin de toutes les choses; je trouve mon repos—ma paix—dans l'ombre qu'elles projètent sur le desert la vie—et ma consolation je la trouve dans le braiement melodieux de mon maître! Voilà! Que voulez vous? Il faut bien vivre quand on a eu le malheur d'être né.—

Mercredi prochain[1] me verra sur l'onde (plus ou moins) bleue. Nous arriverons a Port Adelaide vers la mi-janvier.[2] Ecrivez moi en Decembre en adressant Mr J. Conrad. Chief officer. Ship "Torrens". Port Adelaide South Australia. Dites moi tout ce que Vous faites et autant de ce que Vous pensez que Vous jugerez convenable. Envoyez moi le Figaro qui contiendra Votre ouvrage.[3]

Et toujours—et malgré tout croyez moi Votre admirateur bien sincère et Votre neveu très devoué

J. Conrad.

19 October 1892
London

My very dear Aunt,

You are laughing a little at your nephew in comparing him to the late Hamlet (who was, I believe, mad). Nevertheless, I allow myself to say that apart from his madness he was an altogether estimable person. Thus I am not offended by the comparison. I do not know where you found any signs of my contempt for mankind. This proves to me that, to make a generalization, one might well say even those who know us best know us very little. The philosopher who said 'Know thyself' was, I believe, probably befuddled (having supped with Greek ladies – which was a philosophical custom of the day), since I cannot admit him to be stupid. A philosopher cannot be stupid. Correct? One quickly gets to know oneself. The difficulty comes in knowing others. I hasten to assure

[1] The 26th; he did indeed leave the day before.
[2] Conrad arrived on 30 January.
[3] Either 'Joujou', which appeared in the *Figaro illustré* for 29 July 1893, or *Popes et popadias*, which appeared in the *Revue des Deux Mondes*, not *Figaro illustré*. As we noted above, Conrad appeared to confuse the two journals.

you (before my departure, which will occur on the 25th of this month) that I love humanity as much as you do, without a doubt, but in a different way, perhaps. Nevertheless, you know, humanity doesn't care a jot. I feel scorn for no one, for I don't want to have the favour returned. I am not enough of a philosopher to endure (calmly) the contempt of those who differ from me. And note well that kicks from an ass's hoof hurt very badly. One of the constant considerations of my life has been to avoid them. I hereby notify you that I respect the ass (with a capital A). I take this chance to declare my confession of faith. Long ears are eternal, the beginning and end of all things. I find my repose, my peace, in the shade they cast across the desert of life – and I find my consolation in the melodious braying of my master! There! What more can you want? When we have had the misfortune to be born, it's highly necessary to go on living.

Next Wednesday will see me riding the (more or less) blue sea. We shall reach Port Adelaide about mid-January. Write to me in December, addressing the letter to Mr J. Conrad, Chief Officer, Ship *Torrens*, Port Adelaide, South Australia. Tell me all you are doing and as much of what you are thinking as you see fit. Send me the *Figaro* containing your work.

And always, and despite all, believe me your very sincere admirer and your very devoted nephew.

J. Conrad

1893

To Marguerite Poradowska

Text   MS Yale; Rapin 109; G. & S. 49

3 Fevr. 1893.
Port Adelaide.
"Torrens".

Ma chère Tante. Merci de Votre bonne lettre et de la Revue.[1]—Les nouvelles de votre succès, de l'appreciation de Vos talents que Vous avez gagnée a la pointe de Votre plume me remplissent de joie. Moi qui a toujours cru—et predit—Votre succès j'en suis très fier mais point du tout surpris.—

Je me suis en quelque sorte précipité sur les "Popes et Popadias" avec impatience et en esperant beaucoup. Dès les premières lignes mes ésperances ont été realisées—puis bien vite depassées. C'est une merveille d'observation qui donne le plus vif plaisir comme telle sans parler du style que je n'ose pas juger; mais il m'est permis de dire qu'il m'a charmé. Vous savez bien peindre. Depuis le passage du bac sous ce ciel ou la tempête se prepare j'ai regardé avec des yeux avides toute cette serie de tableaux dont se compose votre charmante nouvelle. C'est dans des courts recits (short story) que l'on voit la main du maitre. Je ne peux pas dire que vos figures ont du relief.—Pour moi elles sont absolument vivantes: le Prêtre et sa femme, l'enfant cherchant les remèdes pendant une nuit d'orage, le veterinaire, la gran'mère avec le chat ils sont tous là distinct, se mouvant respirant dans l'atmosphère que Vous leur avait crée au millieu des paysages que Vous avez peints.—Du reste c'est rempli des traits charmants—d'observations fines, des choses prises sur le vif. Et les amis de notre vétérinaire qui jouent aux cartes pour le consoler! Ils sont délicieux!

Votre lettre a le ton heureux. La mienne l'aurait aussi si ce n'était pour ma santé qui n'est pas brilliante. J'ai été fort indisposé pendant une quinzaine avant notre arrivée ici.[2] Souvenirs d'Afrique. Aussi je vais prendre un congé (qui commence demain) d'une huitaine que je vais passer aux environs d'Adelaide ou le pays plus élevé jouit d'un climat beaucoup moins chaud qu'au bord de la mer.—

Je n'ai ni plans ni projets. Il est fort probable qu'a mon retour j'irai voir mon oncle; dans ce cas nous nous verrons ma chère et bonne Tante.[3]

---

[1]   The *Revue des Deux Mondes*, for 15 November and 1 December 1892, contained her *Popes et popadias*, published in book form in 1893 as *Les Filles du pope*.

[2]   On 30 January. On this voyage, Conrad confided in a young man from Cambridge, W. H. Jacques, that he was working on a manuscript, *Almayer's Folly*. Conrad describes the episode in *A Personal Record*, pp. 15ff.

[3]   Conrad did not see her on this trip.

S'il y a empêchement je serai fort chagriné car je me suis fait a cette idée là! Je l'ai caressée pendant bientôt 3 ans; c'est le seul petit bout de couleur dans le gris uniforme de l'existence. Et cette même existence commence a me fatiguer tant soit peu. Ce n'est pas le mal present (car je me sens beaucoup mieux en ce moment) mais c'est l'incertitude de l'avenir—ou plutôt la certitude du "gris uniforme" qui m'attend qui cause ce decouragement. Je sais fort bien que ce que je viens de dire—et que je ressens—manque de dignité: mais au moins le sentiment e[s]t vrai—il n'est pas morbide car j'envisage la situation sans aucune amertume. Sans doute il serait plus digne d'envisager sans souffler mot mais—ma foi—on ne peut pas rester toujours perché sur les echasses de ses principes. Me voilà donc descendu par terre—bien par terre—sous Votre œil ami. Ceci en confidence.—

Je baise Vos mains et Vous embrasse de tout mon cœur.

Votre serviteur et neveu devoué

J. Conrad.

J'ai trouvé une lettre seulement de mon oncle.[1] Il se plaint que tout effort le fatigue mais sa santé est assez tolerable.—

3 February 1893
Torrens
Port Adelaide

My dear Aunt,

Thanks for your kind letter and the *Revue*. The news of your success, of the recognition of your talents that you have won at pen-point, fills me with joy. I, who have always believed in and predicted your success, am very proud, but not at all surprised.

I threw myself (in a manner of speaking) on *Popes et popadias* with eagerness and high hopes. From the first lines, my hopes were realized – then very quickly surpassed. It is a marvel of observation, which gives the liveliest pleasure as such, not to mention the style, which I dare not judge – but let me say it charmed me. You are very good at description. Beginning with the ferry-crossing under a threatening sky, I read the entire series of scenes which make up your charming tale with avidity. It takes a small-scale narrative (short story) to show the master's hand. I cannot say that your characters have relief. For me, they are absolutely alive: the priest and his wife, the child in search of medicine on a stormy

---

[1] Now lost.

night, the veterinarian, the grandmother with the cat – all are distinct, living and breathing in the atmosphere you have created for them, in the midst of the landscapes you have painted. Moreover, it is full of charming touches – of discriminating observations, of things taken from life. And the friends of your veterinarian who play cards to console him! They are delightful!

Your letter has a cheerful tone. Mine would also but for my health, which is not magnificent. I was severely indisposed for a fortnight before our arrival here. Reminders of Africa. So I am going to take a week's leave (beginning tomorrow) which I shall spend in the vicinity of Adelaide, where the higher ground enjoys a much cooler climate than the coast.

I have neither plans nor projects. Very probably, upon my return, I shall go to see my uncle; in that event, we shall meet, my dear and kind aunt. If there is any obstacle, I shall be most annoyed, for I am set on this plan! I have cherished it for almost three years. It is the only speck of colour amid the uniform grey of existence. And this same existence begins to weary me a little. What causes this discouragement is not my current ill-health (for at the moment I feel much better) but the uncertainty of the future – or, rather, the certainty of the 'uniform grey' awaiting me. I know very well that what I have just said – and what I feel – lacks dignity; but at least the feeling is true – it is not morbid, for I regard the situation without any bitterness. Doubtless, it would be more dignified to view it without breathing a word, but, to be sure, one cannot always remain perched on the stilts of one's principles. Thus I have come down to earth, all the way down, under your friendly eye. This in confidence.

I kiss your hands and embrace you warmly.

Your devoted servant and nephew
J. Conrad

I found only one letter from my uncle. He complains that all effort tires him, but his health is tolerable enough.

To Marguerite Poradowska

Text   MS Yale; Rapin 111; G. & S. 51

17 Mai 1893—
Capetown.

Ma très chère Tante.

Merci de votre lettre ou vous me reprochez mon silence. Je présume qu'en ce moment vous avez lu ma première épitre de Pt. Adelaide[1] qui en Vous donnant la date de notre arrivée aux Colonies Vous explique mon long silence.—

Je Vous ai déjà dit ce que je pense des "Popes et Popadias"—je me resume ici:—c'est un petit chef-d'œuvre. J'aimerai bien de lire le roman français que vous desirez de voir couronné si j'ai bien compris Votre lettre.[2] Et il le sera chère Tante et fidèle amie. Tout Vous réussira car Vous méritez le succès.

Et chacun de Vos succès est une joie pour moi et aussi une gratification de ma vanité de prophète de bonnes choses: car j'ai vécu dans la foi de Vos merites que le monde reconnait seulement aujourd'hui. Aussi ai-je eu le bonheur de Vous connaître avant que le monde et Vous fassiez si bonne connaissance et ce sera toujours un doux souvenir dans la vie a venir, longue ou courte, de loin ou de près!

Votre vie s'aggrandit. Votre horizon s'elargit de toutes les possibilités d'une grande agglomeration des natures humaines dont la monotone diversité se chiffre par l'infini; ma vue est circonscrite par le cercle sombre ou le bleu de l'onde et le bleu du ciel se touchent sans se rapprocher. Me mouvant dans ce cercle parfait inscrit par la main du Createur et dont je suis toujours le centre je suis de yeux la ligne ondoyante de la houle—le seul mouvement dont j'ai la certitude et je pense a Vous qui vivez dans l'agitation des esprits ou les tempêtes qui ragent s'elevant au souffle des idées; et de loin je partage Vos joies—et je suis prêt a partager Vos deboires tout en faisant de vœux pour qu'ils Vous soient epargnés.

Pensez a moi toujours comme votre très devoué ami et neveu

J. Conrad.

Arrivé ici hier.[3] Partons demain. a Londres fin Juillet.[4] Fin Août

---

[1] Probably the previous letter, 3 February, or else one that has been lost.
[2] *Le Mariage du fils Grandsire.*
[3] On 16 May, after a 56–day voyage.
[4] On the 26th, according to Jean-Aubry.

espère etre en route pour Ukraine via Paris. Si Vous y êtes alors. Sinon au retour. Ecrivez a c/o. Messrs. Barr Moering. 36 Camomile St. E.C. London.

17 May 1893
Capetown

My very dear Aunt,

Thanks for your letter reproaching me for my silence. I presume that by now you have read my first letter from Port Adelaide, which, in giving you the date of our arrival in the Colonies, explains my long silence.

I have already told you what I think of *Popes et popadias* – I shall sum it up here. It is a little masterpiece. I should indeed like to read the French novel that, if I have properly understood your letter, you want to see win an award. And it will, dear Aunt and faithful friend. You will succeed in everything, for you deserve success.

And each of your successes is a joy to me and also a gratification of my vanity as a prophet of good things. For I have lived with faith in your talents, talents which the world is recognizing only now. Thus I have had the good fortune of knowing you before you and the world became so well acquainted: in all my life to come, long or short, near at hand or far away, that will always be sweet to remember.

Your life is broadening. Your horizons are enlarging with all the possibilities of a great agglomeration of humanity whose monotonous variety is measured by infinity; my view is circumscribed by the sombre circle where the blue of the sea and the blue of the sky touch without merging. Moving within this perfect circle inscribed by the hand of the Creator, a circle of which I am always the centre, I keep my eyes on the undulating line of the swell, the only movement of which I am certain, and I think of you who live in the tumult of the spirit, where the storms are blown to fury by the inspiration of ideas. And from afar I share your joys – and I am ready to share your disappointments, while fervently wishing that you may be spared them.

Think of me always as your very devoted friend and nephew
J. Conrad

Arrived here yesterday. We leave tomorrow. London end of July. End of August, hope to be en route for the Ukraine via Paris. If you are there then. Otherwise, on my return. Write c/o Messrs Barr, Moering, 36 Camomile St, E.C. London.

To Marguerite Poradowska

Text   MS Yale; Rapin 112; G. & S. 52

Kazimierówka. 14 Sep^t 93.—

Ma chère et bonne Tante.

Tout est arrivée comme vous vous êtes doutée quand a mon voyage en
Ukraine. J'ai trouvé Vos bonnes lettres (2) a Londres donc ne sachant ou
vous trouver et sur d'un autre côté que Vous n'êtes plus a Paris je suis
parti par la route Hollandaise, qui est la plus courte, puisque—Vous
comprenez bien—j'étais très préssé de voir le meilleur des oncles.[1]
J'avais l'intention de vous écrire a temps pour que Vous puissiez trouver
ma lettre en arrivant a Paris.

Je vivais donc paisiblement ici heureux de me sentir si près de
l'affection si sure envers moi, si precieuse pour moi—de mon oncle
quand on m'a remis votre 3ème lettre (via Londres) dont le contenu—a
Vous dire vrai—m'a étonné tant soit peu. Il est parfaitement vrai que
Marysieńka se marie;[2] mais au nom de toutes les folies qu'ai je a faire moi
dans cette galère—matrimoniale! Du reste j'ai peine a croire que Vous
parliez serieusement de la chose dans Votre lettre car il a du Vous
sembler etrange de voir un individu se precipiter comme ça tout d'un
coup du fond de l'Australie—sans dire gare a personne—au fond de
l'Ukraine pour se jeter dans les bras de—c'est très drôle toute cette
affaire-là.

La petite M se marie avec Mr Rakowski fils d'un voisin de mon oncle.
Il a été ici quelques jours avant mon arrivée pour annoncer la chose
officielement a mon oncle. M. a fait un bon mariage (ou fera) vu toutes
les circonstances—car elle était gouvernante chez ces braves gens qui on
dit en sont fort épris—toute la famille.

Je vois avec regret que vous êtes tant soit peu "unsettled". Ce n'est
sans doute que le moment de réaction après le travail continu de l'hiver.
Tout passe. J'espère que Votre prochaine lettre parlera de nouvelles
ésperances, de nouvelle ardeur, et de nouveaux succés. Quand a moi j'ai
été fort souffrant et au lit pendant 5 jours. Il fait bon d'être malade ici. (si
on doit etre malade) Mon oncle m'a soigné comme un petit enfant. Il
baise vos mains et parle toujours de Vous avec la plus grande estime et
amitié.—

Je reviens a Londres vers la fin septembre sans m'arreter nulle part.

---

[1] On the journey from the Netherlands to the Ukraine, Conrad lost the still incomplete
manuscript of *Almayer's Folly*; it was found and returned by a railway porter. See *A
Personal Record*, p. 19.

[2] Marie Ołdakowska, Mme Poradowska's niece by marriage. Cf. Conrad's remarks in the
letter of 26 September 1890.

Je passerais par Amst[erdam] probablement.—Je suis pressé de rentrer et de me trouver une occupation car j'ai quitté le "Torrens" pour de bon.[1]—

Aussitôt mon retour je Vous ecrirai. En attendant je Vous embrasse bien fort et suis toujours Votre affectionné neveu et ami très fidèle

J. Conrad.

Mes devoirs très respectueux a Mme Votre Mère.

14 September 1893
Kazimierówka

My dear and good Aunt,

Everything has occurred as you suspected regarding my trip to the Ukraine. I found your kind letters (2) in London; so, not knowing where to find you, and yet sure on the other hand you were no longer in Paris, I left by the Dutch route, which is the shortest, since – as you can well understand – I was very anxious to see the best of uncles. I intended to write in time for you to find my letter on arriving in Paris.

I was living here peacefully, happy therefore to feel myself so close to my uncle, whose affection for me is so sure and so precious, when I was handed your third letter (via London) whose contents, frankly, rather surprised me. It is perfectly true that Marysieńka is getting married; but in the name of all the follies, what have I to do with this matrimonial affair! However, I can hardly believe that you could speak seriously of the matter in your letter, for it must have seemed strange to you to see someone suddenly rush from the depths of Australia, without warning anyone, to the depths of the Ukraine in order to throw himself into the arms of – the whole idea is ludicrous.

Little M. is marrying Mr Rakowski, son of a neighbour of my uncle. Several days before my arrival, he was here to announce the matter officially to my uncle. M. has made a good marriage (or will make one), everything considered – for she was a governess with these worthy people, who are said – the entire family – to be much taken with her.

I am sorry to see that you are rather 'unsettled'. It is doubtless only a momentary reaction after your continuous work during the winter. Everything passes. I hope your next letter will speak of new hopes, new

---

[1] According to the certificate of discharge, on 26 July 1893. Conrad, apparently, had hoped to gain the command of the *Torrens* when Captain Cope intended to move to a steamship, but nothing came of this desire.

energy, new success. As for me, I have been very unwell and in bed for five days. This is a good place to be ill (if one must be ill). My uncle has cared for me as if I were a little child. He kisses your hands and always speaks of you with the greatest respect and friendship.

I shall return to London about the end of September without stopping anywhere. I'll probably travel via Amsterdam. I am in a hurry to return and find work, having left the *Torrens* for good.

As soon as I return, I shall write to you. Meanwhile I embrace you heartily and am always your affectionate nephew and very faithful friend

J. Conrad

My very respectful regards to your mother.

To Marguerite Poradowska

Text   MS Yale; Rapin 113; G. & S. 54

5 Nov 93.
17 Gillingham Street
[London]

Ma Chère Tante.

J'espère que Vous voudrez bien me pardonner mon long silence. Je n'ai pas d'excuse à Vous offrir car je suis en ce moment sans occupation et depuis mon retour de Pologne j'ai passé les journées dans une désésperante oisivité.[1] Vous qui decrivez les choses et les hommes, et par consequent avez levé un coin du voile Vous savez bien qu'il y a des moments ou la pensée s'endort, les mois s'enfuient,[2] ou l'Espoir lui même semble mort. Je passe par un de ces moments là. Il me semble que je n'ai rien vu, que je ne vois rien, que je ne verrai jamais rien. Je jurerais qu'il n'y a rien que le vide en dehors des murs de la chambre ou j'ecris ces lignes. Certainement ceci ressemble au commencement d'une imbécilité incurable. Qu'en pensez Vous? Dans tous les cas Vous voyez bien que je ne suis meme pas digne de votre colère.—

Très humblement toujours

Votre très devoué

J. Conrad.

---

[1] See *A Personal Record*, pp. 7ff., for Conrad's description of this period of 'disheartening indolence'.

[2] Could be *mots s'enfuient*, 'words flee'.

5 November 1893
17 Gillingham Street [London]

My dear Aunt,

I hope you will kindly forgive my long silence. I have no excuse to offer you, for I am presently out of work, and since my return from Poland I have spent my days in disheartening indolence. You who describe things and men, and consequently have raised a corner of the veil, know very well there are moments when the mind slumbers, the months slip away, when hope itself seems dead. I am experiencing one of these periods. It seems to me I have seen nothing, see nothing, and shall always see nothing. I could swear there is only the void outside the walls of the room where I am writing these lines. Certainly, this resembles the beginning of incurable imbecility. What do you think of that? In any event you will clearly see that I am not even worthy of your anger.

Very humbly, ever your very devoted
J. Conrad

To Marguerite Poradowska

Text MS Yale; Rapin 114; G. & S. 54

26. Nov. 1893
[London]

Tante cherie.

Je quitte Londres demain a bord du vapeur anglais "Adowa" qui est loué par la Comp^nie Franco-Canadienne. pour service entre ports Français et Canadiens.[1] J'ai reçu ma nomination au poste du "second officer" ce matin tout a fait a l'improviste[2] de sorte que j'ai a peine le temps de ramasser mes affaires en toute hate et me precipiter a bord car mon service commence ce soir a 11^h

Il était temps. Je commencais a tomber dans une melancolie très noire. Effet d'oisivété.—Je suis charmé avec "Joujou".[3] C'est tout a fait et delicieusement "shocking". Ou diable avez Vous trouvé cela!?

---

[1] Conrad signed on formally on 29 November. He describes the episode in *A Personal Record*, pp. 6ff.

[2] Conrad's need for a position is underscored by his having taken a second officer's berth when he held a master's certificate.

[3] Mme Poradowska's tale which appeared in the *Figaro* 'Supplément littéraire' for 29 July 1893.

Excusez langage marin. Je Vous embrasse bien fort. Je serai dans un port
français après demain d'ou avant depart Vous enverrais un mot.[1]

Je suis comme toujours et pour toujours Votre très devoué neveu
J. Conrad.—

c/o Barr Moering & C°.
72. 73. Fore Street
E.C.

26 November 1893
[London]

Much-loved Aunt,

I leave London tomorrow on board the English steamer *Adowa*, which
the Franco-Canadian Company has chartered for service between
French and Canadian ports. I received my appointment to the second
officer's berth this morning, quite unexpectedly, so that I've hardly had
time to collect my gear hastily and dash on board, as my service begins
this evening at 11.

It was about time. I was starting to fall into a very black melancholy.
Result of idleness. I am charmed with 'Joujou'. It is altogether and
delightfully shocking. Where the devil did you find it? Pardon the
nautical language. I embrace you most warmly. I shall be in a French
port the day after tomorrow and shall send you a line from there before
sailing.

I am as always and for always your devoted nephew
J. Conrad

c/o Barr, Moering & Co.
72/73 Fore Street
E.C.

---

[1] The *Adowa* arrived in Rouen on 4 December.

To Marguerite Poradowska

Text MS Yale; Rapin 115; G. & S. 55

> 6. Dec. 93.
> S.S. "Adowa".
> à Rouen.

Chère Tante.

Juste une ligne pour Vous dire que me voilà en France. Nous croyons partir Samedi[1] pour La Rochelle, et ensuite à Halifax (Amerique du Nord).[2]

Ecrivez moi un petit mot a La Rochelle.

Il faut adresser:

M[r]. Conrad. 2[d] Off. S.S. "Adowa"

   La Rochelle.

      La Palisse.

J'aimerai bien a avoir de Vos nouvelles avant de quitter l'Europe.

Ma santé est assez bonne. Et la Votre?!

> 6 December 1893
> S.S. *Adowa*, at Rouen

Dear Aunt,

Only a line to tell you I am here in France. We expect to sail on Saturday for La Rochelle and then to Halifax (North America).

Drop me a line at La Rochelle.

Write to:

Mr Conrad, 2d Off. S.S. *Adowa*,

   La Rochelle,

      La Palisse.

I should very much like to have news of you before leaving Europe. My health is reasonably good. And yours?

---

[1] 9 December.

[2] The *Adowa* was to transport French emigrants to Canada, but the project fell through.

To Marguerite Poradowska

Text   MS Yale; Rapin 115; G. & S. 55

18 Dec. 1893
"Adowa" a Rouen.

Ma chère Tante.

Vous serez etonnée de recevoir une lettre d'ici, mais il parait que
Cie Franco Canadienne n'a pas tenu ses engagements envers notre
Armateur et par conséquent notre départ a été remis. En ce moment il y a
un procès qui va se juger a Paris vendredi prochain,[1] question des
dommages-interêts; mais dans tous les cas l'affaire est manquée et nous
n'irons plus au Canada—Aussitot le procès fini nous retournerons en
Angleterre, pour y charger pour l'Inde, le Golfe persique.—que sais-je
moi?—Rien n'est certain excepté notre ignorance de nos mouvements
futurs.—

Il ne semble pas naturel d'être en France sans Vous voir! J'ai eu des
envies de m'echapper pour courir a Paris—même l'envie de quitter le
navire tout a fait mais j'ai du abandonner tout ces rêves.—Le fait est que
[je] ne peux pas me permettre ce petit luxe d'affection. Du reste on ne me
laisserait pas partir. Enfin! Que voulez Vous? Il n'y a pas des nécéssités
agréables. Elles sont toujours dures—. Vous savez la phrase est
stereotypée. Pourquoi? Très drôle tout de même. Du reste j'ai eu
l'honneur de remarquer dans plusiers de mes lettres que la vie est faite a
l'envers. J'en ai fait un article de foi, et je me resigne.—

Ecrivez moi un petit mot ici pour me consoler. Voulez Vous me rendre
un service? Oui! Na[tu]rellement! Eh bien Vous qui connaissez tant de
monde peut-être connaissez Vous quelqu'un de l'administration du
Canal de Suez. Je voudrai bien savoir comment on s'y prend pour
obtenir le poste de pilote du Canal.—Je ne crois pas que c'est bien
difficile mais encore il faut savoir comment.—Et si Vous pouvez
apprendre cela Vous pourrez aussi savoir combien cela se paye. J'ai dans
l'idée que ce n'est point l'Eldorado.—

Pardon pour mon sans gêne et merci mille fois a l'avance mais
n'oubliez pas que la chose n'a pas d'importance et ne Vous donnez pas
trop de peine. Toujours Votre très devoué

Conrad

---

[1] 22 December.

18 December 1893
Adowa at Rouen

My dear Aunt,

You will be surprised to receive a letter from here, but it appears the Franco-Canadian Company has not kept to its agreement with our shipowner, and consequently our sailing has been postponed. Now there is a hearing in Paris next Friday to settle the damages; but, in any event, the venture is a failure, and we shall not be going to Canada. When the lawsuit is over, we shall return to England, to load there for India, the Persian Gulf – what do I know about it? Nothing is certain except our ignorance of our future movements.

It seems unnatural to be in France without seeing you! I have had the urge to escape, to run off to Paris – even the urge to resign from the ship altogether – but I have had to abandon all those dreams. The fact is I cannot permit myself this little luxury of affection. Besides, they wouldn't let me go. So! What can one do? There are no agreeable necessities. They are always harsh. You know the phrase is stereotyped. Why? Very funny all the same. Nevertheless I have had the honour to remark in several of my letters that life is upside down. I have made this an article of faith, and I am resigned to it.

Write me a short note to console me. Do you want to do me a favour? Yes! Naturally! Well, you who know so many people perhaps know someone in the administration of the Suez Canal. I should very much like to know how to go about obtaining a post as a Canal pilot. I don't believe it is very difficult, but one must know how. And if you can find that out, you will also be able to discover how much it pays. I have an idea it's hardly Eldorado.

Forgive my bluntness and many thanks in advance, but remember the matter is of no importance and don't give yourself too much trouble. Always your very devoted

Conrad

To Marguerite Poradowska
Text MS Yale; Rapin 116; G. & S. 56

20 Dec. 1893.
S.S. Adowa
à Rouen.

Chère Tante.

Je viens de recevoir Votre lettre. Merci mille et mille fois pour le livre que Vous promettez,[1] pour Votre prompte reponse, pour les bonnes paroles d'amitié que Vous m'ecrivez.—Pourquoi êtes-Vous en colère contre la pauvre compagnie qui n'en peut mais? Moi je leur pardonne Il fait un temps épouvantable dans l'Atlantique est il fait mieux au port qu'en dehors. C'est vrai que la vie ici n'est guère amusante mais comme je suis payé pour m'embêter!... Tout de même ça ne mène a rien et je commence a me sentir vieux. Il faudrait se caser quelque part si on a l'idée de vivre. A vrai dire je n'en vois pas la nécéssité—mais d'un autre côté je ne suis point préparé a prendre de l'arsenic ou me jeter a la mer. Donc il faut que je me case.

Je fais—ou on fait pour moi—des demarches pour m'obtenir un emploi a la pêche de perles sur la côte d'Australie.[2] L'idée me sourit mais la chose est loin d'être facile de sorte que meditant sur la vanité des choses ici-bas—et surtout des promesses—j'ai pensé au Suez.—Le travail est leger. On n'est pas trop loin et je suppose qu'on y gagne sa vie. J'ai pas de pretensions a autre chose.—

J'attends le livre avec impatience. Est-ce le roman Lillois? Ou l'histoire du fou?[3]

Encore une fois merci! Embrasse bien fort

Votre très devoué neveu

J. Conrad

20 December 1893
S.S. *Adowa* at Rouen

Dear Aunt,

I have just received your letter. Ever so many thanks for the book you promise me, for your prompt response, for the kind words of friendship you send me. Why are you angry at the poor Company, which can't do anything else? Personally, I forgive them. There is a terrible storm in the Atlantic, and it is better in port than outside. It's true that life here is scarcely amusing, but I am paid for my boredom!... All the same, this leads to nothing and I am beginning to feel old. One ought to settle down if one wants to live. To be frank, I do not see the necessity of that – but, on the other hand, I am not at all ready to take arsenic or to throw myself into the sea. So I must get settled.

[1] Mme Poradowska's *Le Mariage du fils Grandsire*, which Conrad received on 6 January 1894.

[2] Like the Suez plan in the 18 December letter, this project came to nothing.

[3] It was the Lille novel. The other was a 'Simple récit', adapted by Mme Poradowska from the Polish of Sophie Kowerska, and published in the *Revue des Deux Mondes* for 1 August 1889.

I am taking steps – or having them taken for me – to get a position in the pearl fisheries off the Australian coast. I rather fancy the idea, but the thing itself is far from easy, so that, thinking of the vanity of things here below, and especially of promises, I thought of Suez. The work is light. One is not too far away, and I suppose one can earn one's living there. I have no pretensions to more.

I am awaiting the book impatiently. Is it the novel about Lille? Or the story of the madman?

Thanks once again! A warm embrace.

Your very devoted nephew

J. Conrad

To Marguerite Poradowska

Text MS Yale; Rapin 117; G. & S. 57

25 Dec^{er} 1893.

"Adowa" à Rouen

Ma chère Tante.

Vous êtes vraiment trop bonne pour Vous donner tant de peine pour Votre vaurien de neveu. Je Vous remercie un million de fois. Je Vous envoi ici le brouillon de mon Etat de service (N° 1.). Voulez Vous bien corriger les fautes. Et quand a la lettre au president je ne sais trop comment l'ecrire. Voici mon idée; qu'en pensez Vous? (N° 2).[1]

Je Vous envoi en même temps mes souhaits de la nouvelle année. Entre nous c'est une ceremonie puisque Vous devez savoir que pas une journée de ma vie (et de la votre) ne se passe sans que je ne Vous souhaite tous les bonheurs possibles et imaginables. Et il y en a si peu! Si peu! Mais ça ce n'est pas de ma faute.—

Ainsi Justine a juré!!!—Et moi qui pensais a . . . Enfin! j'ai de la guigne! C'est a ne pas s'y tromper!! La vie est un desert depuis que j'ai lu Votre lettre. Il n'y a que l'idée du Canal qui m'empêche de me suicider. Justine ou le Canal; le Canal ou Justine.[2] Je ne sors pas de là.—

C'est une fameuse tuile qui Vous tombe sur la tête que les Jonakowski[3]. . . dans cette galère? Dites! ma Tante: le papa ferait un bon cocher de fiacre pusiqu'ils sont des si grand seigneurs. Encore faut-il de

---

[1] Neither document has turned up; both were part of Conrad's plan to obtain a post as pilot on the Suez Canal.

[2] She remains unidentified.

[3] Conrad also spells the name Yonakowski. The family is mentioned by him in a letter of 20 May 1895, and by Mme Poradowska in a fragment of a letter dated 9 June 1890, but never sent. No more of the family is known, however, beyond their objectionable claim to kinship.

l'honnetété pour se faire une carrière comme cocher de Fiacre et le père est—vous savez un peu... douteux d'après ce que j'ai entendu dire.—

J'ai l'honneur de Vous faire savoir que la tribu des sauvages qui vient d'envahir Paris m'est très peu "cousine". Je ne veux pas que ce gens là m'appellent "charmant garçon." C'est une impertinence.—

Je Vous embrasse bien fort avec toute la gratitude, toute l'affection que Vous meritez et je suis toujours Votre très devoué neveu et serviteur

J. Conrad.

25 December 1893
Adowa at Rouen

My dear Aunt,

You are really too kind for giving yourself so much trouble on behalf of your good-for-nothing nephew. I thank you a million times. I am sending you here the rough copy of my service record (No. 1). Will you please correct the mistakes? And as for the letter to the president, I do not really know how to write it. Here is my idea. What do you think of it? (No. 2).

At the same time I send you my best wishes for the new year. Between ourselves, it is only a formality, since you must know that not a single day of my life (and of yours) passes without my wishing you all possible and imaginable happiness. And there is so little of it! So little! But that is not my fault.

So Justine has promised!! ... And I, who was thinking of – well! I have some rotten luck! No mistake about that!! Life has been a desert since I read your letter. Only the thought of the Canal saves me from suicide. Justine or the Canal; the Canal or Justine. I do not go beyond that.

What exceptionally bad luck for you that the Jonakowskis are here – what on earth for? Tell me what *you* think: Papa would make a good public coachman, since coachmen are so lordly. Still, to make a career of driving hackney-carriages, one must be honest, and the father is a shade ... dubious, so I've heard.

I have the honour to inform you that the tribe of savages which has just invaded Paris is hardly 'cousinly' to me. I do not like these people calling me 'charming boy'. It is an impertinence.

I embrace you warmly with all the gratitude, all the affection you deserve, and I am always your very devoted nephew and servant

J. Conrad

1894

To Marguerite Poradowska

Text MS Yale; Rapin 121; G. & S. 58

1er Janvier 1894.
à Rouen.

Chère Tante.

Voilà mes souhaits de Nouvelle Année. J'ai attendu le jour exprès pour qu'il n'y ai pas d'erreur. Je pense a Vous en commencant cette année! Je Vous ecris cela dans un sale petit Café. Nous sommes (tous a bord) dans une dèche tellement complète qu'après avoir vainement essayé d'emprunter dix sous a touts mes camarades j'en ai pris mon parti et je viens d'assomer un monsieur (qui du reste m'est completement etranger) pour voler son porte-monnaie. Il est là, etendu, au coin de la rue pendent que je jouis des fruits de mon industrie. Il laisse sans doute une veuve et plusieurs petits enfants; triste; mais que voulez Vous? Il faut bien que j'affranchisse cette lettre! et puis il avait l'air bête!

Je veux mon livre!!!!!!!!!!! Non! Votre livre. Je l'attends. Il me le faut; et plus vite que ca, encore!—Je ne comprends pas votre hesitation. C'est pour m'agacer probablement. Vous avez réussi————. (ici une crise de nerfs)————

Ah je suis mieux. Un petit verre de cognac m'a remis. Je ne peux pas aller voir l'Evêque.[1] Je n'ai pas de vetements convenables et puis a quoi bon? Aimez Vous cet evêque? D'après ce que Vous en avez dit j'en doute. Eh bien ni moi non plus.

Je Vous embrasse de tout mon cœur et suis toujours. Votre très devoué neveu et serviteur

J. Conrad.

1 January 1894
Rouen

Dear Aunt,

Here are my good wishes for the new year. I have waited for the right day so as to make no mistake. As this year begins, I think of you! I am writing to you in a dirty little café. Everyone on board is so utterly hard up that, having tried in vain to borrow ten sous from all my shipmates, I accepted the inevitable and have just felled a gentleman (what's more, a total stranger) in order to steal his wallet. He lies there sprawling at the corner of the street, while I enjoy the fruits of my labour. No doubt he leaves a widow and several little children. Sad – but what can you expect? I needed a stamp for this letter! And besides, he looked like a fool!

---

[1] The elusive Bishop mentioned in the letter for 15 May 1890.

I want my book!!!!!!!!!!!! No! Your book. I am waiting for it. I must have it, at once, if not sooner! I do not understand your hesitation. It is probably to torment me. You have succeeded————. (here a nervous fit)————

   Ah, I am better. A little glass of cognac has restored me. I cannot go to see the Bishop. I do not have the correct clothes, and then what would be the good? Do you like this Bishop? According to what you've told me, I doubt it. Well, neither do I.

   I embrace you most warmly and am always your very devoted nephew and servant

J. Conrad

To Marguerite Poradowska

Text   MS Yale; Rapin 122; G. & S. 59

Dimanche.[1] 2[h]ap:midi. [7 January 1894]
[Rouen]

Ma chère Tante

   Voici encore un des mes epanchements inspirés par des liqueurs spiritueuses debitées au detail. Du reste on s'en aperçoit par le papier,[2] et puis—sans doute—il se degage un délicat parfum d'ivrogne de cette élégante missive. N'est-ce pas?—

   Hier soir je me suis echappé du navire pour le pélérinage de la gare. J'ai mon colis 4 mille et quelque chose. Voyez un peu une œuvre d'art appelée: colis No: 4000 etc etc!! J'ai dit a l'individu au guichet: "Monsieur votre lettre d'avis est une infamie"—"Plait-il?"—"Une infamie; vous êtes des scélérats des bourgeois. Comprenez-Vous?— Non—repondit-il—mais Vous êtes un anarchiste, Vous! Ou est Votre bombe? La-dessus comme il criait "au secours!" je m'enfuis et je me precipite dans un fiacre. "Cocher"—dis-je—"je suis pressé, detelez votre cheval; la voiture roulera plus vite."—"Fameuse idée. s'ecriat-il.—Et voilà comment j'ai echappé aux agents de police altérés de mon sang.[3]—

---

[1]   This letter falls between the one for 1 January when Conrad had not yet received Mme Poradowska's *Le Mariage du fils Grandsire*, and the one for 9 January, when Conrad announced he was leaving Rouen. The only Sunday was 7 January.

[2]   Cheap, squared paper.

[3]   During the preceding two years, there had been several anarchist bombings. In the most recent of these, 9 December 1893, a fragmentation bomb was thrown from a balcony of the French Chamber of Deputies; Vaillant, the man responsible, went to his execution calling out 'Vive l'anarchie!' The Greenwich explosion, whose echoes are heard in *The Secret Agent*, occurred soon after the date of Conrad's letter, on 15 February.

Il etait tard. Je n'ai lu que le premier chapitre.[1]—Je ne puis—même si j'ose—juger. Mais des les premières pages je suis en presence du charme de Votre individualité. C'est bien Vous!

Je n'ai pas le temps de lire le livre d'une traite mais j'aurais le plaisir de le savourer.—

—Reçu Votre carte. Merci mille fois. Vous ecrivez l'anglais très gentillement.—Si Vous ètes une petite fille bien sage je Vous laisserais lire mon histoire d'Almayer quand je l'aurai fini.[2]—

Je Vous embrasse bien fort

Votre devoué neveu

J. Conrad.

Sunday. 2 p.m. [7 January 1894]
[Rouen]

My dear Aunt,

Here is another one of my outpourings inspired by spirituous liquors sold at retail. One can tell that by the paper, however, since a delicate perfume of drunkenness no doubt wafts from this elegant missive. Isn't that so?

Yesterday evening, I escaped from the ship for the pilgrimage to the station. I have my parcel No. 4000 and something. Just imagine a work of art called Parcel No. 4000, etc. etc.!! I said to the person at the window: 'Sir, your letter of notification is an outrage.' 'I beg your pardon?' 'An outrage. You are bourgeois scoundrels. Do you understand?' 'No,' he replied, 'but you are an anarchist, that's what you are! Where is your bomb?' Thereupon, while he was shouting, 'Help!' I fled, throwing myself into a cab. 'Driver,' I said, 'I am in a hurry, unharness your horses; the cab will go faster.' 'Fine idea,' he cried. And that is how I escaped the police officers who were thirsting for my blood.

It was late. I have read only the first chapter. I cannot judge, even if I dared. But from the first pages, I am in the presence of your charming individuality. It is really you!

I do not have time to read the book at one sitting, but I shall have the pleasure of savouring it.

Received your card. Ever so many thanks. You write English very

---

[1] Of *Le Mariage du fils Grandsire.*

[2] Conrad completed *Almayer's Folly* on 24 April 1894; while in Rouen he worked on Chapter x. See *A Personal Record*, p. 3.

gracefully. If you are a well-behaved little girl, I shall let you read my story of Almayer when I have finished it.

I embrace you most warmly. Your devoted nephew

J. Conrad

To Marguerite Poradowska

Text   MS Yale; Rapin 123; G. & S. 60

9th Jan 1894
[Rouen]

Chère Tante. Nous quittons Rouen demain pour Londres. Ecrivez moi là bas c/o Barr Moring 72 Fore Street. Embrassade. Très occupé. Tout a Vous.

J. Conrad.

9 January 1894
[Rouen]

Dear Aunt,

We are leaving Rouen tomorrow for London. Write to me there c/o Barr Moering, 72 Fore Street. A hug. Very busy. Yours

J. Conrad

To Marguerite Poradowska

Text   MS Yale; Rapin 123; G. & S. 61

20 Jan.[189]4
[letterhead: Barr, Moering]

Ma chère Tante.

En arrivant a Londre[1] j'ai trouvé votre lettre dont je Vous remercie mille et mille fois.—Vous avez raison. Les Polonais sont paresseux. Je Vous dirais que je ne comprends pas trop bien comment je pourrais Vous aider.[2] Je n'ai pas de nouvelles de Pologne.—J'echange une lettre ou deux par mois avec mon oncle. Nouvelles de famille etc etc.—

Je lis le fils Grandsire avec delices.—C'est charmant et c'est characteristique, c'est vivant. Je finirai le livre demain et je Vous en

---

[1] On the *Adowa*, 12 January.
[2] According to Rapin and Gee and Sturm, by supplying details for her forthcoming novel, *Marylka*.

parlerai dans ma prochaine.— Je suis fort ennuyé d'avoir a quitter l'"Adowa".[1] C'etait bien commode d'avoir une occupation près d'Europe. J'ai bien peur que je serai forcé de partir pour un long voyage dans très peu de temps.—

Ne Vous abrutissez pas! Vous en parlez avec une legereté qui me scandalise. C'est serieux savez Vous. Rien de plus facile que de se rouiller.—Dites? Vous êtes donc un Genie universel? D'ou vient cette connaissance de bric-a brac, des vieux livres et vieux tableaux?[2]

A bientot (sur papier)

Votre très devoué

J. Conrad.

20 January 1894
[letterhead: Barr, Moering]

My dear Aunt,

On arriving in London, I found your letter, for which I thank you a thousand-fold. You are right. Poles are lazy. I must say I do not quite understand how I could help you. I have no news from Poland. I exchange a letter or two a month with my uncle. Family news, etc. etc.

I am reading *Le fils Grandsire* with delight. It is charming and characteristic; it is alive. I shall finish the book tomorrow and speak of it in my next letter. I am very annoyed to have to leave the *Adowa*. It was very convenient to have a position close to Europe. I am much afraid I shall very soon be forced to go on a long voyage.

Don't become stultified! You speak of this with a levity which shocks me. It is serious, you know. Nothing is easier than to rust. Tell me, have you become a universal genius? Where did you come by this knowledge of bric-à-brac, of old books and old pictures?

Until our next encounter (on paper)

Your very devoted

J. Conrad

---

[1] The discharge is dated 17 January.
[2] Michel, of *Le Mariage du fils Grandsire*, woos the daughter of a dealer in old curiosities.

To Marguerite Poradowska

Text MS Yale; Rapin 124; G. & S. 61

2 Fev^r 1894
17. Gillingham Street
London. S.W.

Chère Tante.

J'ai fini le livre il y a quelque temps, puis j'ai relu plusieurs passages en attendant que je le relise en entier.[1]—

Mon appreciation de Votre livre—de tout livre—est purement émotionale.—De l'ouvrage, du travail, de la ciselure—si je puis m'exprimer ainsi—je ne peux guère juger; et comme l'émotion est une affaire personelle mon jugement ne peut qu'être incomplet et bien souvent incorrect. Vous voyez donc que je perd la joie de "celui qui sait" et voit l'œuvre d'art dans son entier.—Mais il m'est permis—heureusement—de m'oublier dans la contemplation des images charmantes, d'écouter la musique des mots écrits; de vivre la joie, de respirer dans l'air, de partager les joies et les douleurs, les espérances, et les regrets qui remplissent ce coin de l'Univers que Votre plume de Magicienne a crée. Et il est bien vivant, Votre petit coin du monde, avec le silencieux tumulte des passions, et le cri de douleur final. Le vrai cri celui là—qui n'est qu'un murmure de l'âme fatiguée dans la lutte vers la Terre Promise.—

La note de l'ouvrage c'est son triste charme—mais les details ont fait ma joie—Quelle serie d'images charmantes! Le retour des Cloches; le voyage au cimetière la jeune fille se drapant dans le voile leger et fragile comme son rêve de bonheur, la scène avec Rose. Mais pourquoi enumerer? Il faudrait reciter le livre entier.—

Et les coup de crayon de maître! Il y en a qui ont fait tout simplement mon bonheur. La tante Colombe qui mange son thon a la lueur d'une bougie. Positivement je l'aime la tante C. Et Mme Grandsire et Catherine, et le vieux brocanteur diplomatique. Je les aime tous. En lisant certains passages je battais des mains comme on applaudit au spectacle. Et combien de figures sympathiques avez Vous reussi a produire! Au fait il n'y en a pas une qui ne soit sympathique a sa manière, car elles sont toutes si vivantes et tout a fait humaines!—

Si j'ai mal compris et mal apprecié il ne faut pas trop m'en vouloir. Il

---

[1] *Le Mariage du fils Grandsire*, just published by Hachette. The setting is Lille and its environs in the years leading up to the Franco-Prussian war. Michel Grandsire marries against the wishes of his family, his wife deserts him, he joins the army; gravely wounded, he is nursed by his childhood sweetheart.

vaut mieux entendre mal qu'être sourd; il vaut mieux entrevoir que ne rien voir du tout. Le Createur connait ses creatures. Nous autres nous levons un coin de voile et regardons les âmes de Votre imagination a travers le brouillard de nos defauts, de nos deboires et de nos regrets. Il est permis de se tromper quand il y en a tant qui ferment les yeux et se bouchent les oreilles! Votre devoué J. Conrad

> 2 February 1894
> 17 Gillingham Street
> London S.W.

Dear Aunt,

I finished the book a while ago; then I went over several passages while awaiting the chance to reread it entirely.

My appreciation of your book, of any book, is purely emotional. Of the craft, the workmanship, the chiselling, if I may so put it, I can scarcely judge. And as emotion is a personal affair, my judgement can only be incomplete and often incorrect. So you see I miss the joy of 'one who knows' and sees the work of art in its entirety. But I am at liberty – happily – to lose myself in the contemplation of entrancing images, to listen to the music of written words, to live the joy, breathe the air, partake of the joys and sorrows, the hopes, and the regrets which fill this corner of the Universe created by your magical pen. And your little corner of the world is very lively, with its silent turmoil of passions, and its final cry of woe. That one is the true cry – which is only a murmur of the soul exhausted in its struggle toward the Promised Land.

The tone of the work is one of sad charm – but the details gave me joy. Such a series of charming images! The return of the bells; the journey to the cemetery; the young girl wrapping herself in a veil as light and fragile as her dream of happiness; the scene with Rose. But why list them all? One would have to reproduce the entire book. And the master-strokes! There are some which altogether delighted me. Aunt Colombe eating her tuna by candlelight. I positively love Aunt C. And Mme Grandsire and Catherine, and the diplomatic old second-hand dealer. I love them all. While reading certain passages, I clapped my hands as one applauds at the theatre. And how many sympathetic characters you have succeeded in producing! In fact, there is not one there who is not attractive in some particular way, for they are all so alive and altogether human!

If I have misjudged or misunderstood, do not be too cross with me. It is better to hear badly than to be deaf; it is better to see imperfectly than to see nothing at all. The Creator knows his creatures. We others raise a corner of the veil and look at the denizens of your imagination through the fog of our faults, or disappointments, and our regrets. One may be permitted to make a mistake when there are so many who close their eyes and stop their ears. Your devoted

J. Conrad

To Marguerite Poradowska
Text   MS Yale; Rapin 126; G. & S. 63

18 Fevrier 94.
17 Gillingham St.

Ma chère Tante.

Je viens de recevoir une depêche de Pologne. Mon oncle est mort le 11 de ce mois[1] et il me semble que tout est mort en moi. Il semble emporter mon ame avec lui. J'ai été malade depuis quelques jours et je commençais a me retablir un peu quand j'ai reçu cette nouvelle.[2]

Je Vous embrasse de tout mon cœur
J. Conrad.

18 February 1894
17 Gillingham Street

My dear Aunt,

I have just received a telegram from Poland. My uncle died on the 11th of this month, and it seems as if everything has died in me. He seems to have carried my soul away with him. I have been ill for several days, and I was beginning to recover a little when I received this news.

I embrace you very warmly
J. Conrad

---

[1] Tadeusz Bobrowski died on the 10th (29 January by the Russian calendar). For the depth and breadth of his relationship to Conrad, see Najder's *Conrad's Polish Background: Letters to and from Polish Friends.*

[2] According to Jean-Aubry (1, p. 157), Conrad received a telegram on the very day of his uncle's death.

To Marguerite Poradowska
Text   MS Yale; Rapin 126; G. & S. 63

2 Mars 1894..
17 Gillingham St.

Ma chère Tante.

Je suis très faché de Vous savoir indisposée et la nevralgie surtout! J'en sais quelque chose de sorte que je puis Vous plaindre en connaissance de cause.[1]—

Je suis un peu comme un animal sauvage; je cherche a me cacher quand je souffre soit de corps soit d'esprit et en ce moment je souffre de deux.

Le pire est que dans l'inactivité a laquelle je suis condamné en ce moment je ne puis guère oublier ma souffrance. L'oubli est une belle chose mais difficile a trouver.

Si je puis je viendrai a Bruxelles pour une petite visite[2] mais je ne sais pas si je le pourrai. Ce n'est pas l'envie qui me manque. Je cherche a me trouver une occupation et je n'ose pas quitter Londres en ce moment de peur de manquer une chance.—

Croyez Vous bon que l'on repondra a ma demande d'emploi a Suez?[3] Même pour refuser. ou faut-il prendre le silence comme un refus? Je voudrai bien savoir ce que Vous en pensez.—

Merci de vos bonnes paroles. Vous ne pouvez savoir combien Votre affection m'est précieuse! Je Vous embrasse bien fort

Votre devoué ami et neveu

J. Conrad.—

2 March 1894
17 Gillingham Street

My dear Aunt,

I am very troubled to learn you are indisposed, and with neuralgia of all things! I know something of that, so I can pity you from experience.

I am a little like a wild animal; I try to hide myself when I suffer either in body or in mind, and at present I am suffering in both.

---

[1] See Conrad's letter for 27 February 1891, in which he complains of neuralgia and rheumatism.

[2] Conrad probably went to Brussels, carrying with him the first ten chapters of *Almayer's Folly*, whose completion he announces to Mme Poradowska on 24 April.

[3] Conrad began to speak of a Suez venture in his letter for 18 December 1893. Nothing came of it.

The worst is that in the idleness to which I am now condemned I can scarcely forget my suffering. Oblivion is a good thing, but difficult to find.

If possible, I will come to Brussels for a short visit, but I do not know if I can. It's not that I don't want to. I am looking for a job, and I dare not leave London now for fear of missing an opportunity.

Do you think anyone will respond to my request for employment at Suez? Even to refuse? Or must I take the silence as a refusal? I should like to know what you think about this.

Thank you for your kind words. You cannot know how precious your affection is to me! I embrace you most warmly.

Your devoted friend and nephew

J. Conrad

To Marguerite Poradowska

Text   MS Yale; Rapin 127; G. & S. 64

Jeudi.[1] [29 March or 5 April 1894]
Londres.
17. Gillingham Street
SW

Ma très chère Tante.

Pardonnez-moi de ne pas avoir ecrit plus tot mais je suis en train de lutter avec Chap XI; une lutte a mort Vous savez! Si je me laisse aller je suis perdu! Je Vous ecris au moment de sortir. Il faut bien que je sorte quelquefois Helas! Je regrette chaque minute que je passe loin du papier. Je ne dis pas de la plume car j'ai ecrit fort peu, mais l'inspiration me vient en regardant le papier. Puis ce sont des echappées a perte de vue; la pensée s'en va vagabondant dans des grands éspaces remplis des formes vagues. Tout e[s]t chaos encore mais—lentement—les spectres se changent en chair vivante, les vapeurs flottantes se solidifient et qui sait?—peut-être quelque chose naitra dans le choc des idées indistinctes.—

Je Vous envois la première page[2] (dont j'ai pris copie) pour Vous

---

[1]   The context of the letter places it between the one for 2 March, when Conrad announces his visit to Brussels, and that for 16 April, written on a visit to Elstree. Since the letter came from London, it would not fall within the ten days at Elstree. Possible Thursdays are 29 March or 5 April, as Rapin and Gee and Sturm agree. Other possibilities are 22 March and even 15, for they give Conrad the opportunity for a short visit after his 2 March letter. The later dates are, however, more probable.

[2]   The first MS page of Chapter XI is much revised – words, phrases, entire sentences.

donner une idée de l'apparence de mon manuscrit. Cela Vous est du
puisque j'ai vu le Votre.[1]—J'aime a me conformer a l'etiquette, moi.—
Vous embrasse de tout mon cœur.
Toujours a Vous
J. Conrad.

Donnez-moi adresse a Lille

Thursday, [29 March or 5 April 1894]
London
17 Gillingham Street
S.W.

My very dear Aunt,

Forgive me for not having written sooner, but I am in the midst of
struggling with Chapter XI; a struggle to the death, you know! If I let go,
I am lost! I am writing to you just as I go out. I must indeed go out
sometimes, alas! I begrudge each minute I spend away from the page.
I do not say from the pen, for I have written very little, but inspiration comes to me while gazing at the paper. Then there are vistas that
extend out of sight; my mind goes wandering through great spaces filled
with vague forms. Everything is still chaos, but, slowly, ghosts are
transformed into living flesh, floating vapours turn solid, and – who
knows? – perhaps something will be born from the collision of indistinct
ideas.

I send you the first page (which I have copied) to give you an idea of
the appearance of my manuscript. This I owe you, since I have seen
yours. I for one like to observe the decencies.

I embrace you warmly. Always yours
J. Conrad

Give me your Lille address.

---

[1] On his visit, Conrad discussed her *Marylka*.

To Marguerite Poradowska

Text   MS Yale; Rapin 128; G. & S. 65

16. Avril 94.
[letterhead: Elstree, Herts]

Chère Tante.

Juste un mot pour Vous dire que je suis chez les Sanderson[1] que ma
santé est comme ci comme ça et que le chapitre xi est fini (9.000
mots)—plus long mais bien plus mauvais que les autres. Je commence le
xii dans un quart d'heure.

Veuillez m'apprendre comment Vous allez et comment va l'œuvre.
J'espère que Vos personnages vont bien et s'en vont ou les pousse leur
Destinée et votre plume. Un tout petit mot a mon adresse a Londres
s.v.p.—J'y retourne Vendredi prochain.[2]

Vous embrasse bien fort

Votre très devoué neveu
J. Conrad.

16 April 1894
[letterhead: Elstree, Herts]

Dear Aunt,

Just a note to tell you I am at the Sandersons', that my health is so-so,
and that Chapter xi is completed (9000 words) – longer but much worse
than the others. I am beginning Chapter xii in a quarter of an hour.

Please let me know how you are and how your work is going. I hope
your characters are well and go wherever your pen and Destiny impel
them. A brief note to my address in London, please. I am returning there
next Friday.

I embrace you most warmly.

Your very devoted nephew
J. Conrad

---

[1] Conrad was staying with his friend Edward Lancelot ('Ted') Sanderson, son of the
headmaster of Elstree, a Hertfordshire preparatory school. Sanderson met Conrad in
March 1893, sailing from Adelaide. Sanderson and his friend from Harrow, John
Galsworthy, had gone to the South Seas in quest of an interview with Robert Louis
Stevenson, whom, incidentally, they never found. They returned on the *Torrens*, on which
Conrad was the first mate. Sanderson became headmaster of Elstree in 1911, after ten
years' residence in Africa. Conrad dedicated *An Outcast of the Islands* (1896) to Sanderson,
and *The Mirror of the Sea* (1906) to his mother.

[2] 20 April.

To Marguerite Poradowska

Text   MS Yale; Rapin 129; G. & S. 65

24 Avril 1894
11$^{h.}$ Matin.
[London]

Ma chère Tante.

J'ai la douleur de Vous faire part de la mort de M. Kaspar Almayer qui a eu lieu ce matin a 3^h

C'est fini! Un grattement de Plume ecrivant le mot de la fin[1] et soudain toute cette compagnie des gens qui ont parlé dans mon oreille, gesticulé devant mes yeux, vécu avec moi pendant tant d'années devient une bande des fantômes qui s'eloignent, s'affacent se brouillant; indistincts et palis par le soleil de cette brillante et sombre journée.—

Depuis que je me suis reveillé ce matin il me semble que j'ai enseveli une part de moi-même dans les pages qui sont là devant mes yeux. Et cependant je suis content—un peu.—

Je vous enverrais les deux Chap^{tres}[2] aussitot typés.—

Merci de Votre lettre[3]

Je Vous embrasse de tout mon cœur.

Toujours Votre fidèle et devoué
J. Conrad.

24 April 1894
11 a.m.
[London]

My dear Aunt,

I regret to inform you of the death of Mr Kaspar Almayer, which occurred this morning at 3 o'clock.

It's finished! A scratching of the pen writing the final word, and suddenly this entire company of people who have spoken into my ear, gesticulated before my eyes, lived with me for so many years, becomes a band of phantoms who retreat, fade, and dissolve – are made pallid and indistinct by the sunlight of this brilliant and sombre day.

Since I woke this morning, it seems to me I have buried a part of

---

[1] The words 'The End', with 'April 1894' beneath them, appear on the last page of the MS of *Almayer's Folly*.

[2] Conrad means Chapters XI and XII, although he sent only Chapter XI, as we discover from Conrad's letter of 8 September 1894.

[3] A letter Conrad found upon his return to London.

myself in the pages which lie here before my eyes. And yet I am – just a little – happy.

I shall send you the two chapters as soon as typed.

Thanks for your letter.

I embrace you warmly.

Always your faithful and devoted

J. Conrad

To Marguerite Poradowska

Text   MS Yale; Rapin 130; G. & S. 67

[late April? 1894][1]

[London]

reçu votre Post-Card.

La seule demarche c'est d'envoyer la demission au ministère [de] la guerre.—On peut s'absenter. Generallement, on demande un congé quand on donne sa demission. Alors on s'absente. Une fois donnée on ne peut pas retirer sa demission. ou c'est très difficile je pense. Nous decidames pour Brześć mais Zamość (forteresse)[2] n'est pas loin non plus. L'idée de mettre Lia dans un "szynk" e[s]t bonne.[3] La rencontre est possible là—plutot là qu'ailleurs.

Heureux que vous travaillez. Moi je re-ecrit le 4 premiers chapitres.[4]

Tout a Vous.

J.C.—

---

[1] The content does not allow us to date this carelessly scribbled note with any certainty. While we favour late April, a date in May or even June is very possible. Conrad's references are to Mme Poradowska's *Marylka*, a novella in 24 parts which the *Revue des Deux Mondes* was to publish on 15 February, 1 and 15 March 1895. Those references, together with his allusion to revising the first four chapters of *Almayer's Folly*, permit us to date the note after 24 April, when Conrad indicated he had completed the novel. However, a sequence of letters in May and June also refer to *Marylka* and his revisions of *Almayer*.

[2] Brześć and Zamość are fortified towns near Lublin. The preceding details all refer to Mme Poradowska's *Marylka*. A young Polish officer serving in the Russian army, Thadée Radowski, tries to resign his commission in order to marry Marylka, the daughter of a Polish patriot. Subsequently, she refuses him and he retains his commission.

[3] In Mme Poradowska's novel, Radowski meets a young Jewish girl, Lia, and their first rendezvous occurs in the *szynk*, an alehouse.

[4] Conrad's revisions stressed the theme of paternal love (Gordan, pp. 112–29, 181–2).

[late April ? 1894]

[London]

Received your postcard.

The only procedure is to submit one's resignation to the War Office. It is possible to leave. Generally, one requests permission upon resigning. Then one goes away. Once granted, a resignation cannot be retracted, or at least it is very difficult, I believe. We decided on Brześć, but Zamość (a fortress) is no further away either. The idea of placing Lia in a tavern is good. The meeting is possible there – rather than elsewhere.

Glad you are working. As for myself, I am rewriting the first four chapters.

Yours

J. C.

To Marguerite Poradowska

Text MS Yale; Rapin 132; G. & S. 67

2. Mai. 94.

Londres.

17 Gillingham St

Chère Tante

Je viens de recevoir Votre Lettre.—Bonne Lettre qui fait plaisir, une lettre qui fait comme si on voulait être près de Vous. Comprenez-Vous?—Merci! C'est si bien d'être absolument compris et Vous m'avez compris du commencement jusqu'a la fin

Si Vous y tenez soit pour Wojtek[1]—seulement n'oubliez pas que Wojtek est un diminutif et si Votre Wojtek est un homme grave et sérieux peut être le nom jurera-t-il avec le caractère? Du moment que Vous *voyez* le personnage comme Wojtek il est impossible de changer le nom. Je comprends cela très bien.

Ma santé n'est pas très bonne. J'ai passé dix jours chez les Sanderson a Elstree[2] et ça m'a fait du bien. L'air est très bon là.—Je trouve le travail de remaniement de mes 3 premiers chapitres non seulement désagréable mais absolument pénible. Et difficile avec cela! Et cependant il faut que cela se fasse!

Je Vous enverrai bientôt le dernier Chap:.[3] Il commence avec un *trio*

---

[1] Wojtek (or Woytek) Radowski, a main character in *Marylka*, Mme Poradowska's novel still in progress, and a rival of Thadée. See note for letter of late April? 1894.

[2] In mid-April.

[3] According to the letter of 17 May, Conrad did not send the final chapter (XII).

Nina. Dain. Almayer. et il finit dans un long *solo* pour Almayer qui est presque aussi long que le Tristan–solo de Wagner.[1] Enfin! Vous verrez! Mais je crains fort que Vous ne trouviez la chose fade.—

Je Vous embrasse de tout mon cœur

Votre très devoué

J. Conrad.

2 May 1894
London
17 Gillingham Street

Dear Aunt,

I have just had your letter. A good letter that gives me pleasure, a letter that makes me want to be near you. Do you understand? Thank you! To be so completely understood is a blessing, and you have understood me from beginning to end.

If you insist upon it, let it be 'Wojtek' – only do not forget that 'Wojtek' is a diminutive, and if your Wojtek is a grave and serious man, the name will perhaps jar with the character. From the moment you *see* the character as 'Wojtek', it is impossible to change the name. I understand that very well.

My health is not very good. I spent ten days with the Sandersons at Elstree, and that has done me some good. The air is excellent there. I find the job of revising my first three chapters not only disagreeable but absolutely painful. And difficult as well! And yet it must be done.

I shall soon send you the last chapter. It begins with a *trio* – Nina, Dain, Almayer – and it ends with a long *solo* for Almayer which is almost as long as the solo in Wagner's *Tristan*. Enough! You will see! – but I very much fear that you will find the thing mawkish.

I embrace you warmly.

Your very devoted

J. Conrad

[1] Perhaps King Mark's notoriously long solo (*Tristan*, ii, iii).

1. Conrad's father, Apollo Korzeniowski

2. Conrad's mother, Ewelina Korzeniowska, née Bobrowska

3. Conrad in 1862, holding the whip mentioned in his first letter

4. Conrad, 1873

5. Singapore harbour in the late nineteenth century

6. The *Torrens*, bound for Port Adelaide in November 1892 with Conrad as first mate

7. Spiridion Kliszczewski (also known as Joseph Spiridion), 1915

8. Marguerite Poradowska, c. 1895

9. The *Roi des Belges*, original of 'the battered, twisted, ruined, tin-pot steamboat' in 'Heart of Darkness', and briefly under Conrad's command

and life is long — and art
is so short that no one sees
the miserable thing. Most
of my life has been spent between
Sky and water and now I
live so alone that often I
fancy myself clinging stupidly
to a derelict planet abandoned
by its previous crew. Your
voice is not a voice in the
wilderness — it seems to come
through the clean emptiness
of space. If — under the
circumstances — I hail back
lustily I know You won't
count it to me for a crime.

I am very sincerely

10. A page from Conrad's first letter to Cunninghame Graham, 5 August 1897

11. Wedding photograph of Jessie Conrad, née George,
1896

12. Wedding photograph of Joseph Conrad

13. Constance Garnett in the 1890s, painted by her sister

14. Edward Garnett, *c.* 1895

16. H. G. Wells in the 1890s

15. A. T. Quiller-Couch in the 1890s

17. T. Fisher Unwin, sketched by his office manager, 1915

18.   R. B. Cunninghame Graham: etching by William Strang, 1898

19.   William Blackwood, *c.* 1900

To Marguerite Poradowska

Text MS Yale; Rapin 133; G. & S. 68

Jeudi.[1] [17 May 1894]
[London]

Ma chère et bonne Tante.

Pardon du delai dans ma reponse. J'ai été fort occupé et puis je pensai Vous donner des bonnes nouvelles de moi aujourd'hui. J'etait presque sur—et pourtant je ne suis guère optimiste—d'obtenir le commande-ment d'un navire. Et bien ça a manqué. Au lieu de vous ecrire—comme j'en avais l'intention—la nouvelle d'accomplissement de mon desir—je vous envois—le soupir de regret et le grognement de colère. Enfin! Que voulez vous. Je commence a m'habituer aux deboires de ce genre.—

Pourquoi Vous dites "mon miserable roman"! Je suis sur que ce sera une belle chose. Justement j'ai relu Yaga l'autre jour. Cela m'a donné un plaisir intense. J'ai lu, lentement, et j'ai melé mes rêves a ces pages que j'aime si bien.—

Pardonnez moi de ne pas Vous envoyer mon chap XII. Le manuscrit entier est entre les mains d'un critique assez distingué, Edmond Gosse.[2] Combien de temps le gardera-t-il je n'en sais rien. Du reste comme Vous êtes en ce moment occupée avec Votre ouvrage, j'aime autant ne pas Vous interrompre.—

La question du titre est importante. Ce que Vous dites est parfaite-ment juste. "Cœur de fille" est bien mais un peu long. Ne pensez-Vous pas? Ne pourriez Vous pas trouver quelque chose de plus court: Un terme exprimant une emotion quelquonque par example; "un etat d'ame" comme dit Votre lettre.—

Soit pour Wojtek![3]

---

[1] This letter is clearly later than the one for 2 May; the phrase *'Soit pour "Wojtek"'* shows that they have already discussed the name. The letter comes well before Conrad's of 12 July, when he is pleased that *Marylka* has been well received by the publisher's reader. Since Conrad apologizes for the lateness of his reply, it seems that 10 May, as a possible Thursday (after the Wednesday, 2 May, letter), is too soon. Conrad's preoccupation with revising *Almayer's Folly* keeps the date within mid-May. The 17th seems likely, although a Thursday later in the month is possible. (Gee and Sturm point out, further, that on the wrapper of the manuscript the following note appears: 'Finished on the 22 May 1894'; but they rightly recall that Conrad's dating is unreliable.)

[2] Edmund Gosse (1849–1928), the literary critic and literary adviser, was editing the International Library (a series of foreign novels in translation) for Heinemann. Conrad's novel may have been considered for this series or submitted to him for his private opinion. Gosse remained a good friend of Conrad's in later years and, along with Galsworthy, helped to obtain him a Civil List pension.

[3] As the title of what became *Marylka*.

Je Vous embrasse bien fort. Je n'ecris pas plus long car j'ai le cœur un peu gros de mon mécompte et je ne veux pas *jeremiader*.—

Une autre lettre suivra bientot.

Toujours le votre

J. Conrad.—

Thursday [17 May 1894]

[London]

My dear and kind Aunt,

Excuse my delay in replying. I have been very busy, and had also hoped to give you some good news of myself today. I was almost sure – although I am seldom optimistic – of obtaining a command. And it has all come to nothing. Instead of telling you, as I intended, the news that I had fulfilled my wish, I send you a sigh of regret and a snarl of anger. There we are! What can one do? I am beginning to get used to disappointments of this kind.

Why do you say 'my miserable novel'! I am sure it will be a fine thing. I reread *Yaga* only the other day. It gave me intense pleasure. I read slowly, and I mingled my dreams with these pages that I love so well.

Forgive me for not sending you my Chapter XII. The whole manuscript is in the hands of a rather distinguished critic, Edmund Gosse. I do not know how long he will keep it. Besides, as you are now busy with your own work, I would as soon not interrupt you.

The question of the title is important. What you say is perfectly true. 'Cœur de fille' is good, but rather long, don't you think? Couldn't you find something shorter? For example, a term expressing some particular emotion, 'a state of soul', as your letter says.

Let it be 'Wojtek'!

I embrace you most warmly. I write no more, for my heart is heavy with disappointment, and I don't want to compose a jeremiad.

Another letter will follow shortly.

Ever yours

J. Conrad

To Marguerite Poradowska

Text MS Yale; Rapin 134; G. & S. 70

Mercredi.[1] [June? 1894]
Londres.
17 Gillingham St.

Chère Tante.

Etes-Vous a Paris? Si Vous m'envoyez mot je Vous enverrai le Chap XII et dernier, qui est pret. Comment va Votre roman? Je suis anxieux. Vous n'etes pas malade au moins?!—Je sais bien que mon long silence est une scéleratesse envers la meilleure des Tantes mais Vous savez que j'ai une aptitude naturelle pour le crime. Du reste le metier des bons est de pardonner les méchants. Je m'empresse de dire que Vous appartenez a la première categorie. Je ne suis ni mal ni bien—mais plutôt mal que bien.[2]—Je m'occupe tant que je peux en attendant un travail regulier. Du reste je ne suis ni plus ni moins bête qu'a Bruxelles quand j'ai eu le bonheur de m'infliger sur Vous.[3] Si Vous avez point temps ecrire veuillez m'envoyer mot "Paris". sur carte postale.—

Je Vous embrasse de tout mon cœur.

Votre très devoué

J. Conrad.

Wednesday [June? 1894]
London
17 Gillingham Street

Dear Aunt,

Are you in Paris? If you send me word, I shall despatch the twelfth and last chapter, which is ready. How is your novel going? I am worried. At least you are not ill? I realize that my long silence is villainy toward the best of aunts, but you know I have a natural aptitude for crime. Besides, it is the duty of the virtuous to forgive the wicked. I hasten to say that you belong in the first category. I am neither well nor ill, though rather more ill than well. I spend my time as best I can while awaiting regular work. Anyway, I am neither more nor less stupid than at Brussels when I had

---

[1] The contents point to a date between 17 May (when Gosse had the MS) and 4 July (when Conrad submitted it to Fisher Unwin). The apology for 'mon long silence' rules out a date in May.

[2] Conrad's words are ambiguous: perhaps he refers to the state of his health, perhaps to the state of his soul.

[3] Probably in March.

the pleasure of inflicting myself upon you. If you have no time to write, please send me the word 'Paris' on a postcard.

I embrace you warmly

Your very devoted

J. Conrad

To Marguerite Poradowska

Text   MS Yale; Rapin 135; G. & S. 70

12 Juillet 94.

[London]

Ma chère Tante.

Je suis content de savoir que votre roman a plu au lecteur critique. Du reste je n'en doutai pas—mais je suis bien plus content de savoir que vous êtes bien d'esprit et de corps.

Moi je ne suis pas bien ni de l'un ni de l'autre. J'ai envoyé mon manuscript à Fisher Unwin & Co qui publient une serie des romans anonymes.[1] Pas de reponse encore. Elle viendra sans doute dans la forme de renvoi de ce chef d'œuvre en vue de quoi j'ai envoyé les timbres-poste nécéssaires.—

A vous dire toute la verité je n'eprouve aucun interet au sort d'"Almayer's Folly."—C'est fini. Du reste dans tous les cas cela ne pouvait être qu'un épisode sans conséquence dans ma vie.—

Oui! Il serait bon de se revoir—Mais! . . . . .

En attendant il est bon de penser a Votre vraie et tendre amitié. Cela adoucit bien des choses. Je baise Vos mains.

Votre ami et neveu très affectueux

J. C. Korzeniowski.

J'adresse a Passy quoique Vous n'êtes plus a Paris.[2] J'ai pas d'autre adresse.

---

[1] The MS went to Fisher Unwin on 4 July (see letter to him of 8 September). Calling himself 'Kamudi', Conrad submitted *Almayer* for a series of pseudonymous (rather than anonymous) novels.

[2] Mme Poradowska had gone on a visit to Brussels and Lille.

12 July 1894
[London]

My dear Aunt,

I am happy to learn that your novel has pleased the publisher's reader. Of course, I did not doubt it – but I am all the happier to learn you are well in mind and body.

As for myself, I am well in neither the one nor the other. I have sent my manuscript to Fisher Unwin & Co., who publish a series of anonymous novels. No response yet. It will doubtless come in the form of the return of that masterpiece, in anticipation of which I have enclosed the necessary postage.

To be completely frank, I don't feel any interest in the fate of *Almayer's Folly*. It is finished. Besides, it could in any case be only an inconsequential episode in my life.

Yes! It would be good to see each other again. But! ...

In the meantime, it is good to think of your true and tender friendship. That indeed sweetens many things. I kiss your hands.

Your friend and very affectionate nephew
J. C. Korzeniowski

I am addressing this to Passy, even though you are no longer in Paris. I have no other address.

To Marguerite Poradowska
Text   MS Yale; Rapin 135; G. & S. 71

Vendredi.[1] [20 July ? 1894]
[London]

Ma chère bonne Tante,

J'ai reçu Votre lettre ce matin. Comme vous m'avez ecrit que Vous quitterez Paris pour quelque temps je me suis abstenu de toute correspondence jusqu'a nouvel ordre

Vous voilà dans une periode du "noir"! Je comprends bien ce regret du passé qui s'en va petit a petit marquant sa route par des tombes et des regrets. Il n'y a que cela d'eternel.

---

[1] The dating of this and the following two letters is approximate. All three would appear to precede the letter for 8 August 1894. This letter, tentatively dated 20 July, seems to continue along the same lines as the postscript of the 12 July letter. The handwriting, as well as the stationery, places this and the following letter in 1894. To make time for the two other letters, the Friday of this letter would have to be the 20th.

Cependant rappelez Vous que l'on n'est jamais tout a-fait solitaire. Pourquoi avez-Vous peur? De quoi? Est-ce de la solitude ou de la mort? O etrange effroi! Les deux seules choses qui rendent la vie supportable! Mais soyez sans crainte. La solitude ne vient jamais—et la mort souvent se fait attendre pendant des longues années d'amertume et de colère. Preferez Vous cela?

Mais Vous avez peur de Vous même; de l'être inseparable, toujours a Vos cotés; maitre et esclave; victime et bourreau; qui souffre et fait souffrir. C'est comme ça! Il faut trainer le boulet de son individualité jusqu'a la fin. C'est le [prix]¹ que l'on paye pour le privilege infernal et divin de la Pensée;—de sorte que dans cette vie il n'y a que les Elus qui sont des forçats—la bande glorieuse qui comprend et qui gemit mais qui foule la terre au millieu d'une multitude des phantômes aux gestes maniaques aux grimaces idiotes. Que preferez Vous: Idiot ou forçat?

Je Vous embrasse mille fois

J. Conrad.

Friday [20 July ? 1894]
[London]

My dear, kind Aunt,

I received your letter this morning. As you had written to me that you were leaving Paris for some time, I refrained from all correspondence until further orders.

So you are in a period of 'blackness'! I well understand this yearning for the past which vanishes little by little, marking its route in tombs and regrets. Only that goes on forever.

Remember, however, that one is never altogether alone. Why are you afraid? Of what? Is it solitude or death? O strange fear! The only two things that make life bearable! But be fearless. Solitude never comes – and death keeps us waiting during long years of bitterness and anger. Do you prefer that?

But you are afraid of yourself; of the inseparable being always at your side – master and slave, victim and tormentor – who suffers and causes suffering. That's how it is! Man must drag the ball and chain of his individuality to the very end. It is the [price] one pays for the infernal and divine privilege of thought; consequently, it is only the elect who are convicts in this life – the glorious company of those who understand and

¹ Rapin reads 'ce que'; we join Gee and Sturm in reading 'le que' and assuming a missing word.

who lament, but who tread the earth amid a multitude of ghosts with maniacal gestures, with idiotic grimaces. Which do you prefer – idiot or convict?

> I embrace you a thousand times
>
> J. Conrad

To Marguerite Poradowska

Text MS Yale; Rapin 136; G. & S. 72

> Mercredi.[1] [25 July? 1894]
>
> [London]

Ma chère Tante.

Sans doute Vous avez reçu ma lettre et Vous me croyez fou. Je le suis a peu de chose près. Ma maladie des nerfs me torture, me rend malheureux et paralyse action, pensée, tout! Je me demande pourquoi j'existe? C'est un état affreux. Même dans les intervalles—quand je suis censé d'être bien—je vis dans la peur du retour de ce mal tourmenstant. Selon l'expression arabe appliquée a ceux qui ont encouru le deplaisir du Souverain "je vis dans l'ombre du glaive" et je me demande soir et matin quand tombera-t-il aujourd'hui ou demain ou le jour d'après?

Je n'ai plus le courage de rien faire. J'ai a peine celui de Vous ecrire. C'est un effort; un elan hatif pour finir avant que la plume ne tombe de la main dans l'affaissement du decouragement complet. C'est comme ça! Vous voyez donc que Vous n'êtes pas la seule victime de l'incomprehensible. Je regrette de Vous avoir dit tout cela. Jamais je n'ai dit tant que çela a personne. Vous ferez bien d'oublier ce que vous venez d'entendre.

> Je suis toujours a Vous
>
> J. Conrad

> Wednesday [25 July? 1894]
>
> [London]

My dear Aunt,

Without a doubt you've received my letter and think I am mad. I am almost so. My nervous disorder tortures me, makes me wretched, and paralyses action, thought, everything! I ask myself why I exist. It is a

---

[1] See note on dating for previous letter. If we accept the earlier letter as falling on 20 July, then this, on the following Wednesday, would appear to be a continuation of that mood.

frightful condition. Even in the intervals, when I am supposed to be well, I live in fear of the return of this tormenting malady. According to the Arab expression applied to those who have incurred the sovereign's displeasure, 'I live in the shadow of the sword'; and I ask myself morning and night when it will fall – today, tomorrow, or the day after.

I no longer have the courage to do anything. I hardly have enough to write to you. It is an effort, a sudden rush to finish before the pen falls from my hand in the depression of complete discouragement. That's how it is! You see, therefore, that you are not the only victim of the incomprehensible. I regret having told you all this. Never have I said so much to anyone. You will do well to forget what you have just heard.

I am ever yours

J. Conrad

To Marguerite Poradowska
Text   MS Yale; Rapin 137; G. & S. 73

Lundi[1] [30 July ? 1894]
17. Gillingham St
Londres S.W.—

Chère Tante—Je reponds par retour du courrier pour Vous feliciter— pour Vous dire comme je suis heureux de votre succés![2] Je viens de me lever. J'ai été au lit 10 jours—10 siècles! Je suis toujours malade. C'est d'un monotone!

Je n'ai pas de reponse de Fisher Unwin. Cela peut durer des mois et puis je ne pense que l'on acceptera. Ici, dans ce pays, ou il parait 4 romans par semaine (et quels romans bon Dieu!) on doit faire antichambre très longtemps. Je crois que c'est temps perdu du reste.—

Si Vous n'aviez rien dit a la Revue nous aurions pu peut-être faire paraître Almayer pas comme traduction mais comme collaboration.[3] Ai-je du toupet pour Vous parler comme ça chère Maitre! On dirait que j'ai encore la fièvre.—

---

[1] See notes on dating for the two previous letters. This letter, for Monday, the 30th, appears to complete the 'London depression' that preceded Conrad's return to Champel (letter of 8 August). The reference to Fisher Unwin dates the letter after 12 July, when Conrad sent the manuscript for consideration.

[2] Probably on the acceptance of *Marylka* by the *Revue des Deux Mondes*.

[3] See letters to Unwin (4 October) and Mme Poradowska (18? August). Expecting to be rejected in England, Conrad wanted Mme Poradowska to translate *Almayer* and submit it to the *Revue des Deux Mondes*. If, moreover, the book were called a collaboration (perhaps naming Conrad as the junior partner), her literary reputation might win it some attention. See also Jean-Aubry's *Vie de Conrad*, p. 194.

Je n'ai rien fait—rien entrepris—rien essayé—rien risqué—et par conséquent je n'ai rien excepté la fièvre.—Et celle ci m'a quitté hier me laissant très faible et decouragé. Voila mon rapport.—

Ecrivez moi souvent. Je Vous embrasse de tout mon cœur

Tout a Vous

J. Conrad.

Impossible de rien faire pour le jeune homme[1] J'ai demandé a tout le monde que je connais. Pas mèche! C'est rempli de jeunes français!

Monday [30 July? 1894]
17 Gillingham Street
London S.W.

Dear Aunt,

I am answering by return of post to congratulate you – to tell you how happy I am about your success! I have just left my bed, having been there for ten days – ten centuries! I am always ill. How monotonous!

I have had no response from Fisher Unwin. That could go on for months, and then I do not think they will accept it. Here, in this country, where four novels appear every week (and, good Heavens, what novels!), one must dance attendance for a very long time. I believe it is time lost, in any case.

If you have said nothing to the *Revue*, we might perhaps be able to have *Almayer* appear not as a translation but as a collaboration. Haven't I any amount of cheek to speak to you like this, dear Teacher! One would say I was still feverish.

I have done nothing, undertaken nothing, attempted nothing, risked nothing, and, consequently, I have nothing except the fever. And even that abandoned me yesterday, leaving me very weak and discouraged. That is my report.

Write to me often. I embrace you warmly.

Yours

J. Conrad

Impossible to do anything for the young man. I have asked everyone I know. Nothing doing. Young Frenchmen are two-a-penny.

[1] Identity unknown.

To Marguerite Poradowska

Text   MS Yale; Rapin 137; G. & S. 74

8 Aout. 94.
Champel. près Genève.

Chère Tante.

Je fais de l'hydrothérapie ici et je ne m'en porte pas plus bien pour ça. J'ai quitté Londres si soudainement que je n'ai pas eu le temps de vous ecrire.—

Du reste je n'ai rien a dire. La santé ne vas pas et le moral se démonte tout doucement. Que voulez vous! C'est fatiguant a la fin!

Ecrivez moi un petit mot de Lille pour me dire que Vous êtes bien. Je reste ici jusqu'a la fin de ce mois je crois.[1]

Je vous embrasse.

Votre très fidèle neveu
J. Conrad.

La Roseraie.
Champel. Genève.

8 August 1894
Champel, near Geneva

Dear Aunt,

I am here for hydrotherapy, and I am none the better for it. I left London so suddenly that I had no time to write to you.

Besides, I have nothing to say. My health is not improving, and my morale is gradually falling to pieces. What can one say! It is utterly wearisome.

Send me a short note from Lille to tell me you are well. I shall remain here until the end of this month, I think.

I embrace you.

Your very faithful nephew
J. Conrad

La Roseraie.
Champel, Geneva.

---

[1] Actually, until 6 September.

To Marguerite Poradowska

Text MS Yale; Rapin 138; G. & S. 74

Jeudi.[1] [16? August 1894]
[Champel]

Chère Tante

Je viens de recevoir Votre lettre. Très heureux que Vous avez refusé.[2] Votre santé avant tout. Et puis j'ai peur que la chose n'aurait pas tournée au bien. Si Vous aviez ecrit la verité on Vous aurait ecorché là bas. Vous savez que je n'ai guère de confiance dans mes compatriotes et de Galicie surtout![3] Tout est pour le mieux. Reposez Vous a Lille et a Bruxelles. Ça vaut mieux que de courir les Expositions tant soit peu "farce".—Du reste je suis content que l'on vous a fait cette proposition. Ça montre au moins que l'on apprecie Votre talent et Votre sympathie. Ils ont très bien fait de Vous inviter—Vous avez très bien fait de refuser. Mais soyez très gentille et flattez un peu ces malheureux. Vous savez comme ils se gobent? N'est ce pas?

Forte embrassade. Lettre après demain.—

Votre devoué

J. Conrad.

4[h] après midi
addressez s.v.p.
J. Conrad Esqre
On connait pas d'autre nom ici

---

[1] Postscript and choice of stationery point to a stay at Champel, and the reference to the Exposition in Lwów places the letter in 1894. Mention of Mme Poradowska at Lille and Brussels locates the letter after that for 8 August. Given time for her reply to his of 8 August, *Jeudi* could be the 16th or the 23rd, but the contents of the following letter make the 16th more likely.

[2] Mme Poradowska had been invited to attend and describe the Exposition of Polish art and industry at Lwów (Russian: Lvov; German: Lemberg).

[3] To speculate on the significance of Conrad's remarks is a matter more for the biographer than for the editor. There may have been incidents about which we have no information, or Conrad may have been disguising guilty feelings with irony. For the latter point, Czesław Miłosz has an appropriate comment: 'An immigrant will often, for motives of self-defense, cut himself off completely from his land of origin or show toward it a friendly condescension, thereby contrasting his own success to the miseries of those left behind in the old country' ('Joseph Conrad in Polish Eyes', reprinted in Stallman, ed., *The Art of Joseph Conrad: A Critical Symposium*, East Lansing: Michigan State University Press, 1980, p. 42). Conrad brought in Galicia, the native province of Mme Poradowska's late husband, because its principal city was the scene of the Exposition.

Thursday [16? August 1894]
[Champel]

Dear Aunt,

I have just received your letter. Very happy you have refused. Your health before everything. And then I am afraid the thing would not have turned out well. Had you written the truth, they would have flayed you there. You know I have scarcely any confidence in my compatriots, and especially those from Galicia! It's all for the best. Stay in Brussels and in Lille. That is worth more than gadding about to slightly ridiculous expositions. Still, I am happy they made you this offer. This shows at least that they appreciate your talent and your fellow-feeling. They did very well to invite you – you did very well to refuse. But be very kind and flatter these poor creatures a little. You know how stuck-up they are. Isn't that so?

A warm hug. Letter the day after tomorrow.

Your devoted

J. Conrad

4 p.m.
Please address the letter to
J. Conrad, Esq.
They know me only by that name here.

To Marguerite Poradowska
Text   MS Yale; Rapin 139; G. & S. 75

Samedi.[1] [18? August 1894]
La Roseraie Champel. Genève.

Chère Tante. Puisque Vous êtes assez bonne pour Vous en occuper, parlons de cet imbécile d'Almayer. J'ai envoyé reclamer le renvoi du Ms.[2] et aussitôt mon retour en Angl: je le tiendrais a Votre disposition. Je desire garder mon nom de *Kamudi* (que l'on prononce "Kamoudi")[3]

---

[1] In the previous letter, Conrad promised a 'lettre après demain'; this one, marked only 'Saturday', would appear to be the one promised. It could, as well, be placed on 11 August, following the one for the 8th, but an improvement in his health would seem to need more than three days. If the previous letter belongs to the 16th, then this one belongs to the 18th.

[2] This letter has not turned up. In Conrad's letter to Fisher Unwin for 8 September, he asks if the manuscript is being read and, if not, requests its return as his sole copy.

[3] The pseudonym 'Kamudi' appears on the typescript of *Almayer's Folly* (Gordan, p. 183) and was the name used by Conrad when he submitted the novel to Fisher Unwin for publication in the Pseudonym Library. The novel proved too long for inclusion.

un mot malais qui signifie Gouvernail. Je ne veux pas des grandes
lettres et tout ça. C'est tout-a fait comme Votre bonne amitié de penser
a ces choses là! Avoir Votre beau langage pour exprimer mes pauvres
pensées est un bonheur et un honneur. Ceci n'est pas politesse mais
conviction sincère. Le nom de "Kamoudi" en petites lettres quelque
part suffira. Laissez Votre nom paraitre en titre—une note explicative
suffira pour dire que K. y a collaboré.[1] Voulez Vous? Du reste il me
semble tout drôle de Vous écrire tout cela. J'ai peine a croire a mon
bonheur.—

Vous me faites des offres de service a Bruxelles chez Pechet[2] ou autres.
Je Vous dis franchement que mes ressources sont presque epuisées et
qu'il faut absolument que je trouve une occupation bien vite de sorte que
si Vous pouvez faire quelque chose sans Vous donner trop de peine
j'accepte Votre aide avec reconnaissance Avec Vous je n'ai pas de fiérté,
ni fausse honte ni aucuns autres sentiments que ceux d'affection de
confiance et de gratitude. Si pour commander il faut y mettre de l'argent
je pourrai bien deposer 12.000 fr *au premier Mars 1895 pas avant*.[3] Je suis
prêt a passer un examen en Belgique si la chose est nécéssaire. Ne Vous
donnez pas trop de peine cependant. Je cherche de mon coté et suis sur
de trouver quelque chose de plus ou moins bon. P[lu]tôt *moins* que plus il
est vrai—mais enfin quelque chose!—

Je lis Maupassant avec delices. Je viens de finir le Lys Rouge d'A^le
France.[4] Ça ne me dit rien. Je ne peux pas faire de lecture serieuse. J'ai
commencé d'ecrire—avant-hier seulement. Je veux faire cela tout
court—Disons 20 a 25 pages comme celles de la Revue. J'apelle ça
"Deux Vagabonds" (Two Vagabonds) et je veux decrire a grand
traits—sans ombres ni details—deux epaves humaines comme on en
renco[n]tre dans les coins perdus du monde. Un homme blanc et un
Malais.[5] Vous voyez que les Malais me tiennent. Je suis voué au Borneo.
Ce qui m'ennuie le plus ce que mes personnages sont si vrais. Je le
connais si bien qu'ils m'entravent l'imagination. Le blanc c'est un ami
d'Almayer—le malais c'est notre vieil ami Babalatchi[6] avant qu'il soit

---

[1] This plan died when Fisher Unwin accepted the manuscript on 4 October. See Conrad's
letter to Unwin, 4 October, in which he raises the question of a translation by Mme
Poradowska. Also see Conrad's letter to her, same date.

[2] M. Victor Pécher, the shipowner friend of Mme Poradowska.

[3] Conrad expected 15,000 roubles from his uncle's estate.

[4] Published in 1894 by Calmann-Lévy (Paris). In a letter to Pinker (14 August 1919),
Conrad said his edition of Anatole France's novel was the twenty-seventh, and, although
he did not expect his own work to sell that spectacularly, he did not despair of 'a fair
success with the public'.

[5] This is the first sketch of the eventual *An Outcast of the Islands*.

[6] From *Almayer's Folly*.

arrivé a la dignité du 1ᵉʳ ministre et homme de confiance du Rajah. Voilà. Mais une catastrophe dramatique me manque. La tète est vide et même pour le commencement il y a du tirage! Je ne Vous dis que ça! J'ai envie de lacher tout déjà.—Pensez Vous que l'on peut faire une chose intéréssante sans la femme?!

Je retourne fin Août en Angleterre.[1]—Il me faut m'occuper serieuse-ment de trouver du travail. Ma santé se retablit et comme decidement je ne peux pas mourir il faut s'occuper de vivre—ce qui est fort ennuyeux. (Ceci n'est pas une pose! Je sens cela!)

Ecrivez-moi ici si Vous avez le temps de repondre a la présente. Je Vous previendrais de mon depart.—Donnez moi des nouvelles de Votre santé. Vous avez l'air de dire que ça ne marche pas tout a fait bien et cela me rend inquiet.

Je Vous embrasse de tout mon cœur.—

Toujours à Vous

J. Conrad.

Saturday [18? August 1894]
La Roseraie, Champel, Geneva.

Dear Aunt

Since you have been kind enough to take an interest in the matter, let us speak of that imbecile Almayer. I have requested the return of the manuscript, and immediately upon my return to England I shall put it at your disposal. I wish to keep my name of 'Kamudi' (which is pronounced 'Kamoudi'), a Malay word meaning rudder. I do not want [the pseudonym set in] large type or anything of that sort. To think of these things is altogether characteristic of your friendliness! To have your beautiful language to express my poor thoughts is a joy and an honour. This is not politeness, but sincere conviction. The name 'Kamoudi' somewhere in small print will be adequate. Let your name appear on the title-page – with merely an explanatory note to say that K. collaborated in the book. Do you agree? But it seems very funny for me to be writing all this to you. I can hardly believe my good luck.

You offer to help me in Brussels with Pécher or the others. I tell you frankly my resources are nearly exhausted and I really must find a position very quickly, so that if you can do something without giving yourself too much trouble, I gratefully accept your help. With you I have no pride, neither false shame nor any feelings other than those of

[1] He returned on 6 September, going directly to London.

affection, trust, and gratitude. If I must put up money for a command, I can deposit 12,000 francs *on the first of March 1895, not before*. I am ready to take an examination in Belgium if the thing is necessary. Don't give yourself too much trouble, however. I myself am looking around and am certain to find something more or less suitable. Rather *less* than more, it is true, but at least it will be something!

I am reading Maupassant with delight. I have just finished *Le Lys rouge* by Anatole France. It means nothing to me. I can do no serious reading. I have begun to write – only the day before yesterday. I want to make this thing very short – let us say twenty to twenty-five pages, like those in the *Revue*. I am calling it 'Two Vagabonds', and I want to describe in broad strokes, without shading or details, two human outcasts such as one finds in the lost corners of the world. A white man and a Malay. You see how Malays cling to me! I am devoted to Borneo. What bothers me most is that my characters are so true. I know them so well that they shackle the imagination. The white is a friend of Almayer – the Malay is our old friend Babalatchi before he arrived at the dignity of prime minister and confidential adviser to the Rajah. There they are. But I can't find a dramatic climax. My head is empty, and even the beginning is heavy going. I won't inflict more on you. I already feel like letting everything drop. Do you think one can make something interesting without any women?!

At the end of August, I am returning to England. I must seriously busy myself with finding work. My health is restored, and as I evidently cannot die, I must apply to living – which is very tedious. (I am not striking attitudes! This is how I feel!)

Write to me here if you have time to reply to this letter. I shall warn you of my departure. Give me some news of your health. You imply that it is not altogether good, and that worries me.

I embrace you warmly.

Ever yours

J. Conrad

To Marguerite Poradowska

Text MS Yale; Rapin 140; G. & S. 77

[letterhead: Champel-les Bains près Genève
SOCIÉTÉ ANONYME DE
CHAMPEL-BEAU-SÉJOUR
(Hôtels Beau-Séjour et la Roseraie)]
5th Sept. 94

Chère Tante. Je quitte Champel demain directement pour Londres. De
là, je Vous ecrirai a Bruxelles. Je suis presque completement retabli.
Faut esperer que cela durera.—Donnez moi de Vos nouvelles a 17
Gillingham Street. London.

Je Vous embrasse de tout cœur
J. Conrad.

[letterhead: Champel]
5 September 1894

Dear Aunt,
I am leaving Champel tomorrow, directly for London. From there, I
shall write to you in Brussels. I am almost entirely restored. Must hope it
will last. Send your news to me at 17 Gillingham Street, London.

I embrace you warmly
J. Conrad

To Fisher Unwin & Co.

Text MS Berg (tipped into *Almayer's Folly*, London,
1895); *Saturday Review of Literature*, x, 19 August 1933, 55

8th Sept 1894.

Messrs. Fisher Unwin & C°
Gentlemen,
On the 4th July 1894 there was delivered in your Publg offices of
Paternoster Row a typewritten work.—Title: "Almayer's Folly"; it was
enclosed in brown paper wrapper addressed to J. Conrad. 17 Gillingham
St S.W. and franked for return by parcel post, by twelve 1[d] stamps. The
brown paper package was put between *two* detached sheets of cardboard
secured together by a string. One of the cardboard sheets bore Your
address. The boy mess[ger] produced the usual receipt slip, duly signed,
but I do not remember the name or initials of the signature.—

I venture now upon the liberty of asking You whether there is the slightest likelihood of the MS. (Malay life, about 64.000 words) being read at some future time?[1] If not, it would be—probably—not worse fate than it deserves, yet, in that case, I am sure You will not take it amiss if I remind you that, however worthless for the purpose of publication, it is very dear to me. A ridiculous feeling—no doubt—but not unprecedented I believe. In this instance it is intensified by the accident that I do not possess another copy, either written or typed.—

I beg to apologise for taking up Your time with this matter.

I have the honour to be, Gentlemen,

Your obedient Servant

J. Conrad.

17. Gillingham St. S. W.

To Marguerite Poradowska

Text   MS Yale; Rapin 141; G. & S. 78

8th Sept. 1894

17. Gillingham St. S.W.

Chère Tante.

Merci de Votre lettre anglaise. Vous ecrivez très bien, mais très bien!

Me voilà ici depuis quelques jours. Je me sens assez bien et je cherche une occupation convenable. Les deux Vagabonds dorment.[2] Je ne suis pas satisfait avec moi—même—du tout. Il me manque des idées. J'ai beaucoup brulé. Ce sera à recommencer!

Je viens d'ecrire a Fisher Unwin quand au Almayer. Je leur demande une reponse ou le retour du MS. Quand je l'aurai je Vous enverrai le dernier Chap. que Vous n'avez pas encore lu. Si je pars on tiendra le MS. a Votre disposition chez M.M. Barr. Moring & C° London. 72 & 73. Fore Street. E.C.—Vous ecrirez que l'on Vous l'envois quand Vous Vous sentirez l'envie de commencer.[3]—Quand commence-t-on Votre roman dans la "Revue".[4]—J'ai une impatience pour le lire!

---

[1] T. Fisher Unwin did not write to accept Conrad's first novel until 3 October. As Unwin's reader, Edward Garnett had recommended publication. Garnett had himself been alerted to the manuscript by W. H. Chesson (G., p. 2).

[2] *An Outcast of the Islands.* See Conrad's letters to Mme Poradowska, 29 October–5 November 1894 and 27 December 1894, for comments on the title.

[3] The translation of *Almayer's Folly.*

[4] *Marylka*, whose publication began in the *Revue des Deux Mondes* on 15 February 1895.

Votre idée du roman du pilgrimage e[s]t excellente![1] Seulement n'est-ce pas trop tôt après "Lourdes".[2] On dira que Vous suivez la mode.—Dans un an d'ici je ne dis pas. Je suis sur que Vous ferez quelque chose de tres beau.—N'oubliez pas que chez nous religion et patriotisme se tiennent. On peut tirer parti de ce sentiment complexe. Donnez moi de Vos nouvelles. Je Vous embrasse de tout mon cœur.

Votre devoué

J. Conrad.

8 September 1894

17 Gillingham St S.W.

Dear Aunt,

Thank you for your letter in English. You write very well, very well indeed.

I have been here for some days. I feel reasonably well, and I am looking for a suitable occupation. The two vagabonds slumber. I am not satisfied with myself – at all. I lack ideas. I have burned much of it. I shall have to begin again.

I have just written to Fisher Unwin about *Almayer*. I am asking them for a reply or the return of the manuscript. When I have it, I'll send you the last chapter, which you have not read yet. If I leave, the manuscript will be held for you at Messrs Barr, Moering & Co., London, 72 & 73 Fore Street, E.C. When you feel the urge to start reading, write for it to be sent to you. When does your novel start in the *Revue*? I am impatient to read it!

Your idea for a novel about a pilgrimage is excellent! Only isn't it too soon after *Lourdes*? They will say you are following the fashion. A year from now, it might be a different matter. I am certain you will do something very fine. Don't forget that with us religion and patriotism go hand in hand. One can turn this complex feeling to good account. Give me news of yourself. I embrace you warmly.

Your devoted

J. Conrad

---

[1] *Pour Noémi*, which appeared in the *Revue des Deux Mondes* in 1899 and as a book in 1900.

[2] The novel by Zola (Charpentier–Fasquelle, 1894).

To Marguerite Poradowska
Text MS Yale; Rapin 142; G. & S. 78

2 Oct^{bre} [189]4
[letterhead: Barr, Moering]

Chère Tante.

J'ai reçu Votre Carte hier. Je Vous remercie mille fois de penser a moi. Je suis assez occupé avec les négociations pour divers navires.[1] Rien n'a abouti jusqu'a present. Je ne peux pas obtenir mon manuscript. J'ai réclamé deux fois et chaque fois j'ai eu la reponse que l'on s'en occupe. Je vais attendre quelque jours encore avant de demander le renvoi quand même.—

Je Vous embrasse de tout mon cœur
J. Conrad.

très pressé aujourd'hui. Ecrirai bientôt

2 October 1894
[letterhead: Barr, Moering]

Dear Aunt,

I received your card yesterday. Thank you so very much for thinking of me. I am quite busy with negotiations for several ships. As yet, nothing has happened. I cannot get hold of my manuscript. I have asked twice, and each time I have been told that they are attending to it. I shall wait a few more days before asking that it be returned in any case.

I embrace you warmly
J. Conrad

Very hurried today. Shall write soon.

---

[1] All such plans fell through, and we lack further details. Possible employment through M. Pécher of Antwerp came to nothing, as did Conrad's own negotiations with some Liverpool people about serving on a small barque called the *Primera*. See his letter to Mme Poradowska, 29 October–5 November 1894; also 26 November–3 December 1894.

To T. Fisher Unwin
Text   MS Rosenbach; Unpublished

4th Oct 94.
[London]

Mr Fisher Unwin.
Publisher.
11. Paternoster Row.
Dear Sir.

In reply to your letter of Oct^{er} 3^{d} referring to the MS of "Almayer's Folly" I beg to say that I am disposed to part with the copyright for the sum you mention (£20). I wish however to submit to your courteous consideration the following facts. Last June a regular contributor of the "Revue des Deux Mondes" Mme Marguerite Poradowska saw the MS and proposed to me to translate it into French for the "Revue."[1] She saw afterwards M. Brunetière who promised publication—without—I believe—going into financial details.[2] At any rate I do not know anything about them. I fancy there is nothing in it and I expected no material advantage from it. Nothing decisive has been done and Mme Poradowska who appeared alone in that matter has not even seen the last 2 chapters which were not written at the time. Now I should like immensely to appear in the "Revue" and still more to have the advantage of being translated by such a competent and charming writer. I trust You will see no objection in Mme Poradowska carrying out her plan. I repeat that I think there is very little—materially—in it. The "Revue" does not pay well for translations, but then it is very unlikely that there would be a demand for a translation in any other quarter.—
Awaiting Your decision in that matter I remain
Yours faithfully

J. Conrad.—

17. Gillingham St. S.W.

---

[1] See Conrad's letters to her, 30? July and 18? August, 1894.
[2] Ferdinand Brunetière (1849–1906), French literary critic who opposed Zola and Naturalism, best known for his *Manuel de l'histoire de la littérature française* (1897). In 1893, Brunetière succeeded Buloz as managing editor of the *Revue des Deux Mondes*.

To Marguerite Poradowska
Text MS Yale; Rapin 142; G. & S. 80

4 Oct^{er} 94.
[London]

Ma chère Tante.

On a accepte mon manuscrit. Je viens d'en recevoir la nouvelle. F.U. ne m'offre que £20 pour le copyright.—J'ai ecrit que j'acceptais ces conditions.—Comme il aura *tous* les droits sur l'ouvrage il faudra voir après Votre traduction.[1] J'ai bien peur que F.U. ne demande un prix trop élévé. Je vais tacher de garder le copyright français si je peux. Ce sera matiere a negociation quand je verrai le gerant de la maison.

J'ai pris ce que l'on m'offrait car vraiment le fait même de la publication est de grande importance. Chaque semaine des douzaines des romans paraissent—et il est bien difficile de se faire imprimer.—A presant il ne me manque qu'un navire pour être a peu près heureux.—

Ma santé est assez bonne. J'ai un rhume affreux depuis deux jours et en ce moment ma tête eclate. Vous pardonnerez le decousu de cette lettre. Cet Editeur me dit aussi que si j'ai quelque chose de plus court (25 000 mots) il voudrait le voir. C'est assez flatteur. Je n'ai rien. Les 2 Vagabonds chôment. Je suis trop occupé a courir après les navires. Rien encore de ce coté là.—

Je Vous embrasse de tout mon cœur. Toujours Votre devoué et fidèle

J. Conrad.

4 October 1894
[London]

My dear Aunt,

My manuscript has been accepted. I have just received the news. Fisher Unwin is offering me only £20 for the copyright. I wrote accepting the terms. As he will have *all* rights to the work, we shall have to see about your translation. I am very much afraid that Fisher Unwin may ask too steep a price. I shall try to safeguard the French copyright, if I can. This will be a matter for negotiation when I see the manager of the house.

---

[1] See Conrad's letter to Fisher Unwin for this date.

I have taken what they offered me because, really, the mere fact of publication is of great importance. Every week some dozens of novels appear – and it is truly difficult to get oneself into print. Now, I need only a ship in order to be almost happy.

My health is reasonably good. I have had a frightful cold for two days, and now my head is bursting. You must excuse the disconnectedness of this letter. This publisher also told me that if I have something shorter (25,000 words), he would like to see it. It is rather flattering. I have nothing. 'The Two Vagabonds' are idle. I am too busy chasing ships. Nothing yet on that side.

I embrace you warmly. Always your devoted and faithful

J. Conrad

To T. Fisher Unwin

Text   MS Sutton; Unpublished

8th Oct. [1894]

Dear Sir,

It was understood this morning that I should have the MS of "Almayer's Folly" for a couple of days. Would you kindly—if feasible—give it to bearer of this note. I am going out of town this afternoon and would like to take it with me for final revision.—

Yours faithfully.

J. Conrad.—

To Marguerite Poradowska

Text   MS Yale; Rapin 143; G. & S. 81

10 Oct. 94.
[London]

Chère et meilleure des Tantes

Merci pour Votre carte. Victoire. J'ai le copyright français pour moi tout seul. Que je Vous raconte mon audience.—

D'abord les deux "lecteurs" de la maison[1] m'ont reçu et m'on

---

[1] One of these readers was probably W. H. Chesson. Despite having recommended publication, Edward Garnett does not seem to have been there. He remembered meeting

complimente avec effusion (se sont-ils moqué de moi par hasard?) Puis on m'a conduit en la presence du chef pour parler affaires. Il m'a dit franchement que si je voulais prendre une part dans le risque de la publication je pourrai participer au profits. Sinon on me donne 20 £ et les droits français. J'ai choisi cette dernière alternative. "Nous vous payons très peu—a-t-il dit—mais considerez cher Monsieur que vous êtes un inconnu et que Votre livre appelle a une public très limité. Puis il y a la question du gout. Le Public le goutera-t-il? Nous risquons quelque chose aussi. Nous vous faisons paraître en un beau volume a 6 shillings et vous savez que ce qui parait chez nous reçoit toujours des critique serieuses dans le journaux littéraires. Vous êtes sur d'une longue 'notice' dans la 'Saturday Review' et l' 'Atheneum' sans parler de la presse en general. Voilà pourquoi nous pensons de ne Vous faire paraître que l'année prochaine en Avril pendant la saison. On va imprimer tout de suite pour que Vous puissiez corriger et nous enverrons les 'proof sheets'[2] a Mme Poradowska avant la Noël. Ecrivez quelque chose de plus court— même genre—pour notre Pseudonym Library et si la chose convient nous serons très heureux de puvoir Vous donner un bien meilleur chèque."

Voilà. J'avance tout doucement avec un vagabond sous chaque bras dans l'espoir de les vendre a Fisher Unwin. Traite d'esclaves! Parole d'honneur!

Merci pour Vos efforts avec Mme Pechet.[3] Je n'ai pas eu le temps de m'occuper beaucoup des affaires maritimes car Almayer est venu me rendre visite pour 3 jours.[4] Il me quitte aujourd'hui. Rien a corriger.—

Conrad for the first time in November, at the National Liberal Club – a rendezvous arranged by Fisher Unwin (G., p. 2). On the last Christmas Day of his life, Conrad gave Gertrude Bone a description of the encounter with Garnett, 'so distinguished-looking, with all that black hair'. Garnett was evidently by himself: 'I had gone to meet him to hear what he thought of "Almayer's Folly". I saw a young man enter the room. "That cannot be Edward, so young as that," I thought. He began to talk. Oh yes it was Edward. I had no longer doubts. But I was too frightened to speak. But this is what I want to tell you, how he made me go on writing. If he had said to me "Why not go on writing?" I should have been paralysed. I could not have done it. But he said to me, "You have written one book. It is very good. Why not *write another*?" Do you see what a difference that made? Another? Yes. I would do that. I *could* do that. Many others I could not. Another I could. That is how Edward made me go on writing. That is what made me an author.' (Gertrude Bone to Garnett, n.d., MS, Texas: quoted with minor variations, G., p. 3; see also the Author's Note to *An Outcast*, p. viii.)

[2] Conrad received them on Christmas Eve.
[3] Mme Pécher of Brussels, cousin by marriage of Victor Pécher, the Antwerp shipowner.
[4] In the form either of the MS or of ideas for *An Outcast*.

Ce serait bien gentil de venir a Paris pour Voir Votre pastel.[1] Rien que le pastel Vous comprenez—pas Vous. Oh non! Du tout mais j'ai bien peur que ce plaisir n'est pas pour moi. Pas cette année au moins.— Quand commencez vous a paraitre dans la Revue?[2] Je commence a avoir faim de votre travail. Je Vous embrasse de tout mon cœur et je suis toujours votre affectionné neveu

J. Conrad.

10 October 1894
[London]

Dear and best of Aunts,

Thank you for your card. Victory. I have the French copyright for myself alone. Let me tell you about my interview.

At first the firm's two 'readers' received me, complimenting me effusively (were they, by chance, mocking me?). Then they led me into the presence of the great man in order to talk business. He told me frankly that if I wished to share in the risk of publication, I could participate in the profits. Otherwise, I receive £20 and the French rights. I chose this latter alternative. 'We are paying you very little,' he told me, 'but, remember, dear Sir, that you are unknown and your book will appeal to a very limited public. Then there is the question of taste. Will the public like it? We are risking something also. We are publishing you in a handsome volume at six shillings, and you know that whatever we bring out always receives serious critical attention in the literary journals. You are certain of a long notice in the *Saturday Review* and the *Athenaeum*, not to mention the press in general. That is why we are planning not to publish you until next year, in April, during the season. We shall print immediately, so that you can make corrections, and shall send the proof-sheets to Mme Poradowska before Christmas. Write something shorter – same type of thing – for our Pseudonym Library, and if it suits us, we shall be very happy to be able to give you a much better cheque.'

There it is. I progress very cautiously with a vagabond under each arm, in the hope of selling them to Fisher Unwin. Slave trade! Word of honour!

Thank you for your efforts with Mme Pécher. I haven't had the time to be concerned too much with maritime affairs, for Almayer came to pay me a three-day visit. He leaves today. Nothing to revise.

[1] Pastel portrait of Mme Poradowska by the Dutch artist Schaken.
[2] *Marvlka.*

It would be very pleasant to come to Paris to see your pastel. Only the pastel, you understand – not you. Oh, no! Not at all. But I am very much afraid this pleasure is not for me. Not this year, at least. When do you start appearing in the *Revue*? I am beginning to hunger after your work. I embrace you warmly, and I am always your affectionate nephew

J. Conrad

To Marguerite Poradowska

Text   MS Yale; Rapin 145; G. & S. 82

23 Oct. 94.
17. Gillingham St.

Chère Tante.

J'ai reçu Votre lettre du départ de Bruxelles et j'ai agi en consequence. En ce moment Monsieur Pecher a tous les details nécéssaires. Merci mille fois pour Votre bonté.—

Je n'ai rien de neuf a Vous dire. On ne m'envoit pas les epreuves d'Almayer mais je vais presser ces gens là. Je ne doute pas que vous aurez les "advance sheets"[1] vers la mi-Novembre.

L'autre ouvrage va très doucement.[2] je suis très decouragé. Les idées ne viennent pas. je ne *vois pas* ni les personnages ni les evenements. A vrai dire je suis preocupé de mes plans pour partir et comme ils n'ont pas l'air de se réaliser je suis dans un état d'irritation qui ne me permet pas de m'oublier dans mon récit—par consequent le travail ne vaut rien.—

Et Vous? Qu'allez Vous faire?—Je viens de relire le "fils Grandsire"[3] en ouvrant le livre au hasard et comme ça au hasard j'ai tout lu sans perdre un mot. Decidement je l'aime ce livre avec une drole de tendresse tout-a-fait sentimentale. Je Vous trouve sur chaque page comme je Vous aime le mieux.

Santée assez bien. Je Vous embrasse très fort. Votre J. Conrad.

23 October 1894
17 Gillingham Street

Dear Aunt,

I had your letter about leaving Brussels and have acted accordingly. By this time, M. Pécher has all the necessary details. Thanks again and again for your kindness.

---

[1] Proof-sheets arrived on 24 December.
[2] 'Two Vagabonds'.
[3] *Le Mariage du fils Grandsire.*

I have nothing new to tell you. They have not sent me the proofs of *Almayer*, but I am going to hurry these people up. I've no doubt that you will have the proof-sheets towards mid-November.

The other work goes very slowly. I am discouraged. Ideas don't come. I cannot *see* either characters or events. To be honest, I am busy with my plans for leaving, and, as they seem unlikely to mature, I am in a state of irritation which does not allow me to lose myself in my story – consequently, the work is worthless.

And you? What are you going to do? I have just reread *Le fils Grandsire*, opening the book at random, and, continuing at random, I have read every single word. With an odd and entirely sentimental fondness, I truly love this book. On every page, I find you at your most lovable.

Health quite good. I embrace you very warmly. Your

J. Conrad

To Marguerite Poradowska

Text   MS Yale; Rapin 146; G. & S. 83

[29 October or 5 November 1894]
[London]
Lundi matin[1]

Chère Tante.

Je reponds tout de suite a votre chère lettre. L'idée du roman[2] me plait infiniment. Je suis très heureux de savoir que Vous êtes en train de créer avec plaisir. C'est en quelque sorte une garantie de succés.

J'ai déjà pensé—plusieurs fois que Vous Vous faites une injustice en offrant de traduire Almayer. Du moment que Vous avez un ouvrage qui promet si bien il ne faut pas Vous en occuper. Je parle très serieusement et avec conviction. Ce serait très injuste a Vous et a Votre art créateur. On Vous enverra sans doute les "advance sheets" mais je Vous en supplie mettez les de coté.[3] Si je puis me permettre de juger par moi même—il me serait insupportable de quitter un ouvrage qui me tiendrait au cœur pour—traduire! Ne faites pas ça. Ce serait un crime.—

---

[1] The letter definitely falls within the late 1894 sequence. The date depends on how rapidly Mme Poradowska responded to Conrad's letter of 23 October. If she answered immediately and Conrad then replied, this letter would belong to 29 October; with some delay, 5 November. An even later date is possible, thus moving up the following letters, which are also undated.

[2] *Pour Noémi.*

[3] Mme Poradowska apparently did. In a letter to Unwin, 12 March 1895, Conrad said she was too unwell to undertake the translation. The French translation was eventually undertaken and completed by Geneviève Séligmann-Lui (1919) who also corresponded with Conrad over possible translations from *Tales of Unrest*.

Il Vous faut pour Votre roman une catastrophe non seulement dramatique mais encore characteristique. L'avez Vous? Un petit employé polonais ne ressemble pas un petit employé français (com[m]e Maupassant les connaissait bien!)[1] et si Vous voyez la difference clairement (comme je n'en doute pas) Vous ferez quelque chose de beau. Je suppose que ce sera plutot une etude de femme. N'est-ce pas?

Vous étes trop tard avec Votre avis Madame ma Tante. J'ai peur que je ne sois trop sous l'influence de Maupassant. J'ai etudié "Pierre et Jean"—pensée, methode et tout—avec le plus profond déséspoir. Ça n'a l'air de rien mais c'est d'un compliqué comme mécanisme qui me fait m'arracher les cheveux. On a envie de pleurer de rage en lisant cela.—Enfin!—

Oui c'est vrai. On travaille le plus quand on ne fait rien. Voilà trois jours que je m'assois devant une page blanche—et la page est toujours blanche excépté pour un IV en tête.[2] A vrai dire je suis mal parti. Je me console un peu en pensant que Vous êtes partie du bon pied. Que Voulez Vous? Je ne ressent le moindre enthousiasme. C'est fatal, cela.—

La critique serieuse traite les "Heavenly Twins" de Mme Sarah Grand avec le mepris qui lui est du.[3] Mais!—le livre a passé par 10 éditions et l'auteur a empoché 50.000 francs. Le monde est un sale endroit.—Du rest cette femme est détraquée et bête par dessus le marché. Imaginez Vous un imbecile qui deviendrait fou. C'est d'un triste et d'un affreux. Un vrai cauchemar, quoi!—

Mme M. Wood[4] m'a volé mon titre. Elle vient de publier un livre: "The Vagabonds" et me voilà joliment embêté. Non! Si Vous saviez comme ça m'ennuie Vous auriez pitié de moi.—

Quand a l'idée de cet ouvrage aprésant sans titre comme Vous m'avez indiqué la votre je veux Vous indiquier la mienne. Le motif d'abord c'est une vanité effrenée, feroce d'un homme ignorant qui a du succés mais n'a ni principes ni d'autre ligne de conduite que la satisfaction de sa vanité.—Aussi il n'est même pas fidèle a soi même. D'ou chute, degringolade subite justu'a l'esclavage physique de l'homme par une femme absolument sauvage J'ai vu ça! La catastrophe sera amenée par

---

[1] Conrad much admired the novels and short stories of Guy de Maupassant (1850–93); Rapin provides a good summary of Conrad's immersion in the French writer's work (pp. 146–7, n. 7).

[2] The change in chapter headings makes it impossible to determine what Conrad meant by 'IV'.

[3] Madame Sarah Grand was the pseudonym of Frances Elizabeth McFall, a feminist author; *The Heavenly Twins* was published by Heinemann (1893).

[4] Margaret Louisa Woods.

les intrigues d'un petit etat malais, dont le dernier mot est: empoisonnement. Le denouement est: suicide par vanité encore.[1] Tout cela ne sera qu'esquissé car comme j'ecris pour la "Pseudonym Library" je suis limité a 36 000 mots pour faire un volume.[2] Voilà.—

Rien encore d'Anvers. Je suis en negociations avec des gens de Liverpool. Ils ont un si joli petit navire—et il a un si joli nom! "Primera".[3]—Je pense que cela aboutira mais je ne suis sur de rien.—

Vos lettres sont une grand joie pour moi. Au bout du compte il n y a que Vous au monde a qui je peux tout dire—et Votre sympathie est d'autant plus precieuse. A vous de tout cœur

J. Conrad.—

Monday morning [29 October or 5 November 1894]
[London]

Dear Aunt,

I answer your kind letter immediately. The idea of the novel pleases me exceedingly. I am very happy to learn that you are enjoying the work. In a way, that's a guarantee of success.

I have already thought, on several occasions, that you were doing yourself an injustice in offering to translate *Almayer*. Since you have such a promising book of your own, you should bother with that. I speak very seriously and with conviction. It would be very unjust to you and to your creative work. No doubt they will send you the advance sheets, but I beg you to put them aside. If I may be permitted to judge by my own standards, it would be unbearable for me to postpone a work which grips my heart in order to – translate! Don't do that. It would be a crime.

Your novel needs a climax which is not only dramatic but also characteristic. Do you have it? A minor Polish employee does not resemble a minor French employee (how well Maupassant knew them!), and, if you see the difference clearly (as I am sure you do), you will make something fine. I suppose it will really be a study of woman. Isn't that so?

You are too late with your advice, my splendid aunt. I fear I may be too much under the influence of Maupassant. I have studied *Pierre et Jean*

---

[1] There is neither a poisoning nor a suicide in the completed version of *An Outcast of the Islands*.

[2] *An Outcast* ran to almost three times this length and did not appear in the Pseudonym Library. For this series, see note to letter to Noble, 28 October, 1895.

[3] A barque built in Glasgow. Nothing came of this plan, despite Conrad's optimism about its success.

– thought, method, and all – with the profoundest despair. It seems nothing, but it has a technical complexity which makes me tear my hair. One feels like weeping with rage while reading it. Ah well!

Yes, it is true. One works hardest when accomplishing nothing. For three days, I've been seated before a blank page – and the page has stayed blank except for a 'IV' at the top. I am really on the wrong path. I console myself a little by thinking that you are on the right one. What do you expect? I don't feel the slightest enthusiasm. And that is fatal.

Serious criticism treats *The Heavenly Twins* by Mme Sarah Grand with the scorn it deserves. But! – the book has gone through ten editions and the author has pocketed 50,000 francs. The world is a dirty place. Moreover, this woman is confused and stupid into the bargain. Imagine stupidity gone mad. It is sad and frightful. A real nightmare, indeed!

Mrs M. Wood has stolen my title. She has just published a book called *The Vagabonds* and now I am really furious. No! You would pity me if you knew how that annoys me.

As for the idea of this work, so far untitled: as you have told me yours, I want to tell you mine. First, the theme is the unrestrained, fierce vanity of an ignorant man who has had some success but neither principles nor any other line of conduct than the satisfaction of his vanity. In addition, he is not even faithful to himself. Whence a fall, a sudden descent to physical enslavement by an absolutely untamed woman. I have seen that! The catastrophe will be brought about by the intrigues of a little Malay state where poisoning has the last word. The dénouement is: suicide, again because of vanity. All this will only be sketched, because, as I am writing for the Pseudonym Library, I am restricted to 36,000 words per volume. There it is.

Nothing yet from Antwerp. I am negotiating with some Liverpool people. They have such a pretty little ship, and it has such a pretty name, 'Primera'. I think this will succeed, but I am certain of nothing.

Your letters are a great pleasure for me. In the end, you are the only one in the world to whom I can tell everything – and your sympathy is, therefore, even more precious. Yours with all my heart

J. Conrad

To W. H. Chesson

Text MS Smith (letter pasted into copy of *Almayer's Folly*); Ugo Mursia, *The True 'Discoverer' of Joseph Conrad's Literary Talent* (Varese, Italy, 1971), pp. 5, 11–12

Thursday [mid October–mid November 1894][1]
17 Gillingham St S.W.

Dear M[r] Chesson.[2]

Thanks for your letter. Yes—in Borneo but as a matter of reality in my memory it is only a faded stream.[3]

I regret to see my own stupid finger pointing for ever to the spot on the map. After all, river and people have nothing true about them—in the vulgar sense—but the names. Any criticism that would look for real description of places and events would be disastrous to that particle of the universe, which is nobody and nothing in the world but myself.

Yours very faithfully,

J. Conrad.

To Marguerite Poradowska

Text MS Yale; Rapin 148; G. & S. 85

Mercredi.94. [14 or 21 November 1894]
[London]

Chère Tante.

J'ai lu Votre lettre avec etonnement et encore avec admiration. Quelle fée Vous a donné le don de voir ainsi les évenements compliqués de la vie se dérouler dans l'espace et le temps?—L'histoire des vos creatures est tout ce qu'il y a de plus interéssant. Ça abonde en situations. Vous n'avez donc qu'a faire marcher la plume.—

J'ai eu une longue entreveue avec Monsieur T. Fisher Unwin. Decidement on ne mettra l'ouvrage en type que l'année prochaine en Fevrier.[4] Cela m'est absolument égal. Je n'ai rien a corriger en fait de style ou composition et quand aux fautes d'imprimerie les correcteurs de la maison en prendront bon soin.—Mais j'espère de tout mon cœur et de toute mon âme que je ne serai plus a Londres a cette époque.

---

[1] The letter almost definitely appears to fall within 1894. We have placed it shortly after the time that *Almayer's Folly* was accepted by Fisher Unwin, on the assumption that Chesson, one of the readers, had questioned Conrad about details of the manuscript.

[2] Chesson saw himself as the discoverer of Conrad's talent and later developed a mania that he had 'made' Conrad. He kept extensive diaries, and in these he pasted copies of letters he wrote to Wells and others stressing his role in Conrad's success as a novelist.

[3] The river that, in *Almayer's Folly*, Conrad calls the Pantai was based on the river Berau in Dutch East Borneo, which Conrad had visited as mate of the *Vidar*.

[4] *Almayer's Folly*, which appeared on 29 April 1895.

Le travail ne va pas, et la santé n'est plus aussi bonne. Si je reste plus longtemps a terre tout se gatera, helas! Demain je vais a Anvers pour affaires et je crois que je peux me risquer a faire une visite a M^r. Victor Pechet.[1] Il est trop tard pour Vous demander Votre avis puisque mon voyage a été decidé très soudainement il y a une heure.—

L'autre samedi j'ai passé la soirée avec un de mes amis. Nous avons causé de tout un peu—et nous avons causé de Yaga.[2] Il connait le livre mieux que moi. Nous nous sommes rappelés des scènes qui nous ont empoignés nous avons querrellé la dessus—et nous avons en maint endroit admiré avec une touchante unanimité—nous avons critiqué aussi. Très sevèrement; si Vous saviez Vous trembleriez! La dessus j'ai detérré mon album et nous avons regardé le portrait de l'auteur en soufflant des nuées de tabac avec une solennité exemplaire. La conclusion ou nous sommes arrivés est que livre et auteur sont comme ça—passables—très passables.—Faites pas de gros yeux Madame. Je plaisante. Nous avons dit que c'était très beau et nous l'avons dit avec la plus parfaite sincérité.[3] Vous êtes sure des deux lecteurs au moins dont Vous avez touché le cœur—pas l'écorce—le vrai fond.—

Je Vous embrasse de tout mon cœur. Toujours à Vous.

J. Conrad.

Wednesday [14 or 21 November] 1894
[London]

Dear Aunt,

I read your letter with amazement and with admiration too. What fairy has given you the gift of seeing the complicated events of life thus, as they unfold in space and time? The history of your characters is of the utmost interest. It abounds in situations. You have only to set your pen in motion.

I've had a long interview with Mr T. Fisher Unwin. They will definitely not set the work in type before next year, in February. It's all absolutely the same to me. I have nothing to revise in the way of style or composition, and, as for misprints, the firm's readers will see to them.

---

[1] Pécher, a shipowner.

[2] *Yaga*, Mme Poradowska's fictional sketch of Ruthenian life, which appeared as a book in 1888.

[3] Both Jessie Conrad and Charles Zagórski considered Mme Poradowska a beautiful woman. See Jessie Conrad's *Conrad and his Circle*, p. 70. A photograph of her is reproduced in this volume.

But I hope with all my heart and soul that I shall no longer be in London at that time.

My work is not going well, and my health is no longer as good. If I remain any longer on shore, all will be ruined, alas! I am going to Antwerp tomorrow on business and believe I can risk a visit to Mr Victor Pécher. Since my trip was very suddenly decided upon, only an hour ago, it is too late to ask your advice.

The other Saturday I spent the evening with one of my friends. We chatted a little about everything – and we chatted about *Yaga*. He knows the book better than I. We recalled scenes which gripped us; we argued about them, and we admired many a passage with a touching unanimity. We criticized, also. Very severely. If you knew, you would tremble! Thereupon, I dug out my album, and we looked at the author's portrait while blowing clouds of tobacco-smoke with exemplary solemnity. The conclusion we reached is that book and author are alike – passable, quite passable. Don't look so severe, Madame. I am joking. We said it was very fine, and we said it with perfect sincerity. You are sure of two readers at least whose hearts you have touched – not the surface – the very depths.

I embrace you warmly.

Ever yours

J. Conrad

To Marguerite Poradowska

Text   MS Yale; Rapin 149; G. & S. 87

Lundi.[1] [26 November or 3 December 1894]
17 Gillingham St.

Ma chère Tante.

Pardonnez mon long silence. J'aurais du repondre a Votre bonne lettre il y a bien longtemps, mais je n'avais rien de nouveau et rien d'interessant a dire. Du reste c'est le cas en ce moment. Ceci est seulement pour Vous faire savoir que j'existe encore.—.

Je n'ai pas des nouvelles d'Anvers. Il faut Vous dire que je n'y suis pas allé comme j'en avais le projet. Il y a eu des empêchements. Une affaire qui promettait très bien a manqué au dernier moment. J'en ai machonné l'amertume pendant une semaine entière.—

---

[1] This letter definitely follows the one for 14 or 21 November, when Conrad announced he was leaving for Antwerp the following day, although the exact date cannot be determined. The 'long silence' that Conrad speaks of may be two or three weeks, giving the letter a range from 26 November to 3 December or even after.

Il m'est doux de penser a Vous travaillant sans obstacles et avec joie a cet intéressant ouvrage dont Vous m'avez decrit le plan.[1]—Quand a moi je suis absolument embourbé.[2] Il ya a quinze jours déjà que je n'ai ecrit un seul mot. C'est bien fini il me semble. J'ai envie de bruler ce qui est là. C'est très mauvais! Trop mauvais! Ceci est ma profonde conviction et non pas un cri de stupide modestie. Je me suis débattu assez longtemps comme cela. Voila! Rien de neuf. Rien de rien. Seulement beaucoup de tristesse Santé pas mal.

J[e] V^s embrasse de tout mon cœur. Toujou[rs] Votre devoué

J. Conrad

Monday [26 November or 3 December 1894]
17 Gillingham Street

My dear Aunt,

Pardon my long silence. I should have replied to your good letter long ago, but I had nothing new and nothing interesting to say. And that is still the case. This is only to let you know that I still exist.

I've had no news from Antwerp. I must tell you I did not go there as I had planned. There were some obstacles. A transaction full of promise fell through at the last moment. I ate the bread of bitterness for an entire week.

It is sweet for me to think of you, happy and unhampered, busy with that interesting work whose plan you described to me. As for myself, I am absolutely bogged down. For the previous fortnight I have not written a single word. It's all over, it seems to me. I feel inclined to burn what there is. It is very poor! Too poor! This is my profound conviction and not a cry of stupid modesty. I have struggled like that for a long time. There you are. Nothing new. Nothing whatever. Only much sadness. Health not bad.

I embrace you warmly. Ever your devoted

J. Conrad

---

[1] *Pour Noémi.*
[2] Bogged down on *An Outcast.*

To Marguerite Poradowska

Text   MS Yale; Rapin 150; G.& S. 87

Jeudi.[1] Minuit moins le quart. [6 or 13 December 1894]

[London]

Chère Tante

Je viens de rentrer et je trouve Votre lettre. Je prends ma plume tout de suite pour Vous repondre sous l'impression encore chaude de Votre lettre.

Et puis d'abord en terme general: très bien!—Ensuite quand au details je Vous dis sincerement honetement, d'ami a ami que l'idée du 1er chapitre est très bonne—très jolie très effective. Le devellopement de l'action me semble sans faute absolument. Je vois un tas des situations dramatiques. C'est a Vous de les faire empoignantes et je Vous donne ma parole que je crois en toute conscience que Vous serez absolument a la hauteur de la tâche—car on n'invente pas une charpente comme cela sans se faire une idée des details. Le detail c'est le principal dans un roman comme celui que Vous avez dans la tête. Et puis comme histoire polonaise je vois que vous êtes dans le vrai car Vos femmes auront plus de caractère que les hommes—ce qui chez nous est indubitable. Je suis sur que si Vous commencez a ecrire selon le plan que Vous me donnez Vos personnages prendront leur destinée dans leur mains. Ils seront des personnes vivantes sans nul doute car les evenements les inspireront. Je vous felicite de tout mon cœur—je vous envie un tout petit brin.

Je n'ai rien brule.[2] On parle comme ça et puis le courage manque. Il y en a comme ça qui parlent du suicide! Et puis c'est toujours quelque chose qui manque, tantot c'est la force, tantot la perseverance, tantot le courage. Le courage de reussir ou le courage de reconnaître son impuissance. Ce qui reste toujours ineradicable et cruel c'est la peur de la finalité. On temporise avec le destin, on cherche a tromper le desir, on tàche d'escamoter sa vie. Les hommes sont toujours lâches. Ils ont peur du "jamais plus". Je crois qu'il n'y a que les femmes qui ont le vrai courage.—

Je travaille un peu. J'agonise la plume a la main. Six lignes en six jours. Qu'en pensez Vous? Beau? Eh? Je Vous embrasse de tout mon cœur.

J. Conrad.

---

[1] Conrad seems to be answering a letter from Mme Poradowska in response to his of 26 November or 3 December and the content indicates an immediate answer. Conrad's disclaimer about burning his material confirms the sequence.

[2] In his preceding letter, Conrad had threatened to burn 'Two Vagabonds'.

Thursday, a quarter to midnight [6 or 13 December 1894]
[London]

Dear Aunt

I have just returned and found your letter. I take up my pen immediately, to answer you while the impression of your letter is still fresh.

First, in general terms: very good! Then as to details, I tell you sincerely, honestly, and as a friend that the idea of the first chapter is very good – very fine, very effective. The development of the plot seems to me absolutely faultless. I foresee a series of dramatic situations. It is up to you to make them gripping, and I give you my word that I believe in all conscience you will be absolutely equal to the task – for one cannot devise such a framework without having an idea of the details. Detail is most important in a novel such as the one you have in mind. And then for a Polish story, I see you are on the right path, for the women will have more character than the men, which with us is unquestionably the case. I am sure if you begin to write according to the plan you gave me, your characters will take their destiny into their own hands. Without any doubt, they will be living people, for events will inspire them. With all my heart, I congratulate you; I envy you just a little.

I have burned nothing. One talks like that, but then one lacks the courage. There are those who talk like that of suicide. And then there is always something lacking, sometimes strength, sometimes perseverance, sometimes courage. The courage to succeed or the courage to recognize one's impotence. What remains always cruel and ineradicable is the fear of finality. One temporizes with Fate, one seeks to deceive desire, one tries to play tricks with one's life. Men are always cowards. They are frightened of the expression 'nevermore'. I think only women have true courage.

I am working a little. I agonize with pen in hand. Six lines in six days. What do you think of that? Fine, eh? I embrace you warmly.

J. Conrad

To Marguerite Poradowska

Text   MS Yale; Rapin 151; G. &. S. 88

27 Dec. 1894
17 Gillingham St.

Ma très chère et très charmante Tante.

Mille souhaits de bonheur pour la nouvelle année et succés au nouveau livre![1] La dessus je Vous embrasse très fort.

Je pense si souvent à Vous! Tous les jours. Et je m'imagine Vous voir la plume a la main—la clarté de la lampe sur Votre tête pensive—la feuille blanche devant Vous—et le travail de l'imagination qui fait vivre dans la joie ou dans la souffrance tout ce monde d'âmes sans corps sous Votre front! Vous devez être bien heureuse. Vous voyez Votre œuvre, Vous. Tandis que moi je marche a tatons comme un avantureux aveugle.

La chose est faite. J'ai changé mon titre. Ce sera: "An Outcast of the Islands" Et la chose elle même est changée. Tout est changé excepté le doute. Tout—excepté la peur de ces phantômes que l'on evoque soi même et qui si souvent refusent d'obeir la cervelle qui les a crées.—

Enfin. Voilà le chap. VIII terminé. Encore quatre![2] Quatre siècles d'agonie—quatre minutes des délices et puis la fin—la tête vide—le decouragement et le doute eternel.—

Ecrivez moi un petit mot quand Vous aurez le temps. Rien qu'un mot. Parlez de Vous et du roman. Deux mots. Toujours le Votre

J. Conrad.

Veille Noël reçu 1ere epreuve d'Almayer'[s]Folly. 16 pages.

J'en ai eu horreur. Absolument horreur de la chose imprimée qui a l'air si bête—pire—vide de sens.—

27 December 1894
17 Gillingham Street

My very dear and very charming Aunt,

Ever so many happy wishes for the new year and success with the new book! With that, I embrace you very warmly.

I think of you so often! Every day. And I imagine seeing you, pen in

---

[1] *Pour Noémi.*

[2] In terms of the completed novel, this estimate means little; *An Outcast* comes to 26 chapters, divided into 5 parts of 4 to 6 chapters each.

hand, lamplight on your pensive head, blank paper before you – and the working of your imagination, which brings to life, in suffering or in joy, that whole world of bodiless spirits from beneath your brow. You must be very happy. You see your work, while I feel my way like an adventurous blind man.

The thing is done. I have changed my title. It will be:

An Outcast of the Islands. And the thing itself has been changed. Everything has been changed except doubt. Everything, except the fear of the ghosts which one evokes oneself and which often refuse to obey the brain that has created them.

Here is Chapter viii finished at last. Four to go! Four centuries of agony – four minutes of delight and then the end – an empty head – discouragement and eternal doubt.

Write me a short note when you have time. Only a word. Speak of yourself and the novel. Two words. Always yours.

J. Conrad

Christmas Eve received the first proofs of *Almayer's Folly*.
16 pages.
I was horrified: absolutely horrified by the thing in print, looking so stupid – worse – senseless.

1895

To Edward Garnett

Text MS McMillan; G. 31

Jan 4th 95.
17 Gillingham St.

Dear Mr. Garnett

Coming home after a late prowl I found your good letter.

Le me thank you without delay for this fresh proof of that interest you have been good enough to take in my venture. Whether the book is reset or no the fact of your interference in the matter remains—also the pleasure it has caused me.[1]

I intended to write to you next week but as it is I may say it now. I wanted to ask you to name a day—next week or week after next—in fact when you like—when you would dine with me. I have no engagements— At least no engagements that couldn't be shied overboard at any time without disturbing the harmony of the universe. And would you mind then travelling as far as 17 Gillingham Street? (Victoria). The country is quiet just now hereabouts and the inhabitants have given up the practice of cannibalism I believe some time ago. Name day and hour.— I have no doubt that Mr Chesson will handle A's Folly very tenderly. I shall send on the preface tomorrow (Sat:).[2]

Your book not there yet.[3] You prod my curiosity. To me, attempt is much more fascinating than the achievement because of boundless possibilities; and in the world of ideas attempt or experiment is the dawn of evolution.

Once more thanks! Yours very faithfully
J. Conrad.

---

[1] Garnett's constant solicitude made him the much-loved friend and counsellor of Conrad and many other authors. The book was *Almayer's Folly*, the matter perhaps the omission of a brief paragraph: see the letter to W. H. Chesson, another of Unwin's readers (early January? 1895).

[2] This 'Author's Note' was not used in the Unwin edition.

[3] *An Imaged World: Poems in Prose* (Dent, 1894).

To Edward Garnett
Text   MS Indiana; G. 32

Tuesday evening. [8 January 1895]
17 Gillingham Street
SW.

Dear Mr Garnett.

Your date and hour will do very well. I shall be in the City on Wednesday week and if You are there also on that day perhaps I may pick you up somewhere on my way to the wild west?[1] If this proposal [is] unacceptable don't trouble to say so. I shall understand if I don't hear from you that I am to wait for you at home at 7 pm.

I have Your book; have read it once and now am strolling backwards and forwards with great delight—amongst Your words, Your sentences and Your thoughts.—

You no doubt have the gift of the "mot juste", of those sentences that are like a flash of limelight on the facade of a cathedral or a flash of lightning on a landscape when the whole scene and all the details leap up before the eye in a moment and are irresistibly impressed on memory by their sudden vividness. But of that more when we meet. Now I want only to say that "An Imaged World" charmed my eyes with a charm of its own—distinc[t]ly.

Yours very faithfully

J. Conrad.

To W. H. Chesson
Text   MS Smith (letter pasted into copy of *Almayer's Folly*); Unpublished

Wednesday [early January? 1895][2]
17 Gillingham St. S.W.

Dear Mr. Chesson.

In reference to paragraph (of 2 sentences) left out in the setting of Almayer I must own that the fault is mine entirely. The typescript is in error not the printer. If it can be rectified without too much trouble I would be very glad.

As to the literary notices of the publication, I understand that you

---

[1] Garnett's visit to the wilds of Pimlico was arranged for 16 January.
[2] The only certainty is a date somewhere between the acceptance of *Almayer's Folly* in October and its publication on 29 April. We place the letter in early January because the first proofs had arrived on Christmas Eve, and (in the hope of publication in early March) the rest were probably sent in quick succession.

were good enough to undertake their composition.[1] I am quite content to be in your hands but it struck me that perhaps a suggestion from me would meet with your approval. Could you not say something about being a "civilized story in savage surroundings?" Something in that sense if not in those words—As to that preface[2] (which I have shown you) I trust it may be dispensed with, but if it must appear you are quite right—"*aversion from*" not "aversion for" as I wrote—and stuck to like a lunatic. You will correct?

Yours very faithfully,
J. Conrad.

Remember me to Mr. Garnett

To Marguerite Poradowska

Text MS Yale; Rapin 156; G. & S. 89

Mercredi.[3] [30 January or 6 February 1895]
17 Gillingham St
London S W.

Ma chère Tante.

Je ne Vous demande pas pardon de mon long silence. Vous savez que ce n'est pas parce que je n'ai pas pensé a Vous—et Vous devez savoir que je pense a Vous tous le jours. Seulement j'ai été plongé dans ce decouragement que tout le monde connait mais qui me connait mieux—je crois sans vanité—que tout le reste du monde.—

Avez Vous travaillé? Etes Vous contente de Votre travail? Voila les questions qui se posent devant moi chaque jour et qu'une petite lettre de Vous pourrait résoudre un beau matin. Ce n'est pas que je désire Vous voler Votre temps si précieux—mais je puis bien Vous demander deux ou trois ligne—comme charité. Charité belle dame!—Cette espèce de mendicité n'est pas interdite, Voyons!—

Quand a moi "tout passe, tout lasse".—Je viens d'écrire xi en tête d'une page blanche et blanche elle restera peut etre dix jours ou je ne me connais pas.— Vous voyez mon idée du travail. Drôle! n'est ce pas? Je

---

[1] Conrad presumably means the advance publicity rather than the reviews.

[2] Although dated 1895, this 'Author's Note' was not published until the Collected Edition of 1921. By that time, the manuscript belonged to John Quinn, the collector of Conradiana.

[3] Two facts appear to locate this letter in late January or early February: Conrad's reference to Chapter xi of *An Outcast*, for which he needed time after the completion of Chapter viii, cited in the 27 December letter; and his reference to a long silence since his last letter. Further, matters of paper and handwriting assign this letter to a period no earlier than 1894. Other possibilities are 23 January or 13 February.

n'ai pas été très bien cette quinzaine. Ni sommeil ni appetit. Pas malade
du tout du reste.—

> Je Vous embrasse de tout mon cœur
> Tout a Vous J. Conrad.

> Wednesday [30 January or 6 February 1895]
> 17 Gillingham Street
> London S.W.

My dear Aunt,

I ask no forgiveness for my long silence. You know it's not because I
haven't thought of you; you must know that I think of you every day. But
I have been plunged in that despondency everyone knows, yet which
knows me better (I speak without vanity) than anyone else in the world.

Have you been working? Are you pleased with your work? These are
the questions, recurring every day, that a short letter from you could
resolve one fine morning. Not that I want to steal your so precious time,
but I could well ask you for two or three lines – as charity. Charity, lovely
lady! This kind of begging is not forbidden, is it, now?

As for me, 'everything passes, everything wears out'. I have just
written 'xi' at the head of a blank page, and blank it will remain, perhaps
for ten days – or I don't know myself. You see my idea of work. Amusing
– isn't it? I have not been well this fortnight. Neither sleep nor appetite.
Not at all ill.

I embrace you warmly.

> Yours
> J. Conrad

To Marguerite Poradowska
Text   MS Yale; Rapin 157; G. & S. 90

> Samedi[1] [23? February 1895]
> 17. Gillingham St
> London S.W.

Chère Tante.

Pour Vous expliquer pourquoi je ne Vous ai pas encore remercié pour

---

[1] The date is fairly certain. The reference to *Almayer's Folly* puts the letter before the first
week in March. The reference to Mme Poradowska's *Marylka* places the letter after 15
February, when the first instalment of her novel appeared. The first Saturday after the
15th is the 16th, a possible but not probable date. The 23rd would have given Conrad
time to read the instalment.

"Marylka" il faut Vous dire que j'etais au lit, assez arrangé, chez mon ami Hope[1] tandis que Votre livre m'attendait a Londres. Je suis revenu hier seulement.—

Chère et bonne, Vous avez massacré ce pauvre livre! Et Brunetière— qui est le seul coupable—est aussi un imbecile.[2] Mais ce qui reste est bien delicieux, et il y a l'espace, le souffle du vent dans Votre description des champs ukrainiens.[3] C'est etonnant! Vous n'avez jamais été la? N'est-ce pas?

Je ne me trompe pas si je pense que la scène: Père et fille, a été abregée?[4] Dites? Tout est bien, très bien—sans aucune flatterie. Neanmoins j'aimairais bien abreger Brunetière disons: d'une tête. (L'imbecile!).—

Alm: parait premiere semaine de mars.[5] "The Outcast etc etc" fait son petit bonhome de chemin au millieu des pleurs et des grincements des dents usuels. C'est ma nature d'etre misérable, un décavé de la morale, un banqueroutier du courage. Je devrais partir pour Terre-Neuve pour affaire,[6] mais je ne me sens guère en état et le voyage est remis.—

Ecrivez-moi quand le cœur Vous en dit. Je Vous embrass[e] bien fort. Toujours a Vous.

J. Conrad

Vous connaissez mon culte Daudet.[7] Croyez Vous que ce serait ridicule de ma part de lui envoyer mon livre—moi qui a lu tous les siens sous tous les cieux? Ce n'est pas pour qu'il le lise—simplement un acte d'hommage car après tout il est un de mes enthousiasmes de jeunesse qui a survecu—même qui a grandi.

Qu'en pensez-Vous?

Dites moi comment va Votre livre. J'ai une envie de pousser une pointe jusqu'a a Passy—pour voir le manuscrit.

Mon editeur me parle d'une traduction française. Que dois-je faire?

Ah mon Dieu. Comme tout est noir noir noir. Ceci est un de mes mauvais jours. Faîtes pas attention. Embrassade.

---

[1] G. F. W. Hope, who lived in Essex.
[2] The literary critic who had succeeded Buloz as editor of the *Revue des Deux Mondes*.
[3] Chapter II of the novel.
[4] Chapter IV.
[5] Not until 29 April.
[6] Nothing came of this project.
[7] Conrad often referred to Daudet, and also wrote an article upon his death, originally published in the *Outlook* (9 April 1898) and later included in *Notes on Life and Letters* (1921).

Saturday [23? February 1895]
17 Gillingham Street
London S.W.

Dear Aunt,

To explain why I have not yet thanked you for *Marylka*, I must tell you that I was in bed, in rather poor shape, at the home of my friend Hope, while your book awaited me in London. I returned only yesterday.

My dear and good Aunt, you have mangled this poor book. And Brunetière, who is alone responsible, is, moreover, an imbecile. But what remains is very delightful, and there is space, the blowing of the wind in your description of the Ukrainian countryside. It's astonishing. You have never been there? Isn't that so?

I am not mistaken in thinking the scene between father and daughter has been shortened? Is that right? It's all good, very good – without any flattery. Nevertheless, I should indeed like to shorten Brunetière by, let us say, a head. (The imbecile!)

Almayer will be published the first week in March. *The Outcast, etc. etc.* goes on its foolish little way in the midst of the usual wailing and gnashing of teeth. My nature is to be miserable, morally beggared, bankrupt of courage. I should be leaving for Newfoundland on business, but I hardly feel well enough, and the trip is postponed.

Write to me when you feel inclined. I embrace you warmly.

Ever yours

J. Conrad

You know my Daudet worship. Do you think it would be foolish of me to send him my book – I who have read all his, in all weathers? It's not so that he might read it – simply an act of homage, for after all he is one of my youthful enthusiasms that has survived – and even grown.

What do you think about this?

Tell me how your book is going. I am tempted to make a detour as far as Passy – to see the manuscript.

My publisher speaks of a French translation. What should I do?

Good God! How black, black, black everything is! This is one of my bad days. Pay no attention. Kisses.

To Edward Garnett

Text   MS Virginia; J–A, I, 173; G. 33

Friday [8 March 1895][1]
17 Gillingham St. S.W.

Dear Garnett.

I send You 4 chapters of the "Outcast" who—as you will perceive—is very much so. More than ever.—Your talk yesterday put so much life into me that I am reluctantly compelled to suspect You of good nature. Do not be offended for I do not mean any harm in charging you with such a "bourgeois" (or Philistine) failing. Even our friends are not perfect! This world is a dreary place and a prey to minor virtues. A dreary place—unless a fellow is a Willems of some kind[2] and is stuffed full of emotions—without any moral— when he may discover some joviality or other at the bottom of his load of anguish. But that's a lottery; an illegal thing: the invention of the Devil.—

In chap. XII beginning with the words "And now they are—" are the two pars in the new style.[3] Please say in the margin what you think. One word will do. I am very much in doubt myself about it; but where is the thing, institution or principle which I do not doubt?!

I shall advise You by autograph of my return from the Cont. because the fashionable intelligence of the Pall Mall neglects me in a most unaccountable way.[4] Till then

Vale

Yours   J Conrad.

To T. Fisher Unwin

Text   MS Yale; Unpublished

Brussels.
Hotel Royal Nord.
12 March 95.

Dear Mr Unwin.

As you have been good enough to mention to me several times Your willingness to arrange for a French translation of Almayer's Folly I venture now to ask you for Your good offices in that matter.[5] My aunt is

---

[1] Date supplied by Garnett.

[2] The chief character of *An Outcast of the Islands*.

[3] Conrad had shifted from past to present tense but returned to the old style when Garnett apparently disapproved. The passage in question begins on p. 135.

[4] Ignored, no doubt, by the *Pall Mall Gazette* (an evening newspaper), Conrad returned from the Continent on 15 March.

[5] Not until 1919 was *Almayer's Folly* to appear in a French translation.

too unwell to undertake the work now, and she will be too busy with her own forthcoming novel to make any arrangements for the future—unless a very remote one; and this does not meet my views.

I have sent the proof sheets to Paris to "Th: Bentzon" (Mme Blanc)[1] who writes on England and America in the Revue des Deux Mondes and knows the literature and institutions of both countries. My aunt (who is her colleague on the staff of the "Revue") is writing to her to day asking her to read the work and if possible to write a short appreciation of it. It would be a good thing—only I am afraid it is not in the traditions of the 'Revue' to publish anything of that kind. They do have, now and then, an analysis of the work of more known men; but in my case I am afraid it would be too much of an uphill drag to obtain Brunetière's[2] (who is a dried-up mummy) consent. Still we shall try; for the thing is well worth trying.—

I return to town next week[3]—for the *18th*. Isn't the 18th the date for the appearance of a certain Immortal work?![4]

I warn you that if I am disappointed I shall—surely—have some kind of a fit; and if I die on your office-carpet the Conservative papers will have big headlines. "Horrible cruelty of a well-known Publisher"[5] and not even the bravery of the young men of the Daily Chronicle shall save You from popular fury.

The above frivolity of expression disguises very deep feeling. In common mercy to a suffering fellow creature let it be the 18th without fail.

I am—in great anguish—

Yours very faithfully

J. Conrad.

---

[1] 'Th. Bentzon' was the pseudonym of Marie Thérèse (de Solms) Blanc (1840–1907), a prolific journalist and novelist, author of *The Condition of Woman in the United States*, 1895.
[2] Brunetière, the editor.
[3] On the 15th.
[4] Unwin had set back the publication date of *Almayer's Folly* from the first week in March to the 18th. Actual publication was still six weeks off.
[5] Unwin's politics were Liberal.

To Edward Garnett

Text MS Colgate; J–A, 1, 173; G. 34

Friday morning [15 March 1895][1]
17 Gillingham St.
S.W.

Dear Garnett

I arrived from Brussels about an hour ago and found Your letter. I've read it with my hat on rug over the arm, and umbrella handle by its tassel-string to my finger. Then I undressed, unpacked and before breaking bread read once more. I could not have had a more charming welcome. To be read—as you do me the honour to read me—is an ideal experience—and the experience of an ideal; and as I travel from sentence to sentence of your message I feel my unworthiness more and more. Your appreciation has for me all the subtle and penetrating delight of unexpected good fortune—of some fabulously lucky accident like the finding of a gold nugget in a deserted claim, like the gleam of a big diamond in a handful of blue earth.

Theory is a cold and lying tombstone of departed truth. (For truth is no more immortal than any other delusion.) Yet a man is nothing if not perverse.—That's why Willems[2] lays* buried under my pet theory even while I stand by, lamenting and grinning with blue spade in my hand.

I cannot weep, by all the devils! I cannot even sneer at my dead. All you say is true. All. Absolutely—and the only thing I can think of is to administer to myself a moral bastinado—say five hundred on the soles of my unsteady and erring feet.—

Having propitiated You by the barbarous cruelty of my punishment I prof[f]er my request. Will you meet me next Thursday? any time after six. Or name a day and the time that would suit You best. We shall *not* talk of Willems. Just simply dine—feast of body—not of soul. Soul be hanged!

Yours very faithfully

J Conrad.

This is only to let you know that letter and MS received—also that your words have not fallen into barren ground. The crop will ripen in good time. You shall see.—

[1] Garnett's dating is affirmed by Conrad's return from Brussels, which occurred on the 15th.
[2] Of *An Outcast.*

To T. Fisher Unwin

Text   MS Yale; Keating 11

Thursday. [28 March 1895][1]
[Elstree]

Dear Mr. Unwin.

I do not want to make myself a nuisance—at least not very much, but since I have been staying with my friends here I became aware that the expectation of Almayer's Folly is unsettling this glorious and free country. All the people that have been told to look out for the book in March are writing letters full of anxiety and tears to know when—Oh! When! they will be able to get the immortal work.[2] Letters by every post. They come from North and west and south and east—they are as numerous as the raindrops—as persistent and loud as the wild west wind.—

Not being able to say anything definite I find I am becoming unpopular. One lady even hinted in her letter that she believed there was no such book and never would be. You will ruin my career at its very outset by a too prolonged delay. Can You? Will you? give me a date so that I can appease the universal thirst for information—and be called blessed by [an] anxious and enthusiastic crowd of respectable and intelligent people.—Do! If you can.—

I am working as conscientiously as a penny-in-the-slot machine;[3]— and about as fast. Likewise the quality of my work comes up to the standard of the mechanical Supply C°—

Meantime I remain Yours

Very faithfully

J. Conrad.

Address:
c/o Rev. L. Sanderson.
Elstree.
Herts.

---

[1] In his letter to Mme Poradowska, 2 April, Conrad indicates that he has just returned from Elstree, where he has been staying with the Sandersons. Since the stay lasted for ten days, Conrad must have written to Unwin on 28 March, which was the only Thursday in that period.
[2] The original publication date was early March. The actual date was 29 April.
[3] On *An Outcast*.

To Marguerite Poradowska

Text MS Yale; Rapin 158; G. & S. 92

2^d Avril 1895.
[London]

Ma chère Tante.

Je ne comprends pas du tout. C'est la premiere lettre de Vous que je recois depuis mon depart.[1] Je viens de rentrer d'Elstree ou j'ai passé 10 jours dont 4 au lit.[2] Je repons tout de suite car je suis très inquiet. Vous etes evidemment malade d'ame car Vous avez surmené le corps. Voila d'ou le degout et le decouragement . Je souffre avec Vous car je sais que rien n'est plus cruel que le desepoir intime qui Vous fait souffrir. On est si seul. Que puis-je dire? Rien que des mots d'affection vraie. Votre lettre m'a bouleversée absolument.—

Je Vous dis moi que Votre Roman est bon—que le plan, l'idée sont excellents.—Dans ma lettre qui est perdue je Vous parlais de Marylka. Je Vous ai dit comme la scène de la noce est saisissante.[3] Et aussi j'ai parlé de la fin calme, tranquille promesse de paix. C'est très joli très joli. Mais le prochain livre sera beau. Je le sens. J'en suis sur. Courage. Vous avez là une magnifique mine des diamants—des situations ou Vous pourrez mettre tout Votre charme et toute Votre force. Votre cœur parlera lui même j'en suis sur!—Certain!!—J'ai obtenu le livre.[4] Je vous l'envoie demain. Pensez a moi qui Vous aime bien qui souffre et se rejouit avec Vous. En toute hâte

toujours le votre

Conrad.

Mes compl^{ts} a Mme Votre Mère. J'ai été bien fâche de la nouvelle de sa maladie. Le fait est que je suis parti assez inquiet de son êtat et je me demandai chaque jour... enfin tout est bien

2 April 1895
[London]

My dear Aunt,

I do not understand at all. This is the first letter I've had from you

---

[1] From Brussels, where he had been from 8 to 15 March.

[2] At the Sandersons'.

[3] *Revue des Deux Mondes*, 15 March 1895; Chapter XXIII. Rapin summarizes this and the following scene, p. 159, n. 1 and 2.

[4] An advance copy of *Almayer's Folly*, which was not to be published for another four weeks.

since my departure. I have just returned from Elstree, where I spent ten days, four of them in bed. I am answering immediately because I am very worried. You are evidently sick at heart from having overworked your body. Thus, your disgust and discouragement. I suffer with you, for I know nothing crueller than the deep despair that makes you suffer. One is so alone. What can I say? Nothing but words of true affection. Your letter has absolutely staggered me.

I tell you myself that your novel is good – that the plan and the idea are excellent. In my missing letter, I spoke to you of *Marylka*. I told you how striking the wedding scene is. And I spoke also of the calm ending, a tranquil promise of peace. It is very pretty, very pretty. But the next book will be splendid. I feel it. I am certain of it. Courage. You have there a magnificent diamond mine – situations into which you can put all your charm and all your power. Your heart itself will speak, I know it! I am sure of it! Certain!! I have obtained the book. I shall send it to you tomorrow. Think of me who love you well, who suffer and rejoice with you. In all haste,

Always yours

Conrad

My regards to your mother. I was very upset by the news of her illness. The fact is that I left feeling uneasy about her condition, and I wondered about it every day ... at last all is well.

To Marguerite Poradowska

Text   MS Yale: Rapin 159; G. & S. 93

Vendredi Saint[1] [12 April 1895]
17. Gillingham St.
Londres S.W.

Chère Tante.

Merci de Votre bonne lettre ou Vous me dites tant des charmantes choses.—Je suis très heureux de savoir que le livre plait a Votre mère et Votre belle sœur.[2]

Je ne suis pas encore publié mais c'est pour ce mois pour sur. On ne peut pas me donner la date definitive encore. La maison Mac Millan de

---

[1] Because of references to *Almayer's Folly* and *An Outcast*, the year must be 1895. Good Friday fell on 12 April.

[2] Mme Émile Gachet, now ailing, and Mme Charles Gachet.

New York se charge de la publication en Amerique et a cause de la loi sur le Copyright il faut attendre qu'ils soient prêts la-bas[1]—

J'en suis a mon 17ème chap. Il y en aura vingt je pense sinon vingt-et-un.[2] Je donne bonne mesure cette fois-ci.—

Je vois que Vous êtes mieux. Cela s'aperçoit au ton de Votre lettre et cela me fait du bien... Je n'ai pas besoin de Vous recommander d'avoir du courage, du courage, toujours du courage. Je suis convaincu que Vous avez une belle œuvre en main.[3] Une belle œuvre! Vous la voyez bien aussi, sous bien des aspects. Il s'agit maintenant de choisir le point de vue definitif. Decision faite veuillez—sans tarder—m'en faire part. Je pense aussi souvent a votre roman qu'au mien. Plus peut-être. Je n'exagère pas. C'est vrai! Je Vous embrasse de tout mon cœur. Tout a Vous et toujours

J. Conrad.

Good Friday [12 April 1895]
17 Gillingham Street
London S.W.

Dear Aunt,

Thank you for your kind letter telling me about so many charming things. I am very happy to learn the book pleases your mother and sister-in-law.

I have not yet been published but shall be this month, for certain. They cannot give me a definite date yet. The Macmillan Company of New York is undertaking the American publication, and, because of the copyright law, we must wait until they are ready over there.

I am on my 17th chapter. I think there will be twenty, if not twenty-one. This time I am giving good measure.

I see you are better. That is clear from the tone of your letter, and it does me good ... I needn't urge you to have courage, courage, always courage. I am convinced you have a fine book in hand. A fine book! And you see it well from every point of view. Now it's a matter of settling on one of them. Once the decision is made, please let me know without delay. I think as often of your novel as of my own. More often, perhaps. I'm not exaggerating. It's true! I embrace you warmly. Ever yours

J. Conrad

---

[1] Macmillan published only this one novel by Conrad. Unwin was to publish in England on the 29th.
[2] In all, *An Outcast* contained 26 chapters.   3 *Pour Noémi.*

To Marguerite Poradowska
Text   MS Yale; Rapin 160; G. & S. 93

30 Avril
1895
17. Gillingham St.
SW.

Ma bonne et chère Tante.

Je ne suis pas bien du tout. Je sors de mon lit et je pars pour Champel faire de l'hydrotherapie pour me remettre. Ceci Vous explique mon long silence. Vous savez quand je ne suis pas bien j'ai des accès de melancholie qui me paralysent la pensée et la volonté. J'ai toutefois beaucoup pensé a Vous et a Votre livre—*le livre* a venir.[1] Une fois l'idée genérale arretée il faut Vous laisser guider par l'inspiration du moment. Vous êtes trop artiste pour faire fausse route. *Vous* pouvez craindre de Vous fourvoyer dans une impasse—mais *moi* qui Vous juge "d'en dehors" je suis absolument sans crainte de Vous voir faire fausse route. J'ai la plus parfaite confiance dans Votre inspiration mais aussi je trouve Vos doutes, Vos hesitations absolument naturelles. Que je connais ça! Ma pauvre, chère Marguerite!

L'idée de paraître en polonais est assez bonne. Je doute qu'il y aie de l'argent la dedans; cependant on peut essayer.—Ecrivez donc a Angèle![2] Je crois que Vous Vous trompez dans Vos idées la dessus. Peut-être n'ont-ils pas reçus les numeros de la R?[3] Qui sait?

Je n'ai pas vu Fisher Unwin encore rapport a la traduction. Aujourd'hui. Pars demain. Vous ecrirais de Champel—semaine prochaine.

Toujour et tout a Vous
Conrad.

30 April 1895
17 Gillingham Street
S.W.

My kind and dear Aunt,

I am not at all well. To set myself up again, I am quitting my bed and

---

[1] *Pour Noémi.*

[2] Mme Poradowska's niece, Aniela Zagórska. Conrad probably thought that she would undertake the translation of *Almayer's Folly* into Polish. Later, her daughter, also called Aniela, translated the novel under the title *Szaleństwo Almayera* (Warsaw, 1928). The younger Aniela became the principal translator of Conrad's works into Polish.

[3] The three numbers of the *Revue* containing *Marylka*.

going to Champel for hydrotherapy. This explains to you my long silence. You know that when I'm not well I have attacks of melancholy which paralyse my thought and will. Nevertheless I often think of you and your book, *the* coming book. Once the general idea is settled, you must let yourself be guided by the inspiration of the moment. You are too much of an artist to go astray. *You* can be afraid of losing your way in a dead end, but *I*, who judge you from without, am absolutely without fear of your going astray. I have the most perfect confidence in your inspiration, but I also find your doubts, your hesitations absolutely natural. How well I know them, my poor, dear Marguerite!

The idea of appearing in Polish is quite good. I doubt if there will be any money in it; one can, however, still try. Write to Angèle by all means! I think your ideas on that subject are mistaken. Perhaps they did not receive the numbers of the *Revue*. Who knows?

I have not seen Fisher Unwin yet about the translation. Today. Leave tomorrow. Will write to you from Champel – next week.

Ever yours

Conrad

To Edward Garnett

Text   MS Colgate; G. 35

May 1st 1895
17 Gillingham St
6. Am.

Dear Garnett

I am going to look for Willems[1] in Switzerland. It is written. I go! Today at 9 am.

I resolved yesterday. Called on F[isher] U[nwin] who says Henley[2] can't read more than 60 pages of the immortal work[3]—after which he "lays it down". Despair and red herrings! Suicide by thirst on Henley's doorstep—no. Emigration to Champel and hydropathy when return with Alpenstock branded (untruthfully) "Monte Rosa" and brain the sixty-page-power Henley. Cause célèbre. Fame. Therefore I go Tuan![4]—

Seriously, I find I can't work. Simply can't! I am going to try what

---

[1] Of *An Outcast*.
[2] William Ernest Henley (1849–1903), the poet, critic and highly influential editor of the *New Review*. Henley was later to serialize Conrad's *The Nigger of the 'Narcissus'*, in the *New Review* for August–December 1897. See Conrad's long letter to Henley, 18 October 1898.
[3] *Almayer's Folly*, published two days earlier.
[4] A Malay honorific.

mountain air combined with active firehose (twice a day)[1] will do for divine inspiration. I shall try it for about 3 weeks and maybe the lenient gods will allow me to finish that infernal Manuscript.[2] Sorry can't send you the 4 chap. Just came from type—not corrected. I shall (must) take them with me and when back administer to you the whole of the poison in one large (and therefore merciful) dose.

I take advantage of Your friendly disposition towards my unworthy self to ask you for news of Alm[ayer] in about a fortnight. Speak true talk to him who has been raised from the dust by Your merciful hand—that is: say what *You* think of the chances.

Yours ever faithfully

J. Conrad.

Address J. Conrad.
La Roseraie
Champel.
Genève

To T. Fisher Unwin
Text   MS Texas; Unpublished

2^d May. 1895

Champel les Bains

Genève.

Dear Mr Unwin.

I send you my address in case you have something very good to tell me at some future time. Also a request for the expedition of more copies. I give the addresses on last page so that you can send them to the publish^g dept^t.[3] Sorry to give you all this trouble.

Yours very faithfully

J Conrad.

La Roseraie.
Champel-les-Bains
Genève

---

[1] The Champel cure involved being buffeted by jets of water.
[2] *An Outcast* was completed on 16 September 1895.
[3] The list of addresses has not survived.

To Marguerite Poradowska
Text   MS Yale; Rapin 161; G. & S. 94

2^d May. 95
Champel

Chère Tante.

Je viens d'arriver ici—et je me sens mieux déjà. Ecrivez moi un mot bien vite pour me dire comment Calmann Levy[1] a repondu a Votre lettre.

Je viens d'écrire a F. Unwin pour commander divers envois de mon livre et j'en fais envoyer une copie a Mr. Buls.[2] Ecrivez lui un mot pour dire que le livre vient de Votre part. Autrement il sera surpris.

Les journaux ecossais (quotidiens) ont commencé les critiques de ma "Folie". C'est court, journalistique mais très louangeur! Surtout le "Scotsman" grand journal d'Edimburg est presque enthusiasmé.[3] Le "Glasgow Herald" parle avec une bienveillance plus contenue.

Apresant nous attendons les Quotidiens de Londres et *surtout* les revues hebdomadaires non politiques. La première edition de 1100 copies est vendue.[4]

Voilà toutes les nouvelles.

Parlez moi de Vous—de Votre travail—de Vos projets

Vous embrasse bien fort

Votre Conrad

la Roseraie
Champel les Bains
Genève

2 May 1895
Champel

Dear Aunt,

I have just arrived here – and feel better already. Write me a note quickly to let me know how Calmann-Lévy answered your letter.

[1] The Paris publisher to whom *Marylka* was submitted.

[2] Charles Buls (1837–1914), Burgomaster of Brussels and author of several art books, courted Mme Poradowska before her marriage and after the death of her husband (information in Gee & Sturm, from Mlle Aniela Zagórska).

[3] The review in the *Scotsman* begins: 'Dr Joseph Conrad's story, *Almayer's Folly*, is a remarkable book, which will probably attract all the more attention because its author's name is new to readers of novels, and because its scene of action lies in regions as yet little, if at all, visited by novelists' (29 April 1895).

[4] Not the case. After vigorous promotion by Unwin's traveller, booksellers took up almost the whole edition, but sales to the public went very slowly. See Garnett, p. 16.

I have just written to F. Unwin to order various consignments of my book, and I had a copy sent to Mr Buls. Write him a note saying the book comes from you. Otherwise, he will be surprised.

The Scottish dailies have begun to review my *Folly*. Brief, journalistic, but full of praise! Above all, the *Scotsman*, the major Edinburgh paper, is almost enthusiastic. The *Glasgow Herald* speaks with a more restrained benevolence.

Now we are waiting for the London dailies and, *especially*, the non-political weeklies. The first edition of 1100 copies has been sold.

That's all the news.

Tell me about yourself – your work, your projects.

Warmest embraces

Your Conrad

La Roseraie
Champel les Bains, Geneva

To Mr Newton
Text   MS Northwestern; Unpublished

4th April[1] 1895. [4 May]
Geneva.

Dear Mr Newton[2]

On the day after I had the pleasure of meeting you in Fenchurch street I left London for the continent. I have written yesterday to my Publisher instructing him to send you a copy of my work.[3] I have no doubt he will do it without delay but I wanted to explain to you why there is nothing written from the Author on the flyleaf of the book. As You see it was nothing but stress of circumstances that prevented me from signing Your copy. Necessity—not neglect. I was called away so suddenly that I had no time to call at Fisher Unwin's and do my whole duty by You—for which unfortunate occur[r]ence I crave Your indulgence.

---

[1] 'April' is a mistake. Conrad arrived at Champel on 2 May; see letter to Marguerite Poradowska of that date.

[2] It is not clear whether this is Edward Newton (a director of Methuen, the publishing house), or his father, John. John Newton, whom Tadeusz Bobrowski called 'that kindhearted Professor' (Najder, p. 64), tutored Conrad for the second mate's exam. He ran a Navigation School at the Well Street Sailors' Home (cf. notes to letter to Vernon Weston, 26 May 1896).

[3] *Almayer's Folly.*

Believe me, Dear Mr Newton, with the greatest esteem, Yours very faithfully

J. Conrad.

La Roseraie.
Champel
Genève.

To Marguerite Poradowska
Text   MS Yale; Rapin 162; G. & S. 95

6. Mai. 95
"La Roseraie". Champel
Geneve.

Chère et bonne Marguerite.

Je viens de recevoir Votre lettre. Elle m'a fait bien plaisir. Je vois là que Vous êtes mieux et surtout libre d'esprit.

C'est ça! Ecrivez ecrivez. Je veux avoir une douzaine des chapitres a entendre a Paris. Je m'arrête un jour exprès pour le roman point pour autre chose.

Quand a moi je continue a ecrire et cela n'en finit pas. Je crains les longueurs mais je ne sais pas comment leur echapper.

Pardonnez ma courte lettre Je ne Vous en aime pas moins Vous savez.
Embrasse bien fort

J. Conrad.

Vous avez eu tort de dire a Buls que c'est moi.[1] De Vous c'etait naturel. De moi plutot une impertinence. Ne croyez Vous pas?—

6 May 1895
'La Roseraie', Champel, Geneva

Dear and kind Marguerite,

I have just had your letter. It gave me great pleasure. I see from it you are better and, above all, free from care.

That's it. Write, write. I want to listen to a dozen chapters in Paris. I am stopping one day, expressly for the novel – for no other reason.

As for myself, I continue to write, and the writing never ends. I am afraid of being tedious but don't know how to avoid it.

[1] See letter to Mme Poradowska, 2 May, and to Buls, 12 May.

Excuse my short letter. I don't love you any the less for it, you know.

Warmest embrace

J. Conrad

You were wrong to tell Buls I sent it. From you it was natural. From me, rather an impertinence. Don't you think so?

To Edward Garnett
Text   MS Yale; G. 36; Keating 23

12th May 1895
Champel. Geneve.

Dear Garnett.

Thanks for your friendly letter. It gave me great pleasure tho' your Highness was pleased to jest, and notwithstanding sombre allusions to "dead Lions" which by a fatal association of ideas caused me to think of myself as a "live donkey." Still, being alive is something.—I shall let you know when I come back—but I do not for a moment wish to suggest the propriety of you hiring a few of the unemployed to bestrew the path of my fourwheeler with rushes and thistles.—I wish to return to London incognito. Respect this! (as in the formula of the edicts of that poor dear Emperor of China)

I am working every day:—tolerably bad work.[1] Like poor Risler the Elder's cashier "I haf' no gonfidence".[2]—Some people I have sent the book to wrote very kindly. They seem rather surprised—and I am amused.—

I dread the moment when you shall see my "Outcast" as a whole. It seems frightful bosh. I never felt like that even in the first days of my "Folly".

Meantime I live lazily and digest satisfactorily. At my age that last is important. Do not laugh. Your time will come—Slowly I hope.[3]

I see You have lighted Your camp fire in a new place. I shall dwell here for another fortnight.

Yours ever

Conrad.

---

[1] On *An Outcast*. Conrad later told Pinker he had completed one-third of the novel at Champel. He was to finish it in a little more than four months.

[2] In Alphonse Daudet's *Fromont jeune et Risler aîné* (1874).

[3] Garnett was eleven years younger than Conrad.

To Charles Buls

Text MS Yale; Rapin 162; G. & S. 96

12th Mai 1895.
Champel.
Geneva.

Monsieur.

Il m'est très difficile de Vous exprimer le plaisir avec lequel j'ai lu Votre lettre si bienveillante. Certes en vous envoyant mon livre[1] je n'ai pas eu la plus lointaine pretention d'occuper autant de Votre temps—temps precieux a Vous même et aux autres. Tout au plus je me permettais d'espérer que Vous voudrez bien y jeter un coup d'œil dans Vos rares moments perdus.

Aussi j'ai ressenti une certaine confusion a la vue de Votre lettre—de cette preuve de l'attention serieuse dont Vous avez bien voulu m'honorer. Je Vous assure que je suis très conscient de l'insuffisance de mon mérite en cette matière. Seulement je me dis qu'avec Votre habitude de juger les hommes et les choses—et le bon cœur aidant—Vous avez peut etre aperçu là ce desir de bien faire qui est le seul motif au monde qui peut faire excuser bien des erreurs et toutes les ambitions.

Je m'empresse d'écrire a ma bonne Tante pour la remercier aussi. C'est grâce a Elle que j'ai l'honneur d'être jugé par Vous: et c'est encore grâce a Elle que je puis me rendre bien compte de la haute valeur de ce jugement.—

Veuillez agréer Monsieur l'assurance de ma gratitude et de ma considération la plus distinguée.

Jos Conrad.

12 May 1895
Champel, Geneva

Dear Sir,

It is very difficult for me to express the pleasure with which I have read your so friendly letter. Most certainly in sending you my book, I did not have the slightest claim to taking up so much of your time – time precious to you and to others. I permitted myself at the very most to hope that you would glance at it in your rare moments of idleness.

---

[1] *Almayer's Folly.* Conrad had wanted Buls to think of the book as a gift from Mme Poradowska. M. Buls's courtship of Conrad's 'aunt' may have caused additional embarrassment.

Thus I felt a certain amount of shame on seeing your letter – this proof of the serious attention with which you have kindly chosen to honour me. I assure you that I am very conscious of my lack of merit in this matter. Still, I tell myself that with your experience in judging men and affairs – and with the aid of your good nature – you have perhaps noticed there that wish to do well which is the sole intention in the world which can indeed excuse many errors and all ambitions.

I hasten to write to my good aunt to thank her also. It is because of her that I have the honour of being judged by you; and it is once again owing to her that I can indeed realize the high value of this judgement.

Please accept, Monsieur, the assurance of all my gratitude and esteem.

Jos Conrad

To Marguerite Poradowska
Text   MS Yale; Rapin 162; G. & S. 96

13 Mai. [1895]
[Champel]

Chère Petite Tante.

Je vous envois mon brouillon de lettre que j'expedie par même poste a M Buls. Quand je Vous verrais a Paris je Vous montrerais la sienne. Elle est superlativement charmante, bienveillante et indulgente. J'en suis littéralement tous confus. C'est encore a Vous que je dois ce plaisir—qui est bien grand. Je Vous embrasse—sur les deux joues. On le ferait a moins. J'attends une lettre de Vous chaque jour. Et *le roman?*[1] Parlez. Ecrivez

Toujours a Vous

J. Conrad.

13 May [1895]
[Champel]

Dear little Aunt,

I send you the rough draft of the letter to M. Buls, which I am posting at the same time. When I see you in Paris, I'll show you his. It is superlatively charming, friendly, and indulgent. I am, literally, taken

[1] *Marylka.*

aback. Once again, it is to you that I owe this pleasure, which is very great. I kiss you – on both cheeks. One would do it for less. I wait for a letter from you each day. And *the novel?* Speak. Write.

Ever yours

J. Conrad

To T. Fisher Unwin
Text   MS Yale; Keating 11

18th May 1895
Champel
Genève.

Dear Mr. Unwin.

Thanks very much for the cuttings which have been sent to me from Your office. Norman[1] has been very kind and I wrote to tell him that I trust I have done nothing against the etiquette of journalism.

I have since received many cuttings from the Agency. The provincial press is very good to me so far. The "Realm" so-so but with evident good will. But the poor old "World" kicks at me (in 15 lines) like a vicious donkey.[2] It is severe blame (perhaps deserved) but, I think, no criticism in the true sense of the word.

I trust You are well. I am living on here in a state of continual exasperation with myself and my work. Yesterday snow fell. Jura are all white.[3]

Yours faithfully,

J. Conrad.

I have rec^d 2 copies and acct for the lot. I write to day home directing them to send You cheque for £1.0.5. Mr Buls (an artistic burgomaster) wrote me a warm letter of commendation.[4]

---

[1] Unidentified person in the Unwin office.
[2] The review in the *World* begins: '*Almayer's Folly*, by Joseph Conrad, is a dreary record of the still more dreary existence of a solitary Dutchman doomed to vegetate in a small village in Borneo.' It concludes: 'Altogether the book is as dull as it well could be' (15 May 1895). The *Realm* commented: 'The story itself is crude and ill-arranged, and yet tantalisingly full of rich workmanship' (10 May).
[3] The Jura mountains, north of Geneva.
[4] See preceding letter and Conrad's to Buls, 12 May.

To Marguerite Poradowska

Text   MS Yale; Rapin 163; G. & S. 96

le 2oth May [189]5.
[letterhead: Champel]

Chère Tante.

Toutes mes felicitations. Je n'ai rien vu dans les journeaux ou—Vous pensez bien—je Vous aurai ecrit tout de suite pour Vous dire—pour essayer de Vous dire—toute la joie que j'eprouve a l'occasion de vos succès.[1]

Pas de "Figaro"[2] mais il m'attend a Londres sans doute. Si Vous m'envoyez votre exemplaire ici je Vous le rendrai dans quelques jours quand j'aurai le bonheur de Vous voir a Paris. Bientot je Vous enverrais la date de mon arrivée.[3]

Toute la presse de province a parlé avec bienveillance—d'aucuns avec enthusiasme de ma "Folie".[4] Un grand journal de Londres a parlé aussi tout ce qu'il y a de plus gentil.[5] Vous verrez ça. J'ai les coupures. Du reste les critiques se font attendre. Il y a evidemment qui hesitent a se prononcer mais les plumes jetées au vent flottent dans la direction voulue. Je travaille peu et mal—*très* mal.

Et Vous? Un petit accès de calme ou vent contraire—Votre changement de chapitre e[s]t très bien. Magnifique idée. Nous causerons longuement—très longuement. Une causerie—je trouve—me remets a l'ouvrage. En est-il de même avec Vous. Sinon je serais muet comme une carpe. Je ne Vous parlerai que par signes.—

Vous savez! Pas de Jonakowski d'aucune espèce.[6]—Pourquoi etes Vous tombée et pourquoi cet imbecile de Jonak n'etait pas là pour Vous soutenir puisqu'il est toujours fourré chez Vous quand on n'en a pas besoin?

Je vais assez bien Pas trop. Du reste Vous verrez bientôt

Toujours a Vous

J. Conrad.

---

[1] *Les Filles du pope (Popes et popadias)* had just received the French Academy's Jules Favre Prize. The news had been announced in French newspapers for 15 and 16 May.

[2] The *Figaro* 'Supplément littéraire' of 27 April 1895 contained a brief travel sketch by Mme Poradowska, 'Vers Lemberg'. Lemberg is the German name for Lwów.

[3] On 2 or 3 June.

[4] For samples, see Gordan, pp. 271ff., and Sherry (*Conrad: the Critical Heritage*, Routledge and Kegan Paul, 1973), pp. 47ff.

[5] Possibly the *Daily Chronicle* of 11 May 1895.

[6] The objectionable family mentioned in the letter of 25 December 1893.

20 May 1895
[letterhead: Champel]

Dear Aunt,

My warmest congratulations. I saw nothing in the papers, or, as you well know, I should have written to tell you at once – to try to tell you about all the joy I feel on the occasion of your success.

No *Figaro*, but it is probably waiting for me in London. If you send me your copy here, I shall return it in a few days, when I have the pleasure of seeing you in Paris. I shall soon send you the date of my arrival.

The entire provincial press has spoken favourably, some enthusiastically, of my *Folly*. A big London newspaper has also spoken in the most pleasant terms. That you will see: I have the clippings. Otherwise, the critics are keeping me waiting. There are evidently those who hesitate to make any decision, but straws tossed into the wind are floating in the right direction. I am working little and badly, *very* badly.

And you? A moment of calm or a contrary wind? Your revision of the chapter is very good. Magnificent idea. We shall chat at length, great length. A chat, I find, sends me back to work. Is it the same for you? If not, I shall be quiet as a mouse. I shall speak to you only by signs.

You know! No Jonakowski of any sort. Why did you fall and why, since he's always intruding on you when you don't need him, wasn't that imbecile of a Jonak there to help you up?

I am fairly well, but not excessively so. Anyway, you will soon see.

Ever yours

J. Conrad

To Marguerite Poradowska

Text MS Yale; Rapin 164; G. & S. 97

25th May 1895
[Champel]

Ma chère Tante—

Je viens de recevoir le Figaro. Mille fois merci. J'ai lu Lemberg.[1] Mais c'est charmant! Absolument charmant recit dans la vivacité et clarté de description. Depuis le premier paragraphe jusqu'au dernier. Tout y est. Tout! Mais enfin etes Vous allée à cette exposition ou non?[2] Moi j'ai

---

[1] See preceding letter.
[2] The Exposition of Polish art and industry held at Lemberg (Lwów) in 1894. Mme Poradowska's sketch of Lemberg included a description of the Exposition.

cru que Vous aviez refusé—mais je commence a douter. Je viens a Paris vers 2 ou 3 Juin du reste j[e] Vous ecrirai avant de quitter Geneve. Pardonnez si je finis. Je ne suis guère bien aujourd'hui. C'est passager.

Toujours votre

J.C.

Vous m'intriguez apropos de Gaba?[1] Qu'a-t-elle ecrit? Faudra me montrer.

25 May 1895
[Champel]

My dear Aunt,

I have just received the *Figaro*. Ever so many thanks. I have read 'Lemberg'. It is charming! A report absolutely charming in the liveliness and clarity of its description. From the first paragraph to the last. Everything is there. Everything! Well, did you finally go to that exhibition or not? I thought you had refused, but I begin to doubt it. I am coming to Paris around 2 or 3 June, though I shall write to you before leaving Geneva. Excuse me if I stop. I am not too well today. A passing ailment.

Ever yours

J.C.

Are you trying to interest me in Gaba? What has she written? You must show me.

To Paul Briquel

Text MS Meykiechel (Émilie Briquel's diary copy); Unpublished

Jeudi 30 mai 1895
[Champel]

Chér Monsieur[2]

Votre lettre à Mademoiselle votre sœur vient d'arriver, deux heures

---

[1] Gabriela Zagórska, Mme Poradowska's sister-in-law.

[2] Conrad met the Briquels, a family from Lorraine, at Champel in early May. They, too, were staying at La Roseraie. Paul had just put together his first collection of poems. His sister, Émilie, impressed Conrad by the range of her knowledge, and there seems to have been a romantic attachment between them, ended by her engagement to a local doctor on 10 February 1896.

avant mon départ.[1] Je me permets de vous écrire ces quelques lignes pour vous dire combien je vous suis obligé de la peine que vous vous êtes donné pour trouver une épigraphe pour mon prochain livre. Je suis emerveillé de votre mémoire et de la variété de vos lectures, car enfin, pour trouver un choix pareil à celui que vous m'avez envoyé il faut avoir lu beaucoup et bien.[2]

J'espère un jour avoir le plaisir de faire votre connaissance.

Le sort m'a favorisé d'une manière toute spéciale en me permettant de rencontrer ici, Madame votre Mère et Mademoiselle Emilie. Leur accueil plein de charme et de bienveillance sera un souvenir durable et précieux entre tous ceux que j'ai collectionné dans ma vie vagabonde.

Je me permets de dire: Tout à vous.

J. Conrad

Thursday, 30 May 1895
[Champel]

Dear Sir,

Your letter to your sister has just arrived, two hours before my departure. I allow myself to write these few lines to tell you how very obliged I feel for the trouble you have taken to find an epigraph for my next book. I am amazed by your memory and the variety of your reading; to come up with a quotation like the one you sent me, one must indeed be well and widely read.

I hope some day to have the pleasure of meeting you.

Fate has favoured me in a quite special way by allowing me to meet your mother and Mademoiselle Émilie here. Among all the memories I have collected in my wandering life, their charming and kindly welcome to me will remain lasting and precious.

I take the liberty of signing myself: Sincerely yours,

J. Conrad

---

[1] Conrad returned to London on 4 June.
[2] Paul Briquel suggested a line from Victor Hugo, but because of an oversight, it was not used. See Conrad's letter to Émilie, 14 November 1895.

To Edward Garnett

Text   MS Colgate; J–A, I, 174; G. 37

Friday. 7th June 95
17. Gillingham St. SW

My dear Garnett.

You must think me as faithless as Willems and think of me as hiding the blackness of my soul in epistolary silence.

I came back last Tuesday[1] and called upon the Enlightened Patron of Letters. Meant to call again in Pater*^{er}* Bdgs.[2] yesterday to see you. I received in the morning an invitation *by wire*!!!!! to dine with the E.P.L. and had to waste all day to find a man, just to tell him I could not see him. Do you understand the pathos of the situation? I had accepted the electric invitation having forgotten a very good fellow that was coming to smoke with me in the evening. It was easier, then, to put him off than the Patron.—

So I have added the festive and hospitable board of "my publisher" to my other experiences—and life seems tolerably complete. What else may I expect? What else that is new? Don't you think, dear Garnett, I had better die? True—there is love. That is always new—or rather startling being generally unexpected and violent—and fleeting. Still one must have some object to hang his affections upon—and I haven't. Oh! The world—since this morning—is one big grey shadow and I am one immense yawn. Do come to the rescue early next week and put some heart into me with your dear, precious brazen flattery. Will you? If so—please say so. Say when, and I shall try to go to sleep till then.—

The Patron has sent me McCarthy's letter.[3] I was as pleased as a dog with two tails till the notion came that it may be the white-bearded one's small joke. Perhaps the venerable man of politics felt frivolous. The latter seems to me at times as weird and unreal as Irving's knighthood. Isn't it funny? The whole thing is so c[h]aracteristic of the art, or profession or priesthood—or by whatever name you call playacting. I have smiled several times. Mr.—Brodribb in the part of Sir Henry Irving![4] Hang it.

---

[1] On 4 June, from Champel via Paris.

[2] Paternoster Buildings, near Saint Paul's, was the headquarters of T. Fisher Unwin, Conrad's publisher and Garnett's employer. Not without irony, they often referred to Unwin as the Enlightened Patron of Letters, the Patron, or the E.P.L.

[3] Justin McCarthy (1830–1912), British historian, novelist, journalist and Member of Parliament.

[4] Sir Henry Irving (born John Henry Brodribb; 1838–1905), the actor–manager, had just received his title in the Birthday Honours; he was the first actor to be knighted.

Now if that astonishing Lord Rosebery[1] gives a peerage to Sir John Falstaff and names Bardolph Secretary of state it will put the finishing touch to the fairy tale of the most misty and elusive administration of this practical country. I have 6 more chapters for you and the end is not yet.[2]

Yours

J. Conrad.—

To Paul Briquel

Text MS Meykiechel (telegram, Émilie Briquel's diary copy); Najder (1972)

[8 Juin 1895]
[London]

Lettres seulement aujourd'hui, merci. J'écris demain à Champel, laissez votre adresse à Mürsch,[3] mes souhaits pour le voyage.

Conrad

[8 June 1895]
[London]

Letters [came] only today. Thanks. Shall write tomorrow to Champel, leave your address with Mürsch. Wishing you a good journey.

Conrad

To Émilie Briquel

Text MS Meykiechel; *Nouvelles*; Najder (1972)

Dimanche 10 Juin 1895[4]
17, Gillingham Street
London. S.W.

Merci, mille fois, chère Mademoiselle Emilie de Votre bonne et charmante lettre. C'est a mon retour d'Elstree ou j'ai passé trois penibles journées (pour l'affaire que vous savez) que j'ai trouvé chez Barr Mo[e]ring l'enveloppe avec entête de Champel. J'ai bondi dessus avec un enthousiasme plus facile a comprendre qu'a décrire et puis d'un autre saut "vigoureux" j'ai atteint le bureau du télégraphe pour vous dire—d'une façon plus ou moins "desordonnée"—pourquoi j'ai tant tardé à répondre.

---

[1] Archibald Philip Primrose, Fifth Earl of Rosebery (1847–1929), a Liberal, was Prime Minister from 1894 to 1895.

[2] *An Outcast.*

[3] A functionary at La Roseraie, the hotel–pension at Champel.

[4] Sunday was really the 9th. The sequence of events described here does not match that of the letter to Garnett, 7 June.

Vous m'avez fait un bien grand plaisir par cette phrase où vous dites qu'il Vous semble "que nous avons perdu un véritable ami". "Perdu"— j'espère que non; mais "véritable ami" sont des mots qui me rendent très fier. Une amitié c'est encore la chose la plus précieuse que l'on puisse trouver dans le pèlérinage de la vie, et le voyageur qui en trouve sur son chemin a lieu de se croire favorisé par le Ciel. Nos amitiés sont le but et la récompense de la vie; elles nous tiennent dans le droit chemin—et leur souvenir, joyeux et doux, accompagne le fortuné pèlerin; marche à ses côtés, compagnon infatigable et fidèle, parmi les froides pierres de cette succession des vastes solitudes dont se compose notre existence.

Monsieur Votre Frère[1] m'a écrit une lettre bien intéressante et bien remarquable. En ce moment je n'ai ni le temps ni l'esprit assez libre pour Lui répondre comme il le mérite. Il a les généreux enthousiasmes, et les généreux découragements—de son âge—qui sont le privilège des âmes d'élite—des âmes jeunes qui savent penser. Je vous en prie veuillez Lui dire "merci" de ma part. Merci: mot banal ou profond selon celui qui parle et celui qui entend. Je suis fort occupé—pas de mon livre par exemple![2] Je pense que la réussite est certaine. Ce brave Francis, une fois éloigné de son étonnante épouse, montre toute la bonté de son rude cœur. Mais l'épouse! C'est le diable. (Je vous demande pardon.) Enfin! On verra. Cet après-midi j'y vais me mettre à quatre pattes devant cette femme. J'ai confiance en ma diplomatie. Je vais mentir, faire des courbettes, m'aplatir. On ne s'arrête pas à des vétilles quand il s'agit de sauver une famille. Francis m'encourage—me pousse. Il a une peur bleue de sa femme. Moi pas!

Je suis fort reconnaissant à Madame Votre Mère du bon souvenir qu'Elle me garde. Veuillez Lui présenter mes hommages les plus respectueux et croyez-moi, chère Mademoiselle Emilie, toujours Votre dévoué et très obéissant serviteur.

Jph Conrad

Bien fait! le billard! Vous n'avez pas dit qui gagne aux dominos. Donc vous perdez? Pas vrai? Eh?

Dites bonjour pour moi au père Mursch. Cela lui fera plaisir. Voulez-vous? Merci.

---

[1] Paul.
[2] *An Outcast*. The identity of Francis is not known. His wife sounds oddly like Mrs Peter Willems of *An Outcast*.

Sunday, 10[9?] June 1895
17 Gillingham Street
London S.W.

A thousand thanks, dear Mademoiselle Émilie, for your kind and charming letter. On my return from Elstree, where I spent three painful days (on account of the affair that you know about), I found the envelope from Champel at Barr Moering's. I leaped at it with an enthusiasm easier to understand than to describe, and then, with another 'vigorous' bound I reached the telegraph office to tell you – in a more or less 'disordered' fashion – why I am so late in answering.

You have given me great pleasure by saying that in your opinion 'we have lost a true friend'. 'Lost' – I hope not; but 'true friend' are words which make me very proud. Friendship is still the most precious thing to be found during life's pilgrimage, and the traveller who finds it on his way can consider himself favoured by heaven. Our friendships are the aim and reward of life; they keep us on the straight path – and their memory, joyous and sweet, accompanies the lucky pilgrim – walks beside him, an indefatigable and faithful companion, among the cold stones of this succession of vast solitudes which makes up our existence.

I had a most interesting and remarkable letter from your brother. At the moment I have neither the time nor the peace of mind to answer him in the way he deserves. He has the abundant enthusiasms and the abundant dejections – typical of his age – which, for a select few, are a spiritual privilege – the privilege of young people who know how to think. I beg you to say 'thank you' to him on my behalf. 'Thank you' – words banal or profound, depending on who speaks and who listens. I am extremely busy – but not on my book for a change! I think success is assured. This worthy Francis, once removed from his amazing wife, displays all the kindness of his impetuous heart. But as for his wife! She's the devil. (I beg your pardon.) Anyway, we shall see. This afternoon I am going on all fours in front of this woman. I trust my diplomacy. I shall lie, cringe, and abase myself before her. When it comes to saving a family, we must not be deterred by trifles. Francis encourages me – pushes me ahead. He is terrified of his wife. I am not!

I am most grateful to your mother for remembering me kindly. Please give her my respectful regards and believe me, dear Mademoiselle Émilie, always your devoted and very obedient servant.

Jph Conrad

Good show! Billiards! You've never told me who wins at dominoes.

Does that mean you're losing? Not possible. Eh? Say hello from me to
Papa Mürsch. That will please him. Do you mind? Thanks.

To Marguerite Poradowska

Text   MS Yale; Rapin 164; G. & S. 98

11 Juin 95.
17. Gillingham St.
London. S.W.

Ma Chère Tante.[1]

Pardonnez mon infâme silence,[2] mais j'avais tant d'ennuis! Et puis je
ne voulai pas Vous donner le noir de mes soucis. J'ai emporté un si bon et
si charmant souvenir de Vous—de Vous gaie et tranquille dans Votre
nid parmi les oiseaux.

J'ai arrangé mes affaires—au moins pour quelque temps et je me suis
remis a ecrire: fort encouragé par les *sept colonnes et demie* du "Weekly
Sun" ou T. P. O'Connor[3] m'a enterré sous une avalanche des
compliments, des admirations, d'analyse et de citations, tout ça avec un
enthousiasme qui lui faire dire bien des betises tout - a fait absurdes.
Enfin cela pose un individu puisque le "Sun" se fait une specialité de ce
genre de notes litteraires—et je suis content.

Parlez moi bien vite de Lemerre[4]—et de votre ouvrage. Avancez
Vous?

Je Vous embrasse bien fort. Toujours a vous
J. Conrad.

---

[1] This is the last extant letter of Conrad to Marguerite Poradowska until 16 April 1900.
There is evidence, however, that Conrad and Mme Poradowska continued to correspond
in this period (see letter to Aniela Zagórska, 20 December 1897). The question is why she
suppressed or destroyed his letters. We can only conjecture that Conrad tried to enter
into a greater intimacy and perhaps suggested marriage before he proposed to Jessie
George. This would possibly explain at least the suppression of his 1895–6 letters.

[2] Conrad had not written for a week, since his 4 June return to London after visiting Mme
Poradowska in Paris.

[3] Editor of the *Sun* and *Weekly Sun*, and a Member of Parliament. Conrad later published
Nostromo in *T. P.'s Weekly*. In the 9 June *Weekly Sun*, O'Connor called *Almayer's Folly* a
'startling, unique, splendid book' and cited Conrad as a writer of genius.

[4] A Paris publishing firm, to which, Gee and Sturm suggest, *Marylka* had probably been
submitted after its rejection by Calmann-Lévy.

11 June 1895
17 Gillingham Street
London S.W.

My dear Aunt,

Excuse my shocking silence, but I have had so many worries. And then I did not want to bestow on you the gloom of my troubles. I carried away such a good and charming memory of you, of you gay and tranquil in your nest among the birds.

I have set my affairs in order, at least for the time being, and I have gone back to writing, strongly encouraged by *seven and a half* columns in the *Weekly Sun*, where T. P. O'Connor has buried me under an avalanche of compliments, admiration, analysis, and quotations, all of it with an enthusiasm which certainly makes him say some quite ridiculously stupid things. That, of course, puts one in the right position, since the *Sun* specializes in that type of literary notice – and I am satisfied.

Tell me right away about Lemerre, and about your work. Are you making progress?

I embrace you very warmly. Ever yours
J. Conrad

To Jane Cobden Unwin
Text   MS Chichester; Curreli

Gillingham St. S W
17th June 1895

Dear Mrs Unwin,[1]

I have no engagement for Wednesday[2]—unless perhaps one with myself: an engagement to work[3]—which may be broken with impunity and satisfaction. I hasten therefore to accept Your kind invitation with an absolutely remorseless pleasure. I am, dear Mrs Unwin, Your very faithful and obedient servant

Jph Conrad

---

[1] Jane Cobden Unwin (1851–1949), active in feminist and Radical causes, was the daughter of Richard Cobden, the apostle of Free Trade. She married T. Fisher Unwin in 1892.
[2] 19 June.
[3] Presumably on *An Outcast*.

To Edward Noble

Text   MS Rosenbach; Privately printed;
J–A, I, 175

Monday evening. [17 June 1895][1]

[London]

My dear Noble,

Just got your letter—as I dress to go out to dinner—but I must answer—if only a few words—at once.

I am inexpressibly touched by the appreciation,[2] more touched by the manner of its expression. I am also immensely flattered by Your good opinion which You state with such evident sincerity—with no ring of reservation in it.

I thank You with all my heart. Letters like yours are rewards of all trouble—of a sweet trouble if You will—but still a trouble. It is made up of doubt, of hesitation; of moments silent and anxious when one listens to the thoughts—one's own thoughts—speaking indistinc[t]ly deep down somewhere at the bottom of the heart.

Why do you misjudge so blindly Your own personality? And why do You belittle Your own temperament? You have Your own distinct individuality that may—and in time will—appeal to hundreds, thousands or millions—as blind fate shall will it. And it is an individuality that will stand wear and tear that has resistance and power—while I shall be used up in [a] short and miserable splutter of dim flame. It's so. Hope is the best and the worst of life. Half of it comes from God and half from the devil, but it behoves men to take gifts and curses with a steady hand and an equable mind—because of such is made up Fate—the blind, the invincible.—

I should like to see the beginning of your novel very, very much. Shall drop you a line. Thanks for all your kindness. My duty to Mrs Noble and my love to Miss Noble.

Yours in haste

J. Conrad.

---

[1] The envelope is postmarked 17 June, a Monday. (Jean-Aubry mistakenly has '17 July'.)

[2] Apparently of *Almayer's Folly*. A sailor beginning to write fiction, Noble was in a sense a younger version of Conrad.

To Edward Noble
Text MS Rosenbach; Privately printed

Tuesday [18 June 1895][1]
[London]

Dear Noble.

I think that in my hurried note of yeste^dy I have omitted to give you the address of the Yellow Book[2] people. I do so now. The name of the editor is—I think—*Harland*,[3] but the Publisher is—*John Lane* The "Bodley Head", Vigo Street.[4]

Those People are very aest[h]etic very advanced and think no end of themselves. They are all certainly writers of talent—some of very great talent. I am glad you had the idea to try there. You need not put yourself under any restraint as to subject or treatment of it, but send what you have most original and simple. Good luck with you.

Yours faithfully

J Conrad.

To Paul Briquel
Text MS Meykiechel (Émilie Briquel's diary copy);
Unpublished

[Received in Fribourg, 3 July 1895]

Chèr Monsieur

Je profite du premier instant de liberté pour répondre à votre lettre. J'ai été fort occupé. Il faut s'agiter dans sa cage jusqu'au jour où la porte sera ouverte sur le vide qui nous entoure.

Vous avez sur moi l'advantage de la jeunesse[5] et aussi l'avantage de savoir bien des choses que je ne connais pas. Vous avez lu bien des livres. Moi, je n'ai lu que la grande page, la page, énorme, monotone et remplie d'une vie passée tout en dehors de moi dans l'oubli de l'individualité, au contact avec les forces mystérieuses et variées qui bataillent contre notre

---

[1] Postmark.
[2] An illustrated quarterly periodical published in London, in book form, from 1894 to 1897. Its contributors included Wilde, Beerbohm, Yeats, James, Symons and many others of the first rank. Among its illustrators were Beardsley, Rothenstein and Sickert.
[3] Henry Harland, who was editor for the entire thirteen volumes; Aubrey Beardsley was art editor of the first four volumes, being succeeded by John Lane.
[4] The first volume appeared under the imprint of Elkin Mathews and John Lane; for the third volume the publisher was John Lane alone.
[5] When the thirty-seven-year-old Conrad met Émilie in May, she was twenty, and Paul was seventeen.

volonté.[1] Et voilà! Je conclus que c'est là la seule possibilité du bonheur. Dans las tâche accomplie, dans l'obstacle vaincu, n'importe quelle tâche, n'importe quel obstacle; là est le vrai refuge de l'homme fourvoyé sur cette terre, car la raison est faible, et courte, et la volonté est éternelle et forte.[2] Il faut servir le maître qui est le plus fort, le maître sans caprices, qui ne se trompe jamais. Et ne pensez pas que je prêche l'égoïsme. Il faut accomplir des tâches ennuyeuses, pénibles et répugnantes, il faut faire marcher le monde sans se préoccuper de l'éternelle Erreur, car Elle est remplie des vérités qu'il faut faire triompher. Voilà la pensée de mon ignorance. Je vous la dis. Peut-être vous servira-t-elle dans la vie. Dans tous les cas, elle ne peut pas vous nuire. Croyez-moi tout à vous.

J. Conrad

Rappelez-moi au souvenir bienveillant de Madame votre Mère et de Mademoiselle Emilie. J'espère que tout va bien et que la santé de Madame Briquel s'améliore à Carlsbad d'une façon durable.

[Received in Fribourg, 3 July 1895]

Dear Sir,

I am taking advantage of the first free moment to answer your letter. I have been terribly busy. One must keep moving in one's cage until the day when the door opens into the surrounding void.

You have the advantage of youth over me, and also that of knowing many things with which I am not acquainted. You have read many books. I myself have read only the one great page, the enormous and monotonous page filled by a life passed entirely outside myself, oblivious of my own individuality, in a struggle with the mysterious and varied powers which oppose our will. So you see! I have arrived at the conclusion that *there* lies the sole chance for happiness. In a task accomplished, in an obstacle overcome – no matter what task, no matter what obstacle. There, the baffled wanderer over the earth can find his

---

[1] A fine piece of Conradian rhetoric from a well-read man who found individuality impossible to subdue. Possibly there are echoes in this sentence of his explorations in Schopenhauer.

[2] Cf. *The Mirror of the Sea*, p. 24: 'Efficiency of a practically flawless kind may be reached naturally in the struggle for bread. But there is something beyond – a higher point, a subtle and unmistakable touch of love and pride beyond mere skill; almost an inspiration which gives to all work that finish which is almost art – which *is* art.'

true refuge, since reason is feeble and short-lived and will is everlasting and strong. One must serve the stronger master, the master who is not capricious, who never makes mistakes. And don't think I am preaching egoism. One must accomplish tasks which are boring, painful and repulsive; one must keep the world going without worrying about eternal Error, for it is full of truths whose triumph we must assist. What I am telling you is the thought born of my ignorance. Perhaps it will be of some use to you in later life. In any case, it can't do you any harm. Please believe me, sincerely yours

J. Conrad

Please give my best regards to your mother and sister. I hope all is well with them, and that Carlsbad will bring a lasting improvement in Madame Briquel's health.

To T. Fisher Unwin

Text   MS Leeds; Unpublished

9th July 1895.
[letterhead: Elstree, Herts.][1]

Dear Mr Unwin.

I am very sorry that your arrangements do not allow you to join in my cruise. I trust that at some future time I may have better luck, and secure your company.

Thanks very much for sending me Miss Cape's letter.[2] All appreciation is very welcome but appreciation of the kind she is pleased to give me is very rare—and so the more precious.

I will call on You when on my way to the north.[3] I am rather seedy just now.

Yours faithfully

J. Conrad

---

[1] Conrad was staying with his friend Ted Sanderson.

[2] Harriet Capes praised Conrad's work and began a long friendship with the writer; their correspondence lasted almost until Conrad's death. He dedicated *A Set of Six* (1908) to her, and she compiled *Wisdom and Beauty from Conrad* (1915).

[3] Presumably to join Hope's yacht, the *Ildegonde*.

To Edward Garnett

Text MS Free; G. 39

[10–15 July 1895][1]
17. Gillingham St.

Dear Garnett.

Can we meet this week? Any day but Saturday and any time from 6. p.m. And if not this week then let it be the next where all the days belong to me.—

I suffer now from an acute attack of faithlessness in the sense that I do not seem to believe in anything, but I trust that by the time we meet I shall be more like a human being and consequently ready to believe any absurdity—and not only ready but eager.—Perhaps I will be able then to let you see 2 more chapters. I would like You to see them before I write any more.—I have now 400 pages of MS. and the end is not yet!

Still I think that 50 pp more ought to see the end of the coming failure.

Yours ever

J. Conrad.

To Émilie Briquel

Text MS Meykiechel; *Nouvelles*; Najder (1972)

17 Gillingham Street, London
S.W.
14 Juillet 1895

Chère Mademoiselle Briquel,

Votre lettre est certainement la plus charmante missive qu'un auteur ait jamais reçue. Vous dire combien je vous en sais gré et combien je l'aprécie me serait impossible. Votre jugement a beaucoup de poids, je vous assure, car, après tout, nous écrivons pour nos amis, pour la pensée et le cœur de ceux qui nous connaissent, et non pas pour les pontifes inconnus qui prononcent des critiques (généralement fausses) dans les journaux.

Votre appréciation me flatte, me remplit de joie et aussi de tristesse et de regret. La tristesse de me savoir très peu digne de votre indulgente critique—le regret de ne pas avoir fait mieux. Mais c'est Votre capacité

---

[1] The month and year are not in question. The sole evidence in the letter to support a possible dating between 10 and 15 July is Conrad's indication of progress on *An Outcast*. In a letter of 14 July to Émilie Briquel, Conrad mentions that he is wrestling with Chapter XXIII, with Chapter XXIV remaining. This would coincide with his final sentence to Garnett here, that he needs about another 50 pages of manuscript to complete the novel.

pour acquérir une langue étrangère qui me remplit de stupeur et d'admiration. Comment! Déjà! Il y a deux mois à peine que Vous avez reçu le livre! Vraiment je ne sais ce qu'il faut admirer le plus, la vivacité de Votre esprit ou la force de Votre volonté; Votre talent, ou Votre persévérance!

Et croyez bien que je suis fort touché par cette preuve de votre intérêt dans le livre, d'un intérêt beaucoup plus grand qu'il ne le mérite;[1] par la preuve si décisive et concluante de Votre sympathie. Traduire n'importe quoi est un travail ingrat, mais traduire et conquérir en même temps une langue est un travail que peu de personnes auraient le courage d'entreprendre. Vous parlez d'autorisation—moi je voudrais Vous parler de ma gratitude, seulement je ne peux guère l'exprimer comme elle devrait l'être pour Vous faire comprendre au juste le sentiment que j'éprouve. Je Vous dirais simplement que Vous m'avez fait éprouver un des plus vifs plaisirs de ma vie.

J'ai reçu Votre lettre avant-hier et j'ai écrit tout de suite à mon éditeur. J'ai sa réponse ce matin. Il a fait quelques démarches vers la traduction—qui n'ont pas, du reste, abouti. On n'en fera plus! Puisque Vous avez commencé ce sera Vous—ou personne. Vous voilà bien attrapée—prise au piège! Hein?—Mais serieusement je suis assez egoïste pour désirer Vous voir finir cette traduction quoique ma conscience me crie de Vous avouer—de Vous persuader que le livre n'en vaut pas la peine. Je n'en fait rien, et je vis dans l'espoir que Vous allez continuer.

Je suis très sincerement heureux des bonnes nouvelles que Vous me donnez de la santé de Madame Votre Mère. Veuillez Lui presenter de ma part mes hommages le plus respectueux. J'en suis aux prises—corps à corps—avec le Chapitre XXIII de mon nouveau livre.[2] Puis viendra le XXIV—et puis le deluge. Le deluge des doutes, des remords, des regrets, et de peur ou je vais nager jusqu'au moment ou un critique charitable me tendra une perche, composée des louanges. Sinon je me maisse aller au fond et on n'entendra plus parler de moi. J'espère que Monsieur Votre frère ne se formalisera pas de ma bête de lettre. J'y ai mis mes pensées en forme de théorie de la vie qui n'a d'autre mérite que d'être sincère et d'être appuyée par l'expérience de mon inutile existence. Elle est aussi—je crois—assez honorable. J'espère qu'il ne pense pas que je me

---

[1] *Almayer's Folly*, which Mlle Briquel thought of translating into French. Nothing came of this plan. We recall Conrad's correspondence with Mme Poradowska (see letter of 30 July? 1894) about a translation.
[2] *An Outcast.*

suis permi de donner des conseils! Loin de là. Sa lettre à lui a simplement ouvert un canal pour le courant de ma pensée. Voilà tout.

Je serre la main de Monsieur Votre frère. Croyez-moi, Mademoiselle, toujours Votre très humble, très dévoué et très obéissant serviteur.

Jph Conrad

P.S.—L'affaire de mon ami a marché à souhait. Mme Francis me trouve un homme charmant. Elle m'innonde d'invitations que je n'accepte plus.[1] Suis-je assez ingrat! Le 24 de ce mois je pars pour un tour en yacht dans la mer du Nord.[2] Une absence de quinze jours.

14 July 1895
17 Gillingham Street, London
S.W.

Dear Mademoiselle Briquel,

Your letter is undoubtedly the most charming missive an author ever received. It would be impossible for me to describe how deeply grateful and appreciative it made me feel. I can assure you that your judgement carries a lot of weight because, after all, we write for our friends, for the minds and hearts of those who know us, and not for the unknown pundits who pronounce (generally false) opinions in the newspapers.

Your appreciation flatters me, fills me with joy but also with sadness and regret. Sadness – because I know myself scarcely worthy of your lenient judgement; regret – at not having done better. But it's your gift for mastering a foreign language which leaves me dumbfounded and full of admiration. How can it be? Already? It is hardly two months since you received the book! Truly I don't know what to admire more: the liveliness of your intellect or the power of your will; your talent or your perseverance!

And believe me, I am deeply touched by this proof of your interest in the book, of an interest far greater than it deserves; by the firm and unquestionable proof of your understanding. Translating, no matter what, is an ungrateful task, but translating and having at the same time to conquer another language is a task which only few would have the courage to undertake. You talk of [my] permission – I would rather tell you of my gratitude, except that I hardly know how to express it in such a way as to make you fully understand my feelings. I shall simply say you

[1] See note on letter of 10 June.
[2] On Hope's yacht, *Ildegonde*.

have given me one of the greatest pleasures I have ever experienced in my life.

Your letter reached me the day before yesterday and I wrote immediately to my publisher. I received his reply this morning. He had taken some steps regarding the translation – but it all came to nothing, anyway. No more shall be taken! Since you have begun, it shall be you – or nobody. Now you are really trapped – caught in a snare. Eh? But, seriously, I am enough of an egoist to want to see you finish this translation although my conscience is crying out to tell you – to persuade you the book is not worth the trouble. I am doing nothing of the kind, and I live in the hope you will continue.

I am indeed sincerely glad to hear the good news of your mother's health. Please give her my most respectful compliments. I am now wrestling – at the closest of quarters – with Chapter XXIII of my new book. Then comes Chapter XXIV and then – the deluge. The deluge of doubts, remorse, regrets and fear amidst which I shall swim until some charitable critic offers me a refuge built on flattery. Otherwise, I shall let myself go to the bottom and will never be heard of again. I hope your brother will not take offence at my stupid letter. It contained my thoughts in the form of a theory of life which has no other merit than that of being sincere and supported by the experience of my own futile existence. It is also, I think, quite honourable. I hope he does not think I've allowed myself to give him advice! Far from it. His letter simply opened a channel for the stream of my thoughts. That's all.

A handshake for your brother. Believe me, Mademoiselle, always your very humble, devoted and obedient servant.

Jph Conrad

PS. The affairs of my friend have been settled satisfactorily. Mme Francis finds me a charming man. She overwhelms me with invitations which I no longer accept. How ungrateful of me! On the 24th of this month I am going on a yachting cruise in the North Sea. A fortnight's absence.

To Émilie Briquel

Text MS Meykiechel (Émilie Briquel's diary copy);
Unpublished

[Received 29 July 1895][1]
Harwich
Bureau des Postes

Chère Mademoiselle Briquel,

Je viens de recevoir Votre lettre et cela de Monsieur Votre Frère. Je suis ici dans le yacht "Ildegonde" et nous partons pour la Norvège dans une heure.[2] Pardonnez ce gribouillage, j'écrirai le 7 ou le 8 aôut, si j'existe alors.[3] Merci mille fois pour Votre bonne petite lettre. Toujours Votre dévoué serviteur

[J. Conrad]

[Received 29 July 1895]
Harwich
Post Office

Dear Mademoiselle Briquel,

I have just received your and your brother's letters. I am here on the yacht *Ildegonde*, and in an hour we are leaving for Norway. Please forgive the scrawl; I shall write on 7 or 8 August if I am still alive. A hundred thanks for your charming little note. Always your devoted servant

[J. Conrad]

To E. L. Sanderson

Text J–A, I, 176[4]

24 Aug. 1895.
17, Gillingham Street, S.W.

My dearest Ted,

Yesterday I came home rather late from a dinner with that Enlightened Patron of Letters,—Fisher Unwin,—and found your welcome letter looking up at me reproachfully from the table. I only then clearly realized what ages we have not spoken to each other. Till that

[1] Received on that date according to Mlle Briquel's copy of Conrad's letter.
[2] Apparently they got no further than the Dutch coast.
[3] Conrad's next (extant) letter to her was dated 26 August.
[4] The original for this letter has not turned up, and in printing from Jean-Aubry's copy, we note many divergences from Conrad's usual style of punctuation, and the absence of a formal ending. There may be other errors as well. (Of Conrad's 74 letters to the Sandersons, this is the only one for which there is no original.) For a biographical note, see letter to Mme Poradowska, 16 April 1894.

moment (my life has been so strangely full lately)[1] I have,—often thinking of you,—said to myself: "I shall write to-morrow: it's but one short day more." And so, wondering vaguely what your address might be, I have let the time slip by:—all regardless of the stealthy approach of Eternity which waits not for a day,—and knows everybody's address.

Then coming home (as related above) with a fixed intention to write before I slept,—there was your letter. Into the hot, noisy and dissipated night of my neighbourhood I shouted "Hooray,"—read your letter with a pang, ... and went to bed.

Flesh is weak: and spirit is but of little account.

So you had a tussle with the old enemy! You speak of it slightingly with the affectation of those who come off victorious,—and I rejoice to know that you can speak of it so. Still, my dear Ted, the wise man does not get wet (unless under the stress of extreme necessity), because wet brings dysentery:—the infamous thing! The wise man is also careful of his food. You tell me who grooms and drives the horse (happy horse!—I present my humble duty to the distinguished groom), but I yearn to know who does your cooking for you? That's the thing! my dear boy. What and how you eat! Believe my wisdom (I don't mind telling you in confidence that I have lately torn out by the roots a good many white hairs). Remember likewise that dysentery (like salmon) lurks in water: in the babbling brook and the smooth-flowing river—and is caught without a fly. A tumbler will do. Avoid this form of your beloved sport.—Your idea of elevating yourself above the low-ranging microbe by means of a pair of stilts is very praiseworthy, and I commend it heartily. For, that is your motive,—is it not?—since I cannot comprehend a man of your gravity and idealistic tendencies taking to such ungainly exercises except for weighty,—nay, imperative,—reasons.

I am inexpressibly happy to hear such a good account of your Mother and Father. I shall not write to dear Mrs. Sanderson for another week. I want to enjoy to the full my privilege and for that I must shake off the various trammels of mind, which worry me now,—and shall worry for a few days more.

We extended our cruise[2] to the Dutch coast, having strong winds and moderately heavy seas all the time. We lived mostly in oilskins and all our various guests that came from time to time were very seasick. The last two days were ideally beautiful. We spent them at the mouth of the

---

[1] With several activities: the completion of *An Outcast*; an increasingly serious courtship of Jessie George, his future wife; contacts with a growing circle of friends; and a continuing search for a command or other business outlets.

[2] In Hope's yacht.

Thames from Rochester to Burnham and then to Harwich where we left the yacht for good.

That was on the 7th and ever since I have been extremely busy and half the time in Paris.[1] I have crossed the Channel six times (three trips) in a fortnight. I got back from my last flight on the 21st, having accomplished my purpose. As you may imagine Willems[2] has been considerably neglected during that time and is not dead yet. I had, really, no time to attend to that murder.

Yesterday I sold him. I've sold him for about 12½ per cent. royalty, and fifty pounds cash payable on the 1st of December. I have half serial and American rights. F U wants to get the book accepted for a serial by some magazine or newspaper. I hate the idea but have given in to his arguments. My opinion is he shall not be able to place it.[3] As a book it will be a 6/.- edition uniform with *Almayer*!

Strangely enough I also had a great disturbance of internal machinery,—very much like dysentery,—with a slight fever. It left me depressed. I could take no rest, for I could not let go what I had in hand out of regard for other people. I travelled in a Pullman and generally pampered myself—and so went through,—but it left me rather flabby and cynical.

All this came about unexpectedly (I do not mean the illness but the occupation) and in a rather curious chain of circumstances. First of all I was induced to look up and make use of my old French acquaintances for the sake of a very good fellow called Rorke (of Rorke's Drift) whom I knew some years ago and who is Hope's brother-in-law. That man owned some 150 claims on the Roodeport gold reef for the last 6 or 7 years.[4] Of course he tried many times to sell, but during the period of depression (since 1889) nobody would look at them. Now the boom came a few months ago and a French Syndicate approached Rorke (out there in Johannesburg) and actually concluded the sale, paid £500 deposit and induced Rorke to part with documents. Then various hitches occurred.

[1] On business for a friend. The precise nature of this business is identified by Conrad below. There is no indication that Conrad tried to see Mme Poradowska at this time; there is, in fact, a five-year gap in their letters, which may be attributable to his courtship of Jessie. Baines speculates (p. 171) that Conrad courted and married Jessie on the rebound from Mme Poradowska.

[2] Of *An Outcast*.

[3] Unwin was not.

[4] Hope had extensive interests in South Africa. John Rorke held claims on the Roodepoort Farm, ten miles W of Johannesburg. In 1895, speculative interest in the gold-rich Witwatersrand was rampant. On 31 August the *South African Empire* (London) noted that 'the people still throng into the market; the doors of the brokers are invaded, clerks are worked off their heads' (p. 23: '"The Boom": Will It Continue?').

Rorke waited, paying meantime the Statutory licences,—to keep his title to the claims. For that purpose he parted with every penny he could scrape,—sold his freehold, farms, etc., etc.: and at the end of last June found himself without a penny, with his documents somewhere on the Continent of Europe,—so that he could not sell to anybody else. He wrote a despairing letter to Hope praying to be saved. There was no time to lose. The unsophisticated Rorke was at his last gasp. As the Syndicate was in Paris, I went over there on the 8th and looked up people I know or used to know. They were good enough to remember me with apparent pleasure. I enlisted many influential and sympathetic people for my cause. Pascalis of the *Figaro*,—Guesde (a deputy) and the bankers, Jullien and Epstein. All acquaintances of my young days.[1] We found out (to my intense satisfaction) that the French Syndicate were all Germans. We sat upon them with an order from the President from the X court and ascertained that they have been trying to sell already to some shady people in London. The documents, reports and plans were also in London. Epstein got very interested and proposed to come back with me. Agreed. He snored ignobly all the way. At 8.30 in Victoria. At 10 in Hope's office. At 3 P.M., same day, the London people (called Thompson) parted with all the papers for the sum of £100! They had no more chance, of course, to float a company than any crossing sweeper. As a matter of fact they are penniless Jews. They tried to bluff and bully,—but collapsed before a firm attitude. Next day Epstein, Hope and I met some people of good standing here and before evening a Memorandum of Association of an Anglo-French Syndicate was signed by which they agreed to buy Rorke's claims for £8000 cash and 25,000 shares. We cabled Rorke the terms and he cabled consent. Meantime power of attorney for Hope arrived from Africa. We concluded the sale. On the 11th Aug. I was on my way back to Paris with Epstein. He snored all the way. For two days there was much cabling and rushing about. In

[1] And ranged across the political spectrum. Pascalis wrote for a Conservative daily, and Guesde (who represented the industrial town of Roubaix in the Chamber of Deputies from 1893 to 1898) was already famous as an eloquent and militant leftist. Guesde (1845–1922) was born Jules Mathieu Basile, but on starting a career as a Radical journalist changed his name to protect his parents. Evading imprisonment for his articles defending the Paris Commune, Guesde exiled himself to Switzerland and Italy from 1871 to 1877. On returning to France, he founded the Socialist weekly *Égalité* and organized a mass movement of industrial workers. He knew both Marx and Bakunin personally, but his patriotic beliefs led to an eventual estrangement from the internationalist section of the left. It is surprising, to say the least, to find him enlisted in the cause of rescuing a South African mining syndicate. Presumably Conrad made these acquaintances in Marseilles between 1874 and 1878. Although Guesde was in exile for most of this time, he acted as foreign correspondent for a Radical Marseilles newspaper.

my two trips I managed to get rid of £117. On the 14th (evening) I left Paris with a check of the French Syndicate of £4,000 in my pocket. On the 15th the English half was paid up and £8,000 less expenses (some 370 pounds) were cabled through African Banking Corporation to the unsophisticated Rorke,—and we all sat down and wiped our perspiring brows.—Epstein (previously unknown to me) is a very straightforward Jew and the French part is in very good hands. The English undertaking is practically floated and shall be put on the market within the next fortnight as Rorke–Roodeport Gold-mine.[1] There are two Rhodesia directors on the board and the thing is sound. Of course I do not make anything. My expenses are paid and I shall take 200 shares as acknowledgment of my services. They wanted to give me 1,000, which I declined. Yet I must say I was very smart. Nobody was more surprised than myself!

On the 16th while I sat patting myself on the back I received a cable from a man called Maharg—also an old acquaintance of mine, who is now in Johannesburg.[2] Dazzled by my success with Rorke that fellow offered me the selling of 50 claims on the black reef next to the Minerva Mine (whose shares stand now at 20 per cent. premium). He was so certain of the value of that property that he did not want any cash for it. Was content to get paid in shares only,—but there were conditions about working capital and such like,—all calculated to guarantee the safety of future investors,—and therefore difficult to obtain from the common, garden kind of promoter. After a due amount of reflection I took the thing up. You know that I wanted funds for the base purpose of carrying on a wretched and useless existence. The thing was as honest as such things can be. In fact exceptionally so. It is a first-class property and offered cheap. I could with all due care for my honour (which is my only hereditary property) take it up. And I did so. I went over to Paris again but ultimately I have sold it here in London to people of high repute. It was exciting and interesting work and I had a glimpse into curious depths! Very curious![3]

---

[1] The Prospectus for Rorke's Roodepoort Ltd is dated 6 September; the subscription list was to open on the 12th. According to the Prospectus, Rorke held 46 claims at Roodepoort; either the French syndicate held the rest, or Conrad's figure of 150 is wildly exaggerated. For the 46 claims Rorke was to be paid £80,000 (not £8000).

[2] Hugh Meharg (not Maharg), who had offices on Simmons Street, was the Johannesburg secretary of Rorke's Roodepoort.

[3] As usual, Jean-Aubry omits the closing formalities. We can only assume that nothing else has been left out.

To Émilie Briquel

Text   MS Meykiechel; *Nouvelles*

26 Août 1895
17 Gillingham St. London S.W.

Chère Mademoiselle Briquel,

Il y a trois jours je suis rentré de mon voyage—car je peux bien appeler un (petit) voyage une promenade en yacht qui comprend la circumnavigation des îles Shetland et de Orcades. Des journées entières nous avons passé sans voiles de cape, dans la brume et les grosses mers de l'Atlantique. La petite "Ildegonde" (qui est un côtre de 23 tonneaux de jauge) dansait sur les hautes lames comme une coquille de noix. Pendant deux magnifiques semaines j'ai vécu secoué au large avec la triste chant de la brise dans le gréement s'élevant au-dessus l'accompagnement de la voix immense et monotone des grandes vagues déferlant sans cesse dans un infini de ciel gris et de l'eau verte, et de l'écume d'une éclatante blancheur.

Nous sommes rentrés dans un bon petit coup de vent en fuyant devant avec trois ris dans notre voile. Avec cette voilure réduite la brave "Ildegonde" a fait 273 milles marins en 34 heures. Pendant ce temps nous ne quittâmes point le pont—nous étions mouillés jusqu'au os—et il était impossible d'allumer le feu dans notre cuisine microscopique. Nous avons vécu d'eau fraîche et des biscuits. C'était charmant. Jamais je ne me suis si bien porté. Il est très évident qu'il me faut ça!

Comme vous pensez bien, j'ai fort négligé mes affaires et en ce moment-ci j'ai du travail pardessus la tête. Le livre tire à la fin.[1] Mais j'ai d'autres soucis. Je pense reprendre la mer cette année-ci. Je veux m'acheter un navire et en prendre le commandement pour un voyage de 2 à 3 ans. Tout ça c'est des projets.[2]

J'espère que Vous êtes bien tous. Voulez-Vous me dire cela en un petit mot? Pardonnez l'incohérance de cette lettre. A bientôt une missive moins "désordonnée". Mes devoirs les plus respectueux à Madame Votre Mère. Je suis toujours votre très humble et très dévoué serviteur.

J Conrad

[1] Conrad was to finish *An Outcast* on 16 September.
[2] Conrad continued to look forward to a further sea career, but nothing developed. This latest attempt involved an appeal to Edward Garnett to ask Charles Booth, a friend of his wife's. Garnett quotes Booth's letter of 22 February 1896: 'The plan of a captain taking a share of the vessel he commands with the management is I believe common, but such work lies outside of my own experience. Such vessels are often called "family ships" being got up in that way amongst those who are related to each other. The Welsh do it a good deal and the Norwegians still more. It needs for success a closer eye for small economies than is found amongst the English' (G., p. 17).

Je vais écrire à Monsieur Votre frère aussitôt que j'aurai un moment réellement libre—veux dire: libre d'esprit. Merci de sa bonne lettre.

26 August 1895
17 Gillingham St, London S.W.

Dear Mademoiselle Briquel,

I returned three days ago from my voyage – because I might well call a yachting cruise that included sailing round the Shetland and Orkney Islands a (short) voyage. We spent entire days without trysails, amidst the fog and heavy seas of the Atlantic. The little *Ildegonde* (which is a 23-ton cutter) danced on top of the high waves like a nutshell. For two glorious weeks I was buffeted in the open sea, with the wind's melancholy song in the rigging rising above the accompaniment of the immense and monotonous voice of huge billows ceaselessly breaking in an infinity of grey skies, green water and dazzling white foam.

On our way back we had a good wind, and we flew along with three reefs in our sails. With sails thus shortened, our fine *Ildegonde* covered 273 nautical miles in 34 hours. All that time we never went below – we were wet to the marrow – and it was impossible to light the fire in our microscopic kitchen. We subsisted on fresh water and biscuits. It was delightful. I have never felt so well. Obviously, that's what I need.

As you rightly suppose I have badly neglected my affairs, and at the moment I am up to my ears in work. The book draws to its close. But I have other worries. I have been thinking of going back to sea this year. I want to buy a ship and command it for a voyage of two to three years. This is all just an idea.

I hope you are all well. Would you tell me so in a little note? Forgive the incoherence of this letter. A less 'disordered' missive soon. My most respectful regards to your mother. I remain always your very humble and devoted servant

J Conrad

I shall write to your brother as soon as I have a really free moment – I mean: free mind. Thanks for his kind letter.

To Edward Garnett

Text J–A, I, 179; G. 39[1]

17. Sep. 1895
17 Gillingham Street S.W.

Dear Garnett

It is my painful duty to inform you of the sad death of Mr Peter Willems late of Rotterdam and Macassar[2] who has been murdered on the 16th inst at 4 p.m. while the sun shone joyously and the barrel organ sang on the pavement the abominable Intermezzo of the ghastly Cavalleria.[3] As soon as I recovered from the shock I busied myself in arranging the affairs of the two inconsolable widows of our late lamented friend and I am glad to say that—with the help of Captain Lingard[4] who took upon himself all the funereal arrangements—everything was decently settled before midnight. You know what strong affection I had for the poor departed so you won't be surprised to hear that to me—since yesterday life seems a blank—a dumb solitude from which everything—even the shadows—have completely vanished.

Almayer was the last to go,[5] but, before I succeeded in getting rid of him, he made me perfectly wretched with his grumblings about the trouble and expense connected with the sad event and by his unfeeling remarks about the deceased's little failings. He reviled also Mrs Willems, who was paralysed with grief and behaved more like a cumbersome dummy than a living woman. I am sorry to say he wasn't as sober as he ought to have been in these sad conjectures and as usual he seemed not aware of anybody's grief and sufferings but his own—which struck me as being mostly imaginary. I was glad to see him go, but—such is the inconsequence of the human heart—no sooner he went than I began to regret bitterly his absence. I had for a moment the idea to rush out and call him back but before I could shake off the languor of my sorrow he was gone beyond recall.

There's nothing more to tell you except that the detailed relation of the heartrending occurrences of the last two days will be deposited tomorrow in Paternoster Bdgs for your perusal.[6]

---

[1] Text from Garnett; Jean-Aubry's copy is remarkably similar.
[2] The Outcast himself.
[3] Mascagni's *Cavalleria rusticana* (1890) – another story of illicit passion with a bloody ending.
[4] A peripheral character in *An Outcast* and *Almayer's Folly*; the main character of *The Rescue*.
[5] The last section of *An Outcast* is devoted to Almayer's drunken complaints.
[6] At Fisher Unwin's office.

I can write no more! Assured of your precious sympathy I shake tearfully your trusty hand.

Yours ever

J. Conrad

To Edward Garnett

Text   MS Berg; J-A, I, 180; G. 41

Tuesday. [24 September 1895][1]
[London]

Dear Garnett

I got Your letter and the MS.[2] about an hour ago and I write at once under the impression of your criticism—of your kind and truly friendly remarks. I want to tell you how much I appreciate your care, the sacrifice of your time, your evident desire to help me. I want to tell you all that but do not know how to express myself so as to convey to you clearly the sense of the great obligation, of my indebtedness towards you. You gild the pill richly—but the fact remains that the last chapter is simply abominable. Never did I see anything so clearly as the naked hideousness of that thing. I can also see that You do faithfully try to make the best of it with a delicacy of feeling which does honour to your heart however much it may be wrong from an ethical standpoint.

I am glad you like the xxIII chapter. To tell You the honest truth I like it myself. As to the xxIV[3] I feel convinced that the right course would be to destroy it, to scatter its ashes to the four winds of heaven. The only question is: can I?

I am afraid I can't! I lack the courage to set before myself the task of rewriting the thing. It is not—as you say—a matter of correction here and there—a matter of changed words—or lines—or pages. The whole conception seems to me wrong. I seem to have seen the wrong side of the situation. I was always afraid of it. For months I have been afraid of that chapter—and now it is written—and the foreboding is realised in a dismal failure.

Nothing now can unmake my mistake. I shall try—but I shall try without faith, because all my work is produced unconsciously (so to speak) and I cannot meddle to any purpose with what is within

[1] In his previous letter to Garnett, Conrad indicated that he was depositing the manuscript of *An Outcast* on the 18th at Fisher Unwin's. By the following Tuesday, the 24th, Garnett had responded.
[2] Of *An Outcast.*   3 The final chapter.

myself—I am sure you understand what I mean.—It isn't in me to improve what has got itself written.—

Still with your help I may try. All the paragraphs marked by You to that effect shall be cut out. For Willems to want to escape from *both* women[1] *is* the very idea. Only—don't you see—I did not feel it so. Shame! The filiation[2] of feelings in Willems on the evening when Aïssa speaks to him arises from my view of that man—of the effect produced upon him by the loss of things precious to him coming (the loss) after his passion is appeased. Consequently—his deliberate effort to recall the passion as a last resort, as the last refuge from his regrets, from the obsession of his longing to return whence he came. It's an impulse of thought not of the senses. The senses are done with. Nothing lasts! So with Aïssa. Her passion is burnt out too. There is in her that desire to be something for him—to be in his mind in his heart—to shelter him in her affection—her woman's affection which is simply the ambition to be an important factor in another's life. They both long to have a significance in the order of nature or of society. To me they are typical of mankind where every individual wishes to assert his power, woman by sentiment, man by achievement of some sort—mostly base.

I myself—as you see from this—have been ambitious to make it clear and have failed in that as Willems fails in his effort to throw off the trammels of earth and of heaven.

So much in defence of my view of the case. For the execution I have no word to say. It is very feeble and all the strokes fall beside the mark. Why?—If I knew that—if I knew the causes of my weakness I would destroy them and then produce nothing but colossal masterpieces— which no fellow could understand! As it is I am too lazy to change my thoughts, my words, my images and my dreams. Laziness is a sacred thing. It's the sign of our limitations beyond which there is nothing worth having. Nobody is lazy to accomplish things without any effort—and things that can only be attained by effort are not worth having.—

In the treatement* of the last scenes I wanted to convey the kind of placidity that is caused by extreme surprise. You must not forget that they all are immensely amazed. That's why they are so quiet—(At least I wanted them to be quiet and only managed to make them colourless). That's why I put in the quiet morning—the immobility of surrounding

---

[1] Mrs Willems and Aïssa, the island woman with whom Willems has a passionate, self-destructive affair.
[2] French for 'connection' or 'relationship'.

matter emphasised only by the flutter of small birds. Then the sense of their position penetrated* the [ir] hearts—stirs them.—They wake up to the reality. Then comes violence: Joanna's slap in Aïssa's face, Willems' rush, Aïssa's shot—and the end just as he sees the joy of sunshine and of life.—

Forgive me this long rigmarole. I wanted you to see what I meant—and this letter itself is a confession of complete failure on my part. I simply could not express myself artistically. It is a small loss to me and I notice that the world rolls on this morning without a hitch.

Once more, thanks. I shall set to at once and grub amongst all these bones. Perhaps! Perhaps!

Yours ever

J. Conrad.

P.S. on Friday[1] at 7. with joy.

To Émilie Briquel

Text MS Meykiechel; *Nouvelles*

1er oct 1895
17 Gillingham St. London S.W.

Chère Mademoiselle Briquel,

Je couvre ma tête avec des cendres, je déchire mon paletot, j'enlève mes souliers—pour un rien je me mettrais une corde au cou—pour approcher le tribunal de Votre miséricorde. L'Indigne (c'est moi) ose à peine prendre la plume pour répondre a Votre si bonne lettre du 8 septbre. Quand je regarde la date en tête de cette page j'ai la sensation d'avaler un morceau de fer rouge. Puis-je m'attandre au pardon?

Si Vous saviez comme j'ai été occupé! D'abord j'étais occupé à être malade. Ce n'est pas une occupation bien active (puisque j'étais au lit une semaine) mais c'est étonnant comme cela fatigue! Puis—selon mon imbécile d'habitude de faire plusieurs choses à la fois—je me suis empêtré dans toutes sortes d'affaires (mines d'or, mines de charbon, un navire pour faire la pêche aux baleines dans le sud—on n'est pas tant idiot... enfin!)[2] Vous concevez que pendant que je me donnais le luxe

---

[1] On 27 September.

[2] For a glimpse of Conrad's August business ventures, see letter to Sanderson, 24 August. His chief activity in the first half of September was the completion of the first draft of *An Outcast.*

des névralgies variées dans une chambre aux rideaux tirés, le Diable (qui est très obligeant) s'est mêlé de toutes ces magnifiques affaires, de sorte qu'à présent—étant sorti au soleil—je ne m'y retrouve plus. C'est comme un écheveau qui aurait passé entre les pattes d'un jeune chat. J'ai manqué des rendez-vous, les personnes à qui je me suis fié ont fait des boulettes tout à fait colossales, mes idées ont été mal expliquées—ce n'est qu'explications, récriminations, abomination et désolation. On m'a fait prendre des engagements absolument impossibles, et on veut me faire avaler des histoires fantastiquement improbables. J'ai mes mains pleines et ma tête est bourrée des chifres, des faits, des théories, des lourdes vérités et des mensonges légers mais vénéneux. N'importe! Je finirai bien par me débrouiller là-dedans et—du reste—j'aime à me battre de toutes les façons: contre les éléments ou contre les hommes. La lutte c'est la vie—et pour moi le plaisir est justement dans la lutte même—jamais dans la victoire—ou dans les résultats de la victoire. Jamais je n'y pense. C'est bête, n'est-ce pas? Mais c'est la seule idiosyncrasie qui me rend différent d'un vulgaire aventurier. Merci de toutes les nouvelles que vous me donnez. Je suis très heureux d'apprendre que Madame Votre Mère est dans un état de santé tolérable. Mlle Simon[1] est bien bonne de se rappeler son humble professeur de billard. Je Lui présente mes hommages. Quelle singulière idée de votre violoniste de se marier avec un Turc. Enfin elle est au mois originale—mais quand au bonheur, c'est une autre affaire, à moins que son Turc ne soit considérablement frelaté; dans ce cas il y a encore l'espoir d'une vie supportable. Mon livre paraîtra en novembre je pense.[2] J'ai une peur affreuse. Nous verrons! Mais je m'attends à des éreintements nombreux et cruels. Je vais prendre des toniques et manger des choses fortifiantes pour me préparer pour le choc!

Encore une fois pardonnez mon silence—Force majeure, Vous savez! Croyez-moi toujours Votre très humble serviteur et ami très dévoué

Jph Conrad

Mes devoirs à Madame Votre Mère. Bonne poignée de main pour Monsieur Briquel.

---

[1] Unidentified.
[2] Because of various delays, including a fire in which the printer's plates for the American edition were destroyed, *An Outcast* did not appear until 16 March 1896.

1 October 1895
17 Gillingham St, London S.W.

Dear Mademoiselle Briquel,

I cover my head with ashes. I rend my outer garment, I take off my shoes – for two pins I would put a rope around my neck – to approach the tribunal of your mercy. The worthless wretch (myself) hardly dares pick up his pen to answer your so very kind letter of 8 September! Looking at the date on the top of this page, I feel as if I were swallowing a piece of red-hot iron. May I expect forgiveness?

If you knew how busy I have been! First, I was busy being ill. It is not a very active occupation (since I have spent a week in bed), but it is surprisingly tiring! Then, according to my idiotic habit of doing many things simultaneously, I became involved in all sorts of affairs (gold-mines, coal-mines, a Southern whaler – one is not such a fool ... after all!). While I was enjoying the luxury of assorted neuralgias in a room with drawn curtains, the Devil (who is most obliging) interfered in all these splendid affairs so that, you understand, having now come out into the sunshine, I cannot find my way about. It is like a skein which has gone through a kitten's paws. I've missed a number of engagements, people I trusted have committed colossal blunders, my ideas have been badly explained – and now there are only explanations, recriminations, abomination and desolation. I am being made to take on absolutely impossible commitments and forced to swallow fantastically improbable stories. My hands are full and my head is crammed with figures, facts, theories, heavy truths, and light but poisonous lies. Never mind! I shall manage to disentangle myself eventually, and, besides, I enjoy fights of all kinds: against the elements or against men. To live means to struggle, and for me the pleasure consists in the struggle itself – never the victory, or the results of the victory. I never think about it. It's silly, isn't it? But it is the only peculiarity that distinguishes me from a common adventurer. Thank you for all the news you've given me. I was very happy to learn that your mother's health is tolerable. Mlle Simon is indeed kind to remember her humble teacher of billiards. I pay her my respects. What a strange idea of your violinist's to marry a Turk. It is at least original – but as for happiness, that's another matter, unless her Turk is watered down a little. In that case, there could still be some hope for a tolerable existence. My book will come out in November, I think. I am terrified. We shall see! But I expect many a cruel slating. I shall take a tonic and eat fortifying foods to ready myself for the shock.

Once more please forgive my silence – force majeure, you know! Believe me always your very humble servant and devoted friend

Jph Conrad

My respects to your mother. A warm handshake for M. Briquel.

To T. Fisher Unwin

Text MS Rosenbach; Unpublished

22^d Oct. 95.
17 Gillingham St. S.W.

Dear Mr Unwin.

I forgot to give up the dedication of the "Outcast".[1] I send it on now. I am off to-morrow morning. Trust to find You well when I return.

Yours very faithfully

J. Conrad.

To Edward Noble

Text MS Rosenbach; Privately printed; J-A 1, 182

17 Gillingham St S. W
28 Oct. 95.

My dear Noble

I received Your discouraged letter this morning and can assure You I felt very sorry for Your disappointement* ending the long-drawn hope.

It is hard to say anything. You must remember that true worth is never recognised at once. If Macmillans refused then some other house should be tried. Why not send on to F. Unwin—it might do for the pseudonym series[2]—or Autonym if you do not like the idea of a "nom de guerre".

You shall get certainly a careful consideration. Do make them purely river stories (about 30–40 thousand words).

Only my dear Noble do not throw yourself away in fables. Talk about the river—the people—the events, as seen through your temperament.[3] You have a remarkable gift of expression, the outcome of an artistic

---

[1] To Conrad's young friend, Edward Lancelot Sanderson. There is no further inscription.
[2] Fisher Unwin liked to bring out series of books in cheap and uniform bindings. This series ran from 1890 to 1903 for a total of fifty-six pseudonymous volumes.
[3] There is the suggestion here of Conrad's own handling of such phenomena in 'Heart of Darkness'.

feeling for the world around You, and You must not waste the gift in (if I
may say so) illegitimate sensation—You remember perhaps what I said
about the vampire story. A capital thing—wonderfully well put, as far as
the impressionism of the thing went—only—only to me all the charm, all
the truth of it are thrown away by the construction—by the mechanism
(so to speak) of the story which makes it appear false. Do not be angry
with me. I have thought your letter over many times during the day and
now I put down here my exact thoughts—right or wrong. You have any
amount of stuff in you but you (I think) have not found your way yet.
Remember that death is not the most pathetic—the most poignant
thing—and you must treat events only as illustrative of human
sensation—as the outward sign of inward feelings—of live feelings—
which alone are truly pathetic and interesting. You have much
imagination; much more than I ever will have if I live to be a hundred
years old. That much is clear to me. Well, that imagination (I wish I had
it!) should be used to create human souls; to disclose human hearts—and
not to create events that are properly speaking *accidents* only. To
accomplish it you must cultivate your poetic faculty—you must give
yourself up to your emotions (no easy task) you must squeeze out of
yourself every sensation, every thought, every image—mercilessly,
without reserve and without remorse; you must search the darkest
corners of your heart, the most remote recesses of your brain;—you must
search them for the image, for the glamour, for the right expression. And
you must do it sincerely, at any cost; You must do it so that at the end of
your day's work you should feel exhausted, emptied of every sensation
and every thought, with a blank mind and an aching heart, with the
notion that there is nothing—nothing left in you. To me it seems that this
is the only way to achieve true distinction—or even to go some way
towards it. It took me 3 years to finish the "Folly".[1] There was not a day
I did not think of it. Not a day. And after all I consider it honestly a
miserable failure. Every critic (but two or three) overrated the book. It
took me a year to tear the "Outcast" out of myself and—upon my word
of honour—I look on it (now it's finished) with bitter disappointement.*
Judge from that whether my opinion is worth having. I may be on the
wrong track altogether. I say what I think and from a sincere desire to see
You succeed—but I may be hopelessly astray in my opinions.

  Meantime you should try F. Unwin. 11. Paternoster Buildings E.C.

[1] In all, Conrad spent five years on the manuscript, from 1889 to 1894. By '3 years' Conrad
may have meant more or less sustained effort, beginning with his first voyage to Australia
on the *Torrens*, 25 November 1891.

I shall see Garnett (the reader) and mention your manuscript and Your name to him. He is young but very artistic. He is also a very severe critic. Of course Your book will be judged strictly on its merits. I am sure you would not wish for anything else.

Keep a good heart. You have many stories by you. Rewrite some of them from an inward point of view. In that point of view anything may be made interesting, and the faculty to do it is in you—or I am much mistaken.

I have just finished correcting my proofs. A ghastly occupation. I come out in November—25th or 30th.[1] I shall send you a copy of course.

Believe me my dear Noble Yours very faithfully

J. Conrad.

To Edward Noble

Text   MS Rosenbach; Privately printed; J–A, I, 184

2d Nov. 95
17. Gillingham St

Dear Noble

I have Your letter in answer to mine. Your argument is perfectly just and your point of view perfectly legitimate. There's nothing to say on my part in the way of controversy. On one point I think You misunderstand me. When I speak about writing from an inward point of view—I mean from the depth of Your own inwardness. I do not want you to drag out for public inspection the very entrails of your characters. Lay bare your own heart and people will listen to you for that—and only that is interesting. Everyone must walk in the light of his own heart's gospel. No man's light is good to any of his fellows. That's my creed—from beginning to end. Thats my view of life—a view that rejects all formulas dogmas and principles of other people's making. These are only a web of illusions. We are too varied. Another man's truth is only a dismal lie to me. I am telling you things that I would never dream of telling anybody but I don't want to speak to You from the shelter of any false pretences.

You can see now how little anything I may say is worth to anybody. Good luck to You!

Yours very sincerely

J. Conrad

My compliments to Mrs. Noble and my love to Miss Noble.

---

[1] *An Outcast of the Islands* was eventually published in March of the following year.

To Émilie Briquel

Text MS Meykiechel; *Nouvelles*; Najder (1972)

14 Nov. 1895
17 Gillingham Street, S.W.

Chère Mademoiselle Briquel,

Vous m'avez fait grand plaisir avec Votre bonne lettre d'où je vois que Vous Vous amusez et que tout va bien chez Vous.

Il fait bon de savoir que nos amis s'amusent et sont heureux quand on est dans une période de mal-chance. Pour ma part j'en ai assez de ce globe imbécile qui roule, roule, bêtement, sans savoir pourquoi. Imaginez vous—j'ai un procès sur les bras maintenant![1] Rien n'est plus étranger à mes goûts et à mes habitudes! Cependant me voilà fourré là-dedans et j'en suis tout ébahi.

Mais ce n'est pas tout! Il est arrivé à mon pauvre livre un lamentable accident. J'étais innondé d'épreuves pendant mon indisposition et j'ai fait de mon mieux corriger la chose sans délai. La page du titre avec dédicace et 1-er chapitre sont arrivés la dernière. Là-dessus je fais mes corrections du chapitre (étant au lit) et je demande a un de mes amis qui était là de voir la page du titre. Il regarde, me dit que c'est bien et, à ma demande, marque le tout "pour la presse" et renvoit le paquet. Je n'y pense plus. Avant-hier je reçois une note, qui me prie de passez chez l'Editeur pour voir le premier exemplaire. J'y vais. Je regarde. Très joli, très bien. Puis je regarde le titre. Malheur et malédiction! Il y a un (ou *une*) épigraphe en Espagnol—une citation de Calderon en deux lignes. Je fais un tapage! On me montre le manuscrit. C'était vrai! Vous savez que j'ai eu une certaine difficulté à choisir l'épigraphe. Sur la page il y en avait plusieurs mis là pour voir l'effet au crayon et à la plume; entre autres ce malheureux Calderon. J'avais oublié de passer ma plume dessus. La citation de Victor Hugo choisie par Votre Frère[2] n'y était pas, car mon intention était de l'inscrire sur la page d'épreuve avant de passer pour la presse. (Je voulais choisir la place et le genre de lettres à employer et il me fallait voir la page pour cela.) J'avais oublié de corriger! Mon ami naturellement n'a pris garde qu'ai l'effet général de la chose—à la couleur, etc. etc. Moi, avec ma névralgie, je n'y pensais plus. Quel malheur. J'ai demandé à changer, mais il y a déjà 4.000 exemplaires[3]

---

[1] Possibly connected with Conrad's dealings in South African gold shares. See Conrad's letter to Sanderson, 24 August 1895, for details.

[2] See letter to Paul, 30 May. *An Outcast* appeared with an epigraph from the seventeenth-century Spanish playwright Pedro Calderón de la Barca: 'Pues el delito mayor / del hombre es haber nacido' (*La vida es sueño*, I. ii).

[3] More probably under 3000: see n. 2 opposite.

d'imprimés et la page est stéréotypée. Il n'y avait rien à faire. Mais je suis fort chagrin. Ma foi tant pis! Cet épigraphe est bête mais il faut passer par là. Je demande bien pardon à Monsieur Briquel pour lui avoir donné tant de mal pour rien. Mais au prochain livre Victor Hugo y passera—ou j'y laisse ma tête. Dans dix jours l'impatient public aura ce chef-d'œuvre.[1] C'est le relieur qui n'est pas prêt. La 1ère édition sera de six mille.[2]

Voilà. J'ai tout dit. Mes devoirs les plus respectueux à Madame Votre Mère. Bonne poignée de main à Monsieur Votre Frère. Croyez-moi, chère Mademoiselle Emilie, toujours Votre très dévoué et très obéissant serviteur.

Jph Conrad.

P.S. Mes amitiés à ce brave "Notaire Savoyard"[3] si vous lui écrivez.

14 November 1895
17 Gillingham Street S.W.

Dear Mademoiselle Briquel,

It was a great pleasure for me to get your kind letter, from which I see you are enjoying yourself and all goes well with you.

It does us good to know our friends are enjoying themselves and are happy when we, ourselves, are going through a period of ill-luck. For my part I have enough of this idiotic globe of ours which turns and turns stupidly, without knowing why. Just imagine – I find myself now with a lawsuit on my hands! There is nothing more alien to my tastes and habits! Yet, here I find myself involved in it and feeling quite dumbfounded.

But that is not all! A sad accident has befallen my poor book. I was deluged by proofs during my indisposition and was doing my best to correct them without delay. The title-page with the dedication and the first chapter arrived last. I made my corrections to the chapter (lying in bed) and asked one of my friends who happened to be there to look at the title-page. He looks, tells me all is in order, and, at my bidding, marks the lot 'for the press', and sends the parcel off. I don't give it another thought. The day before yesterday I receive a note requesting me to call on the

---

[1] In fact, four months' time: 16 March.
[2] Actually 3000.
[3] This person, whoever he was, must have reminded Conrad and his friends of the unctuously benevolent Vicaire Savoyard in Rousseau's *Émile*.

editor to see the first copy. I go. I look. Very nice. Very good. Then I look at the title. Hell and damnation! There is an epigraph in Spanish – a two-line quotation from Calderón. I make a row! They show me the manuscript. There it is! You know I had a certain difficulty choosing the epigraph. To see the effect, a number of them were written on the page in pencil and in pen; among them was this wretched Calderón. I had forgotten to cross it out. The quotation from Victor Hugo chosen by your brother was not there because it was my intention to write it on the proof-page before passing it to the press. (I wanted to choose the layout and the typeface, and for that I had to see the page.) I had forgotten to correct it! Naturally, my friend paid attention only to the general effect – the colour, etc. While I, with my neuralgia, never gave it a thought. What bad luck. I asked them to change it, but 4000 copies had already been printed and the page is in stereo-plates. There was nothing to be done. But I am most annoyed. It is too bad! This epigraph is stupid but must be tolerated. My deepest apologies to M. Briquel for having bothered him for nothing. But Victor Hugo will get into the next book – or I perish in the attempt. In ten days' time the impatient public will have this masterpiece. It is the binder who is not ready. The first edition will be six thousand.

Well, I have told you everything. I commend myself to your mother. A hearty handshake for your brother. Please believe me, dear Mademoiselle Émilie, always your devoted servant

Jph Conrad

In case you write to him, my regards to our fine 'notary from Savoy'.

To Edward Noble

Text MS Rosenbach; Privately printed

Thursday night [28 November 1895][1]
[London]

Dear Noble

I've just dined with Garnett (F[isher] U[nwin]'s reader) and it so happens that I can disclose to you the inner working of this affair for I had him to dinner on purpose to put an artful question.[2] You do not in the least take up my time. I have loads of it just now. I should have

[1] The envelope is postmarked 29 November, a Friday.
[2] Conrad had asked Edward Garnett to consider Noble's collection of stories for publication by Fisher Unwin.

written to you to night in any case. I am only sorry that I have no better news to write. Garnett told me what he reported. It comes to this that he recommended to F.U to take the stories with a view of placing them in some magazine (F.U. has a good connection) first—just to see how they will strike people. And then—reported Garnett—they may be published in a vol: He told me that he did not feel justified in going further—and of course I could not argue the matter further with him. Moreover he is absolutely fair and knows no other conscience but that of pure art—yet he must be careful in recommending and is so, unless his enthusiasm is touched.—

Let Your knowledge of the report guide you in Your answer. I consider it my duty to tell you it is *not* a *very strong* report. The proposal to share expenses is made to everybody—as a matter of course—but in my case he offered alternative terms to buy right out. (For a song.) Be cautious. You know what is in his mind and you may work out some arrangement.

My new book is burnt in that great fire at the printers.[1] I mean the stereo-plates. I shall not come out now till March. I am very sick over it. The "Folly" goes into 2^d edition this season. Good luck to You. Yrs sincerely

J. Conrad

To Émilie Briquel

Text   MS Meykiechel; *Nouvelles*; Najder (1972)

17 Gillingham Street, S.W.
29 Déc. 1895

Chère Mademoiselle Emilie,

Veuillez accepter mes souhaits très sincères pour l'année qui s'approche. Je Vous souhaite—à Vous et aux Votres—la santé, la paix de l'âme, la réalisation de toutes les espérances, la félicité de l'imprévu fortuné. Et si le Maître de nos âmes, le Maître Miséricordieux et Clément veut bien entendre la voix d'un solitaire et aveugle pécheur, il vous donnera de longues années paisibles et douces, une existence seraine et digne, l'abri des affections sûres, le support des cœurs courageux et droits. Enfin je Vous souhaite le bonheur—en un mot—mais c'est un mot que l'on ose à peine prononcer, la chose semble si grande, si éloignée, si insaisissable, le vœu semble si audacieux et si futile!

Veuillez présenter à Madame Votre Mère mes hommages les plus

---

[1] The plates of the American edition of *An Outcast* were destroyed by fire in New York.

respectueux. Priez Monsieur Votre Frère d'accepter—avec une forte poignée de main—mes souhaits pour Son succès dans la vie qui s'ouvre devant lui, et croyez-moi toujours—chère Mademoiselle Emilie—Votre très humble et bien obéissant serviteur.

Jph Conrad

P.S. Je voulais vous envoyer mon livre—mais malheureusement il y eu un incendie à New-York et toute l'édition américaine a été brûlée. Comme il faut publier le même jour des deux côtés de l'Atlantique pour assurer les droits de l'Auteur (copyright) nous sommes forcé d'attendre ici la réimpression en Amérique. Je ne parais que fin février, j'en suis désolé.[1]

29 December 1895
17 Gillingham Street S.W.

Dear Mademoiselle Émilie,

Please accept my very sincere wishes for the approaching year. I wish you – and all your family – health, peace of mind, realization of all hopes, the joy of unexpected happiness. And if the Master of our souls, the merciful and clement Master, is well disposed to hear the voice of the lonely and blind sinner, he will give you long years, years peaceful and sweet, a life serene and noble, protected by unwavering affections and supported by courageous and honest hearts. In fact, I wish you, in a word, happiness; but that is a word which one hardly dares pronounce, the thing seems so great, so distant and imperceptible, the wish appears so presumptuous and futile!

Please be so kind as to convey to your mother my most respectful regards. Ask your brother to accept, together with a hearty handshake, my wishes for success in the life which opens before him, and believe me always, dear Mademoiselle Émilie, your most faithful servant.

Jph Conrad

PS. I wanted to send you my book, but, unfortunately, there was a fire in New York and the entire American edition was burned. As, to protect the author's copyright, publication must take place on the same day on both sides of the Atlantic, we are forced to wait for the American reprint. I shan't come out before the end of February; I feel heartbroken.

---

[1] Conrad had already told Noble that *An Outcast* would be appearing in March. Appleton's did not bring out the American edition until August.

1896

To T. Fisher Unwin

Text   MS Rosenbach; Unpublished

Wednesday. [29 January 1896][1]
17 Gillingham St S.W.

Dear Mr Unwin

Herewith I return the proofs of preliminaries sent to me this morning. If You will kindly glance at the "Opinions of the Press" page, You will see the kind of my objection to the manner of its placing. Now, I trust that You will not think me fanciful. But whether I am to incur, or not, that horrible odium I must strongly protest against the abominable advertisement being put opposite my dedication.[2] A dedication, for me, is a serious thing. It is an offering of my thoughts given in affection and esteem to someone whose friendship I consider a good fortune and a privilege. Such an offering—if made at all—should be made with some regard to form. I consider that in this case the form is disregarded. Not that I do not prize exceedingly all the kind and indulgent things said in the press;—but I own that I do not think it correct to put an advertisement opposite a dedication. Of course I assume that the folding of the sheets as sent to me is correct. Otherwise I would be making a fuss for nothing.

Excuse me bothering You personally, with that matter.

I am, dear Sir, Yours very sincerely
J. Conrad

To T. Fisher Unwin

Text   MS Rosenbach; Unpublished

1st Febr. 1896
[London]

Dear Mr Unwin

Thanks for the cheque. Thanks also for your answer to my letter about the Dedication of the absurd Outcast. It appears from another letter—also signed by You—that I opened the sheets wrong. As a matter of fact I just looked at them as they were folded when received.

---

[1] In the following letter, dated 1 February, Conrad thanks Unwin for having answered his letter about the dedication of *An Outcast*. That places this letter, marked Wednesday, earlier, and the most likely Wednesday is 29 January. We assume that Unwin responded by return of post.

[2] The following letter clarifies Conrad's error in thinking that an advertisement and his dedication to E. L. Sanderson had been juxtaposed.

Not being skilful in such matters I viewed the thing from all sides and came to a wrong conclusion. I am very sorry but I am sure You won't mind my appeal to you.

I am, dear sir

Yours sincerely

J. Conrad.

Enclosed receipt for cheque.

To Edward Garnett

Text   MS Sutton; G. 44

Saturday. [22 February 1896][1]

[London]

My dear Garnett

Thanks for Your letter. It gave me great pleasure in the expression of Your belief; the greater because I went away from our last interview with, somehow, an impression within me that You thought me hopelessly wrong headed. That feeling, taken together with my horrible inability (for the last fortnight) to write a line imbued me with a sense of insecurity. Yet such is the cast iron impudence of my soul, that I was less depressed than You may think by the ominous sounds from without and from within. I can be deaf and blind and an idiot if that is the road to my happiness—but I'm hanged if I can be mute. I will not hold my tongue! What is life worth if one can not jabber to one['s] heart's content? If one can not expose one's maimed thoughts at the gate of some cemetery or some palace; and from the disgusted compassion of the virtuous extract the precious penny? for all my talk of anxiety, of care for the future—and such like twaddle—I care very little for the course of events. The unexpected always happens. And if there is no room for one in this world, there is—I suspect—a place for everyone in the shadowy spaces of the next.

Nevertheless I am very grateful to You for your efforts on my behalf.[2] They will not be—in any case—wasted: for they have awakened feelings, stirred up sentiments, caused emotions. Caused pleasure, called out hope, gratitude, doubt; shaped uncertainty into amusing outlines—and touched the heart. So, I apprehend, as work of art they are complete and

---

[1] Date from Garnett.
[2] Garnett identifies these as attempts to find Conrad a command. See note on letter to Émilie Briquel, 26 August 1895.

successful—and no mere failure in securing their ends can destroy the fact of a higher success.

I shall turn up on Tuesday[1] at the concert. There's nothing I desire more than to be made known to Mrs Garnett[2] of whom I am unable as yet to think otherwise than as the incomparable translator of an incomparable novelist.[3] An image, that, gracious, inexpressibly interesting and charming but not quite satisfying to the base human nature, the vestiges of which (I am sorry to say) I have not yet been able to cast off utterly! Alas!

I am, dear encourager, Yours ever

J. Conrad

To Mme Briquel

Text MS Meykiechel; Najder (1972)

17 Gillingham Street

London SW

7. Mars 1896

Chère Madame Briquel.

Je viens d'arriver ici d'Ecosse,[4] et dans ce moment j'ai fini la lecture de Votre lettre, si charmante, si aimable, et, surtout, contenant une si bonne nouvelle.[5]

Les hautes qualités de Mademoiselle Emilie, Votre bonté le gracieux et amical accueil dont Vous avez daignée m'honorer à Champel resteront toujours parmis les plus précieux souvenirs de ma vie.

Devant Mademoiselle Votre fille s'ouvre la contrée paisible et douce des charmantes promesses. Je Lui souhaite des paysages ensoleillés, la fraîcheur de l'ombre sereine sur le chemin de la vie, les brises tièdes d'un eternal printemps. Si le bonheur ici-bas etait distribué selon le mérite je n'aurai aucun doute sur son avenir. Je fais de vœux pour que le Ciel Miséricordieux Lui donne des années longues et prospères pour faire la joie des siens et pour répandre le bonheur autour d'Elle par l'exercice des dons précieux de cœur et d'ésprit dont Il—l a douée.

Croyez, Chère Madame, que je comprends et que j'apprécie haute-

---

[1] 25 February.

[2] Constance Garnett (née Black, 1862–1946), the well-known translator of Turgenev, Tolstoy and Dostoyevsky.

[3] Turgenev, the sole Russian novelist for whom Conrad had an abiding affection.

[4] Where he had been seeking a command.

[5] Of Mlle Briquel's engagement – an event that Conrad probably regarded with mixed feelings.

ment la bienveillance qui a dictée les expressions, si pleines d'amitié, de Votre lettre. Je regrette de ne pas pouvoir, en ce moment y repondre longement. Je suis surchargé des besognes diverses—mais je voulais sans tarder, envoyer mes felicitations à Vous et a Mademoiselle Emilie.

Moi aussi, je me marie.[1] Mais c'est une longue histoire que Vous me permettrez de Vous raconter dans ma prochaine lettre qui suivra dans quelques jours.[2]

Croyez Moi, Chère Madame, toujours Votre très reconnaissant et fidèle serviteur

Jsph Conrad.

7 March 1896
17 Gillingham Street
London S.W.

Dear Madame Briquel,

I have just returned here from Scotland and finished reading your letter, so charming, so amiable, and, above all, bringing such good news.

The high qualities of Mademoiselle Émilie, your kindness, and the gracious but friendly reception with which you were pleased to honour me at Champel will always remain among the most precious recollections of my life.

A sweet and peaceful country of charming promises opens up before Mademoiselle, your daughter. For her I wish landscapes bathed in sunlight, cool and untroubled shade on the pathways of her life, and the mild breezes of eternal spring. Were happiness on this earth distributed according to merit, I should have no doubts about her future. I pray merciful Heaven to grant her long and prosperous years to be the joy of her family and to spread happiness all around by exercising the precious gifts of heart and spirit with which she has been endowed.

Believe me, dear Madame, I understand and deeply appreciate the kindness which dictated the so friendly words of your letter. I am sorry that, for the moment, I cannot answer you at length. I am overburdened with various tasks, but I want to send my best wishes to you and Mademoiselle Émilie without delay.

---

[1] Conrad married Jessie George on 24 March. They may have been introduced by G. F. W. Hope, although Jessie (in her *Joseph Conrad as I Knew Him*, p. 41) implies that she had not known him previously.

[2] If Conrad did indeed write again, none of the letters has survived.

I also am getting married. But this is a long story which, if you will allow me, I shall relate in my next letter, following in a few days' time.

Believe me, dear Madame, always your grateful and devoted servant

Jsph Conrad

To Karol Zagórski

Text J–A, I, 184; *Pion* (Warsaw, 1934), no. 50; Najder
215

17, Gillingham Street,
London, S.W.
10th March, 1896.

My dear Karol,

Once again I am posting to you my masterpiece (this time the second one).[1] Last year I sent three copies of my novel to Poland. Two of them reached their destinations. The third one, destined for you and your wife—presumably did not. I am trying again, hoping that this time both the book and the letter will reach you.

At the same time, I announce solemnly (as the occasion demands) to dear Aunt Gabrynia[2] and to you both that I am getting married. No one can be more surprised at it than myself. However, I am not frightened at all, for as you know, I am accustomed to an adventurous life and to facing terrible dangers. Moreover, I have to avow that my betrothed does not give the impression of being at all dangerous. Jessie is her name; George her surname.[3] She is a small, not at all striking-looking person (to tell the truth alas—rather plain!) who nevertheless is very dear to me. When I met her a year and a half ago she was earning her living in the City as a 'Typewriter' in an American business office of the 'Caligraph' company. Her father died three years ago. There are nine children in the family. The mother is a very decent woman (and I do not doubt very virtuous as well). However, I must confess that it is all the same to me, as vous comprenez?—I am not marrying the whole family. The wedding will take place on the 24th of this month and we shall leave London immediately so as to conceal from people's eyes our happiness (or our stupidity) amidst the wilderness and beauty of the coast of

---

[1] *An Outcast of the Islands.*
[2] Zagórski's mother, Gabriela.
[3] Jessie was very much alive when Jean-Aubry reproduced this letter; he makes several tactful excisions from the following sentences.

Brittany where I intend to rent a small house in some fishing village—probably in Plouaret or Pervengan (near St. Malo). There I shall start working on my third opus,[1] for one has to write in order to live. A few days ago I was offered the command of a sailing vessel[2]—the idea had pleased my Jessie (who likes the sea) but the terms were so unsatisfactory that in the end I refused. The literary profession is therefore my sole means of support. You will understand, my dear Karol, that if I have ventured into this field it is with the determination to achieve a reputation—in that sense I do not doubt my success. I know what I can do. It is therefore only a question of earning money—"Qui est une chose tout à fait à part du mérite littéraire".[3] That I do not feel too certain about—but as I need very little I am prepared to wait for it. I feel fairly confident about the future.

I hope that on the day of my wedding all of you—who are my whole family—will join me in your thoughts. I kiss the hands of my dear Aunt and ask for her blessing. I commend myself to your heart and to that of your wife.

Your loving

Konrad Korzeniowski

To Edward Garnett

Text G. 45

17 Gillingham St

Wednesday. [11 March 1896[4]]

Dear Garnett.

Please let me know where to find you. I do not know your Rwy station. Also let me know about what time we may put in an appearance on Monday.[5]

Yours ever

J. Conrad

---

[1] Probably 'The Sisters'. Jean-Aubry (I, p. 185, n. 1) mentions 'The Rescuer', but it is more likely that that novel followed Conrad's false start upon 'The Sisters'.

[2] Likely to be the *Windermere*, which Conrad, Jessie and Hope saw at Grangemouth. Jessie describes it in *Joseph Conrad and his Circle* (p. 19) as a desolate sight: 'In fact, there was a brooding air of ill-omen about the ship.' She reports that four years later it went down off Dover with all hands lost.

[3] 'Which is a matter quite apart from literary merit.'

[4] Date supplied by Garnett, confirmed by the reference to a forthcoming visit.

[5] Conrad was to visit the Cearne, the Garnetts' secluded house near Limpsfield on the Kent/Surrey border, with Jessie George, his fiancée; they were to marry on 24 March.

To Jane Cobden Unwin

Text   MS Chichester; Unpublished

17. Gillingham Street
S.W.
20th March 1896.

Dear Mrs. Unwin.

I thank You most sincerely for Your gift.[1] It will be most precious to me as an outward and visible sign of Your and Your Husband's kindness towards my undeserving self. Not that I was blind before. I trust I knew how to appreciate the gracious cordiality that meets one under Your roof and the unvarrying* friendliness of Mr Unwin in all his relations with an undistinguished beginner; but I must say that this last manifestation of Your joint goodwill has caused me a special and a heartfelt pleasure.

And I assure You, dear Mrs. Unwin, that in the rocky solitudes of the Brittany sea-coast I shall often hear again the words of true kindness[2] You have been pleased to say to me on the evening when I dined at Your house.

Believe me, dear Mrs Unwin, Your most obedient and faithful servant.

J. Conrad Korzeniowski

To Edward Garnett

Text   J–A, i, 185[3]; G. 45

Monday [23/24 March 1896]
[London]

Dear Garnett

I am very glad you wrote to me the few lines I have just received. If you spoke as a friend I listened in the same manner—listened and was only a little, a very little dismayed. If one looks at life in its true aspect then everything loses much of its unpleasant importance and the atmosphere becomes cleared of what are only unimportant mists that drift past in imposing shapes. When once the truth is grasped that one's own personality is only a ridiculous and aimless masquerade of something hopelessly unknown the attainment of serenity is not very far off. Then there remains nothing but the surrender to one's impulses, the fidelity to

[1] A wedding present.
[2] Conrad and his fiancée planned to spend their honeymoon in Brittany.
[3] Text from Garnett.

passing emotions which is perhaps a nearer approach to truth than any other philosophy of life. And why not? If we are "ever becoming—never being" then I would be a fool if I tried to become this thing rather than that; for I know well that I never will be anything. I would rather grasp the solid satisfaction of my wrong-headedness and shake my fist at the idiotic mystery of Heaven.

So much for trifles. As to that other kind of foolishness: my work,[1] there you have driven home the conviction and I *shall* write the sea-story—at once (12 months). It will be on the lines indicated to you. I surrender to the infamous spirit which you have awakened within me and as I want my abasement to be very complete I am looking for a sensational title. You had better help O Gentle and Murderous Spirit! You have killed my cherished aspiration and now must come along and help to bury the corpse decently. I suggest

THE RESCUER

A Tale of Narrow Waters[2]

Meditate for a fortnight and by that time you will get my address[3] and will be able to let me know what your natural aptitude for faithlessness and crime has suggested to you.

My dear Garnett you are a perfect nuisance! Here I sit (with ever so many things to do) and chatter to you (instead of being up and doing) and what's worse I have no inclination to leave off. (Surrender to impulses—you see). If I was not afraid of your enigmatical (but slightly venomous) smile I would be tempted to say with Lingard: "I am an old fool!" But I don't want to give you an opportunity for one of your beastly hearty approvals. So I won't say that, I will say: "I am a wise old man of the sea"—to you.

Tell Mrs. Garnett with my most respectful and friendly regards how grateful I am to her for the kind reception of myself and Jessie.[4] I commend myself to her kind remembrance and look forward to my next visit to your hermitage, with pleasure unalloyed by the fear of boring her to death. I have the utmost confidence in her indulgence—and the goodness of her heart will come to the rescue in the distress of her mind.

---

[1] 'The Sisters': after Garnett's adverse comments, Conrad abandoned this uncompleted novel.

[2] Having been taken up and given up many times, *The Rescue: a Romance of the Shallows* eventually appeared in 1920.

[3] In Brittany.

[4] See letter of 11 March.

As to you I of course do not care what happens to you. If you expire on your own hearthstone out of sheer "ennui" and weariness of spirit it will only serve you right. Goodbye my dear friend.

I am Yours ever

J. Conrad.

24th March, 1896.[1]

To E. L. Sanderson
Text MS Yale; Unpublished

28th March 1896
Hotel de France.
Lannion
(Côtes-du-Nord)

Dear Ted.

My first letter from this place[2]—where we arrived yesterday at 3 pm. is for You. To day it's raining—and as I have been sitting smoking bad French cigarettes which I extract one by one from the gorgeous cigarette case—it struck me that [I] could no better employ my time than in writing to the dear donor of that cheerfully glittering object.

Perhaps by this time You have the portraits. I told the photographer to send them to You as they were not ready on the day of my departure. I should like to imagine the expression of Your countenance while You contemplate the presentement* of myself—and my fate. But beyond the attitude of its being friendly I can imagine nothing. Yet there are so many shades of friendliness!

I am fixed here for a week. As soon as this beastly rain leaves off we shall hunt all over the country for some small cottage in a romantic situation. Both Jess and I hanker awfully after the Ile de Brehat which is about ½ a mile from the mainland on the side of Paimpol—(16 miles from here). If it isn't too wild we may set up our tent there. I want to be out of the way of absurd French tourists that stream through better known places during July and August. I have a mortal terror of them.

---

[1] Apparently, Conrad started writing on the 23rd, the eve of his wedding, and finished on the 24th. Garnett notes that with the letter came photographs and a card inscribed 'Mr and Mrs Conrad with sincere expressions of deep esteem and great regard'.

[2] Lannion is on the northern coast of Brittany, twenty miles NW of Guingamp.

Tell dear Mrs Sanderson[1] that—up to to-day—we had most glorious and warm weather. On the slopes of ditches there are great quantities of ridiculous yellow flowers growing in bunches. Jess is delighted with these—plants, must I call them? and made a kind of botanical collection of miserable looking specimens during a long walk we took yesterday afternoon. She, with an air of conferring a great favour, directs me to put some of that dismal rubbish into this letter "for Mrs Sanderson"—which with many apologies I am compelled to do. I dare say she attaches some mystical meaning to that apparently imbecile act—because other samples of vegetation are this moment being sent out to her mother—together with an unnecessary tear—which I pretend not to see. I suppose she's home-sick a little. But your mother will understand better the inwardness of these things. With love from both of us I am Yours ever   J.C.K.

I am going to work. The title of the new tale will be: *The Rescuer. A tale of narrow waters.* It is the same I have talked over with Your mother some time ago under the title of Carimata.[2]

To Katherine Sanderson
Text   J–A, I, 187[3]

6th April, 1896.[4]
Lannion.
Côtes-du-Nord.

Dear Mrs. Sanderson,

The joyful sight of your dear missive brought, besides the sense of satisfaction, a small pang of remorse. I am glad to say your first letter to me as a man married and done for has not miscarried. I had it one day after dispatching to you my dismal note with the news of Jessie's indisposition,—and how grateful I was for it and how much cheered by it,—words cannot express.

My very best thanks for your gracious kindness to my wife and myself. The dear girl is herself again,—nearly,—and so am I. For I must tell you,

---

[1] Ted's mother.

[2] A hill or mountain in *The Rescue*; also the Straits between Borneo and Sumatra.

[3] Yale's collection of 73 letters to the Sandersons does not include those to Ted's mother. The punctuation of Jean-Aubry's transcription is not typically Conradian.

[4] An auction catalogue lists 5 April, but in the absence of the original letter, we must accept Jean-Aubry's reading.

that,—unaccustomed as I am to matrimonial possibilities,—I was alarmed,—not to say horribly scared! However she had convincing proofs of my nursing qualifications: and no doubt in a year or two I will be disposed to take things with much more composure,—not to say coolness. But I must tell you under seal of confidence that I would not go through such three days again for a diamond mine! I am delighted to think Miss Monica[1] liked the wretched *Outcast* book. Please tell her so. I have a great opinion of her mental powers and of her judgment. This last you had better not tell her, for of all people of the world I should like her the least to think me gushing. I had a few reviews. Nothing remarkable. The *Illustrated London News* says I am a disciple of Victor Hugo, and is complimentary![2] Very! So are the Irish papers,—the *Whitehall Review* and the *World*.[3] But there is plenty of criticism also. They find it too long, too much description,—and so on. Upon the whole I am satisfied. To-morrow we take possession of the home on Île-Grande. I have written 11 pages of the *Rescuer*.

Believe me always your most obedient and affectionate servant.

Letter to dearest Ted soon. Beg him to excuse delay. My great love to him.

To Edward Garnett

Text   MS Yale; J–A, 1, facsimile pp. 186–7; G. 48

9th April..96.
Monsieur J. Conrad.
chez M*me* Coadon. March*de* des Granits.[4]
à Ile-Grande.
par Lannion.
(Côtes-du-Nord).

Dear Garnett.

The above rigmarole is my address for the next six months.

I am thirsty and hungry for news of you. Not for anything long—

---

[1] The eldest of Ted Sanderson's sisters.
[2] In the *Illustrated London News* (4 April 1896), James Payn wrote: 'Yet on or about him [the Outcast] the finest thoughts of our author are shed; they are often very striking, now sublime, and now grotesque, reminding us of the utterances of a writer who has had, to my knowledge, no other disciple, Victor Hugo.'
[3] The *World* criticized *An Outcast* rather severely, saying that 'The worst faults of the romance are its redundancy and the absence of greatness of any kind in the persons concerned' (1 April).
[4] 'March[an]de des Granits': granite merchant.

you know—but just for a few lines. Just be for once immorally charitable and drop me a line quick.

Have You got our portraits? Jess has been somewhat unwell for three days but is now all right. She is a very good comrade and no bother at all. As a matter of fact I like to have her with me.

We [have] got a small house all kitchen downstairs and all bedroom upstairs on as rocky and barren [an] island as the heart of (right thinking) man would wish to have. And the people! They are dirty and delightful and very Catholic. And most of them are women. The men fish in Iceland, on the Great banks of Newfoundland and devil know[s] where else. Only a few old old fellows forgotten by the capricious death that dwells upon the sea shuffle about amongst the stones of this sterile land and seem to wonder peevishly at having been left so long alive. More inland the country is charming and picturesque and unexpected. I like it much!

Tell me what do You think of the title and matter of the story.[1] "The sisters" are laid aside.[2] Have you seen any notices of the "Outcast" How do they strike You? I had some. They struck me all of a heap so to speak. Ought I to wish myself dead? Or only insane? Or What? Do tell me. By same mail I write to the Patron?[3] Is he very sick at the very thought of me? Or cocky? Or rampagious? Or fishyti icyty, dummy li indifferent? Does he exist at all? Do you all fellows really exist—have ever existed? Is London a myth?

We both send our love to you both—and to the hope of the House of Garnett.[4]

Yours ever and everywhere
J Conrad.

P.S. I have written 15 pages of the dullest trash! ... immense success!!

---

[1] 'The Rescuer'.
[2] On Garnett's advice.
[3] T. Fisher Unwin.
[4] David, born in 1892.

To Edward Garnett

Text MS Virginia; G. 49

Monday. [13 April 1896][1]
[Île-Grande]

Dear Garnett.

I am sending you MS already[2]—if it's only 24 pages. But I must let You see it. I am so afraid of myself, of my likes and dislikes, of my thought and of my expression, that I must fly to You for relief—or condemnation—for anything to kill doubt with. For with doubt I cannot live—at least not for long.

Is the thing tolerable? Is the thing readable? Is the damned thing altogether insupportable? Am I mindful enough of Your teaching—of Your expoundings of the ways of the reader? Am I blessed? Or am I condemned? Or am I totally and utterly a hopeless driveller unworthy even of a curse?

Do tell the truth. I do not mind telling you that I have become such a scoundrel that all Your remarks shall be accepted by me without a kick, without a moan, without the most abject of timid whispers! I am ready to cut, slash, erase, destroy; spit, trample, jump, wipe my feet on that MS at a word from You. Only say where, how, when. I have become one of the damned and the lost—I want to get on!

If you can't make [it] out have the thing typed to see how it looks and tell me the cost—or tell Mrs Gill in Ludgate Hill N° 35 to send J. C.'s. c/t[3] to Barr, Moering 72 & 73 Fore Street E.C. who will pay. Then keep this. I have a copy. May I go on in this style? Tell me soon. I trust this will reach you on Thursday. Remember us to Mrs Garnett.

Yours, J.C.

---

[1] There is no reason to question Garnett's dating.
[2] Of 'The Rescuer'. Garnett praised this first chapter. (See Garnett's letter to Conrad, 26 May 1896, in Jean Aubry's *Twenty Letters*.)
[3] Account.

To E. L. Sanderson
Text   MS Yale; J–A, I, 188

14 April 1896
Ile – Grande
par Lannion
(Côtes - du - Nord)

Dear Ted.

At last from my new (and very first) home I write you to say that I am quite oppressed by my sense of importance in having a house—actually a whole house!!—to live in. It's the first time—since I came to years of discretion—that such an event happened in my life.

Jess is immensely amused by the kitchen (the fire place alone is big enough for her to live in) and spends most of her time there trying to talk with the girl (who is a perfect treasure). The kitchen is the most splendid and the best-furnished appartement* of the palace—and the only way in or out, anyhow. So we see it pretty often. Our sticks and caps have their domicile there altogether.

The coast is rocky, sandy, wild and full of mournful expressiveness. But the land at the back of the wide stretches of the sea enclosed by the barren archipelago, is green and smiling and sunny—often even when the sea and the islets are under the shadow of the passing clouds. From beyond the rounded slopes of the hills the sharp spires of many village-churches point persistently to the sky. And the people that inhabits these shores is a people of women—black-clad and white-capped—for the men fish in Iceland or on the banks of Newfoundland. Only here and there a rare old fellow, with long white hair, forgotten by the successive roll-calls of the sea, creeps along the rock bestrewn beeches* and looks sad and useless and lone in the stormy landscape. The first Chap: of the "Rescuer" is gone to London yesterday.[1] I want Unwin to have a sample to show the Mag: Editors.—Write to me about yourself as I write to You about myself—so we shall have the illusion of nearness.

Yours with love Jph Conrad

---

[1] See Conrad's letter to Garnett, 13 April; his 24 pages of manuscript probably constituted the first chapter in its initial draft.

To Constance Garnett

Text MS Sutton; G.50

April 17th 1896.
Ile-Grande par Lannion
(Côtes-du-Nord)

Dear Mrs. Garnett

We are both much grieved to hear of Edward's illness.[1] These bad tidings, the first bad tidings of any sort which we received since we commenced our lonely life here, touched me very profoundly. I can measure the depth of my friendship and affection for Your husband by the painful disturbance of my thought since I have read your letter.

It is very good of You to have written! And I trust You will soon write again. Let me beg You to discard formulas in Your intercourse with me. You cannot have much heart or time for long messages. Just only a word or two—literally—and may it be "much better"!

I must demand of You, if not in the name of my friendship, then in the name of the interest dear Edward always showed me—thereby conquering my gratitude and affection.

We shall both wait with the greatest impatience for news from the Cearne.[2] I assure You that my wife's concern is very genuine and very great. She sends her best love and best wishes for a rapid recovery.

You are to a certain extent reassuring—but the news was so unexpected and so painful that I shall wait here, looking at the sea, with a heavy heart, till I hear again from You.

Believe me dear Mrs Garnett

Your most faithful and most obedient servant
Jph. Conrad

---

[1] Typhoid.
[2] The Garnetts' house in the country.

To T. Fisher Unwin

Text   MS Rosenbach; Unpublished

22^{d} April.
1896.
Ile-Grande
par Lannion
Cote du Nord
France

Dear Mr Unwin.

Forgive me for not acknowledging the cuttings and your letter sooner. I was in [a] vein of work (and also loafing) and as usual allowed full license to my unbridled passions.

To day I am chastened—so to speak—by the wholesome "slating" of the "National Observer."[1] No doubt the man is right. Everybody generally is. But no man likes to hear his child (no matter how defformed*) criticised and I am no exception to the rule.

Of course nothing said, one way or the other, will alter my own private opinion of my second effort. I am condemned for not being like Kipling (that was a stupid phrase of the Spectator's (?)) but as I never tried to be, I can't pretend to be much upset by that.[2]

I *was* upset by a letter from Mrs Garnett telling me of his serious illness. Through the community and also diversity of ideas I have become much attached [to] the man. Mrs Garnett writes hopefully but I am anxious to hear some positive news of improvement.

I wonder if you will think me very cheeky if I venture to ask you whether You could get for me a Malay Vocabulary, Mal–Eng and Eng–Mal?[3] There has been one published late in the eighties (in Sing[apo]^{re})—and perhaps it could be obtained in London. I find I've forgotten many words. I don't put, as You know, much language-colour

---

[1] Part of the unsigned review reads: 'Mr. Conrad does not possess Mr. Kipling's extraordinary faculty of making his natives interesting. We are sorry not to be able to write more appreciatively of what is evidently a careful and conscientious piece of work, but as it stands, *An Outcast of the Islands* is undeniably dull. It is like one of Mr. Stevenson's South Sea stories, grown miraculously long and miraculously tedious. There is no crispness about it and the action is not quick enough, a serious charge to make against a book of adventure. Even schoolboys will probably have some difficulty in getting through it and we fear adults will find it impossible' (vol. 15, p. 680; 18 April 1896).

[2] The review was highly favourable, calling Conrad a writer of genius (30 May 1896).

[3] For Conrad's work on the 'Rescuer' manuscript.

in my books, but I like to be correct—and now poor Garnett is so ill I have no one to turn to for such matters.

I commend myself to the kind remembrance of Mrs Unwin and . remain, dear Sir, Yours Very faithfully

Jph Conrad.

P.S. The "New[cas]^{tle} Chron[icle]" is enthusiastic about my psychology and very pleased all round. But the "Aberdeen F[ree] P[ress]" extols my English—and that is a real, a great pleasure; for I *did* try to earn that kind of notice.[1]

To Constance Garnett
Text G. 51

25th April 96
Ile Grande

Dear Mrs Garnett

Your welcome letter brought immense relief—how great you can hardly realize! I am truly grateful to you for sending me the good news.[2]

You have some sore trials to pass through with both the men of your house ill at the same time. I trust the dear little fellow[3] does not suffer much—and will soon get over the tonsilitis. I thought it was a disease of grown people and I am very sorry to hear he is precocious in such an infortunate* manner.

Dear Edward will have—no doubt—to leave London for a time to finish off his convalescence. I wish we had been nearer—and in a less uncivilized place—to beg all three of you to come to us. This sea air here is quite tonic—a rare thing. I am afraid it would be too far to travel for an invalid? But if you ever thought of it!—I would come to St Malo to lead you in triumph to *the* Island. The only island! And after all we manage to live not only decently but pretty comfortably. And I would promise

---

[1] To which we might add part of the unsigned review in the *Glasgow Herald*: 'there is distinction in [his] style. Mr. Conrad's books might be read for it, apart from any story at all ... *An Outcast of the Islands* is a book of singular and indefinable power; to be read carefully, some times even with labour, but always beautiful in its style, rich alike in passion and in pathos' (19 March 1896). The *Aberdeen Free Press* thought that 'Mr. Conrad's English gets into one's veins' (30 March).

[2] Garnett's recovery.

[3] David, aged four.

never to speak to Edward of books but entertain him only with light anecdotes and digestible short riddles—or even keep silent—mute as a fish. No sacrifice would be too great.

My wife rejoices at the news and sends her best love.

I am dear Mrs Garnett

Your most faithful and obedient servant
Joseph Conrad

To H. G. Wells

Text   MS Illinois (incomplete); Unpublished

May 18th—1896
Ile-Grande.
près Lannion
Côtes-du-Nord

Dear Sir.

I trust you will forgive whatever may be unusual or incorrect in my writing to you.[1] I do not know whether it is considered improper for the criticised to address his critic, in writing; but, it seems to me, there can be nothing very reprehensible in the expression of simple gratitude: and that is the only object of this letter.

I have tried to tell myself that gratitude has nothing to do there; that You have written all your thought regardless of pain or pleasure for the—more or less—thin-skinned creature behind the book. Such considerations and also the sense of my insignificance should have deterred me from this—say—intrusion. But I own I have been so moved by the evidence that a man of letters had thought it worth his while to give more than a passing thought to my endeavour that I prefer to throw myself upon your indulgence, of which Your review of my book is such a signal proof.

I wish to thank You for the guidance of Your reproof and for the encouragement of your commendation. You have repeated aloud and distinctly the muttered warnings of my own conscience. I am proud to

---

[1] When Conrad wrote this letter, he did not know that it was Wells he was addressing. He was responding to an unsigned review of *An Outcast of the Islands* in the *Saturday Review* for 16 May 1896, in which the reviewer said: 'Subject to the qualifications thus disposed of, "An Outcast of the Islands" is, perhaps, the finest piece of fiction that has been published this year as "Almayer's Folly" was one of the finest that was published in 1895.'

think that, writing in the twilight of my ignorance, I have yet seen dimly the very shortcomings which You point out with a hand so fine and yet so friendly.[1]

If I did not attach the greatest value to Your criticism I would not ask You now to let me add a word more. It is this: it seems to me, from the last paragraph of the review that you suspect my faults to be the outcome of affectation—of a deliberate insincerity of expression. That would[2]

To T. Fisher Unwin

Text MS Leeds; Unpublished

22^d May. 1896.
Ile Grande.

Dear Unwin.

Thanks for your kind letter and the cutting. I am still awfully shaky and my left hand remains for the present useless.[3]

I wrote a short note to the critic of the Sat. Rev.[4] I don't believe either in greatness or in the dishonour of his last paragraph.[5] But I am thankful to him for *all* he says. I can see the beam in mine own eye and am not afraid to own it. I feel idiotically elated by the Sat. Rev: giving a special article. Surely it does not happen to every beginner!—

There is at present in London a short story of mine which I have forwarded to a friend.[6] I am afraid You may have enough for a time of my lucubrations. That's why I did not send direct to you. Should you like to look at it I shall wait till I hear from you before starting it on its travels. It's a story of Brittany. Peasant life. Not for babies. 9.000 words on the outside. Fancy it, not at all bad. Please say.

There is about 20.000 of the "Rescuer" in typescript but have not done anything to it while unwell for fear of doing badly.

---

[1] The reviewer had spoken of Conrad's use of a 'dust-heap of irrelevant words ... His sentences are not unities, they are multitudinous tandems, and he has still to learn the great half of his art, the art of leaving things unwritten.'

[2] The last part of this letter has not survived.

[3] Apparently from gout.   [4] H. G. Wells. See preceding letter.

[5] Wells had ended his review with: 'Only greatness could make books of which the detailed workmanship was so copiously bad, so well worth reading, so convincing, and so stimulating.'

[6] 'The Idiots', a short story of 10,000 words, rejected by *Cosmopolis*, but accepted by the *Savoy* and published in October 1896. This is the first of the works that resulted from Conrad's initial impasse on the 'Rescuer' manuscript. The friend was probably Adolf Krieger.

Could you tell he how poor Garnett is. Haven't heard from his wife for days. I am very anxious.

With kindest regards for Mrs Unwin I remain always Yours very faithfully

Jph Conrad.

To Edward Garnett
Text   MS Texas; J–A, I, 189; G. 52

Sunday, 22 May. 1896.[1]
Ile Grande.

My dear Garnett.

I swear by all the gods that I haven't had such a smashing day since I came here—as to-day. I could not believe my eyes! If you knew how many bitter speculations hesitating hopes, frightened longings I have known since Your wife's last letter! On Friday I could not stand it any more and wrote F[isher] U[nwin] asking for news about you. We— Jessie and I—used to spend our evenings in dismal suppositions as to what happened in the Cearne, and came to the ghastly conclusion that you were no better, Mrs Garnett had broken down—and the end of the world seemed—to me—somehow within sight. We are both rejoiced![2] We have danced with loud shouts round your letter. We are hoarse and very tired. I sit down to answer! I haven't anything to say for the moment! There is nothing to say except that I am glad. Glad like a man relieved from rack or thumb screw—that kind of profound inexprimable* satisfaction. Your letter is so cheerful that I feel you must be in the state of real convalescence. I tell you what. I simply did not dare to write again to your wife. I kept quiet like a man who afraid to start an avalanche keeps deadly still on a narrow ledge—and waits.

It is good of you to think of me—to write to me—and such a long letter too! Don't you read the Resc[uer]: read nothing but Rabelais—if you must read. But I imagine you so weakened by disease that the bare effort of looking at the page must make you pant. However I trust that Mrs Garnett has some control over your actions—and will withhold this letter if she thinks it necessary.

[1] The manuscript reads thus, even though Sunday in May 1896 fell on the 24th, not the 22nd. Garnett has 24 May, Jean-Aubry 22 May. Conrad may have begun the letter on Friday, 22 May, and continued it into Sunday, adding the day later.
[2] At Garnett's recovery from typhoid.

Any amount of reviews![1] Heaps! It's distracting if one could take it all in. But one does not—fortunately. You are the best of invalids to send me the commented *Sat[urday] Rev[iew]*.[2] I had seen it! I was puzzled by it but I felt confusedly what you say in your letter. Something brings the impression off—makes its effect. What? It can be nothing but the expression—the arrangement of words, the style—Ergo: the style is not dishonourable. I wrote to the reviewer. I did!! And he wrote to me. He did!! And who do you think it is?—He lives in Woking. Guess. Can't tell?—I will tell you. It is H. G. Wells. May I be cremated alive like a miserable moth if I suspected it![3] Anyway he descended from his "Time-Machine"[4] to be kind as he knew how. It explains the review. He dedicates his books to W. Henley—you know. I have been rather ill. Lots of pain, fever etc etc. The left hand is useless still. This month I have done nothing to the Rescuer.—but I have about 70 pages of that most rotten twaddle. In the intervals of squirming I wrote also a short story of Brittany. Peasant life. I do not know whether it's worth anything. My wife typed it and it is in London now with a friend. I shall direct him to send it to you soon. The worst of it is that the Patron knows of it. I don't know why I told him about it. I never know what to write to that man. He numbs me like an electric eel. I want to know (when you are quite well) what you think of it. The title is: *The Idiots*. (10.000 words.)—This is all the news. I've been living in a kind of trance from which I am only waking up now to a sober existence. And it appears to me that I will never write anything worth reading. But you have heard all this before. To-night I shall go to bed with a light heart at last. Do not tire yourself writing. It's enough for me at present to know you are getting on. I shall write tho' whenever the spirit moves me or loneliness becomes insupportable. Jess sends her love. My affc^te regards to Mrs Garnett. Always yours,

Jph Conrad.

---

[1] Of *An Outcast of the Islands*.
[2] See Conrad's letter of 18 May to the reviewer (Wells). Wells responded, divulged his name, and the correspondents began a friendship that lasted for more than ten years.
[3] Woking was famous for its Necropolis and Crematorium.
[4] *The Time Machine* was published as a serial in 1894 in the *National Observer* (edited by W. E. Henley), and as a book in 1895. For a while, Wells became a member of the group of writers known as 'Henley's young men' or the 'Henley Regatta'.

To H. G. Wells

Text MS Illinois; Unpublished

25th May. 1896.

Ile-Grande.

Dear Sir.

If I praised highly the review before I knew who wrote it—it becomes still more precious now, when the name of my kind appreciator is known.[1] Strangely enough—about five months ago—when turning over the last page of the "Wonderful Visit" in the full impression of the extraordinary charm and suggestive realism of that book,[2] I remember reflecting—with contemptible bitterness—that a mind which could conceive and execute such work was absolutely beyond my reach. That to a man who could think and write so anything I could do—or attempt to do—would probably never seem worth a second glance. Its a shameful confession but You know how difficult it is for a common mortal to kick himself free of his own clamorous carcass. However it appears that the feeling (besides being base) was uncalled for. I am immensely surprised. But You can imagine how delighted I must be!

I do not know the titles of your unsuccessful books. I have only read the "Time Machine" the "Wonderful Visit" the "Bacillus" volume of short stories[3]—and I am informed to day that "Dr Moreau"[4] is just now on his way to my island. I expect to have the delight of his acquaintance to-morrow. Your book lay* hold of me with a grasp that can be felt. I am held by the charm of their expression and of their meaning. I surrender to their suggestion, I am delighted by the cleanness of atmosphere by the sharp definition—even of things implied—and I am convinced by the logic of your imagination so unbounded and so brilliant. I see all this—but the best I am probably unable to see.

Pardon this uncouth outburst of naïve enthusiasm.* I am, alas, forty and enthusiasms are precious to me and to be proud of. I am also very thankful to those who can raise them in my battered brain. I did not intend to bore you really. Thanks for the kind words of your letter. Believe me Yours very faithfully

Jph Conrad.

---

[1] Wells had written to Conrad (May 1896). See *Twenty Letters*.
[2] *The Wonderful Visit*, published in 1895.
[3] *The Stolen Bacillus* (1895).
[4] *The Island of Doctor Moreau* (1896).

To Vernon Weston

Text   Copies Yale; J–A, I, 190[1]

Île-Grande, par Lannion
26 May 1896

Dear Mr. Weston,[2]

I have just got your card and hasten to thank you and all friends for your kind thought and good wishes.[3] I am not likely to forget my early days in Well Street and the good will shown to a stranger by all there—and especially by your late Father, who so kindly assisted me in becoming (I hope not altogether an unworthy) British subject; and your own uniform friendliness.

Kindly give my best regards to Mr. Newton[4]—my only Teacher—and Mr. Bastard my first Watch-Officer.[5]

I trust everybody is well and happy.

I expect to be in London in October when I shall make a point of calling on you.

I see some newspapers prophesy that my seagoing days are over. It is not my feeling. I do hanker after the sea—it's only the want of opportunity that keeps me on shore. I am now writing my third novel.[6] It is an occupation of much trouble, and little profit, and a man can't live on praise alone. I get enough of that.

To Edward Garnett

Text   MS Colgate; G. 54

2[d] June 1896.
Ile Grande

Dear Garnett.

Don't think me an ungrateful beast. I have read Your criticism of the first chapter with profound thankfulness and I surrender without the slightest demur to *all* your remarks.[7] It is easy to do so because they

---

[1] The original is unknown; Yale has two copies, one of them incomplete.

[2] Vernon Weston succeeded his father, J. E. Vernon Weston, as manager of the Sailors' Home, Well (now Ensign) and Dock Streets, London E.1. In 1886, the elder Weston may have helped Conrad obtain his naturalization papers. (Original identification of the Westons was by Hans van Marle of Amsterdam.)

[3] On his marriage.

[4] See letter to Newton (or his son), [4 May] 1895.

[5] H. J. Bastard, second mate on the *Duke of Sutherland*, on which Conrad served as an ordinary seaman from 12 October 1878 to 19 October 1879.

[6] 'The Rescuer', on which Conrad had reached an impasse.

[7] On the early pages of 'The Rescuer'.

express my own thought. Yes! The first page *is* bad. You see what I wanted to say is by no means easy and I wrote it out in a perverse mood. But still I think something of the kind ought to be said—more concisely—in other words. As to its not being in tone with the rest it only shows what a many-toned fellow I am. But oh! Can't I be bad! Can't I! It's perfectly rotten, that paragraph, and when one touches it the putrid particles stick to the fingers. I shan't touch it for a while for my gorge rises when I look at it.

As to the "lyr[ic]ism" in connection with Lingard's heart. That's necessary! The man must be episodically foolish to explain his action. But I don't want the word. I want the idea. Could You help me to shape it in an unobjectionable form. The passage or two marked as superfluous (the coconut etc) ought to be cut out. I know they are not necessary. I don't care for them.

The Patron got hold of my short story.[1] It's a most damnable occurrence— but You should not indulge in typhoid fevers discomposing recklessly your friends. I wrote to him instructions to forward it to you. I *would not* have it published unless You see and pass it as fit for the twilight of a popular magazine.[2] I want to know what you think of it with an absurd intensity of longing that is ridiculous and painful. Often I think of the thing with shame—less often with pleasure—but I think of it every day. And every day The Rescuer crawls a page forward—sometimes with cold despair—at times with hot hope. I have long fits of depression, that in a lunatic asylum would be called madness. I do not know what it is. It springs from nothing. It is ghastly. It lasts an hour or a day; and when it departs it leaves a fear.

Let me know how You get on. Jess is very proud of Your references to her and sends her love to both of you.

I am with the greatest affection always yours
Jph Conrad.

---

[1] 'The Idiots', which Adolf Krieger had delivered to Unwin's office while Garnett was ill.
[2] The story was eventually published in the *Savoy*.

To Edward Garnett

Text G. 56

[6 June 1896[1]]
[Île-Grande]

Dear Garnett

Blessings on your head for the letter with the "Lucas" enclosure.[2] Today I heard from the *Cornhill*. A letter signed by Charles L. Graves writing by desire of the Editor.[3] Asks for short stories. Serials full up to 1899 (I will be dead before then). Short stories at £1.1 per 500 words (that is one page). Very nice letter. Says they are ready to give the most "sympathetic consideration" to anything I may send.[4]

I wrote to F[isher] U[nwin] urging him to forward "Idiots" to you. Have you got them? What do you think? O! My friend speak the truth if you do tear my entrails through my palpitating flank! from you even torture is sweet. It seems to me I am intruding too much into your life. In this matter too, friend, speak to me unveiled words.

As soon as part I of the stupid *Rescuer* is finished I shall send it straight to you. I am gnawing my fingers over the end of it now. If you knew how idiotic the whole thing seems to me you would pity me. You would weep over me. Oh the unutterable, the inevitable Bosh! I feel as if I could go and drown myself—in a cesspool at that—for twopence.

I used to have swollen veins in both legs after my return from the Congo. If you hobble now then the initial pain is over. But do refrain from overdoing it in your gambols—as I did then and had to go through the whole fiendish performance "da capo."[5]

Postman waits. We two send our love to you three. Think of me with indulgence.

Yours ever   J. Conrad.

---

[1] Date from Garnett. The letter falls before the one to Unwin for 7 June, where Conrad mentions the letter from the editor of the *Cornhill Magazine*.
[2] E. V. Lucas (1868–1936), journalist, essayist, critic. He was a writer for the *Globe* and later joined Methuen as a reader.
[3] St Loe Strachey. The letter, held by the Lilly Library of Indiana University, is dated 3 June.
[4] Conrad published 'The Lagoon' in the *Cornhill* for January 1897.
[5] Musical term: once more from the beginning.

To T. Fisher Unwin

Text MS Yale; Unpublished

7ʰ June. 1896.
Ile Grande
par Lannion.

Dear Mr Unwin.

I had a letter from the Edʳ of the *Cornhill* asking for short stories which he offers to insert and pay for at the rate of £1.1. per page of about 450 words.

I think this *Cornhill* is not a bad mag. to appear in—and, if You have not placed the "Idiots" yet, we might try there. But I am not in a hurry in the least, and in any case would like Garnett to have a look at the story before sending it off.

I trust You are well. I am better now—and doing work—of sorts.

Faithfully yours

Jph Conrad.

To Edward Garnett

Text MS Yale; G. 57

10 June 1896.
Ile Grande.

My dear Garnett.

I send you to-day a registered envelope containing all that there is of the *Rescuer*. It is the whole of the first part. You will see that I have given up dividing it into chapters—formally. I think I had better divide the thing into parts only.[1] Say five. Then in places—where necessary and proper—a wider interval between the paragraphs will mark the subdivisions of the parts; this arrangement will give me more freedom I think.

I do not know what to think of the pages I am sending you. Mostly they fill me with dismay. But I don't know why they should have that effect. I have been thinking, meditating a great deal, and hoped to have much to say to you in justification of my work. And now I have nothing to say. Cannot find two consecutive sentences in my head.

Will anybody in the world (besides you) have the patience to read such twaddle—I wonder! Will you tell me the truth about it? Here I have used up 103 pages of manuscript to relate the events of 12 hours. I have

[1] When the novel did appear, twenty-three years later, Conrad had redivided parts into chapters, the first part containing four chapters.

done it in pursuance of a plan. But is the plan utterly wrong? Is the writing utter bosh? I had some hazy idea that in the first part I would present to the reader the impression of the sea—the ship—the seamen. But I doubt having conveyed anything but the picture of my own folly.—I doubt the sincerity of my own impressions.

Probably no more will be written till I hear from you. If You think I am on a wrong track You shall say so and I may try some other way. Meantime I live with some hazy notions of scenes of passion and battle—and don't know how to get there. I dream for hours, hours! over a sentence and even then can't put it together so as to satisfy the cravings of my soul. I suspect that I am getting through a severe mental illness. Enough of this.

I am ever Yours

Jph Conrad.

Can the *Idiots* be printed without dishonour?

To Aniela Zagórska
Text Translations Yale; J–A, I, 191; Najder 216[1]

12.6.1896.

Ile-Grande—par Lannion

My dear Cousin,

Forgive my long silence: I have been ill. I had an attack of rheumatism in my hand and foot. This attack not only kept me in bed for two weeks, but it has so shaken me that I still feel giddy. What's more my hand is swollen, which doesn't make writing easy.

I cannot express to you, my dearest Aniela, what a great pleasure your letter has given me—seeing the news you sent me of you all and your so very artistic appreciation of my book.[2] The expressions in your letter inspire me with confidence and the desire to continue my work. I again read your letter today and it is with a fresh sense of gratitude that I send you my thanks.

Please forgive me for not being able to write a longer letter today. I am not yet recovered either in body or in mind. Fortunately before I was taken ill I was able to finish the first part of my new novel.[3] Naturally my

---

[1] Letter in French and English translations; Polish original unknown. Najder's text is based on a collation of the French and English versions.

[2] *An Outcast.*

[3] 'The Rescuer'.

illness has made my wife very tired, but otherwise she is well. As for me, I feel better and better every day.

My dearest—I wish to be remembered to you all. I hope that you will find a moment to write to me. We shall stay here for three months longer.

Your very affectionate brother and servant,

K. N. Korzeniowski.

To Edward Garnett
Text   J–A, I, 191[1]; G. 58

19th June 1896
Ile Grande

My dear Garnett.

I got your letter today. Need I tell you how delighted I am with your approval?[2] The warm commendation is to me so unexpected that if I had not a perfect confidence in your sincerity I would suspect that the despondent tone of my accompanying letter induced you perhaps to force the note of satisfaction with my effort. However, if I don't believe in the book (and I don't somehow) I believe in you—in you as a last refuge: somewhat as an unintelligent and hopeless sinner believes in the infinite mercy on high.

Since I sent you that part 1st (on the eleventh of the month) I have written one page. Just one page. I went about thinking and forgetting—sitting down before the blank page to find that I could not put one sentence together. To be able to think and unable to express is a fine torture. I am undergoing it—without patience. I don't see the end of it. It's very ridiculous and very awful. Now I've got all my people together I don't know what to do with them. The progressive episodes of the story *will* not emerge from the chaos of my sensations. I feel nothing clearly. And I am frightened when I remember that I have to drag it all out of myself. Other writers have some starting point. Something to catch hold of. They start from an anecdote—from a newspaper paragraph (a book may be suggested by a casual sentence in an old almanack). They lean on dialect—or on tradition—or on history—or on the prejudice or fad of the hour; they trade upon some tie or some conviction of their time—or upon the absence of these things—which they can abuse or praise. But at any rate they know something to begin with—while I don't. I have had some

---

[1] Text from Garnett.
[2] Of the first part of the 'Rescuer' manuscript.

impressions, some sensations—in my time:—impressions and sensations of common things. And it's all faded—my very being seems faded
and thin like the ghost of a blonde and sentimental woman, haunting
romantic ruins pervaded by rats. I am exceedingly miserable. My task
appears to me as sensible as lifting the world without the fulcrum which
even that conceited ass, Archimedes, admitted to be necessary.

I know the Patron has the *Idiots.* I trust he has sent them to you but I
haven't heard from him at all. I did write to the *Cornhill* a suitable answer
and informed the Patron of their offer.

Thanks with all my heart for the time, the care, the thoughts you give
to me so generously. I am getting so used to your interest in my work that
it has become now like a necessity—like a condition of existence. Why
don't you tell me how you are? How are the veins—for I trust that is now
the only trouble and I long much to know that it is over.

My affectionate regards to Mrs Garnett. I am ever yours
Joseph Conrad

I am nearly right. Had a 3 days' cruise along the coast.[1]

To T. Fisher Unwin
Text   MS Leeds; Curreli

3ᵈ July 1896.
Ile Grande
par Lannion.

Dear Mr Unwin.

I must thank you for some more cuttings relating to the "Outcast",
and especially for that from the *Indian Magazine* which caused me great
pleasure by its level-headed appreciation.[2]

We had a few days ago the very great pleasure of seeing Mrs
Brooke[3]—who passed through Lannion with Miss Ashton. As we owe
that pleasure to Your wife I beg you to express to Mrs Unwin my very

---

[1] In *La Pervenche*, which Conrad hired from a retired shipmaster in Lannion.

[2] The *Indian Magazine and Review*, the journal of the National Indian Association,
London, had reviewed (in June 1896) both *Almayer's Folly* and *An Outcast of the Islands*
in a single article. S. Mario Curreli has traced this review and discovered that the
reviewer identified the original of Tom Lingard, this as early as 1896. Such identification became the basis of later, and much fuller, research by Jerry Allen and Norman
Sherry.

[2] Minnie Brooke was a friend of Mrs Unwin. Her husband, the Reverend Arthur Brooke,
rector of Slingsby, Yorkshire, had conducted the Unwins' wedding ceremony.

sincere thanks for remembering and mentioning to Mrs Brooke the locality of our "idyllic happiness". I have for Mrs Brooke (tho' I have seen Her only twice) the greatest regard and consideration. I don't mean to boast of my discrimination; for my feelings, in that matter, are more trustworthy being from the first instinctive—and that Lady's fundamental goodness is so graciously near the surface that only the hopelessly blind would fail to perceive it. Thinking as I do—Mrs Unwin will easily understand that I was immensely gratified at the opportunity she has kindly given me to introduce my wife to Mrs Brooke. I trust those Ladies arrived home "all well"—as we say at sea.

May I (modestly and with diffidence) inquire about the fate of the "Idiots"?[1] It is not impatience but curiosity only—I assure you.

I have made the acquaintance here of the local poet who is very mad (and also an inspector of a Fire Insurance Company) and who bestowed upon me three vols of his immortal works.[2] I wish to bombard him with at least one copy of my masterpieces. I must therefore beg You either for a copy of "Folly" or the "Outcast" whichever is more handy. The poet is going to impart to me some Breton documents—I don't know of what nature. Still there may be material for something in them. My wife has been ailing—and is better. I have no disease but laziness. Work goes slowly. I am dear Mr Unwin Yours most faithfully

Jph Conrad.

To Edward Garnett

Text   MS Sutton; G. 60

10th July. [1896][3]
Ile Grande.
par Lannion.

My dear Garnett.

I did not write sooner from (would you guess it?) a sense of delicacy—was afraid to take up too much of your time in fact! But hang it all it's more than (my) human nature can stand. I must let out a howl upon things in general—which are things that interest me in particular.

I guess (from the aspect of heavenly bodies and from T. Fisher Unwin's letter) that You are tolerably well. Would like to be sure. Have

[1] The story was to be refused twice, by *Cosmopolis* (ostensibly because of excessive length) and by the *Cornhill*.

[2] Possibly the M. le Goffic mentioned by Jessie Conrad in *Joseph Conrad as I Knew Him*, p. 27.

[3] Garnett supplies no year, but place and content indicate 1896.

no conscientious objections to postcards. Am used to hardships and privations of all kinds. Think that 1½ line from You would do me good! Leave you to draw inferences!

Why am I fooling thusly while there is a pain in my back to which a jab with a carving-knife would be a soothing application? I also have just learned that the Cosmopolis refuses my short story[1] (twice) (twice refuses). So says T.F.U. But he also says you are pleased with it. Is he only gilding the pill? Provisionally I am consoled—but I would like to be sure.

If you have no further use for it please send the 1st part *Resc[uer]* to *G.F.W. Hope 18. Ironmonger Lane. E.C.* I want him to look over the seamanship of my expressions.[2] He is instructed to return it to you. I trust I will live long enough to finish that story but at the pace I am going now I am preparing for myself an interminable old age. I am now setting Beatrix, her husband and Linares (the Spanish gent) on their feet.[3] It's a hell of a job—as Carter would say.[4] However I trust you will find that they stand firmly on their pins when I am done with them. I am trying to make all that short and forcible. I am in a hurry to start and raise the devil generally upon the sea. Jess is not very well but apart from that she is a very good girl. I mention this because I think you might like to know. We send our very best love.

Yours ever Jph Conrad

To Edward Garnett

Text   MS Sutton; G. 61

22 July 96.
Ile—GRANDE

My dear Garnett.

Your letter was like dew on parched grass. I look different to-day. I feel different. I am glad You are taken care of in such an ideal way, but I don't enjoy the news of Your stiff legs. And what is that ominous and startling little sentence "Bills rolling in?"—Ah! my dear Garnett God keep us all!

---

[1] 'The Idiots'.

[2] For a time a keen amateur yachtsman, Hope had been a professional sailor. See notes to letter to Thys, 28 November 1889.

[3] In the published version (*The Rescue*, 1920), these characters first appear in part III; Beatrix has been renamed Edith Travers and Linares, d'Alcacer. The plot concerns the efforts of Tom Lingard to recover Mr Travers's yacht, which has run aground in the Malay Archipelago.

[4] Mate of the stranded yacht.

What are you going to write? What? Why hint, and not explain? If You send me a book let it be Your book—one of your books—for I know now the *Imaged World*[1] pretty nearly by heart.

Don't you spoil me! Don't you? After reading your letter I don't touch the ground for three days. Then I get a fall—when I begin to hear myself.

Cosmo asked for a story. I was then writing a story especially for you.[2] I was polishing, perfecting, simplifying. It's finished. I send it to you first of all. It's yours. It shall be the first of a vol ded to you[3]—but this story is *meant* for you. I am pleased with it. That's why you shall get it. I am sure You will understand the reason and meaning of every detail, the meaning of them reading novels and the meaning of *Carlier not* having been armed.[4] The story is going by this post. After reading send please to *F[isher] U[nwin]*. If any passages are—de trop—then strike out. I mean it. I don't want anything incompatible with the general method of the thing—but am befogged myself now. Thanks for your hint about the "*Savoy.*"[5] I shall wait yet. Don't like to snatch the thing from the Patron who seems to be trying his best. How is your wife and boy? You don't say. We are so so. There is very little more of Rescuer written. I could not. Misery! Write to us. Yours ever Jph Conrad

I have had a lot of worries. A man I love much had been very unfortunate in affairs and I also lose pretty well all that remained.[6]

Jess sends love to you all.

---

[1] Garnett's 'Poems in Prose', published in 1894.
[2] 'An Outpost of Progress', at first called 'A Victim of Progress', written in July in about three weeks, and eventually published in *Cosmopolis*.
[3] Conrad dedicated his first volume of short stories, *Tales of Unrest*, to Adolf Krieger: the dedication of *The Nigger of the 'Narcissus'* is to Edward Garnett.
[4] In the story, two Europeans fritter away their time at an African trading-post. Kayerts shoots Carlier and then hangs himself.
[5] Arthur Symons had asked Garnett for a contribution from Conrad, and 'The Idiots' appeared in October 1896. (See G., p. 62, n. 2.)
[6] G. F. W. Hope, Conrad's longest-standing English friend, had invested heavily in a South African mining company; for an account of Conrad's involvement, see the letter to Sanderson, 24 August 1895. The failure of these interests meant the loss of most of Conrad's capital. According to Jessie Conrad, they had feared this failure as early as March 1896, but, until a director of the company was lost in the wreck of the *Drummond Castle* (17 June), they had hoped that some of the investment might be salvaged (*Joseph Conrad and his Circle*, pp. 27–31).

To T. Fisher Unwin

Text MS Yale; Keating 60–1

22^d July. 96.

Ile Grande

par *Lannion*

Dear Mr Unwin.

Thanks for Your unwearied endeavours to place my story. I am very much touched but suspect that you must have about enough of me and of my 'masterpieces'.

The acceptance of my story would have given me pleasure. But its refusal is not without its compensations[1]—for it is exactly what I did foresee. It shows me that I have judged the work rightly. I am not ashamed of it for all that. Bad or good I cannot be ashamed of what is produced in perfect single mindedness—I cannot be ashamed of those things that are like fragments of my innermost being produced for the public gaze.

But I must live. I don't care much where I appear since the acceptance of such stories is not based upon their artistic worth. It is probably right that it should be so. But in that case there is no particular gratification in being accepted *here* rather than *there*. —If the 'Savoy' thing asks for my work—why not give it to them? I understand they pay tolerably well (2g[uinea]s per page?). The only thing I wish is that your right to reproduce in a volume should be perfectly clear. You said you would—yourself. And it has been a great pleasure for me to hear it. And I feel that the stories will be worth[y] of your imprint—even if stones are cast at them. But I should like to sell them. If you think I am greedy then consider I am greedy for very little after all. And if you knew the wear and tear of my writing you would understand my desire for some return. I writhe in doubt over every line.—I ask myself—is it right?—is it true?—do I feel it so?—do I express all my feeling? And I ask it at every sentence—I perspire in incertitude over every word!—Perhaps you will smile over all this fuss. But I am sure You will not smile unkindly. After all it is my work. The only lasting thing in the world. People die—affections die—all passes—but a man's work remains with him to the last.

—You will soon receive a story for the *Cosmo*.[2] I suspect that they won't take it after all. I send it to Garnett for the reason that it refers (in

---

[1] The refusal of 'The Idiots' by *Cosmopolis*.

[2] 'An Outpost of Progress', which appeared in the *Cosmopolis* for June–July 1897. Unwin was the London publisher of this *International Monthly Review*.

its execution) to a certain discussion we had on matters of art and
I should like to know whether I have succeeded in achieving my purpose—my artistic purpose. The effect produced on him will tell me that.

—It is a story of the Congo. There is no love interest in it and no
woman—only incidentally. The exact locality is not mentioned. All the
bitterness of those days, all my puzzled wonder as to the meaning of all I
saw—all my indignation at masquerading philanthropy—have been
with me again, while I wrote. The story is simple—there is hardly any
description. The most common incidents are related—the life in a lonely
station on the Kassai. I have divested myself of everything but pity—and
some scorn—while putting down the insignificant events that bring on
the catastrophe. Upon my word I think it is a good story—and not so
gloomy—not fanciful—alas! I think it interesting—some may find it a
bore!If the *Cosmo* won't take it (it is as long as the other) I shall put it by.
A day may come for it. I wonder you find time to read my letters! Thanks
once more. Yours very faithfully

Jph Conrad.

My most respectful and affct^nte regards, Mrs Unwin. I ought to thank
you for the Cobden number of the Dly News.[1] I was immensely pleased
to be remembered in that way.

To Minnie Brooke
Text   MS Texas; Unpublished

29th July. 1896.
Ile-Grande.
p. Lannion.

Dear Mrs. Brooke.

It was a very great kindness on Your part to remember me and to write
to me—and a most unexpected pleasure for me to read Your interesting
and friendly letter.[2]

Do not suspect me of indifference as to the fate of the travellers. I did
not of course presume to ask You to give me news of Your safe return

---

[1] Mrs Unwin was the daughter of Richard Cobden (1804–65), Liberal and Free Trader.
The *Daily News* was a devoutly Liberal paper. On 29 June, it reported the Cobden Club's
celebration of the fiftieth anniversary of the repeal of the Corn Laws; Unwin was among
the celebrators.

[2] At the instigation of her friend Jane Cobden Unwin, Minnie Brooke had met the
Conrads in Brittany.

but I wrote to Mr Fisher Unwin shortly after your departure and in that letter made inquiries as to Your safe arrival—naturally supposing that you would see Mrs Unwin in London—In which it appears I was wrong. It explains why I did not hear from Mr Unwin of your safe arrival. My wife and I watched the weather with great interest on the day we supposed You would be crossing the channel—and we often remember Your visit—so short but so charming.

I am very sorry the train went before you could say what—I haven't the slightest doubt—the kindness of Your heart would have dictated; and I would have treasured your words as much as I treasure all the friendly expression of Your letter. I thank You most sincerely for Your remembrance, for Your kind wishes, for the hope You are pleased to express of meeting with us again.

We are going to stay here till the end of September—and then we return home direct through St Malo. I think that for the winter we shall take a small cottage somewhere near London. I should have of course preferred a palace but a cottage is more economical. My wife thinks it will be charming—but I am not so sure of that. Still I am older and have less illusions than she has, so, probably, she is right. At any rate there will be work and solitude—and I am used to such company.

Will you kindly transmit to Mrs Unwin the expression of my most sincere and respectful regard; and pray believe me dear Mrs Brooke Your very grateful, faithful and obedient servant.

Jph. Conrad.

My wife sends her affectionate regards. She has been just tolerably well in health, but her spirits are high. She believes in me, in the future, in happiness. Poor girl!

To Edward Garnett

Text   MS Sutton; G. 63

5th Aug. 96.
Ile Grande. Lannion

My dear Garnett

I've sent you 10 days ago a short story which I trust You received all right.[1] It was registered. Since then—that is since I had Your last letter—I have been living in a little hell of my own; in a place of torment

---

[1] 'An Outpost of Progress'.

so subtle and so cruel and so unavoidable that the prospect of theological damnation in the hereafter has no more terrors for me.

It is all about the ghastly "*Rescuer*". Your commendation of part I plunges me simply into despair—because part II *must* be very different in theme if not in treatment and I am afraid this will make the book a strange and repulsive hybrid, fit only to be stoned, jumped upon, defiled and then held up to ridicule as a proof of my ineptitude. You see I must justify—give a motive—to my yacht people the artificial, civilized creatures that are to be brought in contact with the primitive Lingard. I must do that—or have a Clark Russel[l] puppet show[1] which would be worse than starvation. Now the justification that had occurred to me is unfortunately of so subtle a nature that I despair of conveying it in say 20 pages well enough to make it comprehensible. And I also doubt whether it would be acceptable (if conveyed) to a single creature under heaven—not excepting even—especially!—You. Besides I begin to fear that supposing everything conveyed and made acceptable (which seems impossible) supposing that—I begin to fear that I have not enough imagination—not enough power to make anything out of the situation; That I cannot invent an illuminating episode that would set in a clear light the persons and feelings. I am in desperation and I have practically given up the book. Beyond what you have seen I cannot make a step. There is 12 pages written and I sit before them every morning, day after day, for the last 2 months and can not add a sentence, add a word! I am paralyzed by doubt and have just sense enough to feel the agony but am powerless to invent a way out of it. This is sober truth. I had bad moments with the Outcast but never anything so ghastly—nothing half so hopeless. When I face that fatal manuscript it seems to me that I have forgotten how to think—worse! how to write. It is as if something in my head had given way to let in a cold grey mist. I knock about blindly in it till I am positively, physically sick—and then I give up saying—to morrow! And tomorrow comes—and brings only the renewed and futile agony. I ask myself whether I am breaking up mentally. I am afraid of it.

In desperation I took up another short story. I must do something to live and meantime perhaps a ray of inspiration may come and light me along the labyrinth of incertitudes where I am now lost. I wrote the *Outpost of Progress* with pleasure if with difficulty. The one I am writing now I hammer out of myself with difficulty but without pleasure. It's called *The Lagoon*—and is very much Malay indeed. I shall send it to the

---

[1] Early reviewers often compared Conrad with Clark Russell, a novelist of marine melodramas such as *The Wreck of the 'Grosvenor'*.

Cornhill straight[1]—or else through F[isher] U[nwin]—You must be sick of my short stories. And yet they cost me in a sense more than *Outcast* did. I wrote the *Outpost of Prog.* thinking of you. It was during the time when I had not heard of you for nearly six weeks—and you were very much in my thoughts. I made there an effort at conciseness—as far as in me lies—and just managed it short of 10.000 words. Do You find it very bad? I can't bear to look at my MS. of it. Everything seems so abominably stupid. You see *the belief* is not in me—and without the belief—the brazen thick headed, thick skinned immovable belief nothing good can be done. I am worrying you with my jeremiads. Perhaps you are at work! What are you going to write? You stirred my curiosity by the hint that you are going to begin—but what? I dare not ask You to write to me but if you knew how intensely miserable I am you would forgive my intrusions.

We return in October. We must take a labouring cottage somewhere not too far from town. Perhaps I will be able to do something then. But I doubt it. I doubt everything. The only certitude left to me is that I cannot work for the present. I hope You never felt as I feel now and I trust that you will never Know what I experience at this very moment. The darkness and the bitterness of it is beyond expression. Poor Jess feels it all. I must be a perfect fiend to live with—but I really don't care who suffers. I have enough of my own trouble.

Yours ever

Jph Conrad

My wife sends her love.

To T. Fisher Unwin

Text   MS Leeds; Unpublished

9th Augst. 1896.
Ile-Grande.
Lannion.

Dear Mr Unwin.

Your letter with cheque for £12.10 receive[d] to-day. I need not tell you how much I appreciate your promptitude in sending me the good

---

[1] 'The Lagoon' appeared in the *Cornhill* for January 1897. Conrad made relatively few corrections to the typescript (Garnett, p. 65, n. 1).

news. I am very pleased to be taken up by the Baron[1]—and I am also pleased with the cheque.

I thought that about this time You were out of town. That is why I have sent to the *Cornhill* direct a short story of about 5.000 words.[2] I don't think it so good—or rather I think it is considerably worse than the one I wrote with the fear of *Cosmo* before my eyes. The *Cornhill* you know wrote to me here. So I thought I might send on straight to them. I reserved in my letter to the Editors, the right to publish in a volume. The short story like a fell disease got me under—and the *Rescuer* has to wait. But I am thinking of him and perhaps he will be all the better for it in the long run.

I am sorry to miss making the acquaintance of Mr Becke.[3] Strangely enough I have been, only the other day, reading again his *Reef and Palm*. Apart from the great interest of the stories what I admire most is his perfect unselfishness in the telling of them. The sacrifice of his individuality in the interest of the work. He stands magnificently aloof from the poignancy and humour of his stories. A thing I could never do—and which I envy him. I haven't seen yet the First Fleet Family and have a great curiosity.[4]

I had a charming letter from Mrs Brooke. I suppose Mrs Unwin is in Yorkshire now. We return in October—to live in a .cottage in the country. A perfectly idyllic but also no doubt a hateful kind of existence.

Yours very faithfully
Jph Conrad.

---

[1] Baron Tauchnitz put out a series, in Germany, called *Collection of British Authors*; the Baron published *Almayer's Folly* and *An Outcast of the Islands* and then ignored Conrad until *The Secret Agent* was published. In a letter to J. B. Pinker (10 October 1907, Berg), Conrad wrote: 'To be excluded from the Tauchnitz collection *is* a distinction for Joseph Conrad whose place in English literature is made. To come at the call of Baron Tauchnitz after 8 years of neglect is not to be thought of. None of my work shall appear *with my consent* in the Tauchnitz collection unless the head of that eminent firm agrees to include at least four works mentionned* above [*Lord Jim, Nigger, Youth, Mirror of the Sea*], which he was ill-advised enough to neglect.'
[2] 'The Lagoon', which ran closer to 6000 words.
[3] Louis Becke, a minor romancer, specializing in tales of the South Pacific, with whom the reviewers frequently compared Conrad. (See Gordan, pp. 272, 284, 295.)
[4] Unwin had just published *A First Fleet Family* by Becke and W. J. Jeffery.

To T. Fisher Unwin

Text   MS Yale; Unpublished

14th August
1896
Ile Grande.
p. Lannion.

Dear Mr Unwin.

I hasten to thank You for the *First Fleet Family* received to day. It is a very unexpected pleasure. Really Your kindness is unwearied showing itself in great things and in little things with quite a rounded perfection of friendliness which I have done nothing to deserve.

As I said in my last letter I made sure You would be out of town. If I have done wrong by sending my short story[1] direct to the *Cornhill* that belief must be my excuse. As a matter of fact I have already written a short note to the Editor asking him to send the story to you after perusal—which note was dispatched together with the MS. The first page of the MS. has also the direction: J. Conrad c/o T. Fisher Unwin Esqr and your address so that they have no excuse if the story does not reach You in case of rejection.

I thank You very much for undertaking to place my stories on the terms You mention. It is I am convinced a most advantageous arrangement for me and I look upon it as further proof of your goodwill. Whatever You do in that matter will be—I am sure—the best that could be done.

I am glad to think the story has a chance of acceptance by the *Cosmo*.[2] The delay in publication[3] does not affect me beyond measure tho' I see it would put off the appearance of a volume of stories far into the next year. The cutting in two does worry me a little. I don't think the story is strong enough right through to stand cutting. All the sting—so to speak—is in the tail and the first half read by itself would appear strangely pointless perhaps. But all those matters are left to your discretion and I sit still and am thankful—anyhow. I am Yours very sincerely,

Jph Conrad.

---

[1] 'The Lagoon'.
[2] 'An Outpost of Progress'.
[3] It appeared in June–July 1897.

To Edward Garnett

Text   MS Colgate; J–A, I, 193; G. 66

14th Augst 1896
Ile Grande.

Dear Garnett.

Thanks ever so much for your letter—or rather for Your two letters. I suppose you are now in possession of my howl of distress. Perhaps the not unnatural exasperation of a man condemned to read such lamentations has subsided somewhat and You will be able to look at this missive with a—comparatively—kind eye.

You are right in your criticism of *Outpost*. The construction is bad. It is bad because it was a matter of conscious decision, and I have no discrimination—in artistic sense. Things get themselves written—and you like them. Things get themselves into shape—and they are tolerable. But when *I* want to write—when *I* do consciously try to write or try to construct then my ignorance has full play and the quality of my miserable and benighted intelligence is disclosed to the scandalised gaze of my literary father. This is as it should be. I always told you I was a kind of inspired humbug. Now You know it. Let me assure You that your remarks were a complete disclosure to me. I had not the slightest glimmer of my stupidity. I am now profoundly thankful to find I have enough sense to see the truth of what You say. It's very evident that the first 3 pages kill all the interest. And I wrote them of set purpose!! I thought I was achieving artistic simplicity!!!!!!! Now, of course, the thing—the res infecta[1]—is as plain as a pikestaff. It does not improve my opinion of myself and of my prospects. Am I totally lost? Or do the last few pages save the thing from being utterly contemptible? You seem to think so—if I read your most kind and friendly letter aright.

I must explain that that particular story was no more meant for You than the *Idiots*—that is *all* the short stories (*ab initio*)[2] were *meant alike* for a vol to be inscribed to *you*.[3] Only then I had not heard from You so long that you were naturally constantly in my thoughts. In fact I worried about it thinking of the treachery of disease and so on. And then I thought that the story would be a good title-story—better than the *Idiots*. It would sound funny a title like this: *Idiots and other Stories*. While *Outpst of Progress and Other Stories* sounds nice and proper.[4] That's why Your name

---

[1] Latin: 'the imperfect thing'.
[2] Latin: *ab initio*: from the beginning.
[3] The volume of short stories was dedicated to Adolf Krieger.
[4] The volume was called *Tales of Unrest*.

has been typed by my devoted wife on the title page of the infamous thing. The question is—is the inf. thing too infamous to go into the vol.—I leave it to You.

Meantime the E. P. of L[1] has bombarded the *Cosmo[polis]* with it. It appears it will do. At any rate the secretary of the *Cosmo* accepts and refers to his editor who is away. The price put upon that ghastly masterfolly by the E. P. of L is £50. which seems to be also agreed to provisionally. I must say that the Patron has behaved generally in a friendly manner which is touching. He writes often and seems to want really to push me along. I will want a lot of pushing I fear.

I've sent a short thing to the *Cornhill*.[2] A malay tells a story to a white man who is spending the night at his hut. It's a tricky thing with the usual forests river—stars—wind sunrise, and so on—and lots of secondhand Conradese in it. I would bet a penny they will take it. There is only 6000 words in it so it can't bring in many shekels ... Don't You think I am a lost soul?—Upon my word I hate every line I write. I wish I could tackle the *Rescuer* again. I simply *can't*! And I live in fear that is worse than mortal. But I have told you all that.

Yours ever Jph Conrad.

To Jane Cobden Unwin
Text   MS Texas; Unpublished

August 20th 1896.[3]

Ile-Grande

I wish to add a word to my wife's letter to tell you, dear Mrs Unwin, that I am very much touched by Your gracious kindness.[4] Besides I owe You thanks for the visit of Mrs Brooke[5]—a most charming and comforting incident of our stay here. The only thing I regret is that it was such a short visit. I had a delightful letter not very long ago, from Slingsby Rectory[6] and I trust my reply conveyed a part, at least, of what I felt. Believe me dear Mrs Unwin Your most obedient and faithful servant

J. Conrad Korzeniowski

[1] Unwin, the Enlightened Patron of Letters.
[2] 'The Lagoon'.
[3] The address, the date, and the first part of the letter are in Jessie Conrad's hand.
[4] In sending three books.
[5] See letters to T. Fisher Unwin, 3 July, and Mrs Brooke, 29 July.
[6] Mrs Brooke's husband, the Reverend Arthur Brooke, was rector of Slingsby, in the North Riding of Yorkshire.

To T. Fisher Unwin
Text   MS Berg; Unpublished

Ile Grande.
par Lannion.
22° Augst
1896.

Dear Mr Unwin.

I enclose here the letter I had yesterday from the *Cornhill*. To my great surprise they accept the story.[1] Now I know exactly in what business relation I stand to you I send You their letter—in case you wish to make any remarks or objections. Perhaps you will communicate with them. They do not say anything as to when I am going to appear. There is also the question of proofs. I should like to see them—but as I am leaving here soon and You are more likely than any one to know my whereabouts perhaps You would let them send the proofs to You and transmit them to me—either here or in England. I do not know myself yet for certain what my address in England will be, but would of course let you know at once on my return.—

—I have read the First Fleet Family[2]—with interest tempered by disappointement.* It is not Mr Becke who disappoints me. The trouble is that I cannot find Mr Becke in the book. There are glimpses of him here and there. I can find there his knowledge of ships, of the sea, of seamanship and of seamen—but there is very little of those masterful touches of his. Frankly the book surprises me. I do not know of course what he set himself to do. If he aimed at producing the effect of a personal narrative, of a diary with its self disclosures and the commonplace flow of ideas of such a man as the sergeant—he has absolutely succeeded. But *why* he should attempt such a feat passes my comprehension. It is a book full of possibilities which are never realized, in deference—as it seems to me—to the consistency of the man who is supposed to tell the story. But why he should tell the story and why Mr Becke should take that idiotic weight upon his shoulders I cannot imagine. The book tells of human characteristics. It tells of imperfect thought, of impotent effort; it speaks of error, suffering, desire, hope, failure. It speaks of life—but it has no more life in it than a catalogue. Everything in it is quite true and even obtrusively possible—but not a single episode, event, thought, word; not a single pang of joy or sorrow is inevitable. The end is an outrage on the reader's intelligence not because the squire's daughter marries the

[1] 'The Lagoon'.
[2] *A First Fleet Family* by Louis Becke and Walter Jeffery.

sergeant but because she marries that sergeant. It would be just as logic[al] to say she married a crossing sweeper or the King of Monomatapa.[1] Everything is possible—but the note of truth is not in the possibility of things but in their inevitableness. Inevitableness is the only certitude; it is the very essence of life—as it is of dreams. A picture of life is saved from failure by the merciless vividness of detail. Like a dream it must be startling, undeniable, absurd and appalling. Like a dream it may be ludicrous or tragic and like a dream pitiless and inevitable; a thing monstrous or sweet from which You cannot escape. Our captivity within the incomprehensible logic of accident is the only fact of the universe. From that reality flows deception and inspiration, error and faith, egoism and sacrifice, love and hate. That truth fearlessly faced becomes an austere and trusted friend, a companion of victory or a giver of peace. While our struggles to escape from it—either through drink or philanthropy; through a theory or through disbelief—make the comedy and the drama of life. To produce a work of art a man must either know or feel that truth—even without knowing it. It must be the basis of every artistic endeavour. But I am far away from the *Family* and I suppose you are asking yourself whether I am sober or whether I am trying to escape from the inevitableness of life. The fact is I am furious with Mr. Becke. He is a strong man. He is not afraid to look up to heaven or look down into another place. He knows the earth the sky and the vagaries of human hearts. And he has [a] voice. He can sing a song vigorous and stirring—"instead of which" (as a famous Irish Judge once said) he associates himself with two (two O! Lord!) casual and blind vagabonds for the purpose of going about grinding sweet tunes out of a barrel organ for the entertainment of Unbelievers and Philistines.

As the history of the early times of the colony[2] the book fails through lack of convincing detail. We get tantalizing glimpses of tremendous possibilities. We glance into gloom or into sunshine but we are not allowed to look into anything. Then what an immense, absorbing thing Mr Becke could have done by working out the escape in the boat along the coast! Mr Becke knows better than any man what could have been done with it. Who stayed his hand—or what? Drew–Jeffrey[3]—or simply weariness. My opinion of Mr Becke is not in any way affected by that book. I don't see him there. His hand might have—no doubt did; the

[1] A great empire reported by Portuguese sailors in the early sixteenth century as lying inland from Sofala (Mozambique).
[2] New South Wales.
[3] Sergeant William Dew (not Drew), the narrator of the novel, and Walter Jeffery (not Jeffrey), Becke's collaborator.

tittle* page says so—written some pages of the MS. but his own particular self had nothing to do with that production. The book does not hold, does not grip. There is not a startling thought or a startling event in it. It is but a sweet tune played without expression. It is neither vigourous* nor dreamy. It is solid and somnolent. It can be read however with a calm satisfaction, and, as soon as read, it is forgotten.

The above impertinent rigmarole is only to show You that I am not afraid, even if heavens should fall on me. I do think tho', on consideration, that I owe an apology to Mr Becke for judging his work and to You for the lenght* of this letter. I am always Yours most faithfully

Jph Conrad.

[On the verso of the *Cornhill* letter (Yale), Conrad wrote:]
P.S. I have not answered this.

We shall be back in London on the 28th of Septer. I suppose You will not be in town then. We have taken a small cottage in Essex—about one hour by rail from town.

J.C.

To Edward Garnett?

22^{d} Augst [1896]
Ile Grande.
noon.

[Kept at Yale with the letter to Garnett of 9 April 1896 are fragments of one dated 22 August. Since it has been torn neatly down the middle, the text is beyond restoration.]

To T. Fisher Unwin
Text   MS Leeds; Unpublished

11.30 pm [18 September 1896][1]
Friday.
[Île Grande]

Dear Sir.[2]

I have been thinking over the *Cosmo[polis]* business.[3]

It seems to me that the thing should be treated not from the point of view of promise made but in the aspect of the demand formulated by you.

---

[1] Date in margin, in another hand: 'J. Conrad 18.9.96.'

[2] Although this is not Conrad's usual form of salutation for T. Fisher Unwin, this letter is clearly directed to the firm. There is the chance that the letter was addressed to an unidentified person in the Unwin office; the tone of the letter, however, indicates a continuing dialogue with Unwin.

[3] About 'An Outpost of Progress'.

A certain sum has been asked for the story—and there is an end of it. The demand has been made in my name and I do not want to haggle over the value of my work as if I had been selling a pig at a fair. This is my idea of the thing: from those people either £*50* or the story returned.

In great haste Yours faithfully
Jph Conrad.

I shall leave home at 10 a.m. so after that hour there's no use in wiring to my address. I do not mind meeting Mr Ortmans[1]—but really do not see the use of it.

To Edward Garnett

Text   MS Sutton; G. 68

[end of September 1896[2]]
17 Gillingham St.
London SW

Dear Garnett

We are here! I feel better since I know myself near You. I have a great tongue-itch. When are You coming up to London?

My wife wishes to get things straight for our cottage.[3] I have ordered her to get everything ready for work there in a week's time. Her efforts are superhuman. I sit still and grumble. Today we go to Stanford to measure rooms for carpets. To morrow I'll be in London and probably budge not till I go and take possession.

When? How? Will you see me. Are you well? Have you time? Have You the wish?

Speak!

Our best love to All of you.

Yours ever
J. Conrad.

---

[1] Editor of *Cosmopolis*, a new and ambitious international monthly published in seven cities. Ortmans wrote to Conrad on 27 June 1897: 'I am very sorry to hear from Paris that the enclosed cheque has been kept nearly three weeks by the fault of one of my clerks. I thought it had reached you long ago' (CWW, pp. 332, 395). See also Conrad's note to Adolf Krieger, 28 June 1897.

[2] Garnett gives September 1896; if we accept September, and do not move the date into early October, then it must be 28, 29 or 30 September. Conrad's note to Unwin (22 August) indicates a return to London on the 28th. The Conrads moved to Essex in early October.

[3] In Stanford-le-Hope, Essex, near the Thames estuary, five miles NE of Tilbury and not far from Gravesend, the locale of the *Nellie* in 'Heart of Darkness'. To Conrad's disgust, the first house in Essex was not a cottage but a semi-detached villa. (See Jessie Conrad, *Joseph Conrad and his Circle*, p. 42.)

To Edward Garnett

Text   MS Colgate; G. 69

Stanford-le-hope.
16th oct. 96.

My dear Garnett.

Thanks for the book and Your letter. It cheers me. By the same post I have received documents from the Patron[1]—to sign. I must tell you about them.

In a letter he points out to me that he has incurred expense on account of securing American copyright of my 3 stories. He strongly insists upon that point. Further on he bespeaks more matter; to complete 60.000 words for a 6/- volume. On serial rights he agrees to pay me *90 per cent* of them as arranged before. So far good!

As to the volume. There are the usual claims for royalties. The first 2.000 copies bring me in 10% on published price. After *2000 copies* the royalty is to be 12% on pub. price, and after *4.000 copies* the royalty is to be 15% on net proceeds of sales. There is the usual clause about thirteen copies going to the dozen.

He wants the work delivered in *March* 97 at the latest.[2] He engages himself to publish within *six* months of delivery.

That also is all right. But then he says: on account and in *anticipation* of such royalties the *pub* shall pay to the *Auth* £25 *on 31 Dec 96* and £25 *on 31 March. 97*.

Now I do not think that satisfactory. What do You think? It's exactly what he advanced on the *Outcast*. Ought I not to get more? I want £100 (in two payments if he likes). Can I honestly ask for it? Am I worth that advance?—I shall not write to him till I *hear from you*.

I am glad Smith Elder think of me.[3] I do not see however how I can send my address to them and what would be the use—if they think me entirely in the hands of *T. F[isher] U[nwin]* I do not want to leave him if he gives me enough to live on. If cornered I would try to escape of course. It's simply a matter of "to be or not to be".

I do hesitate about H. James.[4] Still I think I will send the book. After all it would not be a crime or even an impudence.

---

[1] Unwin.

[2] *Tales of Unrest*, which came to include 'Karain: A Memory', 'The Idiots', 'An Outpost of Progress', 'The Return', 'The Lagoon'. All but 'The Return' were serialized.

[3] The publishers of the *Cornhill Magazine*. They were interested in book rights to Conrad's works.

[4] See Conrad's letter to James, following.

Excuse me dear Garnett for interminably worrying You with my affairs. You are my "Father in Letters" and must bear the brunt of that position.

We send our love to you all.

Yours ever

Jph Conrad.

To Henry James

Text   MS Texas; Unpublished[1]

16 Octr. 1896.
[Stanford-le-Hope]

To Henry James.

I address You across a vast space invoking the name of that one of Your children You love the most. I have been intimate with many of them, but it would be an impertinence for me to disclose here the secret of my affection. I am not sure that there is one I love more than the others. Exquisite Shades with live hearts, and clothed in the wonderful garment of Your prose, they have stood, consoling, by my side under many skies. They have lived with me, faithful and serene—with the bright serenity of Immortals. And to You thanks are due for such glorious companionship.

I want to thank You for the charm of Your words, the delight of Your sentences, the beauty of Your pages! And, since the book before You has obtained some commendation, (for men have been good to an erring brother) I trust that You will consent, by accepting this copy, to augment the precious burden of my gratitude.

Jph. Conrad.

---

[1] On 27 October, Conrad sent James a copy of *An Outcast of the Islands* with this 'letter' inscribed on the flyleaf. This letter–inscription began the long relationship between Conrad and James. When *The Spoils of Poynton* appeared, James sent Conrad, in February 1897, one of the first copies, with the inscription: 'Joseph Conrad, in dreadfully delayed but very grateful acknowledgement of an offering singularly generous and beautiful'. (Two excellent descriptions of the relationship are available: in Leon Edel's *Henry James*, Vol. v: *The Master: 1901–16* (Philadelphia: Lippincott, 1972), the chapter called 'A Master Mariner'; Ian Watt's 'Conrad, James and *Chance*,' in *Imagined Worlds: Essays on some English Novels and Novelists in Honour of John Butt*, edited by Maynard Mack and Ian Gregor (Methuen, 1968.)

To T. Fisher Unwin

Text   MS Yale; Keating 42

Stanford le hope.
Essex
19th Oct. 1896.

Dear Unwin.

As you see I have meditated upon Your communication for more than a day.[1] It has interfered fiendishly with the work upon my last story.[2] But it had to be meditated over and the result of the aforesaid meditation is embodied in the alterations marked in red ink upon the copy of agreement which I return for Your final decision.

I am very sensible of Your readiness to secure my American rights and very much cheered by the fact that with Your great knowledge of such matters You think it worth while. From snips of enlightened criticism reaching me across the pond I would think it a very hopeless undertaking.

As to my demands, which You might think excessive it's just this: I can't afford to work for less than ten pence per hour and must work in a way that will give me this magnificent income. I don't like to give up anything I have taken hold of and intend to stick to scribbling till I am fairly convinced of my wisdom or my folly. I will see it out—but I do not wish to see it out at Your expense. After all my work has some value but if people won't have any of it I can do one or two things less gentlemanly (save the mark) but not a whit less honourable or useful. But I have no time to lose and must look about quickly so as not [to] be left standing between two stools occupied by better men.

Should you entertain my modifications I wish to tell you that I would like to try *W. Henley* with my "*Nigger*"[3]—not so much for my own sake as to have a respectable shrine for the memory of men with whom I have,

---

[1] See Conrad's letter to Garnett, 16 October.

[2] Probably *The Nigger of the 'Narcissus'*, which Conrad worked on during the autumn, having reached another impasse with 'The Rescuer'.

[3] William Ernest Henley, of the *New Review*. Conrad must have been fairly well along with *The Nigger* by this time, since he had begun it in Brittany in June 1896, a fact which he noted for John Quinn when he sold him the manuscript many years later. Conrad's memory may have been at fault, but Jean-Aubry reports at least ten pages written before the end of September. We can assume thirty or forty pages by the time of this letter. *The Nigger* was begun as a long short story, and Conrad probably intended it to complete the four-story volume he was planning for Unwin.

through many hard years lived and worked. The Story will contain 25.000 words *at least* and shall be ready very soon.

> I am ever Yours most faithfully,
>
> Jph Conrad.

The *Idiots* are well spoken of—but Smithers had not had the courtesy to send me a copy of his magazine.[1] I shall write to him.

To Edward Garnett

Text G. 70

> Sunday [25 October 1896][2]
> Stanford-le-Hope

Dear Garnett

Thanks for your note on Thursday. I think I will want your advice very much. I've written to F[isher] U[nwin] exactly in the terms suggested by you *that is*. *£100* in two payments.[3]

> *12 1/2* % for the first 3000 copies.
> *15* % for everything over 3000 c.
> *one half* American rights.
> *90* % of serial rights.

And I have had yesterday an answer which I literally transcribe."—I have read it very carefully and have studied the returned agreement. But I have had to put it away on file. I did not send this agreement without serious consideration—and I must leave my proposal as originally drafted. I have no more to say, except that perhaps I made a blunder in copyrighting the stories. If at any time you wish to see me, please let me know so that I may be in office and disengaged.

"With kind regards sincerely yours.

_____ "

He is touched by my allusion to the American rights—evidently. I had said that: "judging from the idiotic tone of press comments over there I would have thought the Am. rights hardly worth anything. I am glad

---

[1] The *Savoy*, published by Leonard Smithers. Later, Smithers was involved with Cunninghame Graham, publishing his *Aurora la Cujiñí: A Realistic Sketch in Seville* (1898).

[2] There is no reason to question Garnett's dating. Conrad had written on the 16th, Garnett had responded on Thursday (the 22nd), and Conrad answered almost immediately, on Sunday, the 25th.

[3] For a volume of short stories, to be published by Fisher Unwin.

that you with your great experience of such matters have thought it worth while!!"

To the letter of F.U. I replied in effect: That his "non possumus"[1] seems final to me; for the difference between us is more fundamental than a mere question of "*more and less.*" That his passage about the *blunder* seems to imply that, with ingratitude, I did try to put a screw on him. "A suspicion"—I said—"unworthy of you and me." Then I said: Let me know the extent of my liability towards you so that I can discharge it if possible at once—for till I have done so I do not feel a perfect liberty of action. A position I dislike. That as far as the *Nigger* is concerned I shall try to place it for serial publication with Henley or elsewhere but as to a book I know no one, have written to no one and shall not do so till the *Nigger* is finished. And I asked him to tell me how much he spent on Am. rights as quickly as possible. I ended by saying that I do not intend to come to town soon but the first time I did so I would call in a friendly manner etc. etc.

This is a faithful account. I shall not recede from my position an inch. I would rather begin with somebody else. Could you advise me what to do to get these infernal rights taken over by someone.[2] And who? And how to get about it? Is it possible? feasible? And how soon?

The *Idiots* earned some commendation. I begin the Magazine and am very pleased with myself. But Smithers[3] has not sent cheque. I do not appear in the Cornhill for *Nov.*[4] It's a shame. Can Unwin knock the *Cosmopolis* arrangement[5] on the head now if he likes? I've had the proof.

Bash the whole business. I am (as the sailors say to express a state of painful destitution) "I am sitting in the lee scuppers." ... Only it interferes with my *Nigger* damnably. I crawl on with it. It will be about *30,000* words.[6] I must enshrine my old chums in a decent edifice. Seriously, do you think it would be too long? There are so many touches necessary for such a picture?

---

[1] Latin: 'We can't [do it]'.
[2] Garnett introduced Conrad to Smith, Elder and Company, but they made him an unacceptable offer for his work.
[3] Of the *Savoy*.
[4] Not until January 1897.
[5] For 'An Outpost' to be serialized.
[6] As noted, Conrad intended it as part of a volume of short stories.

There! My dear Garnett. I have said all—with trust and relief. To you thanks.

Ever yours

J. Conrad

My kindest regards and my wife's love to Mrs Garnett and the boy.

To Edward Garnett

Text   MS Colgate; J–A, I, 194; G. 73

27. Oct 1896.
Stanford-le-Hope
Essex

My dear Garnett.

I am very much touched by Your promptitude in writing to cheer me up. You ease my mind greatly—and in this juncture no man could do it but you. I have nothing to do but to follow your advice which is the more easy because it accords with my inclination. I am at your disposition on Friday[1] or any other day only, my dearest fellow, invite those men in my name for I can not let you stand my business dinners. I can always break your bread (and argue with you impudently while I do so) in the communion of friendship but this is another matter. You will render me an immense service if you will undertake to arrange everything and let me know of the place of feeding. It seems almost an impertinence to ask you to do that but I know You want to help me. On second thought perhaps it is better that *You* should ask them—(I only know Lucas[2])—but I want you to understand that I *won't* let you pay for it. That's all. Blessings on your head!

Your proposal to introduce me to Longman and also to Heinemann smiles at me.[3] Only I do not want you to give any cause for a grievance to the Patron.[4] He may be of a vengeful disposition. And I would never forgive myself if I was the cause of any inconvenience to you. Perhaps I am an old donkey to mention this but somehow the idea struck me. Don't

---

[1] The 30th, probably to arrange for publication rights to *The Nigger*.
[2] E. V. Lucas, of the *Globe*. (He later helped Conrad obtain a 50 guinea award from the *Academy*.)
[3] To publish *The Nigger*.
[4] Unwin; it was characteristic of Garnett to put the needs of authors before those of his employers.

be angry!—As to Watt I think I ought to know him.[1] It would be a great relief to have someone to do one's "dirty work" as the sailors say of any occupation they dislike.

I must tell You that you have sent me an incomplete letter. There are two *full sheets* (8 pages each) and a half sheet which is evidently a P.S.—The last page of the *full sheets* ends "*Don't however commit*" and there is nothing more! Frightful! I have looked everywhere under tables and chairs and can't find the part which tells me what I mustn't commit. So I am left in a state of trepidation. It is just possible there was something in the envelope which I have burnt. I did look in however before throwing it on the coals. I assure you I will commit nothing of any kind till I hear from You. The P. has not as yet replied to my farewell letter. I won't yield an inch, for my "dander is riz" (as Bret Harte's men say). Thanks a thousand times. I am dear Garnett ever yours

Jph Conrad.

My wife sends Love. I have sent *Outcast* to H James with a pretty dedication; it fills the fly leaf.[2]

To Edward Garnett
Text   G. 74

Sunday. [1 November 1896][3]
[Stanford-le-Hope]

My dear Garnett,

I agree with every word of your letter. Especially about Watt.[4] I shall take care to bring all my MSS. to town. They [are] a beggarly lot anyhow.

My wife is very unwell today so I can't write much because when she is like that I forget half of what I wish to say. I am letting myself go with the *Nigger*. He grows and grows. I do not think it's wholly bad though. Moreover I must have about 55000 words (in all the 4 stories)[5] to go to a Publisher with; Do you think it's enough.

---

[1] A. P. Watt, the literary agent. Nothing came of this, and Conrad first used the services of an agent (James Brand Pinker) three years later.

[2] See Conrad's 'letter' to James, 16 October.

[3] There is no reason to question Garnett's dating. This letter falls into the sequence begun on 27 October and continuing with 6 November.

[4] The literary agent.

[5] Conrad intended to make up a volume consisting of *The Nigger* along with 'The Idiots', 'An Outpost of Progress' and 'The Lagoon'. The three short stories were eventually combined with 'Karain' and 'The Return' as *Tales of Unrest* (1898).

I had a note from the P.[1] sad and tender and with an autograph P.S. but saying nothing to the purpose. I haven't replied yet.

I am worried and stupidly nervous about imaginary things. That's nothing new.

Yours ever

Jph. Conrad.

To Edward Garnett

Text MS Berg; G. 75

Friday. [6 November 1896][2]

[Stanford-le-Hope]

Dearest Garnett.

I have seen Mr Reginald Smith[3]—who received me like a long expected friend. Seriously, I am very pleased with what I saw of him—and now the P. seems more impossible than ever.

R. S. holds now all my material for consideration—till Friday next—at noon; when I shall come up to hear what he has to say. Mr Graves—I asked for him at first—was not there. I left my card and thanks for criticism. I feel much easier in my mind—though positively I know nothing of course—but R. S. talked with enthusiasm about my 2 books which, he affirms, having read.[4] You are right my dear G. They do look upon me as a kind of "hinfant phenomenon".[5] Something at any rate seems to stir their curiosity. For all the good that may come from this I have You to thank. I kept Your advice in mind during the interview. I was dignified and not abjectly modest. We shall see!

Imagine! Two Cambridge dons—Walter Headlam and Dr. Waldstein[6] are so impressed by the Outcast (!!!!!!!!) that they wish to make my acquaintance. In fact Headlam through Mrs. Sanderson (my Elstree friend)[7] invites me to Cambridge. I can't accept just now, but

---

[1] Unwin.

[2] There is no reason to question Garnett's dating.

[3] Of Smith, Elder and Company, the publishers.

[4] Garnett notes that it was a Mr Roger Ingpen, the firm's reader, who was enthusiastic about *The Nigger*.

[5] The stage-name of Miss Ninetta Crummles (in Dickens's *Nicholas Nickleby*).

[6] Walter George Headlam (1866–1908), scholar, poet and editor of classical Greek texts. Charles Waldstein (he later changed his name to Walston; 1856–1927), Lecturer and Reader in Classical Archaeology, director of the Fitzwilliam Museum, and subsequently Slade Professor of Fine Art. Headlam was to be the mentor of Rupert Brooke.

[7] Ted Sanderson's mother.

later on it may be a curious experience. I have not the slightest conception of what it may be like! What do such fellows think and talk about? I have seen some of Headlam's "po'try" in MS. He—I fancy—is not made in the image of God like other men but is fashioned after the pattern of Walter Pater which, You cannot but admit, is a much greater distinction.

Yours ever

Jph Conrad.

To T. Fisher Unwin
Text   MS Berg; Unpublished

Saturday 7th Nov. [1896][1]

[Stanford-le-Hope]

Dear Mr Unwin.

Thanks very much for the acc/t of Am: rights.[2] I see only 2 stories mentioned so conclude that the affair of the Outpost is not yet finally accounted for.

I shall next week take steps about arranging for the pub: of my stories and shall let You know either by letter or, if I come up to town shall call upon You.

By the Bye, it strikes me the "Savoy" ought to pay for that story of mine.[3] I do not want to write to them but if You think a reminder would not be "bad form" perhaps You would give it to them. I have a beastly bill to meet on the 13*th*. One of my Youthful sins coming home to roost.

Most amazing! Two Cambridge dons wish to make my acquaintance![4] If it had not been for the channel through which the invitation to go there reaches me I would think it a practical joke. They say the *Outcast* fetched them! Anyhow I can't go. I work too slow to give myself any holidays of that kind. I am dear Mr. Unwin Yours very faithfully.

Jph Conrad.

---

[1] The year is, of course, established by the sequence.
[2] Scribner's published *Tales of Hearsay* in the United States (1898).
[3] For 'The Idiots', which had appeared in the October issue.
[4] See preceding letter.

To Edward Garnett

Text MS Colgate; G. 76

Friday. 13th Nov. [1896][1]
Stanford-le-hope.

My dear Garnett

I have just returned from my interview with Mr Reginald Smith[2] and, having heard his proposals, seek your advice. He began the conversation by asking how long it would take me to finish the *Rescuer*. I replied: six months or so. Then he said that—They would make me an offer for it at once but they thought it better for them and *for me* that the offer should be made after the book was finished. He put a stress on that—and I said "I thought so too." It cost me nothing to say that. Then as to stories.[3] He said they liked them immensely and went on to advise me to put them by for a time. I said I wished to sell them. He replied that they wished to buy them and made the following proposition. He said. We are prepared to give you *at once* £50 for the right to put them away for a time. (He pointed to the safe) We think it's the best way. When we publish we will give you 20%—and all the American rights—whatever they would fetch. To my demand for a serial publication of the "Nigger" he said in effect that he thought the story too long for the "Cornhill" and generally did not seem to see his way.

Then I spoke about the serial of *Rescuer*. There also he did not say anything definite. Said: We can promise to try but can't promise success. If you finished the book in six months, we would publish you in Sept^{er} next year—but a serial would delay the publication. I pointed out to him that I did not wish to disappear from the scene for such a long time. And I said I would take a week to consider. He agreed. Adjourned till Friday next.

All this passed in the nicest way imaginable—You must understand. I really believe the people mean well and would act generously. After all I can't expect more than the offer they made. Nothing would induce me to go back to F. U.[4] Still it worries me to think that my "nigger" would be locked up for a year or two. More likely two. I feel horribly unsettled. It takes the savour out of the work. And the "N" is not yet quite finished. Then to go on toiling over the *Rescuer* without knowing anything about a

---

[1] The year is established by the sequence.
[2] Of Smith, Elder and Company.
[3] The later *Tales of Unrest*, but including *The Nigger*.
[4] Yet Conrad did feel obliged to give *Tales of Unrest* to Fisher Unwin, who published it in 1898.

reward is distasteful. I am somewhat bothered. I dare say shall feel better to-morrow. Would you tell me what You think? Yours ever

J. Conrad

To Edward Garnett
Text   G. 77

16th Nov. [1896] 10 pm.[1]
[Stanford-le-Hope]

Dear Garnett,

I am greatly refreshed by your letter; and, girding my loins, I have written to Smith exactly on the lines indicated by you, a very nice firm letter.[2] I also am sending the press cuttings. And I shall see him on Friday noon—unless he cancels the engagement in consequence of my letter.

To tell you the truth I do not think they will accept my terms. I do not think they care much for me—really. I rather fancy they fancy themselves very generous as it is—to the obscure scribbler. But I am of your opinion entirely. I had better make a stand now and taste the acrid savour of adventure. I do not know how to thank you enough for your encouragement advice and help. I shut up.

I am going to interview the P. on Friday *11 a m.*[3] Just a call and there is a shadow of an excuse for it too. They have heard of me in Poland, through Chicago (of all the God-forsaken places) and think of trying for translations of *A[lmayer's] F[olly]* and *O[utcast]*. So I am unofficially informed by a Warsaw friend. I can talk to the P. about that a little and size him up meanwhile.

The Vienna[4] at 1.30 Friday. When I shall report.

Yours ever

J. Conrad

---

[1] The year is established by sequence and content.
[2] Rejecting Reginald Smith's terms for publication of Conrad's stories, 'The Rescuer' and *The Nigger*. Conrad requested new terms.
[3] Unwin, on the 20th.
[4] A Soho restaurant.

To T. Fisher Unwin
Text MS Leeds; Unpublished

16th Nov. 1896.
Stanford le hope.

Dear Mr Unwin.

My fault entirely calling at a wrong hour and afterwards being late.

I will be in town on Friday next. I have an appointement* at noon but if it would not inconvenience You I would like to call at 11 am.[1] If I don't hear from You I will take it that I may. I shall bring then the copy of agreement You wish me to return.

Yours very faithfully

Jph Conrad.

To Edward Garnett
Text MS Colgate; G. 78

Saturday [21 November 1896][2]
[Stanford-le-Hope]

Dearest Garnett.

You are worthy* ever so many bricks.

It is a lovely arrangement.[3] Remains to be seen whether the story is good enough—or effective enough.

That I doubt. I also remember days when I did not doubt. So I sit tight now; like a man with a lottery ticket; and hope for unheard-of fortunes. The idea about the P is very good[4]—like all Your ideas. By and bye I shall placate him with a burnt offering of stories. The old Moloch!

The best is that if all fails I can always go back to Smith Elder.—I feel like putting my thumbs in the armholes of my waistcoat.

I shall make sail with the "Narcissus" and expect to make a quick passage. Weather fine, and wind fair.

Yours ever

Jph Conrad.

---

[1] On Friday, the 20th, Conrad was to see Unwin at 11, Smith at noon, and Garnett at 1.30.

[2] Since the letter evidently fits into the sequence concerning publication of rights to *The Nigger*, the Saturday of the heading must be 21 November 1896.

[3] Garnett arranged for Pawling, of Heinemann, to show *The Nigger* to Henley for serialization in the *New Review* and for the firm to consider it for book publication. Subsequent letters to Garnett follow Conrad's progress on the manuscript.

[4] Unwin, the Patron: Conrad later gave him *Tales of Unrest* for publication.

To E. L. Sanderson

Text   MS Yale; J–A, I, 195

21ᵈ* Nov. [1896]¹
[Stanford-le-Hope]

Dearest Ted.

I swear by the lyre of Apollo and by the sandals of all the Muses that I haven't the slightest idea why You suspect me of not liking "An Episode of Southern Seas".²

My dearest fellow I received it one evening just at the moment when my wife was treating me to one of her fainting fits. Well! That business over I read it—read it at once—read it more than once. If my first letter was incoherent, it only reflected the exact state of my mind—which, I hasten to add, was *not caused* by the reading of Your stanzas. I waited till I had something like mental leisure to write to You at lenght;* and the very day I was going to write I received the glad tidings from the north. This for a time, I own, put the verses out [of] my head. And since I had no mental leisure. It is the sorry truth. Hang it all! I *love* the thing. My dearest Ted don't suspect me of being conceited enough to think that my opinion can matter to you one way or another—except for the affection I have for You and You for me. Headlam and Richardson were the men to ask³ and I am proud to know that my instinct, impulse (call it as You like), was right. I thought the poem good at first reading—I mean in point of expression. And I took it as complete. When You said, "I won't finish it" I was surprised and took it for an expression of indifference which I could not encourage. I also wondered what more you would say. I own I was curious, for I could see the idea was completely expressed. And even now I think that if there is something more to say—something which I do not see—which others do not see—but what You see Yourself, You should say it—now, or later on.

I am very glad You are going to send it somewhere. Jess tried very hard to copy correctly and I think that one of the copies is absolutely correct. The other I have corrected according to the manuscript which I keep of course. I want your handwriting and your thought, and Your melody.

---

¹ The content clearly establishes the year as 1896, for later in the letter Conrad speaks of his negotiations with Smith, Elder and Co.
² Poems by Sanderson, in manuscript.
³ Two Cambridge dons. For Headlam, see notes on letter to Garnett, 6 November. Possibly Conrad meant Waldstein (mentioned in the same letter) rather than Richardson.

That I prefer the "grey hour" proves nothing. It simply means that if under irresistible compulsion I had to burn one of the two poems, I would keep the "grey hour". I think it written in a much more spiritual—in a much more "rare" mood. But Your inherent distinction is in both—the same quality of it—the same individual note;— something very fine, a little elusive; something pervading, impalpable and distinct; like, in the morning, the glorious charm of a golden haze. In point of workmanship of course the two are perfectly on a level—I think. And what must strike anyone possessed of a *human* kind (as differentiated from *scholarly*) of discrimination is the perfect genuineness of expression, the straight flow of inspiration, the unfaltering felicity of thought. I say nothing about felicity of phrase. You know there are lines I cherish.

—If I do not talk to you much about my work it only means that I am working—with difficulty, as ever.[1] The more I go on the less confidence in myself I feel. There are days when I suspect myself of inability to put a sentence together; and other days when I am positively incapable to invent anything that could be put into a sentence. Gone are alas! those fine days of "Alm: Folly" when I wrote with the serene audacity of an unsophisticated fool. I am getting more sophisticated from day to day. And more uncertain! I am more conscious of my unworthiness and also of my desire of perfection which—from the conditions of the case—is so unattainable. I would blaze like a bonfire and shall consume myself to give the feeble glimmer of a penny dip—if even so much.

I won't come out in *Corn[hill]* and *Cosmo[polis]*[2] till next year. There will be next year no vol. of short stories. Smith Elder offered me £50 down for the privilege of locking them up till after the publication of the *Rescuer*. They are rather keen to get hold of the *Rescuer* but I have concluded nothing. Their promises were rather vague. But one of the short stories (a pretty long one too—about half the lenght* of Almayer)[3] is now under Henley's consideration for serial publication in the *New Review*. If accepted by Henley then Heineman will publish it afterwards in a small volume. I want £100 for serial and book rights and of course some percentage on the sales. Still I will take any offer (not absurdly low) they may make because I do wish to appear in the *New Review*.

As soon as I get my 2^d proof of story for the *Cosmopolis* I shall send it to you. I want to know what you think of it. I also wished to ask where it could best be cut without spoiling the effect too much. It is too long for

---

[1] On *The Nigger*.
[2] 'The Lagoon' and 'An Outpost'.
[3] *The Nigger*.

one number they say. I told the unspeakable idiots that the thing halved would be as innefective* as a dead scorpion. There will be a part without the sting—and the part with the sting—and being separated they will be both harmless and disgusting. But if they must cut, then You will help me to minimize the disaster. Next week I shall hear from Henley and let you know what the patron of Kipling and Stevenson thinks.[1] I haven't said half of what I intended to say. (To be continued in our next.) Yours ever with love Jph Cd.

To Edward Garnett
Text   MS Virginia; G. 79

Wednesday [25 November 1896][2]
[Stanford-le-Hope]

Dearest Garnett.

I am as You may imagine exceedingly pleased with what Pawling writes.[3] My dear fellow you are the making of me! My only fear is that I will droop with the end of the "Narcissus". I am horribly dissatisfied with the ideas yet unwritten. Nothing effective suggest[s] itself. It's ghastly. I shall, end this week, send you on a good many pages—but the end is not yet. I think I could almost *pray* for inspiration if I only knew where to turn my face.

Yours ever J.C.

To Edward Garnett
Text   MS Colgate; J–A, I, 197; G. 79

Sunday. [29 November 1896][4]
[Stanford-le-Hope]

Dear Garnett.

I send you seventeen pages more—*65–82* of my Beloved Nigger. Send them on to Mr Pawling,[5] but first look at them yourself. I am ashamed to

---

[1] W. E. Henley (the model for Long John Silver) had published Robert Louis Stevenson's essays and stories in *London* magazine (1877–9); later, they had collaborated on plays but quarrelled in 1888. In the nineties, as editor of the *National Observer* and fellow imperialist, Henley had brought out Kipling's *Barrack-room Ballads*.

[2] Letter-card, date on postmark.

[3] Pawling (of Heinemann) passed on what Henley had said: 'Tell Conrad that if the rest is up to the sample it shall certainly come out in the *New Review*.' Conrad quoted this statement in his Note to *The Nigger* in the Collected Edition, calling it 'The most gratifying recollection of my writer's life!' (p. x.).

[4] The sequence relating to *The Nigger* establishes the Sunday of the heading as 29 November.

[5] Of Heinemann, acting as go-between with Henley.

think how much of my work You have not seen. It is as if I had broken with my conscience, quarreled with the inward voice. I do not feel very safe.

Of course nothing can alter the course of the "Nigger". Let it be unpopularity if it *must* be. But it seems to me that the thing—precious as it is to me—is trivial enough on the surface to have some charms for the man in the street. As to lack of incident well—it's life.[1] The incomplete joy, the incomplete sorrow, the incomplete rascality or heroism—the incomplete suffering. Events crowd and push and nothing happens. You know what I mean. The opportunities do not last long enough.

Unless in a boy's book of adventures. Mine were never finished. They fizzled out before I had a chance to do more than another man would. Tell me what you think of what you see. I am going on. Another 20 pages of type—or even less—will see the end, such as it is. And won't I breathe! Till it's over there's no watch below for me. A sorry business this scribbling. Thanks. Yours ever

J Conrad.

My wife sends her love to all.

To Edward Garnett
Text   MS Sutton; G. 80

[2 December 1896][2]
[Stanford-le-Hope]

Dearest Garnett.

I have returned with a will. I do not think I can give the whole on Friday but a good piece off the end I can.

Will You lunch with me on Friday 1.30 Ang-Am?[3] I shall be there to time and with a handful of paper in my pocket.[4] Some of that must be in MS. for I won't let my wife sit up to type. There will be enough to see the last headland anyhow.[5] So I suppose Henley likes it.

Thanks my dear fellow.

Yours ever

J. Conrad.

[1] Life on a capsized ship is scarcely uneventful, yet some reviewers were indeed to complain that nothing happened in *The Nigger*. See Watts, pp. 51–2.
[2] The sequence affirms Garnett's dating.
[3] The 4th, at the Anglo-American Restaurant, New Bond St.
[4] Further MS pages of *The Nigger*.
[5] Literally as well as metaphorically: towards the end of the book the *Narcissus*, having made the last headland, is towed upstream to a London berth.

To T. Fisher Unwin

Text   MS Yale; Unpublished

Sunday. [6 December 1896][1]
[Stanford-le-Hope]

Dear Mr Unwin.

Thanks so much for sending me Casements letter.[2] I am glad to see he remembers me.

I will write to him when I have leisure.

I trust Mrs Unwin is better now. I think of coming to town this week and shall call on you trusting that if You are very busy You will send me away without ceremony. I don't want to be a nuisance.

Yours faithfully

Jph Conrad.

I return Casement's letter. I suppose Smithers is all right?[3]

To Edward Garnett

Text   J–A, I, 198[4]; G. 81

Monday morning. [7 December 1896][5]
[Stanford-le-Hope]

Dear Garnett.

Of course—as old Pendennis used to say—I am *monstrously* pleased to see Pawling, monstrously pleased begad![6] You are raising for yourself a fine crop of ingratitude—for I don't see any other course of action opened for me.

---

[1]   Unwin's note on the manuscript indicates '7.12.96.', probably from the postmark. The 7th was a Monday, making Sunday the 6th.

[2]   Conrad met Roger Casement (1864–1916), the reformer and insurrectionist, at Matadi in the Congo, on 13 June 1890. He was apparently quite struck with the Irishman, for he wrote in his diary: 'Made the acquaintance of Roger Casement, which I should consider as a great pleasure under any circumstances and now it becomes a positive piece of luck. Thinks, speaks well, most intelligent and very sympathetic' (*Last Essays*, pp. 238–9). At the time of this meeting, Casement was employed by a commercial firm in the Congo, and in 1898 was to become British Consul in the Congo Free State. The only surviving letters from Conrad to Casement were written between December 1903 and September 1904.

[3]   Smithers, of the *Savoy*, was reputed to have a hand in the pornography business. See Sir Max Beerbohm's *Mainly on the Air* (Heinemann, 1957 edition), pp. 98–100.

[4]   Text from Garnett.

[5]   Once again, the sequence confirms Garnett's dating.

[6]   Pawling of Heinemann, presented here with a bow to Thackeray.

Shall I meet you at Compton Street?[1] I suppose it is the place where we had dinner together once or twice. At the back of Palace music-hall. If you don't write I shall take it as it being so. It seems an awful thing to sleep in a Museum right alongside fellows who have slept for 2000 years or so, but I am brave.[2] Now I have conquered Henley[3] I ain't 'fraid of the divvle himself. I will drink to the success of the *Rescuer*, I will even get drunk to make it all safe—no morality! I feel like, in old days, when I got a ship and started off in a hurry to cram a lot of shore-going emotions into one short evening before going off into a year's slavery upon the sea. Ah! Tempi passati.[4] There were then other prejudices to conquer. Same fate in another garb.

Yours ever

J. Conrad.

I shall look for you downstairs first. But I will be in Monico's entrance-hall at 5.30 for a vermouth. Won't you call in?

To Edward Garnett

Text   MS Sutton; G. 82

19 Xer [December] 96.

[Stanford-le-Hope]

Dear Garnett

Ever since I left You in the rain and mud of Oxford Street I have been at work.[5] I had some real bad days but since last Monday I am going on all right. I think the pages just written won't dishonour the book—Your book which you try to coax into bloom with such devotion and care. And the thing is dramatic enough. It will be done by the 7th Jan.[6] Not before!

We are off to Cardiff on Monday.[7] I take my MS with me. I shall not stop writing unless I am stumped by something, when the only remedy is to wait.

May this next year be a better one to You all than the last! My best wishes go to the Cearne[8] if my poor sinful body must go to Wales—that is if Cardiff is in Wales?

---

[1] At the Restaurant d'Italie, Old Compton Street, Soho (J–A, 1, 198).
[2] As Keeper of Printed Books, Edward's father, Dr Richard Garnett, occupied a house on the premises of the British Museum. Conrad had been invited to stay the night.
[3] *The Nigger* was to be serialized in the *New Review*, whose editor was W. E. Henley.
[4] Italian: 'times gone by'.
[5] On *The Nigger*.
[6] Actually on the 17th.
[7] To spend Christmas with Spiridion Kliszczewski and his family.
[8] The Cearne: the Garnetts' house in the country.

I go on then with my work feeling very swimming somehow, like a man before a fall. "Absit Omen!"[1] I shall buy chickens, make them sacred, watch the auspices of the sky, the flight of crows—the agitation of planets. Never was ambitious scoundrel of republican Rome more anxious about the signs of [the] future. And if I knew of a temple anywhere—of an undesecrated temple within the land—I would go scattering flowers, offer sacrifices, and, prostrate on marble floors at the foot of lofty columns, beseech the gods.

Yours ever

Jph Conrad.

To Karol and Aniela Zagórski

Text   J–A, I, 198; *Droga* (Warsaw, 1928), no. 6;
Najder 217

Stanford-le-Hope, Essex
20th December, 1896

My dear Karol and Aniela,

The first Christmas is approaching which I am or shall be spending in the married state. And now, no longer singly so to speak, but jointly we send you our heartfelt wishes for your happiness, peace, and successes both great and small—for the latter constitute the essence of the joy of life. And we both beg our most gracious and dear Aunt that at this moment when families are united—if only for a moment, if only in thought—she should graciously remember us in her heart, which has known those whose memory guides our lives.

I planned to come to Poland[2] for the holidays—by Poland I mean you. It was a vague and timid plan although the desire behind it was warm enough. I did not write about it—I scarcely allowed myself the thought that perhaps it might be possible. Nevertheless the disappointment is acute. There will be no holiday for me this year, but I console myself with the thought that there is next year and will be other years—and wishes sometimes (although not often) are fulfilled. In the meantime I must work, for praise does not feed a man (not to speak of a man's wife!). Therefore I have been writing, writing endlessly—and now the sight of an inkwell and of a pen fills me with anger and horror;—but I go on writing! Do not be angry at the long periods of silence. The above is a sample of my state of mind,—and why should I fill your ears with the

---

[1] 'Let the [evil] omen be absent.' Conrad sees himself as a Roman augurer.
[2] In the original Polish, *kraj* – 'homeland'.

sound of my complaints? You can be sure that if there was any reason for self-congratulation I should at once come running to wag my tail!

Confidently, but I hope not brazenly, I commend myself to your hearts.

From the depth of my soul, your brother and servant.

Konrad Korzeniowski.

I hope that this is not effrontery. I kiss the hands of Cousin Angèle, I embrace her and kiss my little cousins, after the fashion of a seaman, on both cheeks.[1]

To E. L. Sanderson

Text   MS Yale; Unpublished

22 Dec 1896.
Stanford-le-Hope.

My dear Ted.

We leave here in a few hours for Cardiff. I have been writing against time and inclination to the very last minute almost. But the last words written in the house must be for You. If I have not written before I have thought of You—of both of You of course.[2] May happiness and peace be Yours for the next year, for all the years.

This will be surely the most enchanting Christmas of Your life—but I am certain that in the fulness of your joy you will find a moment to think of me—if for no other thing but because Your joy is so much my joy.

I am still under the charm of that short glimpse I had of Your Fiancée. And I like to picture to myself You both cycling, walking together dreaming daylight dreams in the clear and pale sunshine of the winter. May the sunshine never fail! May all the dreams come true! And may I, a man from a far country but in heart very near You always have a share of Your thoughts.

I am dear Miss Helen's most affectionate and faithful servant, and Yours ever with love

Jph Conrad.

My wife sends greetings and best wishes to both.

[1] The text of this postscript (omitted by Najder) is taken from Jean-Aubry, who must have had access to the original before it was lost. Angèle was the younger Aniela, the Zagórskis' daughter.
[2] Sanderson had become engaged to Helen Watson, daughter of the Sheriff-Substitute of Dumfries and Galloway, Scotland.

To Minnie Brooke

Text MS Harvard; Unpublished

Monday. [1896?][1]

Dear Mrs. Brooke.

It is very good of You to come. Any day this week—but the sooner the better, for we are impatient to see You. If You will drop a line the day before I will be at our station. If You prefer me to meet You at Fenchurch Street[2] I would of course come up to act as escort. You do not change anywhere.

Excuse the shortness of this note. It is altogether out of proportion to the extent of our satisfaction at the prospect of seeing You. Jess sends her great love.

I am dear Mrs Brooke always your most faithful and obedient servant.

Jph Conrad.

---

[1] Dating is arbitrary. The Conrads had seen Mrs Brooke in Brittany in July 1896.
[2] The London railway station.

1897

To T. Fisher Unwin

Text MS Leeds; Unpublished

1st Jan. 1897
Stanford le hope.

Dear Mr Unwin.

I returned home today and found your letter about Smithers' cheque.[1]
It surprised me rather for I was under the impression that the price was
to be 30/- per page, but as your letter says explicitly "as agreed" there is
nothing more to say. I have no doubt the words have been counted
correctly. At any rate I shall not count them—so must take his tale.

With kind regards and best wishes for the New Year I am

Yours faithfully.

Jph Conrad.

To T. Fisher Unwin

Text MS Colgate; Unpublished

3 Jan. 1897.
Stanford le Hope.

Dear Mr Unwin.

Your letter and acc/^t to hand. I have counted the words—and only
differ by fifty from Smithers' number.[2] I must have made a mistake
somewhere—but anyhow it's of no importance.

As I told you it was my intention to do I have submitted the MS of the
"Nigger" to Henley. He has seen two thirds of that story and has
accepted it as a serial for the *N[ew] R[eview]* A price has been mentioned
and things talked over, but nothing in writing has passed as yet—and
nothing will pass till the story is finished; which—I am sorry to say—it*
is not yet. I have expanded it considerably and it will take at least 4
numbers of the Review.[3]

Of course if I had not supposed the thing tolerably good I would not
have tried in that quarter—and I am very glad to see my own opinion
backed by such distinguished authority. I always had a great admiration
for the man. I also think that in book form the story may show elements
of popular success. Amen!

With the other stories I have done nothing of course.[4] If the "Nigger"

---

[1] For 'The Idiots', published in the *Savoy*.   2 See previous letter.
[3] W. E. Henley began publishing it in his *New Review* in August; the last instalment,
followed by Conrad's Preface, appeared in the December issue.
[4] The future *Tales of Unrest*, of which *The Nigger* was supposed to be part. Unwin published
the volume.

329

has some success their value will improve by keeping. And, as I've told you, I would write, say, two others (a story of smuggling and another of intrigue) which *if you wish* You shall have absolutely on your own terms—that is if the aspect of affairs is such (after the publication of the Nigger) that it would make it worth your while to publish a volume of short stories. If *not* then at the end of this year (and we cannot know much before how the "Nigger" will turn out) I confidently expect to be in a position to take up the Am. Rights of the 3 short tales so without inconvenience to myself—which would be the case if I had to do it now. Consequently I propose that out of the amount You have in hand now I should pay what I owe you for books supplied (*£3.6.1*) and as for the rest of the acc/ᵗ remain your debtor for some time longer. If the *Cosmopolis* means to cut my "Outpost" in two I should be very much obliged if they would send me another proof.[1] I would like to perform the operation myself. Still, I think it a great pity.

I won't be now in town till I come up with my completed MS for Henley—sometime about the middle of the month. I have sent You my copy of agreement as You desired me to do. Have you received it?

With kind regards

Yours faithfully

Jph Conrad.

To Edward Garnett

Text   MS Yale; G. 83

Sunday. [10 January 1897][2]
[Stanford-le-Hope]

Dearest Garnett.

Nigger died on the 7ᵗʰ at 6 pm.; but the ship is not home yet. Expected to arrive tonight and be paid off tomorrow.[3] And the End! I can't eat.—I dream—nightmares—and scare my wife. I wish it was over! But I think it will do! It will do!—Mind I only think—not sure. But if I didn't think so I would jump overboard.

Thank You both for Your kind letter. I am not so absorbed as not to

---

[1] 'An Outpost of Progress', which did appear in two issues of *Cosmopolis*, for June and July 1897.

[2] A postmarked envelope affirms the date. In his next letter to Garnett, dated 19 January, Conrad indicates he has been in bed for two days, 'A cheap price for finishing that story'—suggesting a 17 January completion date.

[3] In the book's final scene, the members of the crew receive their wages.

think of You every day. I think of you captive and desolate within the magic circle of dates.

May the gods help You. I am all right—have sold myself to the devil. Am proud of it. My wife sends love to all.

Ever Yours

J. Conrad.

To Edward Garnett

Text MS Colgate; G.83

Tuesday. 19 Jan 1897
Stanford-le-Hope

Dear Garnett.

Thanks for the book, and, before all, thanks for the MS. of *London*.[1] I did not dare to ask. I didn't know whether you cared to let anybody read your work in fragments, and, besides, it is a monstrous thing for the children to call their father to account—to litterary* account which is more terrible than a trial for a crime.

I have soaked in the three fragments. I began with *London Bridge*—then the *Lark's song*—and, last, I have read the *Thames' mouth*. And I am proud to see that it is just what I expected in kind—and most delicious in quality. The *Thames* gives us the measure of your quality of observation. The *Bridge* discloses the manner of your seeing, and the *Lark* the far-reaching minuteness of Your thought—the masterfulness of your sympathy with life. You do not jump on me. You grow—so to speak —around me. Your sentences luxuriate in Your own atmosphere, they spring up on every side—till at last the picture is seen through the crafty tracery of words, like a building through leaves, both distinct—and hidden.

And one is willing to see it so—and not otherwise. There the straight wall, there the clean line of an angle, the slope of a roof, the arch of a gateway, the fragment of a column. Sentences stand out as ornamental cornices, arabesques catch the sunlight—and there are niches of misty shadow. Both light and gloom are snared in your phrases. They wave before our eyes in the stir of sentences—and one feels the greatness, the mistiness of things amongst which lives a crowd—a crowd mysterious and so terribly simple—ground to dust by the present, and with a future of ashes and dust.

[1] Garnett's series of sketches of London scenes, which he never completed.

Yes. "Flicker of wind and pause of mist!" It is almost symbolic and ominous coming after the solid impression of the "contest of men interlocked with matter"—the mortal in alliance with the immortal, to make "utility in the gross." It is very good—wonderfully good. "The material . . . gripped moulded . . . by man" and the sudden disclosure in the following sentences that man after all hardly masters and marks the surface while the material grinds, smashes men into chips. I could take it all page by page—not because you have written it—but because it is what it is—and find a train of thought in every three lines. Indeed that suggestiveness is absolutely fatal to the thing as you very well know—surely. The air is too "thick with the amazing advantages of competition" for your prose to ring in it. It is too human, too much like a song in a haze. It shall die like the hurrying crowd it describes—but like the crowd it is a fact—a wonderful fact!—I must stop, or I would go on for ever. You may believe me I haven't lost one of your epithets, sentences, lines. The apostrophe to London is splendid. But then!. . .

I have been in bed two days. A cheap price for finishing that story.[1] Haven't heard from Pawling yet.[2] I send you back the *Bridge*. [I shall][3] keep the other two another 24 hours. Shall write again then. [My][4] kind regards to Mrs. Garnett. Jess sends her love.

Ever yours

J. Conrad.

To Edward Garnett
Text   MS Sutton; G. 85

Thursday. [21 January 1897][5]
[Stanford-le-Hope]

Dear Garnett.

I was glad to hear from you. Thanks ever so much for the books which I fear will be wasted upon me. You know how rebellious I am to verse. It's like a curse laid on me. I send back the two other fragments—and I would write at lenght[6] about them but my wife is laid up and

---

[1] If we accept Conrad's statement here, *The Nigger* was, as we have already noted, finished on 17 January. On the wrapper of the manuscript which he sold to John Quinn, Conrad, many years later, indicated 7 February as the date of completion. The manuscript itself is dated '19 Febr. 1897'.

[2] Of Heinemann.   [3] A conjecture: the MS is torn.   [4] Another conjecture.

[5] The reference to 'two other fragments', which Conrad had promised to return within 24 hours (on Tuesday, the 19th), places this Thursday letter on 21 January, Garnett's dating.

[6] Conrad originally wrote 'length', but then substituted his customary misspelling.

consequently I am unable to think. For her neuralgia distracts me more than it does herself.

Why do you speak of "extenuating circumstances". I did not look for an excuse for You. not I. I love such criminals—and I would rather rob a man of a last shred of honour—than take any of Your guilt from You. As a matter of fact the more I look at Your pages the more I cherish your misdeeds. I wish I could sin in such a way. I have brought upstairs yesterday *"The Imaged World"*[1] and have been looking through it. I haven't seen it for at least a month. And now I see plainly many things in it: amongst others, that You are incorrigible. And I would sooner see You hanged by Philistines than reformed. That's the whole truth. It may not be friendly to say so but at any rate it is not the villainy of concealment. The *Lark is* a chapter! It is a most poetical idea—a strangely complete vision—expressed with continuous felicity of phrase. That's what it is! I envy your writing—the single minded expression, without a thought for the deaf and blind of the world. And when I remember that while You were looking at *The Thames* while You were drinking in the impressions that are now before me expressed on paper—I was bothering You with my chatter. I feel I have forfeited my right to live—that I owe my existence to Your magnanimity alone. But I do not for all that forswear my chatter. Here are 4 pages of it already!—I can't send the *Nigger*. It's too illegible! I haven't heard yet from S. P.[2] but I suppose it's all right anyhow. He seemed so positive when I saw him. I've sent him a suggestion for a title. What do you think of it?

Yours ever

J Conrad.

THE FORECASTLE

A Tale of Ship and Men.

How [will] this do? It's rather late to ask your opinion for I've already sent a slip to P. I really daren't inflict on You my MS. Will You send me some more of yours? Don't think me cheeky. I would like to see it.

---

[1] Garnett's published volume of prose poems (actually entitled *An Imaged World*). The pieces Conrad cites, however, are from the unpublished volume of London sketches.

[2] Sydney Pawling of Heinemann, the firm that did publish *The Nigger*: eight copies to secure copyyright in 1897; in 1898, a normal edition.

To Helen Watson

Text MS Yale; J-A, 1, 199

Stanford-le-hope
27th Jan. 1897.

Dear Miss Watson

Thanks very much for the "Outpost"—and still more for your kind
note. I am delighted to hear You both had such a happy time. I've heard
already from Ted; he is in a state [of] perfect felicity, and has already
begun to count days to Easter.[1] I trust the beginning of your new life of
content and peace shall not be too long delayed.[2] It is a great trial to
him—this waiting. Women have a more penetrating vision, and a
greater endurance of life's perversities. But man longs for the actual—
because he is less able to look afar into days and years.

I understand the 'Fortune' is to be *the* house. I am very glad. I would
rather see You live in a tent on the lawn than sharing the big house with
another household.[3] This is said with all respect to every individual of
both households. No doubt you understand me. It is almost incredibly
good of You to think and talk of me when You have one another to
contemplate and comment upon. But I am more than delighted—I am
much touched by the unselfishness of Your thoughts. And yet it is what I
expected! The greater the affection the more exacting it is; and I only
hope that later on You will not find I exact or expect too much!

The story just finished is called "The Nigger: A Tale of Ship and
Men". Candidly, I think it has certain qualities of art that make it a thing
apart. I tried to get through the veil of details at the essence of life.[4] But it
is a rough story—dealing with rough men and an immense background.
I do not ask myself how much I have succeeded; I only dare to hope that
it is not a shameful failure; that perhaps, here and there, may be found a
few men and women who will see what I have tried for. It would be
triumph enough for me.

Once more thanks for Your thought—for your gracious words. I am,
dear Miss Watson, Your most affectionate and obedient servant

Jph.Conrad.

My wife's thanks for Your inquiries. She is a little brighter now and
sends her love.

---

[1] When he would be able to see his fiancée: cf. the letter to Ted Sanderson (also of 27
January).
[2] They did not actually marry until 1898.
[3] The newly-weds were to live in Elstree, but in a house of their own; Ted was one of twelve
surviving children.
[4] Statements echoed in the Preface to *The Nigger*, written in the coming August.

To E. L. Sanderson

Text   MS Yale; J-A, I, 200

27th Jan. 97.

[Stanford-le-Hope]

Dearest Ted.

I've just finished a letter to Miss Watson—acknowledging receipt of "Outpost" and thanking her for a charming note she sent with it. I am happy with Your happiness and together with You suffer from the delay of Your wishes. Not that I think the sweetness of expectation will change to bitterness but I do not like to think you are gnawing at your heart—and I know that in a more or less decorous way it is what You are engaged upon.

I suppose that, at Easter, Mehemet-Ali (on whom I invoke the blessings of the Prophet) will undertake the rôle of Cupid again.[1] O! lucky mortal whose love is served by princes! I never could understand before the advantages of Egyptian occupation; but since Your engagement I see the hidden wisdom of the inscrutable Gladstonian policy of many years ago.

I wish You would come and talk things over. I have a certain compunction in asking a man to go to the end of [the] civilized world, just to talk. Still when I think of it I see that I would ask you to do more difficult things for my sake. When you find time, do come. Galsworthy did come last Sunday and returned safely none the worse for his desperate adventure.[2] And what's more he had the pluck to volunteer for it too! Now, what do You think of that! Are You fired with envy and emulation?

I did not explain (being naturally muddle headed) what I wanted Your advice upon *re* "Outpost." It is not cutting down; it's cutting *in two* that bother[s] me. They want to publish in two numbers (March–April)[3] and I do not see *where* it can be cut. The sting of the thing is in its tail—so that the first instalment, by itself will appear utterly meaningless—and by the time the second number comes out people would have forgotten all about it and would wonder at my sudden ferocity. Henley likes my story but there is some hitch about the Review.

---

[1] Conrad's reference is to the Mohammed Ali (1769–1849) who warred in the Middle East until checked by the European powers; his line, made hereditary, continued into the period of British occupation. The reigning Khedive in 1897 was Abbas Hilmi. Sanderson's connection with the princes of Egypt is unknown.

[2] Sunday was the 24th. Before Conrad met them both on the *Torrens*, Sanderson was already a friend of Galsworthy's.

[3] Delayed by the appearance of Kipling's 'Slaves of the Lamp', 'An Outpost' did not appear until the June–July issue of *Cosmopolis*.

What I do not know but expect to hear soon. My wife is anxious to see you under our temporary roof and sends her regards

Ever Yours J. Conrad.

To E. L. Sanderson
Text   MS Yale; Unpublished

2ᵈ Febr. 97.
[Stanford-le-Hope]

Dearest Ted.

I did not know that yesterday You had a new year all to yourself. I hasten to send my best wishes; And may your 30th Year be an 'annus mirabilis'—the beginning of new life and complete peace—a year to be remembered amongst all the years of a long and prosperous life.

I am sorry I worried You with my unlucky story. Well, You know, my life is all stories now, something preoccupied and shadowy and I think more illusive even than other existences. And so it goes on, from story to story, from fiction to fiction in an unceasing endeavour to express something of the essence of life. Fata Morgana! A quest without end and with little satisfaction. An unnequiped* traveller stumbling in a desert in pursuit of [a] mirage!

Do come when You can and feel like it. I am rather lonely here when I come to think of it. With love, ever Yours

Jph. Conrad.

To Edward Garnett
Text   MS Free; G. 87

[2 or 4 February 1897][1]
[Stanford-le-Hope]

Dear Garnett.

I have made the MS. just a little clearer and send it to you—the last 50 pages.[2] It is still ghastly but I haven't energy enough to recopy them for You. If too difficult do not read. I had a letter from Pawling. It appears from it that the final decision as to serial publication would be taken at some meeting (of directors I suppose) on Monday, (yesterday).

---

[1] Although Garnett, whose dating is generally accurate, suggests the 4th, the reference to 'Monday (yesterday)' indicates the 2nd. In any case, this letter seems to precede those to Unwin and Garnett, 7 February.
[2] Of *The Nigger*.

I haven't heard any more and am anxious. I do nothing yet. Take it easy and so on. But am collapsed for a time. I will let you know as soon as I know my fate.

Ever Yours

Jph. Conrad

Do You know of anybody who could introduce me to the London Library.[1] A member is necessary. I enclose form.

P.S. In the list of members I see *Lucas* (Edward Verrall). 21. Bisham Gardens. Highgate. Is he the Lucas I've seen[2] and who writes for the *Cornhill?* If so perhaps You could ask him to sign that form.

To Edward Garnett

Text MS Sutton; G. 88

Sunday. [7 February 1897][3]
[Stanford-le-Hope]

My dear Garnett.

Thanks for the book and Your letter. I do not know whether I am to be sorry or to rejoice at your publishers shying from Your London.[4] It is a damnable thing in one sense and glorious in another. I envy you almost in a way You may imagine a scoundrel envying the serenity of honourable power. But it is obvious that dishonesty (of the right kind) is the best policy: and henceforth my concern shall be to discover and steadfastly pursue a dishonest and profitable course. With characteristic cynicism I inform You that I shall seek illumination in Your misfortunes—and advice from Your sophisticated mind—which, incapable as it is to serve (and distort) Your pure art, can yet direct and mould my deliberate and conscienceless villainy. The fate of the Lark—The Bridge—The River—and of many other admirable chapters which I haven't seen shall be a lesson to me—a lesson in the virtues of shallowness, imbecility, hypocrisy*—as instruments of success.

---

[1] The private library in St James's Square, whose comfortable premises and generous lending policy would be particularly valuable to a writer living out of town.

[2] Garnett had introduced Conrad to Lucas (G. p. 56, n. 1).

[3] There is no reason to question Garnett's dating.

[4] Garnett could not get his London sketches published. Conrad's consolatory remarks echo a favourite Garnett theme: the fate of literary merit ignored by mercenary publishers and a foolish public.

I enclose here a note from Pawling—who is a good fellow.[1] I am glad I kept quiet and refrained from worrying him. I feel very safe in his hands—and I wrote a line to tell him so.

I am thinking of a short story. Something like the Lagoon but with less description. A Malay thing.[2] It will be easy and may bring a few pence. I shall send it to Unwin; ask him to place it (on 10% Com) and look upon it as a further contribution to the Vol. of short stories that is to come in the far future. The *Rescuer* sleeps yet the sleep like of death. Will there be a miracle and a resurrection? Quien sabe![3]

My wife sends her affectionate regards. Ever Yours

Jph Conrad.

To T. Fisher Unwin

Text   MS NYU; Unpublished

Stanford le hope.
Essex
7th Febr. 97.

Dear Mr Unwin.

I return to-day the proof of my story for the *Cosmo[polis]*.[4] I've marked the only place where it can be cut in two. But through you I make an appeal "at misoricordiam"[5] to the Editor not to cut the unhappy thing. It will be a good story ruined if he does.

I am now at a short story (just begun)[6] something in the style of that short tale I wrote for the Cornhill. When finished I shall send it to you as a contribution to the vol of short stories which you eventually may wish to publish. Another 7 to 8 thousand words. I trust that you would place it for me somewhere. I rather think the *Cornhill* might take it as I had some kind of intimation to the effect that they would take my stories there. I hope you and Mrs Unwin are well. I haven't been in town for ages but when I do come out I will call on you. I suppose you are pleased at the

---

[1] He kept in touch with Conrad while trying to arrange for publication of *The Nigger* by Henley in the *New Review* and by Heinemann in book form.

[2] 'Karain'. See letter to Unwin of the same date.

[3] Spanish: 'Who knows!'

[4] 'An Outpost of Progress'.

[5] Properly 'ad misericordiam': 'to mercy'.

[6] 'Karain'. Completed, it ran to almost 15,000 words, published in *Blackwood's* (November 1897).

languid imbecility of the present government?[1] If you are not you must be hard to please.

Yours faithfully

Jph Conrad.

To Edward Garnett
Text J–A, I, 201[2]; G. 89

13th Febr. [1897][3]
[Stanford-le-Hope]

Dear Garnett.

I had this morning a charming surprise in the shape of the "Spoils of Poynton" sent me by H. James with a very characteristic and friendly inscription on the fly leaf.[4] I need not tell you how pleased I am. I have already read the book. It is as good as anything of his—almost—a story of love and wrongheadedness revolving round a houseful of artistic furniture. It's Henry James and nothing but Henry James. The delicacy and tenuity of the thing are amazing. It is like a great sheet of plate glass—you don't know it's there till you run against it. Of course I do not mean to say it is anything as gross as plate glass. It's only as *pellucid* as clean plate glass. The only fault I find is its length. It's just a trifle too long. Personally I don't complain as you may imagine, but I imagine with pain the man in the street trying to read it! And my common humanity revolts at the evoked image of his suffering. One could almost see the globular lobes of his brain painfully revolving and crushing mangling the delicate thing. As to his exasperation it is a thing impossible to imagine and too horrid to contemplate.

I send you some thirty pages of MS.[5] I am heartily ashamed of them and am afraid that this instinct of shame is right. I feel more of a humbug than ever—and yet I lay my shame bare to you because you wish it. My

---

[1] A Conservative administration, led by Robert Cecil, third Marquis of Salisbury (1839–1903), which had come to power in 1895. Robert Rhodes James writes of this period: 'Salisbury was ageing prematurely, tired and vague, increasingly detached from the burdens of office' (*The British Revolution*, Hamish Hamilton, 1976, I, p. 168). In any case, Conrad's remark is typical of his disdainful attitude to government and to any political activity, regardless of ideology.

[2] Text from Garnett.

[3] Year confirmed by James's gift.

[4] In return for the presentation copy of *An Outcast* sent to him on 27 October 1896, James wrote: 'To Joseph Conrad in dreadfully delayed but very grateful acknowledgment of an offering singularly generous and beautiful. Henry James. Feb. 11, 1897' (J–A, I, p. 201).

[5] Of 'Karain'.

wife is this moment reading reverently James' book, and trying honestly to distinguish its head from its tail. Her reverence is not affected. It is a perfectly genuine sentiment inspired by me; but her interest is, I suspect, affected for the purpose of giving me pleasure. And she will read every line! 'Pon my word it's most touching and only women are capable of such delicately penetrating sacrifices. I do nothing but yawn and tear my hair.

Yours ever

J. Conrad.

To E. L. Sanderson

Text   MS Yale; Unpublished

Tuesday. 16th febr [1897][1]

[Stanford-le-Hope]

My dear Ted.

I am not delighted with the news. I trust You have heard already that Miss Helen is better. And I would like to know that and also that You Yourself have got rid of that seediness of which You complain. It seems to me You are facing just now a lot of worries and are thinking of lifting a tolerable sack-full of work. Don't lift beyond your strenght.* It is more manful to recognise one's limitations than to ignore them; and he has the larger wisdom who knows when to desist—at whatever cost to the feelings. If reading the above You murmur "Prosy ass!" You are (to a certain extent) wrong; inasmuch that I understand clearly enough that to natures like Yours to deliberately abstain from impetuous effort towards a cherished aim can not be but a great moral trial. Courageous endeavour is fine but You must refine upon your finest impulses; for the right to break Your heart or your back is no longer Yours. And this is all I have to say to-night. Hope I haven't taken a liberty.

I shall try to come and have a look at you soon. I toil but do no work alas! Can't I ask myself sometimes whether I am bewitched. Enough of this. My affectionate regards to Your dear mother. Ever Yours

Jph Conrad

---

[1] Since Sanderson and Helen Watson are not yet married, the year is clearly 1897.

To Edward Garnett

Text MS Sutton; G. 90

Tuesday [16 February 1897][1]
[Stanford-le-Hope]

My dear Garnett.

I was glad to get your letter. Thanks ever so much for your kind invitation. As a matter of fact we do move in on the 12th by special arrangement[2]—but we both are so anxious to accept your invitation that even had we intended to move on the fifth we would have put off the dismal ceremony. So if Jess (who sends her love) is well we shall see you on the proposed date. I shall be in the mecca on Thursday[3] between 2.30 and 3. Call in if You have time and are not afraid of being bored. My affectionate regards. Yours ever Jph. Conrad

To Edward Garnett

Text MS Berg; G. 90

Friday. [19 February 1897][4]
[Stanford-le-Hope]

Dear Garnett.

I wrote to my literary! friend[5] saying that you promised to give quick attention to his stories. Their title is: "From the Four Corners", his pseudonym I do not know,[6] and he is going to send them (probably early tomorrow) in the usual way.

You have cheered me immensely yesterday—You were so much better than my expectations and from you I always expect more than a little. You know!

I had a note from James. Wants me to lunch with him on Thursday

---

[1] We must accept the accuracy of Garnett's dating. The reference to moving places the letter before 12 March, but it could fall on any Tuesday in February.

[2] The Conrads actually moved on 13 March, to Ivy Walls Farm, an Elizabethan house near Stanford-le-Hope. They moved again at the end of October 1898, this time to Pent Farm, in Kent.

[3] The 18th, probably at The Mecca, a pub near Fenchurch Street.

[4] Once again, we must accept the accuracy of Garnett's dating. Leon Edel places the Conrad–James luncheon meeting on the 25th, 'Thursday next', but apparently uses the Garnett dating as the basis (*Henry James*, Vol. v, *The Master: 1901–16*, Philadelphia, Lippincott, 1972, p. 50).

[5] John Galsworthy, whom Conrad had first met on the *Torrens* in 1893.

[6] John Sinjohn, under which name he published *From the Four Corners* (1897) at his own expense. Garnett's report to Unwin (27 February: Berg) saw the influence of Kipling in these stories: 'The author is a man of action & is *not artist enough* to score a high success in literature, we should judge.'

next[1]—so there is something to live for—at last! He is quite playful about it. Says we shall be alone—no one to separate us if we quarrel. It's the most delicate flattery I've ever been victim to.

I shall try to begin that short story to-day.[2] My heart is in my boots when I look at the white sheets. Offer up a short prayer for me.

Ever Yours

J. Conrad

To Edward Garnett
Text G. 91

[28 February 1897][3]
[Stanford-le-Hope]

Dearest G.

Ecco là![4] I deliver my misguided soul into your hands.[5] Be merciful. I want you, besides as much criticism as you have time and inclination for, to tell me whether the thing is printable. Think of your reputation as well as mine—for once your name appears on the fly leaf on any book of mine you shall be associated in my downfall. People'll say you've patronised an ass. Reflect—Reflect.

And understand well this: If you say "Burn!" I will burn—and won't hate you. But if you say: "Correct—Alter!" I won't do it—but shall hate you henceforth and for ever! Till then

Ever your

J. Conrad.

To Edward Garnett
Text MS Colgate; G. 92

10th March
97.
[Stanford-le-Hope]

My dear Garnett

I write according to promise and Hope shall take the letter to town tomorrow.[6] I have been at Karain and have rewritten all You had seen. A painful task. Strangely, though I always recognised the justness of

---

[1] 25 February.   [2] 'Karain'.

[3] There is no reason to question Garnett's dating. The letter falls before that of 10 March, in which Conrad indicates that he has already revised 'Karain' along the lines of Garnett's comments.

[4] Italian: 'Here it is!'   [5] At least part of the 'Karain' MS.

[6] Conrad's friend G. F. W. Hope, a regular commuter from Essex to London.

Your criticism it is only this evening after I had finished the horrid job that the full comprehension of what you objected to came to me like a flash of light into a dark cavern. It came and went; but it left me informed with such knowledge as comes of a short vision. The best kind of Knowledge because the most akin to revelation.

I have thought of You much. Somehow you have intruded into many moments of my life. You have appeared between lines of print, in the red glow of coals—and in other incongruous places. And I still think that there were several shades of truth in all the impertinences of my talk with you and about you. I think Your mission is to work *for* art—and I know You will work artistically for art—for the very essence of it.

—I haven't heard from Pawling[1] up to now. Could you call? But not from me—I think. See how things shape themselves. I am afraid I may be compelled to ask him to advance me a little cash—say £25. What do you think? There is a blessed old kite which I flew a couple of years ago—and it is coming to roost at the end of this month. Hope—poor devil—is so damnably hard up that I can't call him to the rescue.[2] And if P would do it it would be very convenient. But it isn't strictly speaking a matter of life and death. I wouldn't do anything to shock him—you know.

Write to me what You hear. Do not fear to deal a blow.

My respectful regards to Mrs. Garnett. Jess sends her love

Ever Yours,

Jph Conrad

Stanford-le-hope.
Essex.

To Edward Garnett

Text MS Colgate; G. 93

Friday.
12th March [1897][3]
[Stanford-le-Hope]

My dear Garnett.

I don't know how to thank you for Your exertions.[4] And in fact I won't

---

[1] Of Heinemann, in connection with publishing *The Nigger* in the *New Review*.
[2] Hope's speculation in South African mines had left him short of cash.
[3] The references to Henley and the *New Review* clearly establish 1897 as the year.
[4] Over *The Nigger*.

thank you. You have done enough to earn the blackest ingratitude and you shall not be disappointed of Your reward.

I haven't got the cheque (how pretty the word looks!) but I shall no doubt receive it to night or to morrow. I do not distrust Pawling as you may well imagine. The man who can't appreciate the perversity of the *Spoils of P[oynton]* must redeem himself by the most rectilinear truthfulness. I must say, though, I don't exactly understand my position vis-a-vis of the *N[ew] R[eview]*. Is it a question of "to be or not to be" or the more gross question of time only? To tell You the truth, now Henley has accepted me I don't care much whether I appear or not in the *N. R.* or at least care only for the additional cash it may bring. Otherwise I would like to appear at once in book form and be done with it. It would settle doubts and if it kills hope it would also kill incertitude.

I don't understand the infernal farrago You write about yourself. About Your inability to express yourself etc etc. I can't lay my hands on the letter to quote—everything is upside down (sailors say: Ass upwards) round me here as we shift camp at 7. am. to morrow.[1] But if You mean to say that You do not make yourself understood by me it's an odious libel on both of us. Where do you think the illumination—the short and vivid flash of which I have been boasting to you came from? Why! From Your words, words, words. They exploded like stored powder barrels—while another man's words would have fizzed out in speaking and left darkness unrelieved by a forgotten spurt of futile sparks. An explosion is the most lasting thing in the universe. It leaves disorder, remembrance, room to move, a clear space. Ask your Nihilist friends.[2] But I am afraid you haven't blown me to pieces. I am afraid I am like the Russian governmental system. It will take a good many bursting charges to make me change my ways.

I trust you will persevere, for I feel horribly the oppression of my individuality. I am going on with Karain—and going wrong no doubt!—I'll write soon again. Meantime think tenderly—act brutally—dream sweetly.

Ever yours

Jph. Conrad.

---

[1] For Ivy Walls Farm. See letter to Garnett, 16 February, note 2.

[2] The Nihilists and Anarchists who moved in and out of the Garnetts' lives, partly on account of Constance Garnett's work in Russian literature and her sympathy for revolutionary causes; several political refugees were living near the Cearne.

To Helen Watson

Text MS Yale; J–A, I, 202

14th March
1897.
Stanford-le-hope

Dear Miss Watson,

I trust You will pardon me the delay in answering Your delightful letter—and the most delightful of all was the evidence in your own writing that You are better—but I was finishing another story; a promised and belated story![1] I am so sure of Your generosity that I shall say no more in extenuation.

Languidness was to be expected; only You must permit me to point out that the kind of languidness following upon influenza must not be combat[t]ed otherwise than in spirit; *think* cheerfully—even uproariously!—but do not overtax Your physical powers.

I am right glad to know You like the *Lagoon*. To be quite confidential I must tell you it is of my short stories the one I like the best myself. I did write it to please myself—and I am truly delighted to find that I have also pleased you.

I am sorry to think there is opposition to the *Fortune*.[2] The name is of good omen—and I see no other acceptable alternative but a marble palace on one of the Fortunate Isles. Failing that—it must be *the* Fortune in Elstree.

And I shall come—of course—anywhere—even to a marble palace! Only You must not ruin Yourself in wings. You must trust Ted's love—friends' discrimination and the sincerity of Your own nature. Then indeed we shall not only see wings but even hear music—and a song of serenity and peace.

And here I must end. A mass of neglected correspondence awaits me—and work (but that is always waiting)—and some sad thoughts.

Your letter has cheered me. Thanks for your inestimable friendship and for the proof of your memory. I am, dear Miss Watson, always Your most faithful and obedient servant and friend.   Jph. Conrad.

---

[1] 'Karain', still unfinished.
[2] A house in Elstree, destined to be the home of the Sandersons after their marriage.

To Edward Garnett

Text   MS Yale; G. 94

Wednesday [24 March 1897][1]
Stanford-le-Hope

Dearest Garnett.

I am ashamed of not having written directly I had Pawling's letter. It's that infernal story.[2] I can't shake myself free of it, though I don't like it—never shall! But I can get rid of it only by finishing it coûte-que coûte.[3]

Pawling wrote a very friendly letter but nothing explicit. I have still no idea when I am likely to come out.[4] The cheque for £30 was the only solid fact in the envelope. And after all no man can ask for more.

Do think of Your work. You are the man to think about it. If I venture in the fulness of my affection to expect something from You—You know better what I want than any man alive. See, then, that I get it. Bleed, sweat, writhe, groan, weep, curse. It's no concern of mine. I care too much for you to count your anguish anything but a trifle. I want your very life. Ever yours   Jph. Conrad.

Jess sends her love.

Sorry can't come to town. Can't you come here? Think of some *near* date. For a few days if you could stand it. Is such felicity not for the likes of me?

To E. L. Sanderson

Text   MS Yale; J-A, I, 203

Friday. 26th March [1897][5]
Stanford le Hope

Dearest Ted

I had your letter on the last day of my first year of married life. It was good of You to remember me and even accident was kind by bringing Your missive on an ominous day. A year of anything gone is a great loss, or a great gain—and in any case a fitting opportunity to desire some kind of consolation. At the end of many conventional periods of time one is apt

---

[1] There is no reason to question Garnett's dating, although the 'Wednesday' of the heading could also be the 17th or the 31st. The postmarked envelope is smudged.
[2] 'Karain'.
[3] 'Cost what it may.'
[4] *The Nigger* was to begin in the August *New Review*.
[5] Reference to the publication of 'An Outpost'' establishes the year as 1897.

to think overmuch about one self. A barren occupation! But a friend's voice turns the current of thought into a more fruitful valley in the seamed land of the past.

I need not tell You how sorry I was to hear of the illness at Corsbie West.[1] You did well to go. Well! It's in the past already and it is an easier matter to remember than to bear.

Only the other day I've re-read Miss Helen's letter—*the letter* to me. It is laid away with some of my very particular papers. It is so unaffectedly, so irresistibly charming—and profound too. One seems almost to touch the ideal conception of what's best in life. And—personally—those eight pages of Her writing are to me like a high assurance of being accepted, admitted within, the people and the land of my choice. And side by side with the letter I found the printed paper signed by the Secretary of State. The form of nationalisation and its reality—the voice of what is best in the heart of peoples.[2]

I don't count the weeks since I've seen you. Not now! There are too many. A stream seems to flow between us. Surely it is not a stream of life: I feel like a man in a desert. It is not the deadly stream of ambition, interest, personal thoughts. Let those who live in the world splash in that muddy current. And it is not the black water of forgetfulness. It is but a trickle—a trickle of small worries, of insignificant and vital accidents. I wish I could wade through it and grasp your hand on the other side. Well! In time, in time! The thought is faithful; and that "amicitia "Torrente" inchoata"[3] shall live as long as you and I, dear Ted have eyes to look upon the sea where it was born.

I feel horribly sentimental—no joking matter this, at my age,[4] when one should be grave, correct, slightly cynical—and secretly bored. I am none of those things and feeling my shortcomings withdraw from the gaze of my fellow beings. Now, note the inconsequence of the human animal: I want to rush into print whereby my sentimentalism, my incorrect attitude to life—all I wish to hide in the wilds of Essex—shall be disclosed to the public gaze! Do I do it for money? Chi lo sà![5] Perhaps. Or no!—it would be too indecent. I am in a bad way. Now if I could only attain to become (is that English?) to become a minor Thackeray decency would be preserved and shekels gathered at the same time. Alas!

---

[1] The home of Helen Watson, Ted's fiancée, in Newton Stewart, Wigtownshire.

[2] Conrad was naturalized in 1886.

[3] A punning Latin allusion to their original meeting on the *Torrens*; among the possible meanings are 'in ardent young friendship' and 'the friendship begun on the *Torrens*'.

[4] At 39.

[5] Italian: 'Who knows'.

I have been born too far East where not many cultivate the virtue of reticence.

From the above You will (justly) conclude that I am growling and snarling over my work—and cherishing it at the same time. In short behaving like a dog with a bone. Very true. I am an old dog and nevertheless am tired of the hard road. Preserve us from lying proverbs! A lying prophet must ultimately die but the folly of nations is practically immortal. There is also a French proverb which says that "a wise man does not tie-up his dog with a string of sausages". This one seems rather true—and publishers are wise men.

Galsworthy came here last week. He stayed with me just one hour and forty-five min: by the watch. He wrote since saying he had been in Elstree. I trust Miss Agnes[1] is beyond convalescence now. I was on the point of writing to Mrs Sanderson[2] but refrained for I know that she would answer and I do *not* know how her eyesight is now; so I denied myself that pleasure. Give her my affectionate and respectful regards. We live in the farm house. Jess is busy with the garden. I think I saw her digging with a spade the size of a shoehorn. It reminded me of seaside and children. I've done nothing since finishing the Nigger but am at something now.[3] Lots of writing but not much else in it. The *Outpost* begins in Cosmopolis for April.[14] When you write to Corsbie West spare me the space for a few words of sympathy and the greatest regard. You know how I feel. Write soon to me. Come if You can! With love ever Yours

Jph. Conrad.

To T. Fisher Unwin
Text MS Birmingham; Unpublished

26th March. 1897.
Ivy Walls Farm
Stanford-le-Hope.

Dear Mr Unwin.

Would you spare me a minute of your time and a line of your writing just to say whether I come out in the *Cosmo* for April.

[1] Ted's second oldest sister.
[2] Ted's mother.
[3] 'Karain'.
[14] Not until June.

A friend of mine Jack Galsworthy has been down here to tell me that you are going to publish a vol: of short stories by him.[1] The sly dog never told me he wrote.[2] He is a first rate fellow, clever, has seen the world. I trust the venture will be in every way satisfactory. I wait anxiously.

I am getting on with the luckless "Karain: A Memory." He gives me infinite trouble. I hope he will do credit to his bringing up.

Henry James blocks me in the N. Review.[3] I am learning to be patient, modest and to hold my tongue. But I don't like it!

Yours very faithfully

Jph Conrad.

P.S. Will the *Cosmo* pay me in instalments as I come out—April–May?[4] I wish they would.

To Spiridion Kliszczewski
Text   MS Berg; Unpublished

Ivy Walls Farm

Stanford-le-HOPE

Essex

5th April. 1897

My dear Friend.

My conscience smites me when I think of my neglect in answering Your letter; but I have been very busy—and then we moved to our new abode; and the worst of all my wife has not been well, and, my mind not at ease. She is better now, but I do not think well enough for us to ask Clem to come.[5] We intended to do so about this time all along; but really I think it would be rather dull for him with my wife most of the time in her long chair, and me at the writing table—for I have some pressing work to do. And indeed when is it that work is not pressing!

Life presses upon one with its thousand trifles that go to make up its importance. Not that I complain or have lost hope. On the contrary I feel very hopeful; more so than at any time of my life as I can remember. But still trifles are heavy. Then the unsatisfactory state of my wife's health is

---

[1] *From the Four Corners*, published at Galsworthy's expense.
[2] See Conrad's letter to Garnett, 19 February 1897.
[3] James's *What Maisie Knew* ran in the *New Review* from February to September 1897. Conrad's *Nigger* began in the August number.
[4] Actually June–July, for 'An Outpost'.
[5] One of the Kliszczewski's sons.

not a trifle to me, though she is very plucky and makes light of it.[1] Yet as I said I feel tolerably hopeful about the future.

Could you render me a great service? The facts are these. A story of mine was to appear in a magazine called *Cosmopolis* in two numbers April–May. A week ago I had a letter full of apologies from the secretary saying that Rudyard Kipling's story "Slaves of the Ring" [2] shall appear in the *April* and *May* numbers, while mine (called "An Outpost of Progress") is put off till June and July. This is all very well and I would care little for the delay if it was not that the story will be paid for on publication in the usual way. The *Cosmopolis* is to pay me £45 for that story and I reckoned upon their cheque to settle a couple of outstanding accounts. As it is this payment also is going to be delayed for two months which is very annoying for me. Now could you lend me £20, till June? Of course You know it is not a desperate necessity for I have enough to live on and in May I expect to get a little more; but if I pay those accounts now I shall leave myself without any reserve; and no one knows what may happen. It is easier for me to explain this to You than to anybody else and I had rather ask you for help than the other people to wait. Still should it be inconvenient for You I can ask them to wait or even I can stand strictly on my rights and tell the *Cosmopolis* that as the story was booked for April I require to be paid at once. But that I think, from a business point of view would be inadvisable. That Magazine pays me very well: more than *£2.10* per page; that is £5 per 1.000 words and I intend to sell them more of my work; but if they knew I am in want of money they would try to get the price down. It's human nature—you know. As it is I treat them very cavalierly and am bowed to—and get a good price.

I am sure that you will do what you can for me—only *don't* put yourself out. You see it's more of a diplomatic necessity than anything else. And I can tell you—because I know that you do take a friend's interest in my welfare that I have about £120 worth of work absolutely sold and to be paid for between this and next October. Just now I am finishing another story that will bring £35 certain (as a serial) and another £50 in a few months time (in book form).[3] So, barring a serious illness, I am pretty safe.—My wife (who knows nothing of this) sends her best love to you all. She is always recalling the good time we had last Christmas.[4] She is too

---

[1] From the age of sixteen, Jessie had been intermittently troubled by a painful knee.
[2] Actually 'Slaves of the Lamp'.
[3] 'Karain'.
[4] When the Conrads had stayed with the Kliszczewskis in Cardiff.

languid to write herself just yet but asks me to thank dear Mrs. Spiridion[1] for her letter. We like our farmhouse; and we like to think that we shall see you in it this year. Tell me what is going to be done with Clem. And forgive my cheek. Yours ever

J. Conrad.

To T. Fisher Unwin

Text MS Leeds; Unpublished

14 Ap. 1897.
Ivy Walls Farm
Stanford-le-hope

Dear Mr Unwin.

I am sending you at last "Karain: A memory" the tale mentioned during our last interview—in March I think. I am rather behind with it but it has cost me some reflection—it has been in great part rewritten and is now I think quite satisfactory. The ending is cheerful—a new departure for me.

The matter of Am. copyright I leave entirely to you; and if You still think of publishing a vol of short stories by me you will act to safeguard Your interests there. My feeling is:

That I would like to secure a copyright for the purpose of *not* publishing there. I need not go into the causes of my dislike for that public. They would probably appear absurd. And if you secure the copyright it will be for yourself only.

The story is of 20.000 words or perhaps a little more.[2] It could go into three numbers of a magasine.* It has six chapters. I need not tell you that I am anxious to see it appear very soon.

This story completes 45.000 towards the potential volume. I will try to write another (a London story) of 5 to 7000 words[3] which would complete the vol. I shall send it to you as soon as it is finished. I am also thinking of writing a preface to go with the short stories[4]—if You think it advisable, or at any rate not hurtful.

May I ask You before sending the story out to let Garnett have a look at it. I am writing to him to-day asking him to read at once and give his opinion.

---

[1] Although Conrad often anglicized it, Kliszczewski preferred his Polish surname.
[2] The completed 'Karain' ran closer to 15,000.
[3] 'The Return'.
[4] No such preface exists. Conrad did not write the Preface to *The Nigger* until August.

I trust Mrs Unwin and Yourself are well. I have been abominably
seedy.

I am, dear Mr Unwin,

Yours very faithfully

Jph. Conrad

To Edward Garnett

Text   MS Colgate; G. 95

14 Ap. 97.
[Stanford-le-Hope]

My dear Garnett

Karain gone to Unwin today. In the letter I ask *U* to give the story to
you before sending it out amongst editors. I ask You to read it specially
because it is Your advice that had reshaped it and made it what it is—in
good. I have not got rid of *all* the bad (in the first 15 pages) but I am
nevertheless grateful to you for putting me on the right track. I worked
rather hard. Been seedy. How are you all? Jess sends love. Ever yours
J. Conrad

If you can find out *where* they are going to send it at first tell me.

To Edward Garnett

Text   MS Colgate; G. 96

Tuesday. [20 April 1897][1]
Stanford-le-hope

Dearest Garnett.

The last few lines of Your letter saddened me;[2] for if the smallest world
is the safest from pain yet it is painful to me to learn the manner in which
you take account of Your wealth. Wisdom says: do not fill the vacated
place—never! This is the only way to a life with phantoms who never
perish; who never abandon one; who are always near and depart only
when it is time also for yourself to go. I can tell for I have lived during
many days with the faithful dead.

I suggest it with diffidence—but perhaps it would not be a jar and
perhaps it might be soothing for you to come here for a few days (as many

---

[1] This letter follows directly upon the one for 14 April, when Conrad asked Garnett to read
    'Karain' carefully. There is no reason to question Garnett's dating.
[2] Garnett (p. 96) indicates the death of a friend, Eustace Hartley.

as you like). You need not open your lips for days if You like; You may look at unfamiliar scenery—walk on strange paths. No one shall intrude upon your thoughts unless You consent to the intrusion. That much I can guarantee. We cannot, unfortunately, ask You both—or You three—at the same time owing to as yet deficient accommodation; but perhaps Mrs. Garnett and Bunny[1] would come when the weather is more settled. As to You, if You feel in the least like it just drop me a line the day before so that I can meet the train. This is all said with diffidence.

Thanks for all you say about the story. If it is tolerable it is only because you have recalled me to a tolerable mood. I will not now try to explain what chaotic impulses guided me in writing—but as I wrote I tried to remember what you said. My dear fellow you keep me straight in my work and when it is done You still direct its destinies![2] And it seems to me that if you ceased to do either life itself would cease. For me you are the reality outside, the expressed thought, the living voice! And without you I would think myself alone in an empty universe.

Ever yours

Jph Conrad.

Jess sends her love. She is very anxious you should come.

To E. L. Sanderson
Text   MS Yale; Unpublished

3^d May. 1897.
Stanford-le-hope
Essex.

Dearest Ted

I've not been thinking evil things of You—couldn't do it—simply. But I have been thinking of You, more than once; I have been thinking of You both careering over Galloway[3] and I wished for gentle zephyrs and soft skies for You—and a little for myself, too. I am so inwardly beclouded that a little sunshine from outside was a thing to yearn for.

I exchanged lately a few letters with Your Mother[4] who was good enough to keep me informed as to the state of the invalid—till this last

[1] Their son, David.
[2] Garnett suggested *Blackwood's Magazine* for publication. *Blackwood's* accepted it, for the November 1897 issue.
[3] Helen Watson, Ted's fiancée, came from Wigtownshire, part of Galloway, a moorland region of SW Scotland.
[4] These letters have not survived. For an earlier letter to Mrs Sanderson, see 6 April 1896.

and, I hope, final turn for the better. Then, yesterday, Jack came down here for the night and brought more news of a cheering kind; and we talked of Miss Vi's acrobatic, foolhardy, heroic and altogether touching and charming excursion on the roof.[1] I am immensely impressed—impressed with the thing by itself which was essentially not easy to do—but more by the hint it gives of the faculty in Her to conceive *and perform* enviable feats. It is the faculty that gives value to life—the only one that can affront Fate—the stodgy, sleepy dull fate of the majority of mankind; and weaves thread of gold into the grey stuff of existence.

I am delighted at the good news as to Miss Helen's health.[2] Please remember me to Her most affectionately and tell Her that in deference to Her suggestion the end of my last story[3] if not absolutely of the "happily-ever-after" kind (the subject did not admit of that precise termination) is at least of a hopeful kind. I would have dearly loved to send Her the ms. for perusal but I wanted it at once to beat the wolf away from the door. Ah! My dear Ted, what a ghastly contest it is! But she shall have the proofs as soon (and *if*) anyone buys and prints the thing.

I'll be sending You next week to Elstree the first six sheets of proofs of my *Nigger*. (New Review). And I would want to know—very much—what you think of it all. It seems to me that I must sink or swim with that story. I am pretty well in health.

With love. Ever Yours

Jph Conrad

To E. L. Sanderson

Text   MS Yale; J–A, I, 204

Wednesday. [12? May 1897][4]

[Stanford-le-Hope]

My dearest Ted.

I send you on the *Nigger*. Galsworthy had seen a couple of sheets when he was here last so I let him have the lot first. He returned it to-day and I dispatch it at once to You.

I address it rather to You than to Your dear Mother because I want you to see it first. I know my dear fellow that *You* will never suspect me of

---

[1] 'Miss Vi' was one of Sanderson's younger sisters.

[2] Helen Watson.

[3] 'Karain'.

[4] In his previous letter to Sanderson, dated 3 May, Conrad indicates he will be sending on sheets of *The Nigger*. Wednesday of the following week falls on 12 May. Although 19 May is also possible, the 12th seems reasonably certain.

ingrained coarseness of thought and language. But I want you to read and judge before you hand it over to Mrs Sanderson. Not that I mistrust her comprehension and indulgence but I want to spare to Her (even at the cost of my self-love) any unpleasant experience. Not, perhaps, because I think that the thing is not worth it. I am conceited enough about it—God knows—but He also knows the spirit in which I approached the undertaking to present faithfully some of his benighted and suffering creatures; the humble, the obscure, the sinful, the erring—upon whom rests His Gaze of Inneffable* Pity. My conscience is at peace in that matter and it is with confidence and love that I send the work to You—to read and to judge.

Ever Yours

Jph. Conrad.

Love to all. Write soon again. Now in haste for post.

To Edward Garnett

Text MS Virginia; G. 97

[26 May 1897][1]
[Stanford-le-Hope]

My dear Garnett.

I do not know how to thank you for Your letter about the *Nigger*. It has made me happy and very proud. And I am glad that your name shall be inscribed on something You like.

I saw Pawling yesterday and he was very friendly.[2] He comes for a sail on the 12th June. I trust we shall see You here before that time. I do want to hear you talk and also want to ventilate my naive ideas.

Marius came this morning and I am licking my chops in anticipation.[3] Do come soon. Jess sends her love to you all.

Yours ever

Jph. Conrad

---

[1] On a card accompanying the letter, a note, presumably in Garnett's hand, indicates the date by means of Pawling's visit. Even without this note, however, the letter falls into the late May sequence, when sheets of *The Nigger* were first available.

[2] Conrad was still negotiating with Pawling (and Heinemann) over the manuscript of 'The Rescuer'. See his 2 June letter to Garnett.

[3] Garnett sent Conrad a copy of *Marius the Epicurean* by Walter Pater, a novel whose aesthetic ideas and prose style apparently influenced some of Conrad's own ideas in his Preface to *The Nigger*.

To Edward Garnett

Text MS Yale; G. 98

2^d June. 97
[Stanford-le-Hope]

Dear Garnett.

Wife has not been well, but is better now—much. I did send the 1st part of *Rescuer* to Pawling[1] who seems *very* pleased with it. He is an excellent fellow and you are a super-excellent one to have introduced me to him. Of course I have not written much while Jess was in bed being busy nursing and so on. I *must* go on now with the *Return*[2]—then shall jump upon the *Rescuer*. The *Nigger* is bought in the states by the Batchelor syndicate for serial and by Appleton for book.[3] I begin in the August Number of the New R. (26th July). Jess sends her love to you both. When are you coming. I can't ask you same time with Pawling on account of sleeping accommodation. He comes on the 11th–12th.[4] Can't You come this week? I shan't go in the boat[5] this Whitsuntide. Ever Yours,

Jph Conrad

To T. Fisher Unwin

Text MS Indiana; Unpublished

2^d June 1897
Stanford-le-Hope
Essex.

Dear Mr Unwin.

Thanks very much for the *Cosmo[polis]*.[6] To see my story again was like meeting a long lost friend. My thanks to whom thanks are due for the good position of same.

It's about time we heard from Blackwood about *Karain*.[7] It's either good enough for them or not good enough—and it can be seen at once.

---

[1] For consideration by Heinemann.

[2] 'The Return' grew to 20,000 words, one of Conrad's longest stories, and was never serialized.

[3] The Bachellor Syndicate did not succeed in serializing *The Nigger* in the United States; it was published in book form (as *The Children of the Sea, a Tale of the Forecastle*) by Dodd, Mead, not by Appleton the American publishers of *An Outcast*.

[4] Friday and Saturday.

[5] Hope's yacht.

[6] The June issue, with Conrad's 'An Outpost of Progress', first part.

[7] On 6 May, unknown to Conrad, David Meldrum recommended to William Blackwood that they publish the story. Accordingly, *Blackwood's* made an offer for 'Karain', which Conrad refused, requesting £40. On 17 July, Blackwood agreed (Blackburn, pp. 3–5).

No need to meditate more than a month. If it is refused do not send it a-begging—rather let me have it back. It may be a good spec[ulation] for me to lock it up for a time.

I am, dear Mr Unwin, very faithfully Yours

Jph. Conrad

To Wincenty Lutosławski

Text   MS Warsaw; *Przekrój* (Warsaw), 18 January 1981;
Illg

9 June 1897.[1]
Ivy Walls Farm.
Stanford-le-Hope.

Dear Sir

I received your card today and I was very pleased to hear from a compatriot.[2] Hence, I hurry with the reply. My name is Korzeniowski. My Grandfather[3] had a village in Podolia and also administered the estate of Mrs *Melania* (if I remember the name well) Sobańska.[4] In 1856, my Father, Apollo, married Ewelina Bobrowska, the daughter of a squire in the Ukraine, and a sister of Stefan Bobrowski[5] whose name you most probably know. I was born in the country but my parents went to Warsaw (at the end of the year 1860)[6] where my Father intended to start a literary fortnightly.[7] After the period of social unrest and demonstra-

---

[1] Translations of this letter and that of 11 June were made by Tadeusz Sławek and revised by Dr Krystyna Dietrich. The notes are based in part on those of Jerzy Illg, which appear in *Conradiana*, XIV (1982), 3–22.

[2] When he wrote to Conrad, Wincenty Lutosławski (1863–1954), Polish philosopher and zealous nationalist, was studying in London. Lutosławski later taught in Cracow, Geneva, Lausanne, London, Paris and Wilna, where he held the chair of philosophy from 1919 to 1928. In his work, he attempted to combine Platonism with the belief that Poland is the Messiah among nations. His *The Origin and Growth of Plato's Logic* (Longman's, 1897), published in English, established the chronology of Plato's work. An unstable man, he suffered a number of nervous breakdowns.

[3] Teodor Korzeniowski was a landowner and soldier. A veteran of the Napoleonic wars, he also fought in the uprising of 1831, winning the Cross of Military Virtue. He died on his way to join the insurgents during the uprising of 1863.

[4] In fact it was Conrad's father who administered the Sobańska estate.

[5] Conrad's uncle (1840–63) was a leader of both the militant 'Red' faction of Polish nationalists and the clandestine National Government. He died in a duel stage-managed by Conservative enemies (Najder, p. 7).

[6] Apollo Korzeniowski arrived in Warsaw in May 1861; his wife and son joined him at the beginning of October.

[7] *Dwutygodnik* (*The Fortnightly*), modelled on the *Revue des Deux Mondes*. The project was a cover for his political activities (Najder, p. 5).

tions (caused by the recruitment)[1] which occured then, my Father was imprisoned in the Warsaw Citadel,[2] and in the courtyard of this Citadel – characteristically for our nation – my childhood memories begin. In 1862 we were moved to Perm and later to Vologda. Then, as an act of mercy, we were allowed to settle down in Czernigów. My Mother died there.[3] My Father, who became seriously ill, received a permit to leave for Algiers in 1868. We stopped in Galicia. During this period his health improved and this allowed him to participate in starting a daily newspaper called *The Country*.[4] If I remember well, the editor-in-chief was Count Chłapowski (Mrs Modrzejewska's[5] husband) and the first meetings of the editorial board also belong among my childhood memories. My father died in Cracow in 1869. A few months later the late Stefan Buszczyński,[6] his friend and one of my guardians, published a little booklet called *A Little-Known Poet*.[7] My Father was writing a drama entitled *Comedy* which the critics charged with being an imitation of Gribojedov.[8] Later he wrote a comedy in verse called *For the Beloved Penny*.[9] He translated *Chatterton* (A. de Vigny), *Légende des siècles*, *Travailleurs de la mer*[10] – some of Shakespeare's comedies.[11] After his death I was taken care of by my Uncle Tadeusz Bobrowski.[12] He was a man of great virtue and constancy who had a strong influence upon people's minds and was greatly valued by all the citizens of the

[1] The authorities' plan to conscript young revolutionaries into the Russian army.

[2] On the night of 20 October 1861. He was convicted by a Russian military court of organizing demonstrations, provoking riots, and writing subversive pamphlets.

[3] On 18 April 1865.

[4] *Kraj*, a liberal magazine, began publication in March 1869.

[5] Helena Modrzejewska (1840–1909), known in the English-speaking world as Modjeska, was an actress particularly famous for her Shakespearean roles.

[6] Buszczyński (1821–92), Apollo's literary executor, was a poet, dramatist, literary critic, journalist, historian, and fervent nationalist.

[7] *Malo Znany Poeta* (Cracow, 1870). In English, the full title reads: *A Little-Known Poet: his Attitude before the Last Uprising, his Banishment and Death. A Fragment of the Recent History of Southern Poland*.

[8] The Russian playwright (1795–1829), best known for his satirical comedy *The Misfortune of Being Clever. Komedja* was published in 1855.

[9] *Dla Milego Grosza* (1859).

[10] The version of de Vigny's play came out in 1857. Apollo Korzeniowski translated only fragments of Victor Hugo's massive volume of poems, *La Légende des siècles*; they appeared, posthumously, in 1874. The translation of Hugo's novel was never published.

[11] The only surviving translation is of *The Comedy of Errors* (1866). According to Conrad (letter to Garnett, 20 January 1900), his father also translated *Much Ado about Nothing, As You Like It, Two Gentlemen of Verona*, and *Othello*.

[12] Tadeusz Bobrowski (1829–94) qualified as a lawyer in St Petersburg, but spent his life as a rural landlord in the Ukraine. Sceptical, antiromantic, a substitute father, and the self-elected interpreter of family history, he had a deep influence on Conrad's life and attitudes.

Partitioned Provinces[1] for his wisdom and love of his country and its people. His memoirs have been deposited for a five-year period in the Ossoliński Library in Lwów as directed in his will.[2] He himself died three years ago. The present generation remembers him – but death and oblivion follow even the best! I have been writing too much about the dead! But it seems to me that by writing about those who are no longer living I will show you, Dear Sir, in the best way the one who lives. 'Comme c'est loin – tous ça!'[3] I left Cracow in 1874. I was then seventeen, now I am forty years old! In these twenty-three years I have visited my Uncle in the Ukraine twice.[4] I have lived amongst strangers but not with strangers, and wandering around the world I have never left 'The Country of Remembrances'.[5] Well, I think it is enough. Thank you, Dear Sir, for your kind communications, and I remain

Respectfully yours,

Konrad Korzeniowski

To Wincenty Lutosławski

Text   MS Warsaw; Illg

11 June [1897].
Stanford-le-Hope.

Dear Sir,

A thousand thanks for your letter and the books. I am not even trying to tell you how pleased I was with the package you sent me. Although I think of myself as mentally unworthy of such a gift, still there are things which the Polish soul, even when living in darkness, can understand.

Your kind offer to visit me makes me very happy. Unfortunately I shall not be at home tomorrow since I cannot put off a project which was planned a long time ago. But on *Sunday*, i.e. the day after tomorrow and any day till the 18th of this month I shall be at home. Would it be possible for you to spare me for instance a part of Sunday? There is a train which arrives here at *3.20*, so it most likely leaves London around 2. The *A.B.C. Guide* (which I cannot find at the moment – and I want very much to send my reply with the morning mail) will instruct you as to the departure time. The price is *3/2d* for a 3rd class return ticket. In the evening there is a train to London at 7.55, or if you could stay overnight,

[1] Poland.
[2] They were published in 1900.
[3] 'How distant all that is!'
[4] In 1890 and 1893.
[5] A stock phrase rather than a quotation.

the morning train leaves here at *8.30* – The London Station is *Fenchurch Street*.

Perhaps you could kindly announce your arrival with a post card which if sent off on Saturday evening will reach me on Sunday morning.[1]

Thank you once again and with a hearty handshake I remain

Respectfully yours

Konrad Korzeniowski

To Edward Garnett
Text   MS Colgate; G. 98

Friday. [11 June 1897][2]

[Stanford-le-Hope]

My very dear Garnett

You are a brick to send me your wife's admirable translations of Prose poems.[3] Won't I have a real good time with them tonight!

I trust You are well. I am so so—horribly irritable and muddle-headed. Thinking of *Rescuer*; writing nothing; often restraining tears; never restraining curses. At times thinking the world *has* come to an end—at others convinced that it has not yet come out of chaos. But generally I feel like the impenitent thief on the cross (he is one of my early heroes)—defiant and bitter.[4]

---

[1] Conrad gave his elaborate directions in vain. Lutosławski turned up ravenously hungry and six hours late. Having dined, he went straight to bed and, the next morning, raced off to the station at a disconcertingly early hour. Conrad, in whose presence the messianic Platonist had stripped stark naked, thought the visit 'a positive nightmare!' (Jessie Conrad, *Joseph Conrad and his Circle*, pp. 53–5). This encounter, albeit at the gallop, had important consequences. Two years later, in the Polish journal *Kraj* (March and April 1899), Lutosławski published his version of the meeting. Although claiming to justify the emigration of gifted Poles, he gave an unflattering and thoroughly misleading account of Conrad's motives for writing in English. According to Lutosławski, Conrad felt that his talents were not up to the lofty task of writing in Polish; by writing in English, furthermore, he could make more money. The article provoked various denunciations of Conrad as a fortune-hunting renegade; the most vicious of these ('I felt, when reading about him, something slippery and disgusting coming up in my throat'), in the pages of *Kraj*, came from the prominent novelist Eliza Orzeszkowa (1842–1910). She may also have sent Conrad himself a vituperative letter. In any case, as Conradians have often argued, such charges of desertion were to rankle in his mind for many years to come (Najder, pp. 2–23; Morf, *The Polish Shades and Ghosts of Joseph Conrad*, pp. 91–2). Conrad corresponded again with Lutosławski in 1911.

[2] Aside from Garnett's attribution, the date can be established from Pawling's visit, which Conrad had announced, in his 2 June letter to Garnett, as coming on 11 June.

[3] Constance Garnett's translations of Turgenev's *Dream Tales and Prose Poems*, which Heinemann published in 1897.

[4] Conrad returned to this theme in a letter to Cunninghame Graham, 7 January 1898; see also Watts, p. 62.

Pawling[1] comes to-day. Wish could have had you here. Mind you come soon. Jess sends her love to you both. She has been seedy. My kindest regards to Mrs Garnett and love to the boy.

Ever Yours

J. Conrad.

To T. Fisher Unwin

Text MS Leeds; Unpublished

20 June. 97
Stanford-le-Hope

Dear Mr Unwin.

I've finished reading *Liza of Lambeth*.[2] It is certainly worth reading—but whether it's worth talking about is another question. I at any rate have nothing to say except this—that I do not like society novels—and Liza to me is just a society novel—society of a kind. I am not enough of a democrat to perceive all the subtle difference there is between the two ends of a ladder. One may be low and the other high—a matter of pure chance—just as the ladder happens to be stood-up. The principal thing is that the story gets on a rung and stays there; and I can't find it in my heart to praise it because the rung happens to be low. Rungs are artificial things—that's my objection. There is *any amount* of good things in the story and no distinction of any kind. It will be fairly successful I believe—for it is a "genre" picture without any atmosphere and consequently no reader can live *in* it. He just looks on—and that is just what the general reader prefers. The book reminds me of Du Maurier's drawings[3]—same kind of art exactly, only in another sphere. Now, I could never get up any enthusiasm about Du Maurier's cleverness; but it may be because I am blind. I am dear Mr Unwin Yours very faithfully

Jph. Conrad.

---

[1] Partner of William Heinemann.

[2] Somerset Maugham's 'Naturalistic' novel of life in the London slums, published by Unwin in 1897, which drew on his experiences as a medical student.

[3] George du Maurier (1834–96), novelist best known for *Peter Ibbetson* (1892) and *Trilby* (1894), and illustrator of upper-class foibles for *Punch*.

To Helen Watson
Text   MS Yale; J–A, 1, 205

27th June 1897.
[Stanford-le-Hope]

My dear Miss Watson.

It is a real sorrow for me to hear such news of poor Ted;[1] but it was very friendly and very dear of You to write. I am very grateful to you for the friendship and the confidence. The pang of regret comes when one realizes one's helplessness to remedy the ills of the people one loves. Dear Ted takes life hard as higher natures always do—for him relief must come from changed circumstances for it will never come from within. He is not the man to abandon the ethical position in which his sensitive conscience has placed him for his fight with life. He has no idea of sparing himself. My comfort is in thinking that, for a time a[t] least, You are by his side. But I can imagine how large a part of suffering falls to your share. One hates to preach a lower creed. I have ventured before to do so to him—at a personal risk, you will own—and I did it earnestly if without belief in my success. Abnegation and bitter self forgetfulness are not always right. They are not always right even in the noblest cause. I've said so without fear because of my affection for him. In such a saying one runs the risk of being misunderstood. A man's duties are wide and complex; the balance should be held very even lest some devil should be done when nothing but good is contemplated. These are truisms which choice characters—like Ted—do not condescend to see.

It seems too hard to have nothing to offer You but words. One would like to *do* something. And one is too far, and one is blind—and sympathy is only the refuge of helplessness. If You can't help him no one—no one—can. But I am sure You help him—and much more than You think or would believe if the secret of hearts could be put into words. I trust You will let me know soon how he progresses. Without the slightest exaggeration I may say that since this morning I am very miserable about both of You. Let me entreat You—as Ted's friend—to spare yourself any very trying fatigue. The knowledge that You are near *and Well* will make him more happy than the knowledge You are over-exerting Yourself for his sake. You must sacrifice the best of Your impulses to do the most good.

—It is very good of You—at this anxious time—to think and speak of my book.[2] The pleasure of your appreciation—which I prize so

---

[1] He had influenza, with depressing psychological side-effects.
[2] *The Nigger*, which Miss Watson was reading on proof-sheets.

highly—is overshadowed by the news You send. I must however assure
you that there was no *intention* of levity in my treatment of the cook.[1] I did
not try—and I trust I did not make him—ridiculous. Nothing was
further from my thoughts than irreverence. It would have been untrue to
my convictions. The worst that can be charged against me is artistic
failure—failure to express the mixed sentiments the man (whom I knew)
awakened in me. I close to catch the post. I am dear Miss Watson your
most obedient, faithful friend and servant.

Jph Conrad

My wife has been very seedy. She is very sincerely grieved at the news
and begs You to accept her kindest regards and sympathy.

To Adolf Krieger[2]

Text MS Ogilvie; CWW 395 (facsimile on end-papers)

[28 June 1897][3]
[Stanford-le-Hope]

Dear Boy. This is Ortman's[4] sweet note. Wish he would write every
day—or at least every month. Sent[5] me a chique* for £7 so that I may pay
my rent. No sooner one gets something pretty that* one must break into
it. This is a brutal world—my masters!

How *are* you? And How's Johnny?

We exist with difficulty here. Jess wants to be remembered to You and
your wife. The *Sat[urday] Review* notices my story in the *Cosmo[polis]* with
great discrimination.[6]

Ever Yours,
Jph Conrad.

[1] The cook is a religious fanatic and a chronic pessimist.

[2] Conrad's friendship with Krieger dated back to 1880. Krieger helped him find jobs and
lent him money; indebtedness eventually led to a coolness between them. See *CWW*, pp.
327–34.

[3] The date is reasonably certain, for Ortmans's note to Conrad is dated 28 June, and
Conrad seemed in haste to inform Krieger that the delay in repaying his debt was not his
fault. According to Sherry, Conrad remained in Krieger's debt for some years (*CWW*,
p. 333).

[4] Sherry transcribes the name as Ortinari. Frederick Ortmans edited *Cosmopolis*, a polyglot
monthly. He published work by Stevenson, James, Gosse, George Moore, Mommsen,
Andrew Lang and Anatole France.

[5] Sherry reads 'send': the last letter is indeed ambiguous.

[6] 'The author has placed his two forlorn and unconscious figures on the scene with the
dignity of a fine pathos. So far it looks as if Mr. Conrad's story must lose as much as Mr.
Kipling's gained by the division into two parts' (*Saturday Review*, 26 June, p. 726).
Kipling's 'Slaves of the Lamp' had come out in the April and May issues of *Cosmopolis*.

To T. Fisher Unwin
Text   MS Leeds; Unpublished

2^d July 1897.
Stanford-le-Hope.

Dear Mr Unwin.

Thanks for the N^o of the *Cosmo*. The end of the story is not half-bad. Two days ago I had a cheque from Mr Ortmans to whom I wrote directly of course.[1]

And what about my *Karain*?[2] It's nearly two months since the Blackwood Maga. is meditating over it.* Have You suggested them a price? However I've been meditating also during that time and if they want it now it shall be £50. (nearly 20.000 words. cheap).[3] If not I shall receive the story back with perfect serenity of mind. They have been thinking too long about it. The story is too good to be sat upon in that manner and the Maga[4] does not fill me with so much respect and awe as all this comes to.

I would be infinitely obliged to you if You would get from them an answer or the story back.

I am, dear Mr Unwin Yours very faithfully
Jph Conrad.

To T. Fisher Unwin
Text   MS Leeds; Unpublished

12th July 97.
[Stanford-le-Hope]

Dear Mr Unwin.

I owe You an apology for my mistake as to the number of words. I can't imagine how I got muddled over it—but the fact is Messrs: Blackwood are perfectly right: 16.000 is the correct reckoning.

I am very much obliged to them for their offer. I've made up my mind not to let *Karain* go for less than *£40*. This, I suppose, closes the matter. I am anxious to have the story back *as soon as possible*. I am, dear Mr Unwin, very faithfully Yours

Jph. Conrad.

---

[1] See preceding letter.

[2] See Conrad's letter to Unwin, 2 June 1897. On 17 July Blackwood agreed to Conrad's terms.

[3] In his next letter to Unwin, Conrad set a price of £40 when he discovered the story ran to 16,000, not 20,000, words. It really came to under 15,000.

[4] *Blackwood's Edinburgh Magazine* was widely and simply known as 'Maga'.

To T. Fisher Unwin

Text MS Texas; Unpublished

18 July 97.
Stanford-le-Hope.

Dear Mr Unwin.

I am willing to let Messrs: Blackwood have the refusal of any short stories I may write, on the understanding that:

1° Messrs: Blackwood shall accept or reject within a fortnight from reception of the MS.

2° In case of acceptance the story shall be printed within four months from the date of acceptance.

3°. This arrangement relates only to serial rights.

The story entitled: The Return I am writing now is *excluded* from this arrangement.

Messrs Blackwood should also be informed that for some time to come I am not likely to write any short stories.[1]

Under these conditions I shall be most happy to forward my MSS of short stories to Messrs: Blackwood.

I am, dear Mr Unwin, very faithfully Yours
Jph. Conrad.

Messrs: Blackwoods letter enclosed.

PS. I see they ask for my address. Please send it to them for I am anxious to see the proofs.

To Edward Garnett

Text MS Colgate; G. 99

18th July 97.
Stanford-le-Hope.

My dear Garnett

I suppose that after reading this you will think that "the kindness of Providence for an undeserving reptile has reached a point where it is open to criticism." (Mark Twain)[2]

---

[1] Within a year, Conrad had sent Blackwood 'Youth' and started work on *Lord Jim*, which he began as a short story.

[2] *Life on the Mississippi* (1883), Chapter IV: 'the plurality of Providence for an undeserving reptile had reached a point where it was open to criticism'.

The facts are these: After I saw you off that day I turned to tramp home and got halfway there when my Private Devil got into me. This P. D. suggested the refusing of Blackwood's offer and argued with me all the morning. He ended by convincing me—as You might expect—so I wrote to the Patron[1] that £40 was my price for Karain and nothing less would do. The truth is that my P. D wanted to annoy the Patron who advised me to accept the Scotch offer. This is the secret of my P. D.'s activity.

Yesterday the Patron forwarded me a letter from B'woods, which says that they accept my terms on the understanding that I shall give them the refusal of any short story I may write. As soon as I recovered from the shock I wrote saying I would be most happy to agree if Messrs. Blackwood undertake to decide upon the MSS written a fortnight from reception and in case of acceptance print within four months. This is a distinct good turn in my affairs—and like everything else good I owe it to you—for did you not advise to try Blackwood? I hope you won't be angry with my cheek. Success justifies the means—don't you know.

Jess was very crestfallen to find you gone and scolded me for not wiring her on Sat. to come back at once. I assured her of your complete forgiveness—was I right? I go on groping through the *Return*[2] I feel helpless. That thing has bewitched me. I can't leave it off.

Ever yours

Jph Conrad

I shall send Educ. Sentimentale on Tuesday.[3] Remember me to your wife. I did not know she translated Tolstoi. I shall get it at once from the L[ondon] L[ibrary].

To E. L. Sanderson

Text   MS Yale; J-A, 1, 206

19th July.
1897
[Stanford-le-Hope]

Dearest Ted

I heard from Galsworthy that you have returned from Lowestoft and that You are better. I want to offer my congratulations on recovery and

---

[1] T. Fisher Unwin.
[2] Conrad completed 'The Return' on 24 September 1897.
[3] Flaubert's *L'Éducation sentimentale* (1870).

also to tell you that I did not write before because I was in such a frame of mind that an epistle of mine would have been rank poison to a man depressed by influenza. Just now I also feel better—at any rate well enough not to endanger Your health by my writing.

I am glad to say that the 'Blackwood Maga.'' accepted my last short story which is called *Karain*. They demurred at first to my price but I stuck to it heroically (while I felt very vile all the time)—tho'—really—£2.*10* per thousand words of my painful prose is not extortionate. What do you think?

At last Wm Blackwood wrote himself saying he would accept my terms on the understanding that I should give him the first refusal of any short story I may write! This, coming from Mod[ern] Athens,[1] was so flattering that for a whole day I walked about with my nose in the air. Since this morning however it occurred to me that Blackwood won't help me to write the stories—and with me, I see, the trouble is not in the publishing; it is in the writing—Alas!—I've been 10 weeks trying to write a story of about 20 pages of print.[2] I haven't finished yet! And what I've written seems to me too contemptible for words. Not in conception perhaps—but in execution. This state of affairs spells Ruin—and I can't help it—I can't!

Tell Miss Watson all about *Karain*. A letter of her's* had something to do with the shaping of that story. She informs me your taste has grown so hopelessly depraved that you can no longer conceal Your craving for my prose. I understand even that You have refused all other literary food. I am sorry for You my dear Ted. You'll starve. However I'll do my best and You shall have the proofs as soon as practicable.

There is no other news—unless the information that there is a prospect of some kind of descendant may be looked upon in the light of something new.[3] I am not unduly elated. Johnson[4] says it may mend Jess' health permanently—if it does not end her. The last he does not say in so many words but I can see an implication through a wall of words. This aptitude* does not contribute to my peace of mind—and now, when I think of it, there is nothing very shocking in my not being able to finish a short story in three months. The old practitioner here, tho', is very cheerful about it. Well! we shall see—in December I believe.

[1] Edinburgh, the Athens of the North.
[2] 'The Return', which ran to 50–60 pages of print.
[3] A son, Borys, was born on 15 January 1898.
[4] Presumably a specialist, since Conrad also refers to the local doctor.

Here's a letter all shop and family. As soon as You feel up to it do write dear old chap. I want to know what you do—what You think—how it is with you generally. With love Yours Ever.

Jph Conrad

My most affectionate regards to Mrs. Sanderson. Remember me to all.

To E. L. Sanderson

Text   MS Yale; Unpublished

26 July [1897][1]
[Stanford-le-Hope]

Dearest Ted.

Just a word to thank you for your letter. I've been beastly seedy. Fever, gout sore throat—a regular assortment of ailings. My temper is bad, both my feet in flannel a pillow at my back—how is one to write any kind of letter under such conditions?

Let me know how you find Aldershot—and *do*, dear Ted, take care of your health. Respect the casket of Your soul—even on altruistic grounds.

It seemed I had so much to say—and I have no doubt—but I am too stupid for anything just now. To-day I have no more ideas than if I had been born blind and deaf. There seems to be nothing inside and outside of me. Still I am not utterly annihilated yet for I remember, with a faint inward stir that the first instalment of the "*Nigger*" appears to-day.[2] Whisper "good luck" to it old chap when you see it on a bookstall.

With love, ever Yours

Jph Conrad.

To T. Fisher Unwin

Text   MS Leeds; Unpublished

26th July 97
Stanford le Hope

Dear Mr Unwin

I have both your letters of the 22[d] & 23[d] inst: with their enclosures. Thanks very much for forwarding me Mrs Brunnow's letter.[3] Old friendships find one out after many years—and it is always a pleasure.

[1] The year is established by the reference to the first instalment of *The Nigger*.
[2] In the *New Review* succeeding parts appeared from August to December.
[3] See notes on letter to Janina de Brunnow, 9 August 1897.

I have been very seedy lately and the short story is not complete yet.[1] I think I will try the Yellow Book with it.[2]

I must thank you for your patience in the negociation* with Blackwood. I fear You thought—and perhaps still think me—a very unreasonable person.

I am, dear Mr Unwin, very faithfully Yours
Jph Conrad

Excuse this scrawl but I write in bed.

To R. B. Cunninghame Graham

Text MS Dartmouth; J-A, i, 207; Watts 45

5th Aug 1897.
Stanford-le-Hope.
Essex.

R. B. Cunninghame Graham Esq[r]

Dear Sir.

You've given me a few moments of real, solid excitement. I scuttled about for the signature—then laid the letter down. I am a prudent man.[3] Very soon it occurred to me that you would hardly go out of your way (in the month of August) to kick an utter stranger. So, I said to myself "These—no doubt—are half-pence. Let us see" and—behold! it was real gold, a ducat for a beggar—a treasure for the very poor! You'll ruin yourself; but (I am a white man) what does it matter to me as long as the profit is mine.

And I feel distinc[t]ly richer since this morning. I admire so much Your vision and your expression that your commendation has for me a very high value—the very highest! Believe that I appreciate fully the kind impulse that prompted you to write.

Mr Kipling has the wisdom of the passing generations—and holds it in perfect sincerity.[4] Some of his work is of impeccable form and because of that little thing he shall sojourn in Hell only a very short while. He

---

[1] 'The Return'.

[2] For Conrad's opinion of the *Yellow Book*, see his letter to Edward Noble, 18 June 1895.

[3] And Graham, by reputation, was not. A paradoxical Scottish aristocrat, Socialist, and traveller in far places, Graham started a lifelong friendship with Conrad by expressing his admiration of 'An Outpost of Progress', which had just appeared in *Cosmopolis*.

[4] Rudyard Kipling's 'Slaves of the Lamp' had been serialized in the April and May numbers of *Cosmopolis*.

squints with the rest of his excellent sort. It is a beautiful squint; it is an useful squint. And—after all—perhaps he sees around the corner? And suppose Truth is just around the corner like the elusive and useless loafer it is? I can't tell. No one can tell. It is impossible to know. It is impossible to know anything tho' it is possible to believe a thing or two.

Pray do not regret Your letter; I mean to hold my beliefs—not that I think it matters in the least. If I had your eyesight, your knowledge and your pen it would matter.[1] But I haven't. Nevertheless I shall persist in my beastly attitude. Straight vision is bad form—as you know. The proper thing is to look round the corner, because, if truth is not there—there is at any rate a something that distributes shekels. And what better can you want than the noble metals?

You did not expect such a "tuile sur la tête"[2] as this in answer to your letter. Well! it's only five pages at the most and life is long—and art is so short that no one sees the miserable thing.[3] Most of my life has been spent between sky and water and now I live so alone that often I fancy myself clinging stupidly to a derelict planet abandoned by its precious crew. Your voice is not a voice in the wilderness—it seems to come through the clean emptiness of space. If—under the circumstances—I hail back lustily I know You won't count it to me for a crime.

I am very sincer[e]ly delighted to learn that you can stand my prose. It is so hard to realise that I have any readers!—except the critics, who have been very kind and moral, and austere but excessively indulgent. To know that *You* could read me is good news indeed—for one writes only half the book; the other half is with the reader.

Believe me, dear Sir, very faithfully Yours

Jph. Conrad

---

[1] In the 1890s, Graham began a prolific career as a writer. Some of his essays and stories had appeared in the *Saturday Review*, to which Conrad subscribed (Watts, p. 46). By the date of this letter, Graham had published two books: *Notes on the District of Menteith* (1895), an idiosyncratic guide to his home territory; and *Father Archangel of Scotland* (1896), a collection of his and his wife's essays and tales.

[2] An avalanche (literally, 'a tile on the head').

[3] A rueful twist to Horace's maxim, *ars longa vita brevis* (art is long, and life is short).

To R. B. Cunninghame Graham

Text MS Dartmouth; J-A, 1, 208; Watts 47

9th Augst 1897
Ivy Walls Farm
Stanford-le-Hope
Essex.

Dear Sir.

I was delighted to see your handwriting which—by the bye—I had not the slightest difficulty in reading—this time.[1]

Of course I would be most happy to come whenever you say the word; and I'll be still happier if your recklessness carries you as far as Stanford. I presume bohemianism has no terrors for you. It isn't pretty at my age but it's one of those facts one must face—with concealed disgust. My wife (she's a good girl "et pas du tout gênante")[2] shall cook something and—please God—we may find for you some place to sleep—not absolutely on the floor.

I am both touched and frightened by what you say about being the prophet of my inarticulate and wandering shadow. I can not help thinking with alarm of the day when you shall find me out or rather find out that there is nothing there. How soon will you begin to regret Your magnificent imprudence?—and will you ever forgive me the triumph of Your friends when they assail you with reproaches and a great clamour of "I told you so!"

You understand perfectly what I tried to say about Mr Kipling—but I did not succeed in saying *exactly* what I wanted to say. I wanted to say in effect that in the chaos of printed matter Kipling's "ebauches"[3] appear by contrast finished and impeccable. I judge the man *in* his time—and space. It is a small space—and as to his time I leave it to your tender mercy. I wouldn't in his defence spoil the small amount of steel that goes to the making of a needle. As to posterity it won't smile. Not it! Posterity shall be busy thieving, lying, selling its little soul for sixpence (from the noblest motives) and shall remember no one except perhaps one or two quite too atrocious mountebanks; and the half-dozen men lost in that "bagarre"[4] are more likely to weep than to smile over those masterpieces of our time.

I am very unhappy just now not being able to squeeze three

---

[1] Graham's handwriting was the despair of compositors and friends.
[2] 'And not at all in the way.' Conrad was fifteen years older than his wife.
[3] Rough drafts (properly *ébauches*).
[4] Tussle.

consecutive sentences out of myself. The world however seems to be rolling on without a check—which is of course very offensive to me. I want to ask you a favour. There is a thing of mine coming out in the *New Review*.[1] Being, as you inform me, my "Prophète en titre"[2] I am afraid you must consider it your sacred duty to read everything over my signature. Now in this special case *please don't*. In Nov[er] I shall send you the book[3]—if you allow me—and then you shall see the whole. I am conceited about that thing and very much in love with it, and I want it to appear before you at its best. The instalment plan ruins it. I wouldn't make that fuss if I didn't care for your opinion.

Believe me very faithfully yours
Jph.Conrad

I shall be here from now till the end of time—I fancy. So whenever You are in town and have absolutely nothing better to do drop me a line. I am always ready to drop my work.

To the Baroness Janina de Brunnow
Text *L. fr.* 30; Najder 218

Ivy Walls Farm
Stanford-le-Hope.
Essex.
9 août 97.[4]

Chère Madame,
    Ce brave Fisher Unwin vient de m'envoyer votre lettre, car quant à lui ses principes ne lui permettent pas de communiquer à qui que ce soit l'addresse de ses auteurs. Ainsi c'est donc moi-même qui répond à cette marque de votre bienveillant souvenir.[5] Les miens sont bien vivants! Et la vue de votre signature a réveillé toutes les images du passé dont les

---

[1] *The Nigger.*
[2] 'Titular prophet.'
[3] Heinemann brought it out on 2 December.
[4] The address on the envelope of this now missing letter: Jeanne de Brunnow, à Rudawa, poste Berestowica, Govt de Grodno, Russia (*L. fr.*, p. 30).
[5] See Conrad's letter to Unwin, 26 July 1897. Baroness de Brunnow was born Janina Taube. After the death of her father, she and her six brothers and sisters became wards of Conrad's Uncle Tadeusz. In the early 1870s, Conrad lived in the same house in Cracow as the Taubes. Since Janina was only nine when he left, she is unlikely to have been the austere first love portrayed in the Author's Note to *Nostromo* and a cancelled opening to *The Arrow of Gold*. (See Gustaf Morf, *The Polish Shades and Ghosts of Joseph Conrad*, pp. 78–80, 161–2.)

plus heureux moments ont été dus à la bonté de Madame votre Mère, et
à ces amitiés d'enfance dont on comprend mieux le charme à mesure
qu'on s'en éloigne dans le dur pélerinage de la vie. Merci donc pour votre
bonne pensée!

Le temps qui passe si doucement est bien cruel dans son silence et
quand on voudrait savoir on ose à peine demander. Cependant je
voudrais bien savoir! Et en attendant que vous vouliez bien me parler,
je suis toujours, chère Madame, votre très humble et très dévoué
serviteur.

Jph Conrad Korzeniowski.

9 August 1897
Ivy Walls Farm

Dear Madame,

The worthy Fisher Unwin has just sent me your letter, since, as for
him, his principles do not allow him to give anyone the address of his
authors. Thus it is I myself who answer this sign of your friendly
remembrance. My own remembrances are very vivid! And the sight of
your signature has awakened all the pictures of the past, whose happiest
moments I owe to the goodness of your mother and to those childhood
affections whose attractions one understands better the further one
journeys on the hard pilgrimage of life. Thank you once more for your
kind thought!

Time, which passes so quietly is indeed cruel in its silence, and when I
should like to know, I hardly dare ask. However, I should like to know!
And until you are willing to speak to me, I am always, dear Madame,
your very humble and very devoted servant.

Jph Conrad Korzeniowski.

To Edward Garnett
Text   MS Sutton; G. 100

[August 1897][1]
[Letterhead: T. FISHER UNWIN,
PUBLISHER
11, Paternoster Buildings
London,
E.C.]

My dear Garnett

Do not think me a beast. I have been so very idle and unsettled that I could not find time to send You a line—much less to correct the MS—the next in turn for You to see. To day I go home and shall not come to town till my last short story is finished. I'll then bring it to You in the City.

Till then always and ever yours
Jph Conrad.

To William Blackwood and Sons
Text   MS NLS; Blackburn 4

24th August 1897
Ivy Walls Farm
Stanford-le-Hope
Essex.

Messrs Wm Blackwood & Sons.
Dear Sirs.

Mr Fisher Unwin has communicated to me at the time Your letter accepting my story *Karain*, which, I understand, You intend to publish in October.[2]

I write You direct now to give you my address—for the proofs; and at the same time I venture to ask whether You would do me the favour of sending these as early as is consistent with Your perfect convenience. I

---

[1] The reference to an uncorrected manuscript, which is surely 'The Return', places this letter in August 1897. Conrad's next letter to Garnett, dated 24 August 1897, picks up the sequence. We can assume that this letter falls sometime after 15 August since Conrad's 24 August letter seems to indicate a fairly short span between exchanges.

[2] It appeared in November, in *Blackwood's Edinburgh Magazine*.

make very few alterations, but I like to live for a bit with my work before passing it finally for the press.[1]

> I am, dear Sirs, Yours very obediently
> Jph. Conrad

To Edward Garnett

Text MS Virginia; G. 101

> Tuesday [24 August 1897][2]
> [Stanford-le-Hope]

Dearest Garnett

I am so glad You wrote. You gave me time. I've been a martyr to various worries and can't send you the Return yet. I send You however something else: a short preface to the "Nigger".

I want you not to be impatient with it and if you think it at all possible to give it a chance to get printed.[3] That rests entirely with you. Implicitly the Nigger is *Your* book and besides You know very well I daren't make any move without Your leave.[4] I've no more judgment of what is fitting in the way of literature than a cow. And you must be the herd of that one head of cattle (Ain't I rural in my images? The farm tells. Eh?)

And let me hear the decree soon to ease my mind. On my eyes be it—I shall not draw one breath till your Sublime Highness has spoken to the least of his slaves. We demand mercy.

[1] In his response, Blackwood arranged to postpone the appearance of 'Karain' to give Conrad more breathing space (Blackburn, pp. 4–5). This is the beginning of a substantial correspondence with the Scottish publisher who was to bring out *Youth* (including 'Heart of Darkness') and *Lord Jim*.

[2] There is no reason to question Garnett's dating. Conrad's completion of the Preface to *The Nigger* came in the second half of August, most probably; his letter to Garnett, 28 August, indicates the latter's rapid response to the Preface.

[3] Pawling, of Heinemann, refused to publish the Preface with the novel; consequently, Conrad took it to Henley, who published it following the last instalment of the serial publication, in December 1897. The version Henley published differs in omissions and details from the one Conrad originally wrote, which is the one attached to the Collected and all later Editions. In 1902, however, Conrad apparently had printed for private distribution the text of the Preface as he wished it to appear. This text is basically what Conrad originally wrote in 1897, except for his deletion of one paragraph from the manuscript, to which Garnett had objected. There is, however, the possibility that this 1902 printing was a forgery by Thomas J. Wise, later a collector of Conrad's manuscripts and typescripts.

[4] Conrad dedicated the volume to Garnett, as follows: 'To Edward Garnett/This Tale About My Friends of the Sea.'

Cunninghame Graham has not been. We exchanged a few letters. Tell you all about it when we meet. God be with you brother.

Ever Yours Jph. Conrad.

Jess sends her love

To William Blackwood
Text   MS NLS; Blackburn 5

28th Augst 1897.
Stanford-le-Hope
Essex.

Dear Sir.

Pray believe that I appreciate fully the friendly tone of Your letter and Your readiness to accede to my request in the matter of proofs. As to the month of publication I have only to say that I am made happy by the knowledge the story is to appear whole in the Nov^{er} number—for that is the inference I draw from Your letter. Am I right?

Allow me to express the very real pleasure Your inquiry as to a serial causes me—Not from commercial motives. But without enlarging further upon the state of my feelings I may say I have something "on the stocks". And, since You've had the kindness to broach the subject You'll permit me to reply at some lenght.*

The story I have in hand is entitled *The Rescue: a Tale of Narrow Waters*. I began it last year but after finishing Part 1st laid it aside to write some short stories—one of which (rather unexpectedly) developed itself into a longer work now appearing in the *New Review* and to be published by M^{r} Wm Heinemann in book form next Nov^{er}.[1] However through all these delays the *Rescue* did abide with me very persistently. Strictly speaking the MS is not yet in a form to be submitted to you; nevertheless, encouraged by the interest You are pleased to manifest in my work, I venture to suggest that you should allow me to send You Part 1st—not, of course, for a decision or a promise of any kind but only to give you a view of the subject and the treatment.

If You would consent to look through it at your perfect leisure I would go on writing in the meantime, and by—say—Nov^{er} next the story may be advanced enough to show its quality unmistakably. In any case it would be finished by the end of Jan^{ry} 1898. I would also, with the part 1st send you a short statement—not of events—but of the idea to be worked

[1]   *The Nigger.*

out. And this would enable you in a measure to form an opinion as to whether I am going about it in a promising way—or otherwise.

The truth is I am very much preoccupied with the story. It'll be—apart from its subject—a deliberate attempt to get in some artistic effects of a graphic order—but I mustn't weary You.

As You've been good enough to promise me a letter with the proofs perhaps You would then say Yes or No to the above proposal, which, I trust, You will not consider a trespass upon Your forbearance.[1]

> Believe me, dear Sir very faithfully Yours
> Jph. Conrad.

To Edward Garnett

Text MS Virginia; J–A, I, 210; G. 101

> 1897. 28th Augst
> Stanford-le-Hope
> Essex.

Dearest Garnett

Thanks many many times for your sympathetic and wise letter. I put sympathy first—the gift—the unchanging thing—the most precious to me. But as to your wisdom I am ready to admit without discussion that it surpasses the sagacity of the most venomous serpents.

As You may imagine I do not care a fraction of a damn for the passage you have struck out[2]—that is, the personal part. But I think that the

---

[1] Blackwood told Conrad to send on the first part of *The Rescue* to see if 'from its subject & treatment it is likely to suit the Magazine . . .'.

[2] In going over Conrad's Preface to *The Nigger*, Garnett suggested the deletion of the following paragraph, and Conrad followed his advice: 'It may seem strange if not downright suspicious that so much should be said in introduction to the unimportant tale of the sea which follows. It may also appear the height of conceit or folly since every word of the preface may be brought in judgment against the work it is meant to introduce. But a preface—if anything—is spoken in perfect good faith, as one speaks to friends, and in the hope that the unprovoked confidence shall be treated with scrupulous fairness. And, after all, everyone desires to be understood. We all with mutual indulgence give way to the pressing need of explaining ourselves—the politician, the prophet, the fool, the bricklayer they all do it: and if so then why not the writer of tales who is, as far as I know, no greater criminal than any of these. It is true that the disclosure of the aim otherwise than by the effective effort towards it is a confession of doubt and so far a confession of weakness. Yet in the region of art such an avowal is not so fatal as it would be elsewhere. For in art alone of all the enterprises of men there is meaning in endeavour disassociated from success and merit—if any merit there be—is not wholly centred in achievement but may be faintly discerned in the aim.' The manuscript of the Preface, with this passage crossed out, is at the Rosenbach Library in Philadelphia.

8 lines at the end of the par: struck out conveying the opinion that in "art alone there is a meaning in endeavour as apart from success" should be worked in somehow. And whether Your wisdom lets me keep them in or not I tell You plainly—fangs or no fangs—that there is the saving truth—the truth that saves most of us from eternal damnation. There!

I shall promptly patch the hole you have made and show you the thing with the infamous taint out of it.—If then, there is the slightest chance of it doing some good to the Nigger it shall *not* go to the Saturday or any other Review. Hang the filthy lucre. I would do any mortal thing for Jimmy[1]—you know.

I have a bit of news which I am bursting with. The other day I wrote to Blackwoods asking them to send me proofs[2] early and so on—just to give them my address. Yesterday I had a charming, friendly letter from Wm Blackwood saying he would have the story set up on purpose and at once—asking me whether I would mind the story coming out in Nov[er] instead of Oct. but leaving it to me—and so on in that unheard of tone. At the end he asks me whether I have a long story "on the stocks" and wishes to know whether there is enough of it for him to see with a view to running it as a serial in the magazine. Imagine my satisfaction! I answered in a befitting manner and by and bye shall let him have the *Rescue*. All the good moments—the real good ones in my new life I owe to you—and I say it without a pang; which is also something of which you may boast. O! Wiser than the serpents. You sent me to Pawling[3]—You sent me to Black[ds]—when are You going to send me to heaven? I am anxious to depart soon so as not to be too late for the next batch of immortals—but I don't care to go without an introduction from You. May your days be steeped in serenity and your visions be only of sevenfold Perfection. Yours ever

Jph. Conrad.

---

[1] James Wait, the 'Nigger' of the title.
[2] Of 'Karain'.
[3] Pawling of Heinemann, the firm which owned the *New Review* and was to publish *The Nigger* as a serial.

To Helen Watson

[Address, date and first part of letter in Jessie Conrad's hand.]
Text MS Yale; Unpublished

Ivy Walls Farm
Sep. 2. 1897.

[Joseph Conrad begins]

Let me join my thanks; it was such a pleasure to be remembered—and in such a way[1]—for You did send us a bit of Your own country. I've been very remiss in my correspondence lately. I hope Ted is not angry—but if he is I shall ask you to intercede. I trust life is easier to you now.

Your most obedient friend and servant
Jph. Conrad

To William Blackwood

Text MS NLS; Blackburn 7

Sept 4th 1897.
Stanford le Hope.
Essex

Dear Mr Blackwood.

Thanks for using the word "excellent" in connection with my story.[2] It is consoling to know that Your sympathetic insight, undiscouraged by the imperfections of the accomplished task, can discern the aim—the unattainable aim—of the writer. I shall take a shameless advantage (if need be) of Maga's generosity in the matter of revision. But I don't think there will be much. A passage or two to brace up a little—and a word here and there to change.

I delayed sending You my acknowledgements for the Sep[er] issue. I beg to do so now. The appreciation of Mrs Oliphant's work is just in the right note.[3] It is justice—and discriminating justice—rendered to that serene talent. I think she wrote too much (perhaps it's envy; to me it's simply unconceivable*) but she was ever faithful to her artistic temperament— she always *expressed* herself. She was a *better artist* than George Elliot*; and, at her best *immensely* superior to any living woman novelist I can call to mind. Harris (an old friend of mine—in his work) can write more than

---

[1] Helen Watson had sent the Conrads some Scottish heather.
[2] 'Karain'.
[3] 'Mrs Oliphant as a Novelist.' Margaret Oliphant (1828–97) was a prolific writer of fiction. Her *Autobiography*, published posthumously, describes her struggle to provide for a large family.

a bit.[1] Not to everyone is given to be so graphic and so easy at the same time. Besides his point of view is most sympathetic to me. Blackmore is himself—of course.[2] But professor Saintsbury's paper interested me most—a bit of fundamental criticism most cleverly expounded.[3]

I am delighted to hear You will look at the *Rescue*. I shall dispatch it very soon—but just now I am worried almost to extinction by a short story I've been trying to write for the last three months. It is an old man of the sea to me.[4] I can't shake it off—but I am doing my best to murder it—I must say that for myself. Together with the typed MS I shall send You an explanatory document—concealing nothing and extenuating only very little. And I trust that continuing Your friendly interest You will judge, and say *all* you think. I am, dear Mr Blackwood, most faithfully yours

Jph. Conrad.

To William Blackwood

Text   MS NLS; Blackburn 9

[6 September 1897]
[Stanford-le-Hope]

William Blackwood Esq*re*
Dear Sir.

—This is the first part of the tale. I propose the title of *The Rescue.* instead of *Rescuer* as on the type written page.

—The part contains about 26.000 words. The story is planned in 4 parts. Its lenght* is to be 85–100 thousand words.[5] (The *last* most likely).

—I ought to state at once that what there is of the story has been seen by Mr S. Pawling of the firm of Mr. Wm. Heinemann, when he came to

---

[1] Walter B. Harris (1866–1933), 'During the Armistice: Impressions of the War'. The fighting was between Greece and Turkey. Harris wrote extensively about North Africa, the Balkans and the Middle East. For many years he was *The Times*'s man in Morocco.

[2] R. D. Blackmore (1825–1900), *Dariel: A Romance of Surrey*. He is best known for *Lorna Doone* (1869).

[3] George Saintsbury (1845–1933), 'The Two Tragedies – A Note'. By 1897, the time of this letter, Saintsbury had already established himself as a literary scholar with his extensive contributions on French literature to the *Encyclopedia Britannica* and his *The History of English Literature* (1887). In 1897 he published *The Flourishing of Romance and the Rise of Allegory.*

[4] A monstrous character in *The Thousand and One Nights* whom Sindbad the Sailor carries across a stream; on the other side, the old man refuses to get down and stays clinging to Sindbad's back for weeks. The offending short story was 'The Return'.

[5] *The Rescue* was eventually to contain six parts and come close to 150,000 words, almost double Conrad's estimate.

see me here 3 months ago. The firm proposed to publish the story in book form—a proposal which I of course gladly accepted, without binding myself to any specified time.[1] It would never be before the winter season of 1898 or, perhaps, spring of 1899.

So much in the way of details bearing upon business questions—and now as to the stuff itself.

—The situation 'per se' is not new. Consequently all the effect must be produced in the working out—in the manner of telling. This necessity from my point of view is fascinating. I am sure you will understand my feeling though you may differ with me in the view. On the other hand the situation is not prosaic. It is suitable for a romance. The human interest of the tale is in the contact of Lingard the simple, masterful, imaginative adventurer[2] with a type of civilized woman—a complex type. He is a man tenacious of purpose, enthusiastic in undertaking, faithful in friendship. He jeopardises the success of his plans first to assure her safety and then absolutely sacrifices them to what he believes the necessary condition of her happiness. He is t[h]roughout mistrusted by the whites whom he wishes to save; he is unwillingly forced into a contest with his Malay friends. Then when the rescue, for which he had sacrificed all the interests of his life, is accomplished, he has to face his reward—an inevitable separation. This episode of his life lifts him out of himself; I want to convey in the action of the story the stress and exaltation of the man under the influence of a sentiment which he hardly understands and yet which is real enough to make him as he goes on reckless of consequences. It is only at the very last that he is perfectly enlightened when the work of rescue and destruction is ended and nothing is left to him but to try and pick up as best he may the broken thread of his life. Lingard—not the woman—is the principal personage. That's why all the first part is given up to the presentation of his personality. It illustrates the method I intend to follow. I aim at stimulating vision in the reader. If after reading the *part 1st* you don't *see* my man then I've absolutely failed and must begin again—or leave the thing alone. Of course the paraphernalia of the story are hackneyed. The yacht, the shipwreck, the pirates, the coast—all this has been used times out of number; whether it has been done, that's another question. Be it as it may I think rightly or wrongly I can present it in a fresh way. At any rate as I wish to obtain the effect of reality in my story and also wanted

[1] Nothing, of course, came of that plan. Pawling saw Conrad on 11–12 June.
[2] Conrad's 'primitive', Tom Lingard, who had already appeared, somewhat older, in *Almayer's Folly* and *An Outcast of the Islands*.

the woman—that kind of woman—there was no other way to bring her there but in the time-honoured yacht. Nothing impossible shall happen. I shall tell of some events I've seen, and also relate things I've heard. One or two men I've known—about others I've been told many interminable tales. The French Brig "Amitié" was in 1866 stranded on the coast and attacked by some vagabonds belonging to a certain Haji Saman. I had the story from the captain of the brig. In 1848 an Englishman called Wyndham had been living for many years with the Sultan of Sulu and was the general purveyor of arms and gunpowder. In 1850 or 51 he financed a very lively row in Celebes. He is mentioned in Dutch official documents as a great nuisance—which he, no doubt, was. I've heard several versions of his end (occurred in the sixties) all very lamentable. In the 70^{ies} Lingard had a great if occult influence with the Rajah of Bali. He was a meddler but very disinterested and was greatly respected by the natives. As late as 1888 arms have been landed on the coast of that island—that to my personal knowledge. Thus facts can bear out my story but as I am writing fiction not secret history—facts don't matter.[1]

I think you must have had enough of all this. I don't know whether I've given you any idea at all of what I want to do—of what I am likely to do. But pray believe me that nothing but my appreciation of your kind proposal could have induced me to say so much about the aim of my work—the essential object of it, that is. It is not a prudent thing to do but of course I feel safe with you. Seriously—I would take it as a very real kindness if You would tell me your opinion about the plan—and the manner of execution. This apart from any question of acceptance or rejection. Of course I know I can write—in a way; I also know what I am aiming at—and it is not pure story-telling.[2] To know that my work

---

[1] Norman Sherry, in *Conrad's Eastern World* (pp. 119ff.), provides some of the factual background for these episodes. Sherry suggests (p. 127, n.) that 'something of Lingard's influence and power as Conrad presents it is probably taken from the life of Wyndham'.

[2] Almost twenty-three years later, in a letter to Pinker, Conrad reiterated this view of *The Rescue* and wondered if it might not catch the eye of the Nobel Prize Committee. He wrote: 'There is however another distinction which has been mooted (by the R[oyal] S[ociety for] L[iterature]) and that is the Nobel Prize. That was in the air last year; and as it is an international thing and less in the nature of an honour than of mere reward, we needn't have any scruples about acceptance if it ever comes in our way. And as it is not at all an impossible development I must tell you of the thought which had occurred to me as to the policy to follow.

'I think sincerely that "Rescue" has a particular quality. Novels of adventure will, I suppose, be always written; but it may well be that "Rescue" in its concentrated colouring and tone will remain the swan song of Romance as a literary art. The serial is being extremely well received' (MS Berg; 15 February 1919). Conrad follows with strategies for publishing the novel so as to gain maximum attention from the Committee.

justifies the aim would be encouraging—to be told the reverse would be a lesson. I can only be a gainer by what You say. I feel I must apologize for spreading myself over so many pages. Believe me, dear Mr Blackwood, very faithfully Yours

Jph. Conrad.

6th Sept. 1897.

To William Blackwood

Text   MS NLS; Blackburn 11

11th Sept 1897.
Stanford-le-Hope
Essex.

Dear Sir.

I am very sorry to hear of your indisposition. I trust that by this time You are quite recovered. It was very good of You to think of my work—and of the state of my mind. Pray, believe I am not impatient. I only ventured to write You at such a lenght* about my story on the understanding that you would read at your leisure.[1]

I remain, dear Sir, very faithfully Yours
Jph. Conrad.

Wm Blackwood Esqre.

---

[1] *The Rescue*, Part I, then under consideration for serialization in *Blackwood's*. (See Blackwood's letter to Conrad, in Blackburn, pp. 12–13, for the reasons for his refusal: chiefly that Heinemann was to publish the book form. 'Under my circumstances it would go much against the grain with me to see a serial in Maga brought out by another house.' He suggests that Conrad come to some arrangement with Heinemann.)

To Edward Garnett
Text   G. 103

24th Sept. [1897][1]
Friday
[Stanford-le-Hope]

Dear Garnett.

The Return being accomplished in about 23,000 steps it is natural that I should ask you to come and kick it back again whence it came. The fact is my dear fellow your criticism, even when most destructive,[2] is so shamelessly adulatory that I simply *can't live* without it. As a matter of fact it's about all I have to live upon. Please consider!

Seriously. Am I to send it to you? Are you at leisure and have you the disposition? How much nicer it would be if you could come. Say—on Thursday—or rather on any day after Monday. Eh?—I suppose tho' no such luck. Still—do give a sign of life, so that I know where to pursue you.

I've asked Pawling to send me a copy of the *Nigger* in paper cover—of the copyright issue—you know.[3] They aren't for sale. I thought I would ask you whether you would offer it to your mother who has so kindly consented to be misguided into enthusiasm—by her undutiful son. It would not be the common edition at any rate—and I shall not have any copies "de luxe" to distribute.

What have you been doing? I do want a real talk with you. And now this infernal Return is off my mind we must, we must meet.

Ever yours

Joseph Conrad

To Edward Garnett
Text   MS Sutton; G. 104

1897. 27th Sept.
Stanford-le-Hope.

My dear Garnett.

I was so sure You would write on Sunday that I did send to the P.O. this evening on purpose to fetch your letter. I knew it would be there. And I always—always, want to hear from you.

---

[1] The allusion to 'The Return' establishes the year.
[2] This is Conrad's first letter to Garnett since he acknowledged the latter's criticism and deletion of material in the Preface to *The Nigger* (28 August).
[3] The 1897 edition, of which eight copies were printed for purposes of copyright.

When I wrote to Blackwood I did say exactly what you suggest in your letter. I said that I was under obligation to Wm Heinemann and that the *book* was theirs. My correspondence with Blackwood is very friendly. He sent me proofs "of your excellent story" begging me to do whatever I wanted in the way of correcting "as 'Maga' does not mind the expense of corrections" and so on. Since I sent the *Rescue* (that's the new title) I had a letter from *the firm* saying that Mr. William Blackwood was ill, but would read the story and write to me as soon as he got better. I wrote expressing regret at the news and asking him to take his time over it. I haven't heard since.

I've also exchanged a couple of very friendly letters with Pawling. He is a good fellow. The *N of the "N"* comes out in Nov. sure. P. wrote a personal letter to Scribner offering the *N of the "N"*.[1] The book is being set up. I've sent him a fair copy of the preface with the personal par: taken out as marked by you. It is quite long enough without it. It is certainly much better as expurgated by you. I told P. you said it would do no harm to the book; I also asked him to read it and give me his opinion—from the Public point of view.[2] In the same letter I asked him for the second time to send me the copyright vol. Had no reply yet—of course.

The *Return* completes the Vol. of short stories promised to Unwin.[3] The promise is mine and I would not go back on it. Together it'll be 63000 words. Five stories. I've been casting about for a title—for the whole. I thought of:

Tales of Unrest.

What do you think?

—When I parted with Unwin I said:—you shan't have the *Nigger*— but as you've copyrighted in Am: for me you shall have other stories to make up a vol. I won't touch the Am rights—whatever they are. Otherwise you shall have the *stories on your own* terms.

———

Now, his terms, roughly, were £50 down, & 10% progressing to 15%. I shall propose: £60 down, in two payments one in Jan of £30—the other ½

[1] Dodd, Mead published *The Nigger* in the United States, in 1897, under the title of *The Children of the Sea: A Tale of the Forecastle*.
[2] Pawling rejected the Preface for publication with the book. (For details, see note to Conrad's letter to Garnett, 24 August 1897.)
[3] Originally, this volume was to have included *The Nigger* as a story of about 30,000 words.

on publication. Percentages as he likes (Pawling gives me 15% and
20%) ½ translation rights. Can I ask for these terms. Is it fair to F[isher]
U[nwin]?

I fancy, if the *Nigger* hits, he will make a good thing out of the *vol*:
on such terms. If the *Nigger don't hit* then nothing matters much to me
and *he* would pull a long face at anything—at a gift—at a premium—
anything!

————————

The *Nigger* according to sample sent me by P[awling] makes up to 288
pages. The preface another five or six—if not more. I think it can come
out at 6/-. (My royalties are on *published price throughout*)

Ain't I a sordidly vile old man? At times I am myself amazed at my
impudent desire to be able to live. And at times I feel sick—sick at heart
with doubts, with a gnawing unbelief in myself. It's awful!

The Return! And You—you are jealous! Of what? The subject is yours
as much as ever it has been. The work is vile—or else good. I don't know.
I can't know. But I swear to you that I won't alter a line—a word—not a
comma—for you. There! And this for the reason that I have a physical
horror of that story. I simply won't look at it any more. It has embittered
five months of my life. I hate it.

Now, as to selling the odious thing. It has 23000 words—who would
take it?[1] It won't stand dividing—absolutely not. Shall I give it to Unwin
to place? What Mag: would you advise? *Yellow Book* or Chapman—
perhaps.[2] Eh?

It is not quite typed yet. I shall send it off *to you first* either tomorrow
evening (this letter goes at noon) or Wednesday noon—to the Cearne. I
don't think I'll be in town this week. Come as soon as you can. I am full of
things which I want to disgorge.

Ever yours Jph Conrad.

Jess sends her love to both of you. Perceive that you are still "the best
man in the world" a position that of right should belong to me. But
women are queer—and wives still more so. (This in confidence).

———

[1] No one did.
[2] A curious pairing. *Chapman's Magazine of Fiction* was aimed at a 'family' readership, while
The Yellow Book was, in Conrad's words, 'very aest[h]etic very advanced' (letter to
Edward Noble, 18 June 1895).

To William Blackwood and Sons

Text MS NLS; Blackburn 12

28th Sept 97
Stanford-le-Hope.

Messrs: Wm. Blackwood & Sons
Dear Sirs

I return the proof of Karain—with thanks for Your courtesy in letting me have it so much in advance of its appearance.[1]

I would be very glad to know that Mr Blackwood has recovered from his indisposition. I sincerely hope he has.

Very faithfully Yours

Jph. Conrad

To Edward Garnett

Text MS Sutton; G 107

Wednesday. [29 September 1897][2]
[Stanford-le-Hope]

Dearest Garnett,

I don't know whether to weep or to laugh at your letter. I have already torn out several handfuls of hair. And there seems nothing else left to do.

I am hoist with my own petard. My dear fellow what I aimed at was just to produce the effect of cold water in every one of my man's speeches.[3] I swear to you that was my intention. I wanted to produce the effect of insincerity, or artificiality. Yes! I wanted the reader to *see him think* and then to hear *him speak*—and shudder. The whole point of the joke is there. I wanted the truth to be first dimly seen through the fabulous untruth of that man's convictions—of his idea of life—and then to make its way out with a rush at the end. But if I have to explain that to you—to You!—then I've egregiously failed. I've tried with all my might to avoid just these trivialities of rage and distraction which you judge necessary to the truth of the picture. I counted it a virtue and lo and behold! You say it is sin. Well! Never more! It is evident that my fate is to be descriptive and descriptive only. There are things I *must* leave alone.

This thing however *is*. (the MS has not yet arrived; And the question presents itself: is it to be put away in an unhonoured grave or sent into

---

[1] It appeared two months later, in the November issue.

[2] Garnett's dating. The letter clearly fits between Conrad's letters to Garnett for 27 September and 8 October, the subject matter being 'The Return'.

[3] The protagonist of 'The Return', Alvan Hervey.

the world? To tell you the truth I haven't the courage to alter it. It seems to me, if I do, it will become so utterly something I did not mean. What strange illusions we scribblers have! Probably the thing means nothing anyhow.

Can it be placed as it is in some mag? Perhaps before the book comes out I shall see the true daylight from somewhere and then— and then! I must talk it over with you. I do not want to defend it. I want only to thoroughly understand. Thanks many times. Write when you can.

Ever Yours   Joseph Conrad

To the Baroness Janina de Brunnow

Text   L. fr. 31; Najder 218

Ivy Walls Farm
2 octobre 1897.

Chère Madame,

Veuillez accepter mes excuses les plus humbles pour mon apparente négligence à répondre à votre bonne et charmante lettre de Krynica. La négligence n'est qu'apparente, car je n'ai jamais cessé de penser à vous; mais, imaginez-vous, j'écrivais la fin d'un ouvrage, j'étais en même temps en train d'en corriger un autre pour la presse, tandis que Blackwood, à qui j'avais promis une nouvelle pour son numéro de Novembre prochain, me bombardait avec lettre sur lettre pour avoir le manuscrit.[1] Vous voyez donc que j'étais fort occupé: et par dessus le marché la santé de ma femme me donnait des inquiétudes,[2]—qui, du reste, sont à présent dissippées. Ce n'est qu'aujourd'hui que je parviens à trouver un moment libre pour ma correspondance,—et c'est à vous la première que j'écris. Si vous pouviez voir la pile des lettres sur ma table, qui sont là à attendre ma réponse, vous verriez bien combien ma correspondance avec vous me tient à cœur. Car, quoique je vais peu ou point dans le monde, je suis en correspondence avec un tas de personnes que je ne connais pas,—avec d'autres que j'aime beaucoup,—et avec d'autres encore qu'il faut ménager pour faire son petit bout de chemin dans l'existence. Mais tout cela attendra jusqu'à demain. Il y en a qui ont attendu des mois. Enfin!

Je me suis marié il y a à peu près 18 mois: et depuis j'ai travaillé sans discontinuer. J'ai quelque réputation,—littéraire,—mais l'avenir est rien moins que certain, car je ne suis pas un auteur *populaire* et

---

[1] Respectively, 'The Return', *The Nigger* and 'Karain'.
[2] Jessie was pregnant.

probablement je ne le serai jamais. Cela ne me désole point, car je n'ai jamais eu l'ambition d'écrire pour la toute-puissante populace. Je n'ai pas le goût de la démocratie,—et la démocratie n'a pas de goût pour moi. J'ai obtenu l'appréciation de quelques esprits d'élite et je ne doute pas que je pourrai me créer un public,—restraint il est vrai,—mais qui me permettra de gagner mon pain. Je ne rêve pas de fortune, du reste ce n'est pas dans un encrier qu'on la trouve. Mais je vous avouerais que je rêve la paix, un peu de renommée et une fin de vie vouée au service de l'Art et libre des soucis matériels. Maintenant, chère Madame, vous avez le secret de ma vie.

Je vous remercie de tout mon cœur pour les nouvelles que vous m'avez données. Veuillez présenter mes hommages les plus respectueux à Madame votre Mère à qui je garde avec fidélité les sentiments de gratitude et d'affection acquis depuis bien des années. Rappelez moi au souvenir de vos frères, mes seuls,—à vrai dire,—camarades d'enfance.[1]

Que c'est loin tout çà! Et cependant comme, ça vit dans le cœur. La dernière fois que j'ai vu mon oncle Bobrowski il m'a causé longuement d'Alexandre. Il était l'ainé de notre bande et, pour sûr, le plus raisonnable. Je pense à vous tous bien souvent. J'ai vu Gustave il y a sept ans, et depuis je lui ai envoyé mon premier ouvrage, à son club. Peut-être ne l'a-t-il pas reçu? Madame votre sœur et Arthur ont été toujours bien bons pour moi. Voulez-vous les assurer de ma mémoire? Et ce cher Roman: je suis sûr qu'il a gardé le charme de sa vivacité. Il m'est difficile de me le figurer autrement que comme je l'ai vu pour la dernière fois en 1874. Ah! *Tempi passati!* La vie ne s'arrête pas.

Croyez moi, chère Madame, toujours votre très obéissant et très fidèle serviteur et ami.

J. C. Korzeniowski.

P. S.—Mes cordiales salutations à Monsieur votre Mari que je me rapelle parfaitement quoique je l'ai vu juste cinq minutes ce soir à Varsovie.[2] Si vous permettez je vous enverrai en Novembre le N°. de *Blackwood Magazine* qui aura ma nouvelle.

---

[1] Aleksander, Artur, Roman and Gustaw.
[2] The Baron was a Russian diplomat.

2 October 1897
Ivy Walls Farm

Dear Madame,

Please accept my most humble apologies for my apparent negligence in answering your good and charming letter from Krynica. The negligence is only apparent, for I have never stopped thinking of you; but imagine my position: I was finishing one work and in the middle of correcting another for press, while Blackwood, to whom I had promised a short story for his November number, bombarded me with letter after letter about the manuscript. You see then that I was very busy: and the health of my wife gave me some worries into the bargain – although they are now dispelled. Only today have I succeeded in finding a free moment for my correspondence – and it is you to whom I write first. If you could see the pile of letters on my table awaiting an answer, you would indeed see how vital my correspondence with you is to me. For although I go little or not at all into the world, I am in correspondence with a crowd of persons unknown to me, with others whom I like much, and with still others whom it is necessary to treat with caution in order to make one's little bit of a way within life. But all that will wait until tomorrow. There are some who have waited months.

I got married about eighteen months ago; and since then I have worked uninterruptedly. I have some – literary – reputation but the future is anything but certain, for I am not a popular author and probably I never shall be. That does not sadden me at all, for I have never had the ambition to write for the all-powerful masses. I haven't the taste for democracy – and democracy hasn't the taste for me. I have gained the appreciation of a few select spirits and I do not doubt I shall be able to create a public for myself, limited it is true, but one which will permit me to earn my bread. I do not dream of fortune; besides, one does not find it in an inkwell. But I confess to you I dream of peace, a little reputation, and the rest of my life devoted to the service of Art and free from material worries. Now, dear Madame, you have the secret of my life.

I thank you with all my heart for the news you have given me. Please present my most respectful regards to your mother for whom I loyally retain the sentiments of gratitude and affection acquired over the years. Remember me to your brothers, my sole – to speak truthfully – childhood comrades.

How far away all that is! and yet how it has lived on in my heart. The last time I saw Uncle Bobrowski he talked for a long time of Aleksander.

He was the oldest of our band and certainly the most sensible. I think of all of you very often. I saw Gustaw seven years ago, and since then I sent him my first work, to his club. Perhaps he hasn't received it? Your sister and Arthur have always been very good to me. Please assure them of my remembrance. And dear Roman: I am sure he has kept the charm of his vivacity. It is difficult for me to imagine him other than as I saw him for the last time in 1874. Ah! *Tempi passati!* Life does not stop.

Believe me, dear Madame, always your very obedient and very faithful servant and friend.

J. C. Korzeniowski.

PS. My cordial greetings to your husband, whom I recall perfectly, although I only saw him for a few minutes that evening in Warsaw. If you will allow me, I will send you in November the issue of *Blackwood's Magazine* which will include my short story.

To Edward Garnett

Text MS Sutton; G. 108

8th Oct. 1897
[Stanford-le-Hope]

Best of Men!

How horribly tired of me you must be. Yes. I begin to see—just to see a glimmer. My dearest fellow I am too obtuse for one letter to convince me. But my feelings are fine enough for me to be horrified at the thought of all the time You are wasting upon my unworthy person. Do you know I am at times in the frightful situation of thinking that You are absolutely right in Your blame and—oh horrors!—utterly wrong in Your praise. That there is not a single redeeming line in the story!![1] I can't look at it. It torments me like a memory of a bad action which You—Friend—are trying to palliate. In vain. I am a prey to remorse. I should not have written that thing. It's criminal.

I'm sending it to Chapman to-day.[2]

---

[1] 'The Return'. In his Introduction to 'The Sisters', Ford remarks that Conrad regarded that work and 'The Return' as something 'slightly obscene at which one could only peep in secret'. Conrad himself spoke of 'The Return' disparagingly in his Author's Note to *Tales of Unrest* in the Collected Edition: 'Indeed my innermost feeling, now, is that The Return is a left-handed production.'

[2] See following letter to Garnett for details.

Yes—I see. I am unreal even when I try for reality, so when I don't try I must be exasperating. I feel like a man who can't move, in a dream. To move is vital—it's salvation—and I can't! I feel what you mean and I am utterly powerless to imagine anything else. It's like being bewitched; it's like being in a cataleptic trance. You hear people weeping over you, making ready to bury you—and you can't give a sign of life!—I wish to goodness I could *not* believe You. But I can't. I *feel* all You say and all the same I remain in the dark as though You had spoken an impassioned discourse—in Chinese. I feel—and I can't understand. I am stirred—and I can't grasp my own emotion. It's too awful—without joking.

Perhaps in time—perhaps in time! Who knows? If you don't abandon me in disgust I may yet learn the truth of art—which You possess. Even now I have an imperfect apprehension—for that story has been a heavy trial to me while I was writing it.[1] It has made me ill: I hated while I wrote.

Thanks. Thanks. I must—for a while—think of other things. I can't send you the MS. pages[2] because You *could not* find yourself in them. I can't myself—now. There are heaps of them; whole pages of erasures with perhaps one solitary and surviving line hiding amongst the ranges of scored out words.

When the T S. returns from C & FC.[3] as I feel it will I shall send it to you. I would like your wife to read it. I would like—I have much courage—I would like to know what she thinks.

Blackwood don't give a sign of life about the Rescue.[4] A new serial begins in Oct. It may run six months perhaps. It would give me time to finish mine.

I don't think I will ever write anything more. That shall wear off, but meantime I can't write a word of the Rescue.

I want to make it a kind of glorified book for boys—You know. No analysis.[5] No damned mouthing. Pictures—pictures—pictures. That's what I want to do. And I can do that. Can't I?

I'm going to pull myself together. Shall write You soon. With greatest affection

Ever Yours

Jph Conrad.

[1] In his Author's Note, Conrad repeated this sentiment: 'for I know how much the writing of that fantasy has cost me in sheer toil., in temper, and in disillusionment'.

[2] Of *The Rescue*.

[3] The typescript of 'The Return', from Oswald Crawford, at Chapman and Hall. The initials 'FC' appear to be a mistake.

[4] See Blackwood's letter to Conrad, 28 October (Blackburn, p. 12) and Conrad's response, 30 October.

[5] In contrast to 'The Return'.

To Edward Garnett

Text MS Williams; G. 110

Monday evening [11 October 1897][1]
Stanford-le-Hope
Essex.

Dearest G.

Luckily I walked down to the p.o. and got your letter tonight. I did not come on Thursday as I intended because I positively could not get away for domestic reasons. Then on Friday—most unexpectedly—I *had* to go to town, and, being there, I called on Pawling.[2] He told me he had seen You. I asked him whether You had relieved Your feelings by cursing me to him. At that he smiled with reserve and naturally I did not insist.

My dearest fellow I entreat you to take my letters literally. I never have any arrière-pensée when writing to you—consequently I cannot develop any sarcastic tendency. I do not remember exactly now what I have written in my last letter to You, but I know I wrote guided by what I felt then—what I feel now: a very real gratitude for your friendship, for your appreciation, for your criticism; a gratitude for what you are to me—for what you say to me. Do, in the name of all the gods, do give me credit for being able to say damn You—if such was my thought. I, all along, act on the assumption that *you* would say damn you if such an expression were necessary. That's the true friendship. I wrote that you have the knowledge of artistic effect because I believe you have. You do know. I wish to goodness You didn't. But the more I think of the story the more I feel (I don't see yet) the justice of your pronouncement as to the unreality of the dialogue.[3] Where we differ is there: you say: it is too logical—I say: It is too crude; but I admit that the crudeness (proceeding from want of skill) produces that effect of logic—which is offensive. You see I wanted to give out the gospel of the beastly bourgeois—and wasn't clever enough to do it in a more natural way. Hence the logic which resembles the logic of a melodrama. The childishness of mind coming to the surface. All this I feel. I don't see; because if I did see it I would also see the other way the mature way—the way of art. I would work from conviction to conviction—through inevitable moments to the final situation. Instead of which I went on creating the moments for the illustration of the idea. Am I right in that view? If so the story is bad art. It is built on the same falsehood as a melodrama.

What delighted me was the remark in your 2[d] letter that the phrasing

---

[1] The references to 'The Return' confirm Garnett's dating.
[2] At the Heinemann office.
[3] In 'The Return'.

was good. I did try to phrase well and it was not easy, writing as I did with a constant, haunting fear of being lost in the midst of thickening untruth. I felt all the time there was *something* wrong with that story. I feel it now more than ever. All I've written above is only an honest attempt to understand the failure. It is very important that I should. Am I anywhere near it yet?

I sent the story to Chap[man] & Hall with a letter, subtle but full of assurance. I had an answer by *return of post* from Oswald Crawfurd.[1] He said the story is too long for any single number of the Magazine. But he would like to have my work which he knows and admires. He will read and decide within a fortnight. He thinks it may be used in the Xmas Number, (Here I nearly fell off my chair in a fit of laughter. Can't you imagine the story read by the domestic hearthstone in the season of festivity?)[2] tho' it is somewhat too long even for that. He wants to know my price for serial rights Brit: and Am:

I replied: Delighted he likes my work. Follows a small lecture on art to prove that the story can *not* be divided. (If so the *moral* effect lost.) A hint that the moral effect is nothing less than beautiful. A sentimental phrase about the moral endeavour giving courage to the worker. A declaration that I attach a great importance to the story. Then: my price for serial rights *Brit* & *Am* is £50 and I point out that this is at a rate *less* than what Messrs: Blackwood pay me for my story to appear in their Nov^er Number.—That is perfectly true. £50 works out at about 43/- per thou: while Blackwood pays 45/-

A week has elapsed since and I haven't heard, but the time is not up. I nourish hopes. What do You think?

I haven't heard from Blackwood.[3] When sending back the proof of Karain I asked how was Mr Blackwood and had no answer. I don't think I'll write yet as I have plainly told him to take his time.

I can't get on with the *Rescue*. In all these days I haven't written a line, but there hadn't been a day when I did not wish myself dead. It's too ghastly. I positively don't know what to do. Am I out to the end of my tether? Sometimes I think it must be so.

It did me good to hear that the *Nigger* works miracles. You are a dear fellow to send such news. Pawling after proposing me a paper copy now says he hasn't one. I am horribly disappointed at not being able to carry out my idea of offering it to Your Mother.

---

[1] Editor of *Chapman's Magazine of Fiction*.
[2] 'The Return', a story of marital discord.
[3] About *The Rescue*, Part I.

Heinemann objects to the *bloody's* in the book. That Israelite is afraid of women. I didn't trust myself to say much in Pawling's room. Moreover Pawling is a good fellow whom I like more every time I see him; and it seemed to me he wanted me to give way. So I struck 3 or 4 *bloody's* out. I am sure there is a couple left yet but, damn it, I am not going to hunt 'em up. I've sent the last batch of proofs today. Now the Nigger is cast adrift from me. The book strikes me as good; but I quite forsee it will have no sale.

What do you think of the *Gadfly?*[1] I wrote what I thought to P, who rejoined gallantly. But it comes to this, if his point of view is accepted, that having suffered is sufficient excuse for the production of rubbish. Well! It may be true too. I may yet make my profit of that argument. However I am not "hollow-eyed" and the author of the *Gadfly* is. Women won't play fair—you know. A hollow-eyed man once tried to impress that truth upon me. I think he was right. But the book is very delightful in a way. Look at the logic: He found his mutton-chop very tough *therefore* he arose and cursed his aunt. And the idea of that battered Gadfly in kid gloves finding his revenge in scolding, is—well—feminine, or I have lived all these bitter years in vain. It is perfectly delightful. I don't remember ever reading a book I disliked so much.

I see, the *Tormentor* is booming—in the press.[2] Have you found another nugget of virgin gold for the "patron"? Ah! You do know; you do know. I own that the Standard's review of the *Liza* amazes me.[3] It is no more than justice, but to think the *Standard* could see it! It is the Annus Mirabilis. D'you think I will get my share of loaves and fishes. Eh? Well never mind. The book is written. What worries me now is the unwritten book.

Ever yours   Jph Conrad

Have You enough of *London* to send me. Would you send it? I deserve[4] it for there is hardly a day I do not look into the Imaged World[5]—FOR ITSELF not because you've written it.

---

[1] A novel by E. L. Voynich (Heinemann, 1897); its embittered hero, an Italian revolutionary opposed to both Austrian and clerical domination, has to flee to South America.
[2] A novel by Benjamin Swift, just published by Unwin.
[3] Somerset Maugham's *Liza of Lambeth* (Unwin, 1897).
[4] Reading from Garnett; the manuscript is damaged.
[5] Both the unpublished 'London' and *An Imaged World* (Dent, 1894) are collections of Garnett's prose poems.

To Edward Garnett

Text   MS Sutton; G. 104

[14 October 1897][1]
[Stanford-le-hope]

Dearest G.

It was good to read your letter. I know you've made me and therefore wouldn't be human if you did not take interest in me. But I like to hear you say so—you can't say it too often. It is balm and nectar and sunshine.

I shall be more than delighted to be introduced to your Mother on Friday. You mean on Friday the 22nd.—don't you? But I am ready on any day.

I shall go to town tomorrow to meet P[awling] and Crane.[2] I *do* admire him. I shan't have to pretend.

I'm having a tussle with the *Rescue*. I've sent a long epitome to P. The necessity to write it out has brought me to terms with myself. But it's most damnably hard—all the same. I can't, somehow, swing out—so to speak.

Ever Yours   Joseph Conrad

To E. L. Sanderson

Text   MS Yale; Unpublished

14/10/97.
Stanford-le-Hope

Dearest Ted.

I've read and re-read.[3] To me—were it not so touching—there would seem some thing ludicrous in *You* asking me for remarks—for criticism!—I wish I could tell you critically how much I like these stanzas. But critically I cannot. I can do ignorantly with the naive statement that I love the thing because I feel it lovable.

I send You a typed copy—each stanza on a separate page. If you do your polishing on that copy—then by sending back the corrected leaflets they shall be returned to you typed in their definite shape.

---

[1] The references to Friday the 22nd and the meeting with Crane, as well as the 'tussle with *The Rescue*', establish October as the month and 1897 as the year. For the '14' we must rely on Garnett's dating.

[2] Stephen Crane (1871–1900), whose *The Red Badge of Courage* had been published by Heinemann, showed great interest in meeting the author of *The Nigger of the 'Narcissus'*, which was then appearing in the *New Review* (also under Heinemann's ownership). Pawling arranged a luncheon meeting.

[3] Sanderson had sent Conrad a selection of his poems.

I've no doubt you can improve—if you try; but in my humble opinion
I. II. III. IV. do not want retouching. These I fancy You can only
change—if you touch them—but You would not improve. The *poesy* in
each is *complete*. V. Is all there. It is only on third or fourth reading that a
shadowy dissatisfaction—less than that—a shadowy doubt arises in the
mind about the *complete expression* of the *last* line. I wish to suggest that the
idea of course being left—(it is a charming association of the lovers with
memories of distress and violence) I would suggest whether—again last
line—*massacre* could not be replaced by some expression conveying a less
cruel and a more stirring idea. The idea of combat—of attack—or of
defence. (I feel I'm making an ass of myself.)

But I go on! VI. *First line*. My wife copied faithfully what I take to be
clerical error of Your MS. viz: *it's* where *its* is meant? The typed reading
of the 3^d *line* commends itself to me most of the alternate readings you
give in Your letter.

The idea enshrined in the stanza is most charming, delicate,
suggestive casting a light back on the whole poem. That's why I venture
to ask you to look at the last line—again.

cheer . . . charm

do not seem to have music enough. Or is it only my barbarian ear?

Enough of my twaddle. But I cannot express enough the delight with
which I've read your verses. Forgive me my audacities dear Ted for the
sake of my affection.

Apart from your brotherly appreciation of my preface[1] (for which
thanks with all my heart) your letter seems big with hidden meaning. I
am glad you say things go on *well*.

My congratulations upon Your happy escape from St Mary's.[2] The
place where one lives has much to do with one's happiness. Especially
when one is married.

I've been thinking more than twice of Miss Gery.[3] I had some plunges
in my life too—and shudder at the memory yet. The thing is—will she
lose herself in her work before the change becomes insupportable. I trust
her health, to commence with, is unquestionably right. That's a great
thing too.

Keep me informed dear old chap. With love ever yours Jph Conrad.

A word more about the preface. You understand that, however deeply

---

[1] Preface to *The Nigger*.
[2] Home of the Sanderson family.
[3] One of Sanderson's sisters.

felt, the feeling expressed is not fundamental. One has thoughts that are not for the public. And in so far the preface is superficial. I wanted to say this to You.

To E. L. Sanderson
Text MS Yale; Unpublished

17/10/97.
[Stanford-le-Hope]

Dearest Ted

I had Your letter this morning. All day to-day I've been correcting the last proofs of the Nigger because the printers must have it to-morrow and the sheets have been delayed on their way to me. Now that's off my mind—but You "hardly ever" (classical quotation, is it not?) are out of my mind; so I write to you this evening, for, to-morrow, I must begin the II^{d} part of *The Rescue*, and for a few days letter writing (at least to any purpose) shall be out of [the] question.

So You've been laying a trap for me! I don't know what surprises me most—the fact or the cool impudence of your confession. But, joking apart, my dear Ted you might have obtained a wrong impression of my sincerity. I do not conceal my likes or dislikes which are a matter of feeling. But in criticism I am conscious of my incompetence. Now criticism, unless informed by hardly, honestly acquired knowledge, is either an exhibition of folly or a pure impertinence. I cannot pretend to judge of versification. I do not understand the technique of the craft, I have no knowledge of its rules. I appreciate your stanzas emotionally but not critically. I love the poem; but it is only my perfect confidence in You that could induce me to express any *artistic* opinion upon this or that line. At the very best my opinion can have only the value of a disclosed impression. Impression—and nothing more. Now my impression may be false because my temperament may be rebellious to the vibration of the particular note struck through some dullness, or coarseness, through an inherent inability to respond, of which I, myself, am necessarily unaware. You, knowing me, may forgive a shortcoming of that kind. But for a silly criticism, silly because ignorant, there is no excuse. This conviction makes me cautious not because I would be thought wise through the prestige of silence, but because I care for my dignity, or even because I care for truth—as far as I know it.

Now, I am impressionist from instinct, and speaking purely as such I come back to the line under discussion.

The ocean's hoarse reverberating roar.
This is *much* better—but, strictly from an impressionist point of view, I think some other epithet than *hoarse* would make the line stronger. Something that would convey the notion of the persistent tumultuous voice of the sea.

———————————

Yes "battle with" is just what's wanted.
Last line:————————
—"To glad one heart and soothe. "etc" *feels* to me better than "charm … cheer."
but still I ask once more is it my barbarian ear? I always mistrust my ear; I am never sure even in my own miserable prose.

My wife is delighted to think you are pleased with the type copy. She is naïve. And her appreciation of your verses is also naïve—by no means enlightened. Yet to me it—such as it is—causes me great pleasure. Affectionately

Ever Yours Jph Conrad

To S. S. Pawling
Text MS Berg; Unpublished

21ˢᵗ Oct. 97
[Stanford-le-Hope]

My dear Pawling
Thanks for the *Autumn Announcements.*[1]
I notice both there and in the Sat[urday] Review the title is written: The Nigger of *"the Narcissus."* The ship's name has no *the* in it. Only the word "Narcissus" should be in quotation marks.
I mention this in view of the title-page; and, by-the-bye, would you instruct the printers to send me proofs of *title-page and dedication*?
No matter how You may "cuss" me for worrying You I am Ever

Yours
Jph.Conrad.

---

[1] Presumably Heinemann's autumn publication list, containing Conrad's *Nigger*; Sydney Pawling was a partner in the firm.

To E. L. Sanderson

Text   MS Yale; Unpublished

9 am. [October? 1897][1]
[Stanford-le-Hope]

Dearest Ted

My wife is delighted that you let her type the copy destined for Miss Watson.

The verses shall be sent out from here either to-night or to-morrow morning (I shall inquire at the P.O.) so that they arrive at their destination on Sat: morning[2]—not before and not after.

I had the last stanza typed just now. On *view* and on reading aloud I shall take the liberty to restore the reading

cheer . . charm.

because it is the best.[3] Moreover it is the original reading. The line *as amended* has less cadence and sounds xviii[th] Century-fied. And not the best xviii[th] Century either.

(You may throw a book at my head when You see me.) Some day in a moment of peace and inspiration the *perfectly right* line will come to You. All the rest excellent. I am sorry You're under high pressure again. Try to keep well. I love the little poem.

Ever Yours   Jph Conrad.

To Edward Garnett

Text   G. 115

Tuesday [26 October 1897][4]
[Stanford-le-Hope]

My dear Garnett.

I shall be near Queen Anne's statue before St Paul's[5] at 1 o'clock on Thursday. Do come and lunch with me. I have an amusing and instructive tale to tell—a report to make—and certain documents to show.

---

[1] The letter definitely falls into October 1897 because of its connection with the letters to Sanderson 14 and 17 October. It would appear to fall closer to the middle of the month than the end, but no precise date is possible.

[2] This could mean 16 or 23 October.

[3] A point from the 14 October letter.

[4] Although this letter does fit into a general sequence pertaining to Conrad's hesitant start on part II of *The Rescue*, without Garnett's precise placement of this particular Tuesday we could slide the date forward to 19 October.

[5] And near Fisher Unwin's office.

Chap[man] and Hall (O. Crawford) rejected the Return which I fully expected. Only he need not have been three weeks about it. However I feel cheerful and have at last made a start with the *Rescue*.

Joseph Conrad

Let me know by a word that you've received this.

To William Blackwood

Text   MS NLS; Blackburn 14

29/10/97.
Stanford-le-Hope
Essex.

Dear Sir.

Thanks for the copy of the Nov: number. I need not enlarge upon the pleasure of seeing my story in such a good place.

I turned to *Tennyson* with eagerness.[1] Apart from the interest of details as to Maga's attitude to the rising poet[2] there is value there in things said by the way. With these I am in perfect accord. Here and there I would take exception to a phrase—to the phrase rather than to the thought. Not every man who "waved a cap of liberty on a pike" was a scoundrel. And England had not only given refuge to criminals.[3] There was a greatness in that mistaken hospitality which is the inheritance of all parties. Of course I do not defend political crime. It is repulsive to me by tradition, by sentiment, and even by reflexion.[4] But some of their men had struggled for an idea, openly, in the light of day, and sacrificed to it all that to most men makes life worth living. Moreover a sweeping assertion is always wrong, since men are infinitely varied; and harsh words are useless because they cannot combat ideas. And the ideas (that live) should be combatted, not the men who die.

---

[1] Hallam, Tennyson's son, had just published *Alfred Lord Tennyson: a Memoir* (Macmillan, 2 vols). The review in *Blackwood's* is in Vol. 162, pp. 615–29.

[2] Rudyard Kipling, hailed (with reservations) as a possible successor to Tennyson.

[3] As Conrad well knew. The reviewer had claimed that 'we take a diminished pride in affording an asylum to bloodthirsty ruffians' (p. 621) and had denounced the Liberal Spanish insurgents whom Tennyson and Hallam had aided in 1829–30 as 'dirty rascals' who had 'only to wave a cap of liberty upon a pike to enlist enthusiasm of hundreds of educated young gentlemen' (ibid.). 'Maga' was a notoriously conservative publication.

[4] There speaks the future author of *The Secret Agent* and *Under Western Eyes*. Nevertheless, given his Russian experience, Conrad cannot have appreciated the anonymous reviewer's assertion that 'Continental nations are pretty tolerable judges of their own affairs' (p. 621).

In this combat "Maga" is to the front. In this time of fluid principles the soul of "Maga" changeth not. It informs every page and knows no compromise. It is something. It is, indeed, everything.

Believe me very sincerely Yours

Jph Conrad.

Wm. Blackwood Esqre

To William Blackwood

Text   MS NLS; Blackburn 15

30/10/97.

Stanford-le-Hope.

Dear Mr Blackwood.

Just a word to acknowledge your good letter. I am very glad You are quite recovered now.

I wrote You two days ago. I hope You will forgive any impertinence that may have crept into my letter. I am sure You will.

What You say is important to me and requires consideration. I need not tell You I fully appreciate every kind word You say. Will you allow me some little time to think and see? I am not bound to anyone—strictly speaking, but I think myself under moral obligation to Mr Heinemann.

Mr Unwin has not favoured me with a scratch of the pen (or a single click of the typewriter) for the last 3 months. I knew nothing about the cheque.[1] If I did not acknowledge sooner your prompt payment it was purely for want of information not of "manners".

Believe me, always very sincerely

Yours

Jph Conrad.

P.S. I shall be most happy to make Mr Meldrum's acquaintance.[2] I think of going to town the day after tomorrow, and will call on him—without prejudice of having the pleasure to see him here.

---

[1] Blackwood's cheque to Unwin, intended for Conrad.

[2] They met on 2 November, in the Daniel Lambert Tavern, Ludgate Hill. David S. Meldrum worked in Blackwood's London office as literary adviser. In the margin of this letter, against the paragraph about Unwin, Blackwood noted: 'This is rather good & just as Meldrum expected.'

To T. Fisher Unwin
Text MS Rosenbach; Unpublished

31/10/97.
[Stanford-le-Hope]

Dear Sir.

I've had this morning a letter from Mr Blackwood. In consequence of what he says I think I ought to see you. I shall call at 11.30 to-morrow (Monday). Should you be engaged at that time perhaps you will kindly leave a word in the office what hour would be convenient for a five minute's interview.

I am, dear Sir

very faithfully Yours
Jph Conrad.

To Olivia Garnett
Text MS Colgate; Unpublished[1]

[4 November 1897]
[Stanford-le-Hope]

Madam.

Your son and my friend, whose sympathy criticism and counsel have encouraged and guided me ever since I took pen in hand, has told me that You like this tale. I wish I could have expressed my sense of Your commendation by offering You an unique vellum copy. But since that is impossible—then the other extreme would be better than the middle course. I venture therefore to beg Your acceptance of this plain paper copy of the copyright impression[2]—which, simple as it is, cannot, at any rate, be obtained for money.

I am, Madam,

Your most obedient humble servant
The Author.

4th Nov. 1897

---

[1] Inscription in presentation copy of *The Nigger*.
[2] Only eight were printed.

To Edward Garnett

Text   MS Colgate; G. 115

[4 November 1897][1]
[Stanford-le-Hope]

Dear Garnett

Meldrum thinks B means to take R. without reserve.[2] Also thinks that 250 for serial and 50 for book and 15% 20% are terms B will give. Is going to write informally to find out—like from himself—and let me know early next week.

Thanks for your advice.

Ever Yours

Conrad

To T. Fisher Unwin

Text   MS Yale; Unpublished

5/11/97.
Stanford le Hope
Essex

Dear Mr. Unwin.

I beg to acknowledge receipt of two bills of £25 each at 3[%] at 6 months.

Thanks very much.

I must ask you to give me a few days to correct finally the 4 short stories that have appeared.[3] I shall send You the copies of the Magazines where they appeared.

As to the 5th story *The Return* which has not appeared yet anywhere. I shall send the MS to You as soon as I myself can get hold of the infernal thing. It's knocking about somewhere. I've asked peremptorily for its return. And you shall have it as soon as possible.

The agreement, signed, shall be posted at noon to-morrow. I haven't anybody here to witness my signature, till the evening.

I send you a correct list of stories with the number of words.[4]

Would you like to have for the vol *The Return* as an entirely new story

---

[1] Although the manuscript bears no date, Garnett assigns the letter to 4 November without the square brackets that indicate his own dating. There is no reason to question 4 November, since Conrad met Meldrum in London on 2 November and apparently discussed the information he is sending on to Garnett.

[2] Blackwood had by no means decided to take *The Rescue* without securing the book rights from Heinemann.

[3] For a volume of short stories.

[4] See letter for 8 November.

not published anywhere before?[1] At any rate in this country. I think it much too good for any blamed magazine. If I send it to You at once perhaps You could place it *serially* in some *advanced* Am. Mag: Fossils won't care for it. Anyway if You think that it may be an advantage to the vol: I may drop my search for serial rights here. *Pearson's* have been asking me for some time to give them something.[2] I think it much too good to be thrown away where the *right people* won't see it. Of course I am willing to lose what I may obtain from some periodical; and if You have nothing to propose I feel inclined to try here and there for Another month or so. But in any case You shall have the text as soon as possible.

The above is only a suggestion which I do not in any way push upon Your notice. With kind regards.

> Very faithfully Yours,
>
> Jph. Conrad.

To Edward Garnett

Text   MS Free; G. 116

> 5/11/97.
> [Stanford-le-Hope]

Dearest G.

I had this morning a letter from Pawling so utterly satisfactory to me that there can be no question of even thinking about anyone else as long as he wants me.[3] I am very glad to think that last night the spirit moved me to drop him a postcard where I told him—"I was sorry I worried him about those matters on top of his other worries. That I would write for him rather than for anybody else. That I believed in him implicitly and wished nothing more than to stick to him as long as he would have me." While I wrote the postcard he wrote the letter. And so the truth came out on both sides. He is a good fellow. I trust he will see I am not a hopelessly bad lot. He promises to give £*100* for the next book. To obtain £400 for serial rights. And he writes very nicely. I had rather have his promise than another man's cash down. I shall show—or send you his letter so that you can see how much *you've* done for me.—I have also a paper copy of the *Nigger*. I shall correct it this evening. Do you think it would be breach of etiquette if I send it direct to the Museum.[4] Hadn't I better

---

[1] 'The Return' remained unpublished until *Tales of Unrest* appeared.
[2] *Pearson's Magazine.*
[3] Heinemann promised to publish *The Rescue*; see letter of this date to Meldrum.
[4] For Edward Garnett's mother: she and her husband lived in a Keeper's house at the British Museum.

send it t[h]rough you? I am immensely relieved. I hope I've done with the *selling* business for life.

Ever yours

Jph. Conrad.

The Patron Jew[1] sent bills—agreements etc. etc. I'm done with him.

To David Meldrum

Text   MS Duke; Blackburn 16

5/11/97.

Stanford-le-Hope

Essex.

Dear Mr Meldrum.

I am sorry to have perhaps given You unnecessary trouble yesterday. This morning I had a letter from my friend Pawling which makes it out of question for the book to go anywhere else than to Mr Heinemann. This I have foreseen all along and made—as you remember—no secret of it. I have no doubt Mr Blackwood will understand that it is feeling—not greed—that guides me in that matter. If I was to throw Pawling over the greater success the book would be the greater would be my remorse.

Under those circumstances I can only say that I regret extremely and sincerely that the *Rescue* won't appear in the Maga—since it[s] appearance as a serial there was conditional on the book going to Mr Blackwood.

May I ask you for the return of part Ist which I want to look over. Or shall I write to Mr Blackwood for it? But I hope that the matter ending thus won't prevent friendly relations with Mr Blackwood and with Yourself.

I am, dear Sir, very truly yours

Jph. Conrad

P.S You will let me know in a friendly way what You think of *The Return*. I am very anxious to know your *frank* opinion. And may I, now and then, turn up for a talk?

---

[1] T. Fisher Unwin, whose ancestors were East Anglian congregationalists and Scottish presbyterians.

To Edward Garnett

Text G. 117

[6 November 1897][1]
[Stanford-le-Hope]

Dearest G.

I send you P[awling]'s letter.[2] I replied to it that as long as they stick to me like this I shall stick to them. I trust the selling business is over for life.

I send you a copy of the *N[igger]* for your mother. Present it from me—if you think it isn't too cheeky of me. I've written a few lines there.[3]

Now I can shut my door and work.

Thanks are due to you for introducing me to that good fellow P. I hope he will never regret taking me up.[4]

Remember me kindly to your wife.

Ever yours

Joseph Conrad

Jess sends her love.

To T. Fisher Unwin

Text MS Yale; Unpublished

Monday [8 November 1897][5]
[Stanford-le-Hope]

Dear Mr. Unwin.

I send you 4 stories = 43.000 words ready for press.

Due one more story *The Return* = 22.000 words. The Sat[urday] Review says that the most notable contribution to the current n° of B'wood is my story. It should be the first in the vol.[6]

With kind regards

Sincerely Yours

Jph Conrad.

---

[1] There is no reason to question Garnett's dating.
[2] About Heinemann's publishing *The Rescue*.
[3] Note to Mrs Garnett, 4 November.
[4] Heinemann published Conrad's *Typhoon and Other Stories* in 1903, and brought out the first collected edition in England.
[5] The first Monday after 5 November (see n. 3).
[6] 'Karain', which did appear first.

About the tittle* of the Volume I can say nothing certain. Must think of it. Would You suggest something?

The stories are.

(*Blackwood*).	Karain: A memory.	*18.000*
(Savoy)	The Idiots.	10.000
(Cosmo)	An Outpost of Progress.	9.500
Unpub^d	The Return	23.000
(Cornhill)	The Lagoon	5.300
		about 65.800

This is the order in which, I suggest, they should be placed in the book.[1]

To William Blackwood

Text   MS NLS; Blackburn 18

9th/11/97.
Stanford-le-Hope.
Essex.

Dear Mr Blackwood.

Just a year ago, when I wanted badly to be taken up the Firm of M^r Wm. Heinemann accepted an unfinished work of mine, met all my wishes, and, as things went on, did really much more than I had any reason to expect. I had no introduction to them; I could not boast of even a tolerable sale; my literary achievement amounted in all to two books—praised certainly, but as certainly not successful, in a commercial sense. Under these circumstances they took me up and introduced my work to Mr Henley;[2] and it was its good fortune to please that remarkable man. In that way I secured admission to the pages of the New Review.

Since that time I've been approached from various quarters—with definite and acceptable offers. Under the sense of moral obligation I've refused them all without ever referring to Mr Heinemann. When, however, you did me the honour to ask for my work (I write this phrase as I feel it) I felt justified in departing for once from the conduct my

---

[1] Although in the letter to Unwin, 5 November, Conrad implies that the list of stories is enclosed, the actual list (on a separate sheet) is on the same unusual paper as the letter of 8 November, and is therefore printed with it.

[2] Pawling showed the unfinished manuscript of *The Nigger* to Henley, whose *New Review* Heinemann owned.

obligation dictated. I went to Mr Heinemann. I did not know your terms and I did not ask them for theirs. I simply asked them whether they meant to stick to me. If so I meant to stick to them. But should they have any doubts as to the advisability of—so to speak—keeping me on, there was a flattering and unique opportunity which I could not find it in my heart to sacrifice to my sense of what was due to them. They emphatically declared that their intention is to work for my success here and in America and that their wish is to have the publication of all my books. After the proofs of his goodwill I am bound to take my friend's Pawling (of the firm Wm Heinemann) word. Consequently I am resolved to stick to them with the hope that they will never regret their (and mine) decision.

From first to last, dear Mr Blackwood, this has been no question of money. From You I was sure not only of justice but of generosity. The tradition of Your House made any doubt impossible. On the other hand they had given practical proof that they could be generous. It was simply a question of fidelity—if I may so express it.[1]

This decision is quite compatible with the feeling of a very sincere regret that it will not be my good fortune to appear serially in the pages of Maga. I trust You will continue to me the kind feelings you have been pleased to express. Believe me, dear Mr Blackwood, very faithfully yours

Jph Conrad.

P.S. Till you expressly decline I consider myself authorized to send you any short story or sketch I may write. I have in my mind a study of a Scotch seaman—a humble individual, but whose memory is cherished not only by myself but by many others well on and successful on the road to life.[2]

To Stephen Crane
Text MS Columbia; Stallman 151

16th Nov. 1897.
Stanford-le-Hope
Essex.

My dear Crane.

I must write to you before I write a single word for a living to-day. I was anxious to know what you would think of the end. If I've hit *you* with

[1] 'Fidelity' is an inescapable word in Conrad's writing: see, for instance, the Preface to *The Nigger* (written in August 1897).
[2] Probably MacWhirr of 'Typhoon', or some earlier version of the man and the story.

the death of Jimmy[1] I don't care if I don't hit another man. I think however artistically the end of the book is somewhat lame. I mean after the death. All that rigmarolle* about the burial and the ships coming home seems to run away into a rat's tail—thin at the end. Well! It's too late now to bite my thumb and tear my hair. When I feel depressed about it I say to myself "Crane likes the damned thing"—and am greatly consoled. What your appreciation is to me I renounce to explain. The world looks different to me now, since our long pow-wow.[2] It was good. The memory of it is good. And now and then (human nature *is* a vile thing) I ask myself whether you meant half of what you said! You must forgive me. The mistrust is not of you—it is of myself: the drop of poison in the cup of life. I am not more vile than my neighbours but this disbelief in oneself is like a taint that spreads on everything one comes in contact with; on men on things—on the very air one breathes. That's why one sometimes wishes to be a stone breaker. There's no doubt about breaking a stone. But there's doubt, fear—a black horror, in every page one writes. You at any rate will understand and therefore I write to you as though we had been born together before the beginning of things.[3] For what you have done and intend to do I won't even attempt to thank you. I certainly don't know what to say, tho' I am perfectly certain as to what I feel.

I know it is perfectly right and proper from a ceremonial point of view that I should come to you first. But, my dear fellow, it's impossible. My wife is not presentable just now. And, joking apart, I wouldn't dare let her undertake a journey—even of the shortest.[4] As to myself I would come speedily and I shall come as soon as I can get away with a free mind. Meantime show your condescension by coming to me first. After this week I haven't any engagements. Just drop a postcard saying *I'm coming* and I shall meet the train from Fenchurch Street You have trains at *11.20* am. *1.45* pm. *3.28* pm. *5.5* pm. *5.53* pm *8.13* pm.

[1] James Wait. Crane had written to Conrad on 11 November that *The Nigger* 'is simply great. The simple treatment of the death of Waite [*sic*] is too good, too terrible. I wanted to forget it at once. It caught me very hard ...' (*Two Letters from Stephen Crane to Joseph Conrad*, London, First Edition Club, 1926).

[2] In October, Pawling invited Crane and Conrad to lunch. After the meal, the two authors talked for many hours as they wandered through London, oblivious of their surroundings. Subsequently, Conrad sent Crane an inscribed *Almayer* and proof-sheets of *The Nigger*.

[3] Although Crane was fourteen years younger than Conrad, their personal and professional intimacy was immediate and warm. It lasted until Crane's death in 1900, at the age of twenty-eight.

[4] Crane had invited the Conrads to Ravensbrook, his house near Limpsfield, Surrey, for a Sunday luncheon. Jessie, however, was seven months pregnant.

Last train to town at night is at *8* arrives in London at 9.30. But we can put you up in a bachelor's quarters. I should love to have you under my roof. And come soon for when the circus begins here and then the house is full of doctors and nurses there will be no peace for the poor literary man. Finish to catch the post.

Ever Yours

Jph Conrad.

To William Blackwood

Text   MS NLS; Blackburn 20

24 Nov. 97.
Stanford-le-Hope
Essex.

Dear Mr Blackwood.

I try to catch the return post.[1] Thanks for thinking of me for the Jany number, but I fear it would be impossible for me to come up to time. I am wrestling with the *Rescue* and dare think of nothing else. Yet there are days when I am incapable of writing a line. I had too many such days lately. When anything short gets itself written I shall send it to You at once.

I am sorry You have that bother with your men.[2] There is something inspiring in the idea of the heads of Blackwood doing their own printing. Another episode for the future vols of the firm's history! I've read the two vols.[3] It's *most* interesting and well done too.

Once more thanks. Believe me, dear Mr Blackwood, always most sincerely Yours.

Jph. Conrad

---

[1] Blackwood had asked Conrad for a contribution to the January issue, possibly 'the sketch of the old Scottish Seaman you suggested writing', to be ready by 10 December. (See Blackburn, p. 20.)

[2] During a printers' strike, William Blackwood's nephew, George, ran the presses himself.

[3] *Annals of a Publishing House: William Blackwood and his Sons* by Margaret Oliphant, 1897, 2 vols.

To T. Fisher Unwin
Text MS Duke; Unpublished

1897. 24th Nov.
Stanford-le-Hope

Dear Mr Unwin

Here's the last story of the volume, *The Return* 22.000 words. I had it a few days but concluded You had better have it at once since You desire to have it set up in time. I am not willing to lose what a serial publication would bring but I see that for many reasons the story is not easy to place. As I mentioned in my last letter perhaps some advanced mag^z in the States would print it. The book rights there being yours I thought that if You could secure serial pub^{on} we could come to some understanding as to our respective share in the proceeds. As to this country of course I would like to appear serially. Blackwood is out of the question, and so—but for other reasons—is Pearson. The length of the story is against it. Are You inclined to try what you can do with it? If not perhaps you will kindly send me a set of proofs and I may try my hand at it, tho' I really don't know where to turn. I don't suppose You shall wish to publish before April.[1] This would give me three months to dispose of the story.[2]

I've no title as yet for the *vol.* I was thinking of: *Tales of Unrest* (?) It's a title that embraces all the stories and most of life. However it is only a suggestion. As to the order of the stories in the book I trust You will follow my suggestion, as I have given some thought to the matter. Of course I would advise such order only in case of the vol having a distinct title. If one of the stories is to give the title to the whole then: *An Outpost of Progress* must be first I think. But we shall have many opportunities to talk the matter over.

I trust You are well. With kind regards

Sincerely Yours

Jph. Conrad

---

[1] Unwin published the volume on 4 April 1898.
[2] Conrad could not.

To Edward Garnett

Text MS Morgan; G. 118

26th Nov. [1897][1]

My dear Garnett.

Thanks for letter and books. When I see Crane I shall shake him till he drops the two stories. Cunninghame Graham writes to ask me to dine with him to-night. I shall do so for I am interested in the man and besides it may do me good to be friendly with him. The chiel writes to the papers[2]—you know. I am doing nothing and suspect myself of going crazy. Well, one shall see. Humphry James *is* good.[3] Is he very deep or very simple? And by the bye R. Bridges *is* a poet. I'm damned if he ain't! There's more poesy in one page of "Shorter Poems" than in the whole volume of Tennyson.[4] This is my deliberate opinion. And what a descriptive power! The man hath wings—sees from on high. It is the real thing—a direct appeal to mankind, not to a certain kind of man. It is natural beauty—not would-be beautiful notions. I love him.

Ever yours

J. C.

To T. Fisher Unwin

Text MS Indiana; Unpublished

26th Nov. 97.
[Stanford-le-Hope]

Dear Mr Unwin.

I've offered the story[5] only to O. Crawford for the *Chap[man]^s Mag.* I do *not* wish the story to be offered to Pearson[6] or B'wood.[7] With these exceptions I am perfectly willing to leave success in your hands. As to price: I should like it to be no less than 50/- per *1000* or even say £50 which is less than that rate. Crawford did not think that price too high. He

---

[1] The reference to Crane and Graham establishes the year as 1897.

[2] Graham did indeed, frequently. Conrad had probably noticed his letters in the *Saturday Review*. Chiel: Scots for 'fellow'.

[3] Garnett specifies Humphrey James's *Paddy's Woman* (Unwin, 1897).

[4] Garnett notes that he had sent Conrad *The Shorter Poems of Robert Bridges* (Bell, 1890). Bridges (1844–1930) was to become Poet Laureate in 1913.

[5] 'The Return'.

[6] Of *Pearson's Magazine*, which began publication in 1896.

[7] In this and his previous letter to Unwin (24 November), Conrad's insistence on this point must have been based on Blackwood's rejection of the story for 'Maga'. In his 5 November letter, Conrad had asked Meldrum to let him know 'in a friendly way' what he thought of 'The Return'.

declined on other grounds. This is only my feeling. I shall accept what you can get—and the more the better. Very faithfully Yours

Jph Conrad.

May I have all the proofs when ready?

To Henry James
Text   MS Harvard; *L.fr.* 34

[30 November 1897]
[Stanford-le-Hope]

Cher Maître.[1]

Vous m'avez permis de Vous envoyer mon livre.[2] Le voilà. Il a la qualité d'être court. Il a été vécu. Il est, sans doute, mauvais. Rien de si facile comme de raconter un rêve, mais il est impossible de penetrer l'âme des ceux qui écoutent par la force de son amertume et de sa douceur. On ne communique pas la réalité poignante des illusions! Le rêve finit, les mots s'envolent, le livre est oublié. C'est la grâce miséricordieuse du destin. Mais, Cher Maître, vous m'avez permis de vous envoyer ce livre—et le voici!

Croyez-moi toujours, avec une affection fidèle, Votre très humble admirateur

Jph. Conrad.

30 Nov. 1897

[30 November 1897]
[Stanford-le-Hope]

Dear Master

You gave me permission to send you my book. Here it is. It has the virtue of being brief. It has been lived. It is probably bad. Nothing so easy as recounting a dream, but it is impossible to penetrate the soul of those who listen with its bitterness and its sweetness. One does not communicate the poignant reality of illusions! The dream ends, the

---

[1] Writing in French enabled Conrad to present himself in his most courtly manner; he may also have wanted to imply that he shared with James a reverence for the language of Maupassant and Flaubert.

[2] *The Nigger of the 'Narcissus'.*

words vanish, the book is forgotten. It is the merciful grace of Destiny. But, Dear Master, you gave me permission to send you this book— and here it is.

Believe me always, with a loyal affection, your very humble admirer

Jph. Conrad

To Stephen Crane
Text MS Columbia; Stallman 154

1ᵗ Dec. 1897
Stanford-le-Hope

My dear Crane.

Glad to hear you haven't had your head taken off. We had here on Monday a high tide that smashed the sea-wall flooded the marshes and washed away the Rwy line.[1] Great excitement.

But *my* great excitement was reading your stories. Garnett's right. "A Man and some others" is immense.[2] I can't spin a long yarn about it but I admire it without reserve. It is an amazing bit of biography. I am envious of you—horribly. Confound you—you fill the blamed landscape—you—by all the devils—fill the sea-scape. The boat thing is immensely interesting.[3] I don't use the word in its common sense. It is fundamentally interesting to me. Your temperament makes old things new and new things amazing. I want to swear at you, to bless you—perhaps to shoot you—but I prefer to be your friend.

You are an everlasting surprise to one. You shock—and the next moment you give the perfect artistic satisfaction. Your method is fascinating. You are a complete impressionist. The illusions of life come out of your hand without a flaw. It is not life—which nobody wants—it is art—art for which everyone—the abject and the great hanker—mostly without knowing it.

Ever Yours

Jph Conrad.

---

[1] Stanford-le-Hope is very close to the Thames estuary. Monday was 29 November.
[2] In the *Century* (February 1897).
[3] 'The Open Boat', in *Scribner's Magazine* (June 1897).

To Edward Garnett
Text   J-A, I, 211[1]; G. 118

5th Dec. 1897
[Stanford-le-Hope]

My dear Garnett.

The *Nigger* came out to date[2] I believe but is not advertised in the *Sat. Review*. As soon as I get my copies I shall forward a specimen to the Cearne.[3]

I had Crane here last Sunday.[4] We talked and smoked half the night. He is strangely hopeless about himself. I like him. The two stories are excellent. Of course *A Man and Some Others* is the best of the two but the boat thing interested me more.[5] His eye is very individual and his expression satisfies me artistically. He certainly is *the* impressionist and his temperament is curiously unique. His thought is concise, connected, never very deep—yet often startling. He is *the only* impressionist and *only* an impressionist.[6] Why is he not immensely popular? With his strength, with his rapidity of action, with that amazing faculty of vision —why is he not? He has outline, he has colour, he has movement, with that he ought to go very far. But—will he? I sometimes think he won't. It is not an opinion—it is a feeling. I could not explain why he disappoints me—why my enthusiasm withers as soon as I close the book. While one reads, of course, he is not to be questioned. He is the master of his reader to the very last line—then—apparently for no reason at all—he seems to let go his hold. It is as if he had gripped you with greased fingers. His grip is strong but while you feel the pressure on your flesh you slip out from his hand—much to your own surprise. That is my stupid impression and I give it to you in confidence. It just occurs to me that it is perhaps my own self that is slippery. I don't know. *You* would know. No matter.

My soul is like a stone within me. I am going through the awful experience of losing a friend.[7] Hope[8] comes every evening to console me

---

[1]   Text from Garnett.

[2]   Jean-Aubry reads 'to-day', which makes better sense, but Garnett is usually more reliable.

[3]   Garnett's house.   [4]   28 November.

[5]   'The Open Boat'.

[6]   'Impressionism' was a much-debated term in the nineties, as writers of poetry, fiction and criticism attempted to find a verbal counterpart to Impressionist painting.

[7]   Probably Adolf Krieger, whom Conrad had known since 1880/1. Krieger had helped Conrad obtain a position at Barr, Moering and then worked to find Conrad a post in the Congo. The rift between the two was most likely over money owed by Conrad. Conrad dedicated *Tales of Unrest* to him.

[8]   Conrad's friend and neighbour, G. F. W. Hope.

but he has a hopeless task. Death is nothing—and I am used to its rapacity. But when life robs one of a man to whom one has pinned one's faith for twenty years the wrong seems too monstrous to be lived down. Yet it must. And I don't know why, how, wherefore. Besides there are circumstances which make the event a manifold torment. Some day I will tell you the tale. I can't write it now. But there is a psychological point in it. However this also does not matter.

The *Nigger* is ended and the *N.R.* stops[1] I suppose you've heard already. Henley printed the preface at the end as an Author's note. It does not shine very much, but I am glad to see it in type. This is all the news. No criticisms appeared as yet. I am trying to write the *Rescue* and all my ambition is to make it good enough for a magazine—readable in a word. I doubt whether I can. I struggle without pleasure like a man certain of defeat.

Drop me a line.

Ever yours

Jph. Conrad.

To R. B. Cunninghame Graham
Text MS Dartmouth; J–A, I, 212; Watts 49

6th Dec 1897
Stanford-le-Hope
Essex

My dear Sir

I am horribly ashamed of myself. I ought to have written last week to thank you for the Stevenson.[2] My inadequate excuse is I've been strangely seedy—nothing very tangible, but for nearly a week I have thought not at all and eaten very little—and didn't see the use of doing anything. This may seem to you an impertinent excuse but I assure you it is a very sad and fiendish—well, indisposition, and too real for words. I throw myself on your mercy. I shook myself at the sight of your letter and now what between shame and pleasure I am able to sit there like a galvanised corpse[3] to write this flat and miserable apology.

The 'xmas at sea' is *all* what you said. I was glad of the book and Still more of your thought. I was glad to know I haven't been seen—and

---

[1] The *New Review* ceased publication early in 1898.

[2] Robert Louis Stevenson's *Ballads* (1895), with the poem 'Christmas at Sea' to which Conrad refers later.

[3] Watts (p. 51) points out that this unusual phrase is used by Conrad in *Under Western Eyes* to describe Madame de S—— (p. 222).

forgotten. Only—parce-que c'est Vous![1] There are people from whom I would beg on my knees the favour of an eternal oblivion. Would I get it? Croyez-Vous qu'on se retrouve—la bàs?[2] To me 'la bàs' appears sometimes as a big hole—a kind of malefactors' cavern—very crowded (think how long mankind has been in the habit of dying!) with perspiring Shades—a moral perspiration of squeezed spirits—exhaling the unspeakable meanness, the baseness, the lies the rapacity, the cowardice of souls that on earth have been objects of barter and valued themselves at about two-and-six. But this is morbid—and I sat down intending to produce a good impression! I take it all back and declare my belief in lilies, gold harps—and brimstone, like my Podmore in the "Narcissus".[3]

And à-propos of Podmore—I am afraid the 'Nigger' will bore you. C'est vécu—et c'est bête.[4] There are twenty years of life, six months of scribbling in that book—and not a shadow of a story. As the critic in to-day's Dly Mail puts it tersely: "the tale is no tale at all". The man complains of lack of heroism! and is, I fancy, shocked at the bad language.[5] I confess reluctantly there is a swear here and there. I grovel in the waste-paper basket, I beat my breast. May I hope you at least! won't withdraw your esteem from a repentant sinner?

No man can escape his fate! You shall come here and suffer hardships, boredom and despair. It is written! It is written! You—as a matter of fact—have written it yourself (at my instigation—very rash of you) and I shall be inexorable like destiny and shall look upon your sufferings with the idiotic serenity of a benevolent Creator (I don't know that the ben: Crea: is serene;—but if he is (as they say) then he *must* be idiotic.) looking at the precious mess he has made of his only job. This letter reminds me of something I used to know years ago: Algebra—I think. Brackets within brackets and imbecility raised to the nth power.

I heard of the H & S play through G.B.S. in the SR. More Algebra. Do you understand? I allude in this luminous way to Admiral Guinea.[6] I

---

[1] 'Because it's you!'

[2] 'Do you think people meet again – down there?' Conrad, of course, has Hell in mind.

[3] The ship's cook.

[4] 'It comes from experience – and it's stupid.'

[5] The *Daily Mail* reviewer goes on: 'There is no plot, no villainy, no heroism, and, apart from a storm and the death and burial, no incident. The only female in the book is the ship herself, which Mr. Conrad describes lovingly and with an intimate knowledge of seamanship unrivalled even by Dana or Clark Russell' (7 December 1897). Dana wrote *Two Years Before the Mast*; Russell was a popular maritime novelist.

[6] *Admiral Guinea* by William Ernest Henley and Robert Louis Stevenson. The play opened on 29 November 1897, and was reviewed by George Bernard Shaw in the *Saturday Review* (4 December 1897).

haven't seen a play for years; but I have read this one. And that's all I can say about it. I have no notion of a play. No play grips me on the stage or off. Each of them seems to me an amazing freak of folly. They are all unbelievable and as disillusioning as a bang on the head. I greatly desire to write a play myself. It is my dark and secret ambition.[1] And yet I can't conceive how a sane man can sit down deliberately to write a play and not go mad before he has done. The actors appear to me like a lot of *wrongheaded* lunatics pretending to be sane. Their malice is stitched with white threads. They are disguised and ugly. To look at them breeds in my melancholy soul thoughts of murder and suicide—such is my anger and my loathing of their transparent pretences. There is a taint of subtle corruption in their blank voices, in their blinking eyes, in the grimacing faces, in the false light in the false passion, in the words that have been learned by heart. But I love a marionette show. Marionettes are beautiful—especially those of the old kind with wires, thick as my little finger, coming out of the top of the head. Their impassibility in love in crime, in mirth, in sorrow,—is heroic, superhuman, fascinating. Their rigid violence when they fall upon one another to embrace or to fight is simply a joy to behold. I never listen to the text mouthed somewhere out of sight by invisible men who are here to day and rotten to morrow. I love the marionettes that are without life, that come so near to being immortal!

Here's the end of paper. It is tomorrow already and high time for me to go to bed—to dream, perchance to sleep. You must forgive the writer, the letter, the mistakes of spelling, the obscurity of the grammar—the imbecility of the nth power. Forgive! Forgiveness has been invented to prevent massacres. Yours ever

Jph Conrad.

P.S. I haven't had yet *St Thérèse*.[2] Expect it next week. I have looked lately again at the Best scenery article[3]—and am confirmed in my opinion that your wife has said what is really fundamental, essentially true in the matter—and said it charmingly. Sorry to hear of Hudson's illness.[4] A lovable man—a most lovable man.

---

[1] Conrad's *One Day More* was performed in 1905.
[2] *Santa Teresa: Being some Account of her Life and Times* by Gabriela Cunninghame Graham (1894, 2 vols).
[3] 'The Best Scenery I Know', an article by Gabriela Cunninghame Graham, in the *Saturday Review* (4 September 1897).
[4] W. H. Hudson (1841–1922), the naturalist and novelist, best known, perhaps, for *The Purple Land* (1885) and *Green Mansions* (1904). Although Conrad almost certainly corresponded with Hudson, none of the former's letters has turned up.

To Edward Garnett

Text MS Yale; G. 120

Tuesday [7 December 1897][1]
[Stanford-le-Hope]

Dearest Garnett.

Thanks. It is admirable. I am not speaking of Turgeniev.[2] But surely to render thus the very spirit of an incomparable artist one must have more than a spark of the sacred fire. The reader does not *see* the language—the story is alive—as living as when it came from the master's hand. This is a great achievement. I have been reading with inexpressible delight—not the delight of novelty for I knew and remembered the stories before— but with the delight of revelling in that pellucid, flaming atmosphere of Turgeniev's life which the translator has preserved unstained, unchilled, with the clearness and heart of original inspiration. To me there is something touching like a great act of self-sacrifice and devotion in this perfect fidelity to a departed breath. The capacity to be so true to what is best is a great—an incomparable gift. Thanks many times for the book. I see you put the date 3ᵈ of Dec. Did you know that on that day I went over the rise of forty to travel downwards—and a little more lonely than before. Tell your wife I am deeply grateful to her for the happy moments with the book—yesterday. I am trying to write—what folly!

Ever Yours Jph Conrad.

To ?[a reviewer of the *Nigger*][3]

Text MS Rosenbach; Unpublished

9ᵗʰ Dec. 1897
Stanford-le-Hope
Essex

Dear Sir.

Allow me to thank you for the thought, the indulgence and the lesson of Your criticism of the "Nigger". Permit me also to say—to you alone—a few words of explanation.

I wrote this short book regardless of any formulas of art, forgetting all

---

[1] The presentation copy of the Turgenev volume is dated 3 December; the following Tuesday was the 7th.

[2] *The Torrents of Spring and Other Stories*, by Ivan Turgenev, translated by Constance Garnett (1897).

[3] The identity of the recipient remains unknown.

the theories of expression. Formulas and theories are dead things, and I wrote straight from the heart—which is alive. I wanted to give a true impression, to present and* undefaced image. And You, who know amongst what illusions and self-deceptions men struggle, work, fail— You will only smile with indulgence if I confess to You that I also wanted to connect the small world of the ship with that larger world carrying perplexities, fears, affections, rebellions, in a loneliness greater than that of the ship at sea.

To You, whose mind will sympathise with my feeling, I wish to disclaim all allegiance to realism, to naturalism and—before all—all leaning towards the ugly. I would not know where to look for it. There is joy and sorrow; there is sunshine and darkness—and all are within the same eternal smile of the inscrutable Maya.[1] As to the title of the story it's sheer clumsiness of mind. I could not invent anything else.

One word more. I do not think that vice triumphs. It gets the money only. Donkin is an unhappy man.[2] He is the only one of the crowd who is essentially unhappy. The others may suffer but are not unhappy. Jimmy pays with anguish for his want of courage but, till the last moment, is not unhappy. I tried to make so Donkin alone. In my desire to be faithful to the ethical truth I have sacrificed the truth of the individual: I did not bring out that intimate, invincible self-satisfaction which shields such natures from humiliation and despair. And I leave him faced by the contempt of his fellows and shaking with rage. I tried—I failed!

I trust you will forgive me the lenght* of this letter for it declares, as nothing else could, my high appreciation of Your luminous and flattering notice. I am grateful to you for the blame, for the praise, for the kindness that pervades the whole. To pick out the paragraph You have chosen for quotation is more like the inspiration of a true friend than the perspicuous choice of a benevolent critic. And I am most grateful to you for endorsing the words of the end. Twenty years of life went to the writing of these few last lines. "Tempi passati!" The old time—the old time of youth and unperplexed life!

Believe me very gratefully and faithfully Yours

Jph. Conrad

P.S. A preface intended for the Nigger which in deference to my excel-

---

[1] In Indian philosophy, both the power to generate illusion and illusion (or appearance) itself. Conrad could have met this term in Schopenhauer.

[2] When the crew is paid off, Donkin, malcontent and agitator, receives a bad discharge along with his money.

lent publisher I have withheld has been printed in the last N° of the *New Review* as an Author's note after the final instalment of the story. Is it too much to hope that [you] will find time to look at it?

To T. Fisher Unwin
Text MS Yale; Unpublished

11.12.97.
Stanford le Hope
Essex.

Dear Mr Unwin.

I am sorry I kept the *Return* so long. I send it back now corrected and also the proofs of half the *Karain* story.[1]

I trust You'll be able to place the *Return* as the loss of serial rights would be serious to me.

With kind regard very faithfully yours
Jph. Conrad

To R. B. Cunninghame Graham
Text MS Dartmouth; J–A, I, 214; Watts 52

14 Dec. 1897
Stanford-le-Hope.
Essex.

My dear Sir.

Your good letter cheered me immensely but with my usual brutal ingratitude I've let the days pass without saying so. It was a friendly thought to send me the Glasgow Herald's cutting.[2] It came in the nick of time and send* me to bed at peace with my fellow men.

I've been thinking over the letter you have written me about the *Nigger*. I am glad you like the book. Sincerely glad. It is clear gain to me. I don't know what the respectable (hats off) part of the population will think of it. Probably nothing. They never think. It isn't respectable. But I can quite see that, without thinking, they may feel an instinctive disgust. So be it. In my mind I picture the book as a stone falling in

---

[1] Conrad was correcting the proofs of *Tales of Unrest*.
[2] 'There is no novelist of the day who is more original in his methods than Mr Conrad ... We have nothing but the highest praise for this distinguished contribution to modern literature ...' (9 December 1897).

the water. It's gone and not a trace shall remain. But the words of commendation you and a few other men have said shall be treasured by me as a proof that the book has not been written in vain—as the clearest of my reward.

So You may rest assured that the time you have given to reading the tale and to writing to me has not been thrown away—since, I presume, You do not believe that doing good to a human being is throwing away effort and one's own life. And You have done me good. Whatever may be the worth of my gratitude you have it all; and such is the power of men to show feelings that "helas! Vous ne vous en apercevrez même pas!"[1]

But as I said I've been meditating over your letter. You say: "Singleton with an education".[2] Well—yes. Everything is possible, and most things come to pass (when you don't want them). However I think Singleton with an education is impossible. But first of all—what education? If it is the knowledge how to live my man essentially possessed it. He was in perfect accord with his life. If by education you mean scientific knowledge then the question arises—what knowledge, how much of it—in what direction? Is it to stop at plane trigonometry or at conic sections? Or is he to study Platonism or Pyrrhonism or the philosophy of the gentle Emerson? Or do you mean the kind of knowledge which would enable him to scheme, and lie, and intrigue his way to the forefront of a crowd no better than himself? Would you seriously, of malice prepense cultivate in that unconscious man the power to think. Then he would become conscious—and much smaller—and very unhappy. Now he is simple and great like an elemental force. Nothing can touch him but the curse of decay—the eternal decree that will extinguish the sun, the stars one by one, and in another instant shall spread a frozen darkness over the whole universe. Nothing else can touch him—he does not think.

Would you seriously wish to tell such a man: "Know thyself". Understand that thou art nothing, less than a shadow, more insignificant than a drop of water in the ocean, more fleeting than the illusion of a dream. Would you?

But I hear the postman. Au revoir till next week. I won't now delay my thanks for your good and friendly letters. Yours Ever

Jph Conrad.

---

[1] 'Alas! You will not even notice it!'
[2] Singleton appears semi-literate, but is clearly the backbone of the ship's crew. See also Watts, pp. 54–6.

To Edward Garnett

Text   MS Colgate; G. 121

Friday. 16 X^er 97 [17 December 1897][1]

[Stanford-le-Hope]

My dear Garnett.

I am awfully sorry. I sat at Lyons' upstairs[2] and near the stairs till *4.20* and then had to go, as I could not lose the train and had to buy first something for my wife. Thanks for all you say. Next time we meet we shall have a talk—a real talk. Your friendship is so much part of my life that I refer all my thoughts to you—and to think of You consoles me. I trust we will meet soon. Meantime when I have about 20 pages written, I shall send them to you in *MS*, for, my type operator is as You know off duty.[3] Would you undertake to have them typed for me? What worries me is that Pawling does not advertise me much. I daresay he knows what to do. The *Star* has given me an enthused little notice with special heading.[4] I am glad because I want Pawling to keep cheerful about me. Why the devil does he not send me my free copies. I am ashamed to ask any more. The copy for the Cearne shall be for your wife. You, having the whole, cannot want a part and economy is a great word.

Ever Yours

Jph. C.

To R. B. Cunninghame Graham

Text   MS Dartmouth; J–A, I, 215; Watts 56

20th Dec. 1897.

Stanford-le-Hope

My dear Sir.

Your letter reached me just as I was preparing to write to you. What I said in my incoherent missive of last week was *not* for the purpose of arguing really. I did not seek controversy with you—for this reason: I think that we do agree. If I've read you aright (and I have been reading You for some years now) You are a most hopeless idealist—your aspirations are irrealisable.[5] You want from men faith, honour, fidelity

---

[1] Friday was 17 December.

[2] At a J. Lyons tea-shop.

[3] Jessie Conrad, who usually did her husband's typing, was entering the last month of her pregnancy. The MS was *The Rescue*.

[4] The London evening paper's notice of *The Nigger* called it 'Assuredly one of the most powerful and extraordinary books of the year' (16 December 1897).

[5] Watts (p. 57) points out that Conrad was to say something similar about Anatole France, in his review of *Crainquebille* (*Notes on Life and Letters*).

to truth in themselves and others. You want them to have all this, to
show it every day, to make out of these words their rule of life. The
respectable classes which suspect you of such pernicious longings lock
you up and would just as soon have you shot[1]—because your personality
counts and you can not deny that you are a dangerous man. What makes
you dangerous is your unwarrantable belief that your desire may be
realized. This is the only point of difference between us. I do not believe.
And if I desire the very same things no one cares. Consequently I am not
likely to be locked up or shot. Therein is another difference—this time to
your manifest advantage.

There is a—let us say—a machine. It evolved itself (I am severely
scientific) out of a chaos of scraps of iron and behold!—it knits. I am
horrified at the horrible work and stand appalled. I feel it ought to
embroider—but it goes on knitting. You come and say: "this is all right;
it's only a question of the right kind of oil. Let us use this—for
instance—celestial oil and the machine shall embroider a most beautiful
design in purple and gold". Will it? Alas no. You cannot by any special
lubrication make embroidery with a knitting machine. And the most
withering thought is that the infamous thing has made itself; made itself
without thought, without conscience, without foresight, without eyes,
without heart. It is a tragic accident—and it has happened. You can't
interfere with it. The last drop of bitterness is in the suspicion that you
can't even smash it. In virtue of that truth one and immortal which lurks
in the force that made it spring into existence it is what it is—and it is
indestructible!

It knits us in and it knits us out. It has knitted time space, pain, death,
corruption, despair and all the illusions—and nothing matters. I'll
admit however that to look at the remorseless process is sometimes
amusing.

I've got S[an]^{ta} Teresa at last. I've just finished reading that
wonderful introduction.[2] Of course what I find in it is mostly new to
me—new as impression. It seems as though I were reading of Spain for
the first time. I am delighted and intensely interested. I feel myself in
sympathy with the book. I shall breathe its atmosphere and track its
style for some time now—a charming prospect. As to the style I cant just
yet "locate" its charm. For one thing I find it unexpectedly masculine—
in the best sense. Don't you think so too?—And the Saga! Where haven't

---

[1] For his part in the Bloody Sunday demonstration in Trafalgar Square (13 November
1887), Graham was sentenced to six weeks in gaol; he earned one and a half weeks'
remission for good conduct.

[2] Graham wrote the Preface, his wife wrote the Introduction to her life of the Spanish saint.

you been? I want more of the saga. Why the devil did they divide it? I want the whole Saga and nothing but the Saga.[1] Ever Yours faithfully

Jph. Conrad

P.S. As I may not write before the days of merriment and festivities I enclose herewith my best wishes. May you get as much happiness as is going on this merry planet. May You, without disappointement,* see the accomplishment of *all* Your desires! J.C.

To Minnie Brooke
Text   MS Texas; Unpublished

20.12.97.
Stanford-le-Hope
Essex

Dear Mrs Brooke.

I trust I have not offended beyond forgiveness by my inexcusably prolonged silence. If my pen has been unfaithful my thought has faithfully remembered the kindness of our intercourse. I did not write because often I've been too wretched mentally to write and often had not the peace of mind or even the health.

This year both my wife and I have been ill in turns. She would have written only I always said—'I shall write soon' and did not after all; for there was nothing very good to write—nothing very interesting in the old tale of doubt and struggle. Now in this season of good will I have the courage to approach You in both our names with our best wishes for peace and health—for as much merriment and happiness as can be found on this merry planet; and speaking thus I shall try to forget that the wishes of men are futile—that words have no power—that peace and happiness are not always for the deserving.

We are now in daily expectation of an important event the prospect of which makes my wife very happy and me very anxious.[2] I am glad to say that lately she has been going very well.

That's the most important news. A book of mine came out this month[3] and some critics are shocked at the rough language to be found in its

---

[1] Conrad is referring to Graham's 'Snaekoll's Saga', *Saturday Review* (18 and 25 December). The tale was included in Graham's *The Ipané* (1899). It tells of an Icelandic farmer who tries to ride across a great desert of ice; only the horse, who has presumably subsisted on his owner's flesh, reaches the other side.

[2] Borys was born on 15 January.

[3] *The Nigger.*

pages. However I do get plenty of praise—more perhaps than is good for me.

In the perfect trust in Your indulgence I am, dear Mrs Brooke Your very faithful and obedient servant.

Jph. Conrad.

To Aniela Zagórska

Text Translations Yale: J–A, i, 216; Najder 220[1]

20.12.1897.
Stanford-le-Hope

My dearest Aniela,

I know that you do not forget my existence and I know also that this is not due to my merit, but to your goodness. Silence may be a sin, but it is not always a mortal one; there are circumstances when one may obtain pardon. Naturally, I think that my sins deserve forgiveness. Besides, everybody thinks the same way—from a personal viewpoint, of course. In all sincerity I may add earnestly that there is in me so much of the Englishman, the sailor, and the adventurer, that I do not care to write—even to my nearest and dearest relatives—when things do not go well. This is the reason for my long silence. I do not want to count the months. I prefer to ask you to forget them. We have lived another year. We can say that much! Therefore we must wish one another happiness— ce bonheur dont personne ne connait le premier mot—and wish it sincerely with all our hearts: we must try to forget that man's wishes are seldom fulfilled.

I write here words of affection, words that vanish when once spoken—but the feeling remains. May the next year bring you health, peace, and the realization of your dreams—without disenchantment. And if you think that this is not possible—I shall tell you that my wishes do not reflect the possibility, but my feelings for you all.

My wife joins me in my wishes. She knows you all—as children know the characters in fairy stories, and like children eager for stories, she is always ready to listen, and I (a true story-teller) am always ready to relate. In this way you live two lives. Over there, at Lublin, where life is hard, no doubt—and here in Stanford, Essex, on the banks of the Thames—under the spell of my words: for the one you have never seen, you have the softness of Shadows and the splendour of the Unknown!

---

[1] Najder's text, used here, is based upon a collation of French and English versions of the lost original.

I have worked during the whole year. I have finished two books.[1] One came out a fortnight ago and the other is ready for the press. There we are, And while waiting I live in a state of uncertainty. I enjoy a good reputation but not popularity. And as to money I have none, either. Sad. But things are going better at present. That I shall some day attain material success there is no reason to doubt. But that requires time and meanwhile???

The worst is that my health is not good. Les nerfs, les nerfs! Uncertainty torments me. It is very foolish, no doubt—but what do you expect? Man is stupid.

And this is how I battle with time. At my age that is a serious matter. I fear that 'Before the sun rises, the dew will have destroyed the eyes'.[2]

Enough wailings. A few days ago I had news from good Margot.[3] Her life is not very easy either. I do not know if she has written to you that we expect a baby here. Jessie is very happy with this expected event, which will take place in about a week—if the devil doesn't get involved.[4] Moi je suis plus calme. As a matter of fact, not very "calm" as, possessing a certain amount of imagination—I imagine all kinds of disasters. As I have already had the honour to inform you, man is stupid. I must close, it is already late. I only hear the bells of the ships on the river, which remind me how far I am from you all. Do not forget me whatever happens! I kiss the hands of Aunt Gabriela and yours, dear Aniela. I embrace Karol, whose photo stands on the mantelpiece in the room where I work at my masterpieces.

Yours very affectionately
K. Korzeniowski.

To Edward Garnett

Text   MS Virginia; G. 122

23 Dec. 97.
Stanford-le-Hope

My dear Garnett.

Your letter did my eyes good. I wait anxiously for the Morris book. I've an idea of him. He was an artist and a man of art. The gybes

---

[1] *The Nigger* and *Tales of Unrest* (three of whose stories were written in 1896).
[2] Najder points out that this is a Polish proverb.
[3] Marguerite Poradowska: there is no extant letter from Conrad to his 'aunt' between 11 June 1895, and 16 April 1900.
[4] Borys was born on 15 January.

about Wardour St I've seen and they seemed to me contemptible.[1]

I post tomorrow a copy of the *N[igger]* to your wife. You have the whole edition so can't want a copy. My best wishes to you all—no more sincere today than on other days of the year but this is supposed to be the proper time for expressing durable sentiments in words which, pronounced, vanish and leave no ꞇrace—except in a heart here and there—yours, for instance.

I had a most enthused letter from Quiller Couch. He says the book "*must*" be a success. Is writing about it in the Pall Mall Maga: in February. He says "truthful and heroic"—that's what he says. He has tested it on an old salt and they both conclude that "this *is* a book".[2] I am pleased with that appreciation. The *Dly Chron* gives special article with a leaded heading—but you must have seen it as that is your household idol—isn't it?[3] I am writing the *R[escue]*! I am writing! I am harassed with anxieties but the thing comes out! Nothing decisive has happened yet.

Ever yours Jph. Conrad.

To A. T. Quiller-Couch

Text MS Quiller-Couch; Najder (1970)

23rd Dec. 1897.
Stanford-le-Hope
Essex

My dear Sir.

The best way in which I could prove to you how much I appreciate your letter is to answer it at once. It has reached me an hour ago—and it has made me very happy on this frosty morning.

To a man who has steadily pursued your literary work over the dismal

---

[1] Wardour Street, Soho, now a centre of the British cinema industry, was then a centre of the trade in antique, or spuriously antique, furnishings. William Morris, artist, writer, mediaevalist and Socialist visionary, had died in the previous year; we cannot tell which of his books Garnett was sending to Conrad.

[2] *The Nigger.*

[3] Perhaps Garnett, a bohemian and something of an anarchist, would have turned to the *Chronicle*'s respectable, chapel-going Liberalism only for lack of anything more subversive. Besides, it was his employer's favourite newspaper. The review (22 December) begins: 'There may be better tales of the sea than this, but we have never read anything in the least like it.' At one point, the unsigned review says: 'For, indeed, he has irony, humor, a sense of words, a power of choice, and also a steady sympathy with old mankind – all of them qualities that go to make up a rare and powerful writer.'

ocean of printed matter your letter is of immense significance.[1] It is a sign that endeavour has come somewhere within sight of achievement, that the thought has cast its shadow upon the wall of the cavern and the discriminating eyes of a fellow captive have seen it pass, wavering and dim, before vanishing for ever[2]. The difficulty is in justifying one's work to oneself. One quarrels bitterly with one's own thoughts—then, perhaps, a friend speaks, and for a time all is peace. And yours is, distinctly, a friend's voice.

Writing in a solitude almost as great as that of the ship at sea the great living crowd outside is somehow forgotten; just as on a long, long passage the existence of continents peopled by men seems to pass out of the domain of facts and becomes, so to speak, a theoristical* belief. Only a small group of human beings—a few friends, relations—remain to the seaman always distinct, indubitable, the only ones who matter. And so to the solitary writer. As he writes he thinks only of a small knot of men—three or four perhaps—the only ones who matter. He asks himself: will this one read what I am writing—will that other one? Will Q read these pages? And behold! Q has read the pages. Not only has he read the pages but he writes about them! It is like seeing unexpectedly a friend's face in the crowd at the dock head after a two years' voyage ending with four months at sea.

Twenty years of life, six months of scribbling and a lot of fist-gnawing and hair tearing went to the making of that book. If I could afford it I would never write any more—not because I think the book good, but because it is what it is. It does not belong to the writing period of my life. It belongs to the time when I also went in and out of the Channel and got my bread from the sea, when I loved it and cursed it. Odi et amo[3]—what does the fellow say?—I was always a deplorable schoolboy. But I don't hate it now. It has the glamour of lost love, the incomparable perfection of a woman who has been loved and has died—the splendour of youth. Tempi passati. I need not tell you how delighted I was to hear of the forthcoming *causerie* in the P.M. Mag:[4] You will understand my feeling better if I confess to you that it has been my desire to do for seamen what Millet (if I dare pronounce the name of that great man and good artist in

---

[1] Arthur Thomas Quiller-Couch (pseudonym 'Q'; 1863–1944), the versatile Cornish man of letters, writer of fiction and essays, don and anthologist. His *Oxford Book of English Verse* (1900) was a standard anthology for many years. When Conrad wrote to him, 'Q' had already published eight novels.

[2] An allusion to Plato: *Republic* VII.

[3] 'I hate and I love': Catullus, LXXXV.

[4] In the *Pall Mall Magazine*, February 1898.

this connection) has done for peasants.[1] Of course the ambition is honourable but I am well aware that it may provoke a smile. Still? I am sure, if you smile it will be with indulgence and sympathy. I am concerned for the men—and for the men only. It is a great relief and a great pleasure to know you've taken them up—for it is not to dismiss them at once as "brutes and ruffians". (vide reviews)

The only unkind passage in your letter is that sentence about ("needs no answer"). There is no room now to explain to you what a shock it has given me. And I even yet do not know what you meant exactly. Perhaps you did not want an answer? However, as Belfast shouted before leaping: "Here goes!"[2] and if you once open the envelope you will no doubt read to the end—unless you are made of very stern stuff indeed.

Believe me, dear Sir, very gratefully and faithfully yours

Jph. Conrad

To Helen Watson

Text   MS Yale; Unpublished

23ᵈ Dec 1897
Stanford-le-Hope
Essex

Dear Miss Watson.

My very best, most sincere wishes for the coming year. May it be the beginning of a new and uninterrupted happiness. May You be happy Yourself and may You have the strenght*, the courage, the grace to give happiness to others. A noble and a most difficult task for which the Most High Dispenser of sorrows and joys chooses the best amongst his creatures. I could wish you no more splendid fate.

I had my share of the lovely violets my wife generously telling me [to] have a few on my writing table. I owe You thanks—for, both the scent and the flower itself are my favourites.

I write in a hurry. I am always doing things in a hurry and nothing gets done somehow. As a matter of fact it [is] not so much hurry as trepidation. I am afraid that for some time I'll have to "trepidate" and make [the] best of it.

May I ask You to give my affectionate wishes to dear Ted. This is not a

---

[1] Jean-François Millet (1814–75), the French painter of the Barbizon school and etcher, best known for works such as 'The Reapers', 'The Gleaners' and 'The Sower'.

[2] In *The Nigger*.

base attempt to avoid writing to him. I only want to make my wishes more acceptable by expressing them through You; for Yours is the voice he likes to hear best. I shall write him very soon a letter that will be more like an official report of my acts and thoughts.

Believe me dear Miss Watson your most faithful friend & servant

Jph Conrad.

P.S. I am sending You the *N[igger] of the "N[arcissus]"*. There is much in the book in need of your forgiveness. I declare the intention was blameless; and I only send it to You as a token of very serious and profound regard.[1]

To Stephen Crane

Text   MS Columbia; Stallman 157

24th Dec. 1897.
Stanford-le-Hope.

My dear Crane.

Just a word to wish—from us both—to you and Mrs. Crane all imaginable prosperity and all the happiness that may be found in this merry world.

How are you getting on? I struggle along feeling pretty sick of it all. The New Year does not announce itself very brightly for me—and that's a fact. Well! a bad beginning may make a good ending tho' I don't believe in it much.

Criticisms(!) are coming in. Some praise, some blame, both very stupid.

Yours Ever

Joseph Conrad
t.o.p.[2]

PS Have you seen the Daily Tele: Article by that ass Courtney?[3] He does not understand you—and he does not understand me either.

---

[1] Conrad was very sensitive about the 'off-colour' language in *The Nigger* when he knew women were going to read it, but his diffidence is, in any case, characteristic.

[2] Turn over, please.

[3] In the *Daily Telegraph* (for 8 December), W. L. Courtney wrote that 'Mr. Joseph Conrad has chosen Mr. Stephen Crane [*The Red Badge of Courage*] for his example, and has

That's a feather in our caps anyhow. It is the most *mean-minded* criticism I've read in my life. Do you think I tried to imitate you? No Sir! I may be a little fool but I know better than to try to imitate the inimitable. But here it is. Courtney says it: You are a lost sinner and you had lead* me astray. If it was true I would be well content to follow you but it isn't true and the perfidious ass tried to damage us both. Three cheers for the Press!

Your

J.C.

To E. L. Sanderson
Text MS Yale; J-A, i, 218

26 x^{er} 97. [26 December 1897]
Stanford-le-Hope

Dearest Ted.

We got your card this morning but I was not so covered with confusion as you may imagine—since I had already asked Miss Watson (in a letter sent on Thursday to Corsbie West)[1] to give You from me all the wishes suitable to the season and which friendship may dictate. By that clever move I disarm any resentment You may feel for my apparent neglect to write—and go on to explain that it isn't neglect at all. I simply desired to write you with plenty of time for a long palaver—and it seemed as though I would never get the time! I declare solemnly to You that for all that I haven't done anything for ages. After all perhaps it was not so much time I wanted as freedom of mind. And that seems tonight as far off as ever—but I write anyhow.

Life passes and it would pass like a dream was it not that the nerves are stretched like fiddle strings. Something always turns up to give a turn to the screw. Domestic life would be tolerable if—but that soon will be over.[2] The larger life (including many large hopes) rolls on like a cart

determined to do for the sea and the sailor what his predecessor had done for war and warriors. The style, though a good deal better than Mr. Crane's, has the same jerky and spasmodic quality; while a spirit of faithful and minute description – even to the verge of the wearisome – is common to both...'

Courtney's review represented the kind of academic criticism that made Conrad a life-long enemy of literary analysis. Later reviewers re-emphasized Conrad's so-called reliance on Crane.

[1] On 23 December, to her Scottish home.

[2] Jessie's pregnancy.

without springs—that is jolting one fearfully. It's true also I never knew how to drive. Driving bores me; and yet one must attend to it in a way, to avoid an upset—a dismal death in a ditch. How do you like driving dear Ted? What kind of road have you been travelling over lately? Methinks O! most fortunate of men, whom Egyptian princes serve (tho' not on bended knees)[1] that you also have your share of ruts and jolts. Still You know where You're driving to. A great thing—in fact everything! But I don't—I don't.

The clearest gain so far from the "Nigger" was the other day a letter from Q. The excellent man—may his stars ever be propitious—writes enthusiastically a message short but packed full of sweetness. He is struck in his very vitals by the tale (which the "Standard" indignantly declares is "no tale") and apologises for saying so "in a private letter of thanks" I wrote him back four pages to explain that this apology is the only thing I find it hard to forgive him, but that, otherwise, I am not angry. I hope that my letter got to Fowey Cornwall before the remorse for his indiscretion quite overpowered him.

In this way I am paid for the life and the writing that went up to the making of the book, the "like of which" (the D. Chron: says) "we have never read before". Apart from that I am afraid that Mr. Conrad "who is, in fact, unique" (Pall Mall Gaz:) will not gain much from the book. Yet in a sense it is enough. When writing one thinks of half-a-dozen (at least I do) men or so—and if these are satisfied and take the trouble to say it in so many words then no writer deserves a more splendid recompense. On the other hand there is the problem of the daily bread which can not be solved by praise—public or private.

I went up to town at the beginning of this month to dine with Cunninghame-Graham on his return from the captivity amongst the Moors.[2] We had exchanged 4 or 5 letters before. He is a most interesting man not at all bigoted in his socialistico-republican ideas which I treated to his face which a philosophical contempt. We get on very well. Of course as is often the case the groundwork of his ideas is I may say intensely aristocratic. We talked in two languages.[3] I like him—and I verily believe he likes me.

This is all I can find to say in a hurry. The future is as mysterious as

[1] Cf. letter of 27 January 1897.

[2] Disguised as a descendant of the Prophet, Graham had attempted to reach the forbidden city of Tarudant, in Morocco. High in the Atlas Mountains, he was apprehended by the Kaid of Kintafi, who held him captive for nearly two weeks. Graham tells the story in *Mogreb-el-Acksa* (1898).

[3] In his letters to Graham, Conrad often breaks into French.

ever and every added happiness is another terror added to life. Sometimes I think I am following an ignis fatuus that shall inevitably lead me to destruction; sometimes I try not to think at all. And all the time I am trying to write. Here you have the essence of my existence unveiled.

Good luck to You dear Ted, health and peace of mind. The peace of heart you have—and no one rejoices more at it than I do. Think of me often—write to me sometimes—but only when you feel the need. Our friendship can withstand silence—because silence is not forgetfulness.

My affectionate regards and duty to Miss Watson. I've sent off a copy of the *"N[igger]"* for her. You must wait for Yours a little. With love Ever Yours

Jph. Conrad

P.S. My wife thanks you for your good wishes and joins me in mine for your welfare. She is a good girl—no trouble at all, tho' neuralgia racks her for weeks at a time.

To the Baroness Janina de Brunnow

Text L.fr. 34; Najder 222

31 Dec. 1897
Stanford-le-Hope.
Essex

Chère Madame,

Chez nous l'année est sur le point de finir et je la termine en consacrant les derniers instants du dernier mois à vous écrire. Je fais des vœux bien sincères pour votre bonheur et le bonheur de ceux qui vous sont chers et je nourris l'espoir que quand le jour de Noel et votre nouvelle année viendront,[1] vous daignerez m'accorder quand ce ne serait qu'un instant de souvenir.

Je me demande si vous avez reçu le numéro de *Blackwood Magazine* que je vous ai envoyé il y a à peu près un mois?[2] J'ai bien peur que non. Du reste vous n'aurez pas eu là une bien grande perte: le malheur sera réparé quand je me ferai le plaisir et l'honneur de vous envoyer le volume de cinq contes qui paraitra au mois de mars prochain.[3]

Vous aurez la bonté, chère Madame, de me rappeler au souvenir de

---

[1] According to the Russian calendar.
[2] With 'Karain'.
[3] *Tales of Unrest.*

Madame votre Mère et de toute la famille, ainsi que Monsieur votre Mari à qui je me permets d'envoyer une cordiale poignée de main.

Je suis, chère Madame, votre très dévoué et très obéissant serviteur et ami.

Jph Conrad Korzeniowski.

P.S.—I hear twelve strike on our village church clock. Midnight! May you have many, very many happy years.

31 December 1897
Stanford-le-Hope
Essex

Dear Madame,

For us the year is nearing its end and I will finish it by devoting the last instances of the last month to writing to you. I offer very sincere wishes for your happiness and the happiness of those who are dear to you, and I cherish the hope that, when Christmas Day and your New Year come, you will deign to accord me at least a moment's thought.

I wonder if you have received the number of *Blackwood's Magazine* that I sent you almost a month ago? I fear you may not. Nevertheless you will not have suffered any great loss: your misfortune will be redressed when I have the pleasure and honour of sending you the volume of five tales appearing next March.

Have the kindness, dear Madame, to remember me to your mother and all your family, as well as to your husband, whom I allow myself to send a cordial handshake.

I am, dear Madame, your very devoted and very obedient servant and friend.

Jph Conrad Korzeniowski

PS. I hear twelve strike on our village church clock. Midnight! May you have many, very many happy years.

CORRECTIONS TO THE TEXT

The following slips of the pen have been silently corrected.

Missing full stop supplied

14 Feb. 1890: after '"Marguerite"'; 10 June 1890: after 'Mr Wauters'; 30
Sept. 1891: after 'baise les mains'; 13 Sept. 1892: after 'vous convient'; 26
Nov. 1893: after 'Canadiens', 'il était temps' and 'marin'; 6 Dec. 1893:
after '(Amerique du Nord)'; 20 Dec. 1893: after 'Australie'; 2 May 1894:
after 'fait du bien'; 8 Sept. 1894: after '"Lourdes"'; 4 Oct. 1894 (to
Poradowska): after 'Votre traduction' and after 'Vagabonds chôment';
23 Feb. 1895: after 'de mars'; 12 Mar. 1895: after 'the *18th*'; 15 Mar. 1895:
after 'any other delusion'; 30 April 1895: after 'remettre' and 'volonté'; 2
May 1895 (to Unwin): after 'dep"; 18 May 1895: after '£1. o. 5'; 20 May
1895: after 'vos succès'; 25 May 1895: after 'Tout y est'; 28 Oct. 1895:
after 'nom de guerre', after 'thousand words)', and after 'Paternoster
Buildings E.C'; 2 Nov. 1895: after 'other people's making'; 28 Nov. 1895:
after 'March'; 19 June 1896: after 'old almanack)'; 28 Mar. 1896: after
'from here'; 22 April 1896: after "National Observer"'; 10 July 1896: after
'Ironmonger Lane E.C'; 16 Nov. 1896 (to Garnett): after '*Friday 11 a.m.*';
16 Nov. 1896 (to Unwin: after 'call at 11 am'; 21 Nov. 1896 (to
Sanderson): after 'Southern Seas' and after 'continued in our next'; 6
Dec. 1896: after 'without ceremony'; 19 Jan. 1897: after 'the Bridge'; 16
Feb. 1897 (to Sanderson): after 'I am bewitched'; 27 Sept. 1897: after
'out at 6/-'; 28 Sept. 1897: after 'his indisposition'; 14 Oct. 1897 (to
Sanderson): after 'making an ass of myself'; 30 Oct. 1897: after 'to Mr
Heinemann'; 9 Nov. 1897: after 'on the road to life'; 16 Nov. 1897: after
'8.13 pm' and after 'bachelor's quarters'; 24 Dec. 1897: after 'inimitable';
26 Dec. 1897: after 'never read before'.

Dittography

2 July 1891: a second 'a' before 'a Passy'; 25 Dec. 1893: a second 'le'
before 'père est'; 2 March 1894: a second 'que' before 'dans l'inactivité';
24 April 1894: a second 'de' before 'Plume ecrivant'; 12 July 1894: a
second 'et' before 'de corps'; 18 August 1894: a second 'me' before
'manque'; 12 April 1895: a second 'me' before 'fait du bien'; 10 July 1896:
a second 'from' before 'a sense of delicacy'; 5 August 1896: a second 'so'
before 'ghastly—nothing half'.

Other

10 Oct. 1894: closing quotation marks supplied after 'cheque'; 23 Oct. 1894: closing quotation marks supplied after 'fils Grandsire'; 12 Mar. 1895: opening quotation marks supplied before 'Horrible cruelty'; 18 May 1895: 'state on continual' altered to 'state of continual'; 29 Jan. 1896: 'consider than' altered to 'consider that'; 22 April 1896: parenthesis supplied after 'spectator's'; question mark supplied after 'Eng–Mal'; 22 July 1896 (to Garnett): comma supplied after 'every detail'; 22 July 1896 (to Unwin): 'it it exactly' altered to 'it is exactly'; 21 Nov. 1896 (to Sanderson): comma supplied after 'You see Yourself'; 29 Nov. 1896: 'it it must be' altered to 'if it must be'; 19 Dec. 1896: comma supplied after 'very swimming somehow'; 19 Feb. 1897: comma supplied after 'Four Corners'; 14 Mar. 1897: 'Yours most faithful' altered to 'Your most faithful'; 17 Oct. 1897: closing quotation marks supplied after 'cheer'; 9 Dec. 1897: full stop deleted after 'ethical truth'; 14 Dec. 1897: closing quotation marks supplied after 'même pas'.

INDEX

In Index I, which identifies recipients, only the first page of each letter is cited.

In Index II, an index of names, run-on pagination may cover more than one letter. References to ships and boats are consolidated under 'Ships'; references to newspapers and magazines under 'Periodicals'. References to works by Conrad appear under his name.

A full critical index will appear in the final volume.

INDEX I

Recipients

INDEX II

Names of people, places, ships, organizations and publications